THE DANCE BETWEEN GO.

The Dance between God and Humanity

Reading the Bible Today as the People of God

Bruce K. Waltke

WILLIAM B. EERDMANS PUBLISHING COMPANY

GRAND RAPIDS, MICHIGAN / CAMBRIDGE, U.K.

Published 2013 by

Wm. B. Eerdmans Publishing Co.

2140 Oak Industrial Drive N.E., Grand Rapids, Michigan 49505 /
P.O. Box 163, Cambridge CB3 9PU U.K.

Printed in the United States of America

18 17 16 15 14 13   7 6 5 4 3 2 1

Library of Congress Cataloging-in-Publication Data

Waltke, Bruce K.
      The dance between God and humanity: reading the Bible
      today as the people of God / Bruce K. Waltke.
            pages   cm
      Includes bibliographical references.
      ISBN 978-0-8028-6736-0 (pbk.: alk. paper)
      1. Bible — Criticism, interpretation, etc.
      2. Bible — Hermeneutics.   I. Title.

BS511.3.W35   2013
220.6 — dc23

2013005019

www.eerdmans.com

Contents

Preface   vii

Abbreviations   ix

Introduction: My Philosophy of Christian Education   1

Part I: Biblical Theological Studies

Aims of Old Testament Textual Criticism   23

The Book of Proverbs and Old Testament Theology   39

A Canonical Process Approach to the Psalms   58

Does Proverbs Promise Too Much?   75

Fundamentals for Preaching the Book of Proverbs   89

The First Seven Days: What Is the Creation Account
    Trying to Tell Us?   130

How We Got the Hebrew Bible: The Text and Canon
    of the Old Testament   139

Myth or History? The Literary Genre of Genesis Chapter 1   163

On How to Study the Psalms Devotionally   181

Problematic Sources, Poetics, and Preaching the Old Testament:
    An Exposition of Proverbs 26:1-12   189

Part II: Biblical Theological Themes

Atonement in Psalm 51   203

Biblical Authority: How Firm a Foundation?   212

Cain and His Offering   227

The Dance between God and Humanity   237

Dogmatic Theology and Relative Knowledge   256

Evangelical Spirituality: A Biblical Scholar's Perspective   262

The Fear of the Lord: The Foundation for a Relationship
   with God   282

Hermeneutics and the Spiritual Life   301

How I Changed My Mind about Teaching Hebrew
   (or Retained It)   313

Kingdom Promises as Spiritual   322

Old Testament Texts Bearing on the Problem of the
   Control of Human Reproduction   353

The Phenomenon of Conditionality within
   Unconditional Covenants   366

The Redeemed and the Righteous: A Study in the
   Doctrine of Man as Found in the Psalms   387

Reflections on Retirement from the Life of Isaac   399

The Relationship of the Sexes in the Bible   416

Responding to an Unethical Society: A Meditation
   on Psalm 49   428

Righteousness in Proverbs   441

The Role of Women in the Bible   457

Birds   476

Theonomy in Relation to Dispensational and
   Covenant Theologies   485

The New Testament Doctrine of "Land"   510

Preface

Someone has well said that every choice we make makes us. Every time we enter one vocational door we shut others. After I walked through the wide door of full-time ministry in the Christian Church, I shut doors to becoming a doctor or whatever. Having entered that wide door, I intended to walk through the narrower door of teaching theology until I realized that all I knew about God came down to words about God. And so I entered the door of teaching biblical languages. Providence led me through the very narrow door of teaching Hebrew and the Old Testament. Each choice I made finally made me into an Old Testament professor. I could have entered even smaller doors, such as specializing in Akkadian, or biblical archaeology, or textual criticism. But I kept in mind my ambition to use Hebrew to teach theology, and so I did not further define myself. This collection of essays represents that broader interest in Old Testament research. The book includes essays on archaeology, textual criticism, and a wide range of Old Testament issues, but always with a view to advance theology — that is to say, a true knowledge of reality, which is rooted in God.

What unites the essays is not only their Old Testament subject matter but their evangelical way of knowing reality. The first essay, on epistemology, is foundational to the others. This essay recognizes two ways of knowing reality: experiential knowledge for physical realities and revelation for metaphysics, such as the meaning of history. The former demands cogent reason applied to firm data; the latter demands faith inspired by God upon his revelation, the Bible. Reason and faith are not incompatible, but by themselves they are inadequate for knowing reality. Within that way of knowing, the essays address contemporary issues in Old Testament studies. Is the received text of the Old Testament reliable in light of the variety of texts attested in the Dead Sea Scrolls? How and when was the Old Testament canon formed? Did the Church form the canon or did the canon form the Church? Is the apostle's apologetic that Jesus is the Messiah based on an accredited method of exegesis? Does the book of Proverbs promise too much? How do you preach its isolated sayings? All essays aim to bring glory to the triune God and to enrich the spiritual life of the Church.

Someone once approached me and said: "I hear you are an expert in the Old Testament." I replied: "I wouldn't make such a boast, but I do get paid to teach the Old Testament." When I was graduated from Harvard, President Pusey said to the graduates receiving their Ph.D. degrees: "Welcome to the world of scholars." I wouldn't make such a boast of myself, but I am thankful that the William B. Eerdmans Publishing Company is bringing to a wider readership some of what its editors, in consultation with me, consider to be my best work, and work that they felt had enduring value. The wider readership in view is seminary educated and/or serious readers, but not more narrowly the academic guild of Old Testament scholars. For example, the work that has been most commended by that guild is "The Samaritan Pentateuch and the Text of the Old Testament," in *New Perspectives on the Old Testament* (1970). But its subject is too specialized and its content too erudite for the average seminary graduate. The collection also represents my evolving thought. Though I later qualified my view of an Old Testament perspective on abortion in *Journal of the Evangelical Theological Society* 19 (1976), this collection includes my earlier essay, "Old Testament Texts Bearing on the Problem of the Control of Human Reproduction," in *Birth Control and the Christian* (1969).

A writer sows the seed of research and editors of publishing houses and managers of bookstores water it to its full fruition. Rob Clements, a Regent College alumnus and staff member of the highly respected Regent Bookstore, initiated publishing this collection of my essays about a decade ago. Bill Reimer, the Regent Bookstore manager, agreed with Rob and invested time to prepare copy to be printed by the Regent Bookstore. But Bill, wanting to give the book wider exposure than the Regent Bookstore could provide, generously handed over what he had prepared to a willing Michael Thomson, acquisition editor at Eerdmans Publishing Company. Eerdmans retained some articles, eliminated others, and expanded the base to appeal to the targeted audience. I gladly confess my debt to these and other editors for maximizing my work. Ultimately, it is the Lord who gives the increase. I can testify that he rewards our efforts a hundred fold.

Abbreviations

ABD	*Anchor Bible Dictionary*
AEL	*Ancient Egyptian Literature*
AnBib	Analecta biblica
ANE	Ancient Near East(ern)
ARG	*Archiv für Reformationsgeschichte*
BA	*Biblical Archaeologist*
BAGD	Bauer, W., W. F. Arndt, F. W. Gingrich, and F. W. Danker. *Greek-English Lexicon of the New Testament and Other Early Christian Literature*. 2nd ed. Chicago, 1979
BASOR	*Bulletin of the American Schools of Oriental Research*
BDB	Brown, F., S. R. Driver, and C. A. Briggs. *A Hebrew and English Lexicon of the Old Testament*. Oxford, 1907
BH	*Biblia Hebraica*
BHK	*Biblia Hebraica*. Edited by Kittel.
BHS	*Biblia Hebraica Stuttgartensia*
Bib	*Biblica*
BKAT	Biblischer Kommentar. Altes Testament.
BSac	*Bibliotheca sacra*
BZAW	Beihefte zur Zeitschrift für die alttestamentliche Wissenschaft
CBQ	*Catholic Biblical Quarterly*
DSS	Dead Sea Scrolls
EBC	*Expositor's Bible Commentary*
EEC	*Encyclopedia of Early Christianity*
EncJud	*Encyclopedia Judaica*
ETL	*Ephemerides theologicae lovanienses*
ExpTim	*Expository Times*
G	Greek

GTJ	*Grace Theological Journal*
HALOT	*Hebrew and Aramaic Lexicon of the Old Testament*
HB	Hebrew Bible
HS	*Hebrew Studies*
HSM	Harvard Semitic Monographs
HSS	Harvard Semitic Studies
HTR	*Harvard Theological Review*
HUBP	Hebrew University Bible Project
HUCA	*Hebrew Union College Annual*
IB	*Interpreter's Bible*
IBHS	*An Introduction to Biblical Hebrew Syntax*
ICC	International Critical Commentary
IDB	*The Interpreter's Dictionary of the Bible*
Int	*Interpretation*
ISBE	*International Standard Bible Encyclopedia*
JAOS	*Journal of the American Oriental Society*
JBL	*Journal of Biblical Literature*
JBR	*Journal of Bible and Religion*
JETS	*Journal of the Evangelical Theological Society*
JNES	*Journal of Near Eastern Studies*
JNSL	*Journal of Northwest Semitic Languages*
JQR	*Jewish Quarterly Review*
JSJ	*Journal for the Study of Judaism in the Persian, Hellenistic, and Roman Periods*
JSOT	*Journal for the Study of the Old Testament*
JSOTSup	Journal for the Study of the Old Testament: Supplement Series
JSS	*Journal of Semitic Studies*
JTS	*Journal of Theological Studies*
KBL	Koehler, L., and W. Baumgartner. *Lexicon in Veteris Testamenti libros*
LB	*Linguistica Biblica*
LXX	Septuagint
MT	Masoretic text
NAB	New American Bible
NBD	*New Bible Dictionary*
NIB	*New Interpreter's Bible*
NICOT	New International Commentary on the Old Testament
NIDOTTE	*New International Dictionary of Old Testament Theology and Exegesis*
NIGTC	New International Greek Testament Commentary
OBO	Orbis biblicus et orientalis
OG	Old Greek

OTL	Old Testament Library
OTS	Old Testament Studies
PEQ	*Palestine Exploration Quarterly*
RB	*Revue biblique*
RTP	*Revue de théologie et de philosophie*
SB	Sources bibliques
SBLDS	Society of Biblical Literature Dissertation Series
ScrHier	Scripta hierosolymitana
SJT	*Scottish Journal of Theology*
SP	Samaritan Pentateuch
SVT	*Studi in Veteris Testamenti*
Syr.	Syriac Peshitta
TDNT	*Theological Dictionary of the New Testament*
TDOT	*Theological Dictionary of the Old Testament*
Tg.	Targums
THAT	*Theologische Handwörterbuch zum Alten Testament*
Them	*Themelios*
TSF Bul	*Theological Students Fellowship Bulletin*
TWOT	*Theological Wordbook of the Old Testament*
TynBul	*Tyndale Bulletin*
UBS	United Bible Society
Vg.	Vulgate
VT	*Vetus Testamentum*
VTSup	Supplements to *Vetus Testamentum*
WBC	Word Biblical Commentary
WMANT	Wissenschaftliche Monographien zum Alten und Neuen Testament
WTJ	*Westminster Theological Journal*
ZAW	*Zeitschrift für die alttestamentliche Wissenschaft*

INTRODUCTION:

My Philosophy of Christian Education

President Wright asked me to prepare a personal paper that would address the question: "How does theological education — and the mission of Regent College — call us to, provide for, and compel us toward a life-changing, character-transforming response?" I can best share with you my understanding of theological education, which hopefully fulfills this mission, from the perspective of one engaged in biblical studies. I divided the paper into three parts: theology as propositional truth, theology as spiritual formation, and theology as a "way" of life.

I. Theology as Propositional Truth

Propositional truth. Sound theology must involve propositions about divine matters. If a theological institution is worth its salt it must be committed to truth, which involves in part a linguistic correspondence to extralinguistic "realities" as they are constituted by and known by their creation. Theology sets forth the content of divine realities in propositional form. As we shall see, truth ultimately pertains to a correspondence between behavior and these ultimate realities, but the Bible makes many linguistic assertions about ultimate realities, about God, about human behavior, and about humanity's situation before God. Moses refers to this correspondence between ultimate reality and linguistic expression as "law," the sage refers to it as "wisdom," the New Testament, as "doctrine," and theologians, as "theology."

Previously published in booklet form by Regent College, 1994.

The inadequacy of unaided human reason. Ever since the eighteenth-century Enlightenment, the Western world has held a faith in the power of the human mind and of the scientific method. It has sought to understand and control nature and has believed, almost without question, that anything that could not be understood by unaided human reason and validated by the scientific method was not to be taken seriously.

We can know absolutely, however, only if we know comprehensively. To make an absolute judgment, says Van Til, humanity must usurp God's throne:

> *If one does not make human knowledge wholly dependent upon the original self-knowledge and consequent revelation of God to man, then man will have to seek knowledge within himself as the final reference point.* Then he will have to seek an exhaustive understanding of reality. He will have to hold that if he cannot attain to such an exhaustive understanding of reality, he has no *true* knowledge of anything at all. Either man must then know everything or he knows nothing. This is the dilemma that confronts every form of non-Christian epistemology.[1]

A play does not make full sense as one views only an isolated act or scene. It is not until the final act, until the last word is spoken and the curtain drops, that the play takes on its full meaning. Humans are confined to the tensions of the middle acts; without revelation they are not privy to their resolution in the final act.

This partiality condemns itself. It makes all the difference in the world whether good or evil will finally triumph or go on indefinitely in an unresolved stalemate. Without revelation humanity cannot answer the fundamental questions of its existence.

The human mind, employing the scientific method, to be sure can determine the "truthfulness" of statements pertaining to empirical data, whether or not they cohere with the physical world. That method can answer questions of proximate origins (How did A arise out of B, if it did?), but it cannot answer the question of ultimate origins (How and why did the law governing that A arises out of B originate?). What is incomprehensible within this epistemology is how impersonal nature can be comprehensible to us. Philosophy and/or theology deals with primary causality, with a First

---

1. Cornelius Van Til, *A Christian Theory of Knowledge* (Philadelphia: Presbyterian and Reformed, 1969), p. 17. Emphasis his.

Cause; science deals with secondary causality, restricted to finite factors. The scientific method got humanity to the moon by overcoming its ignorance of physical laws, but once a man stood on the moon the mystery of humanity's existence on this good earth became even more profound. Science answers questions with as much mathematical precision as possible, questions about "when" and "how" within the finite world, but it cannot overcome mystery; it cannot decide ultimate meaning and without that light establish a credible ethic. "The function of setting up goals and passing statements of value transcends the domain of science," said Albert Einstein.

Since unaided human reason and the scientific method cannot validate ultimate "truth," many moderns deny its existence. The presupposition of the Enlightenment at best leads to agnosticism. It leaves humanity only with valuations, what certain people at certain times have thought good, not that which is eternally good. According to this point of view we can be certain only that the meanings and values embraced by one generation will be discarded by the next.[2]

Yet this presupposition confronts the human spirit with a contradiction; that spirit yearns for absolute certainty, meaning, and values. All human beings want to see things holistically and within that frame of reference to commit themselves to something enduring. "He has also set eternity in the hearts of men," says the Teacher, "yet they cannot fathom what God has done from beginning to end" (Eccles. 3:11).

The Spirit's conviction that the Bible is truth. By showing the inadequacy of unaided human reason I have sought to establish negatively and indirectly the necessity of divine revelation, a proposition that entails that God is there and that he has spoken. The Bible's own claim to be the Word of God is too well known to require elaboration here.[3]

What is not as well known is that the truthfulness of the Bible depends on the convicting work of the Holy Spirit, not on human reason. My apologetic above has sought to show the inadequacy of unaided human reason and the need for revelation. The conviction that the Bible is God's Word, however, comes from the Holy Spirit, not human reason. If the Holy Bible's claim to represent "truth" must be validated by finite, fallible human reason, then, even if it is inspired revelation of "truth," humanity could not know it and so must continue to despair of attaining the meaning and values it seeks.

The Holy Spirit revealed the truth to the extent that God was pleased

2. Harvey Cox, *The Secular City* (London: SCM, 1965), p. 31.
3. See my article, "What I Would Change in Teaching Hebrew," *Crux* (Spring 1994).

to make it known to humanity, inspired its expression in infallible Scripture, and must bear witness to its truthfulness. The church throughout its history has heard the voice of God in Scripture (John 10:3-6; 2 Cor. 3:14-18; 1 Thess. 1:4-6; 2:13; Heb. 10:15). That truth finds articulate expression in the Reformers. The *Scots Confession* of 1560, the first confession of the Scottish Reformed Church, states:

> Our faith and its assurance do not proceed from flesh and blood, that is to say, from natural powers within us, but are the inspiration of the Holy Ghost; whom we confess to be God, equal with the Father and with his Son, who sanctifies us, and brings us into all truth by his own working, without whom we should remain forever enemies to God and ignorant of his Son, Christ Jesus. For by nature we are so dead, blind, and perverse, that neither can we feel when we are pricked, see the light when it shines, nor assent to the will of God when it is revealed, unless the Spirit of the Lord Jesus quicken that which is dead, remove the darkness from our minds, and bow our stubborn hearts to the obedience of his blessed will.[4]

Calvin in his justly famous *Institutes* wrote:

> The testimony of the Spirit is more excellent than all reason. For as God alone is a fit witness of himself in his Word, so also the Word will not find acceptance in men's hearts before it is sealed by the inward testimony of the Spirit. The same Spirit, therefore, who has spoken through the mouths of the prophets must penetrate into our hearts to persuade us that they faithfully proclaimed what had been divinely commanded.[5]

There is also the apostle Paul's prayer:

> I keep asking that the God of our Lord Jesus Christ, the glorious Father, may give you the Spirit of wisdom and revelation, so that you may know him better. I pray also that the eyes of your heart may be enlightened in order that you may know the hope to which he has called you, the riches of his glorious inheritance in the saints, and his incomparably great power for us who believe. (Eph. 1:17-19)

4. The Scots Confession (Presbyterian Church [USA], *The Book of Confessions* [New York and Atlanta: Office of the General Assembly, 1983], 3.12).

5. *Institutes*, I.7.4.

Christian epistemology is grounded in God's revelation in the Bible through the Holy Spirit, who revealed the truth, inspired its writing, and illuminates its meaning. Humans cannot manipulate this process. God is not a parrot.

Conclusion. In sum, theology based on biblical studies both constitutes the basis of Regent College and determines an essential part of its mission. At the least it must educate each generation of the church in the Holy Scripture's propositional truths, derived from an accredited exegetical method. To achieve this mission it is dependent on the Holy Spirit. Furthermore, the church has reflected on this revelation for over two millennia and given it expression, depending on its historical context, in creeds and various theological formulations. Certainly, educated students ought to know their historical heritage and their place in that history. If we are not committed to the disciplines of theology, biblical studies, and church history, we are unfit to govern and lead this institution.

II. Theology as Spiritual Formation

Introduction to exegesis and spirituality. "Exegesis" aims to construct an accredited method to lead out of the text what its original author intended; "hermeneutics" aims, in addition to determining what the text meant, to decide what it means today. In this paper the terms are used somewhat interchangeably.

What, then, is an accredited exegetical method? I have already argued that the Holy Spirit plays a determinative role in revealing, inspiring, and certifying the truth. Here I argue that the Holy Spirit plays an essential role in the human spirit for the correct exegesis of Holy Scripture.

Unfortunately, however, many theological educators set up a tension between the student's spiritual formation and exegetical competence. Courses on exegesis are divorced too frequently from those on spirituality. Students come away confused, and sometimes professors in these disciplines misunderstand each other. Those teaching spirituality fear that those teaching exegesis, who must to some extent subvert the students' confidence in their interpretations of Scripture and their theology learned in church, harm the students' spiritual lives, and those teaching exegesis wonder if their counterparts are authentic in their use of Scripture.

The crisis in exegesis. Historically, orthodox theologians confess that the Holy Spirit must illumine the Bible's meaning. "No-one knows the thoughts

5

of God except the Spirit of God," says Paul (1 Cor. 2:11b). The apostle argues that only as we are in step with the Spirit can we know the things of God. Luther commented: "For if God does not open and explain Holy Writ, no one can understand it. . . ."[6] Similarly Calvin, in the Catechism of the Church of Geneva (1541), wrote:

> Our mind is too weak to comprehend the spiritual wisdom of God which is revealed to us by faith, and our hearts are too prone either to defiance or to a perverse confidence in ourselves or creaturely things. But the Holy Spirit enlightens us to make us capable of understanding what would otherwise be incomprehensible to us, and fortifies us in certitude, sealing and imprinting the promises of salvation on our hearts.[7]

The Chicago Statement of Faith continues the tradition: "The Holy Spirit, Scripture's divine author, both authenticates it to us by his inward witness and opens our minds to understand its meaning."[8] Orthodox exegetes subscribe to this doctrine but mostly ignore it in practice. Most textbooks on exegesis written by evangelicals during the past decade or so tend to emphasize and refine the grammatico-historical method — that is, to decide the meaning of the Bible's original linguistic expression within their historical context — and to neglect the role of the Holy Spirit and the spiritual qualifications of the interpreter.[9] I do not name these works by dedicated servants to condemn

---

6. *Luther's Works,* American Edition, ed. J. Pelikan (St. Louis: Concordia, 1956), 13.17.

7. T. F. Torrance, *The School of Faith* (London: James Clarke, 1959), p. 23, P113.

8. Short Statement No. 3, J. I. Packer, *God Has Spoken* (Toronto: Hodder & Stoughton, 1979), p. 143.

9. D. A. Carson, *Exegetical Fallacies* (Grand Rapids: Baker, 1984). Carson deliberately refrains from a sustained discussion of the Holy Spirit's role in the exegetical task because it "involves a shift to a hermeneutical focus that would detract from the usefulness of this book as a practical manual." If, however, the Holy Spirit's role is crucial to the interpretation of the Bible, then the practice of interpreting the Bible cannot neglect this spiritual aspect or sidestep it as "impractical." This is a common "scholarly fallacy." All of the following books by evangelical exegetes fall prey to this fallacy:
- W. M. Dunnett, *The Interpretation of Holy Scripture* (New York: Thomas Nelson, 1984).
- W. L. Liefeld, *New Testament Exposition: From Text to Sermon* (Grand Rapids: Zondervan, 1984).
- J. B. Green, *How to Read Prophecy* (Downers Grove, IL: InterVarsity, 1984).
- W. Kaiser, *Toward an Exegetical Theology* (Grand Rapids: Baker, 1981).

(list continues on p. 7)

them; they are too well written, too brilliant, and too full of an excellent spirit for that. I reluctantly mention them only to document the widespread neglect of the most important factor in exegesis. My own teaching has been flawed by the same imbalance. When I first taught exegesis, about thirty years ago, a student asked me the relationship between the Spirit's illumination and the grammatico-historical method in interpreting the Bible. I was so dull, I had not even thought of the question and had no answer.

One notes a trend to depreciate the interpreter's spiritual qualifications from the Reformers to their sons. The Reformers finely balanced the "scholarly" and "spiritual" factors in exegesis. Art Lindsley, formerly the director of Ligonier Institute, notes:

> I have not found anything in modern writing on hermeneutics that even comes close to the thoroughness of John Owen's work on illumination. William Whitaker in his *A Disputation on the Holy Scripture* (Cambridge: The University Press, 1588) devotes significant space to this subject. Compare this with the amount of space to the subject in conservative texts such as Milton Terry, *Biblical Hermeneutics;* Bernard Ramm, *Protestant Biblical Interpretation;* Louis Berkhof, *Principles of Biblical Interpretation.*[10]

Herbert Jacobsen, a Methodist writer, echoes this sentiment: "It puzzles me at times that the literature on hermeneutics, at least in the Protestant tradition, does not deal more extensively and seriously with this personal dimension. When the Reformation began, there seemed to be a much more balanced approach to hermeneutics than there is today."[11]

- G. R. Osborne, *The Hermeneutical Spiral* (Downers Grove, IL: InterVarsity, 1991); *Handbook for Bible Study* (Grand Rapids: Baker, 1979).
- Douglas Stuart, *Old Testament Exegesis: A Primer for Students and Pastors* (Philadelphia: Westminster, 1984).
- H. Vandergoot, *Interpreting the Bible in Theology and the Church* (Lewiston, NY: Edwin Mellen, 1985).
- P. Yoder, *Toward Understanding the Bible* (Newton, KS: Faith and Life Press, 1978).
- A notable exception is George Martin's *Reading Scripture as the Word of God* (Ann Arbor, MI: Servant Books, 1982).

10. Art Lindsley, "The Role of the Holy Spirit: Response," in *Hermeneutics, Inerrancy, and the Bible,* ed. Earl D. Radmacher and Robert D. Preus (Grand Rapids: Zondervan, 1984), p. 491, n. 1.

11. Herbert Jacobsen, "On the Limitations of Hermeneutics," in *Interpreting the Word of God,* ed. S. J. Schultz and M. A. Inch (Chicago: Moody, 1976).

Two reasons suggest themselves for the diminished role of the Holy Spirit in exegesis: the Enlightenment and Scottish pragmatism. The former, with its emphasis on unaided human reason and the scientific method, saw no need for supernatural enlightenment for the accurate interpretation of the Bible. One should read the Bible, according to the legacy of this tradition, as any other book. J. A. Ernesti, one of the clearest and most influential writers on exegetes in evangelical theological institutions during the last century, affirms that Scriptures can be properly explained without resorting to prayer. According to him: "Pious simplicity of mind is useless in the investigation of Scriptural truth."

Fred H. Klooster, on the other hand, points his finger at Scottish realism: "This separation between knowledge and faith has been promoted by the use of Scottish realism in the Old-Princeton apologetic and appears in the new context in Pannenberg's theology."[12] The scientific method of exegesis apart from the interpreter's spiritual formation seems to work. Those of us who attend the annual Society of Biblical Literature conference often find better exegesis in the learned papers offered there than from the pulpit on Sunday morning. Yet, I have never heard a prayer offered at that learned society. By contrast, I have never gone to a Sunday-morning worship service — which included the preaching of the Word — without participating in prayer.

Head knowledge versus heart knowledge. It is commonly taught that scientific exegesis can determine the text's meaning but only the Spirit of God can internalize it. Henry Virkler represents the distinction: "The unbeliever can *know* (intellectually comprehend) . . . the truths of Scripture using the same means of interpretation he would use with non-biblical texts, but he cannot truly *know* (act on and appropriate) these truths as long as he remains in rebellion against God."[13] Lindsley agrees: "It is possible [for a non-Christian] to grasp an idea [of Scripture] with the mind," he writes, "but not to have a deep sense of its truth, goodness or beauty."[14] While this distinction in exegesis obviously has some validity, it actually distorts the exegetical method and its objects.

Developing an accredited exegetical method by the nature of the Bible. Any subject must generate its appropriate method of study. The well-known

12. Fred H. Klooster, "The Role of the Holy Spirit in the Hermeneutic Process: The Relationship of the Spirit's Illumination to Biblical Interpretation," in *Hermeneutics, Inerrancy, and the Bible,* ed. Radmacher and Preus, p. 462.

13. Henry A. Virkler, *Hermeneutics, Principles and Processes of Biblical Interpretation* (Grand Rapids: Baker, 1981).

14. Lindsley, "The Role of the Holy Spirit: Response," p. 488.

verse, "All Scripture is inspired by God and is profitable for doctrine . . ." (2 Tim. 3:16), entails that Bible study involves three objects at the same time: the divine Author, "God," the "inspired" human author, and the text, "all Scripture." The first two objects are personal, the last impersonal. Each demands an appropriate approach. Furthermore, an accredited exegetical method must satisfy all three objects at the same time. Immanuel Kant, radically distinguished between *Erklärung,* knowing impersonal (i.e., nonvolitional) objects, and *Verstehen,* knowing personal (i.e., volitional) objects. For the former the scientific method is appropriate; for the latter it is inappropriate. To understand objects that lack volition one distances oneself from them, attempting to become as detached and as dispassionate as possible. On the other hand, to know a person involves passion; one must commit oneself to another.

In addition to satisfying all three objects, an accredited method of exegesis will also take into account the depravity of the human knower and the sovereignty of God. Consideration is given to each of these five criteria.

1. An Accredited Exegesis Aims to Open the Exegete to an Encounter with God

Exegesis aims, I stated, to uncover a text's intention. Through the inspired author's text God aimed to disclose himself. The text was never intended as an end in itself; to make it such falsifies the aim of exegesis. Solomon boldly combined his teaching, the book of Proverbs, with knowing God. "My son, if you accept my words . . . then you will find the knowledge of God" (Prov. 2:1-5). "Knowledge of God" is the Hebrew word for "theology," the study of divine matters, but the Hebrew term does not mean the same thing as the English gloss. Plato and Aristotle employed theology in the sense of "science of divine things." "Quite differently," says Terrien, "the Hebrew expression . . . 'knowledge of God,' points to a reality which at once includes and transcends intellectual disquisition."[15] It designates the involvement of a person's total personality with God. Solomon substantiates his claim: "For the LORD gives wisdom, and from his mouth come knowledge and understanding" (Prov. 2:6). Solomon's mouth became God's mouth. The scientific method, which we traditionally call the grammatico-historical method, is appropriate for

15. Samuel L. Terrien, *The Elusive Presence: Toward a New Biblical Theology* (San Francisco: Harper & Row, 1978), p. 40.

understanding the text, but inappropriate for the principal aim of Christian understanding of Scripture, *the knowledge of God.* Conservative exegetes have downplayed the role of the Holy Spirit in exegesis because they have forgotten the object of its study. Charles Wood explains:

> In an earlier age, the claim which this thesis advances [i.e., that the aim of Christian understanding of Scripture is to know God] might simply have been taken for granted, so that the statement of it would have been superfluous. Today it would not occur to many interpreters to describe the goal of their efforts in this way. Not that they would necessarily deny the claim if it were proposed to them. They might well assent to it then as a proper theological statement of the eventual telos [the goal/end] of the exegetical labours from a Christian standpoint. But to grant the truth of the claim at some level of abstraction or at some stage of eschatological remoteness is one thing; to give it a place in one's ongoing reflections upon the practice of interpretation is another.[16]

John Frame concurs:

> Listening to Scripture is not merely a transaction between ourselves and a book, even a very extraordinary book; rather, in Scripture we meet God *Himself.* For Protestants (at least those outside "charismatic" circles), no experience offers a more profound closeness with God.[17]

Jürgen Moltmann helpfully distinguished between knowledge as power and knowledge in wonder:

> The motive that impels modern reason to *know* must be described as the desire to conquer and to dominate. For the Greek philosophers and the Fathers of the church, knowing meant something different: it meant knowing in *wonder.* By knowing or perceiving one participates in the life of the other. Here knowing does not transform the counterpart into the property of the knower; the knower does not appropriate what he knows. On the contrary, he is transformed through sympathy, becoming a participator in what he perceives. Knowledge confers fellowship. That

16. Charles M. Wood, *The Formation of Christian Understanding: An Essay in Theological Hermeneutics* (Philadelphia: Westminster, 1981).

17. John Frame, *Spiritual Formation* (Philadelphia: Westminster, 1981), p. 221.

is why knowing, perception, only goes as far as love, sympathy and participation reach. Where the theological perception of God and his history is concerned, there will be a modern discovery of Trinitarian thinking when there is at the same time a fundamental change in modern reason — a change from lordship to fellowship, from conquest to participation, from production to receptivity.[18]

We must consciously change the exegete's psychology from knowing in power to knowing in wonder. Without that psychology we cannot know God who speaks to his people through the Bible.

2. Accredited Exegesis Empathizes with the Human Author

The personal dimension of the human author requires a personal/spiritual approach to the Scriptures. Superior intellectual talent and superb education — though not to be despised — cannot render one fit to encounter the human author. To understand an author, a reader must come to meet the author with empathy. We may have competent knowledge of the text's philology, forms, and rhetoric, yet be incapable of knowing what the text means. Without empathy for the authors of Scripture, we cannot understand them. James Houston notes the interaction between the knowing subject and the object to be known:

> We are always experiencing two landscapes at the same time: the landscape before our eyes — the phenomenal world — and the landscape in our minds, what the poet Gerard Manley Hopkins has called "inscape." The one is constantly interacting upon the other. If therefore, we conceive the world to be a desert, then we make it such.[19]

An unsympathetic reader distorts an author's meaning. Patrick Fairburn lays down a sympathy with an author as his first rule to be followed in the interpretation of particular words and passages.

> The first we shall notice is one that bears on the state of mind of the interpreter — *he must endeavour to attain to a sympathy in thought and*

---

18. Jürgen Moltman, *The Trinity and the Kingdom of God: The Doctrine of God* (London: SCM Press, 1981), p. 9.

19. James Houston, *I Believe in the Creator* (London: Hodder & Stoughton, 1979), p. 1.

feeling with the sacred writers, whose meaning he seeks to unfold. Such a sympathy is not required for the interpretation alone of the inspired writings; it is equally necessary in respect to *any* ancient author. Language is but the utterance of thought and feeling of one person to another, and the more we can identify ourselves with the state of mind out of which that thought and feeling arose, the more manifestly shall we be qualified for appreciating the language in which they are embodied, and reproducing true and living impressions of it. . . . Not a few of them have given proof of superior talents, and have brought to the task also the acquirements of a profound and varied scholarship. The lexicography and grammar, the philology and archaeology of Scripture, have been largely indebted to their inquiries and researches; but, from the grievous mental discrepancy existing between the commentator and his author, and the different points of view from which they respectively looked at Divine things, writers of this class necessarily failed to penetrate the depths of the subjects they had to handle, fell often into jejune and superficial representations on particular parts, and on entire books of Scripture never once succeeded in producing a really satisfactory exposition. . . .

Hence it is laid down as a fundamental point by a distinguished German theologian — by Hagenbach in his Encyclopedia, that "an inward interest in the doctrine of theology is needful for a Biblical interpreter. As we say that a philosophical spirit is demanded for the study of Plato, a poetical taste for the reading of Homer or Pindar, a sensibility to wit and satire for the perusal of Lucian, a patriotic sentiment for the enjoyment of Sallust and Tacitus, equally certain is it, that the fitness to understand the profound truths of Scripture, of the New Testament especially, presupposes, as an indispensable requisite, a sentiment of piety, an inward religious experience. Thus is it ever true, that the Scriptures will not be rightly and spiritually comprehended, unless the Spirit of God become Himself the true interpreter of His words, the *angelus interpres,* who will open to us the real meaning of the Bible."[20]

Occasionally scholars who make no claim to being led by the Spirit read the text with more perspicacity than those who claim such leading because they read it more diligently and more empathetically.

Let me illustrate the need for a right disposition for understanding Scriptures from two personal experiences.

20. Patrick Fairbairn, *Hermeneutical Manual* (1858), pp. 63f.

In a question period that followed a lecture on Genesis 3 by a professor at Harvard who taught me more about the biblical text than any other teacher, a student pushed him to identify the "seed of the serpent" and "the seed of the woman" in Genesis 3:15 and the nature of their antipathy. To my astonishment my respected professor interpreted the text with such crass literalness that, according to him, the passage presented in mythical form the eternal antipathy between snakes and humanity, nothing more. I wondered how such an interpretation was possible. Obviously the fast-talking serpent is extraordinary — it talked, was diabolical, and knew of heavenly matters. My professor, I suggest, missed the text's meaning because he lacked spiritual empathy with its author. Harold Bloom's *The Book of J*[21] also illustrates the need for spiritual empathy. Bloom deconstructs traditional interpretations of J in every episode he selects for commentary. Regarding the Gift of the Bride Story (Gen. 2:18-25), he says that, "J is not in the business of endorsing marriage as such, let alone of considering Yahweh the establisher and sanctifier of marriage." Rather, Bloom suggests that J is writing a satire on marriage. About the Serpent and the Fall Bloom says that Yahweh, not the Serpent, is culpable. He explains Cain's murder of Abel as "a murder provoked by the arbitrariness of Yahweh." The infamous "sons of god" in Genesis are not condemned in J, rather she has "a wry appreciation of those mythic men and women." In J's Tower of Babel Story, "Yahweh is an antithetical imp or sublime mischief-maker, in no way morally or spiritually superior to the builders of Babel." For the patriarchs, "J has no particular affection just as her attitude toward Yahweh is hardly marked by reverence or by awe." Sinai is "one of J's most extraordinary ironies, because it plainly shows us a Yahweh who is not only at the verge of going out of control but who keeps warning Moses to tell the people to watch out, because their God knows that he is about to lose all restraint." And on and on.

How are such interpretations possible? In a critical review of his book I argued that Bloom's J and "her god" derive from Bloom's imagination, not from the biblical text, in spite of his protests. Consider first that J is just like him apart from gender; both are irreligious, ironic, humorous, and interested in literary characters, not religion, politics, or theology.[22] Consider too that for 2,500 years, not even the most astute readers of the biblical text rec-

21. Harold Bloom, *The Book of J.* Translated from the Hebrew by David Rosenberg (New York: Grove Weidenfeld, 1990). For a full review see Bruce K. Waltke, "Harold Bloom and the Book of J," *JETS* 34, no. 4 (1991): 509-20.

22. Bruce Waltke, "Harold Bloom and 'J': A Review Article," *JETS* 34 (1991): 509-20.

ognized the personality and style of J until Bloom found his own image in J. Finally, consider how unique J would be in her world. No other Ancient Near Eastern author treats with bemused detachment his or her nation's deity and its ancestral founders. Bloom's reflections on the text reveal *his* mental landscape, not J's. Textual and philological errors in exegesis pale in their significance in comparison to Bloom's blunder due to his lack of empathy.

Empathy with the inspired author is also necessary so as not to emphasize the wrong things. John Owen noted that apart from the Spirit, people are "inclined to all things that are vain, curious, superstitious, carnal, suited unto the interests of pride, lust and all manner of corrupt affections."[23] An honest reader of the learned journals in biblical studies must acknowledge this fact. Preunderstanding *(Vorverständnis)* is now widely accepted but not treated adequately in exegetical textbooks. Modern hermeneutics would express the attempt to bring the interpreter's thoughts and feelings into those of the author as the merging of two horizons. The importance of shared preunderstanding was not unknown to earlier generations. Says Carl Michalson:

> Preunderstanding *(Vorverständnis)* was not unknown to Wesley. Probably it was known to him, technically, in German before it was in English, even though Locke and Shaftesbury gave the notion its earliest philosophical development. It was Oetinger, however, who gave to the experience of "presentiment" and "taste" the German translation *Vorempfindungen.*[24]

We must have a "taste" for truth to find it.

3. Accredited Exegesis Loves Truth

The *impersonal nature of the biblical text* is the third factor that calls for a right spirit in an accredited exegesis. Epistemology, the science that studies the theory of knowledge, has shown that knowing always involves a knower, a knowable content, and some "laws of thought" or criteria for determining what is true about the knowable content. To know the text's content the knower must come to it with a love for truth.

23. John Owen, *Works* (London: T. & T. Clark, 1862), IV:118-234.
24. C. Michalson in W. McCown and J. E. Massey, eds., *Interpreting God's Word for Today* (Anderson, IN: Warner, 1982), p. 26.

Many orthodox exegetes prefer the exegesis of scholars who make no appeal to the Spirit's illumination, because they often find more honest scholarship in their writings than in those who confess the illumination of the Spirit. This is most disturbing. A few years ago a prominent American fundamentalist remarked to the press that the standards of truth are different for the press than for the church. Even that statement condemned him; he should have said forthrightly, "higher," not "different." The scientific method requires a spirit that loves truth. B. Ramm states, "No matter how accurately a lens may be ground, unless the glass is crystal-pure the image passing through the lens will suffer distortion."[25] Along a similar vein, Terry notes that the scientific method operates best when it is free from "prejudice, preconceived opinions, engagements by secular advantages, false confidences, authority of men, influences from parties and societies."[26] Through God's common grace scholars who make no appeal to the Spirit's illumination attain this ideal to a relatively higher degree. Though perhaps motivated by love for self, not for God, they nevertheless research the text assiduously and write about it indefatigably.

4. The Depraved Nature of the Knower

The nature of the human knower demands the work of the Holy Spirit to interpret and/or exegete the text. Because of our innate depravity our minds have been darkened (Rom. 1:18-22; Eph. 4:17-18; 1 John 1:8). We suppress the truth (Rom. 1:18), and we aim to justify our behavior, including our unbelief and unethical conduct (Prov. 14:12; 16:25). Satan continues to deceive us with half-truths, calling into question God's goodness and truthfulness (Genesis 3). Sin has destroyed our ability to do what is right (Rom. 7:13-25). We must come to the text with a pure conscience. Thus, apart from God's regeneration and the work of the Holy Spirit we cannot hear the text clearly.

When Balaam went to God honestly desiring to know whether he should go with the Midianites to put a curse on Israel, God said: "Do not go with them." Later, however, when Balaam was enticed by the lure of more silver and gold and pressured by men more numerous and of higher status, he returned to see whether God would change his mind. At that point God deluded him, telling him to go with them. However, God was so angry with the

---

25. B. Ramm, *Protestant Biblical Interpretation,* 7th ed. (Boston: Wilde, 1975), p. 7.

26. Milton S. Terry, *Biblical Hermeneutics* (New York: Eaton & Mains, 1968), p. 202.

seer he nearly killed him (cf. Num. 22:2-35). The lesson is clear: unless we come to God's word with an honest heart to hear the truth, God may delude us. Jesus said: "If anyone chooses to do God's will, he will find out whether my teaching comes from God or whether I speak on my own" (John 7:17).

The account of the confrontation between the prophet Micaiah and King Ahab in 1 Kings 22 also illustrates the failure to see truth clearly because of unbelief. Acceding to Jehoshaphat's request that they seek a prophet of the LORD besides others to determine whether to go to war with the Arameans or to refrain, Ahab sent a messenger to fetch Micaiah son of Imlah. The messenger instructed Micaiah to let his words agree with the others. When the prophet arrived in Ahab's presence and was asked by him the LORD's mind, God deluded Ahab again even as he had through the false prophets. "Attack and be victorious," Micaiah said, "for the LORD will give it into the king's hand" (v. 15). But when the king said to him, "How many times must I make you swear to tell me nothing but the truth in the name of the LORD?" (v. 16), Micaiah answered, "I saw all Israel scattered on the hills like sheep" (v. 17). Even then the word of God failed to enlighten Ahab's darkened understanding. Trusting in his own techniques, he marched off to his death; his chariot was washed at the pool where the prostitutes bathed, and dogs licked up his blood (v. 38).

Both of these accounts imply that we will get out of the Bible what we want. If we want God to rubber-stamp our opinions through the Bible, he may delude us, bringing us into judgment.

5. The Sovereignty of God

Finally, *the nature of the Revealer of the Scriptures* demands that the exegete have proper spiritual qualifications. God has hidden himself in Scripture and must sovereignly show himself to us. We cannot make God talk through the scientific method. As the Lutheran scholar David Steinmetz says:

> Scripture is not in our power. It is not at the disposal of our intellect and is not obliged to render up its secrets to those who have theological training, merely because they are learned. Scripture imposes its own meaning; it binds the soul to God through faith. Because the initiative in the interpretation of Scripture remains in the hands of God, we must humble ourselves in His presence and pray that He will give understanding and wisdom to us as we meditate on the sacred text. While we may

take courage from the thought that God gives understanding of Scripture to the humble, we should also heed the warning that the truth of God can never coexist with human pride. Humility is the hermeneutical precondition for authentic exegesis.[27]

More particularly, God has hidden the revelation of himself in Jesus Christ both in his physical presence at his advent and in his textual presence in Scripture.[28] In the words of Fred Klooster, Jesus is "the pneumatically Christological theocentric message of Scripture."[29] While Jesus walked among people, most thought he was a great prophet. When Peter, however, confessed him to be the Son of the living God, Jesus said, "This was not revealed to you by man, but by my Father in heaven" (Matt. 16:17).[30] Earlier in his ministry the Lord Jesus praised his Father for having hid divine matters, including his identity, from the wise and learned and revealing it to little children (Matt. 11:25). Regarding this revelation Jesus said: "If anyone chooses to do God's will, he will find out whether my teaching is from God or whether I speak on my own" (John 7:17).

Saul the Pharisee, with the rest of his countrymen, had a veil over his heart when he read the text of the Old Covenant until Christ took it away in his turning to the Lord (2 Cor. 3:14-16). After his conversion and call to be an apostle, if we may generalize from his behavior at Corinth, he reasoned in the synagogues relatively unsuccessfully in terms of numbers, trying to persuade Jews and Greeks that Jesus was the Christ (cf. Acts 18:4). Salvation belongs to the Lord; it entails the Spirit's illumination of the text. Klooster writes:

> The confession of the inherent authority of Scripture is basic to all sound biblical interpretation. This confession alone does not guarantee faithful biblical interpretation, however. Many Jews of Jesus' day claimed to acknowledge the authority of Moses and of the Old Testament, but they did not really believe the Old Testament since they rejected Jesus as the Christ of Scripture. Jesus denounced that unbelief. (John 5:45-47)[31]

27. David C. Steinmetz, "Luther as an Interpreter of the Bible," *Archiv für Reformationsgeschichte* 70 (Beiheft: Literaturbericht, 1973), p. 71.

28. Cf. Eph. 2:12-13, 18; Luke 24:27; John 5:45-47.

29. Klooster, "The Role of the Holy Spirit in the Hermeneutic Process," p. 453.

30. See A. B. Bruce, *The Training of the Twelve* (Grand Rapids: Kregel, 1971 [reprint of 1894 edition]), p. 42.

31. Klooster, "The Role of the Holy Spirit in the Hermeneutic Process," pp. 453f.

This illumination is the believing exegete's intuitive experience. Says John Calvin: "I speak of nothing other than each believer experiences within himself — though my words fall far beneath a just explanation of the matter."[32]

Conclusion

The mission of Regent calls us to the transformation of our spiritual lives through the Holy Spirit. Tragically, our college is somewhat unique within evangelicalism in focusing on this indispensable aspect of theological education. Paradoxically a symbiotic relationship exists between Scripture and the spiritual life. A right spirit is necessary for the interpretation of Scripture, and Scripture so read nourishes the spirit.

III. Theology as a "Way" of Life

If truth consists of correspondence between linguistic expression and ultimate reality, more fundamentally it consists of a correspondence between behavior and that ultimate reality. Jimmy Johnson, head coach of the Dallas Cowboys, said before the Super Bowl: "It's not what we say that counts, it's how we play." That's good theology. To be sure, we need sound propositions, but these ultimately function to ensure sound behavior. This seems so obvious that it scarcely needs explanation, elaboration, or validation. "Knowledge of God," inadequately glossed as "theology," designates more than the involvement of a person's total personality in the presence of the Lord. B. Childs notes that God is known through doing his will: "The knowledge of God is defined throughout as obedience to his will which has a content."[33]

The Bible consistently demands action, not words. God was pleased to validate his own character in the acid test of history, in the time-space-matter continuum. He did not content himself merely in propositional truths about himself. Jesus draws his famous Sermon on the Mount to its conclusion with these sobering words: "Therefore every one who hears these words of mine and puts them into practice is like a wise man who built his

32. *Institutes*, I.7.5.
33. Brevard S. Childs, *Old Testament Theology in a Canonical Context* (Philadelphia: Fortress, 1986), p. 51.

house on the rock" (Matt. 7:24). At the end of his ministry he commends the preaching of the teachers of the law and the Pharisees who "sit in Moses' seat" but condemns them for their failure to practice what they preached: "So you must obey them and do everything they tell you. But do not do what they do, for they do not practice what they preach" (Matt. 23:3).

Jews were marked out by three practices: circumcision, sabbath, and kosher-laws, not by their confessions. Christians are to be marked out, says Jesus, by the way in which they love each other, not only by their confession that "Jesus is Lord." "Not everyone who says to me, 'Lord, Lord,' will enter the kingdom of heaven, but only he who does the will of my Father who is in heaven. Many will say to me on that day, 'Lord, Lord, did we not prophesy in your name, and in your name drive out demons and perform many miracles?' Then I will tell them plainly, 'I never knew you. Away from me, you evildoers'" (Matt. 7:21-23). On the day of judgment we will be judged by our works, not only by our words.

The quintessential expression of biblical ethics is "do to others as you would have them do to you" (Matt. 7:12). Christianity thinks of itself as a "faith"; the Bible thinks of the covenant people as following *a way, a halakhah*, a life-path. The word "faith" refers to faithfulness to the Lord, not so much to a belief system. The book of Proverbs alone uses the metaphor "seventy times," and Jesus referred to himself as "the way, the truth, the life." The metaphor denotes a traversable road, or movement on a road leading to a destination, and connotes at one and the same time "course of life" (i.e., the character and context of life), "conduct of life" (i.e., specific choices and behavior), and "consequences of that conduct" (i.e., the inevitable destiny of such a lifestyle).

The mission of Regent College certainly involves a commitment to the "way" of Jesus Christ, a way that compels the transformation of lives and cultures into conformity with the ultimate realities he taught and which Regent College reformulates for its world. The College's interdisciplinary disciplines and the disciplines of practical theology are essential to the realization of that mission. Tragically, its commitment to the integration of Christian "faithfulness" with the marketplace, arts, and sciences is rare in Christian education. Under God's good hand Regent has been raised up in this generation to give leadership in spiritual formation and in integrating Christian thought with practice. These two components, so vital to sound theological education, are largely overlooked in many Christian theological institutions. Regent dare not lose its vision or, having called others to the task, falter in the race.

PART I

Biblical Theological Studies

Aims of Old Testament Textual Criticism

Textual criticism of the Hebrew Bible is living through a period of reconceiving its discipline. Historically, text critics, whether they worked on Homer, Moses, Isaiah, Paul, or Shakespeare, tried to produce a text as close as possible to the text that left the author's hand. They agreed that to reconstruct such a text the critic must assess the history of the text's transmission in light of available MSS; expose additions, omissions, and other corruptions; and eliminate them. Today, however, not all text critics of the Hebrew Scriptures aim to establish a text that most nearly represents the author's original intentions. This essay identifies five aims of contemporary textual critics of the Hebrew Bible, critically appraises the views, and draws a conclusion.

I. Restore the Original Composition

Before the advent of modern biblical criticism, OT text critics conceived their task in terms of intentions of inspired charismatic figures such as Moses, David, Solomon, and Isaiah. They aimed to rid the text of the historical clutter that came to be attached to these writings, and by eliminating the contaminations of other authorial interventions, they hoped to recover as much as possible the *ipsissima verba* of the inspired person. Their aim was

---

Previously published in *Westminster Theological Journal* 51, no. 1 (Spring 1989): 93-108. Reproduced by permission.

like that of Tanselle in modern text criticism: "to establish the text as the author wished to have it presented to the public."[1]

This goal had the advantage of being in accord with the nature of great literature; viz., it was the product of a literary genius. It had the disadvantage of not recognizing editorial additions to the text.[2]

II. Restore the Final Text

With the advent of historical and source criticism the text critic of the Hebrew Bible conceptualized the task differently, though the practice remained essentially the same. More and more scholars came to regard the received text not as the *ipsissima verba* of one particular charismatic figure, but as the final redaction of earlier oral and written sources, the *ipsissima verba* of a final redactor.[3] They distinguished between the oral and written processes that went into making the final text of a biblical book and the processes by which the final text, once established, was handed down or transmitted. Higher critics aimed to recover the genetic processes by which the final version of a text came into existence, and text critics aimed to recover the processes of its written transmission so as to restore it to its final, and in that sense original, pristine purity. "The final text," says F. E. Deist, "is the end product of the genetic processes and, at the same time, the starting point of the processes of written transmission."[4] Even though rhetorical criticism, the most recent trend in biblical criticism, puts an emphasis on what the text says instead of on what happened behind the text,[5] it still mostly views the text critic as one who works out textual errors from the text's final intentions by revealing the history of their emergence. Though the text critic who seeks

1. C. Thomas Tanselle, "The Editorial Problem of Final Authorial Intentions" (1976), reprinted in Tanselle's *Selected Studies in Bibliography* (Charlottesville: University Press of Virginia, 1979), p. 314.

2. For scribal practices in editing the text, see M. Fishbane, *Biblical Interpretation in Ancient Israel* (Oxford: Clarendon, 1985), pp. 44-88.

3. For an attempt to debunk the prevailing view that the text passed through a long and often complicated oral prehistory before arriving at the final text, see Bruce K. Waltke, "Oral Tradition," in *Inerrancy and Hermeneutic,* ed. Harvie Conn (Grand Rapids: Baker, 1988), pp. 117-36.

4. F. E. Deist, *Toward the Text of the Old Testament* (Pretoria: D. R. Church Booksellers, 1978), p. 24.

5. See the excellent article by Tremper Longman III, "The Literary Approach to the Study of the Old Testament: Promise and Pitfalls," *JETS* 28 (1985): 385-98.

to restore a final text is not as innocent as one who seeks to restore an original composition, yet he accepts the notion of one authentic text to which the extant MSS bear witness.

Text critics of this persuasion think of the scribes as contaminators of an authoritative text through the intentional and unintentional changes they introduced into it. Furthermore, since no MS preserves the original final text, these critics restore an eclectic, archetypical text by scientifically classifying the MSS into recensions, spotting errors, and artfully removing them.

Unquestionably this has been the prevailing aim of the modern critics of the Hebrew Bible. It may be thought that the editors of the Hebrew Bible do not have this aim in view because they do not publish an eclectic text but a specific Masoretic MS. Formerly such editors used the basic single text of Jacob ben Hayyim;[6] presently they use the Leningrad Codex B 19A (L),[7] or the Aleppo Codex.[8] Here one must distinguish the editor's goal in textual criticism from his necessity to prepare copy-text. For practical and traditional reasons the editors of *BHK* and *BHS* chose a specific Masoretic MS that they judged to be the "best" as a copy-text, but they nevertheless had in mind restoring an original text, as can be seen in their considering and evaluating deviant readings in their apparatus. In *BHK* there are two apparatuses, the first with variants not considered superior to L and the second with variants considered more or less preferable to L. *BHS* combined these two into one apparatus, but there is no difference in purpose and no great degree of difference in judgment, though it contains fewer conjectures. The Hebrew University Bible Project (HUBP), however, differs significantly from these editions because it disallows conjectural emendation altogether (see below).

That the reconstruction of an eclectic original (or final) text has been the prevailing view can be seen in the English versions (EV). Translators of the EV offer an eclectic text as the copy-text and indicate in their margins their sources other than the Masoretic text (MT) and important differences from it. Although the EV mostly render the MT, all offer an eclectic text, sometimes preferring one textual tradition, sometimes another, and sometimes opting for a conjectured emendation.[9]

---

6. Ernst Würthwein, *The Text of the Old Testament* (Grand Rapids: Eerdmans, 1979), pp. 37f.

7. Cf. *Biblia Hebraica Stuttgartensia (BHS)*, ed. K. Elliger and W. Rudolph (1967-1977).

8. M. H. Goshen-Gottstein, ed., *The Book of Isaiah*, The Hebrew University Bible (Jerusalem: Magnes, 1975-).

9. See L. H. Brockington, *The Hebrew Text of the Old Testament: The Readings Adopted by the Translators of the New English Bible* (Oxford: Oxford University Press, 1973);

This approach has the disadvantage of minimizing the contribution of the original religious, literary "genius," but it does handle more adequately editorial additions. A text critic of the Hebrew Bible does not need necessarily to distinguish between original compositions and final texts. It seems more prudent for him to interpret his rationale not in terms of the more subjective original authorial intentions but in terms of the more objective final text.

The attempt to reconstruct a nonextant final text has sometimes been ridiculed as a will-o'-the-wisp enterprise. Critics reconstructing an archetypical text have rightly defended themselves by noting that the attempt has the heuristic value of removing many and possibly most intentions of later contributors who have bedeviled the intentions of the final text.

As will be shown, however, several learned voices are arguing that serious problems underlie the theory of final intentions when it is applied to some of the literature of the Hebrew Scriptures.

III. Restore the Earliest Attested Text

Textual criticism classically operates in two areas: finding and removing errors from extant MSS and conjecturally emending the text where the extant evidence defies reasonable exegetical expectations. However, scholars associated with HUBP and the United Bible Societies' Hebrew Old Testament Text Critical Project do not aim to reconstruct the final text but a secondary stage, the earliest attested form of the text (c. second century BC). Limiting their work to textual options actually extant in ancient texts and versions, they concomitantly eliminate scholarly conjectures from consideration in text criticism.[10]

To be sure, there has been a healthy and growing caution on the part of

---

cf. the NAB appendix offering textual notes on the OT. For the NT, see R. V. G. Tasker, *The Greek New Testament* (London: Oxford University Press, 1964), and B. M. Metzger, *A Textual Commentary on the Greek New Testament* (London and New York: United Bible Societies, 1971). For a critique of Brockington's work, see D. F. Payne, "Old Testament Textual Criticism: Its Principles and Practice," *TynBul* 25 (1974): 99-112.

10. See vols. 1-3 of the *Preliminary and Interim Report on the Hebrew Old Testament Text Project* (Stuttgart: United Bible Societies, 1973), pp. 197-377. The first of five projected volumes was published in 1982: Dominique Barthélemy, *Critique textuelle de l'Ancien Testament* (OBO 50, no. 1; Fribourg: Éditions Universitaires/Göttingen: Vandenhoeck & Ruprecht, 1982). For critiques of this work, see Albert Frey, *RTP* 117 (1985): 197-207.

commentators away from the extremes of Duhm and the "eccentricity in the later work of Cheyne"[11] in having recourse to emendation.[12] Würthwein's first rule for making a decision about the original text is: when MT and all other witnesses offer a text that is unobjectionable, that makes sense, and has been preserved without a variant, "we may naturally assume that the original text has been preserved by the tradition, and that it should be accepted implicitly. It may seem strange that this point requires statement here, because it seems so obvious. But anyone acquainted with the history of Old Testament scholarship will not consider it unnecessary."[13] It is with good reasons the church has confessed that "by His singular care and providence," the text has been "kept pure in all ages."[14]

Nevertheless, the posture of these two committees against subjectivism is too radical. Sanders defended the stance of the UBS project not by disallowing conjectures but by taking them away from text critics. "Conjectures about a non-extant Urtext of any biblical passage," he wrote, "have their place elsewhere in biblical study . . . but not in text criticism in *sensu stricto*."[15] To be sure, conjectural criticism is rooted in exegetical expectations and therefore is only secondarily connected with textual criteria,[16] but the emendations themselves need to be acceptable from a textual point of view. For that reason, conjectural criticism has classically been the purview of competent text critics.

Implicit and explicit evidence establishes the need and validity of judicious conjectural emendations. Centuries separate the earliest attested MSS and the final text. The Greek translations of Hebrew Scriptures were made mostly in the century between 250 BC and 150 BC. The bulk of Qumran Scrolls belong to the first centuries BC and AD, though F. M. Cross dated one poorly preserved Qumran MS to the mid-third century BC. Judging by ex-

---

11. See Sidney Jellicoe, *The Septuagint and Modern Study* (Oxford: Clarendon, 1968), p. 320.

12. Cf. W. F. Albright in *The Old Testament and Modern Studies*, ed. H. H. Rowley (London: Oxford University Press, 1952), p. 25: "We may rest assured that the consonantal text of the Hebrew Bible, though not infallible, has been preserved with an accuracy perhaps unparalleled in any other Near-Eastern literature."

13. Würthwein, *Text of the Old Testament*, p. 116.

14. Westminster Confession of Faith 1.8.

15. John Sanders, "Text and Canon: Concepts and Method," *JBL* 98 (1979): 5-29, p. 12.

16. See M. Margolis, "The Scope and Methodology of Biblical Philology," *JQR* 1 (1910-11): 19, cited by E. Tov, *The Text-Critical Use of the Septuagint in Biblical Research* (Jerusalem: Simor, 1981), p. 33.

tant evidence a few readings were added, lost, or corrupted over this extended period of time. J. M. Sprinkle rightly complained against the UBS project: "What we as students of the Hebrew Bible actually want . . . is not a later stage of the text but the original."[17]

The Qumran MSS validate conjectural emendations by containing original readings not found in the traditional MSS. For example, 4QSam[a] contains about three lines introducing chapter 11 of 1 Samuel heretofore known only partially in Josephus.[18] Furthermore, these MSS, which were discovered relatively recently, occasionally confirm judicious conjectures by earlier scholars. Cross wrote: "No headier feeling can be experienced by a humanistic scholar, perhaps, than that which comes when an original reading, won by his brilliant emendation, is subsequently confirmed in a newly-found MS."[19]

IV. Restore Accepted Texts

Canonical critics do not aim to restore an archetypical text; they stress instead the social relations that exist in literary production. A dialectic, they note, always exists between the text and the community as each shapes and reshapes the other. These text critics do not necessarily deny the existence of a final text, but for them it is a chimera because between its creation and the time the text was stabilized in the proto-rabbinic period (c. AD 70) it existed in many accepted texts. John Sanders noted: "There is no early biblical manuscript of which I am aware no matter how 'accurate' we may conjecture it to be, or faithful to its *Vorlage,* that does not have some trace in it of its having been adapted to the needs of the community from which we, by archaeology or happenstance, receive it."[20]

No scholar familiar with the data disagrees with Sanders's observation. For example, in the rabbinic tradition behind MT one finds the *tiqqune*

---

17. J. M. Sprinkle, *JETS* 28 (1985): 469.

18. Frank Moore Cross, "The Ammonite Oppression of the Tribes of Gad and Reuben: Missing Verses from 1 Samuel 11 found in 4QSamuel," in *The Hebrew and Greek Texts of Samuel* (Jerusalem: Academon, 1980), pp. 105-20. Note also Terry L. Eves, "One Ammonite Invasion or Two? 1 Sam 10:27–11:2 in the Light of 4QSam[a]," *WTJ* 44 (1982): 308-26.

19. Frank Moore Cross, "Problems of Method in the Textual Criticism of the Hebrew Bible," in *The Critical Study of Sacred Texts,* ed. W. D. O'Flaherty (Berkeley Religious Studies Series, Graduate Theological Union, 1979), p. 37.

20. Sanders, "Text and Canon," pp. 5-29.

sopherim (that is, scribal notations that the text had been changed for theological reasons); in the Greek tradition the text was altered to protect the sanctity of God and to accommodate it to Greek philosophy;[21] and in the Samaritan recension, Deuteronomy 27:4 with the reading "Mount Gerizim" (contra "Mount Ebal" in the received text) was interpolated along with other passages after Exodus 20:17 so that its tenth commandment calls for worship on Mount Gerizim (cf. John 4:19-22).

The welter of conflicting readings in the Qumran scrolls prior to the fixing of the text sometime between 70 BC and AD 100 also suggests to canonical critics that the text was fluid and flexible, capable of being moderately adjusted and made relevant to the times. According to them, restraints on the text, such as the canonical proscription against adding or taking away from the text (cf. Deut. 4:2; 31:9ff.; Josh. 24:25-26; 1 Sam. 10:25), were balanced with the need to shape it in accordance with what communities thought God was doing in their times. Canonical critics think it is wrongheaded to restore a nonexistent final text from a hodgepodge of secondarily shaped accepted texts; such a procedure would result in a ludicrous potpourri of reworked texts from widely differing eras and localities. P. R. Ackroyd seemingly defines text as the many levels of understanding with its rich and varied materials.[22]

In the view of these scholars, all the text critic can hope to do is to isolate a number of textual layers and/or traditions belonging to varying communities of faith. Brevard Childs put it succinctly:

> A basic characteristic of the canonical approach in regard to both its literary and textual level is its concern to describe the literature in terms of its relation to the historic Jewish community rather than seeing its goal to be the reconstruction of the most original literary form of the book, or the most pristine form of a textual tradition.[23]

Canonical critics vary, however, in their practice. The more liberal, such as Ackroyd and Sanders, celebrate the diversity of accepted texts and so do not prefer one accepted text over another. The more conservative, like Childs, argue for the priority of the rabbinic text stabilized at about AD 100. In

21. For example, see Gillis Gerleman, "The Septuagint Proverbs as a Hellenistic Document," *OTS* 8 (1950): 15-27.

22. P. R. Ackroyd, "An Authoritative Version of the Bible?" *ExpTim* 85 (1973-74): 376.

23. Brevard S. Childs, *Introduction to the Old Testament as Scripture* (Philadelphia: Fortress, 1979), pp. 96f.

Childs's view the text critic aims to restore from later corruptions in the rabbinic and Masoretic tradition the most pristine form of that text. He wrote:

> The first task of the Old Testament text critic is to seek to recover the stabilized canonical text through the vehicle of the Masoretic traditions. This process involves critically establishing the best Masoretic text which is closest to the original text of the first century.[24]

Childs is interested in the text's recensional history in the prestabilization period, not to recover the original text but to provide a perspective by which critically "to measure the range of mechanical errors" in MT, which is his canon. In short, Childs modifies the second approach: to restore the Masoretic final text.

Canonical critics help us to see the scribe not merely as a transmitter of the text but as a publishing editor, striving to keep the Scriptures clear and relevant to successive generations. For too long, critics have seen scribes as culprits responsible for separating later audiences from the original text when in fact they should be seen as helpful publishers, making the text accessible, intelligible, and sometimes even freshly relevant to their immediate audiences. This understanding of early scribal practices ameliorates the unfortunate tendency to call all "secondary" readings "spurious." To the extent that these "improvements" communicate truth they are "genuine" readings. In fact, modernized readings may be even more "genuine" than an early one that no longer communicates the original meaning. Even as translations of the Hebrew Bible are the Word of God to the extent that they convey the message contained in the Hebrew expression of it, so also these modernizations should be recognized as Scripture.

This socialization of the text also gives perspective on the use of the OT in the NT. As is also well known, the apostles were not hidebound to any one textual tradition; their writings preserve readings from the rabbinic tradition, the Septuagint,[25] and the proto-Samaritan texts.[26] Although the apostles were fully conscious of canonical Scripture, they also had a freedom in citing and interpreting it. (The so-called Apocrypha and Pseudepigrapha, which can also be dated to the period before the stabilization of the text, also

---

24. Childs, *Introduction to the Old Testament*, p. 101.

25. Cf. the high respect for the text of the LXX in the Epistle to the Hebrews.

26. Bruce K. Waltke, "Prolegomena to the Samaritan Pentateuch" (Ph.D. diss.; Harvard University, 1965), pp. 20-59.

show a similar mindset.) The Word of God came to them through divergent texts, just as the Word of God comes to the church today through varying translations. Between the original composition or final text and the stabilization of the text there is no evidence that a text that lacks editorial intervention was prima facie more sincere than one that doesn't.

Textual critics are indebted to canonical critics for giving them a more generous attitude towards scribes, but they must resist the temptation to lower their sights from the high ideal of recovering final text(s) that emerged in Israel before prophecy ceased in Israel.[27] Although the transmitters of the text at this early stage may have thought of themselves as editors, rather than as merely copyists, nonetheless their conception of *their* task ought not to dictate the text critic's conception of his task. Scribes seek in varying ways to transmit and disseminate the text; text critics seek to restore an original text.

The functions of scribes and text critics became confounded after the text became stabilized at the turn of the first century AD, for after that time scribes no longer sought to modernize and relativize the text but only to preserve it. Thereafter scribes sought to restore the text by means of the *ketiv-qere* (i.e., alternative traditional readings), *sebir* (i.e., expected readings to be rejected), and *tiqqune sopherim* traditions.[28] Later on the Masoretes added the Masorah, the vowels, and the accents to preserve it.

There is always the need in humanities for critics to restore the original (or final) text. The original author's (or redactor's) wishes and intentions are obviously matters of importance. Although scribal editors played an important role in transmitting a living text, nevertheless, the original text demands to be heard in its own right. In spite of an editor's best intentions, his activity does separate later audiences from original authors. Literary critics make a sharp distinction between a scholarly or critical edition of a literary work on the one hand and a modernized or noncritical edition on the other. Each has its place.

The canonical approach to textual criticism not only lets down the humanities, it is also theologically unsound. During the creative period both "truth" and "falsehood" came into the text. Scribal changes during the time

27. Cf. A. J. Petrotta, "Old Testament Textual Criticism: Some Recent Proposals," *Theological Student Fellowship Bulletin* (April 1981): 9.

28. See Dominique Barthélemy, "Les Tiqqune soperim et la critique textuelle de l'Ancien Testament," *International Organization for the Study of the Old Testament: Congress Volume* (VTSup 9; Leiden: E. J. Brill, 1963), pp. 285-304; S. Talmon, *Qumran and the History of the Biblical Text,* ed. F. M. Cross and S. Talmon (Cambridge, MA: Harvard University Press, 1975), pp. 321-400.

of the text's fluidity were sometimes more than incidental modernizations; they also contained substantive changes both in theology and history. Did the Ten Commandments contain the prescription to worship on Mount Gerizim or not? Although some critics think the Jews changed the text in Deuteronomy 27:4 from Mount Gerizim to Mount Ebal in order to embarrass the Samaritans,[29] few aside from the Samaritans accept it as the tenth commandment. A frivolous scholar says that this kind of question is neither possible nor proper, but a serious one aims to recover the original authorial intention. A serious historian wants to know whether the biblical historian recorded in Exodus 12:40 that Israel spent 430 years before the exodus in just Egypt (so MT) or in Egypt and Canaan (so LXX and SP). These and many other issues cannot be obfuscated by celebrating the variants or by arbitrarily opting for a text that all agree has errors in it. Liberal canonical critics are in danger of relativizing truth and absolutizing conflicting faiths.

Finally, Sanders's verdict that no early biblical MS has no trace of having been socially adapted entails that he has in mind a purer original to which he is comparing the MS. Is it not better theory and more useful practice to reconstruct the purer original than to accept the contaminated text?

V. To Reconstruct Final Texts

According to other contemporary text critics of the Hebrew Scriptures the MSS and versions reflect varying stages or versions in the editing of the final text, the relative value of which the text critic is incompetent to judge. This approach differs from the aim of restoring "accepted texts" by distinguishing creative, literary readings from "confessional" and "mechanical" readings. Whereas the former approach attenuates the line between canon and confessions, this approach attenuates the line between literary criticism and textual criticism and opens the door to the possibility that more than one form of a text may exist within the canon.

Critics who recognize "original literary variants" in contrast to "secondary transmissional variants" give a more accurate insight into the nature of parallel passages in the OT. As is well known, parallel passages in the OT (cf. 2 Sam. 22 = Ps. 18; 2 Kings 18:13–20:19 = Isa. 36–39; 2 Kings 24:18–25:30 =

---

29. For a defense of the SP, see R. H. Pfeiffer, *Introduction to the Old Testament* (New York: Harper & Brothers, 1941), p. 102; for a defense of MT, see James Alan Montgomery, *The Samaritans: The Earliest Jewish Sect* (Philadelphia: J. C. Winston, 1907), p. 35.

Jer. 52; Isa. 2:2-4 = Mic. 4:1-3; Ps. 14 = 53; 40:14-18[13-17] = 70; 57:7-11 = 108:1-5; and the parallels between Samuel-Kings and Chronicles and the Pentateuch and Chronicles) contain glaring differences.

It is well known that 2 Samuel 22 and Psalm 18, for instance, are the same psalm in slightly different forms. Adele Berlin latches onto S. Talmon's suggestion that "it is not a question of which is correct, but a matter of comparing alternate [sic!] forms which were equally acceptable to the ancient poet."[30] She compares these variants:

> From the palm of all his enemies and from the palm [Hebrew, *kap*] of Saul. (2 Sam. 22:1)
> From the palm of all his enemies and from the hand [Hebrew, *yad*] of Saul. (Ps. 18:1)
> When I am in distress I call to YHWH; and to my God I call [Hebrew *qārā'*]. (2 Sam. 22:7)
> When I am in distress I call to YHWH; and to my God I cry out [Hebrew *šāwa'*]. (Ps. 18:7[6])
> For who is a god except YHWH? And who is a rock except [Hebrew *mibbalʿâdê*] our God? (2 Sam. 22:32)
> For who is god except YHWH? And who is a rock beside [Hebrew *zûlātî*] our God? (Ps. 18:32[31])

Just as scribes modernized and contemporized the text after the time when tradition held that the spirit of prophecy had ceased in Israel, sometime between Ezra and the Era of Contracts (that is, the time of the Seleucids),[31] so also during the time of the writing of the Hebrew Scriptures authors and/or later editors reworked texts. Sometimes they modernized it, as in the case of the Chronicler in his use of Pentateuchal sources;[32] other times they gave it fresh meaning, as can be seen in a comparison of Psalm 40:14-18[13-17] with Psalm 70. The variants in these psalms with reference to the divine name —

30. Adele Berlin, *The Dynamics of Biblical Parallelism* (Bloomington: Indiana University Press, 1985), p. 69. For Talmon's bibliography, see footnote 46.

31. Cf. J. Weingreen, *Introduction to the Critical Study of the Text of the Hebrew Bible* (Oxford: Clarendon, 1982), pp. 73-75.

32. M. Cross and D. N. Freedman, *Studies in Ancient Yahwistic Poetry* (SBLDS 21; Missoula, MT: Scholars Press, 1975); cf. G. Weil, "La nouvelle édition de la massorah gedolah selon le manuscript B 19a de Leningrad," *Note e Testi* (Florence: Olschki, 1972), p. 329. Note the comment from about 100 BC in 1 Maccabees 9:27: "There had not been such great distress in Israel since the time prophets ceased to appear among the people."

the former reading "the LORD" in the "a" verset and "God" in the "b" verset, and vice-versa in Psalm 70 — are as Boling noted "genuine variants."[33] The synoptic variations between Isaiah 2:2-4 and Micah 4:1-3 may be compared to a preacher who uses the same sermon or illustration more than once in varying social contexts. The Masoretes retained these early editings of the text, either by the authors themselves (see below) and/or by later editing scribes, and so should the text critic.

Although occasionally variants in synoptic passages may be due to scribal error that crept into one and/or the other parallel texts, the former attempt of text critics to assimilate the two and to get back of both to an Urtext was ill-conceived.[34]

The book of Jeremiah confronts the text critic with a striking instance of two texts that circulated in different forms, not within the Masoretic tradition but between the extant Masoretic and Greek witnesses to that text. Compare, for example, the MT of Jeremiah 27:1-7 (the full passage below) with the LXX:

> *Early in the reign of Jehoiakim*[35] *son of Josiah king of Judah, this word came to Jeremiah from the LORD:* This is what the LORD said to me: "Make a yoke out of straps and crossbars and put it upon your neck. Then send word to the kings of Edom, Moab, Ammon, Tyre and Sidon through the envoys who have come to Jerusalem to Zedekiah king of Judah. Give them a message for their masters and say, 'This what the LORD *Almighty,* the God of Israel, says, Tell this to your masters: With my great power and outstretched arm I made the earth *and its people and the animals that are on the face of the earth,* and I give it to anyone I please. Now I will hand *all these* lands over to my servant Nebuchadnezzar king of Babylon to serve him and even the beast of the field *I will give to him* to serve him. *All nations will serve him and his son and his grandson until the time for his land comes; then many nations and great kings will subjugate him.'"*

This sample illustrates the well-known fact that the LXX of Jeremiah is one seventh shorter than the MT of that book.[36] Not only does the LXX of Jere-

---

33. Robert G. Boling, "Synonymous Parallelism in the Psalms," *JSS* 5 (1960): 250.

34. Gillis Gerleman, "Synoptic Studies in the Old Testament," *Lunds Universitets Årsskrift* (N. F. Avd. 1) 44 (1948): 34, 69f.

35. Read "Zedekiah" with a few Hebrew MSS and Syriac.

36. For other examples of additions and slight differences between the two versions of

miah differ from the MT of that book with regard to length, it also locates Jeremiah's oracles against the foreign nations (chaps. 46–51 in MT) following Jeremiah 25:13. Finally, and most instructively, the few and tiny fragments of the Qumran scroll, 4QJer, exhibit the main characteristics of the LXX,[37] demonstrating that the varying versions to some extent existed in Hebrew texts.

Sven Soderlund[38] categorized earlier scholarly proposals to explain these variations, viz.: (1) "The abbreviation theory" (i.e., the Greek text is an abbreviated or mutilated version of the Hebrew; so K. H. Graf, C. F. Keil, and C. von Orelli); (2) "the editorial theory" (i.e., the two texts derive from two different editions of the book produced by Jeremiah himself, the shorter version done in Alexandria, the longer taken to Babylon; so Eichhorn, cf. A. Van Selms, and T. W. Overholt); (3) "the expansion theory" (i.e., the LXX is the best witness to the text of Jeremiah, the MT having suffered greatly from expansion, conflation, and interpolation in the course of transmission; so F. C. Movers, A. W. Streane, and J. G. Janzen); and (4) "the mediating view" (i.e., it is impossible to generalize on the relative priority of the two texts, but instead, each reading has to be evaluated on its own merits; so F. Hitzig, W. Rudolph, and J. Bright).

Janzen[39] made some progress toward eliminating the first and last options, and Sven Soderlund[40] effectively called into question Janzen's explanation, the third option. Emanuel Tov's solution is best: these versions of Jeremiah reflect not recensions (changes in the text after the establishment of a final canonical text) but early editions of the book.[41] He contends that the same is true of Joshua,[42] in a shorter version of the story of Goliath,[43]

Jeremiah, see E. Tov, *Text-Critical Use,* pp. 190-92, 297-98; "L'incidence de la critique textuelle sur la critique littéraire dans le livre de Jérémie," *RB* 79 (1972): 189-99; and "Exegetical Notes on the Hebrew *Vorlage* of the LXX of Jeremiah 27 (34)," *ZAW* 91 (1979): 73-93.

37. J. Gerald Janzen, *Studies in the Text of Jeremiah* (HSM 6; Cambridge, MA: Harvard University Press, 1973), pp. 173-84.

38. Sven Soderlund, *The Greek Text of Jeremiah: A Revised Hypothesis* (JSOTSup 47; Sheffield: JSOT Press, 1985), pp. 11f.

39. Janzen, *Studies.*

40. Soderlund, *Greek Text,* pp. 198-248.

41. E. Tov, "L'incidence"; see also "Some Sequence Differences between the MT and the LXX and Their Ramifications for Literary Criticism of the Bible," forthcoming in *JNSL.*

42. E. Tov, "The Growth of the Book of Joshua in the Light of the Evidence of the LXX Translation," in *Studies in the Bible: 1986* (ScrHier 31; Jerusalem, Magnes, 1986), pp. 321-39.

43. E. Tov, "The Composition of 1 Samuel 1618 in the Light of the Septuagint Version," in *Empirical Models for Biblical Criticism,* ed. J. H. Tigay (Philadelphia: University of Pennsylvania Press, 1985), pp. 97-130.

and in Ezekiel.[44] Soderlund makes the important point: "It is important not to lose one's perspective: whether in the longer or shorter version, the book of Jer still speaks to us with power and conviction which should not be obscured in the course of an otherwise legitimate and necessary text critical enterprise."[45]

S. Talmon[46] earlier claimed that in the case of synonymous readings one should not be preferred to the other. Similarly, M. Goshen-Gottstein[47] held that any two or more readings that cannot be established as primary and secondary should be regarded as true alternatives, and M. Greenberg[48] reckoned with "irreducible variants going back to plural primary versions."

Though these critics have not sought to support their view from analogies in the Qur'an and in modern literature, it finds support in these quarters. Widengren contended that Muhammad not only contributed directly or indirectly to putting the Qur'an into writing but that he also made some interpolations in the text.[49] Regarding modern literature, Hans Zeller[50] suggested that texts frequently exist in several versions, no one of which can be said to constitute itself the final one. Jerome J. McGann agrees: "Many works exist of which it can be said that their authors demonstrated a number of different wishes and intentions about what text they wanted to be presented to the public, and that these differences reflect accommodations to changed circumstances, and sometimes to changed publics."[51]

---

44. E. Tov, "Recensional Differences between the MT and LXX of Ezekiel," *ETL* 62 (1986): 89-101.

45. Soderlund, *Greek Text*, p. 248.

46. S. Talmon, "The Variant Readings of IQIsᵃ," *Auerbach Jubilee Volume* (Jerusalem, 1956), pp. 147-56 [Hebrew], cited by Tov, *Text-Critical Use*, p. 311; "Synonymous Readings in the Textual Traditions of the OT," in *Studies in the Bible* (ScrHier 8; Jerusalem: Magnes, 1961), pp. 335-85; "The Textual Study of the Bible — A New Outlook," in *Qumran and the History of the Biblical Text*, pp. 321-400.

47. M. Goshen-Gottstein, "The History of the Bible Text and Comparative Semitics," *VT* 7 (1957): 195-201; cited by Tov, *Text-Critical Use*, p. 311.

48. M. Greenberg, "The Use of Ancient Versions for Interpreting the Hebrew Text," *Congress Volume: Göttingen 1977* (VTSup 29; Leiden: E. J. Brill, 1978), pp. 131-48; cited by Tov, *Text-Critical Use*, p. 311.

49. Geo Widengren, *Literary and Psychological Aspects of the Hebrew Prophets* (Uppsala Universitets Årsskriff 10; Uppsala: Lundequistska, 1948), p. 49.

50. Hans Zeller, "A New Approach to the Critical Constitution of Literary Texts," *SB* 28 (1975): 231-64.

51. Jerome J. McGann, *A Critique of Modern Textual Criticism* (Chicago and London: University of Chicago Press, 1983), p. 32.

Varying final texts may be the product of an original author, a view-point similar to the first goal, or of editorial activity, a viewpoint similar to the second goal. From the text critic's view, the difference is immaterial. This goal attenuates the line between literary criticism and text criticism, for the text critic for the first time is now giving the literary critic textual attestations of the editorial process with which the latter heretofore has worked only theoretically.

The theory should not be rejected out of hand on theological grounds. There is no reason why the Spirit may not have inspired men to write varying editions of the same book; in fact, the parallel passages in the Bible suggest that he did. The theory does entail, however, modifying the notion of an "original autograph." On the other hand, the theory should not be latched on to too quickly, for parallels in Ancient Near Eastern literature show that in the course of transmission texts were usually expanded and sometimes condensed.[52]

Tov thought that at "a certain point in time, the literary growth of the biblical books necessarily ended, at least for those who accepted the present canonical form of the books as final," after which point "the actual textual transmission began."[53] His goal, therefore, is ultimately to restore the *Urtext*. "At the beginning of the textual transmission, we thus posit one copy which incorporated the final literary product, and this text may, for the sake of convenience, be called the *Urtext* of the biblical books. The *Urtext*, then, is the ultimate goal of our text-critical analysis." In theory, however, there is no compelling reason why a text could not exist in more than one final canonical form.

VI. Conclusion

Theology and the humanities depend on text critics, who scientifically collect and compare variants, then select the "best" readings or even conjecture emendations where all texts prove exegetically senseless and/or nonsensical in order to artfully reconstruct final texts. Conjectured readings, however, lack the authority of an assured Hebrew reading: "Est conjectura, non vero scriptura." This task of the text critic must be kept distinct from scribes and publishers who modernize and interpret old texts.

---

52. See bibliography cited by Soderlund, *Greek Text*, p. 201.

53. Emanuel Tov, "Criteria for Evaluating Textual Readings: The Limitations of Textual Rules," *HTR* 75 (1982): 429-48.

The text critic's aim will vary according to the nature of the book. If a book had but one author, then the critic will aim to restore his original composition; if it be an edited text, then the critic will seek to recover the final, canonical text. If he turns up more than one final text, he will turn his data over to the literary and canonical critic to determine whether the text is in process of developing into a final canonical text or whether it existed in more than one canonical form. Before reaching this conclusion however, the text critic must make every effort to distinguish between "literary" and "transmissional," or "creative" and "mechanical," or "redactional" and "scribal" additions. Judith Sanderson, following Gesenius and this writer, established some criteria for detecting editorial and scribal additions in the late second temple period as exhibited in the text of 4QpaleoExodM.[54] Text critics will need to continue their historic practice of identifying later haggadic and confessional additions and glosses brought into recensions. Some problems will remain beyond solution *(crux interpretum)*, and the verdict *non liquet* ("unsolved") must be accepted.

Although these conclusions are unremarkable, until this writer drew them he was even more perplexed by the data and the debate.

---

54. Tov, "Criteria," pp. 431-54. Judith E. Sanderson, *An Exodus Scroll from Qumran: 4QpaleoExodM and the Samaritan Tradition* (HSS 30; Atlanta: Scholars Press, 1986).

The Book of Proverbs and Old Testament Theology

Hartmut Gese wrote, "It is well known that the wisdom literature constitutes an alien body in the world of the Old Testament."[1] This implied consensus is founded on two superficial observations: the striking similarities between the book of Proverbs and the ancient, panoriental wisdom literature,[2] and the lack of reference in Israel's wisdom circles to national Israel's election and covenants.

In an earlier article this writer surveyed the affinities of the book of Proverbs with the international sapiential literature in its literary forms, arrangement, and contents.[3] On account of these striking parallels Preuss went so far as to suggest that Israel's wise men attempted to shape Israel into the image of their pagan environment.[4]

---

1. Hartmut Gese, *Lehre und Wirklichkeit in der alten Weisheit* (Tübingen: Mohr [Siebeck], 1958), p. 2, cited by James L. Crenshaw, "Prolegomenon," in *Studies in Ancient Israelite Wisdom,* selected by James L. Crenshaw (New York: Ktav, 1976), p. 2.

2. See Bruce K. Waltke, "The Book of Proverbs and Ancient Wisdom Literature," *Bibliotheca Sacra* 136 (July-September 1979): 226-38.

3. Waltke, "The Book of Proverbs and Ancient Wisdom Literature," pp. 226-38.

4. Horst D. Preuss, "Erwägungen zum theologischen Ort alttestamentlicher Weisheitsliteratur," *Evangelische Theologie* 30 (1970): 393-417, cited by Crenshaw, "Prolegomenon," p. 2.

Previously published in *Bibliotheca Sacra* 136 (October-December 1979): 302-17. Copyright © 1979 by Dallas Theological Seminary. Used with permission. The author is delighted to express his indebtedness to students in an Old Testament seminar on Proverbs (Spring 1979) who contributed to his thinking for this article. Papers deserving recognition include Nigel Biggar, "Wisdom in Weakness"; Kathy Brown, "Wisdom's Veil"; and Judy Krzesowski, "The Power of Words."

In contrast to the scholarly success in showing the comparative similarity of Israel's wisdom with its pagan environment, Old Testament theologians proved unable to integrate the book of Proverbs into the rest of the Old Testament, which builds around Israel's covenants and its history of salvation. In the heyday of the biblical theology movement Wright commented that "in any outline of biblical theology, the proper place to treat the Wisdom literature is something of a problem."[5] Rylaarsdam put the problem this way: "This striking neglect of Jewish history and religion by the canonical wisdom writers clearly indicates that the Hebrew Wisdom movement had not yet been integrated into the national movement."[6] The attempts of Eichrodt to integrate wisdom into "covenant" and of von Rad into salvation history have proved notable failures.[7] Kaiser's recent proposal to relate wisdom to the rest of the Old Testament by the common concept of "the fear of God/ Lord" also fails because he relates this theme to "promise," which he seems to define in terms of Israel's organic covenantal history.[8] Wisdom writers do not mention Israel's covenants or national promises culminating in the Messianic age.

Moreover, according to others there is a strain of wisdom in the Old Testament whose posture is summed up as "humanism," meaning here the ability to attain one's goal through proper education and mental discipline.[9] This alleged strain belonging to the age of the so-called "Solomonic Enlightenment" differs from the prophets not only in its universalism over against their national particularism, but in its very soul and spirit. McKane, who accepts this view, says that it is "this-worldly and has no commitment to ethical values."[10] Fichtner stated the view thus:

> In the spiritual history of Israel, there are so few completely antithetical phenomena as prophecy and ḥokmah (wisdom). Two worlds stand in total opposition: the proclaimer and the admonisher who is seized by God and laid completely under claim and who carries out his lofty and dan-

5. G. Ernest Wright, *God Who Acts* (London: SCM Press, 1952), p. 115.

6. J. Coert Rylaarsdam, *Revelation in Jewish Wisdom Literature* (Chicago: University of Chicago Press, 1946), p. 20.

7. Cf. Crenshaw, "Prolegomenon," p. 1, and notes from criticisms from many sides.

8. Walter Kaiser, Jr., *Toward an Old Testament Theology* (Grand Rapids: Zondervan, 1978), pp. 168-71.

9. For example, H. Gressman, "Die neugefundene Lehre des Amenemope und die vorexilische Spruchdichtung Israels," *Zeitschrift für Altes Testament* 41 (1924): 289-91.

10. William McKane, *Prophets and Wise Men* (London: SCM Press, 1965), p. 1.

gerous mission to his people without any personal considerations, and the clever and prudently worldly-wise sage who goes his peaceable way cautiously looking right and left and who instructs his protégés in the same wise style of mastering life. To appreciate this vast difference one has only to read a few sentences from the book of Amos and then a few from Proverbs 10 or 27![11]

If one assumes that these morally neutral wise men contributed to the book of Proverbs, it follows that the prophetic attack against the wise who made themselves independent of Yahweh included these men (cf. Isa. 5:19-24). According to many liberal critics, the prophets made war against the priest with his magic; McKane now adds that they made war against the shrewd sage with his strength of mind.

But others have made a start in challenging this distorted picture. They have noted that a distinction cannot be established in the book of Proverbs between an older, profane, and secular wisdom and a younger so-called distinctively Israelite strain of wisdom that transformed and supplemented the former. Accordingly, the Proverbs are *not* alien to the concepts and spirit of the rest of the Old Testament. Priest argued that the prophetic age and the age of wisdom occurred simultaneously and that there existed "a common religious tradition in early Israel from which prophets, priests and wise men selected specific emphases without necessarily rejecting those emphases chosen by other groups."[12] According to this view prophet and sage together expressed the totality of Israel's faith, which neither could do alone. But Priest did not attempt to demonstrate their common inspiration, and until that is done his thesis lacks conviction. Weinfeld showed a clear connection between wisdom and Deuteronomy both in specific legislation and even in identical wordings (cf. Deut. 4:2; 13:1[12:32] and Prov. 30:5-6; Deut. 19:14 and Prov. 22:28; Deut. 25:13-16 and Prov. 20:23).[13] But he gave pride of place to wisdom and proposed that the Deuteronomists were schooled in wisdom circles. Moreover, he restricted his attention to specific verbal and

11. Johannes Fichtner, "Isaiah among the Wise," in *Studies in Ancient Israelite Wisdom,* p. 429. Most recently D. Kent Clark sides with those who pit prophet against sage ("Between Prophet and Philosopher," *New Blackfriars* 58 [1977]: 267-72).

12. John F. Priest, "Where Is Wisdom to Be Placed?" in *Studies in Ancient Israelite Wisdom,* p. 281.

13. Moshe Weinfeld, "The Wisdom Substrata in Deuteronomy and the Deuteronomic Literature," *Deuteronomy and the Deuteronomic School* (Oxford: Clarendon, 1972), pp. 244-74.

ethical parallels, some of which are also met in non-Israelite wisdom. But in spite of these limitations it is a start in the reverse direction.

The vein of this article is to demonstrate that the sages and the prophets were true spiritual yokefellows sharing the same Lord, cultus, faith, hope, anthropology, and epistemology, speaking with the same authority, and making similar religious and ethical demands on their hearers. In short, they drank from the same spiritual well. Noth[14] and von Rad[15] have shown the close connection between the book of Deuteronomy and the works of the so-called "former prophets," and Westermann[16] has demonstrated that the accusations, threats, sentences, and promises found in the "classical" prophets correspond with similar literary forms in Deuteronomy. Thus this writer here uses the term *prophetic* more broadly to include the book of Deuteronomy along with the literature traditionally attributed to the prophets.

The Same LORD

According to Manley, God's personal name, Yahweh, occurs in the book of Deuteronomy either alone or in various compound expressions 593 times, and his generic title, Elohim, twenty-four times.[17] In the book of Proverbs, the tetragrammaton occurs alone forty-six times and thirty-eight times in various combinations for a total of eighty-four times, and the appellative Elohim appears five times. Thus the distribution of the two common epithets for Israel's deity occurs in about the same proportion in Deuteronomy and Proverbs. The distinct meaning of these two names is widely recognized: whereas the title Elohim contrasts God with man in their natures, the name Yahweh presents God as entering into a personal relationship with human beings and revealing himself to them. More specifically Yahweh is God's covenantal name, and by using this name the sages present themselves as teachers within Yahweh's covenant community even though they never mention Israel or the covenant. In short, the sages present themselves as spokesmen for the same God who encountered Israel through Moses and the prophets that succeeded him.

14. Martin Noth, *A History of Pentateuchal Traditions,* trans. Bernard W. Anderson (Englewood Cliffs, NJ: Prentice-Hall, 1972).

15. Gerhard von Rad, *Studies in Deuteronomy* (London: SCM Press, 1953), pp. 74-91.

16. Claus Westermann, *Basic Forms of Prophetic Speech* (Philadelphia: Westminster, 1967).

17. G. T. Manley, *The Book of the Law* (London: Tyndale, 1957), p. 37.

Also, the wise men ascribe the same attributes and actions to Yahweh as those ascribed to him by the prophets. According to both circles he is the Creator of the cosmos (Deut. 10:14; Isa. 40:21-22; Prov. 3:19-20) and of all humankind (Deut. 4:32; Isa. 42:5; Prov. 14:31; 29:13). He is the same living God who will avenge wrong (Deut. 32:35, 40-41; Nahum 1:2; Prov. 25:21-22) and the same spiritual being who comforts men and knows man's ways (Deut. 23:14; Jer. 16:17; Prov. 5:21; 15:3). According to both, he is the sovereign Lord directing history (Deut. 4:19; 29:4, 26; Isa. 45:1-13; Prov. 16:1-9, 33; 19:21; 20:24 et passim) and is yet present in it, withholding and giving rain (Deut. 11:13-17; Hag. 1:10-11; Prov. 3:9-10), disciplining his children (Deut. 8:5; Isa. 1:4-6; Prov. 3:11-12), and in his mercy answering their prayers (Deut. 4:29-31; Isa. 56:7; Prov. 15:8, 29). According to both sources he is merciful (Deut. 4:31; Isa. 63:7; Prov. 28:13), wise (Isa. 11:2-3; 31:2; Prov. 8:22-31), delights in justice and hates iniquity (Deut. 10:17; Isa. 1:16-17; Prov. 11:1; 17:15), and has aesthetic-ethical sensibilities (Deut. 22:4-11; 23:10-14; Jer. 32:35; Prov. 3:32; 6:16-19; 11:20; 15:9 et passim).

To put the matter the other way around, there is no difference between the way God is described in the prophetic literature and the way he is described in the book of Proverbs.

The Same Religious System

Scholars frequently allege that Israel's preexilic prophets and wise men both took a critical stance toward Israel's religious systems with its sacred site, personnel, sacrifices, and institutions (cf. Amos 5:25-27; Hos. 6:7; 12:9; Isa. 1:10-15; Jer. 7:22; and Prov. 15:8, 29; 20:25; 21:3, 27; 28:9; 31:2).[18] But in fact neither is critical of the cultus per se; instead they are critical of religious ritual devoid of ethical behavior. In fact, the prophets were zealous for a worship established in righteousness (Isa. 43:22-24; 44:28; 56:4-7; Ezek. 45:13–46:24; Zeph. 3:18 et passim), and the sages assumed its existence. Perdue has argued persuasively that Proverbs 15:8 does not say the Lord accepts prayer as a valid practice and rejects sacrifice, but rather that the verse condemns both prayer and sacrifice offered by the wicked.[19] He also argued that Proverbs

---

18. Space does not permit entering the debate here regarding this relationship. For the purposes of this article it is simply noted that since the turn of the century scholars have recognized many affinities in the language, style, and thought of these two sources.

19. Leo G. Perdue, *Wisdom and Cult* (Missoula, MT: Scholars Press, 1977), p. 156.

21:3 and 27 are not lambasts of the wise against religious sacrifices — though they could be regarded in this light — but aphorisms affirming with their spiritual peers (the priests and the prophets) that ethical behavior is more important than religious ritual.[20] In addition to prayers and sacrifices the sages referred to the sacred vow (20:25; 31:2), the sacred lots (16:33), and the firstfruits (3:9). In short, although the wise men did not initiate the cultus, they assumed it, and with the prophets and priests they attempted to correct it by an emphasis on the priority of ethical behavior. There is no reason to assume that the sages had in view a religious system differing from the one referred to in the Law and prophets.

The Same Inspiration

As stated above, according to the prevailing consensus, preexilic prophetic proclamation is grounded in a claim to revelation, whereas preexilic sapiential counsel is founded in human experience and reflection. Fichtner stated this view bluntly: "The prophet speaks in large measure on the basis of the authority conferred with his commission and tells his hearers 'God's Word'; while the wise man — especially in the earlier period! — gives advice and instruction from tradition and his own insight without explicit or implicitly assumed divine authorization."[21] Zimmerli in his pioneering study exploring the structure of Israelite wisdom also underscored the anthropocentric character of wisdom thought.[22] According to him, instead of speaking with a categorical, prophetic word (dābār), the wise men offered deliberative, debatable counsel ('ēṣâ); instead of appealing to the Creator's authority, they appealed to what is in man's best interest as the justification for their validity; instead of issuing commands, they sought to compel assent. Cazelles presented the same view. "Wisdom is the art of succeeding in human life, both private and collective. It is grounded in humanism, in reflexion [sic] on and observation of the course of things and the conduct of man."[23] For Couturier the wisdom tradition began as "the totality of life experiences transmitted by a father to his son, as a spiritual

---

20. Perdue, *Wisdom and Cult*, pp. 161-62.

21. Fichtner, "Isaiah among the Wise," p. 430.

22. Walther Zimmerli, "Concerning the Structure of Old Testament Wisdom," in *Studies in Ancient Israelite Wisdom*, pp. 179-99.

23. Henri Cazelles, "Bible, sagesse, science," *Revue d'Histoire des Religions* 48 (1960): 42-43, cited by Crenshaw, "Prolegomenon," p. 4.

testament."[24] And Rylaarsdam claimed, "the wisdom seeker must rely entirely on his natural human equipment."[25]

But to defend this view one must divide up the sayings in the Proverbs into earlier secular and humanistic sources and its later religious context, which was added to validate the strictly utilitarian approach, or into categories of wisdom, as Crenshaw does. For him there are "court wisdom," which has a "secular stance," and "scribal wisdom," which has a "dogmatico-religious" stance along with still other sources.

But in the author's discussion of the history of the wisdom tradition in the preceding article, it was argued that there is no compelling evidence for this construction in either Israelite or non-Israelite wisdom texts.[26] Rankin likewise concluded, "We have no reason to assume, in the absence of actual evidence, that at any time there was in Israel a purely secular proverb literature. From the very outset in Israel's wisdom writings the religious sanction of right conduct, the motive supplied by the idea of God's blessing and cursing was present."[27] Priest noted: "Even if, and this is by no means beyond dispute, there was a movement from the secular to the divine in the wisdom of those countries (around Israel), such a shift had already taken place by the 15th century at the latest, well before the inception of Israel's wisdom."[28] Priest also noted that even in Ben Sirach, unquestionably later than Proverbs, maxims appear, which, if they had been found in Proverbs would have been assigned by many scholars to the earliest strata since they are obviously "secular" in content and orientation. He concluded, "It is simply impossible to demonstrate that the earliest strata are secular and the latest religious."[29]

As the above discussion implies, critics concur that the canonical form of the book of Proverbs has a religious stance and that its teachings are grounded not in humanism but in revelation. Thus in the sayings constituting the hermeneutical context for interpreting the book it is stated that the Lord brought forth wisdom before the creation (8:22) and that "from his mouth came knowledge and understanding" (2:6). Agur assumed canonical limits to revealed wisdom: "Every word of God is flawless; he is a shield to those who take refuge in him. Do not add to his words, or he will rebuke you

24. Guy P. Couturier, "Sagesse babylonienne et sagesse israelite," *Sciences Ecclésiastiques* 14 (1962): 309.

25. Rylaarsdam, *Revelation in Jewish Wisdom Literature,* p. 667.

26. Waltke, "The Book of Proverbs and Ancient Wisdom Literature," pp. 226-38.

27. Oliver S. Rankin, *Israel's Wisdom Literature* (Edinburgh: T. & T. Clark, 1936), p. 69.

28. Priest, "Where Is Wisdom to Be Placed?" p. 278.

29. Priest, "Where Is Wisdom to Be Placed?" p. 278.

and prove you a liar" (30:5-6). Without this revelation man casts off restraint and perishes (29:18).[30]

But how was this revelation mediated to the sages? God spoke audibly to Israel at Sinai out of the fire (Deut. 4:33), to Moses face to face (Exod. 3:2-4; 5:22-23; 34:10), to the prophets in visions (Isa. 1:1; Jeremiah 1; Ezekiel 1), and to Job out of a whirlwind (Job 38:1–42:6). But to Solomon, apart from the vision granted him at Gibeon (1 Kings 3), God did not speak audibly. Instead of having the revelation mediated to him, Solomon spoke with the authority of an anointed king, as the son of God (2 Sam. 7:14). An indirect parallel in Egypt may be instructive here. In Egypt no legal code existed, and this absence is attributed by various Egyptologists — though without consensus — to the fact that the word or command *(mdw, wd)* of the reigning king was regarded as actual law and no written law could have existed beside it.[31] So likewise in Israel, it was probably sufficient that God's courtier spoke as his anointed representative. The royal sage won truth by reflection on what he saw (Prov. 24:30-34) and what he perceived by faith (cf. 15:3). It was the glory of God to conceal the matter; it was Solomon's glory as an anointed king to find it out (25:2). Moreover, the Spirit of God rested on him (cf. 1 Sam. 16:13), the Spirit of wisdom and understanding (cf. Isa. 11:1-2; Prov. 1:23). In short, the same Spirit that inspired Moses and the prophets worked effectually in Solomon and Israel's other courtiers (1 Kings 4:29-34; 2 Tim. 3:16), and the circumcised of heart have heard his voice in those writings.

The Same Authority

Crenshaw on firm grounds censured Zimmerli for eroding the ground of wisdom's authority.[32] According to Crenshaw, the wise man's counsel carried the same authoritative weight as the prophet's word. His study of the meaning of the root *'ēṣâ* and the sociological setting in which the wise men gave their teachings verify his position. Moreover, the biblical aphoristic litera-

---

30. The mention of revelation *(ḥazâ)* and law *(torâ)* probably refers to the sayings of the wise that are otherwise attributed to Yahweh and called torah (Prov. 2:6 and 1:8 et passim).

31. John A. Wilson, *The Culture of Ancient Egypt* (Chicago: University of Chicago Press, 1956), p. 49.

32. James A. Crenshaw, "Prophetic Conflict," *Beihefte zur Zeitschrift für die alttestamentliche Wissenschaft* 125 (1976): 116-23.

ture claimed authority. If indeed "wisdom" denotes a fixed order informing the creation,[33] then, as Hermission has argued, man is not the measure of all things but is measured against the creation in which he is placed,[34] and cosmology not anthropology is more central to the book's thought structure, as Schmid contended.[35] More central to wisdom's thought than anthropology is the reckoning with a Creator who through wisdom established the cosmos (3:19-20; 8:22-31; 16:11) and upholds with power the moral order in it (10:3; 16:4; 22:12 et passim). The book calls on the faithful not to trust the order but the God who stands behind it (3:5; 16:3; 22:19).

But it took an inspired sage "to search out" this fixed order (25:2) and give it expression. By giving it expression it can almost be said that he created it. Cassirer wrote: "In a realistic sense, what happens in language is that the world is given material expression. Objects are only given form and differentiation in the word that names them."[36] He moved a step even closer to hypostatization when he reasoned: "Language's power is released when a word is actually spoken. The act of speaking the word frees the concept's potentials as it reveals the world to man. Each spoken word has unlimited and sovereign power over the scope of its thought."[37] Even as Adam joined the Creator in naming and thereby defining the animals, so the Israelite king took part with him in coining proverbs revealing his truth. Moreover, it is important to note the arresting comment added to Genesis 2:19: "And whatever the man called each living creature, that was its name." In a similar way Israel's king, needing no specially mediated audible revelation, coined the rules of moral and social behavior with authority. Thus the wise man both discovered, created, and maintained order in the personal and social spheres of life. Obviously their words, by transforming ontological reality into epistemological categories, carried inherent weight.

This idea of wisdom as a revealed fixed order does not correspond badly with the sages' references to their teachings as "law" *(torâ)* and "commandments" *(mṣwt)* and their demand that the hearer give them his ear. Zimmerli called attention to this terminology so similar to the Mosaic law.

---

33. Waltke, "The Book of Proverbs and Ancient Wisdom Literature," pp. 226-38.

34. H. J. Hermission, *Studien zur israelitischen Spruchweisheit*, WMANT 28 (1968).

35. H. H. Schmid, "Wesen und Geschichte der Weisheit," *Beihefte zur Zeitschrift für die alttestamentliche Wissenschaft* 101 (1966).

36. E. Cassirer, *Language and Myth*, trans. Susanne K. Langer (New York: Harper & Brothers, 1946), pp. 80-81.

37. E. Cassirer, *The Philosophy of Symbolic Forms*, trans. Ralph Manheim (New Haven: Yale University Press, 1953-1957), pp. 107-8.

Not only is the entirety of wisdom admonition repeatedly referred to as torah (1:8; 3:1; 13:14; 28:4, 7 et passim) — with the same designation as the Law which is authoritative admonition *kat 'exochēn* — the correspondence also appears in the designation of individual admonitions of the wise, when they often occur as commands *mṣwt* (2:1; 3:1; 4:4; 6:23 et passim).[38]

Fichtner also recognized that this wisdom spoke with a word no less authoritative than that of Law.[39]

Moreover, like Moses and the prophets the sages demanded to be heard. Zimmerli noted this fact along with other additional features that lead to the conclusion that the wisdom teacher spoke with authority.

> Again and again, it is stressed that everything depends on "hearing" — the high value of the *'zn šm't* ("ears that hear") is underscored a number of times (15:31; 25:12) since *'zn* ("ear") above all is the principal entrance for wisdom. Wisdom's precepts can be simply termed *leqaḥ* (that which is to be accepted 1:5; 4:2; 9:9; 16:21, 23 . . .); obedience to the wise commandment can be designated *lqḥ* "learning/doctrine" (cf. *lqḥ mṣwt* ["authoritative doctrine"] 10:8 etc.). Moreover, when the picture of education in the Egyptian scribal schools is considered and certain aphorisms of Proverbs concerning the education of the young man to wisdom are compared with it (13:24; 22:15; 29:15; 23:13f.; and to the last see Aḥikar 81f.), then they seem to round out the picture of how wisdom-precept is authoritative-command in the strictest sense.[40]

It is amazing in the light of this clear evidence that Zimmerli later reversed himself in the same article.

In short, the attempt to construct a model contrasting a prophetic authoritative word from God against tentative, human counsel is false. The wise man spoke with the same authority as the prophet.

---

38. Zimmerli, "Concerning the Structure of Old Testament Wisdom," p. 179.

39. J. Fichtner, "Die altorientalische Weisheit in ihrer israelitisch jüdischen Ausprägung," *Beihefte zur Zeitschrift für die alttestamentliche Wissenschaft* 62 (1933): 82ff.

40. Zimmerli, "Concerning the Structure of Old Testament Wisdom," p. 179.

The Same Anthropology

Moses complained about the sinful depravity of the elect and privileged nation: "For I know how rebellious and stiff-necked you are. If you have been rebellious against the LORD while I am still alive and with you, how much more will you rebel after I die?" (Deut. 31:27). Jeremiah castigated man with his famous words: "The heart is deceitful above all things and beyond cure. Who can understand it?" (Jer. 17:9). The sage observed that man was both foolish and wayward: "Folly is bound up in the heart of a child, but the rod of discipline will drive it far from him" (Prov. 22:15). "Stop listening to instruction, my son, and you will stray from the words of knowledge" (Prov. 19:27). Solomon's life tragically bore out his own proverb.

The Same Epistemology

When this writer spoke of the wise men as searching out the fixed order, and even in a sense creating it, he did not mean to imply that they thought with the Greek philosophers that this order could be known as some objective reality apart from man. Prophet and sage concur that their doctrines could not be "understood" simply by the hearing of the ear; they had to be understood in the heart. Thus, for example, Moses commented on his own generation: "But to this day the LORD has not given you a mind that understands or eyes that see or ears that hear" (Deut. 29:4). Thus, though not without ambiguity, he exhorted the people, "Circumcise your hearts, therefore, and do not be stiff-necked any longer" (10:16). The Lord judged Isaiah's generation by hardening their hearts beyond understanding: "He said, 'Go and tell this people: "Be ever hearing, but never understanding; be ever seeing, but never perceiving." Make the heart of this people calloused; make their ears dull and close their eyes. Otherwise they might see with their eyes, hear with their ears, understand with their hearts, and turn and be healed'" (Isa. 6:9-10).

The sages shared the same skepticism about man's ability to understand without "wisdom" already resident in the heart: "The way of a fool seems right to him, but a wise man listens to advice" (Prov. 12:15). "There is a way that seems right to a man, but in the end it leads to death" (14:12).

Thus only the weak, the humble, the teachable — in contrast to the arrogant, the proud, and mockers — are capable of "understanding." "A fool finds no pleasure in understanding, but delights in airing his own opinions"

(18:2). The mocker "does not listen to rebuke" (13:1b) and "resents correction; he will not consult the wise" (15:12).

By contrast, "with humility comes wisdom" (11:2). Thus the sages' epistemology resolves itself to trust in the Lord and to love him. "Trust in the LORD with all your heart and lean not on your own understanding; in all your ways acknowledge him, and he will make your paths straight. Do not be wise in your own eyes; fear the LORD and shun evil" (3:5-7). "Whoever loves discipline loves knowledge, but he who hates correction is stupid" (12:1).

Probably it was for this reason that the wise referred to their proverbs as enigmas, riddles, and dark sayings (1:6). Knowledge, for them, was not a matter of intellectual control, but openness of heart. Like the parables of Jesus, they obfuscate reality to the unbelieving heart but reveal it to the faithful.

Pascal's debunking of Descartes's human pretensions to autonomy in epistemology and Pascal's demand for a submissive spirit in order to comprehend divine mysteries harmonize with the demands of the prophets and the sages. Pascal wrote, "What amazes me most is to see that everyone is not amazed at his own weakness. Man is quite capable of the most extravagant opinions, since he is capable of believing that he is not naturally and inevitably weak, but is, on the contrary, naturally wise."[41]

According to saint, prophet, and sage, one must first make himself open and available to understand the divine Word.

The Same Spiritual Demand

Both prophet and sage, therefore, concentrated their address to the human heart. Its spiritual condition in the final analysis determined the success or failure of their teaching. Moses knew that the Lord had sealed the fate of Pharaoh and Sihon when he had made their hearts obstinate. The sage admonished, "Above all else, guard your heart, for it is the wellspring of life" (Prov. 4:23). Deuteronomy mentions the heart forty-five times; Proverbs refers to it fifty-three times.

Moreover, both prophet and sage made a similar claim on the heart. Moses said, "And now, O Israel, what does the LORD your God ask of you but to fear the LORD your God, to walk in all his ways, to love him, to serve the LORD your God with all your heart and with all your soul" (Deut. 10:12). This

---

41. Blaise Pascal, *Pensées* 374.

command "to fear God" is found many times in Deuteronomy (4:10; 5:29; 6:2, 13, 24; 8:6; 10:12, 20; 13:5[4]; 14:23; 17:19; 28:58; 31:12-13) and in the prophetic literature based on it. Indeed, the prophet historian evaluates Israel's king on the basis of his heart (cf. 1 Kings 11:4). It is well known that the motto of Proverbs is in 1:7: "The fear of the LORD is the beginning of knowledge."

Becker concluded from his study of this term in the Law that the fear of the Lord denotes "reverence of Yahweh and the special aspect of loyalty to Him as the covenant God."[42] Without question it denotes along with other terms a commitment to Yahweh and his covenant, and thus it is correctly designated a "covenant formula."[43] Stähli noted that it is used in conjunction with the commands to "love" (Deut. 10:12), "hold fast" (10:20), "walk in His ways" (8:6), "follow after" (13:5[4]), and "serve" (6:13).[44] In contrast to love, which denotes a spontaneous commitment out of appreciation, fear denotes a commitment out of awe and respect. This fear is not the numinous dread of a moment, but a lifetime stance of submission in reverent awe. Such an attitude is an essential spiritual condition of the heart if a human being hopes to have a personal relationship with a God whose name and deeds are "terrible" (Exod. 34:10; Deut. 4:34; 28:58; Mal. 1:14; 3:23[4:5]) and who is "great" and "holy" (2 Sam. 7:22; 1 Chron. 16:25; Ps. 99:3; 145:6).

In Proverbs the expression occurs in parallel with humility before God (15:33; 22:4) and unfailing love and fidelity to him (16:6) in contrast to pride and arrogance (8:13; 18:12) and rebellion (1:7). This appropriate submissive attitude of commitment issues in life (10:23; 19:23), security (14:26), and spiritual enrichment (15:16), and enables one to avoid calamity (16:6; 24:21).

Since the religious issue resolves itself to the heart, both prophet and sage divide all men into only two categories: the righteous/wise and the wicked/foolish. Until one understands that the heart is central to man's spiritual condition, the biblical division into rascals and saints will appear overly simplistic. Rengstorf cogently observed: "But the basis of the distinction in both the prophetic and wisdom circles is not to be found in the immoral or ungodly mode of life, but much deeper. . . . The basis of the distinction is the fundamentally different religious attitudes."[45] The pious

---

42. J. Becker, *Gottesfurcht im Alten Testament* (1965), p. 85, cited by H. P. Stähli, *Theologisches Handworterbuch zum Alten Testament* (Munich: Chr. Kaiser Verlag, 1971), I:774.

43. Cf. K. Baltzer, *Das Bundesformular* (Neukirchen-Vluyn: Neukirchener Verlag, 1964), pp. 22-23, 46-47.

44. Stähli, *Theologisches Handworterbuch*, p. 774.

45. Karl Heinrich Rengstorf, "ἁμαρτωλός," in *Theological Dictionary of the New Testament*, I:321.

are committed in their hearts to God; the ungodly are not. As the Lord Jesus Christ expressed it, "He who is not with me is against me" (Matt. 12:30).

Sages, prophets, and saints know that there is but one religious command: "Serve the LORD" (Josh. 24:24).

The Same Ethical Demands

The phrase "the fear of the Lord" presents a paradox in both the prophetic and the sapiential literature: It is at one and the same time both the source and the substance, the cause and the effect. On the one hand, the term denotes the spiritual prerequisite for all ethical behavior, namely, a commitment to God out of awesome reverence for him. On the other hand, it denotes the objective content of that which he demands through his spokesman whether it be the priest with the law, or the prophet with the word, or the wise man with his counsel (cf. Jer. 18:18). Thus the sage promised, "My son, if you accept my words . . . then you will understand the fear of the LORD and find the knowledge of God" (Prov. 2:1-5). Stähli noted that in Proverbs "the fear of the Lord" is a close parallel to terms for wisdom and can almost be used as a synonym for knowledge (1:29; 2:5; cf. Isa. 11:2; 33:6; Job 28:28).[46] In Deuteronomy and the prophetic literature the fear of the Lord is both taught and learned (Deut. 31:12; 2 Kings 17:7, 25, 28, 32-39, 41).

The content of the fear of the Lord overlaps in the prophetic and aphoristic literature. This point is conceded even by Fichtner.

> Without question, there are various points at which the views of the pre-exilic prophets seem to be directly compatible with those of the wise men of the Book of Proverbs. Further areas of ethical admonition were cultivated by both groups. I need only mention here their active championship of righteousness and charity toward the *personae miserabiles* (Amos 5:7; Hos. 5:11; Isa. 1:21ff.; Mic. 2:2; Jer. 22:17 *et passim*, and Prov. 3:27; 14:21, 31; 22:9; 28:27; 29:14 etc.).[47]

In addition, Fichtner noted that both circles condemned the use of false weights and measures, partisanship and corruption, disrespect for elders,

---

46. Stähli, *Theologisches Handworterbuch,* p. 776.
47. Fichtner, "Die altorientalische Weisheit," p. 430.

etc. Weinfeld cataloged parallels regarding ethical behavior in Proverbs and Deuteronomy.[48]

But these commonalities do not prove that the sages were drinking from an Israelite heritage. Weinfeld tried to trace the flow of thought from non-Israelite to Israelite wisdom and from there to Deuteronomy. More particularly, Fensham notes, "the protection of widow, orphan and the poor was the common policy of the ancient Near East."[49] But Fensham also cogently observed that in Mesopotamia the same ethical values find expression in the legal and the wisdom literature and that both forms of texts present their similar ethical demands in the religious context in which Shamash (the sungod) upholds the course of justice. For example, in the prologue to the Code of Hammurabi (1728-1686 BC) the statement is made that "the strong are not allowed to oppress the weak, so that the sun (Utu-Shamash, god of justice) may rise over the people."[50] The same statement occurs in the epilogue. Moreover, Shamash is called on to maintain justice in the land. Thus, as in the Bible, religion and social ethics are closely connected.

Fensham then turns his attention to the Babylonian wisdom literature and finds the same religio-ethical context: "The idea that the poor man is protected by Shamash and that this is expected as a way of life amongst his people, occurs frequently in Babylonian wisdom literature."[51] Thus Old Babylonian law and wisdom share the same religio-ethical system. Moreover, it is arresting to observe that though the ancient Mesopotamian lawgiver and sage share the same spiritual convictions, they do not quote each other.

From this Mesopotamian analogy it seems plausible to suppose against Weinfeld that the Israelite sage derived his ethical convictions not by borrowing from his pagan neighbors but rather by his common belief with the other authors of the Old Testament that Yahweh as the Judge of all men will reward the righteous and punish transgressors. Murphy remarked, "In the concrete, the sage was a Yahwist, and the worshiper of Yahweh found that the wisdom of the sages fitted in with his tradition."[52]

In any case, the book of Proverbs is in the biblical canon not because it

---

48. Weinfeld, "The Wisdom Substrata in Deuteronomy and the Deuteronomic Literature," pp. 244-74.

49. F. Charles Fensham, "Widow, Orphan, and the Poor in Ancient Near Eastern Legal and Wisdom Literature," *Journal of Near Eastern Studies* 21 (1962): 129-39.

50. Fensham, "Widow, Orphan, and the Poor," p. 130.

51. Fensham, "Widow, Orphan, and the Poor," p. 131.

52. Roland E. Murphy, "The Kerygma of the Book of Proverbs," *Interpretation* 20 (1966): 12.

contains ethical values similar to those demanded by pagan sages but because Yahweh encounters the faithful in it with his commandments to fear him and to love human beings made in his image.

The Same Hope

Murphy tersely concluded, "The kerygma of wisdom can be summed up in one word: *life*."[53] He proceeded by stating that "life and death . . . are central in the doctrine of the Old Testament sages."[54] Kaiser underscores the connection between the fear of the Lord and life (10:27; 14:27; 19:23; 22:4).[55]

Life may refer to sheer existence in many days (3:16; 28:16), or the quality of realizing the highest possible good in this existence,[56] or even existence beyond the shadow of death (12:28).[57]

The Law and the prophets set forth this same hope (Deut. 8:1; Isa. 55:1-3; Ezek. 33:19; cf. John 17:3). Moreover, in Proverbs as in the rest of Scripture this hope does not function as a mere "profit motive" within a eudaemonistic philosophy of life. Instead it denotes the enjoyment of life's potentials in the will of God, and thus all material gain possesses sacramental value as a benefit given from him.

The Same Faith

In Romans 12:19-20 the Apostle Paul strings together Deuteronomy 32:35 and Proverbs 25:21-22 to support his exhortation to the saints at Rome that they show kindness to their persecutors rather than seeking revenge. This Pharasaic practice was dubbed by Longenecker as "pearl stringing": "bringing to bear on one point of an argument passages from various parts of the Bible in support of the argument and to demonstrate the unity of Scripture."[58]

---

53. Murphy, "The Kerygma of the Book of Proverbs," p. 9.

54. Murphy, "The Kerygma of the Book of Proverbs," p. 10.

55. Kaiser, *Toward an Old Testament Theology*, p. 171.

56. "It refers to all the assets — emotional, physical, psychological, social, spiritual — which permit joy and security and wholeness" (Walter Brueggemann, *In Man We Trust* [Atlanta: John Knox Press, 1972], p. 15).

57. Waltke, "The Book of Proverbs and Ancient Wisdom Literature," pp. 226-38.

58. Richard N. Longenecker, *Biblical Exegesis in the Apostolic Period* (Grand Rapids: Eerdmans, 1975), p. 115.

Without question both Proverbs and Deuteronomy teach the common norm that a man not avenge himself.[59]

But it may escape the casual reader's attention that this ethical behavior is based on the common faith verbalized in Proverbs 20:22 that Yahweh will avenge wrong. Commenting on Proverbs 20:22 and 24:29 von Rad observed, "Behind the very serious exhortation not to requite evil done to one . . . , not to take matters into one's hand when found with evil men . . . there does not lie . . . a lofty ethical principle, but something else, namely faith in the order controlled by Yahweh."[60] Robinson put this common faith behind the aphoristic sayings in this way: "There is almost always present a confidence that Yahweh is active in man's life."[61]

Out of this common belief to trust God rather than to seek one's personal revenge, both prophet and sage call the righteous to prayer (Deut. 4:32; Isa. 12:4; Prov. 15:8; 15:29). Both prophet and sage call on their hearers to trust the living, righteous, powerful Creator.

Conclusion

Several points may be noted in concluding this study.

1. The commonality observed between the prophet and the sage is not intended to minimize the obvious differences in their lifestyles, fate, purpose, literary forms, and manner of receiving and delivering revelation. One cannot imagine the sages who speak in the book of Proverbs going about in a loincloth like Isaiah or eating dung-baked bread like Ezekiel or thundering out invectives like the shepherd of Tekoa. The wise men did not arraign the nation before the Lord's bar of justice and accuse them of breaking his covenant. But in spite of these differences, it is maintained that they shared the same theology.

2. This notion of unity with diversity fits well with the belief that the Creator is also the Lord of the canon. Kaiser stated this point well: "To introduce the topic of the integration of truth, fact, and understanding is to appeal

---

59. The reference to "burning coals of fire on the head" should be interpreted on the basis of an Egyptian expiation ritual, according to which a guilty person, as a sign of his amendment of life, carried a basin of glowing coals on his head (S. Morenz, *Theologische Literaturzeitung* 78 [1953]: 187-92).

60. Gerhard von Rad, *Wisdom in Israel* (New York: Abingdon, 1972), p. 95.

61. H. W. Robinson, *Inspiration and Revelation in the Old Testament* (London: Oxford University Press, 1946), p. 252.

to the unity of truth made possible by the one Who created a UNI-verse. Thus the doctrinal base for any norms of truth and character [is] grounded ultimately in a doctrine of Creation and the person of the Creator."[62]

3. This article has not attempted to inquire into the common source from which both the classical prophets and the royal sages drank, but it seems plausible to suggest that it originated with Moses and even more particularly in the covenant he mediated between Yahweh and Israel "in the desert east of the Jordan" (Deut. 1:1). As noted, Weinfeld reversed the field by arguing for the priority of the wisdom literature and the dependence of Deuteronomy on it. The priority of one over the other cannot be proved as yet by empirical data, but no hard evidence exists to turn upside down the prima facie witness of the Bible that the addresses attributed to Moses preceded the book of Proverbs. This primary witness finds support in the assumption that both Yahweh and his cultus were well known by the sages. Moreover, the borrowing of individual non-Israelite sayings by wise men does not support the notion that these pagan sources shaped the Israelite sage's philosophy. Those he borrowed were probably consonant with his faith in Yahweh, which he already possessed.

If recent scholarship is correct in its view — and there is no reason to think otherwise — that the prophets were not innovators but reformers harking back to Israel's covenantal heritage, then why should one not suppose the same for their spiritual peers, the sages? The close affinity between Proverbs and Deuteronomy finds a plausible explanation in the Law's injunction that the king "write for himself on a scroll a copy of this law" (Deut. 17:18). Kaiser commented that the similarities noted by Weinfeld "do illustrate the point that wisdom was not cut off conceptually or theologically from materials which we have judged to be earlier than sapiential times."[63]

4. Old Testament theologians must find another center than covenant, salvation, history, cultus, or even promise — if this be understood in terms of promises to the patriarchs and Israel — to accommodate wisdom. As Toombs has commented, "As long as Old Testament theology is represented exclusively in terms of history, institutions and cultus of the Hebrew people, it will exclude the wisdom literature by definition."[64] Kaiser's suggestion of looking to "the fear of the Lord" as an expression common to both is helpful,

---

62. Kaiser, *Toward an Old Testament Theology*, p. 175.

63. Kaiser, *Toward an Old Testament Theology*, p. 166.

64. Lawrence E. Toombs, "Old Testament Theology and the Wisdom Literature," *JBR* 23 (1955): 195.

but it is more apropos to define it in terms of its own use, that is, not as a reference to promise but to a commitment to serve Yahweh as Lord.

5. Although prophet and wise man occasionally express identical ethical norms, such as not removing a neighbor's landmarks (Deut. 19:14; Prov. 22:28) and showing concern for the disenfranchised, for the most part their areas of ethical concern remain distinct. Kidner introduced his superb commentary by calling attention to these differences: "There are details of character small enough to escape the mesh of the law and the broadsides of the prophets, and yet decisive in personal dealings. Proverbs moves in this realm, asking what a person is like to live with, or employ; how he manages his affairs, his time and himself."[65]

For wisdom, man needs both the priest with his *torâ*, the prophet with his *dābār*, and the sage with his *'ēṣâ* (cf. Jer. 18:18). But above all he needs to enter into a personal relationship with him of whom Isaiah predicted, "The Spirit of the Lord will rest on him — the Spirit of wisdom and of understanding, the Spirit of counsel and of power, the Spirit of knowledge and of the fear of the LORD" (11:2).

---

65. Derek Kidner, *Proverbs* (Downers Grove, IL: InterVarsity, 1964), p. 5.

A Canonical Process Approach to the Psalms

Dr. Charles Lee Feinberg is one of our Lord's rare and precious gifts to his church. He uniquely brings to the proclamation of Jesus as Messiah those strengths of his commitment to the Christian faith, his many spiritual gifts, his Jewish heritage, and his studies with W. F. Albright. As I thought about offering a small token of my affection and appreciation for Dr. Feinberg, who preceded me in the teaching of Semitic languages and Old Testament exegesis at Dallas Theological Seminary, it seemed fitting that it pertain to the proclamation of Jesus as Messiah and to the exegesis of the Old Testament.

Throughout the history of the church, Christians have found meaning and significance in the Old Testament in the conviction that the Old Testament foretold an age of salvation to come, and that this age had come with the advent of Jesus of Nazareth. That conviction that the Old Testament promised an age of salvation, including a regenerated people under a restored king of the Davidic line, is based solidly on the teaching of the New Testament. For example, Peter said in his temple sermon: "Indeed, all the prophets from Samuel on, as many as have spoken, have foretold these days" (Acts 3:24; see also 1 Pet. 1:10-11).

The writers of the New Testament saw Jesus as the fulfillment of prophecies not only in the prophetic literature *sensu stricto,* but also in specific statements in the book of Psalms that they treated as though they belonged to the prophetic literary genre. The early church, for example, re-

---

Previously published in *Tradition and Testament: Essays in Honor of Charles Lee Feinberg* (Chicago: Moody Press, 1953), pp. 3-18.

garded the sufferings of Christ at the hands of Herod and Pontius Pilate as the fulfillment of Psalm 2:1-2 in precisely the same way as they saw his death on the cross as the fulfillment of Isaiah 53. After rehearsing the psalm,

> Why do the nations rage
>   and the peoples plot in vain?
> The kings of the earth take their stand
>   and the rulers gather together
>   against the Lord and against his Anointed One,

they concluded: "Indeed Herod and Pontius Pilate met together with the Gentiles and the people of Israel in this city to conspire against your holy servant Jesus, whom you anointed. They did what your power and will had decided beforehand should happen" (Acts 4:27-28). At Pentecost, Peter regarded Psalms 16 and 110 to be just as prophetic as Joel 2 and used all three texts indiscriminately to prove that God predicted Jesus' death, resurrection, ascension, and the pouring out of his Spirit.

But since the apostolic era, the church has not agreed about the extent and the nature of the psalms that speak of Jesus Christ. Those who employ the allegorical method of imposing Christian doctrine upon the psalms without considering their meaning and significance to the audiences for whom they were originally composed have tended to see Jesus in almost every verse of every psalm. Augustine, who dominated all subsequent interpretations of the Psalter in the Western church, was never surpassed in seeing Christ everywhere. According to Augustine, our method of interpretation should be "Him first, Him last, Him midst and without end."[1] Thus, for example, he says that the blessed man of Psalm 1 "is to be understood of our Lord Jesus Christ."[2] Adhering to the same approach, Bonaventure commented on Psalm 3:5,

> I laid me down and slept
>   and rose again:
>   for the LORD sustained me,

---

1. J. M. Neale and R. F. Littledale, *A Commentary on the Psalms: From Primitive and Mediaeval Writers* (London: John Masters, 1884), p. 77.

2. Saint Augustine, *Expositions on the Book of Psalms*, A Select Library of the Nicene and Post-Nicene Fathers of the Christian Church, ed. Philip Schaff, 8 vols. (New York: Christian Literature Co., 1888), 8:1.

"Our blessed LORD is speaking. He laid him down in the sepulchre. He slept His sleep of three days; He rose up again on the third day from the dead."[3]

Those scholars, on the other hand, who reject the unrestrained Alexandrian method of interpretation and who opt instead for the Antiochian principle that every passage has only one literal, historical meaning, have tended to minimize the messianic element in the psalm. Those employing this approach, which is the most widely accredited method among Protestants, can be classified further into three broad categories: the precritical or noncritical expositors, the literary-historical critics who deny any real predictions, and the literary-historical critics who see the psalms cited in the New Testament with reference to Jesus as containing both direct prophecies and indirect prefigurements of Christ.

The precritical or noncritical expositors — represented by such writers as E. W. Hengstenberg,[4] A. C. Gaebelein,[5] David Baron,[6] David Cooper,[7] and the late J. B. Payne[8] — tend to limit the number of messianic psalms to the approximately fifteen psalms cited in the New Testament with respect to Jesus Christ, and they regard them as direct prophecies of Christ. J. B. Payne divided these psalms into two groups: those that predict the messiah in his glory (Psalms 2, 8, 45, 72, 89, 110) and those that foretell his passions (Psalms 16, 22, 40, 41, 69, 109).

But most scholars today disdain an approach that ignores a psalm's historical context and meaning. Noncritical scholars by their "prooftexting" actually discredit the claims of Jesus in the eyes of literary and historical critics.

The literary and historical critics who deny there is any real prediction in the Psalter explain the messianic element in the psalms, which they limit to statements about an ideal, future son of David, as reflections of the natural and nationalistic aspirations of the late postexilic Jewish community who hoped for the return of the Davidic political conditions. Wellhausen wrote: "The theocratic or messianic hope was the hope that the conditions of Da-

3. Neale and Littledale, *A Commentary on the Psalms*, p. 107.

4. E. W. Hengstenberg, *Christology of the Old Testament* (Grand Rapids: Kregel, 1828, 1970).

5. Arno C. Gaebelein, *The Jewish Question* (New York: Our Hope, 1912).

6. David Baron, *Types, Psalms and Prophecies* (New York: American Edition of Missions to Jews, 1948, 1907).

7. David Cooper, *Messiah: His First Coming Scheduled* (Los Angeles: Biblical Research Society, 1939).

8. J. B. Payne, "Psalms," in *Zondervan's Pictorial Encyclopedia of the Bible*, ed. Merrill C. Tenney, vol. 4 (Grand Rapids: Zondervan, 1975), pp. 940-43.

vid's times might return." Moreover, for him prophecies are "not predictions . . . but announcements of aims."[9] Most recently R. E. Clements continued to show Wellhausen's influence when he wrote: "The main essential of the 'messianic' hope was . . . derived from the expectation of the restoration of the Davidic family to the kingship of a renewed Israel after the Babylonian exile."[10] He then added: "We find that not one of the texts which the New Testament appeals to in support of such a hope can, from a strictly historical-critical point of view, be held originally to have been intended in the way in which it was later taken. . . . Yet, in spite of this certainty about their original meaning, it is precisely these texts which have formed the seedbed of the messianic hope."[11]

Whereas the noncritical approach tends to discredit the messianic claims of Christ by its neglect of history, this approach discredits the New Testament by untying, or at least loosening, the bond connecting the New Testament with the original meaning of the Old Testament.

The literary-historical critics who see the messianic psalms pertaining to the sufferings and the glories of the Christ as containing real predictions and indirect prefigurements of Jesus, reject both the Montanistic theory of inspiration, which represented the biblical writers as passive instruments of the divine Spirit, and the attack upon the credibility of the New Testament witness. These men insist on the literal, historical sense as the only proper sense, but they recognize that the psalms contain real predictions in that they present an ideal that was only partially real in ancient Israel, but which became actual in the life of Christ. C. A. Briggs put it this way: "The psalms embraced the vision of a reality beyond the impression of the senses, a vision which guided Israel to an ever deeper understanding of the reality."[12] H. H. Rowley found the vision of a king whose kingdom would extend to "the ends of the earth" (Ps. 2:8), whose "divine throne [is] for ever and ever" (Ps. 45:6 [7]), and who would "live while the sun endures, and as long as the moon, throughout all generations" (Ps. 72:5) went beyond pious optimism or flattering hyperbole. He wrote, "While they may have been royal psalms, used in the royal rites of the Temple, they were also 'messianic.' They held before

---

9. Julius Wellhausen, *Prolegomena to the History of Israel* (Edinburgh: A. & C. Black, 1885), p. 415. See also G. R. Berry, "Messianic Predictions," *JBL* (1926): 232-38.

10. Ronald E. Clements, *Old Testament Theology: A Fresh Approach* (London: Marshall/Morgan and Scott, 1978), p. 150.

11. Clements, *Old Testament Theology*, p. 150.

12. Charles Augustus Briggs, *Messianic Prophecy* (New York: Scribner's, 1886), p. 63.

the king the ideal king both as his inspiration and guide for the present, and as the hope of the future."[13]

Franz Delitzsch,[14] followed closely by Kirkpatrick,[15] analyzed the messianic psalms into five classes: (1) typical, that is, psalms that refer primarily to the circumstances of the time but which God also intended to prefigure some feature in the life of Christ (see Psalms 34; 69); (2) typico-prophetic psalms, in which not only the sufferings of the psalmist were typical of Christ's sufferings, but the records of them were so molded by the Spirit of God as to predict the sufferings of Christ even in circumstantial details (see Psalms 22; 40); (3) Jehovic psalms, that is, those that prepared men's minds for God's incarnation in this world and his victory over evil (Psalms 18; 50; 58; 93; 96-98); (4) indirectly messianic psalms, those that pertained to David's seed and thus indirectly to Jesus Christ as the son of David (see Psalms 45; 72); and (5) purely predictive (Psalm 110). Concerning this last reference Delitzsch wrote: "Among all the Davidic psalms there is only a single one viz. Ps cx, in which David . . . looks forth into the future of his seed and has the Messiah definitely before his mind."[16]

But while this approach maintains a balance between history and prophecy, it fails to give a consistent and comprehensive method for identifying the messianic element in the psalms. For the most part these expositors limit the typical element in the psalms to those cited in the New Testament, because apparently they are afraid of allowing the typical method of interpretation to degenerate into the unrestrained allegorical method. But this method cannot adequately explain why, for example, the New Testament (John 2:17) cites Psalm 69:9, "zeal for your house consumes me," as a reference to Christ, but not Psalm 3:1, "How many are my foes." In all fairness, it seems as though the writers of the New Testament are not attempting to identify and limit the psalms that prefigure Christ but rather are assuming that the Psalter as a whole has Jesus Christ in view and that this should be the normative way of interpreting the psalms.

I conclude, therefore, that both the nonhistorical and undisciplined allegorical method of interpreting the psalms and the Antiochian principle of allowing but one historical meaning that may carry with it typical signifi-

13. Harold Henry Rowley, *The Faith of Israel* (Philadelphia: Westminster, 1957), p. 192.

14. Franz Delitzsch, *Biblical Commentary on the Psalms,* trans. Francis Bolton (Grand Rapids: Eerdmans, 1952), pp. 68-71.

15. A. F. Kirkpatrick, *The Book of Psalms* (Cambridge: Cambridge University Press, 1916), pp. lxxvi-lxxxv.

16. Delitzsch, *Biblical Commentary on the Psalms,* p. 66.

cance are inadequate hermeneutical principles for the interpretation of the psalms. In place of these methods, therefore, I would like to argue for a canonical process approach in interpreting the psalms, an approach that does justice both to the historical significance(s) of the psalms and to their messianic significance. Indeed, I shall argue that from a literary and historical point of view, we should understand that the human subject of the psalms — whether it be the blessed man of Psalm 1, the one proclaiming himself the son of God in Psalm 2, the suffering petitioner in Psalms 3–7, the son of man in Psalm 8 — is Jesus Christ.

By the canonical process approach I mean the recognition that the text's intention became deeper and clearer as the parameters of the canon were expanded. Just as redemption itself has a progressive history, so also older texts in the canon underwent a correlative progressive perception of meaning as they became part of a growing canonical literature.

My indebtedness to Childs's[17] canonical approach is obvious. But I distinguish the approach advocated here from his, especially as he represents it in *Introduction to the Old Testament as Scripture* (1979), in at least these three ways:

1. Childs does not clearly distinguish the stage of literary activity in the development of the text from changes that take place through scribal activity on the text. This is due to the fact that he has no clear definition of inspiration. But by the "canonical process approach" I have in mind that development of the text and canon that took place under the Spirit's inspiration in contrast to those changes that took place through scribal copying.

2. Childs reckons with tracing the development of the tradition through historical criticism, another term he does not define, though recognizing that all too often the procedure is arbitrary and as such leads to inconclusive and nugatory results. One of the frequent presuppositions underlying historical criticism is the denial of supernatural activity as a cause effecting an event. Childs allows the possibility of a divorce between Israel's religious history and the canonical witness to that history. By canonical process I have no such division in mind and clearly affirm God's supernatural intervention in Israel's history.

3. Childs lays emphasis on the authority of the Jewish text achieved at about AD 100. I lay emphasis on the meaning of the Hebrew Scriptures within the context of the New Testament.

In contrast to canonical criticism — represented also in the writings of

17. Brevard S. Childs, *Biblical Theology in Crisis* (Philadelphia: Westminster, 1970).

J. Sanders[18] and R. E. Clements[19] — according to which the ancient texts were reworked in the progressive development of the canon in such a way that they may have lost their original historical significance, the canonical process approach holds that the original authorial intention was not changed in the progressive development of the canon but deepened and clarified. I agree with Childs's emphasis on the unity of the text and the value of rhetorical criticism, and with his minimizing the recovery of original literary unities apart from their canonical form, but I would emphasize that canonical texts in their earlier stages in the progressively developing canon were just as accurate, authoritative, and inspired as they are in their final literary contexts.

The canonical process approach is similar to the approach known as *sensus plenior* in that it recognizes that further revelation brought to light a text's fuller or deeper significance, but it differs from that approach in several ways.

First of all, in contrast to the normal sense of *sensus plenior* that God intended a fuller meaning in a text than that intended by the human author,[20] the canonical process approach does not divorce the human authorial intention from the divine intention. According to the canonical approach, the original poets presented their subjects in ideal forms, that is, in prayer and in praise fully acceptable to God. Progressive revelation, however, fleshed out this vision and made clearer the exact shape of the ideals always pregnant in the vision.

Second, *sensus plenior,* although insisting that the text's true historical significance was always present in the mind of God, tends toward an allegorical method of interpretation by regarding later writers as winning meanings from the text quite apart from their historical use and significance. By contrast, the canonical process approach underscores the continuity of a text's meaning throughout sacred history along with recognizing that further revelation won for the earlier text a deeper and clearer meaning.

18. James Sanders, *Torah and Canon* (Philadelphia: Fortress, 1972).

19. Clements, *Old Testament Theology,* p. 150.

20. Raymond E. Brown defined *sensus plenior* as "that additional, deeper meaning, intended by God but not clearly intended by the human author, which is seen to exist in the words of a Biblical text (or group of texts, or even a whole book) when they are studied in the light of further revelation or development in the understanding of revelation." Cited by William Sanford LaSor, "The *Sensus Plenior* and Biblical Interpretation," in *Scripture, Tradition, and Interpretation,* ed. W. W. Gasque and W. S. LaSor (Grand Rapids: Eerdmans, 1978), p. 270.

And third, the canonical process approach consciously recognizes and represents the distinct stages in that winning of the clearer and deeper significance of older texts through the discernment of the stages in the development of the canon rather than viewing the New Testament writers as "supernaturally" discovering the fuller, divine meaning of the text.

In the case of the Psalms we can identify at least four distinct advances in the meaning and significance of many specific psalms, and the exegete must keep these four stages in view in his interpretation of them. We can liken the four stages to four lookout points on a mountain. From each successively higher vantage point the vista becomes more full or complete. So also in the four successive stages of the canonical approach to these psalms the text's significance becomes more and more complete, and at the last stage the fullest meaning of the text is finally won.

The four distinct points in the progressive perception and revelation of the text occasioned by the enlarging of the canon are: (1) the meaning of the psalm to the original poet, (2) its meaning in the earlier collections of psalms associated with the first temple, (3) its meaning in the final and complete Old Testament canon associated with the second temple, and (4) its meaning in the full canon of the Bible including the New Testament with its presentation of Jesus as the Christ.

I was surprised recently in rereading Delitzsch's commentary on the Psalms to discover that he had come to a similar position almost a century ago. He wrote:

> The expositor of the Psalms can place himself on the standpoint of the poet, or the standpoint of the Old Testament church, or the standpoint of the church of the present dispensation — a primary condition of exegetical progress is the keeping of these three standpoints distinct, and, in accordance, therewith, the distinguishing between the two Testaments, and in general between different steps in the development of the revelation, and in the perception of the plan of redemption.[21]

Unfortunately, however, Delitzsch too sharply distinguished the standpoints and failed to recognize the genetic and organic connection between them in the development of the revelation. But in recognizing three distinct stages in the revelation he anticipated my own awareness of the need for identifying stages in the progress of revelation and apprehension of many psalms.

21. Delitzsch, *Biblical Commentary on the Psalms*, p. 64.

This canonical process approach to the interpretation of the Psalms rests on at least four convictions.[22]

First, it assumes that the people of God throughout history are united by a common knowledge and faith (certainty in the knowledge). Although the community's knowledge is expanded during the time that the canon is taking shape, the former knowledge and faith is not changing. To preserve the "givenness" of its faith, Israel was instructed to remember her heritage, both by recital and ritual at the Passover and Firstfruits festivals in the spring and at the Tabernacles festival in the fall (Exod. 12:26-27; 23:14-17; Deut. 16:1-17; 26:1-11; 31:10-13). Moreover, the people of God preserved other tokens of their history by preserving relics such as an omer of manna (Exod. 16:32) and by erecting memorials such as the stones at Gilgal (Josh. 4:20-24). From the call of Abraham to the close of the Old Testament era, each succeeding generation passed on its common faith by circumcising its male infants. In short, each succeeding generation of the believing community was shaped by its unchanging past history, and the knowledge added to it was consistent with that heritage. This is one reason we can confidently say that the progressive revelation by clearer perceptions of earlier texts was an organic and genetic unity.

Second, this approach accepts the biblical witness that God is the ultimate author of the progressively developing canon. He inspired elect individuals to add to that revelation already received through their own unique experiences with God in the progress of sacred history. Because of that common, divine inspiration we have further reason for affirming the continuity in the progressive revelation and grasping of the canonical literature. Moreover, because God is the author of the whole Bible, any piece of literature within it must be studied in the light of its whole literary context.

Third, this approach rests on the conviction that as the canon developed, lesser and earlier representations were combined to form greater units that are more meaningful than their component parts. Therefore, the full meaning of an earlier and smaller text cannot be gained without interpreting it in the light of the entire Bible.

Finally, this approach presupposes that the canon closed with the addition of the last book of the New Testament. Thus the received Scriptures constitute the final literary framework within which any given text must be interpreted.

---

22. I am partially indebted here to Adolf Schlatter, "The Theology of the New Testament and Dogmatics," in *The Nature of New Testament Theology*, ed. Robert Morgan (London: SCM, 1973), pp. 117-66.

Now that we have broadly sketched the canonical process approach with its four organically connected stages of interpretation and the four convictions that undergird it, let me now apply the approach to the Psalms.

First of all, we ask what the psalm meant to the original poet. Here it is important to note that the human subject of most of the psalms is a king. Two lines of evidence lead to this unmistakable conclusion: the external evidence of the so-called superscriptions and the internal evidence of the psalms themselves. The Masoretic text identifies King David as the author, and presumably the human subject, of seventy-three psalms; the LXX attributes eighty-four psalms to him.

There are many good reasons for accepting Gesenius-Kautzsch-Cowley's (par. 129 c) contention that the preposition l^e in the phrase $l^e dāwid$ in these headings designates authorship even as in Arabic, and that the phrase accordingly should be translated "by David." First, many Old Testament traditions from both the preexilic and postexilic periods present David as a composer and a promoter of Israel's psalmody. In the book of Samuel, for example, it is claimed for the psalm numbered as Psalm 18 in the English version that "David sang to the LORD the words of this song" (2 Sam. 22:1). The same statement is found in the heading to Psalm 18 after the phrase $l^e dāwid$. Moreover, the superscriptions of fourteen psalms specify the incident in David's life that prompted him to write the psalm. The Chronicler claims that David assigned the Levites to various musical guilds in order to beautify the Mosaic ritual with music, and associates David with Israel's psalmody (1 Chron. 16:1-43).[23] Then too, one of Israel's earliest writing prophets complained that the men of the Northern Kingdom whiled away their time strumming on their harps like David (Amos 6:5). The same persuasion regarding Davidic authorship persists in both the early Jewish tradition and the New Testament. Ben Sirach (c. 190 BC) put the tradition into poetry: "In all that he [David] did he gave thanks to the Holy One, the Most High, with ascription of glory; he sang praise with all his heart, and he loved his maker" (Eccles. 47:8-9; cf. Josephus, *Contra Apion* VII:305-6). The New Testament cites David as the author of Psalms 2, 16, 32, 69, 109, 110. In the case of the last reference, Jesus identified the Messiah as greater than David on the assumption that David wrote it (Matt. 22:43-44). There is no need to chronicle the numerous contributors to this orthodox opinion after the close of the canon.

---

23. W. F. Albright, *Archaeology and the Religion of Israel* (Baltimore: Johns Hopkins University Press, 1953), pp. 125-26, and H. Ringgren, *Theological Dictionary of the Old Testament,* 3:164, also connect David with Israel's psalmody.

Furthermore, the literature from the Ancient Near East tends more and more to support this unanimous biblical and ancient tradition by pointing to the antiquity of the Psalms. H. Gunkel demonstrated that Israel's hymns closely parallel in their forms the hymns of ancient Egypt and Mesopotamia.[24] Parallel Sumerian hymns contain musical notations as unintelligible to Sumeriologists as the musical notations in the Psalter are unintelligible to Hebraists.[25] S. Mowinckel has demonstrated from internal evidence that the psalms were sung in the cultus of the first temple,[26] and M. Dahood backed up his conclusion with linguistic evidence from the Ugaritic texts, though he marred his work by overextending the argument.[27]

In addition to the evidence of the superscriptions that King David is the author of about half the Psalter, and presumably the human subject of these psalms, there is the internal evidence of the psalms themselves. No one disputes the form-critical researches of H. Gunkel that Psalms 2, 18, 20, 21, 45, 72, 89, 101, 110, 132, 144 are royal psalms. But more significantly John Eaton[28] has followed up the work of H. Gunkel, S. Mowinckel, and others in showing that the supplicant in the so-called psalms of lament (c. fifty psalms) is also a king. Eaton wrote,

> Gunkel identifies the following. All nations attend to the psalmist's thanksgiving (Pss. 18:50; 57:10; 138:1, 4; 119:46). His deliverance has vast repercussions (22:28f.). He invokes a world-judgment to rectify his cause (7:7, 9; 56:8; 59:6[5]; 59:9[8]; cf. 43:1). He depicts himself as victorious over the nations through God's intervention (118:10-12). He confronts armies (3:7; 27:3; 55:22[21]; 56:2f.; 59:6; 72:4; 109:3; 120:7; 140:3, 8). He is like a bull raising horns in triumph (92:11[10]).
>
> To these items from Gunkel . . . we may add considerably. The speaker vows continual psalmody. He stands out before the vast festal congregation (22:26[25]; 40:10f.). His head is raised on high. . . . His glory receives special mention. . . . He is blessed with superabundant life. . . . His designations of God as his helper are often related to war-

24. Hermann Gunkel, *Einleitung in die Psalmen*, completed by Joachim Begrich (Göttingen: Vandenhoeck & Ruprecht, 1933).

25. Samuel Noah Kramer, *The Sumerians* (Chicago: University of Chicago Press, 1963), p. 207.

26. Sigmund Mowinckel, *The Psalms in Israel's Worship*, 2 vols. (New York: Abingdon, 1962).

27. Mitchell Dahood, *Psalms*, vol. 1 (New York: Doubleday, 1966).

28. John H. Eaton, *Kingship and the Psalms* (London: SCM, 1976).

fare. . . . Enemies, military and national in character, aim at him personally rather than at his country and people.[29]

We conclude, therefore, that transcending the various types of psalms
so laboriously analyzed and classified by Gunkel stands the more significant
fact that in the original composition the king is the human subject of the
psalms, whether they be lament, acknowledgment, and praise, or belong to
various other types of psalms.[30] Furthermore, we must bear in mind that the
king is presented idealistically and prays to God and praises him through the
inspiration of God's Spirit.

We now move to the second standpoint in our canonical approach to
the Psalms by asking the question: What did these psalms mean in their earlier canonical collections mentioned in such passages as 2 Chronicles 29:30
and Psalm 72:20 and used in connection with the worship of the first temple?
Here too we come to the conclusion that the living king continued to be understood as the human subject of many of these songs of praise and petition.

In the first place, the Davidic covenant, alluded to several times in the
Psalms (most especially Psalm 89), provides us with a firm basis for the conviction that the individual in view in many psalms was the son of David. According to this covenant, God promised David a son whose house and kingdom would endure forever before God and whose throne would be
established forever (2 Sam. 7:12-16). In the light of such a promise it would be
most surprising if David did not intend his many and varied types of royal
psalms to be used by and for the house of David at the house of the LORD. Almost certainly these royal psalms had a royal significance in Israel's cultus.

Second, those scholars sensitive to the extensive royal interpretation of
the psalms universally recognize that the king represented the people.

29. Eaton, *Kingship and the Psalms*, pp. 23-24.
30. Although I have argued here that *lᵉdāwid* means "by David," other proposed interpretations of the phrase do not undermine the thesis that the original composition had an
ideal king in view. Mowinckel (1:77f.; 2:98-100) argued that *dawidum* originally meant a
chief or king, especially among semi-nomadic groups. Elsewhere he argued ("Psalm Criticism Between 1900 and 1935," *VT* 5 [1955]: 18) that the phrase meant "destined for the (cultic)
use of David" (= the reigning king). D. R. Ap-Thomas ("Saul's 'Uncle,'" *VT* 11 [1961]: 244f.)
also read *dwd* as a title of office, more specifically "deputy, ruler, governor." Eissfeldt (*Old
Testament Introduction* [1965], p. 451) interpreted the phrase "in praise of David's exploits."
Dalglish (*Psalm Fifty-One* [Leiden: E. J. Brill, 1962], p. 240) interpreted the preposition *l*
more vaguely "of David." Accordingly, it could mean: "a collection belonging to David," a
psalm "for David," etc. (I am indebted here to my student Gordon Brubacher, who is writing
a thesis on the structure of Psalm 68, for bringing these references together.)

Mowinckel wrote, "All that concerned him and his cause also concerned the people; nothing which happened to him was a purely private affair."[31] It would be utterly foreign to the culture of preexilic Israel to suppose that the psalms were democratized in their interpretation. Such an interpretation would be appropriate for texts in our democratic, twentieth-century Western societies, but it would be unthinkable during the monarchy in preexilic Israel.

Third, we believe the living king was understood to be the human subject of most psalms, because in the Ancient Near Eastern literature the king was the patron of the foreign cults (exactly as is the case in Israel) and was the subject of numerous hymns. Gunkel noted that the extant prayers and laments of the Mesopotamian kings are "extraordinarily numerous."[32] Why, then, should we think that Israel would have reinterpreted the psalms at this early period in Israel's history as a reference to the common man or some individual other than the son of David? Directly reinforcing this argument is the universal recognition among students of Ancient Near Eastern languages and literatures that the king played a central role in the religions of the Ancient Near East.[33]

Fourth, it is sufficiently clear that in many psalms not ascribed to David the king is the human subject of the psalm. For example, in Psalm 44, associated with the sons of Korah, is it not most likely that the king represents the defeated army of Israel in prayer before God? Who is a more likely candidate than the king as the speaker of the line, "I do not trust in my bow, my sword does not save me" (v. 6)? It is also instructive to note that in this psalm, as in many others, there is a fluid interchange between the plural pronoun "we" and the singular pronoun "I." This psalm begins, for example, "We have heard with our ears . . . our fathers have told us what you did in their days" followed by "You are my King and my God who decrees victories for Jacob" (v. 4). This change can best be explained on the assumption that the human subject is the king representing the people. In short, although the

31. Mowinckel, *The Psalms in Israel's Worship*, 1:42-61.

32. Gunkel, *Einleitung*, p. 161. Mowinckel makes the same observation: "All this points to the fact that in Israel, as in Babylonia and Egypt, the psalms . . . were originally intended, not for all and sundry, but for the king and the great" (Mowinckel, *The Psalms in Israel's Worship*, 1:77).

33. For a critique of Mowinckel's notion of an annual enthronement festival for Yahweh, of the myth and ritual school, and of the comparative phenomenology approach of the Uppsala school, see my forthcoming article "Israel, Religion of," in *The New International Standard Bible Encyclopedia*, vol. 2.

psalm is assigned to the sons of Korah, the human subject is a king. Does not this also suggest that other psalms not assigned to David were composed for Israel's king?

Fifth, Birkeland[34] has shown that in many psalms the enemies are Israel's international political enemies and that this indicates, as Kraus[35] also argued, that the individual subject is a king.

We conclude, therefore, that most psalms had a royal significance in their cultic use at the first temple.

Now it is important to note that each living successor to David's throne was clothed in the large, magnificent, purple mantle of the messianic vision attached to the House of David. Each king became the son of God through his anointing with Yahweh's Spirit. Of these historical kings Ringgren wrote: "The king is Anointed of Yahweh, he is set up by him and proclaimed his son, he shall maintain right and righteousness in the country, he conveys to his people divine blessings, rain and fertility, he defeats in divine power all enemies, he rules over the whole world, and his throne shall stand eternally."[36] We should also add that ideally he also suffers on behalf of the kingdom of God and wrestles with God in prayer in accordance with the divine imperative: "Ask of me [my son], and I will give the nations as your inheritance" (Ps. 2:8). H. Gressmann[37] pointed out that Israel's association of the reigning monarch with messianic significance found its counterpart in Egypt where the pharaoh was also associated with messianic expectations. But none of David's successors up to the time of the Captivity had shoulders broad enough to fill this ideal mantle that was laid upon him at his coronation as Yahweh's king over Israel.

We conclude, then, that the many types of psalms composed for the first temple and used in it and constituting a part of Israel's canonical literature had a messianic meaning and significance that none of David's successors satisfied up to the time that the house of the LORD was destroyed and the House of David was deported to Babylon.

A third vantage point in interpreting the psalms is gained by now ask-

34. H. Birkeland, *The Evildoers in the Psalms* (Oslo: I. Kommisjon hos J. Dybwad, 1955), pp. 12ff.

35. H. J. Kraus, *Psalmen*, vol. 1 (Neukirchen: Neukirchener Verlag, 1961), pp. 40-53 (Excursus 2).

36. Helmer Ringgren, *The Messiah in the Old Testament* (Chicago: Allenson, 1956), p. 20.

37. Hugo Gressmann, *Der Messias* (Göttingen: Vandenhoeck & Ruprecht, 1929), pp. 1-7, 415-23.

ing the question: What did these royal psalms mean to the editors who gave the Old Testament canon its received shape and substance? Or, to put the matter another way, what do these psalms mean in the broader context of the Old Testament canon compiled during the postexilic period, probably between 400 BC and 200 BC?

Haggai makes it sufficiently clear that the exiles who returned from the Captivity continued to associate the living House of David with the messianic hope. This perception of the matter inherited from the preexilic period is apparent in the LORD's address to the House of David through Haggai:

> Tell Zerubbabel governor of Judah that I will shake the heavens and the earth. I will overturn royal thrones and shatter the power of the foreign kingdoms. I will overthrow chariots and their drivers; horses and their riders will fall, each by the sword of his brother. "On that day," declares the LORD Almighty, "I'll take you, my servant Zerubbabel son of Sheal-tiel," declares the LORD, "and I will make you like my signet ring, for I have chosen you," declares the LORD Almighty. (Hag. 2:21-23)

In sum, the two institutions — the House of David and the house of the LORD — providing Israel with its greatest sense of continuity were revived at the beginning of the postexilic era.

But Zerubbabel and apparently his descendants continued to fall short of the messianic expectation laid upon them, and by about a century later the last of the Old Testament canonical prophets, Malachi, projected the vision of Israel's golden age, when the LORD would come to his people with healing in his wings, to an age beyond his own temporal horizon and on into the eschatological future. Thus, when the Old Testament canon closed, no son of David was sitting on Yahweh's throne, and no living scion of David's line was associated with that hope. Accordingly, we may safely conclude that the royal psalms in the final shape of the Old Testament canon must have been interpreted prophetically precisely as we found them interpreted in the New Testament. This prophetic interpretation of these old texts is not a rein-terpretation of them away from their original, authorial meaning; rather, it is a more precise interpretation of them in the light of the historical realities. Aage Bentzen noted, "It must, however, be acknowledged that the difference between the 'cultic' and the 'eschatological' interpretations of the Enthrone-ment [sic; royal] Psalms is not very great."[38] If one keeps in mind the genetic

38. Aage Bentzen, *King and Messiah* (London: Lutterworth, 1955), p. 37.

and organic unity in the progressive apprehension of these psalms, the following statement by R. E. Clements might prove helpful:

> From the point of view of the messianic interpretation of certain psalms it appears most probable that the same stimulus towards a new dimension of interpretation has been felt. It is in fact possible that those editors who incorporated into the Psalter the texts of royal psalms, which must have appeared obsolete at a time when Judah had no king, do so out of a genuine hope that Israel would again need them. In this case, a dimension of hope was present in the act of retaining compositions which the contemporary political scene made inapplicable in their original sense [*sic*]. The formation of the canon, therefore, must have had its own part to play in projecting the ideas and images associated with the kingship into the future.[39]

The intertestamental literature and the New Testament make clear, however, that the royal dimension of the lament psalms became lost during this period of time, and thus Israel lost sight of a suffering Messiah. Perhaps these psalms now become democratized in the synagogues and interpreted as references to Everyman, as Mowinckel theorized.[40] But that was not their original meaning and significance, and Jesus had to correct Israel's understanding back to their original intention. In brief, the New Testament does not impose a new meaning on these old psalms but wins back for them their original and true significance. We cannot be sure how the editors who compiled the final form of the Old Testament interpreted the lament psalms. It seems plausible to me to suppose that they continued to understand them according to their original meaning. I draw that conclusion on the basis that the progressive development of the canon is a genetic and organic unity, on the recognition that later prophecies, such as Isaiah 53, made it abundantly clear that the one to be exalted by Yahweh over all the nations must suffer and die, and on the certainty that the protoevangelium was understood as a reference to the suffering and triumph of the Messiah over Satan.

Thus we conclude that at this third stage in the development of the canon, the psalms continued to have a royal and messianic significance, but they now carried a predictive meaning as well. Israel must now wait in hope for a future son of David worthy to pray and sing these psalms.

39. Clements, *Old Testament Theology*, p. 151.
40. Mowinckel, *The Psalms in Israel's Worship*, 1:78-80.

With the advent of Jesus Christ this hope was satisfied. Accordingly, within the literary context of the New Testament the psalms find their final and full meaning and perception. From this fourth and highest vantage point we win the full significance of the psalms. Jesus of Nazareth, son of David and Son of God, fulfills these psalms. Those elements in each psalm presenting the king as anything less than ideal, such as his confession of sins, are the historical eggshells from the preexilic period when the psalms were used for Israel's less-than-ideal kings.

We conclude, then, that the Psalms are ultimately the prayers of Jesus Christ, Son of God. He alone is worthy to pray, the ideal vision of a king, suffering for righteousness and emerging victorious over the hosts of evil. As the corporate head of the church, he represents the believers in these prayers. Moreover, Christians, as sons of God and as royal priests, can rightly pray these prayers along with their representative Head. Dietrich Bonhoeffer also reached the conclusion that Jesus Christ is the one praying in the Psalter. "The Psalter," he wrote, "is the prayer book of Jesus Christ in the truest sense of the word."[41]

41. Dietrich Bonhoeffer, *Life Together,* trans. John W. Doberstein (New York: Harper & Brothers, 1954), p. 46.

Does Proverbs Promise Too Much?

Turn with me to Proverbs 3 and we will look at the first ten verses:

> ¹My son, do not forget my teaching,
>   but keep my commands in your heart,
> ²for they will prolong your life many years
>   and bring you prosperity.
> ³Let love and faithfulness never leave you;
>   bind them around your neck,
>   write them on the tablet of your heart.
> ⁴Then you will win favour and a good name
>   in the sight of God and man.
> ⁵Trust in the LORD with all your heart
>   and lean not on your own understanding;
> ⁶in all your ways acknowledge him,
>   and he will make your paths straight.
> ⁷Do not be wise in your own eyes;
>   fear the LORD and shun evil.
> ⁸This will bring health to your body
>   and nourishment to your bones.
> ⁹Honor the LORD with your wealth,
>   with the firstfruits of all your crops;
> ¹⁰then your barns will be filled to overflowing,
>   and your vats will brim over with new wine.

Previously published in *Andrews University Seminary Studies* 34, no. 2 (Autumn 1996): 319-36. Copyright 1996 by Andrews University Press.

The structure here is quite different from that of Proverbs chapter 2. In chapter 2 we had the conditions in verses 1-4, followed by the consequences of knowing God and being able to discern right from wrong. In this chapter we have an alternation of command and promise, or, to put it another way, of command and consequence. In the odd verse we have the command; in the even verse we have the consequences of keeping the command, that is, the promise attached to the command.

Let me exegete these verses a little more closely. Verse 1, the first command, mentions "my son." Let me explain here that "my daughter" is not excluded. It is addressed to all the children, but since the son is expected to take the headship of the home and the wife will be submissive to her husband, it is addressed to the son in particular. Other passages in Proverbs clearly indicate that the female counterpart is included. For example, Proverbs 1:8 says, "Listen, my son, to your father's instruction and do not forsake your mother's teaching." Here both mother and father are involved together in teaching the child. In this book, before you can be a teacher you yourself must first be taught; here we have an inherited wisdom being passed on from generation to generation. There is no idea that the mother is teaching in her own authority, but she has received instruction as a daughter from her parents. So, the mother is put on a parity with the father in the teaching of the children. Again, in Proverbs 31:26, one of the characteristics of the virtuous woman is that she is a teacher in Israel in the home.

> She speaks with wisdom,
>   and faithful instruction is on her tongue.

Very clearly the mother is shown to be a teacher of wisdom, and, if she herself is teaching wisdom, then she must first have been taught.

These poems in praise of wisdom in chapters 1–9 have striking parallels with Egyptian instruction material. Some of the Egyptian proverbs go back to Ptah-Hotep, dated to about 2500 BC (1500 years before Solomon). Again, very similar to this material are the proverbs of Merikare, dated around 2000 BC. Most of this Egyptian wisdom literature antedates Solomon, and, in addition, bears many similarities to Israelite wisdom. But in the Egyptian instruction literature there is never a reference to the mother. The reference to the mother as a teacher in Israel is unique to the Bible. You will not find it in the Akkadian, Sumerian, or Egyptian wisdom.

Let us also note the word "forget." The Hebrew word for *forget* does not pertain so much to a mental lapse as to a moral lapse. We forget God and his word because we feel autonomous; we feel secure without God. What the Bible means by "forget" can be seen quite clearly in Deuteronomy 8:10-14:

> When you have eaten and are satisfied, praise the LORD your God for the good land he has given you. Be careful that you do not forget the LORD your God, failing to observe his commands, his laws and his decrees that I am giving you this day. Otherwise, when you eat and are satisfied, when you build fine houses and settle down, and when your herds and flocks grow large and your silver and gold increase and all you have is multiplied, then your heart will become proud and you will forget the LORD your God, who brought you out of Egypt, out of the land of slavery.

Here the people are warned against feeling secure in their success and prosperity with the result that they forget God because they no longer feel any need of his help. When we become independent there is a danger that we will forget God, forget prayer, and forget the reading of his word.

Sometimes students ask me whether it is necessary to follow the Puritan tradition and have a quiet time with God daily in prayer and reading of Scripture. My answer to that is usually in this direction: If you mean do you need to spend time with God as a religious obligation, as something you have to do, the answer is no. It will probably do you little good. But ask yourself, does the question reflect a spirit of arrogance? Are you not asking yourself, "Can I live the day without God? Can I live the day without prayer?" Jesus said, "Without me you can do nothing." He did not mean that without him you cannot make money; you can make more money without Jesus than with Jesus. You can make money your God; rich people do and they live for money. If you want to make money Jesus just gets in your way because he will say to you that there are better values than money. I found as a student, I could get better grades without Jesus than with Jesus because I could live for my grades and crack straight A's. But if you have to take time for worship and do acts of charity you may not get as good a grade. When he says "without me you can do nothing," he means that without me you can do nothing spiritually worthwhile. We cannot be like Jesus, without Jesus. So when Solomon says "My son, do not forget my teaching," he means do not become so proud that you think you can get on through life without the book of Proverbs. But if we do take his teaching seriously then there is the promise that this "will prolong your life many years and bring you prosperity."

The next command is in verse 3 and the associated promise in verse 4:

> ³Let love and faithfulness never leave you;
>   bind them around your neck,
>   write them on the tablet of your heart.

The author began with himself: "do not forget **my** teaching, keep **my** commands." Now he sees himself as part of a larger community, a covenant community. Love and faithfulness, *ḥesed we*ᵉ*met,* are covenantal terms. Do not leave your commitment to covenantal values. "Love and faithfulness" is a metonymy for the teachings of the covenant community and particularly of this book. The promise associated with the keeping of this command is found in verse 4: "Then you will win favor and a good name in the sight of God and man."

In the next three quatrains the focus of the command is on the Head of the covenant community, the LORD: "Trust in the LORD . . . fear the LORD . . . Honor the LORD . . ." Verse 5 commences, "Trust in the LORD . . ." Here the author is referring to the LORD who stands behind this book. Unless God has revealed himself and defined himself and given content for the focus of our trust, then "trust in the LORD" is platitudinous. It needs definition. He is saying "trust in the LORD who has spoken this wisdom."

Next, he warns us not to be autonomous but to fear the LORD:

> ⁷Do not be wise in your own eyes;
>   fear the LORD and shun evil.
> ⁸This will bring health to your body
>   and nourishment to your bones.

I take the promise to refer to both physical and psychological well-being. Bones in Scripture often speak of our psychological well-being. As David would say, "May the bones you have broken rejoice." So if you fear the LORD and are not wise in your own eyes you will experience physical and psychological health.

Finally, the last quatrain speaks of honoring the LORD with your wealth. The Hebrew *kabbēd* signifies that we should honor God, prize him, and give him social weight. That is, by giving to God the best, we show the community that everything we own and have comes from God. "Honor the LORD with your wealth, with the firstfruits of all your crops." That is, don't be like Cain who was guilty of tokenism, who brought from the fruit of his crops but did not give God the firstfruits. In other words, whatever opens the womb, the firstborn belongs to God; whatever opens the ground, the firstfruits of the crops also belong to him. We give these back to God as a way of saying we owe all life to him. With the command, "Honor the LORD with your wealth, with the firstfruits of all your crops" there follows the promise, "then your barns will be filled to overflowing, and your vats will brim over with new wine" (3:10).

Looking at those even verses we begin to see a problem. We have been promised long life and prosperity; we've been promised favor with God and man; we've been promised a smooth path; we've been promised physical and psychological well-being; and we've been promised material prosperity. But these things do not seem true to our experience; these heavenly promises seem to be detached from earth's realities. We as believers are persuaded of the truthfulness of the Bible; we know it's utterly trustworthy, but we are perplexed. This perplexity keeps us from taking this book too seriously.

Many scholars draw a contrast between the book of Proverbs and the books of Job and Ecclesiastes (commonly referred to as *Qoheleth* — the preacher). According to them the book of Proverbs is older wisdom, whereas the books of Job and Ecclesiastes are younger wisdom. Proverbs, they allege, is didactic wisdom, confirming a moral order; Job and Ecclesiastes they call reflective wisdom, which denies there is a moral order. The authors of the younger wisdom are said to have reflected on their experience and decided that the moral order does not exist.

Let us take the book of Job as an example. Job was righteous. He had not broken any laws, and yet he lost everything. He scarcely had a smooth path. His vats were not overflowing with new wine. He had not won favor with God and with man, not even with his three friends. So he says (Job 9:22-24):

> [22]It is all the same; that is why I say,
>   "He destroys both the blameless and the wicked."
> [23]When a scourge brings sudden death,
>   he mocks the despair of the innocent.
> [24]When a land falls into the hands of the wicked,
>   he blindfolds its judges.
>   If it is not he, then who is it?

Job could not find a moral order in this world.

The same problem is raised in the book of Ecclesiastes. Qoheleth is unable to discover a moral order (Eccles. 9:2):

All share a common destiny — the righteous and the wicked, the good and the bad, the clean and the unclean, those who offer sacrifices and those who do not.

> As it is with the good man,
>> so with the sinner;
> as it is with those who take oaths,
>> so with those who are afraid to take them.

The sage in Proverbs has affirmed a moral order; the other wisdom teachers, however, having taken off the lens of faith, say, "We cannot see a moral order with our own eyes; it's not apparent under the sun." The book of Proverbs seems to be contradicted not only by the so-called younger reflective wisdom, but also by our own experience as well. We can identify with Job and Ecclesiastes. Take the great heroes of faith in Hebrews 11. Abel believed God and he died; Enoch believed God and he didn't die; Noah believed God and everybody else died! In those first three examples of faith all three believed God, but the consequences were so radically different. Some of us can identify with Abel. We have a martyr's complex. Others say if you're not like Enoch there's something wrong with you.

The promises in Proverbs also seem to be contradicted by the life of Jesus. When we talk about other people there is always a fudge factor — maybe they had sinned, maybe they weren't righteous, maybe they weren't just. But with the life of Jesus that option is excluded from our thinking. He was perfect. He was without sin. He pleased God perfectly. Did Jesus live a long life? No, he died in the prime of life. Did Jesus win favor with God and man? Maybe when he was twelve, but as he hung upon the cross bearing shame and scoffing, he cried out, "My God, my God, why have you forsaken me?" When he was born there was no room for him in the inn. Shortly thereafter there was the flight into Egypt to avoid death. After his first sermon, they tried to kill him.

Did Jesus have physical and psychological well-being? We are told that he was buffeted upon the cross. His sweat was like great drops of blood, which expressed great distress, as he became our sin bearer. Were his barns filled with plenty and his vats brimming over with new wine? He said, "Foxes have holes and birds of the air have nests, but the Son of Man has no place to lay his head." These promises do not seem to have been fulfilled even in the life of Jesus. So we have a major problem on our hands that needs to be addressed before we proceed with the book of Proverbs.

Let me then turn toward a solution to our problem. First, let me give three solutions that I do not consider viable.

1. Some people actually suggest that the sage is a dullard. He has colored glasses on and cannot see the way things really are. That solution is not an option to me. We have already seen from chapter 24 that he is an astute observer. When he looked at the field of the sluggard, and passed the vineyard of the man who lacked judgment, he saw the thorns and the weeds, and he was very perceptive as to the reality of the fallen creation all around him (Prov. 24:30-34). Again, that he is a keen observer can be seen in Proverbs 23:29-35 when he talks about the drunkard.

2. Most academics say that the whole doctrine expressed in Proverbs is false. If that were true it would morally tarnish Holy Scripture. The sage has claimed that he has a revelation from God — "from God's mouth come knowledge and understanding" (Prov. 2:6) — and he commends the truth. Let me cite some renowned academics who say that Proverbs presents a false doctrine in its teaching on this issue. In a very fine book titled *Wisdom in Israel,* Gerhard von Rad has a chapter on Ecclesiastes that says,

> [T]he most common view of the radical theses of Koheleth has been to see in them a counter-blow to older teachings which believed too "optimistically," or better, too realistically, that they could see God at work in experience. . . . According to the prevailing point of view, it would appear as if he were turning only against untenable statements, as if he were challenging a few, no longer justifiable sentences which presented the divine activity as too rational and too obvious a phenomenon. Such sentences may in fact have existed. . . . This explanation breaks down, however, for the reason that Koheleth is turning against not only outgrowths of traditional teaching but the whole undertaking. Anyone who agrees with him in this can scarcely avoid the conclusion that the whole of old wisdom [i.e., the book of Proverbs] had become increasingly entangled in a single false doctrine. (*Wisdom In Israel* [London: SCM Press, 1972], p. 233)

I read von Rad as saying that the whole undertaking of Proverbs, to discern and set forth an absolute moral order, is false.

Says James G. Williams:

> But the tradition that he [Qoheleth] knows [i.e., the book of Proverbs] is more of a foil for him than anything else; his use of gnomic forms, for example, is often in order to contradict traditional wisdom. (*Those Who Ponder Proverbs: Aphoristic Thinking and Biblical Literature,* Bible and Literature series, ed. D. M. Gunn [Sheffield, UK: Almond Press, 1981], p. 53)

Von Rad is saying that, according to Ecclesiastes, the whole undertaking of Proverbs is false. Williams is saying that Ecclesiastes is written to contradict the book of Proverbs. For me both views are unacceptable because they tarnish Holy Scripture; Jesus himself included Proverbs as part of Holy Scripture that cannot be broken. The Apostles too quoted Proverbs as Scripture.

Some rabbis at the Council of Jamnia in AD 90 called its right to be in the canon into question because of the apparent contradiction in Proverbs 26:4-5, one verse saying "Do not answer a fool according to his folly"; the other saying "Answer a fool according to his folly." The point is, however, they had an underlying assumption that Proverbs was part of Holy Scripture. According to these rabbis Proverbs was regarded as part of Holy Scripture, otherwise there would have been no dispute.

3. Another solution is to suggest that the book of Proverbs gives probabilities, not promises. But Proverbs says that these are commands, these are laws; they represent the created order. I don't know how I would trust in the Lord with all my heart if there were some doubt about the truth of these proverbs. I would want to know whether they are true 99 percent of the time or true 51 percent of the time. If the probability is 99 percent then maybe I'd better obey and not run my chances on the 1 percent. If it is 51 percent, then maybe I'll do it or maybe I won't do it. The book would lose all of its authority on that line of reasoning. Therefore, that solution, I must honestly confess to you, is not open to me as a practical solution to the problem.

Having given three views on Proverbs with which I disagree, I shall now make four positive statements that help me toward solving the relationship between Proverbs' heavenly promises and earth's hard realities.

1. Some proverbs are *partially* validated by our experience. For example, we know from experience that what Proverbs says about the sluggard is true. The sluggard does not usually enjoy abundance (Prov. 24:30-34) or the blessings of Proverbs 3:1-10. He does not have a good name with man, or walk a smooth path, or possess barns filled with plenty, or enjoy psychological well-being.

The same is true of what Proverbs says about the alcoholic. You might turn with me to Proverbs 23:29-35 where we have a poem about the tragic results of substance addiction.

> [29]Who has woe? Who has sorrow?
>   Who has strife? Who has complaints?
>   Who has needless bruises? Who has bloodshot eyes?
> [30]Those who linger over wine,

who go to sample bowls of mixed wine.
³¹Do not gaze at wine when it is red,
when it sparkles in the cup,
when it goes down smoothly!
³²In the end it bites like a snake
and poisons like a viper.
³³Your eyes will see strange sights
and your mind imagine confusing things.
³⁴You will be like one sleeping on the high seas,
lying on top of the rigging.
³⁵"They hit me," you will say, "but I'm not hurt!
They beat me, but I don't feel it!
When will I wake up
so I can find another drink?"

This is a very apt description of the tragic figure of the drunkard. All he wants is another drink, and again, I think we can say that the drunkard does not walk a smooth path, enjoy a life of prosperity, or live a long life. All of what is said here is validated in our experience. Nevertheless, we do find people who appear to live righteously yet who do not seem to find the promises of Proverbs 3:1-10 validated in their experience.

2. The proverbs state truth categorically without qualifier or nuance. An example of this elsewhere in Scripture is Psalm 2:8,

Ask of me,
and I will make the nations your inheritance,
the ends of the earth your possession.

If we had only this verse we might have expected the kingdom of God to come on a balmy breeze. But that promise needs to be qualified by the reality of the rest of the psalter — that this kingdom will come only through tribulations. Psalm 2 is followed by a prayer in Psalm 3 that presents a very different picture:

¹O Lord how many are my foes!
How many rise up against me!
²Many are saying of me,
"God will not deliver him."

In other words, I have to qualify Psalm 2:8 by the reality of Psalm 3:1-2.

The same is true, for example, of Proverbs 22:6, "Train up a child in the way he should go and when he is old he will not depart from it." On one level we are perplexed by the proverb because we all know children who have been raised in the faith and yet they have jettisoned the faith as they have grown older and have walked away from the people of God, and so the proverb seems to be falsified. We need to qualify a proverb like 22:6 by other texts such as Ezekiel 18:20, "The soul who sins is the one who will die. The son will not share the guilt of the father, nor will the father share the guilt of the son." This verse is teaching individual accountability. We cannot push Proverbs 22:6 to such an extreme limit that the parent is responsible for the choices of the child, so that the faith of the child is dependent upon the faith and training of the parent. The child has accountability to make the faith his or her own. All Proverbs 22:6 is saying is that parental training has its effects. We are all the product of our parental training. You cannot extend that principle, however, to make the parent totally responsible for every decision of the child.

3. The Proverbs of Solomon have in view the end of the matter. We need to take account of what is called, in academic terms, *genre effect*. A particular kind of literature will look at things from a given perspective. In the case of Proverbs, the perspective is the final outcome. For example, in Proverbs 24:15-16 the perspective of the writer is clear:

> [15]Do not lie in wait like an outlaw against
> a righteous man's house,
> do not raid his dwelling place;
> [16]for though a righteous man falls seven times,
> he rises again,
> but the wicked are brought down by calamity.

He is conceding that the righteous man falls seven times, but that's a throwaway line, a peripheral point. We would say, though the righteous man is down for the count of ten, he will rise again. By contrast, the perspective of Job and Qoheleth — their genre effect — is the poor guy flat on the canvas. They effectively throw away the end line that he's going to rise again. They focus on the tragic situation; that's their perspective. Solomon in Proverbs is not concerned with the shadows along the trail; he's concerned with how it all turns out. Though the righteous man falls seven times, as in the case of Jesus, he rises again.

4. Solomon looks to a future beyond the grave. If we end the life of

Christ on the cross the book is not true. He died in the prime of life; he did not have long days. But if you read Proverbs in the light of the resurrection, then death is merely a shadow along the trail. It is foreign to this book that death and evil should prevail; it's contrary to its theology.

Let us consider some examples:

In the way of righteousness there is life;
along that path is immortality. (Prov. 12:28)

The Hebrew of the second line *('al māwet)*, which NIV translates as "immortality," is most unusual. Normally for "no" with a noun, such as *māwet*, "death," Hebrew uses *lo'*, but in Proverbs 12:28 it strangely uses *'al*, the form expected with a verb, not a noun. The late Mitchell Dahood, an Ugaritic scholar at the Pontifical Institute, Rome, saw a parallel in the Ugaritic expression *bl mt* [*bl* = Hebrew *'al; mt* = Hebrew *mwt*], which appeared in the clause: "In your life, O father, we rejoice and in your *not dying* [= *bl mt(k)*] we exult" (see M. Dahood, *Biblica* 41 (1960): 176-81; see also Dahood, *Proverbs and Northwest Semitic Philology* [Rome: Pontifical Biblical Institute, 1963], p. 28). Even before the discovery of the Ugaritic texts, the grammarians Gesenius-Kautzsch-Cowley (§152g) conceded the possibility that in Proverbs 12:28 *'al māwet* means "immortality." The Ugaritic texts tend to confirm that option. Dahood further wrote:

Thus the brace *hyym*, "life," // *bl mt*, "immortality," calls for a new translation and exegesis of Prov. 12:28. It also entails the re-examination of those passages, especially in poetry, of an eschatological tenor. Do we do justice to the author's intention when we understand *hyym* merely as temporal life, or must we take it to connote life in the full sense, like *zoe*, "life," in some New Testament passages? (*Ras Shamra Parallels: The Texts from Ugarit and the Hebrew Bible*, ed. Loren R. Fisher [Rome: Pontificium Institutum Biblicum, 1972], 1:82)

Again in Proverbs 14:32 we read, "When calamity comes, the wicked are brought down, but even in death the righteous have a refuge." In this text too there is something of a textual problem. Suffice it to say that in the received text that has been handed down to us, it is apparent that the writer is looking beyond the grave and sees that even in death there is security. Then again in Proverbs 23:18 we have the Hebrew word *'aḥarît*, which looks to a future that outlasts death. Verses 17 and 18 say,

> [17]Do not let your heart envy sinners,
>   but always be zealous for the fear of the Lord.
> [18]There is surely a future hope (*'aḥarît*) for you,
>   and your hope will not be cut off.

Solomon perceives there is a future, but it's opaque in the Old Testament. The truth of immortality had not been demonstrated as it now has been with the resurrection of Jesus Christ. Proverbs 24:19-20 says,

> [19]Do not fret because of evil men
>   or be envious of the wicked,
> [20]for the evil man has no future hope (*'aḥarît*),
>   and the lamp of the wicked will be snuffed out.

After examining the Hebrew word *'aḥarît* in Psalms 37, 49, and 73, Gerhard von Rad draws the conclusion that the term may look to a future that outlasts death. He writes:

> One can never judge life in accordance with the appearance of the moment, but one must keep "the end" in view. This important term, which is so characteristic of thinking which is open to the future, cannot always have referred to death. One can also translate the word by "future." What is meant, therefore, is the outcome of a thing, the end of an event for which one hopes. (*Wisdom in Israel*, p. 202)

Commenting on its meaning in Psalm 49:15 he writes:

> There can, of course, be no thought of deleting it entirely. Neither, however, can the confession be taken to mean that the poet hopes, in an acute situation of need, that is, temporarily, to be saved from death, for it would be impossible to understand the resultant antithesis to the idea that the thoughtless rich must die. The verb in question means (with reference to death) "snatch away." The most likely solution, then, is to understand the sentence as the expression of a hope for a life of communion with God which will outlast death. (*Wisdom in Israel*, p. 204)

That sense also best satisfies the wisdom contexts of Proverbs 23:17-18 and 24:19-20. Life will have the last word in the life of the righteous, but death will triumph over the wicked.

The reason we find Proverbs to be partially validated by experience with regard to the sluggard or with regard to the drunkard is that we live long enough to see the outcomes of their ways of life. There may be times when the sluggard appears to be experiencing no difficulties, but we usually live long enough to see the outcome of his laziness. The same is true with the drunkard. It may seem for a while as though the drinker is enjoying life, but sooner or later his excesses destroy him. But we don't live long enough to see the outcome of righteousness. We have to see the end of the matter by faith. Without that kind of faith we cannot please God. I say that if the book ends with the cross it is false but if it ends with resurrection it is true. The focus of the book is beyond the cross. Jesus too had the same focus: "who for the joy set before him endured the cross, scorning its shame" (Heb. 12:2).

Turn back to Proverbs 3:5-6:

⁵Trust in the LORD with all your heart
    and lean not on your own understanding;
⁶in all your ways acknowledge him,
    and he will make your paths straight.

Trusting God with all your heart takes faith. If you saw it all worked out before your eyes, where's the faith? Just as trusting God involves faith because the outcome is not realized immediately, so faith is necessary to accept the promises of God in this book. I would encourage you to take hold of the promises of this book by faith.

At one time I had a colleague who told me a story of how his grandfather had moved many years ago from the southern part of the United States, where it's warm, to the north, where it's cold. He had heard that rivers freeze over, but he had never seen a frozen-over river and wasn't quite sure it was true. He arrived in northern Pennsylvania in winter, and came across one of our larger rivers called the Susquehanna. It looked as though it might be frozen over. He got down on all fours and timidly tested it out. While he was tentatively testing out the ice he heard a rumbling sound behind him. Here came four horses drawing a wagon. They charged down the bank, across the river and up the other side without hesitation. The grandfather, down on all fours, felt very silly. When I was told that story I thought, this could be a parable of the different stances Christians have to their faith. Some of us are very tentative about our faith, while others are storming ahead, full of confidence in the Lord, fully assured in their hearts.

We are told: "Trust in the LORD with all your heart." We are to trust entirely. "Lean not on your own understanding." We are to trust exclusively. Philosophically that is the only sensible way to live. If we follow the Enlightenment and we trust our rationality, there will be only doubt and confusion about values. Without comprehensive knowledge we cannot make absolute judgments. As Anaxagoras (the first philosopher who quit philosophy) said in the beginning, "My life is too short, my senses delude me, my intellect is too weak, I can be certain of nothing." He is absolutely right. It is sheer stupidity to base your world- and life-view on your finite mind. Finally we are to trust extensively. "In *all* your ways acknowledge him and he will make your paths straight." The text is saying trust in the LORD who stands behind the promises in the book of Proverbs in everything, in all aspects of life that are covered by this book.

May God give us the grace that we might be fully committed and fully assured in our hearts, by his Spirit, which is his good gift to us.

Fundamentals for Preaching the Book of Proverbs

Part 1

Promise for and Difficulties in Preaching Proverbs

In a world bombarded by inane clichés, trivial catchwords, and godless sound bites, the expression of true wisdom is in short supply today. The church stands alone as the receptacle and repository of the inspired traditions that carry a mandate for a holy life from ancient sages. As the course and bulk of biblical wisdom, the book of Proverbs remains the model of a curriculum for humanity to learn how to live under God and before humankind. As a result it beckons the church to diligent study and application. To uncommitted youth it serves as a stumbling stone, but to committed youth it is a foundation stone.

But Proverbs is a briar patch for its expositors. One student confessed that before taking a course on Proverbs he thought some proverbs and sayings were banal and others wrong. For sober theologians the book's heavenly promises of health, wealth, and prosperity seem detached from reality. Some proverbs seem to contradict each other: "Do not answer fools according to their folly" (26:4) is followed by "Answer fools according to their folly" (v. 5).[1] Moreover, whereas the book of Proverbs affirms a righteous order, the books

---

1. Unless noted otherwise, all Scripture quotations are from Today's New International Version.

Previously published as a series of four articles, delivered as the W. H. Griffith Thomas Lectureship at Dallas Theological Seminary, February 6-9, 2007.

of Job and Ecclesiastes deny that reality. How does a preacher preach what seems banal, wrong, or contradictory?

The book seems to be a hodgepodge collection with no rhyme or reason in its grouping of sayings. They jump from one topic to another like scatterbrains in a living-room conversation. Nevertheless, from such an apparent mishmash the expositor is expected to prepare a logically developed and emotionally escalating sermon. No wonder expositors are hesitant to touch the book.

Three Types of Sermons

Preachers of Proverbs can justly and profitably employ the three most common sermonic forms: textual, topical, and expository. In textual preaching the preacher devotes his entire message to preaching one proverb. This is feasible and is arguably a form of expository preaching because each proverb has a distinct message.

In topical preaching the preacher designs his own message, consistent with the book's teachings, by selecting wisdom sayings from various groupings to support his message and then arranging them according to his own logic. Topical preaching is especially feasible in Proverbs because the composition of the book differs so radically from the composition of a sermon that even the expository preacher must translate the original organization of a grouping of proverbs into the quite different form of a homily.

In expository preaching the expositor discerns by form and rhetorical criticism an author's abstract message embedded in a grouping of several proverbs. This abstract meaning serendipitously enriches the meaning of the individual proverbs and protects the vulnerable proverb against abuse. Expository preaching is the queen of sermonic forms.

Exegetical Substance and Sermonic Style

Expository preaching consists of at least seven fundamental components. Four of them pertain to exegetical substance, and three to sermonic style. They are (a) demarcating the textual units by form and rhetorical criticism and selecting which of them to preach, (b) deciding the English version to be used in the pulpit, (c) exegeting the selected text according to the accredited grammatical-historical method of hermeneutics, (d) abstracting the big idea that unifies the grouping of proverbs, (e) translating the big idea into a message in light of its place in the progress of redemption and of the congregation's need, (f) translating the text's structure for which the audience has no reading strategy into the structure of the homily, which the audience intuitively understands, and (g) motivating the congregation to apply the message to concrete situations.

Fundamental Steps in Preaching Proverbs

Demarcating and Selecting Texts

The first fundamental step in preaching the book is demarcating the groupings and selecting the texts to be preached. The present writer's two-volume commentary on Proverbs demarcates the units in Proverbs by form criticism and rhetorical analysis.[2]

Four series of thirteen sermons per year on four biblical books have worked well for the writer because they give the congregation a sense of stable consistency and of appealing variety. For a series of sermons on Proverbs thirteen texts or topics are chosen on the basis of their importance for contemporary issues, their character representative of the book, their display of God's attributes, and their potential to empower the congregation to use the book in their personal or family devotions.[3]

The book of Proverbs has seven sections, marked by editorial notices at 1:1; 10:1; 22:17; 24:23; 25:1; 30:1; and 31:1. Although 22:17 lacks a clear editorial marker, most scholars demarcate 22:17–24:22 as a distinct section in the book.

Collection I: Introduction to the Book (chaps. 1–9)
Collection II: Proverbs of King Solomon (10:1–22:16)
Collection III: Thirty Sayings of the Wise Adapted by Solomon (22:17–24:22)
Collection IV: Further Sayings of the Wise (24:23-34)
Collection V: Further Proverbs by Solomon, Collected by Hezekiah's Men (chaps. 25–29)
Collection VI: Sayings of Agur, Son of Jakeh (chap. 30)
Collection VII: Sayings of King Lemuel (chap. 31)

---

2. Bruce K. Waltke, *The Book of Proverbs: Chapters 1-15* (Grand Rapids: Eerdmans, 2005); and *The Book of Proverbs: Chapters 15-31* (Grand Rapids: Eerdmans, 2006).
3. Waltke, *The Book of Proverbs: Chapters 1-15*, pp. 67-75.

The groupings of sayings within these sections, however, lack clear editorial jackets. These groupings embedded within the collections are like sermons and lectures in a preacher's file without file folders to separate them. Unlike the psalms that are separated by superscripts and subscripts, the textual units within Proverbs must be isolated, as already noted, by form and rhetorical criticism. Chapter divisions in English Bibles are not reliable indicators of the author's groupings, for the chapters were demarcated before form and rhetorical criticism had become a science.

Collection I (chaps. 1–9). This collection includes a preamble (1:1-7), prologue (1:8–8:36), and epilogue (chap. 9). The epilogue functions as a transition between collections I and II.

The book's preamble functions well as the first of thirteen sermons because it sets forth the fundamental information for understanding and preaching the book of Proverbs. Five sermons from the prologue are proportionate to the book's own proportions. Also, the prologue's encomiums to wisdom lay the spiritual foundation for the teachings in the remaining collections.

The importance of the prologue (1:8–8:36) can be inferred from its ruling metaphor, "the way." This metaphor refers to a person's "course of life" (i.e., the character and context of life), "conduct of life" (i.e., specific choices and behavior), and "consequences of that conduct" (i.e., the inevitable destiny of such a lifestyle). Fundamental to conduct is character. To live out the explicit or implicit admonitions of the proverbial sayings in the collections, a person must first prepare his or her heart. As Moses in his three valedictory addresses in Deuteronomy first spiritually prepared the hearts of his audience to trust and love God in Deuteronomy 6–11 before giving the statutes and commandments in Deuteronomy 12–26, so also the lectures and sermons in Collection I in Proverbs spiritually prepare the catechumens to trust and love God before instructing them on behavior in the remaining six collections.

Moreover, the poems of the prologue are highly relevant. The lectures and sermons of Collection I aim to safeguard Israel's youth from the seductive appeals both of wicked men to make easy money and of the femme fatale to indulge in easy sex.

It is prudent to select several sermons from this collection because the poems in this collection come packaged for the preacher and shoehorn the church's foot into the shoe of Proverbs.

Here are six suggested sermons from Proverbs 1–9.

Sermon 1: Unlocking the Book of Life (preamble, 1:1-7).

Sermon 2: Safeguards against wicked men and wicked women (chap. 2). This sermon presents the spiritual essentials to develop the godly mind as defense against the temptations of easy money and easy sex.

Sermon 3: Does Proverbs promise too much (3:1-12)? The sermon sets forth the covenant obligations of God and of the son. The obligations on God's part are promises, not probabilities. But that raises the question of whether the book promises too much and of the wrong thing, namely, health, wealth, and prosperity. The writer's commentary discusses this tension.[4]

Sermon 4: Why bother (3:13-26)? Of the prologue's twelve motivating lectures and sermons, this text offers the most comprehensive argument.

Sermon 5: What's wrong with adultery (chaps. 4-7)? A sermon on the femme fatale, who plays a larger role in the prologue than even Woman Wisdom, can combine the three warnings of the parents in chapters 5-7 into three points of a sermon. The sermon is essential in contemporary culture, in which liberty is desired without law, freedom without form, and lovemaking without marriage.

Sermon 6: Woman Wisdom's final appeal to uncommitted youth (chap. 8). Woman Wisdom addresses her two sermons in 1:20-33 and chapter 8 to simpletons, that is, to children who have passed puberty without making a commitment to the catechism. The preceding four selected texts are the parents' lectures in the home. Of wisdom's two sermons to simpletons, the second is most famous because in the history of Christian teaching the identification of Woman Wisdom with Jesus Christ wrongly became an established doctrine.

Collection II (10:1–22:16). Selecting texts and sermons from this collection is more difficult because the proverbs function on two levels of meaning: individually and collectively. Individually each proverb explicitly or implicitly admonishes the audience toward specific expressions of pious and/or ethical behavior. Collectively they communicate a message greater than the parts. The groupings, however, depend almost entirely on rhetoric, not grammar. Unlike prose and longer poems, they are not held together by syntactic links such as conjunctions and particles.

Not all agree that in Collection II there are meaningful groupings, each of which has a message. If they are right, then the preacher should preach either textual or topical sermons from this section. Expository preaching would be wrong because it would impose messages not intended by the inspired author.

4. Waltke, *The Book of Proverbs: Chapters 1–15,* pp. 107-8.

Good reasons exist, however, for recognizing larger textual units in Collection II, and pastors have found the groupings useful. Nevertheless topical preaching from less clearly demarcated units has its place in a healthy diet of sermons. Congregations respond well to a topical sermon that includes a short exposition of one textual unit at some point in the sermon. If one opts for topical sermons from Collection II, then there are two important topical sermons to represent the teachings of this collection:

Sermon 7: Being money wise (using the grouping of 10:1-5 as one of the texts).

Sermon 8: Wise speech (using 10:6-14 as one of its texts).

Collection III (22:17–24:22). Grouping the sayings in Collection III, the Thirty Sayings of the Wise, is also challenging, but not as challenging as Collection II. After its own preamble (22:17-21), the collection essentially consists of three decalogues of sayings. Since the first decalogue, which is about money, and the second decalogue, which is about being an obedient son, are about topics already dealt with in the series, the congregation will find a healthy variety in the third decalogue.

Sermon 9: Strength in distress (24:3-12). This sermon is especially applicable to awaken the church to its social responsibilities.

Collection IV (24:23-34). Collection IV is too short to call for representation in a separate sermon.

Collection V (chaps. 25–29). Collection V can be analyzed fairly readily with respect to its macro-groupings and micro-groupings. One grouping amenable to expository preaching and relevant to help safeguard youth against the entertainment industry is this:

Sermon 10: How to deal with fools (26:1-12).

Collection VI (30:1-33). Though the prophet Agur intended his collection of inspired sayings to be treated holistically, a sermon can be limited to his autobiographical confession in 30:1-6. That biography is especially applicable to a culture that believes in relative evaluations, not absolute values.

Sermon 11: Christian values versus postmodern evaluations (30:1-6).

Collection VII (chap. 31). The sayings of King Lemuel place two distinct poems together: the noble king (vv. 1-9) and the noble wife (vv. 10-31). Though both are challenging, the preacher is better advised to choose the second of the two because it draws the series to a conclusion with the book's own conclusion. Although most speak well of the noble woman, few will emulate her.

Sermon 12: A noble woman as a paradigm of wisdom (vv. 10-31).

Sermon 13: (A thirteenth sermon on a text or topic from Proverbs can be chosen by the expositor for a concluding message.)

Deciding the Translation

A pastor must wisely choose his translation for all his sermons. All translations (other than the Jehovah's Witnesses *New World Bible*) are faithful and adequate. "Faithful and adequate" means that all translations lead their audience to faith in Jesus Christ — into sound doctrine and never into heresy. A congregation can respond to any message in the book of Proverbs using any English translation.

However, translations are not equal with regard to exegetical accuracy, their targeted audiences, and fluency. In the writer's opinion, the best translation that satisfies these three criteria is Today's New International Version (TNIV), a revision of the New International Version (NIV).

Unlike the as-much-as-possible word-for-word translation of the New American Standard Bible and the English Standard Version (ESV), the TNIV follows the translation philosophy of Chrysoloras, a Byzantine scholar who arrived in Florence in 1397. His roster of pupils reads like a who's who of early Renaissance humanism. Prior to Chrysoloras, medieval scholastic scholars, when they translated from Greek into Latin, practiced a method called *verbum ad verbum* ("word for word"). At its best, this resulted in clumsy, graceless Latin. At its worst, as Chrysoloras pointed out, it could change the meaning of the original completely. So Chrysoloras abandoned the old method. Instead, he taught his students to stick as closely as possible to the sense of the Greek, but to convert it into Latin that was as elegant, fluent, and idiomatic as the original. Chrysoloras's philosophy is true translation.

Having spent forty years in helping produce English translations of the Bible, the writer is amazed at the cavalier manner in which pastors revise a translation on the basis of their own exegesis. If a preacher corrects the TNIV, he implies that he, with his one or two years of studying the Hebrew language, is more competent than a committee of professional exegetes.

Exegeting the Text

Having selected the text and version, the preacher should then exegete the original Hebrew text in order to be authentic. He is God's voice, mediating God's Word to God's people. Knowing the Bible's original languages is essential to being an authentic theologian and preacher. "(1) Language is the means for all discernment and linguistics is the means for all investigation and wisdom; (2) the fulfillment of the commandments depends upon the understanding of the written word, and in turn, the proper knowledge of the language is impossible without the aid of linguistics."[5] Knowing the original languages can help a pastor become a skilled exegete rather than a sloppy theologian and/or preacher.

Proper exegesis includes the following disciplines: (a) establishing the Hebrew text by textual criticism, (b) establishing the literary genre by form criticism, (c) defining significant terms by the use of a concordance, a lexicon, and a theological word book, (d) parsing and deciding the sense of all grammatical forms, (e) identifying and interpreting figures of speech, (f) decoding the author's rhetoric, (g) abstracting the biblical writer's thesis, and (h) locating the text's teaching within the contexts of the progress of redemptive history and of the history of Christian doctrine. A good expositor will involve himself in all these exegetical tasks to the extent of his available time and competence, for these academic disciplines internalize the text in his soul and help it flow from his lips. These fundamental disciplines are learned in seminary, and a seminary that sends forth preachers incompetent to exegete the original text fails Christ and his church and shortchanges its students.

Occasionally, however, one hears of a teacher or an exegete who denies himself the use of a commentary. This is foolhardy. No unaided preacher has the time or competence to give authoritative answers to exegetical questions under the gun of a weekly clock. He may fool his congregation and even himself about his own authority, but this is wrong. To speak competently a preacher must use a good commentary intelligently.

Abstracting the Big Idea

The expositor is now in a position to abstract the big idea of the text. He is concerned primarily with the vital central concept of his text, with the interrelationship of the idea of each proverb that links them to each other, and with the deep underlying convictions that inspired the texts and united them as a composite and yet unitary "witness" to theological truth.[6] To put it another way, the expositor is looking for the groupings' "system" or "structure," a sort of inner grid that can be placed within the material and can be seen to provide some degree of order and coherence.[7] Simply stated, the big

---

5. Bruce K. Waltke and M. P. O'Connor, *Introduction to Biblical Hebrew Syntax* (Winona Lake, IN: Eisenbrauns, 1990), p. 32.

6. James Barr, *The Concept of Biblical Theology* (Minneapolis: Fortress, 1999), p. 7.

7. Barr, *The Concept of Biblical Theology*, p. 334.

idea, as Robinson suggests, consists of both a subject and its complement. The subject answers the question, What is the writer talking about? And the complement answers the question, What is he saying about what he is talking about? The two together form the idea.[8]

Translating the Idea into a Message

W. A. Criswell, the late pastor of the First Baptist Church of Dallas, Texas, said that he considered having a sermon's purpose the most important fundamental step in preaching. He said he kept his purpose in mind throughout the entire sermon, from the attention-grabbing introduction, to its logical development in the body of the sermon, to its climactic emotional appeal and practical application to real and concrete life situations.

What Criswell called a sermon's purpose may also be called its message. The big idea abstracted by exegesis from the text must be translated into a message, for the textual units of the Bible have a character that makes them suitable and able to provide direction to what the human mind brings into relationship with it. The notion of a big idea, though good, is inadequate. The Bible is not interested in impersonal "ideas" and ethical principles. Moreover, the Bible is not simply about divine matters.[9] The Bible is more than concepts about God or ethical principles or Israel's witness to God. The Bible is God's address to his people, and he encounters them through Spirit-filled communicators of his Word. Since the inspired author's "ideas" and "principles" are true, they contain a moral imperative that demands a response. In other words, an "idea" in the Bible is a *message* to be believed and acted on, not merely a notion and/or a guide to proper behavior. A message, then, is not an idea but the expected response to the idea.

The ancient message must be expressed in a way appropriate to the Christian gospel. A faithful Christian today is both similar and dissimilar to an ancient Israelite. Both share in Israel's covenants, and both share the same spirit of faith, love, and hope. But the Christian now understands those covenants in the light of the gospel of Jesus Christ — of his life, death, and resurrection — and he focuses his faith, love, and hope on the triune God: Father, Son, and Holy Spirit. The expositor must formulate his message in the light of that more complete theological knowledge.

---

8. See Haddon Robinson, *Biblical Preaching* (Grand Rapids: Baker, 2001), chapter 2.
9. Gerhard von Rad, cited by Barr, *The Concept of Biblical Theology,* p. 47.

Developing the Message

The wisdom literature for the most part does not come packaged for the preacher. Its literary genres differ more radically from the genre of the homily than any of the other literary genres attested in the Bible, making more difficult the expositor's job of translating the messages as packaged in Proverbs to the homily. The book of Proverbs was composed to be memorized, sung, and meditated on by children in the home under the tutelage of parents, not to be preached as homilies in a church. A word-for-word translation of the Hebrew into English, as in an interlinear, is frustrating and not intelligible to the reader. Likewise retaining the literary styles of the book of Proverbs to develop the sermon often does not yield a sensible message. Congregations intuitively know the appropriate strategy for hearing a sermon, but they are mostly ignorant of the literary strategies for reading Proverbs. Just as the Hebrew of the original book of Proverbs must be translated into smooth English, so also the literary forms of Proverbs must be translated into a flowing homily.

Applying the Message

The response to a message can be actualized and measured only by concrete actions. What does the preacher expect the congregation to do with the message when they step out of the church door back into the world? How will they incarnate the message? Without a clear notion of how to apply the sermon, the congregants will quickly forget the message and not transform it into action. They will have enjoyed the sermon, but little more than that will have been accomplished.

Conclusion

Seven steps are essential in preaching the book of Proverbs. First, by form and rhetorical criticism identify a textual unit within the anthology of proverbs and sayings and select thirteen texts that best represent and communicate the message of the book. Second, use a translation that best represents the text to the average reader of the congregation. Third, exegete the text and then consult a good commentary. Fourth, extract from the text the dynamic idea that explains the relationship of the proverbs in a grouping, including their continuities and discontinuities with each other, and that explains their place in God's progressive revelation.[10] Fifth, translate the text's abstract idea into a relevant Christian message. Sixth, for the development of the message translate the unfamiliar compositional form of the original text into the familiar form of the homily. Seventh, draw the message to conclusion by applying it to real-life situations.

Part 2

To preach Proverbs authentically the expositor should master the fundamentals of preaching (the topic of the first lecture in this series) and understand essential concepts of Proverbs, the topic of this and the next two lectures.

The preamble of Proverbs (1:1-7) reveals these fundamentals. In this lecture I have two objectives: to review and illustrate the fundamentals of preaching by expounding the preamble, and from the superscript of the preamble to reflect on two of the six fundamental concepts the expositor should understand.

An Exposition of the Preamble

The exposition of the preamble entails seven fundamental steps (which were discussed in the first lecture): demarcating the text, choosing the best translation, exegeting the text, abstracting its big idea, transforming that idea into a message, developing the message in sermonic form, and applying it.[11]

First Fundamental: Demarcating the Text

Form and rhetorical criticism demarcate Proverbs 1:1-7 as an intentional grouping. These verses read as follows:

> The proverbs of Solomon son of David, king of Israel: for gaining wisdom and instruction; for understanding words of insight; for receiving

---

10. Gerhard F. Hasel, *Old Testament Theology: Basic Issues in the Current Debate*, rev. ed. (Grand Rapids: Eerdmans, 1975), p. 112.

11. Bruce K. Waltke, "Fundamentals of Preaching Proverbs," *Bibliotheca Sacra* 165 (January-March 2008): 3-12.

instruction in prudent behavior, doing what is right and just and fair; for giving prudence to those who are simple, knowledge and discretion to the young — let the wise listen and add to their learning, and let the discerning get guidance — for understanding proverbs and parables, the sayings and riddles of the wise. The fear of the LORD is the beginning of knowledge, but fools despise wisdom and instruction.

Grammatically verses 1-6 are one sentence: a topic (the proverbs of Solomon, v. 1) followed by a predicate that gives the writer's purpose for the book (vv. 2-6). A superscript modified by purpose clauses also introduces Egyptian wisdom literature. This form contrasts radically with the forms of the following twelve lectures and sermons in Collection 1. Their form consists of an admonition by the lecturer to the addressee to accept his teaching with motivations to heed the lesson.

Rhetorically verse 7 belongs to the preamble. Grammatically it stands apart as a separate sentence from the superscript with purpose clauses in verses 1-6, but its rhetoric firmly attaches it to the preamble. The sequence of *da'at mūsār wᵉḥokmâ* ("to know instruction and wisdom") in verse 2, involving knowledge, wisdom, and instruction, is repeated but with a different syntax in verse 7: "The fear of the LORD is the beginning of knowledge, but wisdom and instruction fools despise."[12]

Thus verses 1-7 may be demarcated by grammar and by form and rhetorical criticism as a unit, and it serves as a preamble.

Second Fundamental: Choosing the Translation

Having established by grammar, form, and rhetoric that verses 1-7 are an intentional preamble to the book, the expositor should choose for his congregation the best translation of the text for accuracy, clarity, and beauty. In verse 2 the New International Version has "for gaining" rather than "to know," found in the New American Standard Bible and the English Standard Version. The Hebrew *da'at* means "to know," but English "to know" normally separates the knower from the object known, whereas the Hebrew term means to experience or internalize the object known. The New Revised Standard Version gets it wrong by rendering *da'at ḥokmâ* "to know about" wisdom. "To gain" more accurately represents the Hebrew than "to know" or "to know about."

12. The last clause follows Hebrew word order more closely than does the rendering in Today's New International Version.

Third Fundamental: Exegeting the Text

The structure of the preamble consists roughly of a superscript (v. 1), a statement of purpose (see "for" in vv. 2-6), and a foundational principle: the fear of "I Am." The prose superscript identifies the literary form of this book, "a proverb," and its author, "Solomon son of David, king of Israel." The structure of the preamble can be analyzed in this way:

I. Superscript (v. 1)
    A. Literary genre (v. 1a)
    B. Author (v. 1b)
II. Purpose of the Book (vv. 2-6)
    A. Summary (v. 2)
        1. The book's substance: to gain wisdom (v. 2a)
        2. The book's style: to understand words of insight (v. 2b)
    B. To gain wisdom (vv. 3-5)
        1. Wisdom defined in terms of ethical behavior (v. 3)
        2. Wisdom with regard to simpletons (v. 4)
        3. Wisdom with regard to the wise (v. 5)
    C. To understand words of insight (v. 6)
III. Essential Spiritual Component to Gain Wisdom (v. 7)

Fourth Fundamental: Abstracting the Big Idea

What is the author's ideological grid that interfaces the superscript (v. 1), purpose (vv. 2-6), and essential spiritual quality (v. 7)? Rudyard Kipling's "six little men" help focus the point.

> I keep six honest serving-men
> (They taught me all I know);
> Their names are What and Why and When,
> And How and Where and Who.

The preamble addresses the fundamental issues raised by Kipling's little men. Verse 1 answers the questions, What is the book's literary form? and Who is its author? Verses 2-6 answer, Why did he write it and for whom? And verse 7 answers the question, What is the spiritual prerequisite for learning this book? In summary, the essential question the preamble answers is, What do you need to know to gain the wisdom of the book of Proverbs? To state the question metaphorically, What is the code of the combination lock that unlocks the gate to gain entrance into the paradise, the wisdom, of the book of Proverbs?

Fifth Fundamental: Translating the Idea into a Message

What fundamental information do readers need in order to profit from this book? The answer to that question — the big idea — must now be transformed into a message to which a response can be given. The big idea calls for a response of a joyful willingness to learn the code: *Be wise; learn the fundamentals that unlock the gate to wisdom. Don't be a fool and ignore it.*

Sixth Fundamental: Developing the Argument

The code of the combination lock has six numbers — that is, six concepts. This lecture develops the first two, which are found in the book's superscript: (a) understanding the book's genre: "proverbs" (v. 1a); and (b) understanding the book's authors, especially "Solomon son of David, king of Israel" (v. 1b). The next lecture develops two more fundamentals: (c) understanding the book's purpose: "to gain wisdom" (v. 2), and (d) understanding the book's addressees: simpletons and those growing in wisdom (vv. 4-5). The final lecture develops the last two: (e) understanding the book's words, and (f) understanding "the fear of 'I Am.'"

Seventh Fundamental: Applying the Message

In the light of these six fundamentals the book of Proverbs should then be preached with integrity.

Fundamental Concepts of Proverbs for Preaching

As noted, the code for the combination lock in the preamble has six numbers that help unlock the book of Proverbs. The first two involve understanding its genre and its authors.

Number One: The Book's Genre

All scholars agree that the sayings in Proverbs are a species of the wisdom genre. But they do not agree on the distinctive characteristic that binds together such diverse works as Job, Proverbs, and Ecclesiastes, all of which belong to this genre.

To understand the nature of wisdom literature two things should be noted: its distinctive mark (inspiration) and the epistemology that informs it (revelation).

Wisdom literature's distinctive mark: its form of inspiration. According to some scholars, wisdom literature is humanistic in its orientation; according to others it is international in scope. Others note that it is nonhistorical, unlike the rest of the Old Testament, or eudaemonistic, that is, "We do good to get good." Still others define it as a human search for order. Kidner focuses on its rational tone. Although wisdom literature contains some of these characteristics, other forms of literature also contain some of them, though not to the same extent. I suggest that its distinctive mark is the nature of its inspiration.

The writer of Hebrews notes that in the Old Testament God spoke in diverse ways. He spoke to Moses in theophany, to the prophets in visions and auditions, and to the sages in their keen observations and cogent reflections on the order of creation. One can observe from Proverbs 24:30-34 how the sage received his inspiration. His laboratory was the sluggard's field. "I went past the field of a sluggard, past the vineyard of someone who has no sense; thorns had come up everywhere, the ground was covered with weeds, and the stone wall was in ruins" (vv. 30-31).

Then in verse 32 he wrote of his keen observation and cogent reflection. "I applied my heart to what I observed and learned a lesson from what I saw."

Then he cited in a proverb the lesson he learned: "A little sleep, a little slumber, a little folding of the hands to rest — and poverty will come on you like a thief and scarcity like an armed man" (vv. 33-34).

The sage, however, did not base his wisdom on what theologians call natural theology. Natural theology is based on God's general revelation in creation, human conscience, and human reason. In natural theology nature itself is God's oracle. God's sages, by contrast, based their theology on God's covenants with Israel, and in light of those covenants they found illustrations in creation that support the values in those covenants.

In other words, the "inscape" of the sages determined how they saw the landscape. As William Blake expressed it, "We see through the eye, not with the eye." What a person is on the inside determines how he sees the world. When Solomon assumed David's throne, Solomon copied by hand Moses' book of the Law under the tutelage of the priest. "When [the king] takes the throne of his kingdom, he is to write for himself on a scroll a copy of this law, taken from that of the Levitical priests. It is to be with him, and he is to read it all the days of his life so that he may learn to revere the LORD his God and follow carefully all the words of this law and these decrees" (Deut. 17:18-19).

Undoubtedly even before becoming king, Solomon had been instructed in Israel's covenants. He and the sages of Proverbs viewed the world while saturated in God's Law and its concern for justice and mercy.

This orientation pervades their writings. They speak of God as "I Am" (*yhwh*), God's name associated with his covenants with Israel. When Solomon discussed the ant as an illustration of discipline and prudence in Proverbs 6:6-11, he turned a blind eye to the disastrous effects of the carpenter ant. Qoheleth and Job temporarily removed the lens of Israel's covenants, spoke of the Lord as *'elohîm*, that is, of God as transcendent, and they observed in the creation the amoral law of the survival of the fittest. Job and Qoheleth, however, in the final analysis extracted wisdom from the created order by finally viewing it by faith through Israel's covenants. Both fell back on "the fear of 'I Am'" (Job 28:28; Eccles. 12:13), which entails special revelation.

The point is that though the sage's form of inspiration differs from that of Moses and the prophets, his writings are inspired. With Solomon's wisdom on his lips, a fictitious father lectures his son: "For the 'I Am' gives wisdom; from his mouth come knowledge and understanding" (2:6).

Wisdom literature's epistemology: its dependence on revelation. Inspiration implies revelation. Moreover, without revelation, there is no absolute or certain knowledge. The finite mind cannot determine absolute truth. Agur made this argument in his autobiographical confession in 30:1-6. Agur, a sage and a prophet, confessed his philosophy of knowledge to an unknown official named Ithiel, who in the canon of Scripture represents all the people of God.

In the third lecture I will argue that by "understanding" and "wisdom" Agur had in mind ethics and social skills, that is, the skill of proper behavior in relationship to God and to one's neighbor. Agur introduced his philosophy of knowledge in a summary statement: "I am weary, God, but I can prevail" (v. 1). In this succinct statement he affirmed that though humans are incapable and weary, they can find wisdom and come to understand how they should live. He did this by constructing a ladder with five rungs of confessions.

Confession 1: Apart from revelation, no one can attain moral and social skills. The first rung of Agur's ladder is made from human experience. The first rung people must climb is an honest confession that on their own as mere mortals they cannot attain proper moral and social skills. "Surely I am only a brute, not a man; I do not have human understanding. I have not learned wisdom, nor have I attained to the knowledge of the Holy One" (vv. 2-3).

Agur's confession contrasts sharply with the self-assurance of the Enlightenment. Its philosophers have full confidence that by reasoning, humankind can determine how to behave. After having been tried for three centuries, the Enlightenment has enabled the human race to achieve what before the Enlightenment would have been regarded as miracles. Remarkably, physicists and engineers have enabled men to walk on the moon. Chemists have eliminated dreaded diseases. But in moral and social skills the Enlightenment is a colossal failure. MacIntyre documented how the Enlightenment moved Western civilization from the Greek virtues to Nietzsche's will for power.[13] In its wake came Nazi genocide and ethnic cleansing. Geneticists, social scientists, and medical practitioners sometimes play God and kill unwanted human beings. Today no human life can be sure it is precious or safe.

Confession 2: Apart from revelation people cannot attain certainty. Whereas Agur made his first rung out of experience, he made his second rung out of his cogent reflection on his confession that human beings on their own do not know how to behave. He set this rung in place by four "who" questions in verse 4. "Who has gone up to heaven [i.e., to see everything holistically and come down to tell us the whole]? Whose hands have gathered up the wind? Who has wrapped up the waters in a cloak? Who has established all the ends of the earth?"

These four "who" questions confirm the current view that human knowledge is relative and uncertain. This is so, Agur reasoned, because without comprehensive knowledge the human race cannot derive certain knowledge.

Engineers used to think damming up rivers was good; now ecologists point out that sometimes dams are bad. People used to think forest fires are always bad; now horticulturalists affirm that they may be necessary. In other words, what was once thought good and wise now with more knowledge turns out to be bad and foolish.

Westminster Theological Seminary, where I once taught, rightly prides itself on its superb library, located prominently on a hill overlooking

---

13. Alasdair MacIntyre, *After Virtue: A Study in Moral Theory,* 2nd ed. (Notre Dame: University of Notre Dame Press, 1984).

the surrounding valleys. Around the library's core of books are the faculty offices. One of our students, however, before coming to Westminster, worked for the department of the United States government that measures concentrations of deadly radon gas in atmospheres. One day he decided to test the amount of radon gas in our library.

The atmosphere normally contains four pico curies of radon gas; each day a chain smoker inhales about two hundred pico curies, and a uranium miner inhales about four hundred pico curies. In fact, the United States government requires uranium miners to take every third year off in order to detoxify their bodies. Our student discovered (and the government confirmed) that the atmosphere of the Westminster library, where my office was located, had a concentration of four thousand pico curies, ten times more than in a uranium mine. The day after the discovery the government sealed the library shut with black and yellow tape, with the words "Danger. Lethal. Keep out!" And my office was in the library building!

The architects who located and designed the library thought they had built wisely, but in truth they built foolishly. Unknown to them, according to geologists, there was a fracture in the earth's crust, forty miles directly below the library, spewing out the largest concentrations of radon gas ever measured in the United States.

Unlike modernity of the past three centuries, postmoderns of the twenty-first century agree with Agur that all unaided human knowledge is relative. But unlike Agur these secularists have drawn the perverse conclusion that there are no moral absolutes by which to evaluate social behavior. According to their philosophy of knowledge, human beings must own up to the reality that they can no longer speak of values; they can only speak of evaluations. In their view no culture is better than another. Their jettison of absolute values has thrown Western civilization over the cliff into a freefall of moral relativity that inevitably ends in death. Postmodernism, cultural relativism, Utopian pacifism, and moral equivalence have filtered down from the media, universities, and government to the general public. And the pernicious wages of such theories are now evident everywhere. For the first time in Western civilization marriage is no longer defined as between a man and woman, and cohabitation of any form is tolerated. The devil is always on the lookout for the moral relativism that signals a latter-day Faust, and it seems that he is finding eager recruits among some prominent spokespeople in the West.

Confession 3: Only the Creator has comprehensive knowledge. In contrast to postmodernists, Agur composed his next three rungs out of faith. To climb above the failed modernity of the first rung that depended on experimentation and reason to determine values, and the deadly postmodernity of the second rung that denies the possibility of establishing absolute values, Agur's third rung calls on God's people to answer the first of two "what" questions: "What is his name?" (v. 4). Agur challenged Ithiel by his assertion, "Surely you know." Surely a catechumen in Israel's faith would know the name of the Creator "who has established all the ends of the earth" and its Sustainer "whose hands have gathered up the wind" and "who wrapped up the waters in a cloak." Believers intuitively answer, "'I Am' is the Creator and Sustainer of the universe." Implicitly since God knows everything from beginning to end, he knows comprehensively and speaks absolute truths.

Confession 4: Israel is God's son. Agur's fourth rung on which one must step to escape from moral and social inadequacy is his second "what" question: "What is the name of his son?" Agur's third rung called on his readers to name the competent teacher. Now he called on them to name the privileged student. Although he said to his original audience, "Surely you know," his later Christian audience may not know. The New King James Version wrongly answers his question by capitalizing Son, presumably a reference to Jesus Christ. The answer to Agur's question, however, must be deduced from the firm lexical evidence that in Proverbs "son" always refers to a student who listens to his teacher. The son whom Agur had in mind is Israel, as can be seen in many Old Testament passages, such as Exodus 4:22, where God called Israel his unique son. The Septuagint of this verse rendered the Hebrew *ben* ("son") with the plural *paideia* ("children"): "What is the name of his children?" thereby interpreting "son" as the children of Israel. Baruch, a sage of the second temple period, answered Agur's two questions in this way: "This is our God, with whom none can be compared. He found the way of understanding and gave it to Jacob his servant and to Israel whom he loved" (Baruch 3:35-36).

In the fullness of time Jesus Christ was born and demonstrated himself to be the quintessential Son of God, and each one who trusts in Jesus Christ is a seed of Abraham and a child of God. In short, the triune God is the believers' Teacher, and they are his children and students.

Agur's challenging questions to identify the God of Israel as the Father-Teacher, who is competent to teach wisdom, and to identify ourselves as his sons-students, radically reshapes the crisis of knowing into a crisis of relationship. The human epistemological crisis in ethics and social behavior is now defined in relational rather than intellectual categories. True wisdom is found in a responsive and receptive relationship with the triune God.

Confession 5: God revealed himself in the Scriptures. The first four steps of the ladder reveal (a) that people have failed to find out how they should behave, (b) that they cannot establish absolute values by which to determine which behavior is good or which is bad, (c) that only the omniscient God of Israel is competent to make such evaluations, and (d) that believers must confess that they are his students. Agur then led his readers to take the fifth and final step out of their own relative and unreliable knowledge to the firm ground of God's absolute knowledge. A person steps on that firm ground when he confesses that the triune God has spoken in the Bible. "Every word of God is flawless; he is a shield to those who take refuge in him. Do not add to his words, or he will rebuke you and prove you a liar" (vv. 5-6). As Childs writes, "As an answer to the inquirer's despair at finding wisdom and the knowledge of God, the answer offered is that God has already made himself known in his written word."[14]

Verse 5 is a citation from a psalm of David: "As for God, his way is perfect: the LORD's word is flawless; he shields all who take refuge in him" (Ps. 18:30). Agur's further confession, "Do not add to his words or he will . . . prove you a liar," warns readers not to add to or subtract from any part of God's Word. The formula is taken from Moses' teaching in Deuteronomy 4:2 and 12:32. In other words, Agur located his own teachings in Proverbs 30 within the framework of the Word of God to the extent that the canon existed in his day.

These reflections on biblical wisdom literature goad the preacher to preach as presenting God's oracles. He is to be like a trumpet, giving a clear and certain sound of God's Word, not the uncertain sound of human wisdom (cf. 1 Cor. 14:8).

The specie of "proverb." The first word of the preamble's superscript narrows the genre of wisdom literature to its specie of "proverb" *(māšāl).* In English a proverb refers to a short, pithy saying that has popular currency, but the Hebrew *(māšāl)* refers to an apothegm that has currency among those who fear "I Am." Solomon's proverb, "Treasures gained from wickedness have no lasting value, but righteousness delivers from death" (10:2, author's translation), is not popular with the masses. Were it popular with the masses, Wisdom would not have to stand at the gate of the city pleading a hearing for her sayings from unheeding simpletons (1:20-33; 8:1-3).

Proverbs, whether in English or Hebrew, call on the hearer to apply the abstracted truth of a proverb to his or her situation. The word *(māšāl)* means

14. Brevard Childs, *Introduction to the Old Testament as Scripture* (Philadelphia: Fortress, 1979), p. 556.

"to be like." Landis, following McKane, says that this noun means "a comparison or analogy [constructed] for the purpose of conveying a model, exemplar, or paradigm."[15] More specifically, this speech-act, as Polk advanced the argument, calls for heightened reader involvement to exercise the imagination in an effort to forge some sort of equivalence or connection between the proverbs and one's situation.[16] "The poet," as Goethe said, "should seize the particulars, and he should, if there be anything sound in it, thus represent the universal."[17] What is important here for the preacher is the awareness that a proverb is a specific example of a universal truth, an example that is to be applied by the preacher to other specifics. In short, a proverb calls for the preacher's application.

How a proverb is applied depends on the reader's response. According to some theorists, the reader's response to a text determines its meaning. But an expositor seeks to establish the author's intention and knows that the reader response, not the author's intention, determines the application of a text. This point may be illustrated from Psalm 49. The sage introduced his proverb with a call for all to hear. "Hear this, all you peoples; listen, all who live in this world, both low and high, rich and poor alike: My mouth will speak words of wisdom; the meditation of my heart will give you understanding. I will turn my ear to a proverb [*māšāl*]; with the harp I will expound my riddle" (vv. 1-4).

After this introduction the sage developed his poem in two stanzas, each consisting of eight verses and each ending with his proverb in refrains that differ by one letter.

"Human beings, despite their wealth, do not endure [*yalîn*]. They are like [*nimšal*] the beasts that perish" (v. 12; Heb., v. 13).

"Human beings who have wealth but lack understanding [*yābîn*] are like [*nimšal*] the beasts that perish" (v. 20; Heb., v. 21).

According to the first stanza and its refrain, all human beings, wise and fools, despite their wealth, do not endure [*yalîn*]. They perish like the animals. The third line of his first stanza reads, "No one can redeem the life of another or give to God a sufficient ransom" (v. 7).

According to the second stanza and its refrain, however, a fool, who by

15. George M. Landis, "Jonah: A *Māšāl*?" in *Israelite Wisdom*, ed. John G. Gammie et al. (Missoula, MT: Scholars Press, 1978), p. 140.

16. Timothy Polk, "Paradigms, Parables, and *Měšālîm*," *Catholic Biblical Quarterly* 45 (1983): 564-83.

17. Johann Wolfgang von Goethe and Johann Peter Eckermann, *Conversations with Eckermann* (New York: M. Walter Dunne, 1901).

definition is without understanding, perishes eternally like the animals. Though all perish — wise and fools — only fools die eternally. The third line of the second stanza distinguishes the fate of the wise in resurrection from the fate of fools in an eternal doom: "But God will redeem me from the realm of the dead; he will surely take me to himself" (v. 15). The author intended to compare and contrast the wise and fools. But readers will hear his proverb in different ways: it will comfort the lowly, sober the high, warn the rich, and console the poor.

In other words, the proverb calls on the preacher to apply the universal truth of the proverb to the circumstance of his audience. The proverb, "Treasures gained from wickedness have no lasting value, but righteousness delivers from death" (10:2), can be used to sober an audience that trusts in its wealth, or to comfort an audience that is suffering for righteousness' sake, or to admonish an audience not to gain money by hurting others but to use their wealth to help the needy. The meaning of the proverb is one; its potential applications are many.

Number Two: Knowing the Human Author

The second number that must be dialed to unlock the book of Proverbs is knowing the human author. The inherent nature of any object to be studied dictates the best method for elucidating its properties. As James Houston, founder of Regent College, reminds his students, "To understand a matter one must first stand under it." Before designing an accredited hermeneutic to study and understand the Scriptures, one must stand under them to determine their essential nature and to let them dictate an accredited method for their study.

The well-known text, "All Scripture is inspired by God" (2 Tim. 3:16, NASB), implies that three inherent qualities of the biblical text must be recognized. Each quality demands that a proper instrument (i.e., method) be fashioned for understanding it. The phrase "by God," a genitive of authorship, names God as the Author; "inspired," which refers to the written text, implies a human author who mediated the revelation; and "Scripture" denotes a text. All three demand an appropriate approach, and these three approaches must be accepted together because the Bible is a unit that is informed by all three. The first two qualities demand a spiritual commitment on the part of the interpreter, and the third paradoxically calls for approaching the text with the detached objectivity of a scientist.

Of interest here is the need to know the human authors of the Scriptures. Superior intellectual talent and superb education, though not to be despised, cannot render one fit to interpret the Scriptures. To understand them, a reader must encounter their authors with spiritual sympathy, not merely with empathy. Fairbairn argued the necessity of reading the text with a sympathetic spirit.

> *He* [the interpreter] *must endeavor to attain to a sympathy in thought and feeling with the sacred writers, whose meaning he seeks to unfold.* Such a sympathy is not required for the interpretation alone of the inspired writings; it is equally necessary in respect to *any* ancient author. . . . The more we can identify ourselves with the state of mind out of which that thought and feeling arose, the more manifestly shall we be qualified for appreciating the language in which they are embodied, and reproducing true and living impressions of it. . . . Not a few of them [interpreters] have given proof of superior talents, and have brought to the task also the acquirements of a profound and varied scholarship. The lexicography and grammar, the philology and archaeology of Scripture, have been largely indebted to their inquiries and researches; but, from the grievous mental discrepancy existing between the commentator and his author, and the different points of view from which they respectively looked at Divine things, writers of this class necessarily failed to penetrate the depths of the subjects they had to handle, fell often into jejune and superficial representations on particular parts, and on entire books of Scripture never once succeeded in producing a really satisfactory exposition.[18]

Fairbairn also adds an excerpt from Hagenbach's Encyclopedia:

> [A]n inward interest in the doctrine of theology is needful for a Biblical interpreter. As we say that a philosophical spirit is demanded for the study of Plato, a poetical taste for the reading of Homer or Pindar, a sensibility to wit and satire for the perusal of Lucian, a patriotic sentiment for the enjoyment of Sallust and Tacitus, equally certain is it, that the fitness to understand the profound truths of Scripture, of the New Testament especially, presupposes, as an indispensable requisite, a sentiment of piety, an inward religious experience.[19]

18. Patrick Fairbairn, *Hermeneutical Manual: or, Introduction to the Exegetical Study of the Scriptures of the New Testament* (Edinburgh: Clark, 1858), pp. 64-66. Italics his.

19. Fairbairn, *Hermeneutical Manual*, p. 66.

To understand Proverbs one must identify with Solomon and the sages. First, they were spiritually sensitive. They viewed their audience as the covenant people of God, and their wisdom enabled them to see beyond what they saw with their eyes and heard with their ears. Their spiritual sensitivity enabled them to see and hear the human heart. Second, they spoke as kings by divine appointment, that is, they spoke their words as oracles from God with the authority of prophets. Their officials spoke similarly. Third, they were brilliant. These proto-scientists probed into astronomy, gemology, psychology, and so forth; they retained knowledge, had a creative imagination, and expressed themselves with wit and a love for wordplay.

Conclusion

Knowledge of the literary genre of the book of Proverbs and of its authors is fundamental for preaching Proverbs. The proverbs are oracles of God on the preacher's lips that allow him to adapt them for the needs of his audience and also to apply them. Moreover, knowing that their authors are godly kings challenges the expositor both to enter into the king's intimate knowledge of the Law — for on assuming the throne kings copied the Law under the tutelage of the priest — and to have the king's wit. These two — understanding the book's literary genre and its author — are fundamental concepts for expounding the book of Proverbs.

Part 3

In the second lecture in this series we learned that the preamble to Proverbs gives the expositor essential information for the book's interpretation and exposition. Its six fundamentals are like the code of a combination lock, which, when dialed, opens the lock and allows the expositor of Proverbs to lead an audience into this paradise of delights, including eating the honeyed leaves of the tree of life and drinking from a bubbling spring of waters of eternal life.

As noted in the previous section, the first number to be dialed is knowledge of the book's literary genre. In the genre of wisdom literature, Proverbs is an inspired revelation from the Creator, and as a collection of maxims the book coins this revelation in short, pithy, memorable statements. These memorable sayings demand that their readers or hearers exercise their imagination in an effort to forge some sort of equivalence or connection between the proverbs and the readers' or hearers' situation.

The second number that opens the lock and gives access to the book's paradise is knowledge of the human author. To understand him, the hearer must share his spirit: his love for Israel's covenants and his wit to see and to speak.

The present section discusses two more code numbers needed to unlock the book.

Number Three: Understanding the Concept of Wisdom

The third code number to unlock the book is understanding the concept of wisdom. The book's purpose is "to gain wisdom"; the Hebrew root translated "wise" (an adjective), "wisdom" (a noun), or "to be wise" (a verb) is the book's key word. It occurs 102 times in Proverbs — almost a third of its uses in the entire Old Testament. The lectures by the parents and the sermons by Woman Wisdom in the prologue admonish the son or simpleton to be wise. So to know what is being talked about in this book an expositor must master the concept of wisdom.

Mastery of this profound term can be gained by noting three things: the uses of the root for "wisdom" in the Old Testament, the word's sevenfold equivalent terms in 1:2-6, and its coreferential terms "righteousness" and "knowledge."

Uses of the Root "To Be Wise"

In biblical texts outside Proverbs the noun "wisdom" is used of technical and artistic skills (Exod. 28:3; 31:6), of the art of magic (7:11; Isa. 3:3), of government (Eccles. 4:13; Jer. 50:35), of diplomacy (1 Kings 5:7 [Heb., v. 21]), and of war (Isa. 10:13). There is enough commonality in these five specific uses of the word to deduce the abstract meaning of "masterful understanding," "skill," or "expertise."

In the book of Proverbs the uses of the root suggest the more specific sense of "social skill" or "masterful understanding of proper social relationships." Skillful relationships involve the skill of relating to God and to all kinds of people in order to enjoy an abundant life and to avoid death. The wise have the social skill to deal successfully with rich and poor, wise and fools, young and old, parent and child, and others.

Synonyms of Wisdom

In 1:1-7 several synonyms of the word "wisdom" are used. Von Rad referred to the Bible's proclivity for heaping up terms for wisdom as a "stereometric" way of thinking to achieve "the desired extension of the conceptual range."[20] The preamble mentions seven terms: "knowledge," "insight," "prudence," "cunning," "discretion," "learning," and "guidance." These virtues come as wisdom's attendants. For as Woman Wisdom says, "I, wisdom, dwell together with prudence; I possess knowledge and discretion. To fear the LORD is to hate evil; I hate pride and arrogance, evil behavior and perverse speech. Counsel and sound judgment are mine; I have insight, I have power" (8:12-14).

Wisdom's Coreferential Term "Righteousness"

Wisdom and its synonyms are neutral with regard to morality. For example, Pharaoh labeled his magicians who had mastered black magic as "wise men" (Exod. 7:11), and though a murderer may be 'ormâ ("cunning," 21:14, author's translation), wisdom dwells with 'ormâ ("prudence," Prov. 8:12). In the book of Proverbs, however, "wisdom" and its equivalents are never used as pejorative terms or even as morally neutral terms, but always as favorable terms. Wisdom and her attendants are protected against misunderstanding by coreferential terms such as "righteousness," "justice," and "equity."

Coreferential terms belong to different semantic domains but speak of the same referent. For example, a person may be referred to as the vice president of the United States by his relationship to the president or as chair of the senate of the United States by his relationship to the senate. Though these are different concepts, he cannot be one without being the other. "Vice president" and "chair of the senate" designate different notions, but they refer to the same person. The same is true of the terms "the righteous" and "the wise." They pertain to the different semantic fields of ethics and intelligence, but they refer to the same person. The wise are righteous and the righteous are wise; they go together like a horse and a carriage. The preamble binds together the coreferential sapiential and ethical terms in verse 3: "for receiving instruction in prudent behavior, doing what is right and just and fair."

Moreover, throughout the book "wise" and "righteous" versus "fool" and "wickedness" are used interchangeably.

20. Gerhard von Rad, *Wisdom in Israel* (London: SCM Press, 1972), p. 13.

"Righteousness" is a social term signifying that people do right by each other as defined by God's covenants with Israel. In a nutshell "righteousness" means "to disadvantage oneself as necessary in order to advantage others," and "wickedness" means "to disadvantage others in order to advantage oneself." A student who takes a reserved book out of the library to get an A, leaving the rest of the class to get a lower grade, is wicked (i.e., a fool). By contrast, a student who resists the temptation to check out a rare book from the library so that his or her classmates have the opportunity to read and write an "A" paper, even if it means he gets a lower grade, is righteous (i.e., wise). Righteousness, the disadvantaging of oneself to advantage others, is counterintuitive. Jesus Christ is the supreme example of wisdom according to this definition.

Wisdom's Coreferential Term "Knowledge"

Another coreferential term for wisdom is "knowledge." The inseparable connection of "wisdom" and "knowledge" can be inferred from their parallelism in 1:7, the so-called key to the book: "The fear of the LORD is the beginning of knowledge, but fools despise wisdom and instruction." The inclusio to this key verse is 9:10. "The fear of the LORD is the beginning of wisdom, and knowledge of the Holy One is understanding." Thus "wisdom" and "knowledge," though different notions, seem to be interchangeable.

To state their inseparable relationship more precisely, "knowledge" is essential to "wisdom" (i.e., to skill). The Wright brothers "miraculously" flew the first airplane because they had worked out the laws of aerodynamics. In Proverbs "wisdom" denotes mastery over social relationships by knowing the deed-destiny nexus — that is, righteous behavior (serving others) tears down strongholds and promotes the life of an individual and a community. The proverbs of Solomon and the sayings of the wise provide the knowledge that, when actualized, affects social skills, wisdom.

Number Four: Identifying the Audience

The fourth number to be dialed in opening the combination lock to wise living is identifying the book's audience. The expositor must understand to whom his text was addressed. The answer in Proverbs is threefold: originally budding officials in Jerusalem's royal court, then all of Israel's youth, and third, all the people of God.

Budding Officials

Before being gathered into the collections that compose the book of Proverbs, its aphorisms were coined by kings and royal officials. The named authors in Proverbs are King Solomon, King Hezekiah's men, King Lemuel, and the court official Agur. The analogous Ancient Near Eastern wisdom literature names both the vizier who coined and collected the sayings, and the budding official, his son or nephew, whom he mentored.

The original court setting of the apothegms explains their dominant royal content. "When you sit to dine with a ruler, note well what is before you, and put a knife to your throat if you are given to gluttony. Do not crave his delicacies, for that food is deceptive" (23:1-3).

Obviously this admonishment is addressed to a court official, not to a normal, run-of-the-mill person. Malchow labeled chapters 28–29 a manual for kings.[21]

All Israel's Youth, Both Wise and Simpletons

When these collections of aphorisms were gathered to make the book of Proverbs, they were democratized for all of Israel's youth, not for just the royal court. In striking contrast to the Egyptian parallel instruction literature, the book of Proverbs names no individual addressee. Rather it addresses all of Israel's youth.

The preamble divides Israel's youth into the two categories of simpletons and wise: "for giving prudence to those who are simple, knowledge and discretion to the young — let the wise listen and add to their learning, and let the discerning get guidance" (1:4-5).

The simpletons are qualified simply by "young" in the parallel line in verse 4, and the "wise" are specified as "my son" in the parental lectures that follow.

The wise. The parents' ten lectures are addressed to their son. Essentially they call on the son "to hear" and "to be wise." The first "lecture" points to their content: "Listen, my son, to your father's instruction, and do not forsake your mother's teaching" (v. 8).

This admonition that begins Collection I, composed of lectures and sermons, comports well with the first proverb of Collection II, which though

---

21. Bruce V. Malchow, "A Manual for Future Monarchs," *Catholic Biblical Quarterly* 47 (1985): 238-45.

not in the form of an admonition, implies it: "A wise son brings joy to his father, but a foolish son grief to his mother" (10:1, NIV).

Advancing from "Listen, my son," which introduces the first lecture, the third lecture is introduced by the exhortation "do not forget." "My son, do not forget my teaching, but keep my commands in your heart" (3:1). "Let love and faithfulness never leave you; bind them around your neck, write them on the tablet of your heart" (v. 3).

A similar progression is evident in the fourth sermon. "Blessed are those who find wisdom, those who gain understanding. . . . She is a tree of life to those who take hold of her; those who hold her fast will be blessed. . . . My son, do not let wisdom and understanding out of your sight, preserve sound judgment and discretion" (3:13, 18, 21).

The son is assumed to be accepting the parents' lectures to be wise. If so, he is wise.

The simpleton. Whereas the son orients himself to the parents' lectures in the home, the simpleton has moved beyond puberty into society without having made a decision to own the catechism.

The word "simpleton" renders the Hebrew *pᵉtî,* which basically means "to be open." A simpleton is complacent. He has heard Israel's worldview and life-view of reality in its covenants and proverbs, but he refuses to commit himself to Israel's covenants and its inherited wisdom based on those covenants. The sage lumps the uncommitted, gullible simpletons, who are open to both wisdom and folly, together with condemned fools and mockers. But there is still hope for him as seen in this appeal by wisdom. "How long will you who are simple love your simple ways? . . . Repent at my rebuke! Then I will pour out my thoughts to you, I will make known to you my teachings. But since you refuse to listen when I call and no one pays attention when I stretch out my hand, since you disregard all my advice and do not accept my rebuke, I in turn will laugh when disaster strikes you" (1:22-26).

At the end of the prologue both wisdom and folly contend for the soul of the simpleton as represented by their rival invitations to their fictitious meals. Woman Wisdom has built a perfect house with seven pillars, large enough to host all who want to enter and dine with her. Hers is a royal banquet of mixed wine (i.e., the catechistic collections that follow). "Wisdom has built her house; she has set up its seven pillars. She has prepared her meat and mixed her wine; she has also set her table. She has sent out her servants, and she calls from the highest point of the city, 'Let all who are simple come to my house!' To those who have no sense she says, 'Come, eat my food and drink the wine I have mixed. Leave your simple ways and you will live; walk in the way of insight'" (9:1-6).

Woman Folly also appeals to the simpletons to come into her house. She pretentiously sits as queen, inviting the simple to drink stolen water (i.e., to enjoy sex outside of marriage), which stands in sharp contrast to Woman Wisdom's strong wine of wise sayings. "Folly is an unruly woman; she is simple and knows nothing. She sits at the door of her house, on a seat at the highest point of the city, calling out to those who pass by, who go straight on their way, 'Let all who are simple come to my house!' To those who have no sense, she says, 'Stolen water is sweet; food eaten in secret is delicious!' But little do they know that the dead are there, that her guests are in the realm of the dead" (vv. 13-18).

In summary, the expositor motivates the youth of his congregation to grow in wisdom with the promise of eternal life, and he threatens the uncommitted with the possibility of death.

Sons and daughters. The wise and simple are reckoned as sons. Are the daughters excluded from the book's audience? Although *ben* can mean "child," the obvious male orientation of the book shows that the son, not the daughter, is in view. Nevertheless Proverbs indicates that daughters were not excluded from being educated in its catechism of aphorisms and that the book has women as well as men in its audience.

The mother is identified along with the father as the authoritative voice in the home. She is mentioned in parallel with the father in 1:8 ("Listen, my son, to your father's instruction and do not forsake your mother's teaching") and in 10:1 ("A wise son brings joy to his father, but a foolish son grief to his mother," NIV). The mention of the mother at these junctures implies that when the father is mentioned in the other terse proverbs, the mother, though not mentioned, is an unstated parallel with the father. Both parents are the authoritative voices in the home before their children. The book's conclusion points to the noble wife and mother as the exemplar of the book's teachings (31:10-31), and she is commended for having faithful instruction on her tongue (v. 26).

For the mother to instruct her household she herself had to know Israel's inherited wisdom. The dissemination of the book's content through the mother means that she herself had to be taught wisdom in the home by her parents and/or by her husband. Deuteronomy 31:9-12 explicitly states that the women were instructed in the book of the Law, and Proverbs implies that they memorized its catechism.

Instead of mentioning his daughter, the father singled out the son because the male offspring was expected to assume leadership in defining the family's identity and values.

All of God's People

When the book of Proverbs was recognized as canonical literature, its audience expanded beyond the royal court and Israel's youth to the entire covenant community, young and old alike. Paul, the apostle to the Gentiles, wrote, "All Scripture is God-breathed and is useful for teaching, rebuking, correcting and training in righteousness, so that all God's people may be thoroughly equipped for every good work" (2 Tim. 3:16-17).

The book sets no age limit on learning wisdom. "Let the wise listen and add to their learning" (Prov. 1:5). What Augustine said of the Bible — "It is shallow enough for a baby to wade in, but deep enough for an elephant to drown in it" — is especially true of Proverbs. In other words, the expositor addresses all the discerning: novitiate and trained, the wise of all ages. There is no time restraint on growing in wisdom.

Excursus: Identification of Woman Wisdom

Since the parents lectured the son in the home and Woman Wisdom preached to the simpletons at the city gate, the expositor should have an understanding of this woman's identity.

First, Wisdom is represented as a woman because abstract nouns, such as *ḥokmâ* ("wisdom"), commonly end with the suffix *â*. This suffix with animate nouns signifies the feminine gender in contrast to the masculine. So when an abstract noun that ends in *â* is personified, as in the case of *ḥokmâ*, it must be personified as a female. Karl Brugmann demonstrated in 1895 that this grammatical phenomenon is true of mythic personifications in all languages. For example, Russians personify the days of the week as male or female on the basis of the day's grammatical gender.[22]

In the two addresses to simpletons at the entrance to the gate, this mythic Woman is unique. She wears a prophet's mantle, carries a sage's scroll, and wears a goddess-like diadem. She preaches and pleads with a prophet's passion, thinks and circulates with "intellectuals," and wields the

---

22. Bruce K. Waltke and Michael P. O'Connor, *Introduction to Biblical Hebrew Syntax* (Winona Lake, IN: Eisenbrauns, 1990), p. 100.

authority of God. The prophetic, sapient, and divine components of her characterization so penetrate each other that she emerges as a unique personality whose only peer is Jesus Christ. Her identification as an incarnate heavenly being who in humility accepts the rejection by the masses of her offer to them of eternal life functions within the canon as a foreshadowing of him who is greater than Solomon.

But she is not Jesus Christ. Rather she is a figurative personification of the book's wisdom that is promoted in its proverbs. According to the preamble, the book's aim is to teach wisdom through these collections of inspired aphorisms. The book's key word, wisdom, refers to the substance of these sayings. Wisdom in this book never refers to anything else. Exegetically the only possible interpretation of her identity is that she is a figurative personification of the book's teaching.

In her famous soliloquy in 8:22-31 Woman Wisdom argues that she (i.e., the wisdom of this book) was born from God's nature, existed before anything else was formed, and saw the whole creation. "The LORD brought me forth as the first of his works, before his deeds of old; I was formed long ages ago, at the very beginning, when the world came to be. When there were no oceans, I was given birth, when there were no springs abounding with water; before the mountains were settled in place, before the hills, I was given birth, before he made the world or its fields or any of the dust of the earth. I was there when he set the heavens in place, when he marked out the horizon on the face of the deep, when he established the clouds above and fixed securely the fountains of the deep, when he gave the sea its boundary so the waters would not overstep his command, and when he marked out the foundations of the earth. Then I was constantly at his side. I was filled with delight day after day, rejoicing always in his presence, rejoicing in his whole world and delighting in humankind."

In other words, because she was begotten from the divine nature, Solomon's teaching derives from God's attributes, and because she was constantly at the Creator's side while he made everything, Solomon's teachings are based on comprehensive knowledge and thus certain values, not contingent evaluations.

Expositors of Proverbs who give Woman Wisdom a voice from their pulpits inferentially wear a prophet's mantle, carry a sage's scroll, and wear a heavenly crown as they proclaim with a clear voice and full lungs God's truth. May they preach as boldly, urgently, and passionately as Woman Wisdom.

Part 4

The preamble to Proverbs presents the code that opens the lock to a gated paradise. The previous two sections have discussed the first four numbers of the code: (1) understanding the literary genre of the book of Proverbs, assuring the expositor that God's authority is stamped on its coined and relevant proverbs; (2) understanding its human authors, especially Solomon, who shared his knowledge of God's ways in witty words; (3) understanding its concept of wisdom, namely, social skills that produce an abundant life of health, wealth, and peace; and (4) understanding its intended audiences: the royal court, Israel's youth, and all the people of God.

The last two numbers of the code are understanding its words (1:6), and understanding the concept of "the fear of 'I Am'" (v. 7).

Number Five: Understanding Its Words

The preamble's summary statement of purpose includes the words "for understanding words of insight" (1:2). In Hebrew, unlike English, "word" refers to an entire sentence — in this case a proverb or saying — not an isolated term within it. Moreover, understanding grammar is essential if one is to be literate. Knowledge of phonology (meaningful sounds), morphology (meaningful terms), and syntax (meaningful combinations of terms) is the means for all discernment. Without knowing grammar, the expositor cannot know the message. Knowledge of Hebrew grammar is essential for interpreting the book of Proverbs accurately, for its sages play with sound and sense in that language.

However, the aphorisms of Proverbs require more than an understanding of Hebrew grammar. Verse 6 expands the summary statement with these words: "for understanding proverbs and parables, the sayings and riddles of the wise" (v. 6).

"Words" of the summary are now specified as "proverbs" and "sayings," which refer to the many statements in the book's seven collections. The proverbs and sayings are further specified as "parables" and "riddles." The words for proverbs, parables, and riddles are used together in Habakkuk 2:6 to describe the same poem, suggesting that "parables" and "riddles" are coreferential terms for the synonyms "proverbs" and "sayings."

The proverbs of Solomon and the sayings of the wise are parables and riddles because they demand the noetic and existential function to relate the proverb to one's own situation. The book's aphorisms call on audiences to

make intuitive critical judgments about their own situations. An example is
Agur's numerical saying in 30:24-28. "Four things on earth are small, yet
they are extremely wise: ants are creatures of little strength, yet they store up
their food in the summer; hyraxes are creatures of little power, yet they make
their home in the crags; locusts have no king, yet they advance together in
ranks; a lizard can be caught with the hand, yet it is found in kings' palaces."

According to the superscript, Agur's inspired sayings were addressed
to Ithiel, a court official (vv. 1-2), whom he warned not to exalt himself above
his superiors (vv. 32-33). Agur, a moral teacher and prophet, was not aiming
to teach Ithiel zoology through this numerical proverb. Rather, the small animals represent a weak and vulnerable official such as Ithiel, who represents
all God's people. Yet the vulnerable creatures (lit., "people") function as a
parable on survival. From the weak ant, one can learn to prepare for the future by making provision ahead of time. The ant also may suggest storing up
these sayings to have them ready on one's lips when needed (22:18), as Jesus
did in having the book of the Law on his lips to defeat the devil.

From the defenseless hyrax or rock badger one can learn to find protection in the crag of a rock, such as trusting God with all one's heart (3:5;
22:19). And from the locust one can learn not to be a maverick but to prevail
in community. And yes, wonder of wonders, a person, though nothing more
than a lizard, may live in a royal palace, even the ivory palace of heaven.

This interpretation is not allegory; it is the intention of the riddle to be
applied in these practical ways.

Whether the riddle refers also to rhetorical criticism is uncertain, but
the expositor of Proverbs must master the book's rhetoric. The first grouping
of proverbs in Collection II (10:1-5) pertains to money. The second grouping
of proverbs in Collection II (vv. 6-14) pertains to communication.

6 Blessings crown the head of the righteous,
  but violence overwhelms the mouth of the wicked
  [ûpî r^ešā^cîm y^ekasseh ḥāmās].
7 The name of the righteous is used in blessings,
  but the name of the wicked will rot.
8 The wise in heart accept commands,
  but a chattering [lit., "lippy"] fool comes to ruin.
9 Whoever walks in integrity walks securely,
  but whoever takes crooked paths will be found out.
10 Whoever winks [lit., "winks the eye"] maliciously causes grief,
  and a chattering [lit., "lippy"] fool comes to ruin.

¹¹ The mouth of the righteous is a fountain of life,
    but the mouth of the wicked conceals violence
    [*ûpî rᵉšāʿîm yᵉkasseh ḥāmās*].
¹² Hatred stirs up dissension,
    but love covers over all wrongs.
¹³ Wisdom is found on the lips of the discerning,
    but a rod is for the back of one who has no sense.
¹⁴ The wise store up knowledge,
    but the mouth of a fool invites ruin.

On first reading, these verses seem a willy-nilly lumping together of unrelated proverbs, but a knowledge of rhetorical criticism suggests that the unit falls into two equal halves, each having four antithetical proverbs (see the word "but" in vv. 6-9 and 11-14) around a janus pivot of synthetic parallels (introduced in Hebrew by "and" in v. 10).

The collection is unified and made more memorable by mentioning two body parts in the first verse of each quatrain. "Head" and "mouth" occur in verse 6, "heart" and "lips" occur in verse 8, and "lips" and "back" in verse 13.

Of these body parts the focus is on those involved in communication. The mouth is mentioned four times (vv. 6, 10 [twice], 14), lips three times (vv. 8, 10, 13), and the sinister eye once (v. 10). Six of the nine verses in the second grouping mention body parts, and of the eleven mentioned body parts, eight refer to organs of communication. The key words "mouth" and "lip" point to the unit's topic of "speech," or more broadly, "communication."

Thematically the first half of the unit (vv. 6-9) focuses on the effects of good and bad communication on oneself. And the second half of the unit (vv. 10-14) focuses on the effects of good and bad speech on others.

The center verse (v. 10) chiastically reverses the pattern, pointing to the pain to others of bad communication in the first line and its pain to oneself in the second line. This unexpected reversal is clearly signaled by repeating the second line of verse 8 in verse 10: "a chattering [lit., 'lippy'] fool comes to ruin." Then other patterns emerge. "Mouth" occurs in the two verses (vv. 6, 11) that introduce the unit's two halves.

Moreover, each of these two verses juxtaposes the "righteous" versus "the wicked." Even more striking is the play in sound and sense in these introductions: "but violence overwhelms the mouth of the wicked" (v. 6) and "but the mouth of the wicked conceals violence" (v. 11). The Hebrew is the same in these two verses. The chiastic parallelism in verse 6 shows that "violence" is the subject, the verb means "cover," and "the mouth of the wicked" is the object. But in verse 11 the chiastic parallelism shows that "violence" is the object (*y^ekasseh* again means "cover"), and "the mouth of the wicked" is the subject. The initial pun links the two halves and signals that the first pertains to the effects of communication on oneself (vv. 6-9), and the second pertains to its effects on others (vv. 11-14).

Moreover, "mouth," a key word in the semantic domain of communication, frames the unit in verse 6 ("the mouth of the wicked") and in verse 14 ("the mouth of a fool").

Unless the expositor wears the glasses of rhetorical criticism in reading the Hebrew text, he cannot see clearly its meaning and its message. To coin a proverb, "To know what a text means, one must know how it means."

The big idea of 10:6-14 may be stated this way: "Good communication heals; bad communication hurts." Of course there is a pun in the thesis: good speech heals oneself and others, and bad speech hurts oneself and others. From that, the message becomes: Learn to speak well and heal a community; avoid bad speech that burns it down.

A sermonic outline can now be developed that faithfully represents the exegetical outline of the text.

I. The beneficial and baneful effects of speech on oneself (vv. 6-10)
   A. Beneficial effects of good speech
      1. People will crown you with blessings during your lifetime (v. 6a).
      2. Your memory will bring blessings on others for generations (v. 7a).
      3. You will walk securely and not be tripped up (v. 9a).
   B. Baneful effects of bad speech
      1. Your violent speech will boomerang (v. 6b).
      2. Your memory will rot and stink (v. 7b).
      3. You will come to ruin (vv. 8b, 10b).

An alternating parallelism exists between A.1 (crown you) and B.1 (come back on you); between A.2 (memory will bring a blessing) and B.2 (memory will stink); and between A.3 (walking securely) and B.3 (come to ruin).

II. The beneficial and baneful effects of speech on others (vv. 11-14)
   A. Beneficial effects of good speech on others
      1. Your righteous speech will be a fountain of life (v. 11a).
      2. Your discerning lips will yield wisdom (v. 13a).

    3. Your wise speech will be a storehouse of knowledge (v. 14a).
  B. Baneful effects of bad speech on others
    1. Sinister speech causes grief (v. 10a).
    2. Hateful speech causes quarrels (v. 12a).
    3. Foolish speech is like a cherry bomb (v. 14b).
III. Conclusion
  A. Accept these commands (v. 8a).
  B. Live by them constantly (v. 9a).
  C. It is a matter of the heart: hate versus love (v. 12).[23]

Number Six: Understanding the Fear of "I Am"

According to the preamble, the final code number for unlocking Proverbs is the mastery of the concept of "the fear of 'I Am.'" Preambles to Egyptian instructive literature contain a code similar to the first five numbers, but this sixth number, understanding "the fear of 'I Am,'" is unique to the Bible. Many call this number *the key* to the book of Proverbs. "The fear of the Lord is the beginning of knowledge, but fools despise wisdom and instruction" (1:7).

"Beginning" means the foundation, on which all is built; it may be likened to the first step of a ladder on which the other steps are built, not to a starting block that the runner leaves behind. Elsewhere "the fear of 'I Am'" is said to be founded on wisdom, not on its coreferential term "knowledge" as here (see 9:10). Probably the correlative term "knowledge" was used in 1:7 to make the pun and an inclusio with 1:2a, which reads, *lᵉda'at ḥokmā ûmîsār* ("for gaining wisdom and instruction"). Verse 7a reads, "The fear of the Lord is *da'at* ('knowledge'); *ḥokmā ûmûsār* ('wisdom and instruction') fools despise."

The expositor can gain mastery of the concept of "the fear of the Lord ['I Am']" by noting that the expression is a collocation of two Hebrew terms, by defining the collocation from its uses, and by exegeting 2:1-5, which analyzes the psychological-spiritual components of "the fear of 'I Am.'"

"The Fear of 'I Am'" Is a Collocation

The combination of *zyʿrat* ("fear") plus *yhwh* ("I Am") yields a distinct meaning. The formula H_2O is not the same as the differentiated two parts of

---

23. For insights from rhetorical criticism see Bruce K. Waltke, *The Book of Proverbs, Chapters 1–15* (Grand Rapids: Eerdmans, 2004), pp. 47-48.

hydrogen and one part of oxygen, and concrete does not exist without mixing cement with water. Even as one will not understand "butterfly" by analyzing "butter" and "fly" independently, so also "the fear of 'I Am'" cannot be understood by studying "fear" and "I Am" in isolation.

Uses of "The Fear of 'I Am'"

From its uses one can deduce that this collocation involves both rational and nonrational aspects of the human psyche. On the one hand "the fear of 'I Am'" includes a rational aspect, an involvement with words of an objective revelation that can be taught and memorized (cf. Ps. 34:11). In Psalm 19:7-9 "the fear of 'I Am'" is equated with "law," "statutes," "precepts," "commands," and "ordinances."

On the other hand, "the fear of 'I Am'" also has a nonrational aspect, an emotional response of fear, love, and trust. The unified psychological poles of fear and love come prominently to the fore in a surprisingly uniform way. Deuteronomy treats "love of 'I Am'" and "the fear of 'I Am'" as coreferential terms (cf. 5:29 with 6:2; and 6:5 with Josh. 24:14). This emotional response finds expression in humility, a brokenness that obeys the Lord. "The fear of 'I Am'" and humility are parallel terms in Proverbs 15:33. "Wisdom's instruction is to fear 'I Am,' and humility comes before honor." And 22:4 reads, literally, "The wages for humility — the fear of 'I Am' sort — are riches, honor, and life." The New International Version glosses the awkward grammar by rendering the verse, "Humility is the fear of the LORD; its wages are riches and honor and life."

The emotional link connecting God's objective revelation with meekness is "the fear of 'I Am.'" The wise humble themselves before God's revelation because they fear and stand in awe of "I Am," who holds their lives in his hand. For the wise "the fear of 'I Am'" and the love of "I Am" are coreferential terms for their spiritual disposition. Both aspects of their psyche are rooted in their faith; they believe he is, that he has spoken in the Bible, that he says what he means, and that he means what he says. They believe his promises and love him; they believe his threats and fear him. Bridges writes that the fear of the Lord is "that affectionate reverence, by which the child of God bends himself humbly and carefully to his Father's law."[24]

---

24. Charles Bridges, *An Exposition of Proverbs* (Evansville, IN: Sovereign Grace Book Club, 1959), pp. 3-4.

Exegesis of Proverbs 2:1-5

"My son, if you accept my words and store up my commands within you, turning your ear to wisdom, and applying your heart to understanding — indeed, if you call out for insight and cry aloud for understanding, and if you look for it as for silver and search for it as for hidden treasure, then you will understand the fear of the LORD and find the knowledge of God."

Accepting the catechism. The first four verses discuss the condition for understanding "the fear of 'I Am,'" and each verse mentions the objective revelation that the mind must engage either by its outward expression ("words," "commands") or by its content ("wisdom," "understanding," "insight"). The revelation in view is the seven collections of Proverbs, which may be referred to as "the catechism."

The first requirement is to accept the catechism, thereby laying the foundation for the heaping up of other components for understanding "the fear of 'I Am.'" "To accept" entails a faith commitment to the catechism. Science philosopher Michael Polanyi argues that true knowledge flows from personal commitment to a set of particulars, as tools or clues, to shape a skillful achievement. True knowledge, he says, does not come from mere detached observation of those tools. From a set of clues a scientist commits himself to a theory that leads to new knowledge. Somewhat analogously, a child knows, discovers, learns, and experiences the skill of riding a bicycle by risking and committing himself or herself to the ride and using skillful actions — not by acquiring facts about a bicycle. One understands "the fear of 'I Am'" and knows God not merely by reading and/or hearing the catechism but by accepting it, that is, by entrusting one's life and behavior to it. This commitment is counterintuitive because it calls on the catechumen to serve others, not self, with the faith that God rewards that lifestyle. In fact, that commitment may involve taking up a cross, or even accepting death, to serve God and others.

Memorizing the catechism with religious affection. In the second condition, "if you store up my commands within you," "commands" escalates "words," and "store up" escalates "accept." "Store up" means to hide or conceal something for a definite purpose (cf. Ps. 119:11), in this case, to receive a religious and ethical education. The notion of storing up implies that one prizes and treats as a treasure what is being stored (see Prov. 2:4). The metaphor alludes to memorizing carefully the catechism. The prologue to the Thirty Sayings of the Wise reaffirms this second component of what it means to fear "I Am," namely, to memorize the catechism with religious affection. "Pay attention and turn your ear to the sayings of the wise; apply your heart to what I teach, for it is pleasing when you keep them in your heart and have all of them ready on your lips" (22:17-18).

Paying attention to the catechism. However, memorization is not enough. One must pay attention to what is memorized. Proverbs 2:2 breaks the syntax between the conditional clauses of verse 1 and verses 3-4 and the consequence in verses 5-19, and so verse 2 constitutes an aside. Literally verse 2 reads, "by making your ear attentive to wisdom you will incline your heart to understanding." This aside has its own condition and consequence, for it implies, "If you pay attention to the wisdom taught in these sayings, you will incline your heart to understanding [piety, vv. 5-8, and ethics, vv. 9-11]."

"To make the ear attentive" is a vivid way of saying "to pay attention." Simone Weil and others argue that moral improvement does not come about by the exercise of the will. "Moral change comes from an attention to the world whose natural result is a decrease in egoism through an increased sense of the reality of someone or something. . . . Change of behaving, *metanoia*, is not brought about by straining and 'will-power,' but a long deep process of unselfing."[25] This psychological process "inclines the heart," a metaphor meaning "to win over the heart." When a student has an increased sense of the reality of the catechism, the truth of the catechism wins over the heart from self-absorption to experiencing the fear of "I Am."

Passionately desiring the truths of the catechism. The fourth component in this heaping up of parallel terms to hear stereophonically what it means to fear "I Am" is to desire them passionately. "Call out for insight and cry aloud for understanding" (v. 3).

"Cry aloud" translates a Hebrew term that refers to a fervent and emotional situation, as when Joseph wept so loudly in his own chambers that Pharaoh's whole household heard him (Gen. 45:2).

Earnestly studying the catechism. The fifth component achieves the desired extension of the conceptual range of what is meant by "the fear of 'I Am.'" "And if you look for it as for silver and search for it as for hidden treasure" (Prov. 2:4). "To seek" means to search for something lost or missed, and when that something is silver and the crown jewels, the desire to fulfill a wish or realize a plan, that searching has an extreme emotional nuance, "to strive after something, to be busy, to be concerned." The metaphor may also imply that a great deal of effort and sacrifice must be expended to get it. "Though it cost all you have, get understanding" (4:7).

25. Iris Murdoch, *Metaphysics as a Guide to Morals* (London: Penguin, 1993), pp. 52-54.

Conclusion

The biblical expositor recognizes that the initial condition leading to "the fear of 'I Am'" is to accept God's good gift (James 1:17). In other words, he depends on God's grace to empower his preaching. Moreover, he takes note of the progress of revelation. In the Old Testament, God encountered his people in the catechism of these seven collections, their memorizing it with religious affection, their "de-selfing" themselves in their paying attention to it, and their passionate yearning and willingness to make sacrifices to realize its truth.

In the New Testament, however, God encounters his people in his own person, in his Son. "The fear of 'I Am'" for the church now involves their engaging these spiritual and psychological processes with reference to Jesus Christ and his teachings. His teachings extend those of the catechism to their fullest range. In Christ's resurrection the abundant life promised in Proverbs reaches its full conceptual range. Jesus Christ brought the full light of the day, and so the expositor preaches the book of Proverbs in the zenith of the day.

The First Seven Days: What Is the Creation Account Trying to Tell Us?

Evangelicals agree that the Bible is the inspired word of God. And they reject in unison any approach that treats Scripture with a profound skepticism regarding its historical credibility. Yet when they read Genesis 1:1–2:3, there is anything but unanimity.

While there seems to be great variety of opinion, we can generally divide evangelical scholars who study the early chapters of Genesis into two groups: *concordists* and *nonconcordists*.

The concordists try to harmonize (or find concord between) Genesis 1:1–2:3 and scientific descriptions of the earth's origins. Some (called *scientific creationists*) harmonize science with their straightforward reading of the Bible. Others (called *creation scientists*) harmonize the Bible with science.

The creation scientists, in turn, are composed of various subgroups: *progressives* (who construe the "days" of Genesis as immense periods of time) and *re-creationists* (who reckon with more than one creation). In addition, there are *transformationalists,* who argue for a pre-Genesis earth and time. They may belong to either kind of concordists. Re-creationists and transformationalists reject the traditional reading of Genesis 1:1-3, which understand those verses to describe the beginning of earth-time, when God created the earth from nothing.

The second group, nonconcordists, may disagree about the meaning of "days" and the syntax of Genesis 1:1-3. But they agree that Genesis teaches neither straightforward history nor science, and needs no reconciliation

---

Previously published in *Christianity Today,* August 12, 1988. Used by permission.

with the kind of history and science devoted exclusively to what can be observed and measured.

Which of these groups you find yourself in depends on how you answer three big questions about the biblical creation account:

- What kind of literature is Genesis 1:1–2:3?
- What does the author mean by the word *day*?
- How are the phrases and sentences of Genesis 1:1-3 related?

Let us examine them in reverse order.

How Is Genesis 1:1-3 Put Together?

Knowing how the various parts of a statement are related can make a big difference in our understanding. For instance, I might write: "I went to my office today. The telephone system wasn't working right. I felt discouraged. I went home early." That is rather inelegant writing, in part because I did not explicitly connect the ideas with words that showed time relationships or cause-and-effect patterns. You would probably read some relationships into that passage — that the malfunctioning telephones caused my discouragement — and you might be right; but you might be wrong.

Likewise, the first few sentences of Genesis are not connected in a clear way. Thus scholars suggest relationships between the sentences and come to different understandings of the text.

One group of scholars sees Genesis 1:2 as contemporaneous with Genesis 1:1. This is a traditional view in which 1:1 recounts God's original creation of the earth, and 1:2 gives us three situations belonging to the same period: (a) the earth was "formless and empty"; (b) there was "darkness over the surface of the deep"; and (c) "the Spirit of God hovered over the waters." Following this line of thought, Calvin commented: "For Moses simply intends to assert that the world was not perfected at its commencement . . ."

All schools of thought see God's activity of 1:3 ("Let there be light") as later than the situation in 1:2. But this school sees all of 1:1-5 (from "In the beginning" right through the end of the first day's creation) belonging to the same chronological grouping.

In its favor, this view has the support of the classic Hebrew grammar, Gesenius-Kautzsch-Cowley. And theologians prefer it to a transformational theory that reads God's "In the beginning" creation of 1:1 as earlier creation attempts than the one described in the six days recounted in the rest of the chapter.

But there are insurmountable problems with this traditional interpretation. This passage contains pairs of words called *syntagms*, words that occur together in various contexts to denote one unique notion. One scholar explained it this way: "In language, as in chemistry, a compound may be found to possess qualities absent from its constituent elements. For example, anyone who does not know what 'broadcast' denotes, will not be able to guess the connotation of the word from its separate elements 'broad' and 'cast'" (U. Cassuto, *A Commentary on the Book of Genesis*).

Let us take the word-pair *heaven and earth*. Like our phrase *night and day*, it is a statement of opposites to indicate totality. *Night and day* means "all the time." Likewise, *heaven and earth* signifies "the entire organized universe" or "the cosmos." Brevard Childs of Yale Divinity School concludes that this syntagm never stands for disorderly chaos, but always for an ordered world. And John Skinner says it is "a Hebrew designation of the universe as a whole . . . the organized universe, not the chaotic material out of which it was formed."

Next let us look at *empty and formless*. This word pair (which reads *tohu wabohu* in Hebrew) is a rhyming syntagm, something like the English phrase *hanky-panky*. It stands for "chaos," and it is the antithesis of the "cosmos" of verse 1. Logically, the disorderly chaos and the orderly cosmos cannot be applied to the same thing at the same time — and thus verses 1 and 2 simply cannot be contemporaneous.

Another way to understand the relationship between the sentences of Genesis 1:1-3 is to see verse 2 as following verse 1 in time.

According to re-creationists, verse 2 tells of a second creation that happened after the original creation recorded in verse 1. The first creation, they say, may have occurred millions of years ago but was reduced to chaos by divine judgment on disobedient spiritual beings; and the second creation happened around 4000 BC. According to this so-called gap theory, most fossils are relics of the first creation.

Although it was the Scofield Reference Bible that popularized and sanctioned this view in 1909, it has its roots in early Jewish tradition and has been held throughout the history of the church. Moreover, the verb translated "was" in verse 2 may mean "became" — "The earth *became* formless and empty." Finally, the condition "formless and empty," when it occurs in other Old Testament contexts (Jer. 4:23; Isa. 34:10), is the result of divine judgment.

But this interpretation faces an insurmountable problem: the "and" that introduces the "formless and empty" description of verse 2 does not imply a subsequent situation (unlike the "and" introducing verse 3: "And [then] God said: 'Let there be light'"). Also, although the formlessness and emptiness in Isaiah and Jeremiah result from God's fury, it is not logically necessary (or even likely) that this chaos arises from his wrath. Peter knows of only two divine judgments on the whole earth: a past flood and a future fire (2 Peter 3:5-7).

A third way to understand the relationship between the Bible's first sentences is to see verse 1 as a dependent clause, with verse 2 as either a parenthesis or the principal clause — as in several recent translations:

> When God began to create the heaven and the earth — the earth being
> unformed and void . . . — God said . . .
> (Jewish Publication Society, 1962)
> In the beginning, when God created the heavens and the earth, the
> earth was a formless wasteland. . . . Then God said . . .
> (New American Bible, 1970)
> In the beginning of creation, when God made heaven and earth, the
> earth was without form and void. . . . God said . . .
> (New English Bible, 1970)

All three endorse a transformational view of creation, entailing a pre-Genesis time and chaotic place.

The eminent scholar of Hebrew Scriptures, Harry Orlinsky, argued that the cumulative evidence — from the study of lexicons, syntax, context, and comparable Near Eastern stories of how the universe began — favors this interpretation. Indeed, no lexical or grammatical objections can be raised against it. But the context and comparison with other Near Eastern creation stories favors the next view we shall examine. Moreover, with two notable exceptions, Jewish and Christian traditions have understood verse 1 as an independent clause.

A fourth way of understanding the relationships in these verses (and perhaps the best way) is to see verse 1 as a summary statement that matches the concluding summary statements of Genesis 2:1: "Thus the heavens and the earth were completed"; and to see verse 2 as a circumstantial clause modifying verse 3.

Thus understood, Genesis 1:1-3 could be translated: "In the beginning God created the cosmos. Now [this is how it happened]. The earth was chaotic . . . , and then God said . . ." Like the third option, this reading also entails a pre-Genesis time and earth.

Read this way, Genesis 1:1-3 would be similar in structure to the introduction of the other creation story in Genesis 2:4-7, as well as with other Ancient Near Eastern tales of how it all began.

An obvious theological observation will be raised against this transformationalist view. Where did the negative conditions originate? The question is best answered with another question: Where did Satan originate? The origins of both moral evil and natural evils (like tornadoes and malaria) remain a mystery in monotheism, and Genesis offers a relative beginning with respect to each. Nevertheless, by comparing Scripture with Scripture, transformationalists should conclude that both evil and matter are temporal in contrast to the eternal (see Jer. 10:16; John 1:3; Col. 1:16).

Since Genesis seems to presume preexistent matter and time, scientific creationists would do better to argue for an old earth rather than a young one.

How Long Are the "Days" of Genesis?

Part of the problem science poses for the interpreter of Genesis is the long periods of time required to lay down the fossil record. Obviously, those who wish to harmonize Bible and science must in some way read the seven days of creation as something other than twenty-four-hour days.

Progressive creationists — who tend to minimize divine, special intervention and to maximize the operation of natural law — make room for the long ages in two ways:

First, some interpret the days of Genesis as successive days on which God revealed his creative process to Moses. Back in the last century, J. H. Kurtz wrote that God revealed his creative process to Moses, through visions of seven progressive scenes of pre-Adamite creation. And in 1936, P. J. Wiseman suggested that God told Moses the story over six days. In this approach, the six visions are presented in logical, but not strictly chronological, order. Wiseman embellishes the theory by noting that Babylonian creation accounts were customarily put on six tables with a concluding colophon. And so in Genesis, he alleges, there was a day of revelation for each tablet followed by the "colophon of Genesis 2:4."

This interpretation of "day" faces the objection that it adds to Scripture. Genesis 1:1–2:3 contains nothing comparable to the introduction in

Genesis 15:1: "And the word of the Lord came to Abram in a vision." And in any case, the verb "made" cannot be changed into "showed" in Genesis 2:2: "And on the seventh day, God ended his work which he had made, and he rested on the seventh day."

Second, some progressive creationists interpret the days as ages, which they correlate with the successive epochs recorded in the geological column. These advocates of the "day age" theory (which W. B. Riley called "The Devil's Counterfeit") argue that the Hebrew word *yom* can have other meanings than "a 24-hour period." For example, in Genesis 2:4, we find the phrase "in the day," referring to the whole creative process recorded in Genesis 1:1–2:3. Gleason Archer of Trinity Evangelical Divinity School also argues cogently that the events recorded in 2:4-25 (the making of Adam, the planting of the garden, the naming of the animals, and the gift of a bride) cannot be squeezed into a sixth twenty-four-hour period.

This view, however, satisfies neither the text nor science. Terence E. Fretheim of Lutheran Northwestern Theological Seminary linguistically validates the assertion that the author of Genesis intended to write of twenty-four-hour days. And Robert C. Newman of Biblical Theological Seminary shows that they were intended to be chronologically successive. Moreover, in Genesis, against scientific understanding, plants precede marine organisms and even the sun, and birds precede insects. Problems, such as the chronological tension of so much happening on the sixth day, are better explained by an artistic-literary approach.

What Kind of Literature Is Genesis 1:1–2:3?

The strongest evidence that Genesis 1:1–2:3 should be read as a historically and schematically accurate narrative is that this traditional interpretation seems to be the plain, normal sense of the passage. When the fourth commandment gives God six days of creation and one day of rest as a pattern for human work and sabbath, it seems to clinch the argument (Exod. 20:11).

But there are two acute contradictions between Genesis and normative science about terrestrial origins: how long the process took, and in what order events took place. These contradictions have driven some biblical scholars to suspect that the passage was not intended to be taken in so straightforward a manner. They have asked just what kind of literature it is, and have compared and contrasted their own preunderstandings with those of the biblical writers. Even if the prodigious research, debates, and diligent publications of the scientific creationists should fully harmonize science with Genesis, Bible scholars can never again read the text through uncorrected lenses.

Former Barrington College President Charles Hummel noted that Genesis 1:1–2:3 is unlike science in these ways:

- Its subject is God, not the forces of nature;
- Its language is everyday speech, not mathematics and technical jargon;
- It is prescriptive (answering the questions who, why, and what ought to be), not descriptive (answering the questions what, how, and what is);
- It is written for the covenant community and is validated by the Spirit, not for a scientific community or validated by empirical evidence.

To pit the biblical claim of Ultimate Cause ("God created the heavens and the earth") against scientific claims of immediate causes is as mischievous as pitting David's theological assertion "You created my inmost being (Ps. 139:13) against genetics. The Bible shows a marked disinterest in the mechanics of creation (compare the one chapter devoted to the origins of the earth and life to the numerous detailed chapters in Exodus, Leviticus, Chronicles, and Ezekiel devoted to recounting the formation of Israel's formal worship system). And certainly science cannot answer questions of the creation's purpose or value.

In addition, nonconcordists say Genesis 1 conflicts with the aims of modern historians, who exclude ultimate cause and stress brute facts. In contrast to that kind of history writing, the Bible editorializes to the point that it rearranges the order of events in order to make theological points. For example, D. J. A. Clines of Sheffield University shows that the Table of Nations in Genesis 10 (which must chronologically follow the scrambling of languages at the Tower of Babel in Genesis 11) was dischronologized for theological reasons. The author wants to present humankind under God's blessing to be fruitful and to fill the earth. And while Exodus (7:14–11:10) reports that God inflicted ten plagues on Egypt, beginning with blood, the poet-theologian of Psalm 105 (vv. 28-36) feels free to reduce the number to seven and begin with darkness (to contrast with God's three miracles in the desert that begin with light). Similar rearrangements of events in the synoptic gospels are well known.

Ronald Youngblood of Bethel Seminary West has demonstrated that Genesis 1:1–2:3 has also been dischronologized. In brute history, he argues, it seems unlikely that God created light and "separated light from darkness" on the first day, or that evening and morning existed on the first three days before he created the heavenly lights to mark off the days.

These obvious incongruities in the text suggest to more and more evangelicals that a literary reading of Genesis 1:1–2:3 is called for. Systematic theologian Henri Blocher of the Faculté Libre de Théologie Évangélique labels the genre as "historico-artistic." According to him, the interpreter should understand "the form of the week attributed to the work of creation to be an artistic arrangement . . . not to be taken literally." "It is possible," he adds, "that the logical order [the author] has chosen coincides broadly with the actual sequence of events of the facts of cosmogony; but that does not interest him. He wishes to bring out certain themes and provide a theology of the sabbath." This approach not only relieves tensions within the narrative itself and with science, but also with the second creation story (Gen. 2:4-25).

Australian scholar N. Weeks offers a plausible objection: "There is no logical reason why the presence of a structure should prove that a passage is not to be taken literally." But Weeks fails to address the tensions within the text as well as the figurative elements we shall note later. And Blocher argues against this objection by applying the philosophical principle that prefers simple solutions to multiplied hypotheses.

R. Clyde McCone, professor of anthropology and linguistics at California State University, also objects to a literary approach. He complains, with some justification, that literary theories shift the focus of study away from God to the text and "present little substantive revelation of God." This may be true of many literary approaches, but it certainly is not necessary.

Even as exegetes call for a literary rereading of the text as an artistic achievement, theologians, professional and self-taught, are calling for a figurative approach. Howard Van Till of Calvin College notes that God's actions in creation "are presented in highly figurative and anthropomorphic language." Even the eminently conservative commentator E. J. Young points to the repeated formulae "God said" and "God called" and reminds us that "God did not speak with physical organs of speech nor did he utter words in the Hebrew language." These expressions and others portray the transcendent God and his activity in human forms so that earthlings may understand him. So nonconcordists ask: In the light of these obvious and numerous anthropomorphisms, is it not plausible to suppose that the first week is also an anthropomorphic representation of the Creator's work and rest, so that the covenant people could bear witness to him and imitate his pattern?

If Moses did not intend to write a straightforward history, but an artistic literary account in anthropomorphic language (so that God's people might imitate him), this would also give us a clue to the meaning of the fourth commandment.

While calling Genesis 1:1–2:3 a literary work, nonconcordists shy away from using the word *myth*. For most people, that slippery term implies a fanciful, untrue story. Besides, there is actually very little similarity between this story and pagan accounts of the beginning and ordering of the universe. Indeed, some have pointed out that Genesis 1:1–2:3 reads like a polemic against pagan cosmogonies.

*   *

Having surveyed the answers to the three big questions, we can draw some conclusions. Perhaps it is best to regard Genesis 1:1–2:3 as a creation story in *torah* ("instruction"), which is a majestic, artistic achievement, employing anthropomorphic language. As H. J. Sørenson said in the *New Catholic Encyclopedia:* "The basic purpose is to instruct men on the ultimate realities to live successfully. It contains 'truths to live by' rather than 'theology to speculate on.'"

Moses intended no distinction between historical data and its theological shaping, and Bible students should resist the temptation to separate the two. Historical critics evaporate history, but nonconcordist evangelicals must take history seriously and compare Scripture with Scripture, a task that some accomplish better than others. In *Literary Approaches to Biblical Interpretation,* for example, Westminster Theological Seminary's Tremper Longman helps readers walk gingerly between the promise and pitfalls of the literary approach to the Old Testament. In *The Fourth Day,* however, Howard Van Till seems to lose his balance when he writes that the primeval history in Genesis 1–11 is not concerned whether the events actually happened.

This literary approach may unsettle some who cling to the Reformers' claim that Scripture is perspicuous. But note: the literary approach to Genesis 1:1–2:3 changes no doctrine of the church while it helps us to see some of them more clearly.

How We Got the Hebrew Bible: The Text and Canon of the Old Testament

1. The Task of OT Textual Criticism, Its Importance and Method

There is always a need in the humanities for critics to restore original texts, be they of Homer or Shakespeare, or of Moses or Isaiah. Many texts of the OT, however, were composed over centuries, not by just an original author, and thus it is too simplistic to say that OT textual criticism aims to recover the original text of the OT. Rather, as we shall argue, "original text" in the OT refers to the text-type that lies behind the MT, the received text. The reconstruction of other critical editions of portions of the OT is the task of literary criticism, not of textual criticism.

Textual criticism is necessary because there is no error-free manuscript. (Even in *BHS*, the standard representation of the MT text, printing errors can be found.) Variants occur more frequently in the medieval manuscripts of the MT tradition, but they are minuscule compared to the variants found in the Dead Sea Scrolls (DSS). In fact, the further back we go in the textual lineage the greater the textual differences. Before the text was fixed at ca. 100 CE it was copied and recopied through many centuries by scribes of varying capabilities and of different philosophies, giving rise to varying readings and recensions (i.e., distinct text-types).

The restoration of the original OT text is foundational to the exegetical task and to theological reflection. For instance, whether the book of Proverbs teaches immortality depends in part on deciding between textual variants in Prov 14:32b. Basing itself on the MT, the NIV renders "even in [their] death *(bᵉmôtô)* the righteous have a refuge," a reading that entails the doctrine of immortality for the righteous. The NRSV, however, basing itself on the LXX, translates "the righteous find a refuge in their integrity *(bᵉtummô),*" a reading that does not teach that doctrine. The consonants of the MT are *bmtw,* and those of the (assumed) *Vorlage* (i.e., the retroverted text lying before a translator) behind the LXX were *btmw.* The slight difference due to metathesis of *m* and *t,* however, profoundly affects the exegesis of that text and the theology of the book.

To restore the original, the text critic must know the history of its witnesses and of scribal practices and must have exegetical competence. In this essay we will consider each of these respectively. The LXX, however, is such an important witness that we treat it separately. Knowledge of the text's history will explain the varying characteristics of the textual witnesses and why we opt for the restoring of the original text behind the MT against other literary editions of OT portions, such as the differences between the MT Pentateuch versus the Samaritan Pentateuch and of the MT Jeremiah versus the Septuagint Jeremiah. We conclude the article with reflections on the reliability of the OT text.

2. History of the Text and Its Witnesses

Because of the varying fortunes of the OT text and of our sources of information about it, its history may be analyzed in six distinct periods: (1) The determinative formative period for the production of OT texts extended from the composition of the Ten Commandments (ca. 1400 BCE or ca. 1250 BCE, depending on the date of the Exodus) to Nehemiah's library (ca. 400 BCE), when, according to 2 Macc 2:13, Nehemiah founded a library and "gathered together the books about the kings and prophets, and the books of David, and letters of kings about sacred gifts," or even to the late fourth century, if one opts for that date for the composition of the book of Chronicles. (2) The canon and text remained open from Nehemiah's library to when the canon was stabilized (ca. 100 BCE). (3) At least two centuries elapsed between the fixing of the OT canon and the fixing of its text, now sometimes called "the Proto-MT" (ca. 100 CE). (4) The labors of the Masoretes (600-1000 CE), who based their work on the Proto-MT, came to a conclusion ca. 1000 CE, when the Masorete Aaron ben Asher produced the authoritative

Masoretic Text, as recognized already on the frontispiece of the Leningrad Codex (1009 CE). (5) The medieval manuscripts of the MT were produced between 1000 CE and the invention of printing (ca. 1500 CE). (6) The Great Rabbinic Bible (ca. 1525 CE) became the standard text of the MT until 1936, when P. Kahle got back to the Ben Asher text by basing the third edition of *BH* on the Leningrad manuscript B19[A] (L). Since the variants that came into the text after 1000 CE are relatively insignificant, we will not discuss the last two periods. N. Sarna has superbly summarized the history of the printed Hebrew Bible.[1]

2.1. From the Ten Commandments to Nehemiah's Library

We have virtually no external, extant data regarding the OT text during its most formative period, aside from two recently discovered silver amulets, about the size of a "cigarette butt," containing the priestly benediction of Num 6:24-26 (ca. 600 BCE). From internal notices within the OT and from our knowledge of the way Ancient Near Eastern literature was composed, we can infer that during this era earlier pieces of canonical literature were collected into developing books. For example, the Bible presents the Ten Commandments as the first piece of canonical literature, that is, literature inspired by God and recognized as such by the faithful (Exod 20:1-19; cf. Deut 5:6-27). To this original core the Book of the Covenant, mediated by Moses, was added (Exod 20:22-23:33), and to this still other pieces were added to make up the book of Exodus. We do not know how or when the book of Exodus, for instance, took its final shape. In a roughly comparable way isolated hymns were collected into books, and these in turn edited to form the book of Psalms. The same dynamic processes were involved in the composition of other books of the Bible. From data both within the Bible and from knowledge of Ancient Near Eastern scribal practices we can infer that during the formation of the OT books, there was a tendency both to preserve and to revise earlier texts.

(a) The tendency to preserve the text. Elsewhere we have argued:

> The very fact that the Scripture persistently survived the most deleterious conditions throughout its long history demonstrates that indefatigable scribes insisted on its preservation. The books were copied by hand for generations on highly perishable papyrus and animal skins in the rel-

---

1. N. Sarna, "Bible Text," *EncJud* 4.831-35.

atively damp, hostile climate of Palestine. . . . Moreover, the prospects for the survival of texts were uncertain in a land that served as a bridge for armies in unceasing contention between the continents of Africa and Asia — a land whose people were the object of plunderers in their early history and of captors in their later history. That no other Israelite writings, such as the Book of Yashar (e.g. 2 Sam 1:18) or the Diaries of the Kings (e.g. 2 Chr 16:11), survive from this period indirectly suggests the determination of the scribes to preserve the books that became canonical. The foes of Hebrew Scripture sometimes included audiences who sought to kill its authors and destroy their works (cf. Jeremiah 36). From the time of their composition, however, they captured the hearts, minds, and loyalties of the faithful in Israel who kept them safe often at risk to themselves. Such people must have insisted on the accurate transmission of the text.

In addition, both the Bible itself (Deut 31:9ff.; Josh 24:25, 26; 1 Sam 10:25; etc.) and the literature of the ANE show that at the time of the earliest biblical compositions a mindset favoring canonicity existed. This mindset must have fostered a concern for care and accuracy in transmitting the sacred writings. For example, a Hittite treaty (of the Late Bronze Age), closely resembling parts of the Torah, contains this explicit threat: "Whoever . . . breaks [this tablet] or causes anyone to change the wording of the tablet — . . . may the gods, the lords of the oath, blot you out." Undoubtedly this psychology was a factor in inhibiting Israelite scribes from multiplying variants of the texts. Moreover, scribal practices throughout the ANE reflect a conservative attitude. W. F. Albright noted, "The prolonged and intimate study of the many scores of thousands of pertinent documents from the ancient Near East proves that sacred and profane documents were copied with greater care than is true of scribal copying in Graeco-Roman times."[2]

(b) The tendency to revise the text. We also argued:

On the other hand, scribes, aiming to teach the people by disseminating an understandable text, felt free to revise the script, orthography (i.e. spelling), and grammar, according to the conventions of their own times. Albright said, "A principle which must never be lost sight of in

2. B. K. Waltke and M. O'Connor, *An Introduction to Biblical Hebrew Syntax* [*IBHS*] (Winona Lake, IN: Eisenbrauns, 1990) 16-17.

dealing with documents of the ancient Near East is that instead of leaving obvious archaisms in spelling and grammar, the scribes generally revised ancient literary and other documents periodically. . . ."[3]

Moreover, the many differences between synoptic portions of the OT show that authors and/or scribes, "the authorized revisers of the text" at this time, felt free to edit earlier works into new, mutually independent, literary achievements (cf. 2 Samuel 22 = Psalm 18; 2 Kgs 18:13-20:19 = Isaiah 36-39; 2 Kgs 24:18–25:30 = Jeremiah 52; Isa 2:2-4 = Mic 4:1-3; Psalms 14 = 53; 40:14-18 = 70; 57:8-12[7-11] = 108:2-6[1-5]; 60:7-14[5-12] = 108:7-14[6-13]; Psalm 96 = 1 Chron 16:23-33; Ps 106:1, 47-48 = 1 Chron 16:34-36; and the parallels between Samuel-Kings and Chronicles). Literary critics, not textual critics, should concern themselves with the differences between these portions of the OT.

(c) The need to emend the text. Accidental textual errors, however, probably corrupted the text during this formative period. In cases where none of the transmitted variants satisfy exegetical expectations, text critics propose a textual emendation (a conjectured variant based on the known variants). The DSS have now validated this procedure in certain instances. F. M. Cross comments: "No headier feeling can be experienced by a humanistic scholar, perhaps, than that which comes when an original reading, won by his brilliant emendation, is subsequently confirmed in a newly-found manuscript."[4] The confusion in Ezek 3:12 of the similarly formed consonants *k* and *m* in the preexilic angular script offers a good illustration of the need for emendation.[5]

All texts: *brwk kbwd-yhwh mmqwmw*
　　"May the glory of YHWH *be praised* in [sic!] his dwelling place" (cf. NIV).
Emendation: *brw[m] kbwd-yhwh mmqwmw*
　　"As the glory of YHWH *arose* from its place" (cf. NRSV).

"Be praised," *brwk*, is attested in all textual witnesses. However, the phrase is unique, awkward, and contextless. Text critics salvage the line by emending

3. Waltke, *IBHS*, 17.

4. F. M. Cross, "Problems of Method in the Textual Criticism of the Hebrew Bible," in *The Critical Study of Sacred Texts*, ed. W. D. O'Flaherty (Berkeley: Graduate Theological Union, 1979) 31-54, esp. 37.

5. J. Kennedy, *An Aid to the Textual Amendment of the Old Testament* (Edinburgh: Clark, 1928) 83-84.

brwk to *brwm*, "when [it] arose." The emendation nicely satisfies exegetical expectations, Hebrew syntax, and the context of the verse (cf. Ezek 10:4, 15-18).

Scholars associated with Hebrew University Bible Project (HUBP) and the United Bible Societies Hebrew Old Testament Text Critical Project disallow conjectural emendations. Their stance serves as a healthy corrective away from the extremes of B. Duhm and the "eccentricity in the later work of Cheyne."[6] However, it is too extreme. J. M. Sprinkle complained: "What we as students of the Hebrew Bible actually want . . . is not a later stage of the text but the original."[7]

2.2. From 400 BCE to 150 BCE

(a) An open canon. Though we possess a good knowledge of the OT's theology, we do not know when or where the OT books were first published or precisely how they gained admission into the very select group of writings that we call the OT. We do know, however, that by the time of the NT the OT canon is closed.[8] Jesus and the apostles held the same OT in hand that Protestants do today. R. Beckwith argues convincingly that Judas Maccabeus, at a date around 164 BCE, gave the OT canon its final shape.[9] The Qumran scrolls, however, reflect a Jewish community that embraced a somewhat different canon, at least to judge from the absence of Esther among them and the very different shape of 11QPs[a] from the MT.[10]

(b) During these two and a half centuries there was also a tendency both to preserve and to revise the text. We can now sketch the history of the text for this period on the basis of the DSS and the LXX (ca. 250 BCE to 150 BCE).

(i) The DSS. By the techniques of paleography, numismatics, and archaeology the DSS are dated from the middle of the third century BCE to the revolt of Bar Kochba (132-135 CE). Most manuscripts were found in the eleven mountain caves just west of Khirbet Qumran. These caves yielded over 200 scrolls of all the books of the Bible, except Esther. The other princi-

---

6. S. Jellicoe, *The Septuagint and Modern Study* (Oxford: Clarendon Press, 1968) 320.

7. A book review on D. Barthélemy, *Critique textuelle de l'Ancien Testament*, vol. 1 (OBO 50; Fribourg, Switzerland: Editions universitaires; Göttingen: Vandenhoeck & Ruprecht, 1982) in *JETS* 28 (1985) 468-70, esp. 469.

8. F. F. Bruce, *The Canon of Scripture* (Downers Grove, IL: InterVarsity, 1988) 28.

9. R. Beckwith, *The Old Testament Canon of the New Testament Church and Its Background in Early Judaism* (Grand Rapids: Eerdmans, 1985) 165.

10. J. A. Sanders, "Two Non-canonical Psalms in 11QPs[a]," *ZAW* 65 (1964) 57-75.

pal sites, Naḥal Ḥever and Wadi Murabbaʿat, yielded texts mostly from the early second century CE. Scrolls were also found at Masada, which fell to the Romans in 73 CE.

(ii) The LXX. According to the pseudepigraphic *Letter of Aristeas* (ca. 130 BCE), the Pentateuch was translated into Greek at ca. 285 BCE by seventy-two translators (hence its title, "Septuagint"). This tradition was later expanded to include all the OT books translated into Greek.

The Question of an Original LXX. P. Kahle argued that a great number of independent Greek translations existed for all the books, and the LXX as we know it now was a creation of the Church. We have argued that studies by M. L. Margolis on Joshua and by J. A. Montgomery on Daniel, as well as the realization that recensional activities to conform the Old Greek to the Proto-MT, which had given the illusion that all these variants could not go back to one original, have led to widening consensus that agrees with P. de Lagarde's view that all the Greek manuscripts go back to one textual tradition.[11]

Character of the LXX. It is impossible to speak generally of the character of the LXX because it is not a uniform translation. Rather, different translators with varying capabilities and philosophies of translation rendered assorted portions of the OT. Elsewhere this writer collected the conclusions of scholars about these translations:

> Swete [drew the conclusion] that the majority of the translators learned Hebrew in Egypt from imperfectly instructed teachers, and Barr . . . that these translators invented vowels for the unpointed text. . . . Except in passages such as Genesis 49 and Deuteronomy 32, 33, the Pentateuch is on the whole a close and serviceable translation of a smoothed Hebrew recension. The Psalter is tolerably well done, though Ervin concluded that the theology of Hellenistic Judaism left its mark on it. About Isaiah, Seeligman concluded, "The great majority of the inconsistencies here discussed must be imputed to the translator's unconstrained and carefree working method, and to a conscious preference for the introduction of variations." He added, "We shall not, however, do the translator any injustice by not rating his knowledge of grammar and syntax very highly." Regarding Hosea, Nyberg found that "it is overly composed of gross misunderstandings, unfortunate readings and superficial lexical definitions which often are simply forced conformity to similar Aramaic cognates.

---

11. *The Expositor's Bible Commentary* [*EBC*], ed. F. E. Gaebelein (12 vols.; Grand Rapids: Zondervan, 1980-82) 1.220-21.

Helplessness and arbitrary choice are the characteristic traits of this interpretation." Albrektson said of Lamentations: "LXX, then, is not a good translation in this book. But this does not mean that it is not valuable for textual criticism. On the contrary, its literal character often allows us to establish with tolerable certainty the underlying Hebrew text. It is clearly based on a text which was in all essentials identical with the consonants of the MT; indeed the passages where it may have contained a variant are notably few." Gerleman said of Job that the translator interprets the text as well as he can, and, with the help of his imagination, attempts to give an intelligible meaning to the original, which he does not understand. He added that the many deviations between the Hebrew and the Greek translations of Job are not the result of an essential difference between the original of the LXX and our Hebrew text. They have come about in the course of translation when the translator has not mastered the difficulties of the original. Swete concluded, "The reader of the Septuagint must expect to find a large number of actual blunders, due in part perhaps to a faulty archetype, but chiefly to the misreading or misunderstanding of the archetype by the translators. . . ."[12]

G. Gerleman evaluated the LXX of Zephaniah thus:

> The *Vorlage* of the Greek translator was not identical with the consonantal text of the MT but close to it. . . . The translator is very free in his interpretation of the MT. His work points to an innumerable number of wrong vocalizations, unfortunate divisions of the text, and superficial lexical definitions. . . . Finally, it seems fairly clear that the capabilities of the translator were not always up to mastering certain words and expressions that are difficult to translate.[13]

This writer reached independently a similar conclusion for Micah as T. Nyberg had for Hosea and Gerleman for Zephaniah.[14] This is not surprising, for J. Ziegler demonstrated the unity of the Septuagint in the Minor Prophets.[15]

12. B. K. Waltke, "The Textual Criticism of the Old Testament," EBC 1.221-22.

13. G. Gerleman, *Zephanja textkritisch und literarisch untersuch* (Lund: Gleerup, 1942) 85-86.

14. B. K. Waltke, "Micah," in *The Minor Prophets*, ed. T. E. McComiskey (Grand Rapids: Baker, 1993) 2.591-764.

15. J. Ziegler, "Die Einheit der Septuaginta zum Zwölfprophetenbuch," in idem,

It is well known that the LXX translator of Proverbs was influenced by Greek ethical thought, especially Stoic, along with early Jewish midrashic tradition, and that he modified a number of proverbs and made additions.[16] J. Barr says of this translation:

> In fact the term "free," as applied to a translation like the Greek Proverbs, must mean something considerably different from what we mean when we speak of "free translation" in a modern context.... For a translator like that of Proverbs free technique meant . . . that after having translated *some* elements in the text in a rather "literal" way, he could then break loose from literality and complete the sentence with a composition so loosely related to the original that it might equally be considered as an original composition rather than a rendering. . . .[17]

However, this writer also noted: "The LXX of Samuel, parts of Kings, and Ezekiel is of special value because the text preserved by the Masoretes of these books suffered more than usual from corrupting influences."[18] With regard to the chronology from Omri to Jehu, J. D. Shenkel concluded that the Old Greek, represented in several manuscripts, preserves the original chronology better than the recensional developments, represented in the majority of manuscripts.[19]

(c) The tendency to preserve the text. Some of the oldest manuscripts of the DSS show a striking similarity with the MT. Their silent testimony shouts out the achievement of scribes to preserve faithfully the OT text. This text-type undoubtedly existed before the time of these scrolls. The many archaic forms within the MT confirm the inference. The studies of M. Martin show that the DSS reveal a conservative scribal tendency to follow the exemplar both in text and in form.[20]

(d) The tendency to revise the text. Though the author of 1 Maccabees

---

Sylloge: Gesammelte Aufsätze zur Septuaginta (MSU 10; Göttingen: Vandenhoeck & Ruprecht, 1971) 29-42.

16. G. Gerleman, "The Septuagint Proverbs as a Hellenistic Document," *OTS* 8 (1950) 15-27; S. Jellicoe, *The Septuagint*, 68, 317-18.

17. J. Barr, *"B'RS-MOLIS:* Prov XI.31, 1 Pet IV.18," *JSS* 20 (1975) 149-64, esp. 158.

18. Waltke, "Textual Criticism," 210-28, esp. 222.

19. J. D. Shenkel, *Chronology and Recensional Development in the Greek Text of Kings* (Cambridge, MA: Harvard University Press, 1968).

20. M. Martin, *The Scribal Character of the Dead Sea Scrolls* (2 vols., Bibliothèque du Museon 44-45; Louvain: Publications universitaires, 1958).

(ca. 125 BCE), for example, recognized that prophecy had ceased in Israel years before his time (cf. 1 Macc 9:27), the text of the OT was still open during this period. Scribes of this era were still the authorized revisers of the text, not just copyists. They continued to expand portions of the OT and to alter it to such an extent that their productions might equally be considered as distinct literary editions rather than as copies. In addition, they continued to revise older texts philologically to make them more intelligible to younger generations.

As a result of their literary achievements the line between literary criticism and textual criticism has become attenuated. The texts of some portions of the OT have come down to us in two forms, attested in both the DSS and in the LXX. There is, for instance, a short form of Jeremiah preserved in 4QJer[b] and in the LXX, and a long form preserved in 4QJer[a] and the MT. In the following example the additions in the long text are noted with italics:

> This is what the *Lord Almighty, the God of Israel,* said to me: "I will break the yoke of the king of Babylon. Within two years I will bring back to this place *all* the articles of the house of the Lord *that Nebuchadnezzar king of Babylon removed from this place and took to Babylon,* and Jeconiah *son of Jehoiakim king of Judah* and *all* the exiles from Judah *who went to Babylon, I am going to bring back to this place,"* declares the Lord. (Jer 28:1-4a)

One is reminded of the editorial comment in Jer 36:32:

> So Jeremiah took another scroll and gave it to the scribe Baruch son of Neriah, and as Jeremiah dictated, Baruch wrote on it all the words of the scroll that Jehoiakim king of Judah had burned in the fire. And many similar words were added to them.

E. Tov established on the basis of the ancient texts and versions the existence of two editions of Joshua, 1 Samuel 16–18, Ezekiel, and Proverbs.[21] The different literary editions of Daniel and Esther are well known. This scribal practice was entirely consistent with known practices of composing books in the ANE. From cuneiform texts (ca. 2000 BCE) to Tatian's *Diatesseron* (ca. 200 CE) one can observe that ANE literatures were composed by supple-

---

21. E. Tov, *Textual Criticism of the Hebrew Bible* (Philadelphia: Fortress, 1992) 314-19.

menting earlier editions of a text with later materials.[22] We drew the conclusion elsewhere that the major contribution of the Samaritan Pentateuch (SP) to biblical studies is to literary criticism, not to textual criticism.[23] For example, it involves the insertion of material from Deuteronomy into Exodus and the extensive repetition of other texts.

The scribal editors not only effected literary changes, they also altered the text for both philological and theological reasons. We noted elsewhere:

> They modernized it by replacing archaic Hebrew forms and constructions with forms and constructions of a later age. They also smoothed out the text by replacing rare constructions with more frequently occurring constructions, and they supplemented and clarified the text by the insertion of additions and the interpolation of glosses from parallel passages. In addition, they substituted euphemisms for vulgarities, altered the names of false gods, removed the phrases that refer to cursing God, and safeguarded the sacred divine name or tetragrammaton (YHWH), occasionally by substituting forms in the consonantal text.[24]

Philological alterations were already taking place at the time of Malachi, the last representative of mainstream OT prophecy. The book of Chronicles in its synoptic parallels with the Pentateuch and Former Prophets as preserved in the MT exhibits similar revisions.[25] Ezra-Nehemiah explicitly states that as Ezra read from the Book of the Law of God, he made it clear and gave the meaning so that the people could understand what was being read (Neh 8:8).

2.3. From 150 BCE to 135 CE

The bulk of the DSS belong to the period between the closing of the canon and the closing of its text. During this time, the Samaritan Pentateuch began a life of its own.

22. See, for instance, *Empirical Models for Biblical Criticism*, ed. J. H. Tigay (Philadelphia: University of Pennsylvania Press, 1976); cf. R. P. Gordon, "Compositions, Conflation and the Pentateuch," *JSOT* 51 (1991) 57-69.

23. *The Anchor Bible Dictionary* [*ABD*], ed. D. N. Freedman et al. (6 vols.; New York: Doubleday, 1992) 5.938-39.

24. Waltke, *IBHS*, 19.

25. A. Kropat, *Die Syntax des Autors der Chronik verglichen mit der seiner Quellen: Ein Beitrag zur historischen Syntax des hebräischen Text* (BZAW 16; Giessen: Töpelmann, 1909).

(a) Samaritan Pentateuch. At ca. 110 BCE scribes of the Samaritans, a sect similar to the Jews apart from its worship on Mount Gerizim instead of at Jerusalem (John 4:19-22), adopted and adapted a distinct recension of the text attested as early as the Chronicler to constitute the SP. They probably accepted only the Pentateuch as their canon because its second division, the Prophets, and its third, the Writings, celebrate Jerusalem.

(b) The tendency to preserve the text. In addition to the evidence adduced above for the tendency to conserve the text, there is a Talmudic notice that the scribes attempted to keep the text "correct" (*b. Ned.* 37b-38a). Moreover, the MT itself preserves the following remnants of scribal concern with preserving the text probably from this era: (i) the fifteen extraordinary points either to condemn the Hebrew letters as spurious or to draw attention to some peculiar textual feature; (ii) the four suspended letters to indicate intentional scribal change or scribal error due to a faulty distinction of gutturals; and (iii) the nine inverted *nuns* apparently to mark verses thought to have been transposed.[26]

(c) The tendency to revise the text. The text was not fixed, however, and continued to be revised. Tov classifies the DSS into five different text-types.[27]

(i) There are the *Proto-Masoretic* texts, which others call "the rabbinic text," during this period. About 60 percent of the Scrolls belong to this type and may reflect their authoritative status.[28]

(ii) The *Pre-Samaritan* texts have the same characteristic features of the SP, aside from the thin layer of ideological and phonological changes the Samaritans added. Basing himself on W. Gesenius (1815), the first to classify the variants between the SP and MT in a thorough and convincing way, the present writer hoped to demonstrate from recent philological and textual research that the SP presents a secondarily modernized, smoothed-over, and expanded text.[29] The theological changes imposed on this text by the Samaritans, though thin, are significant. For example, they were able to make the worship on Mount Gerizim the tenth commandment by combining the first two commandments into one and by inserting texts about Mount Gerizim (Deut 11:29a; 27:12b-13a; 28:4-7; and 11:30) after Exod 20:17, numbering the material from Deut 28:4-7 and 11:30 as the tenth commandment.

---

26. B. K. Waltke, "Samaritan Pentateuch," in *ABD* 5.932-40; for inverted *nuns* also see 6.397.

27. Tov, *Textual Criticism,* 114-17.

28. Tov, *Textual Criticism,* 115.

29. *ABD* 5.936-38.

(iii) About 5 percent of the DSS are *Septuagintal* in character. Some DSS scrolls, most notably Jeremiah (4QJer[b,d]), bear a strong resemblance to the LXX's *Vorlage*.

(iv) The many *nonaligned* DSS are not exclusively close to any one of the types mentioned so far. Tov explains: "They agree, sometimes insignificantly, with MT against the other texts, or with SP and/or LXX against the other texts, but the non-aligned texts also disagree with the other texts to the same extent. They furthermore contain readings not known from one of the other texts."[30]

(v) Tov identifies a group of texts that reflect a distinctive *Qumran practice* with regard to orthography (i.e., spelling, similar to "favor" versus "favour"), morphology, and a free approach to the biblical text visible in content adaptations, in frequent errors, in numerous corrections, and sometimes in negligent script.[31] Tov thinks that only these scrolls were produced at Qumran.

These variant recensions also find parallels in Jewish and Christian literature originating during the time in question, such as the book of *Jubilees* (either early or late postexilic) and, most importantly, the NT (50-90 CE). For example, Stephen's sermon (Acts 7) and Hebrews (chap. 9) are based on the pre-Samaritan recension.

The fall of the Second Temple (ca. 70 CE), the debate between Jews and Christians, and Hillel's rules of hermeneutics all contributed to produce a stable text by about 100 CE. The Naḥal Ḥever and Wadi Murabbaʿat DSS, which date between 100 CE and 135 CE, attest to the Proto-MT.

2.4. From 135 CE to 1000 CE

(a) Other early versions. From ca. 100 CE to ca. 500 CE the official Aramaic Targums (Tg), the Syriac Peshitta (Syr), various recensions of the LXX, and the Latin Vulgate (Vg) were produced. They all have as their common denominator the Proto-MT and so are not as useful witnesses to the early stages of the still open text as are the DSS and the LXX. We need to note here only that the Syriac has been influenced both by the LXX and the targums. Nevertheless, each of these versions sometimes contains an original (i.e., an uncorrupted) reading.

30. Tov, *Textual Criticism*, 116.
31. Tov, *Textual Criticism*, 114.

(i) "Targum" means specifically a translation into Aramaic. When knowledge of Hebrew decreased among the Jewish people during the post-exilic period, targums were created orally and later committed to writing. The targum fragments found at Qumran show that both free and literal targums were made. Scholars are divided about their dates (first to fifth century CE) and their places of origin (Babylon or Palestine). These more or less paraphrastic Targums are of more value for understanding the way Jewish people understood their OT than for textual criticism. For example, the Targum of Isa 52:13 reads: "Behold, my servant, the Messiah."

(ii) Early recensions of the LXX. Some scribes deliberately revised the original LXX, known as the Old Greek (OG), according to the Proto-MT. Prior to Origen (200 CE), who brought this process to completion in his famous Hexapla, Aquila (125 CE), Symmachus (180 CE), and Theodotion (180 CE) revised the OG and/or earlier recensions of it according to this principle. A Greek scroll of the Minor Prophets recovered at Naḥal Ḥever shows that this process had already begun by the middle of the first century BCE. Its distinctive translation techniques enabled scholars to link it up with other texts bearing witness to an early stage of the OG. Justin Martyr in his *Dialogue* complains against the Jew Trypho about the attitude the rabbinate had taken toward the LXX in order to remove an essential arm from the Christian apologist. D. Barthélemy, who brilliantly edited this text, showed that Justin forced himself to use this revision in order to be acceptable to his adversaries.[32]

(iii) Vulgate. Pope Damasus I commissioned Jerome (Hieronymus, 345-420 CE) to produce a uniform and reliable Latin Bible. Jerome based his original translation of the Psalms *(Psalterium Romanum)* on the *Vetus Latina,* namely, Old Latin texts based largely on the LXX. His second translation of the Psalms was based on the Hexapla *(Psalterium Gallicanum).* Dissatisfied with these translations, Jerome finally translated *The Vulgate* ("the common one") from, as he put it, "the original truth of the Hebrew text." However, the Vulgate also includes the Gallican Psalter.

(b) The MT. The Masoretes (600-1000 CE) were groups of Jewish families who produced the final form of the OT text. They added four features to the inherited Proto-MT.

(i) They "hedged in" the consonantal text with a Masorah, consisting of scribal notes in the margin with instructions to assure its precise transmission. Scribal precision in transmitting the consonants before the Masoretes is

---

32. D. Barthélemy, "Redécouverte d'un chaînon manquant de l'histoire de la LXX," *RB* 60 (1958) 18-29.

reflected in the Talmud. R. Ishmael cautioned: "My son, be careful, because your work is the work of heaven; should you omit (even) one letter or add (even) one letter, the whole world would be destroyed" (*b. Soṭa* 2a).[33]

(ii) They added vowel points above and below the consonants to preserve as perfectly as possible the accompanying tradition of pronunciation. These points supplemented the early consonants (*'*, *h*, *w*, and *y*), known as the *matres lectionis* ("mothers of reading"), which were used to mark vowels in the prevocalized stage of the text. A Talmudic anecdote illustrates an acute awareness of the importance of an accurate oral tradition. David reprimanded Joab when he killed only the men of Amalek and not the "remembrance" *(zēker)* of them. Joab defended himself, noting his teacher taught him to read "all their males" *(zākār)*. Joab subsequently drew his sword against his teacher who had taught him incorrectly (*b. Bathra* 21a-b).

A complex body of evidence indicates the MT could not, in any serious or systematic way, represent a reconstruction or faking of the vocalization. Among other things we have argued:

> On the whole the grammar [which depends heavily on vocalization] of the MT admirably fits the framework of Semitic philology, and this fact certifies the work of the Masoretes. When in the 1930s Paul Kahle announced his theory that the Masoretes made massive innovations, Gotthelf Bergsträsser sarcastically observed that they must have read Carl Brockelmann's comparative Semitic grammar to have come up with forms so thoroughly in line with historical reconstructions.[34]

J. Barr demonstrates that the Masoretes were preservers of the oral tradition, not innovators like the LXX translators, by contrasting Jerome's earlier version of the Psalter based on the LXX and his later one based on the Hebrew.[35] The consonants of Ps 102:23-24a [24-25a] are:

'nh bdrk khw [Qere khy] qṣr ymy: 'mr 'ly

The LXX and the Gallican Psalter read this as:

'ānāh[û] bᵉderek kōḥô qōṣer yāmay ᵉmor 'elāy

---

33. Cited by Tov, *Textual Criticism*, 33.
34. Waltke, *IBHS*, 28.
35. J. Barr, *Comparative Philology and the Text of the Old Testament* (Oxford: Clarendon Press, 1968) 213.

"He replied to him in the way of his force; the fewness of my days report to me" (no major English version). The MT and Psalter, "Juxta Hebraeos," however, vocalize:

'innāh badderek kōḥî qiṣṣar yāmāy: 'ōmar 'ēlî

"He broke the strength on the way, he cut short my days. I said, My God . . ." (cf. English versions).

(iii) The Masoretes added a system of conjunctive and disjunctive accent signs to mark the chant or music.[36] These diacritical marks serve to beautify, to add dignity, to denote the stress of the word, which can be as meaningful as the difference between English "pre-sént" and "prés-ent," and, most importantly, to denote the syntactical relationship of words. It makes some difference where one places the accents in Isa 40:3:

The voice of him that crieth in the wilderness, Prepare . . . (KJV).

A voice of one calling: "In the desert prepare . . ." (NIV).

Here, too, the Masoretes are preservers, not innovators, unlike the LXX, whose translators seem to have been flying by the seat of their pants. E. J. Revell suggests that the punctuation was the first feature after the consonantal text to become stabilized in the Jewish biblical tradition.[37]

(iv) The Masoretes also added various paratextual elements — the verse and paragraph divisions and ancient textual corrections. Its variants known as *Kethiv* (K, the consonants of the Proto-MT) and *Qere* (Q, the text they read aloud) are the most important among these last-named. At first the Q readings were optional corrections of the text, but by the time of the Masoretes they had become obligatory. We already noted a preferred Q reading in Ps 102:23 [24]. However, sometimes the K is preferred. Prov 17:27b K (+ the LXX, Syr, Vg) reads *wᵉqar-rûaḥ*, "and cool of spirit," but Q (+ Tg) reads *yᵉqar-rûaḥ*, "precious of spirit," which was variously and dubiously understood to mean "heavy in spirit" (Tg), "sparing of words" (Rashi), and "of worthy bearing" (Saadia).[38] Both K and Q are *hapax legomena*. K now finds

36. S. Haik-Vantoura, *The Music of the Bible Revealed* (Berkeley: BIBAL; San Francisco: King David's Harp, 1991).

37. E. J. Revell, "Biblical Punctuation and Chant in the Second Temple Period," *JSJ* 7 (1976) 181-98, esp. 181.

38. Cited by Tov, *Textual Criticism*, 353.

support from the Egyptian side. L. Grollenberg showed the Egyptians used "hot" and "cold" in a metaphorical sense of two distinct personality types.[39]

The title page of L, the diplomatic text of *BHK* and *BHS*, reads: "Samuel Jacob copied, vowel-pointed, and Masoretically annotated this Codex of the Sacred Scripture from the correct manuscripts that the teacher Aaron b. Moses Ben-Asher redacted (his rest is in paradise!) and that constitute an exceedingly accurate exemplar." In fact, however, L probably contains too many corrections and errors to have served as a synagogue scroll.

2.5. Conclusion

In the light of this history we can now restrict the aim of OT text criticism to that of recovering the original text that lies behind the Proto-MT recension. The witnesses show such diverse text-types for some portions of the OT, like Joshua, Proverbs, and Esther, that they are best regarded as either distinct, literary stages in the development of the text or as distinct compositions. Tov summarizes: "The differences between the textual witnesses show that a few books and parts of books were once circulated in different formulations representing different literary stages, as a rule one after the other, but possibly also parallel to each other."[40] In Tov's view the text critic ought to reconstruct the edition represented in the Proto-MT. Socioreligious and historical reasons validate his view. That recension became the authoritative text within both Judaism and the Church. Tov argues this case for Judaism, but he failed to note that both Origen and Jerome, the two most formative OT text critics in Church history, also established the MT recension for the Church. Our English versions are based on it. "This history," we said, "should not be underestimated in deciding the question, 'What is the original text?' The MT inherently commended itself to both the synagogue and the church. As the canon of the OT emerged in the historical process, so also the MT surfaced as the best text of that canon."[41] B. Childs reached a similar conclusion.[42]

39. L. Grollenberg, "A propos de Prov. VIII,6 et XVII,27," *RB* 59 (1962) 42-43.

40. Tov, *Textual Criticism*, 177.

41. B. K. Waltke, "Old Testament Textual Criticism," in *Foundations for Biblical Interpretation*, ed. D. S. Dockery, K. A. Mathews, and R. B. Sloan (Nashville: Broadman & Holman, 1994) 175-76.

42. B. Childs, *Introduction to the Old Testament as Scripture* (Philadelphia: Fortress, 1979) 96-97.

We do not agree with the theory of P. R. Ackroyd[43] and of J. A. Sanders[44] that the different recensions enjoy equal canonical status. That view is unsatisfying from both a theologian's and historian's point of view. A serious theologian will want to know whether or not the Tenth Commandment prescribes worship on Mount Gerizim, and a resolute historian needs to know whether the biblical historian recorded in Exod 12:40 that Israel spent 430 years before the Exodus in just Egypt (MT) or in Egypt and Canaan (LXX, SP). Both theology and history demand that the critic decide upon an original text.

3. The Practice of Textual Criticism

Texts critics traditionally distinguish between *external criticism* (i.e., the evaluation of the textual witnesses) and *internal criticism* (i.e., the transcriptional and intrinsic probability of the readings themselves). For the former critics need to know the history of the witnesses; for the latter, the kinds of errors scribes make along with a sensitivity to exegetical expectations.

3.1. External Criticism

Before critics can evaluate the variants, those variants must first be collected and collated. Unfortunately, the apparatus in *BHS* still swarms with errors of commission and omission. True variants, we said, are restricted to those that pertain to the editing of the Proto-MT, not to the literary achievements of earlier scribes. For example, the shorter readings of Jeremiah should be passed over. This also applies to Joshua. Compare these variants of the MT and the LXX in Josh 1:1. The MT reads *'ḥry mwt mšh 'bd yhwh*, "After the death of Moses servant of YHWH," but the LXX reads *'ḥry mwt mšh*, "After the death of Moses." The MT of Joshua 1 has more than twelve additional words or phrases that are not found in the LXX, and the LXX rendering of Joshua is about 4-5 percent shorter than the MT. Plausibly the LXX reflects an earlier, shorter stage of the text and in this case should be ignored. Radically dissimilar to his NT counterpart, the OT text critic does not prefer the earlier and shorter readings! In fact, he turns them over to the literary critic.

43. P. R. Ackroyd, "An Authoritative Version of the Bible?" *ExpTim* 85 (1973) 374-77, esp. 376.

44. J. A. Sanders, "Text and Canon: Concepts and Methods," *JBL* 98 (1979) 5-29.

3.2. Intrinsic Criticism

(a) Unintentional errors. Following are a few illustrations of some kinds of unintentional scribal errors. In each case we retrovert the LXX to its Hebrew *Vorlage*.

(i) Confusion of consonants: Scribes confused *b/k, b/m, b/n, g/w, g/y, h/ḥ, w/z, w/y, w/r, k/n, m/s,* and *'/ṣ.* Javan's sons are called *ddnym* ("Dodanim") in Gen 10:4 of the MT, but *rdnym* in Gen 10:4 of the SP, LXX, and in 1 Chron 1:7 of the MT.

(ii) Haplography ("writing once") as a result of homoioteleuton (i.e., words with similar endings), or homoiarcton (words with similar beginnings). The MT for Gen 47:16 reads *w'tnh lkm bmqnykm,* "I will give you for your cattle" (cf. KJV), but the SP and the LXX read *w'tnh lkm lḥm bmqnykm,* "I will give you bread for your cattle" (cf. NIV, NRSV). The scribe may have skipped *lḥm* "bread" not only due to words with similar beginnings and endings but because of the similar sound of *k* and *ḥ.*

(iii) Metathesis (the accidental exchange or transposition of two adjacent letters within a word). The MT of Deut 31:1 reads *wylk mšh,* "and Moses went" (cf. NIV), but 4QDeut[n] and the LXX read *wykl mšh,* "and Moses finished" (cf. NRSV).

(iv) Different concepts of word and verse division. The MT of Hos 6:5 reads *wmšptyk 'wr yṣ',* "and your judgments, light goes forth" (cf. KJV, NASB), but the LXX reads *wmšpty k'wr yṣ',* "and my judgments went forth as light" (cf. NIV, NRSV).

(v) Dittography ("writing twice"). Isa 30:30 in the MT, the LXX, the Tg, the Syr, and the Vg reads *whšmy' yhwh,* "and YHWH will cause to be heard," but 1QIsa[a] reads *whšmy' hšmy' yhwh,* "and YHWH will cause to be heard, to be heard."

(vi) Doublets (conflation of two or more readings). The MT of 2 Kgs 19:9 reads *wyšb wyšlḥ ml'km,* "and he again sent messengers," and the MT of its synoptic parallel in Isa 37:9 reads *wyšm' wyšlḥ ml'kym,* "and when he heard it, he sent messengers." The LXX and 1QIsa[a] of Isa 37:9 read *wyšm' wyšb wyšlḥ ml'kôm,* "and when he heard it, he again sent messengers."

(b) Intentional changes. Following are a few illustrations of some kinds of intentional scribal changes in the text.

(i) Linguistic changes. Scribes sometimes modernized archaic features of a verse. In Num 15:35 the SP replaces the old infinitive absolute construction of the MT *(rāgôm)* for probably the imperative, *rigmu,* stone.

(ii) Contextual changes. In Gen 2:2, according to the MT, the Tg, and the Vg, God completed his work on the seventh day, but according to the SP, the LXX, and the Syr, he finished on the sixth day to avoid making it appear that God worked on the Sabbath.

(iii) Euphemistic changes. In Gen 50:23 the SP changes *'l-brky ywsp*, "upon the knees of Joseph," into *'l-bymy ywsp*, "in the days of Joseph," because it seemed improper that Joseph's grandchildren should be born upon his knees.

(iv) Theological changes. We have already noted how the SP altered the Ten Commandments. Better known are the changes of early names with the theophoric element *ba'al*, "lord," by the derogatory element, *bōšet*, "shame" (cf. 1 Chron 8:33 and 2 Sam 2:8). On the whole, however, theological changes are rare in the MT. G. R. Driver noted: "Theological glosses are surprisingly few, and most are enshrined in the *tiqqunê sōp\u1eb0rîm*, which are corrections of the text aimed chiefly at softening anthropomorphisms and eliminating the attribution of any sort of impropriety to God."[45]

4. Textual Criticism and Exegesis

Variants often impact the exegesis of the text and ultimately, to a greater or lesser extent, Old Testament theology. At the same time, however, the critic must decide between them on the basis of exegetical expectations.

The basic canon for deciding between variants is: That reading is preferable which would have been more likely to give rise to the others. To say this in another way: The variant that cannot be explained away is more probably the original. To apply this canon effectively demands extensive knowledge of the textual witness, scribal practices, exegetical factors, and common sense. P. K. McCarter wisely counsels the text critic to: (1) keep a clear image of the scribe in mind; (2) look first for the unconscious error; (3) know the personalities of your witnesses; and (4) treat each case as if it were unique.[46] Regarding the last he cites A. E. Housman's memorable metaphor: "A textual critic engaged upon his business is not at all like Newton investigating the motion of the planets; he is much more like a dog hunting fleas. . . . They re-

---

45. G. R. Driver, "Glosses in the Hebrew Text of the OT," in *L'Ancien testament et l'Orient: Études présentées aux VIes Journées bibliques de Louvain (11-13 septembre 1954)* (Orientalia et Biblica Lovaniensia 1; Louvain: Publications universitaires, 1957) 123-61, esp. 153.

46. P. K. McCarter, *Textual Criticism: Recovering the Text of the Hebrew Bible* (Philadelphia: Fortress, 1988) 22-24.

quire to be treated as individuals; and every problem which presents itself to the textual critic must be regarded as possibly unique."[47]

Let us illustrate the practice of textual criticism by returning to the metathesis in Prov 14:32b: *wᵉḥōseh bᵉmôtô ṣaddîq*, "and the righteous is *ḥōseh* in his death" (MT) versus *wᵉḥōseh bᵉtummô ṣaddîq*, "and the righteous is *ḥōseh* in his blamelessness" (LXX). The key to deciding the original text lies in a correct understanding of the *qal* participle of *ḥsh*. The lexeme occurs thirty-seven times and always with the meaning "to seek refuge," never "to have a refuge" (*pace* NIV) nor "to find a refuge" (*pace* NRSV). Thirty-four times, not counting Prov 14:32b, it is used with reference to taking refuge in God or under the shadow of his wings (cf. Prov 30:5). The two exceptions are Isa 14:32 and 30:2. In 14:32 the afflicted take refuge in Zion, a surrogate for God; in 30:2 Isaiah gives the expression an exceptional meaning because he uses sarcasm: *laḥsôt bᵉṣal miṣrāyim*, "to take refuge in the shadow of Egypt!" His intended meaning is that the Jerusalemites should have sought refuge in the Lord. The *qal* participle of *ḥsh* or the occurrence *ḥsh* in a relative clause denotes a devout worshipper, "one who seeks refuge in the Yahweh." One other time besides Prov 14:32b the *qal* participle is used absolutely: "[Show the wonder of your love], O Savior of those who take refuge" (*môsîaʿ ḥôsîm*, Ps 17:7). NIV here rightly glosses, "Savior of those who take refuge in you."

J. Gamberoni agrees that the *qal* participle has the same "religio-ethical" sense in Prov 14:32b as in Ps 17:7.[48] O. Plöger[49] and A. Meinhold[50] independently also reached the conclusion that YHWH is the unstated object of *ḥōseh* in Prov 14:32b. W. McKane, citing A. Barucq,[51] recognizes this as the meaning of the MT.[52] The LXX, NIV, NRSV, however, misunderstood the term. The unequivocal meaning of *ḥōseh* nicely satisfies the exegetical expectation of "in his death," but not of "in his righteousness." McKane rejects the MT because, as he says, "I do not believe that the sentence originally asserted this [a belief in the afterlife]." He follows the LXX and renders: "But he who relies on his own piety is a righteous man." His interpretation, however,

---

47. McCarter, *Textual Criticism*, 24.

48. J. Gamberoni in *The Theological Dictionary of the Old Testament*, ed. G. J. Botterweck and H. Ringgren (Grand Rapids: Eerdmans, 1974) 5.71.

49. O. Plöger, *Sprüche Salomos (Proverbia)* (BKAT 17; Neukirchen-Vluyn: Neukirchener Verlag, 1981) 176.

50. A. Meinhold, *Die Sprüche* (Züricher Bibelkommentare; Zürich: Theologischer Verlag, 1991).

51. A. Barucq, *Le Livre des Proverbes* (Paris: Gabalda, 1964).

52. W. McKane, *Proverbs* (OTL; Philadelphia: Westminster, 1970) 475.

violates both the lexical expectations of this word and the exegetical expectation of the book as a whole. Proverbs consistently encourages faith in the Lord (cf. 3:5; 22:19), never faith in one's own piety. In sum, the exegetical expectations of *ḥsh* and of the book favor the MT, suggesting that the corruption occurred in the LXX tradition.

In this treatment we have focused on scholarly competence. Exegetical competence also entails spiritual virtues, as we have argued elsewhere.

5. The Reliability of the OT Text

In the light of the OT text's complex history and the welter of conflicting readings in its textual witnesses, can the Church still believe in an infallible OT? Can it still confess with the Westminster divines: "by His singular care and providence" the text has been "kept pure in all ages" (Westminster Confession of Faith, 1.8)? We argue that in fact this history of the text and its witness and other reasons give the Church good reason to continue to confess *ex animo* both the reliability of the OT text and its purity.

1. In every era there was a strong *tendency to preserve the text,* as argued above.

2. The *antiquity of the MT* can be inferred from both the DSS and from comparative Semitic grammar. There is a continuous witness to the received text-type that lies behind some of the oldest biblical manuscripts at Qumran to the whole versional tradition (apart from some portions of the OG) that stretches from ca. 100 CE to the most modern translations into English and a host of other modern languages and dialects. Moreover, the grammar of this text-type admirably fits the framework of ancient Semitic philology. In fact, it accurately preserves *hapax legomena,* such as *qar-ruaḥ,* "cool of spirit," even though they were not understood later on in the text's transmission.

3. *The MT recension can be distinguished* from the scribal activity that in effect produced other literary editions of OT materials. If the Church confesses that the Holy Spirit superintended the selection of books that comprise the canon of the OT, why should it not confess that the Holy Spirit also superintended the selection of the MT recension? To be sure, the NT authors exhibit the Septuagintal and pre-Samaritan recensions and unique readings, but they also had a freedom in citing noncanonical religious literature. Even though the canon was closed, they felt free to cite noncanonical literature for theological reasons. How much more should we expect them to use texts freely before the text was finalized?

4. One needs to *keep the data in perspective.* A quick count of the textual variants in *BHS* shows that on average for every ten words there is a textual note. The humanists that produced its text-critical notes for recovering an original eclectic text infer that 90 percent of the text in hand is unquestioned. Textual criticism focuses on the problem readings, not on uncontested readings, giving a sense of disproportion to the amount of contaminated text.

5. *The significance of these variants* must be kept in view. In this essay we featured significant variants to make our points, but in truth most variants, including the 10 percent collated in *BHS,* are insignificant and do not affect doctrine. Most text-critical work is boring because the differences are inconsequential. If we restrict ourselves to the MT recension, D. Stuart rightly observes: "It is fair to say that the verses, chapters, and books of the Bible would read largely the same, and would leave the same impression with the reader, even if one adopted virtually every possible *alternative* reading to those now serving as the basis for current English translations."[53] Even if we accepted the earlier and/or other literary editions of portions of the OT, no doctrinal statement within the Protestant tradition would be affected. S. Talmon notes regarding the variants both within and between textual traditions:

> The scope of variation within all textual traditions is relatively restricted. Major divergences which intrinsically affect the sense are extremely rare. A collation of variants extant, based on the synoptic study of the material available, either by a comparison of parallel passages within one Version, or of the major Versions with each other, results in the conclusion that the ancient authors, compilers, tradents and scribes enjoyed what may be termed a controlled freedom of textual variation.[54]

6. Paradoxically, *the variety of texts bears witness to an original text.* Even in those portions of the OT that have been preserved in different literary editions there is still a relatively large consensus and close genetic relation between the manuscripts. This is best explained by a schema that commences with an *Ur*-text. Within the MT tradition, of course, there is a much

53. D. Stuart, "Inerrancy and Textual Criticism," in *Inerrancy and Common Sense,* ed. R. R. Nicole and J. R. Michaels (Grand Rapids: Baker, 1980) 97-117, esp. 98.

54. S. Talmon, "Textual Study of the Bible," in *Qumran and the History of the Biblical Text,* ed. F. M. Cross and S. Talmon (Cambridge, MA: Harvard University Press, 1975) 321-400, esp. 326.

greater agreement and closer genetic connection. The variants within this tradition point unmistakably to an original text from which they sprang. With respect to this agreement R. L. Harris provides an apt illustration of the reliability of the text, in spite of there being no perfect witness to it.[55] He notes how the loss or destruction of the standard yard at the Smithsonian Institution would not enormously affect the practice of measurement in the United States, for a comparison of the multitudinous copies of that yard would lead us to something very close to the original standard.

7. *The correctability of the text* must also be kept in view. Normally an error in the transcriptional process is subject to human correction. In the same way that an average reader can normally correct errors in a book or manuscript, the text critic can correct a textual error in the OT. A good exegete can reduce the number of problematic readings considerably. Moreover, we are the heirs of the work of many competent text critics. Just as electrical engineers can remove unwanted static from a telecommunication signal, so text critics can remove scribal corruptions by their knowledge of the text's history and character and by their exegetical expectations.

8. *The variants in the NT are similar to those found in the DSS.* Our Lord and his apostles confronted OT variants qualitatively similar to the ones that confront us, yet they did not hesitate to rely on the authority of Scripture. These differences did not prevent Jesus from saying that Scripture cannot be broken (John 10:35), nor Paul from confessing that "all Scripture is God-breathed" (2 Tim 3:16). Why should the contemporary Church, which is built upon Christ and his apostles, hesitate any more than they to confess the reliability and inspiration of Scripture?

9. *The variants in the DSS are not qualitatively different from those already known.* The Westminster divines knew the variants in the Samaritan Pentateuch and the ancient versions, which are qualitatively the same as those in the DSS, and yet did not hesitate to confess their conviction that the same Spirit who inspired the OT also preserved it. There are no new data to change this confession.

10. *The preserved OT achieves the work of the Holy Spirit.* Paul says: "All Scripture is God-breathed and is useful for teaching, rebuking, correcting and training in righteousness, so that the man of God may be thoroughly equipped for every good work" (2 Tim 3:16-17). The OT we have in hand does just that.

---

55. R. L. Harris, *Inspiration and Canonicity of the Bible* (Grand Rapids: Zondervan, 1957) 88-89.

Myth or History? The Literary Genre of Genesis Chapter 1

The creation account of Genesis 1:1–2:3 needs desperately to be heard today in the social-science classroom as a viable option in the marketplace of world religions.[1] This biblical creation story provides the foundation for the biblical world- and life-views, its views about God, humans, the creation, and each other, truths that the Spirit uses to convict sinners of sin, righteousness, and judgment and to point to Jesus Christ as the Savior. Biblical values and ethics are based on this account.

Unfortunately, instead of contending that its message be heard in the social-science classroom as an alternative option to the paganism that is coming more and more to the fore in our postmodern world, some Christians, led by "scientific creationists," are contending boisterously that it be taught in the hard-science classroom. This is due to their conviction that the biblical story and scientific data must and can be harmonized. For most, however, the attempt to harmonize the scientific data with a straightforward reading of Genesis is not credible, and as a result the Bible's message is rejected as a viable option in the marketplace of competing world- and life-views.

Whether Genesis 1:1–2:3 should be taught in the social sciences or in the hard sciences depends on its literary genre. If it be a scientific and/or straightforward historical account, then it belongs in the latter; if not, then Christians should be contending that it be given a hearing in the former. In

---

1. I am grateful to Dr. Dennis O. Lamoureux of the University of Alberta for helpful criticisms of my original essay.

Previously published in *Crux* 27, no. 4 (December 1991).

this paper I will attempt to identify its genre in the hope that it will encourage Christians, and especially Christian educators, to see that students again hear this famous story and rightly understand it in the classroom.

Genre identification depends on a text's contents and function. George Brooke[2] reasoned that "[t]he determination of literary genres is assumed by most literate people most of the time; however, when the debate is heated, it is necessary to be precise lest we miss the writer's point, for genre and intention often go hand in hand." In light of the biblical text's literary genre, the reader will be in a better position to decide the compatibility or the incompatibility of this creation account with scientific theories of origin.

Part I: Its Purpose

An author's purpose is determined in part by his perception of his audience's need. Genesis 1:1–2:3 was originally addressed to Israel in the Wilderness of Sinai c. 1400 BC. Both Psalm 8, by David c. 1000 BC, and Psalm 104, a polemic against the Hymn of Aton dated c. 1350 BC, transform our prosaic narrative into poetry and set it to music. Empirical evidence confirms the tradition that our text goes back to Moses, the charismatic founder of Israel.[3]

Through Moses' mediation, Israel, after its Exodus from Egypt, entered into covenant with their Savior, "the LORD," who promised to reward his faithful worshipers with life and threatened the disobedient with death. To undergird this covenant an inspired Moses gave Israel this creation story, allowing only one God, Creator of heaven and earth, who alone deserves worship, trust, and obedience.

Pagan mythologies about the creation continually threatened to annihilate Israel's witness to ethical monotheism. Pantheism, not theism, universally informed their myths, which demanded no moral rectitude. Believing in magic, their liturgical personnel annually mimed their myths, hoping that by reenacting the drama of their lustful gods they would re-create life. Their myths and rituals, such as Babylon's famous *Enuma Elish* with its dramatic rubrics, symbolized the world- and life-views that animated their pagan cul-

---

2. George Brooke, "Creation in the Biblical Tradition," *Zygon* 22 (1987): 233.

3. It is beyond the scope of this paper to discuss the authorship of the final form of the Pentateuch, which was composed of several sources, including both Mosaic and post-Mosaic materials.

tures. God's revelation annihilated them and revealed to Israel new and true symbols by which to live. John Stek[4] argues:

> His [the author of the Pentateuch] pen seemed to break the power of ages-old religious notion[s] that still held many in thrall. He was not grappling with issues arising out of modern scientific attempts to understand the structure, forces, and dimensions (temporal and spatial) of the physical universe. He was not interested in the issues involved in the modern debates over cosmic and biological evolution.

Moses aimed to produce through a true understanding of God a right perception of the universe and humans, including their relationships to God and one another, and to proclaim this truth in the face of false religious notions dominant throughout the world of his day. Conrad Hyers[5] notes:

> In the light of this historical context it becomes clearer what Genesis 1 is undertaking and accomplishing: a radical and sweeping affirmation of monotheism *vis-à-vis* polytheism, syncretism and idolatry. Each day of creation takes on two principal categories of divinity in the pantheons of the day, and declares that these are not gods at all, but creatures — creations of the one true God who is the only one, without a second or third. Each day dismisses an additional cluster of deities, arranged in a cosmological and symmetrical order.
>
> On the first day the gods of light and darkness are dismissed. On the second day, the gods of sky and sea. On the third day, earth gods and gods of vegetation. On the fourth day, sun, moon and star gods. The fifth and sixth days take away any associations with divinity from the animal kingdom. And finally human existence, too, is emptied of any intrinsic divinity — while at the same time all human beings, from the greatest to the least, and not just pharaohs, kings and heroes, are granted a divine likeness and mediation.

The Genesis creation narrative gives the faithful a firm foundation for their covenant with God. Why have no other gods (Exod. 20:3)? Because he

4. John H. Stek, "What Says the Scripture?" in *Portraits of Creation,* ed. Howard Van Till (Grand Rapids: Eerdmans, 1990), p. 230.

5. Conrad Hyers, "Biblical Literalism: Constricting the Cosmic Dance," in *Is God a Creationist? The Religious Case Against Creation-Science,* ed. Roland Mushat Frye (New York: Charles Scribner's Sons, 1983), p. 101.

alone is maker of heaven and earth (Gen. 1:1). Why not murder (Exod. 20:13)? Because humans alone are created in his image (Gen. 1:26-28). Why set apart a day for rest (Exod. 20:8-11)? Because he set it apart (Gen. 2:2-3).

Our text continues to speak to the Christian church, the new Israel, and to separate it on its journey through the "wilderness" to the "promised land" from competing worldviews and values. On the one hand, it girds the pilgrim people against the myths of the Enlightenment: materialism (the philosophical theory that regards matter and its motions as constituting the universe, and all phenomena, including those of the mind, as due to material causes), secularism (the system of political or social philosophical theory that rejects all forms of religious faith and worship), and humanism (the system or mode of thought or action in which human interests, values, and dignity predominate). On the other hand, it also fortifies them against pagan New Ageism, which fails to distinguish adequately between the Creator and his creation and right from wrong.

Part II: Its Content

The Genesis creation story falls into five parts: a summary statement (1:1), the negative state of the earth at the time of creation (1:2), the six days of creation (1:3-31), a summary conclusion (2:1), and an epilogue about the sabbath day (2:2-3). For our purposes we may treat the first two gingerly,[6] not develop the last two at all, and focus on the process and progress of creation during the first six days as recorded in this account of creation.[7]

Summary Statement (v. 1)

Three lines of evidence validate that verse 1 summarizes the rest of the chapter. First, "heaven and earth," is a hendiadys (a single expression of two apparently separate parts) denoting "the cosmos," the complete, orderly, harmonious universe. For example, the hendiadys "kith and kin" indicates all of one's relatives.

6. For a detailed exegesis of Genesis 1:1-2, see B. K. Waltke, "The Creation Account in Gen 1:1-3," *Bibliotheca Sacra* 132 (1974): 25-36, 136-44, 216-28, 327-42; 133 (1976): 28-41.

7. The terms "process" and "progress" are used in their nontechnical senses. The writer rejects Process Theology as unbiblical. Also, he does not infer by these terms that Genesis is teaching evolution. He uses them merely as an economic method to exegete the manner of creation.

More specifically, the hendiadys is a merism, a statement of opposites to indicate totality, like the compounds "day and night," "summer and winter."

Now, the elements of a compound must be studied as a unit, not in isolation. The hendiadys[8] "heaven and earth" cannot be understood by treating "heaven" and "earth" as separate elements any more than "butterfly" can be decoded by investigating "butter" and "fly" in isolation. Umberto Cassuto[9] commented:

> In language, as in chemistry, a compound may be found to possess qualities absent from its constituent elements. Anyone who does not know what "broadcast" denotes, will not be able to guess the connotation of the word from its separate elements "broad" and "cast."

The Sumerian compound *anki,* composed of *an,* "heaven," and *ki,* the "earth," also signifies "universe." The intertestamental book Wisdom of Solomon (11:17) actually renders the merism by the Greek word *"cosmos."* In poetry the stereotyped phrase "heaven and earth" is often split apart. Note how the trope stands as an equivalent of "all things" in Isaiah 44:24:

> I am the Lord who makes *all things,*
> who stretched out the *heavens* by myself,
> who alone spreads out the *earth.*

If verse 1 were translated "In the beginning God created the cosmos," one would see more clearly that it is a summary statement about what God made during the six days of creation, not about what God made before them.

Second, the verb *bara',* "create," for both lexical and grammatical reasons refers to the finished cosmos, not a state before its completion. Regarding its meaning J. Stek[10] commented:

> It is silent as to the utilization of pre-existent materials or the time (whether at the beginning of time or in the midst of time, whether instantaneously or over a period of time) as the means involved. In biblical language, *bara* affirms of some existent reality that God conceived, willed, and effected it.

---

8. Also, a syntagm, a series of different elements forming a syntactic unit.
9. U. Cassuto, *Commentary on Genesis,* vol. 1 (Jerusalem: Magnes, 1961), p. 22.
10. Stek, "What Says the Scripture?" p. 213.

"Create" in Genesis 1 embraces the process and progress of creation over the six days of creation in verses 3-31. Grammatically, it is a telic verb, that is, it refers "to a situation . . . that involves a process that leads up to a well-defined terminal point, beyond which the process cannot continue," according to Cambridge linguist Bernard Comrie.[11] Other telic verbs include "sell" and "die." Although "sell" and "die" include processes up to a definitive point, one has not sold until property is exchanged or died until life finally ceases. "Create" involves the processes narrated for the six days of creation, but the cosmos was not created until, as the summary statement in 2:1 puts it, "the heavens and earth were completed in their vast array."

Third, the grammar of the Hebrew text, as the writer argued in detail elsewhere,[12] favors rendering the first verse, "In the beginning God created the cosmos," not "when God began to create the cosmos." For the purposes of this essay, namely, to decide the literary genre of Genesis 1:1–2:3 and its compatibility or incompatibility with scientific theories of origins, the point of grammar need not be pursued.

In sum, verse 1 is adumbrated in the rest of the chapter.

Earth's Negative State (v. 2)

Verse 2 describes earth's threefold condition when God began to create the cosmos. First, it was *tohu wabohu,* "unformed and unfilled." *Tohu wabohu* is also a hendiadys, not a merism, like *dribs and drabs, spic and span, hem and haw,* signifying "utter chaos." By chaos I do not mean the earth was unstructured in a scientific sense but that it was uninhabitable and uninhabited. "Unformed and unfilled" (= "utter chaos") is the antonym of "heaven and earth" (= the "total cosmos"). E. Jacob[13] wrote: "Where it [*tohu wabohu*] is met (Isa. 34:11; Jer. 4:23), [it] denotes the contrary of creation and not merely an inferior stage of creation." Against Luther and Calvin, the text cannot mean that God created the "heaven and the earth" and what he brought into existence was an "unformed and unfilled" earth. The cosmos of verse 1 and the chaos of verse 2 cannot have coexisted. E. Jacob[14] continued: "Evidently

11. Bernard Comrie, *Aspect: An Introduction to the Study of Verbal Aspect and Related Problems* (Cambridge: Cambridge University Press, 1976), p. 45.

12. Waltke, "The Creation Account in Gen 1:1-3," pp. 221-27.

13. E. Jacob, *Theology of the Old Testament* (London: Hodder & Stoughton, 1958), p. 144, n. 2.

14. Jacob, *Theology of the Old Testament,* p. 144, n. 2.

we must regard Gen 1:2 as a parenthesis which seeks to describe the condition before creation and 1:1 as the heading of the whole chapter." *In sum, Genesis 1 represents the Heavenly King transforming the preexisting chaos into the present cosmos.*

Second, there was "darkness over the surface of the deep." The Bible does not explain the origins of the darkness and of the abyss, both so hostile to life. Other Scriptures (e.g., Isa. 44:24; Jer. 10:16; Ps. 90:2) affirm that God, and inferentially not matter, is eternal. Of Jesus Christ Paul said: "He is before all things, and in him all things hold together" (Col. 1:17). The Genesis creation account, however, teaches only that God brought the pre-Genesis darkness and chaotic waters within his protective restraints, not when or how they happened. The writer of Hebrews says: "By faith we understand that the universe was formed at God's command, so that what is seen was not made out of what was visible" (Heb. 11:3). But in Genesis 1:2, in contrast to verses 3-31, no divine command is heard. The first heaven and earth, in which we earthlings live, exists between the pre-creation chaos (Gen. 1:2) and the new heaven and earth in which there will be no night and no sea (Rev. 21:1-2, 22-25). If one wishes to form a concord between natural theology and Genesis 1, which I for one do not, then let it be noted that the age of the earth cannot be decided by this text and that one must commence one's thinking about cosmic origins with chaotic waters already in existence.[15]

Finally, "the Spirit of God was hovering over the waters." Although the account does not specify the origin of the waters, it instructs us that the Spirit of God was hovering over them to protect and prepare the uninhabitable earth for creation as an eagle hovers over its fledglings (Deut. 32:11) and as the Spirit of God prepares humans to receive the word of God that can make them into new creations in Christ Jesus (2 Cor. 4:6).

The Six Days of Creation (vv. 3-31)

a. The Process of Creation

God segregated the process of creation into six days, each of which essentially consists of six panels: an announcement, "and God said"; a command, "let there be" or its equivalent; a report, "and so God made"; a naming, re-

---

15. Contra Henry Morris, *The Genesis Record: A Scientific and Devotional Commentary on the Book of Beginnings* (Grand Rapids: Baker, 1976), pp. 42-46.

stricted to the first three days, "and he called"; an evaluation, "it was good"; and a chronological framework, "first day," "second day." As we shall argue below, the language is anthropomorphic, representing God in human dress.[16] Moses does not intend to say that God speaks and sees as a human. Behind his figurative anthropomorphisms lie the spiritual realities represented by them.

The *announcement,* "and God said," teaches that the whole world and all that it contains were created according to the plan of the One God and through an agency best represented by "word" (cf. John 1:1-18). The *commandment,* "let there be," expresses the truth that this cosmos came into existence by God's will, which, operating without restraint, overcame the chaos. The *report,* "and so God made," or its equivalent, presents the creed that God is transcendent over everything, including the gathered sea and the darkness. By *naming* the elements on the first three days, the life-supportive systems of sky and/or air, land, and water, God shows that he is the supreme ruler over them. Even the elements of the uncreated state, the abyss and darkness, are under his dominion. His *evaluation,* "and it was good," as William Dumbrell[17] shows, instructs that everything fulfills the divine intention for them. Humans should not fear the good creation but rather the Heavenly King, the universal and absolute monarch, who rules them. The *chronological framework* reveals that God created the cosmos in an orderly and, as will be seen in the discussion on "the progress of creation," logical way.

Cassuto[18] noted the conscious, not the coincidental, use of the important number seven along with the numbers three and ten to structure our text and to determine many of its details. Embedded in Ancient Near Eastern literatures the number six represents incompleteness and the number seven represents resolution, wholeness, completeness. The seven days of creation are marked off by seven paragraphs in the Masoretic text. The ten announcements, "and God said," are clearly divisible into two groups: the first group contains seven divine commands in a jussive form (e.g., "let there be," "let the earth bring forth") enjoining the creation of the creatures, and three imperatives in other grammatical forms for humans. The evaluation, "it was good," appears seven times, being omitted for the second day and repeated twice for the third. The first verse has seven words, and the second fourteen,

---

16. Better than "anthropomorphisms" we should speak of "theomorphisms": humankind's physical aspects represent God's spiritual functions.

17. William Dumbrell, "Creation, Covenant and Work," *Crux* 24, no. 3 (1988): 16-17.

18. Cassuto, *Commentary on Genesis,* pp. 12-15.

twice seven, and so forth. To these Henri Blocher[19] adds the seven completion formulas, "and it was so," and the seven times that a further statement is added (God names or blesses).

b. Progress of Creation

Since the time of Herder (c. AD 1750) students have noted that Genesis 1:1–2:3 represents the creation as occurring in two triads of days, days 1-3 matched by days 4-6:

Unformed	*Unfilled*
1. Light	4. Luminaries
2. Sky/atmosphere and Water	5. Fish and Fowl
3. Land	6. Beasts
Vegetation	Humans

During the first triad God separated the formless chaos into static spheres: light and darkness, the sky and/or atmosphere, water and land; and in the second triad he filled those spheres that house and shelter life with moving forms; that is, in the second triad he populates the first. Each triad progresses from heaven to earth: from light to dry land, from heavenly luminaries to earth creatures. Each triad progresses from a first day with a single creative act, light matched by luminaries; to a second day with one creative act with two aspects, sky and seas paired with fish and birds; to a third day with two separate creative acts, dry land and vegetation coupled with land animals and humans. Each triad ends with the earth bringing forth: first flora and then fauna. The inhabitants of the second triad rule over the static spheres of the first: luminaries over the light, birds over the sky, fish over the sea, beasts over the land that houses them and the vegetation that feeds them, and humans over all living things.[20]

In sum, the Genesis account's remarkably symmetrical representation of the process and progress of creation supports Henri Blocher's[21] claim that

---

19. Henri Blocher, *In the Beginning: The Opening Chapters of Genesis,* trans. David G. Preston (Leicester, UK/Downers Grove, IL: InterVarsity, 1984), p. 33.

20. For further demonstration of the literary artistry of the Genesis creation narrative, see Mark A. Throntveit, "Are the Events in the Genesis Creation Account Set Forth in Chronological Order?" in *The Genesis Debate: Persistent Questions about Creation and the Flood,* ed. Ronald Youngblood (Grand Rapids: Baker, 1986), pp. 36-55.

21. Blocher, *In the Beginning,* pp. 49-59.

it is at the least a magnificent literary-artistic representation of the creation. Is it more?

Part 3: Its Genre

We will judge its literary genre by critically appraising other suggested possibilities.

A Hymn?

Is it a hymn? Hardly, for the poetic mode, the linguistic conventions, and doxological tone of known Ancient Near Eastern hymns are notably absent in Genesis 1.

Cult Liturgy?

Is it a cult liturgy composed for a New Year festival like a typical pagan cosmogony? No. The reconstruction of such a ritual in Israel is a hypothetical fiction. In fact, this account polemicizes against the magic that made those rituals cogent within their social structures. Nahum Sarna[22] said:

> The inextricable tie between myth and ritual, the mimetic enactment of the cosmogony in the form of ritual drama, which is an essential characteristic of the pagan religions, finds no counterpart in the Israelite cult. In this respect too, the Genesis story represents a complete break with Near Eastern tradition. To be sure, there are points of contact between ancient Near Eastern cosmogonies such as creation out of chaos, creation by separation, and creation of opposites, but pantheism, polytheism, and annual recreation through magical myths and rituals, are not among them.[23]

---

22. Nahum M. Sarna, *Understanding Genesis* (New York: Schocken, 1978), p. 9.

23. In a private communication Denis O. Lamoureux calls attention to F. M. Cornford, "Pattern of Ionian Cosmology," in *Theories of the Universe: From Babylonian Myth to Modern Science,* ed. M. K. Munitz (New York: Free Press, 1957), p. 22.

Myth?

Is it myth? Here the answer may be yes or no, depending on one's definition of myth. J. W. Rogerson[24] cataloged twelve different definitions of the term. If one means by myth nothing more than a story that explains phenomena and experience, or a story about God/gods, or a story about him/them as working and having his/their being in this world among humans in the same mode as men speak and work, then Genesis 1 can be labeled "myth," for it satisfies those definitions. In its popular sense, however, "myth" has come to be identified with a fairy tale, imaginary and fantastic events that never happened. As will be shown, the narrator of Genesis 1 connects his creation account with real history, and so the designation "myth" is best rejected. Peter says, "We did not follow cleverly invented stories [Gr. *mythois*] when we told you about the power and coming of our Lord Jesus Christ, but we were eyewitnesses of his majesty" (2 Peter 1:16).

History?

Is it history? Here our answer is both a qualified yes and no. The Genesis creation account sets forth as historical fact that God created the universe with its vast array of moving forms. Furthermore, the author of Genesis links this prologue to the rest of his book structured about ten historical accounts by clearly linking it with his first two accounts. The first account, "the account of the heavens and earth," recounting the origin, development, and spread of sin (2:4–4:26), is unmistakably coupled with the prologue by the addition, "when the LORD God made the earth and the heavens." Likewise, he clearly binds his second account, "the written account of Adam's line" (5:1-32), with 1:26-28 by repeating such crucial terms as "image" and "likeness," and "male and female."

On the other hand, he is just as clearly not giving us in his prologue a straightforward, sequential history. Henry Morris[25] misleads us when he claims "[t]he creation account is clear, definite, sequential and matter-of-fact, giving every appearance of straightforward historical narrative." If not, he argues, it is a blatant deception. The text, however, is begging us not to read it in this way.

24. John William Rogerson, *Myth in the Old Testament Interpretation* (Berlin: W. de Gruyter, 1974).
25. Morris, *The Genesis Record*, p. 84.

First, consider how such a reading creates an *irreconcilable contradiction between the prologue of Genesis and the supplemental creation account in Genesis 2:4-25*. According to the prologue, the first creation narrative, God created vegetation on the third day, fish and fowl on the fifth, and beasts and humans on the sixth. According to the second, a supplemental creation account (2:4-25), however, between the creation of man (2:7) and the creation of woman (2:18-25), God planted a garden (2:8); caused its trees to grow (2:9); caused a heavenly river to flow from the top of Mount Eden through the garden whereupon it divided into four rivers flowing to the four corners of the earth (2:10); put the man he formed into the garden to work it and keep it and placed him on probation (vv. 15-17); and apparently, before he built the woman, formed the birds and animals (v. 19), and the man named them all (v. 20). Gleason Archer[26] exclaimed: "Who can imagine that all these transactions could possibly have taken place in 120 minutes of the sixth day (or even within twenty-four hours, for that matter)?"

Take the trees alone. Even if the orchard in view was planted three days earlier, are we to put our imaginations in fast-forward and see its trees as growing to maturity and bearing fruit within three days? Unlike chapter 1, where one could appeal to apparent age with reference to such things as the stellar bodies, one cannot make a similar appeal to the planted trees. To be sure, God could have caused the trees to grow instantaneously, even as Jesus in a moment turned water into wine (John 2:1-11), but the Genesis narrative, using the verbs "plant" and "cause to grow," gives no indication that an extraordinarily quick growth of trees is intended, whereas John labels Jesus' work as "the first of his miraculous signs." A straightforward reading of the Genesis prologue is improbable in light of its supplementary account of creation.

As so often happens in Scripture, historical events have been dischronologized and reconstructed for theological reasons. For example, the nations listed in Genesis 10 came into existence after the confusion of languages at Babel recounted in Genesis 11, but the writer has dischronologized events in order to put the nations under Noah's blessing, not under Babel's curse.[27] According to Genesis 35:16-18 Benjamin was born in Canaan, but less than ten verses later it lists Benjamin among Jacob's sons born in Paddan-

---

26. Gleason L. Archer, Jr., *A Survey of Old Testament Introduction* (Chicago: Moody Press, 1964), p. 192.

27. David J. A. Clines, *Theme of the Pentateuch* (Sheffield, UK: Department of Biblical Studies, University of Sheffield, 1978), p. 68.

Aram, presumably to represent the youngest patriarch as taking part in the return of all Israel from the exile in Paddan-Aram. Biblical writers display a freedom in representing historical events for theological reasons.

Second, the creation of light on the first day and of luminaries on the fourth confirms our suspicion that Genesis 1 ought not be read as straightforward history. John Sailhamer[28] argues that "the division between 'the day' and 'the night' . . . leaves little room for an interpretation of 'the light' in v. 3 as other than that of light from the sun." A straightforward reading of Genesis 1:4 and 14 leads to *the incompatible notions that the sun was created on the first day and again on the fourth day.* The suggestion that the sun was created on the first day and made visible on the fourth day is unlikely.[29] If "let there be" in verse 3 means "let there come into existence," it should have the same meaning in verse 14, not "let them be visible." More plausibly, Moses, representing God as the Ultimate Source of light and the luminaries as its immediate sources, separates the two sources in this matching pair of triads to educate its audience that God is transcendent, not dependent on means.

Furthermore, *verse 14 cannot be reconciled readily with verses 5, 8, and 13.* Our narrator begs us not to read him in a straightforward, sequential account by marking off three days (vv. 5, 8, 13), each with its own "evening and morning," before narrating that on the fourth day lights were created to separate the day from the night, and . . . to mark . . . days" (v. 14). A sequential reading of the text lacks cogency. How can there be three days characterized by day and night before the creation of the luminaries to separate the day from the night and to mark off the days? Are we clueless?[30]

---

28. John H. Sailhamer, "Genesis," in *Expositor's Bible Commentary,* vol. 2, ed. Frank E. Gaebelein (Grand Rapids: Regency Reference Library, 1990), p. 26.

29. Sailhamer argues that "heaven and earth" in verse 1 expresses "totality" (p. 23), including the celestial bodies. He further renders verse 14 to read "And God said, 'Let the lights [created in v. 1] in the expanse of the sky separate.'" Although a syntactical possibility, his interpretation of Genesis 1:1 curiously entails the creation of everything before the six days of creation rather than a summary adumbrated in those days.

30. Since all six days are based upon the diurnal appearances of the sun, they presumably have the same character. It would be very curious if the first three days were calibrated by a different measure of time from that applied to the last three. All six days are the same as our twenty-four-hour days.

The appeal to "day" in compounds such as "in the day" (Gen. 2:4) and the "day of the LORD" to validate the "Day-Age Theory," the theory that "day" in Genesis 1 does not necessarily denote the twenty-four-hour diurnal day but may designate a geologic age or state, is linguistically flawed. The use of "day" in syntagms, "the ordered and unified arrangement of words in a distinctive way," such as these is clearly different from its use with numerals:

Finally, the language of our creation narrative is figurative, anthropo-morphic, not plain. The writer's vantage point is with God in his heavenly court.[31] As a representation of what has transpired in that transcendent sphere, the narrative must employ metaphor. John Stek[32] observes:

> What occurs in the arena of God's action can be storied after the manner of human events, but accounts of "events" in that arena are fundamen-tally different in kind from all forms of historiography. As representa-tions of what has transpired in the divine arena, they are of the nature of metaphorical narrations. They relate what has taken place behind the veil, but translate it into images we can grasp — as do the biblical visions of the heavenly court. However realistic they seem, an essential "as if" quality pervades them.

H. Ridderbos[33] concurs:

> Is . . . the author not under the necessity of employing such a method, because this is the only way to speak about something that is really be-yond all human thoughts and words?

Even the very conservative theologian E. J. Young[34] admits: "It is cer-tainly true that God did not speak with physical organs of speech nor did he

---

"first day," "second day." The argument is as fallacious as saying that "apple" does not neces-sarily indicate the round edible fruit of the rosaceous tree because this is not its meaning in "pineapple."

31. The "us" in verse 26 is best interpreted as referring to God and the divine beings gathered about him. The first person plural pronoun assumes those antecedents in its two other uses, in Genesis 3:22 and 11:7. In Isaiah 6:8, the only other passage using "us" with ref-erence to God, Isaiah, upon being transported into the heavenly court and overhearing God's consultation with the seraphim, records God using the same mixture of singular and plural first person pronouns as Moses, "Whom shall I send? And who will go for us?" (Isa. 6:8). In spite of the King's use of "us" in his deliberations with His court, He is the sole Actor. He created humans (Gen. 1:26-28) and sent Isaiah (Isa. 6:9). See P. D. Miller, *Genesis 1–11: Studies in Structure and Theme,* JSOT Supplement Series 8 (Sheffield, UK: University of Sheffield Press, 1978).

32. Stek, *Portraits,* p. 236.

33. H. Ridderbos, "The Meaning of Genesis I," *Free University Quarterly* 4 (1955/1957): 222.

34. Edward Joseph Young, *Studies in Genesis One* (Philadelphia: Presbyterian and Re-formed Publishing House, 1964), pp. 55-56.

utter words in the Hebrew language." If the other panels in the process of creation are anthropomorphic representations of creation, is it not plausible to suppose the same is true of the chronological framework, the six days? God lisped so that Israel could mimic him, working six days and resting the seventh (Exod. 20:11). To be sure, the six days in the Genesis creation account are our twenty-four-hour days, but they are metaphorical representations of a reality beyond human comprehension and imitation.

Science?

Is it science? The answer is a qualified yes, but finally no. To be sure, it deals with the life-supportive systems, air, water, land, with heavenly bodies, sun, moon, stars, and with species of plants and animals, but it treats them in a way unlike scientific literature. Contrary to Henry Morris's[35] assertion that "the biblical record, accepted in its natural and literal sense, gives the only scientific and satisfying account of the origins of things," we argue it cannot give a satisfying scientific account of origins for it is not scientific literature.[36]

First, *the subject* is God, not the forces of nature. The canons of the scientific method do not allow supernatural causes to be included in a theory.

Second, *their concerns* differ. The Bible is concerned with ultimate origins (Where did it all come from?), not scientific questions of proximate origins (How did A arise out of B, if it did?). The biblical account makes no sharp distinction between immediate cause and ultimate source. Langdon Gilkey[37] complains: "They [the creation scientists] ignore the (scholastic) distinction between *primary* causality of a First Cause, with which philosophy or theology might deal, and *secondary* causality, which is causality confined to finite factors." When our text says "and God said, 'Let the water teem with living creatures'" (v. 20), and "Let the land produce living creatures," it traces the origins of living creatures back to their ultimate source, God, not explaining how the proximate sources, water and land, produced them. Genesis does not attempt to link phenomenon with phenomenon but

---

35. Henry M. Morris, *The Remarkable Birth of Planet Earth* (Minneapolis: Bethany House, 1978), p. iv.

36. The writer leans heavily in this discussion on Charles E. Hummel, *The Galileo Connection: Resolving Conflicts between Science and the Bible* (Downers Grove, IL: InterVarsity, 1986).

37. Langdon Gilkey, "Creationism: The Roots of the Conflict," in *Is God a Creationist?* ed. R. M. Frye (New York: Charles Scribner's Sons, 1983), p. 60.

with the covenant-keeping God. It is as mischievous to pit a scientific theory of evolution against Genesis as to pit David's account of his ultimate origin, "You [O, God] created my inmost being" (Ps. 139:13), against a geneticist's account of his contingent birth.

Third, its *language* is nonscientific. The account reports the origins of the cosmos phenomenologically, not mathematically or theoretically. From a geocentric perspective, the sun, moon, and stars are "in the expanse of the sky"; from a heliocentric perspective they are not. Scientific and biblical languages about origins, like their contents, also supplement, not oppose, each other. People err, however, when they think scientific language is more "correct" than the Bible's. Both languages are relatively, not absolutely, correct or incorrect, depending on their purposes.

Fourth, its *purpose* is nonscientific. Whereas science aims primarily to answer with as much mathematical precision as possible questions about the "when" and "how" of the origin of physical things, Genesis aims primarily to answer questions about "who" and "why" they were formed, and passes the value judgment, "it was good." To be sure, it tells us that God created the cosmos "in the beginning" and by his word, but its aim is theological, not mathematical precision. Because the intentions differ so radically one can safely say that Genesis does not attempt to answer scientific questions, and scientists cannot answer those addressed in the biblical creation account. Augustine said of that account, "The Spirit of God who spoke through them did not choose to teach about the heavens to men, as it was of no use for salvation." Galileo[38] was more caustic: "The intention of the Holy Ghost is to teach us how to go to Heaven, not how the heaven goes." Pope John Paul II,[39] humbly reversing an earlier papal decree, agrees:

> The Bible itself speaks to us of the origin of the universe and its make-up, not in order to provide us with a scientific treatise, but in order to state the correct relationship of man with God and the universe. . . . Any other teaching about the origin and make-up of the universe is alien to the intentions of the Bible, which does not wish to teach how heaven was made, but how to go to heaven.

---

38. Galileo, "Letter to the Grand Duchess Christina," in *Discoveries and Opinions of Galileo,* ed. and trans. Stillman Drake (Garden City, NY: Doubleday Anchor, 1957), p. 186.

39. John Paul II, "Science and Scripture: The Path of Scientific Discovery," *Origins* 11 (1981): 277-80, with quotation on p. 279.

The biblical goals remain outside the parameters of the scientific method. The purpose of the Bible and of science, like their contents and languages, do not confront one another but complete each other. Persons are impoverished intellectually and spiritually by limiting themselves to either one.

Finally, the biblical and scientific accounts are *validated* in different ways: the former by the Spirit of God, the latter by empirical testing.

Since the biblical narrative is nonscientific, we draw the double conclusion that it cannot be a satisfying scientific account of the origins of things and that it can be supplemented by scientific theories. The Bible and a scientific theory of origins clash only when the latter is set forth as the complete explanation of origins and the former is interpreted as a scientific treatise.

Theology?

Is it theology? In substance yes, for it treats divine matters, but in style no, for the narrative reports God's actions, not reflections upon them.

We come back then to Henri Blocher's suggested genre identification: it is a literary-artistic representation of the creation. To this we add the purpose, namely, to ground the covenant people's worship and life in the Creator, who transformed chaos into cosmos, and to ground their ethics in his created order.

Conclusion

The sixteenth-century Belgic Confession states:

> We know Him by two means: First, by the creation, preservation, and government of the universe; which is before our eyes as a most elegant book, wherein all creatures, great and small, are as so many characters leading us to *see clearly the invisible things of God, even his everlasting power and divinity,* as the apostle Paul says (Rom. 1:20). All which things are sufficient to convince men and leave them without excuse. Second, He makes Himself more clearly and fully known to us by His holy and divine Word, that is to say, as far as is necessary for us to know in this life, to His glory and our salvation.

Now these two books about creation complement one another, but they cannot and should not be harmonized. With the one hand, we salute Henry Morris and other creation scientists for their yeoman work in pointing scientists to the Creator through their researches in his creation. Creation points humans to the Creator; Genesis 1 identifies him as Israel's covenant-keeping God. We hold out the palm of the other hand, however, to caution against the danger of harmonizing scientific studies in natural theology with a straightforward, scientific reading of Genesis 1:1–2:3. These two books clash when scientists, attempting to speak about metaphysical matters, substitute naturalism for creationism, and when exegetes use Genesis to construct a scientific theory of cosmic and biological origins. Natural theology and exegetical theology are both hindered by a continued adherence to the epistemic principle that valid scientific theories must be consistent with a woodenly literal reading of Genesis. Because of the attempt to harmonize Genesis with science, such implausible interpretations of Genesis 1 as "the Restitution Theory," commonly called "the Gap Theory," and "the Day-Age Theory" have vexed biblical exegesis, and scientific theories presupposing a young earth and denying evolution unnecessarily have discredited their advocates, despite their unconvincing protests that they are not influenced by Genesis. Let each book speak its own language and be appropriately exegeted and exposited, and let each in its own way bring praise to the Creator, the God and Father of our Lord Jesus Christ.

On How to Study the Psalms Devotionally

At the end of the summer in which our committee translated the Book of Psalms for the New International Version of the Bible, I felt less devoted to God than at the beginning of the summer when we began our assignment. (No aspersion on the NIV! I suspect translators of all versions have had a similar experience. In my judgment the NIV is the best translation available, and I thank God for giving me opportunity to have a small part in it.) My confession is a wry comment on my depravity and the paradox of faith — God seeking after man and man seeking after God. Is it not ironic that after tirelessly studying some of the most richly devotional literature of the Bible I came away from the study less consecrated to God, less zealous to perform his service, and less aware of the Holy? And does not my experience, reinforced by the experience of most students in biblical and theological studies, show us that in the "quest for holiness" the human dimension must take a place alongside the neo-orthodox emphasis on God's sovereignty and transcendence in revealing himself in his Word and re-creating man through it?

Studying Devotionally

My concern in this essay — to consider ways in which we as the people of God may study the Psalms so that we become more devoted to our Lord — is but a part of the larger issue on how to study any discipline in such a way as to further one's commitment to God. A major temptation confronting any student is

---

Previously published in *Crux* 16, no. 2 (June 1980). Used with permission.

that instead of seeking God in his or her discipline he or she seeks personal achievement and human recognition through it. In a word, we are always in danger of being "worldlings," by which I mean seeking "success" according to secular evaluations instead of according to sacred values. Driven by pride and a desire to advance ourselves in the eyes of others we become self-ambitious, competitive, and foolish "workaholics." Montaigne (1533-1592), the inventor of the modern essay, complained about students in his time: "How many have I seene in my daies, by an overgreedy desire of knowledge, become as it were foolish. Carneades was so deeply plunged, and as I may say besotted in it, that he never had leasure to cut his haire, or pare his nailes. . . ." (See "Of the Institution and Education of Children," in *The Harvard Classics*, vol. 32: *Literary and Philosophical Essays*, 1938, p. 54.) I confess that I identify with Carneades and must turn to my Lord to save me from my folly.

We need to heed this reproof against worldliness by Thomas à Kempis:

> . . . the treating of worldly matters abateth greatly the fervour of spirit: though it be done with a good intent, we be anon deceived with vainity of the world, and in manner are made as thrall unto it, if we take not good head. (*The Imitation of Christ*, I.10; trans. Richard Whitford, 1953, pp. 17f.)

The Preacher coined a proverb that every student would do well to frame and hang over his or her desk:

> Better one handful with tranquility
> >than two handfuls with toil
> >and chasing after wind. (Eccles. 4:6)

Paul provided us with a model:

> Am I now trying to win the approval of men, or of God? Or am I trying to please men? If I were still trying to please men, I would not be a servant of Christ. (Gal. 1:10)

Studying the Bible Devotionally

Having briefly looked at that temptation which greatly abates the fervency of our spirit toward God in academic pursuits, we can more directly address our topic by considering how to study the Bible devotionally. The object of biblical studies is twofold: the literature itself and God who revealed himself in it. (I use "object" with reference to God with some qualms because in the final analysis God is the author who discloses himself to us. On the other hand, the Bible is the revelation of God in the double meaning of that phrase: it is from him [a subjective genitive] and about him [an objective genitive]. With this second sense in view it is appropriate to speak of biblical studies in the way I have.) Because of the dual nature of biblical studies we need to adopt a stance appropriate to both these aspects.

In the first place, then, the incarnation of God in literature exacts a rigorous, scientific investigation of the text. It is highly mischievous to pit a devotional study of the Bible against an academic study of it. A devotional study must include a careful determination of the text (until the invention of the printing press no two manuscripts of the Bible were exactly the same), of the meaning of its words (now from dead languages), of the value of the grammatical forms and their syntactical relations in the discourse, of the figures of speech and the authorial intention behind them, of the historical and cultural milieu shaping the composition, and of its literary forms. Moreover, the exegete must make a conscious attempt to trace the progressive development of the text's meaning as the canon containing it grew. As the ancient text's literary parameters expanded, its meaning became fuller and more precise. With regard to this dimension of exegetical study, often overlooked by those schooled in the grammatico-historical approach, a student should ask of Psalm 2, for example, what this coronation liturgy meant during the first temple when David's sons were installed on Mount Zion to rule over God's kingdom. What did it mean during the second temple when the Old Testament canon took its final shape and there was no king in Israel? And what does it mean in the New Testament when Jesus Christ fulfilled the psalm's vision and assumed his throne in the heavenly Mount Zion (Acts 4:23-27; 13:32-33)? (I have labeled this hermeneutic "the canonical process approach"; see pp. 58-74 of this volume.)

An honest quest for God is obviously more than a scientific inquiry, as we shall argue below, but it is certainly not less. If we attempt in our pursuit for God to pole-vault ourselves directly into the heavenlies and bypass the more difficult climb of biblical criticism (textual, literary, and historical), accredited exegetical procedure (lexical, grammatical, and historical), and biblical theology (the progress of revelation), we shall expose ourselves to inauthentic encounters with the Holy, fall into a mysticism that denies God's incarnation, and despise the apostolic exhortation to study the Scriptures diligently as approved workmen (1 Tim. 4:13-16; 2 Tim. 3:15-17). A student cannot say he or she is devoted to God who carelessly treats the empirical data in which he revealed himself.

Here, however, we must face the reality that we are in the process of growing in our knowledge of accredited exegetical procedure and in our application of it to the literature, and therefore as we improve in our exegesis we mature in our knowledge of God. Our relativism in knowledge should not defeat us but instead spur us on in our quest for God. In addition, we need to bear in mind that the church is a body nurtured by gifted individuals within it (Rom. 12:3-8; Eph. 4:7-16; 1 Cor. 12:1–14:40). In particular, he gave pastors and teachers to guide his church in its understanding of the Bible and, therefore, we need to avail ourselves of their contributions in up-to-date translations of the Bible, in commentaries, in schools, and above all, in the assembling of ourselves together as his temple.

But these disciplines so essential to the devotional study of the Bible must not be undertaken in a spirit of cold academic detachment. Such a spirit is actually hostile to the Scriptures, for, as Adolf Schlatter has shown, the Holy Scriptures call upon us to surrender our wills to its claims (see "The Theology of the New Testament and Dogmatics," in *The Nature of New Testament Theology,* ed. Robert Morgan, 1973, pp. 117-66). Rather we must approach our inspired literature with open hands of faith. Thus, for example, the exegete should receive the textual traditions and his or her tools with heartfelt appreciation that he or she is the heir of all the ages, and he or she should approach the work with a deep sense of dependence on God to help execute this craft with skill. Moreover, with imagination and prayer the student should endeavor to re-create in his/her mind and viscera the historical and spiritual state of his/her spiritual father that authored these texts with the Spirit of God upon him. In sum, we should do our work in the Spirit (1 Cor. 2:9-16), both walking in him (Gal. 5:16) and being filled with him (Eph. 5:18), and neither grieving him (4:30) nor quenching him (1 Thess. 5:19).

But since God is ultimately the object of our contemplation it is obvious that our study must be more than scientific; it must also be artistic. John Warwick Montgomery in his excellent study of the theologian's craft, *The Suicide of Christian Theology* (1970), calls attention to John Ciardi's introduction to literary criticism, *How Does a Poem Mean?* in which the following passage from Dickens's *Hard Times* is quoted:

> "Bitzer," said Thomas Gradgrind, "your definition of a horse."
> "Quadruped. Graminivorous. Forty teeth, namely twenty-four grind-

ers, four eye-teeth, and twelve incisive. Sheds coat in the spring; in marshy countries sheds hoofs too. Hoofs hard, but requiring to be shod with iron. Age known by marks in mouth."

Thus (and much more) Bitzer.

"Now, girl number twenty," said Mr. Gradgrind, "you know what a horse is."

Montgomery cogently commented on this insightful spoof: "'Girl number twenty' knew 'what a horse is' only in a very special and limited way: she knew horses in a formal objective, scientific manner, but not at all in a personal, experiential way — not in the way in which a poet or an artist endeavours to convey knowledge" (pp. 28f.).

But in our approach to meeting God in the sacred page we must come not only as to a living Person, but with awe and joy to his numinous holiness. Before revealing himself to Moses he commanded: "Do not come any closer. Take off your sandals, for the place where you are standing is holy ground" (Exod. 3:5). Are the Scriptures any less holy than the burning bush? The psalmist said:

> He guides the humble in what is right
>   and teaches them his way. (Ps. 25:9)

If we fail to come with the imagination of a saint to the Holy Bible we shall come away from our visit with God in a way similar to the proverbial pussycat's visit to the queen in London:

> "Pussy cat, pussy cat, where have you been?"
> "I've been to London to visit the queen."
> "Pussy cat, pussy cat, what did you there?"
> "I frightened a little mouse under her chair."

Luther nicely combined the scientific with sacred imagination in his biblically based method for theological study in this counsel:

> Let me show you a right method for studying theology, the one that I have used. If you adopt it, you will become so learned that if it were necessary, you yourself would be qualified to produce books just as good as those of the Fathers and the church councils. Even as I dare to be so bold in God as to pride myself, without arrogance or lying, as not being

greatly behind some of the Fathers in the matter of making books; as to my life, I am far from being their equal. This method is the one which the pious king David teaches in the 119th Psalm and which, no doubt, was practised by all the Patriarchs and Prophets. In the 119th Psalm you will find three rules which are abundantly expounded throughout the entire Psalm. They are called: *Oratio, Meditatio, Tentatio.* (Cited by Montgomery, p. 289)

There we have the method: *oratio,* "by prayer"; *meditatio,* "by reading and contemplation"; *tentatio,* "by personal experience."

Studying the Psalms Devotionally

As in all study we must approach the Psalms in our search for God by shunning the worldliness that turns us away from him toward self and our peer group, and as in the study of all Scripture we must approach our hymnbook as both scientist and saint. But in the Psalms, in contrast to the Law and Prophets, we directly encounter God's king/King. Most modern readers of the Psalms identify the human subject of the psalms as Mr. Everyman, but this is not so. The human subject in most of the psalms is the king/King, and we shall never enter fully into its rich devotional material until we realize this.

John Eaton superbly summarized the evidence for an extensive royal interpretation of the Psalms as follows:

1. "The heading *l^edawid* stands over seventy-three psalms (eighty-four in Greek). . . . In spite of problems of detail, this can reasonably be taken as an indication of the large place which royal psalmody has in the collection."
2. "The biblical tradition (1 Chron 15–16; 25:1-8; 2 Chron 29:26f.; Neh 12:36; Amos 6:5; etc.) and later Jewish tradition including one of the Dead Sea Scrolls dated to the first century A.D. unanimously ascribe the Psalter largely to King David. 'The probability must be faced that the view most evident in the Chronicler will have had a genuine basis.'"
3. "Directly reinforcing the preceding argument is the picture of royal responsibility in religion which has emerged from modern studies of [Ancient Near Eastern] kingship."

4. "Many and various have been the suggestions as to who were the original subjects of the 'psalms of the individual' and what their circumstances. But the only 'situation' which is certainly attested is that of the king; it is certain that he is the subject in a number of psalms, and the dispute is only about how many. This cannot be said of the other suggested usages."

5. "Coupled with the preceding point is the general homogeneity of the psalms. . . . There is a prevailing similarity which is in accord with an origin within a restricted royal and national cultus."

6. "Birkeland and Kraus demonstrated that in many instances the psalmist's enemies are national. These references to international and political enemies make most sense if we assume the prayers were composed for a king."

7. "The special problem presented by the psalms where 'I' and 'we' alternate can be resolved by taking account of the representative character of the king" [cf. Pss. 9–10; 44; 60; 66; 75; 102].

8. "Throughout the 'psalms of the individual' there occur motifs or expressions which are royal or at least specifically appropriate for the king. . . . Gunkel (*Einl.*, pp. 147f.) identifies the following. All nations attend to the psalmist's thanksgiving (Pss 18:50; 57:10; 138:1, 4; 119:46). His deliverance has vast repercussions (22; 28f.). He invokes a world-judgment to rectify his cause (7:7; 9; 56:8; 59:6; 59:9; cf. 43:1). He depicts himself as victorious over the nations through God's intervention (118:10-12; 9). He confronts armies (3:7; 27:3; 55:22; 56:2f.; 59; 62:4; 109:3; 120:7; 140:3, 8). He is like a bull raising horns in triumph (92:11; 1 Sam 2:1). He is God's son (2:7; 27:10). . . ."

9. "In many cases the royal interpretation is especially to be preferred because it allows the psalm as it stands to be seen as a consistent and meaningful whole."

10. "It is almost unthinkable that a collection of hymns stemming from the royal temple — one large court enclosed . . . both the LORD's Temple and the king's palace — should not include the petitions and praises of the king." (*Kingship and the Psalms*, 1976, pp. 22-25)

The psalms not only represent the prayers and praises of the historical king, but most of them present the king in Messianic terms. C. A. Briggs put it this way: "The psalms embraced the vision of a reality beyond the impression of the senses, a vision which guided Israel to an ever deeper understanding of the reality" (*Messianic Prophecy*, 1886, p. 63). H. H. Rowley found that the vision of a king whose kingdom would extend to "the ends of the earth" (Ps. 2:8), whose "divine throne [is] for ever and ever" (45:6), and who would "live while the sun endures and as long as the moon, throughout all generations" (72:5), went beyond pious optimism or flattering hyperbole. He wrote that "[w]hile they may have been royal psalms, used in the royal rites of the temple, they were also 'messianic.' They held before the king the ideal king both as his inspiration and guide for the present, and as the hope of the future" (*The Faith of Israel,* 1974, p. 192).

The Father and Jesus reveal to us in the New Testament that our Lord Jesus Christ fulfills the Messianic vision and is the Son of God (Matt. 11:25; 16; 17; Luke 24:44-49; John 1:18). In brief, in reading the Psalms we encounter not only God but the prayers and praises of his Son.

Finally, we need to realize that these ancient royal laments and confessions were not intended for the king's private use apart from the congregation. On the contrary, the king represented the people in them. According to Mowinckel, "All that concerned the king and his cause also concerned the people; nothing which happened to him was a purely private affair" (*The Psalms in Israel's Worship,* vol. 1, 1961, pp. 42-61). We might say that ancient Israel prayed "in the king." But since the Psalter is the prayer book of Jesus Christ in its fullest and truest interpretation, we can also say that his church today prays the psalms in him. Bonhoeffer put it this way: "The Psalter is the vicarious prayer of Christ for his Church. Now that Christ is with the Father, the new humanity of Christ, the Body of Christ on earth, continues to pray his prayer to the end of time" (*Life Together,* 1954, p. 46). But the church today needs to distinguish those elements in the prayer that were shaped by a historical-cultural milieu different from our own. Therefore, we need to keep in mind that the saints under the Old Covenant differed somewhat from the church under the New Covenant. (It is far beyond the limits of this essay to point out these differences.) Bonhoeffer also helpfully commented: "Even if a verse or a psalm is not one's own prayer, it is nevertheless the prayer of another member of the fellowship . . ." (pp. 46f.).

How then shall we study the Psalms? In the first place, let us count ourselves dead to sin (Rom. 6:11), self (Gal. 2:20), and the world (6:14) through the cross of our Lord Jesus Christ; and secondly, let us come into the sphere of the Holy with academic rigor while keeping our bodies in subjection and as a community dependent on him and on one another. Finally, let us come with faith, expecting to meet both God and his Son in these poems of prayer, acknowledgment, and praise inspired by the Holy Spirit.

Problematic Sources, Poetics, and Preaching the Old Testament: An Exposition of Proverbs 26:1-12

Introduction

The Problem of Source Criticism and Preaching the Big Idea

Biblical source criticism, whether it be literary criticism, form criticism, or tradition criticism, is no friend to Haddon Robinson's concept of expositing a text by developing its big idea. To be sure, the techniques involved in identifying sources enable the expositor to isolate discreetly unified smaller texts. However, it calls into question the notion that a final redactor compiled them to communicate unifying concepts in his finished composition or in all of its parts.

Literary source criticism attempts to isolate by changes of literary style and theologies the literary sources that comprise a finished composition. Within the Pentateuch, critics of this school discern at least four distinct and sometimes contradictory documents. The preacher can present the great ideas of the source documents, but not of the whole book, because according to these critics a crude redactor pieced together the sources, contradictions and all. Indeed, a preacher worth his salt should point out these contradictions. That can lead to confusing preaching.

Form criticism is most helpful in identifying sources but presents the preacher with a different problem. This approach groups texts into genres

---

Previously published as "Old Testament Interpretation Issues for Big Idea Preaching," in *The Big Idea of Biblical Preaching: Connecting the Bible to People,* ed. Scott M. Gibson and Keith Willhite (Grand Rapids: Baker, 2003). Used with permission.

that share the same structure, motifs, moods, vocabulary, and so on. For example, in the fifty petition psalms, the psalmist addresses God, vents his complaint that God has abandoned him and the enemy is too powerful, expresses his confidence in God, and then petitions God to deliver him. The trouble is, they all seem to have the same big idea. That can lead to boring preaching.

Tradition critics attempt to trace the historical development of a source from its inception to its final form in the book. This creative process entails that the majority of Old Testament texts contain multiple levels of meaning, reflecting the gradual contribution of new individuals, groups, and generations to the text as they reinterpreted the old heritage for themselves. The preacher's problems with this approach are that critics of this school do not agree on this history and that the preacher must decide the authoritative level of meaning. That can lead to uncertain preaching.

Conservative preachers dismiss a biblical criticism that breaks Scripture apart into contradictory sources and that denies the infallibility and authority of the final text. However, they must own up to the truth that many biblical books are an anthology of sources that seem to be loosely hung together without unifying concepts.

Let me cameo the problem from the book of Proverbs, a parade example of a "loose" anthology. According to Proverbs 25:1, the "men of Hezekiah" compiled the proverbs of Solomon in chapters 25–29. However, it is alleged that sometimes they arranged them by sound, not by sense. For example, "Like a thorn bush [that grows up] in the hand of a drunkard [*shikkor*] is a proverb in the mouth of a fool" (26:9) and "like an archer who wounds at random is he who hires [*shōkēr*] a fool" (26:10) were apparently linked together by their topic, "a fool," and by the sound play of *shikkor* and *shōkēr*, not apparently by sense. The preacher who from this paronomasia abstracts a unifying comment about a fool is engaging in eisegesis, *not* exegesis.

This cameo illustrates the problem with all sorts of Old Testament literature. The historical, prophetic, hymnic, and sapiential all consist of many originally isolated sources. Can preaching based on a great idea move with integrity beyond the textual fragments isolated by source criticism to the larger compilations?

The Contribution of Poetics

Whereas source criticism bedevils preaching the big idea of disparate texts within the finished composition or the composition itself, recent research into the poetics of the Old Testament tends to validate Robinson's popularized homiletical approach. During the last quarter of the twentieth century, scholars have turned their attention to finding the rules by which redactors/authors of the biblical books assembled their sources. "We must first know how a text means," in Adele Berlin's famous phrase, "before we know what it means." Whereas the old critics regard the final text as "crudely" pieced together, critics who employ poetics have come to regard it as artistic, with careful attention having been given to detail. Robert Polzin refuses to speak any longer of redactors of the biblical books but only of their authors.[1]

The new breed of biblical critics has been developing the "grammar" of poetics.[2] Their indefatigable efforts and numerous publications have shown that biblical "authors" artistically gave unity to their work through, among others, the following techniques: (1) inclusio (i.e., marking off a literary unity by matching the end with the beginning); (2) structures of many patterns, such as alternating (ABC::A′B′C′) or chiastic (ABC X C′B′A′ [i.e., the sequences before and after the turning point (called "the pivot") often contrast with one another]); (3) catchwords that stitch the work together; (4) key words that focus its meaning; (5) synonyms; (6) paronomasia (i.e., a play on sound and/or sense); (7) syntax; (8) refrains; (9) janus (i.e., linking sections together with a piece of literature that looks both backward and forward); (10) contrasts and comparisons; (11) logic (e.g., cause and effect); (12) generalization; (13) preparation/foreshadowing (i.e., inclusion of material in one part of the text that serves primarily to prepare the reader for what is still to come). By matching the poetic techniques embedded with the deep struc-

1. Robert Polzin, *Samuel and the Deuteronomist: A Literary Study of the Deuteronomic History,* part 2, *1 Samuel* (San Francisco: Harper & Row, 1989).

2. Foundational works include Robert Alter, *The Art of Biblical Narrative* (New York: Basic Books, 1981); Robert Alter and Frank Kermode, eds., *The Literary Guide to the Bible* (Cambridge, MA: Belknap, 1987); Shimon Bar-Efrat, *Narrative Art in the Bible,* JSOT Supplement Series 70; Bible and Literature Series, no. 17 (Sheffield, UK: Almond, 1989); Adele Berlin, *Poetics and Interpretation of Biblical Narrative,* JSOT Supplement Series; Bible and Literature Series, no. 9 (Sheffield, UK: Almond, 1983); Tremper Longman III, *Literary Approaches to Biblical Interpretation* (Grand Rapids: Zondervan, 1987); Richard L. Pratt Jr., *He Gave Us Stories* (Brentwood, TN: Wolgemuth & Hyatt, 1990); Mark Allan Powell, *What Is Narrative Criticism?* (Minneapolis: Fortress, 1990); Jean Louis Ska, *"Our Fathers Have Told Us": Introduction to the Analysis of Hebrew Narratives* (Rome: Editrice Pontificio Istituto Biblico, 1990); Meir Sternberg, *The Poetics of Biblical Narrative: Ideological Literature and the Drama of Reading,* The Indiana Literary Biblical Series (Bloomington: Indiana University Press, 1985).

ture of meaning, one can discern the abstract meaning that enriches the whole, which is greater than the sum of its parts.

This new breed reads the Old Testament in a way that more closely resembles that of the rabbis than of source critics, but, unlike the ingenious rabbis, they ground their readings in the science of poetics. To be sure, good readers have always, consciously or unconsciously, used poetics to interpret a unified text. The grammar of poetics, however, brings to light that biblical authors deftly used these techniques to unify disparate sources. The fragmentary appearance of their final compositions is only skin deep; poetics shows they had in mind "big ideas" that transcend the isolated sources.

An Exposition of Proverbs 26:1-12

Let us return to our cameo to illustrate how poetics helps uncover the big idea. The larger context of Proverbs 26:9-10 is Proverbs 26:1-12. The key word uniting the composition is "fool."[3] It occurs in every verse except verse 2, which is a proverbial pair with verse 1. At verse 13, the topic shifts from the fool to the sluggard (26:13-16). The key word "fool" gave rise to the title "A Mirror of Fools"[4] for this composition, but a single word like "fool" only "masquerades" as a big idea.[5]

Formally, the composition consists of ten sayings (vv. 1-3, 6-12) and two admonitions (vv. 4-5). Apart from the concluding verse, these ten sayings have essentially the same structure. Their A versets (i.e., the first halves of the verses) present striking negative images from the order of creation to serve as a metaphor of the fool in the social order. "A Mirror of Fools" consists of an introduction, which sounds the theme (vv. 1-3); a body, which develops its two sides (vv. 4-10); and a conclusion (vv. 11-12).[6]

---

3. The repetition of the palatals /k-q-g/ that ripples through the unit in phonological harmony with *kesil* ("fool") also unifies the work. Verse 1 sets the stage: *kaššeleg baqqayiṣ wekammaṭar baqqayṣîr kēn lo' na'weh lᵉkesîl kābôd.* Apart from the prefixes, every word apart from "not fitting"(!), begins with /k-q/.

4. Arndt Meinhold, *Die Sprüche*, in *Zuercher Bibelcommentare* 16, no. 2 (Zurich: Theologischer Verlag, 1991), p. 436.

5. Haddon W. Robinson, *Biblical Preaching: The Development and Delivery of Expository Messages* (Grand Rapids: Baker, 1980), pp. 39f.

6. Cf. Raymond C. Van Leeuwen, *Context and Meaning in Proverbs 25–27* (Atlanta: Scholars, 1988), pp. 88f.

Introduction (vv. 1-3)

Verse 1 functions as a summarization that the body will particularize; it sounds the composition's major theme: "honor is not fitting for a fool."[7] The images of snow in summer and rain in harvest illustrate that honoring a fool occurs in a world out of joint and that to do so is catastrophic. As snow in harvest destroys crops and brings death, an individual or society that honors a fool destroys a life or a culture full of promise.

Verse 2 functions as a comparison and a contrast with verse 1. Uniquely sharing the same syntax as verse 1,[8] it too pertains to what is unfitting vis-à-vis uttering a curse against an innocent person. However, it principally functions as a contrast. On the one hand, glory is not fitting for a fool, because as verse 1 made clear (and the body will make even clearer), giving him social standing will cause great damage. On the other hand, uttering a curse against an innocent person is unfitting but will do no damage, because it has no place to land. A paronomasia (i.e., a play on sound and/or sense) assists the contrast. Hebrew *kābēd*, the root of "glory" [*kābôd*], means "heavy," and Hebrew *qalal*, the root of "curse" [*qᵉlālâ*], means "light." Indeed, in the Semitic languages it can mean "to be flighty," a notion that gives rise to the image of birds flying about without landing.

Verse 3 functions as a climax to the introduction and sounds the positive counterpoint to the negative theme. What is fitting is "a rod for the backs of fools" (v. 3)! The assonance, a form of paronomasia, among *ṣippôr* ("sparrow"), *dᵉrôr* ("swallow"),[9] and *ḥᵃmôr* ("donkey") helps sound both the positive thesis, what is fitting (v. 3), and the negative, what is unfitting (vv. 1-2). In sum, the introduction sounds the thesis along with its counterpoint.

Body: Section 1 (vv. 4-5)

Two admonitions that develop the countertheme of what is fitting for a fool logically form a relatively smooth transition from the introduction to

7. Van Leeuwen says "the idea of fittingness is the poem's central concern" (*Context and Meaning*, p. 100). Although we all stand in debt to Van Leeuwen's brilliant dissertation, "fittingness" is an inadequate summarization.

8. The English versions obscure the unique syntax of *k* + *k* + *ken* "like [snow/a fluttering sparrow] . . . like [rain/darting swallow], so [honor/an undeserved curse . . .]."

9. "Sparrow" and "swallow" are glosses; the precise genre or species of birds is uncertain.

the body. In addition to physically caning the fool to control him, without naming who is responsible (v. 3), the wise son/disciple needs to give the fool a verbal answer (vv. 4-5). His answer, however, must distinguish between what is unfitting (v. 4) and what is fitting (v. 5). It is unfitting to answer with the fool's insolence; the son must not meet "insult with insult" (1 Peter 3:9). Should he reply vindictively, harshly, or with lies — the way fools talk — he too — "yes, even you" — would come under the fool's condemnation. Rather, without lowering himself to the fool's level, and by overcoming evil with good (25:21f.), he must expose the fool's folly for what it is. The wise must not silently accept and tolerate the folly and thereby confirm fools in it.

Body: Section 2 (vv. 6-10)

The five sayings of verses 6-10 return to the introduction's form, using negative images from the created order to develop the negative and major theme. These sayings answer the questions of what is meant by "honor" and why it is "unfitting" for fools. However, they escalate the standards of comparison to striking and ludicrous images to develop the proposition.[10] Instead of drawing images from the impersonal weather (v. 1) and animals (vv. 2-3), these images are drawn from the human realm, from deformed (vv. 6-7) and deranged (vv. 9-10) people. At the pivot stands the absurd stone-slinger (v. 8).

Verses 6 and 7, in addition to the sensible binding of images pertaining to deformed people, are also connected by the images of "feet" *(raglayim)* and "legs" *(shōqayim)*. Both images uniquely share the same syntax, the Hebrew dual number. Verses 9 and 10, in addition to the sensible binding of images pertaining to deranged people, are also connected by the paronomasia of "drunkard" *(shikkor)* and "one who hires" *(shōkēr)*. However, it is now clear the paronomasia assists the sensible binding!

Duane Garrett shows that the compilers arranged these sayings in a chiasm.[11]

10. The images are so creative and absurd they confound pedestrian and prosaic commentators, who want to tame them. Even the NIV alters the normal meaning of verse 9a, "a thorn bush grows up in the hand of the drunkard," to "a thorn bush in the hand of a drunkard." Delitzsch defended the meaning of the NIV from Mishnaic Hebrew, not from biblical Hebrew, and my own research calls into question his lexicography.

11. Duane A. Garrett, *Proverbs, Ecclesiastes, Song of Songs,* The New American Commentary 14 (Nashville: Broadman, 1993), p. 212.

A: Committing important business to a fool (v. 6)
  B: A proverb in a fool's mouth (v. 7)
    C: Honoring a fool (v. 8)
  B′:   A proverb in a fool's mouth (v. 9)
A′:   Committing important business to a fool (v. 10)

The compilers profile the chiasm by repeating verbatim in its inner core "a proverb in the mouth of a fool," an exaggerated form of catchwords, on either side of the pivot. Its outer core pertains to hiring the fool for a job, of which commissioning him to send messages is one part.

In the light of this chiasm, it becomes clear that verse 8 is the pivot and that this focal verse, also the center verse of the body and conclusion, restates with increased volume the composition's big idea: "to honor a fool [is unfitting]." The decibel volume is increased by the pivot's final catchwords, "honor for/to a fool" (*l^{e}kesîl kābôd*), repeating verbatim the final words of the summary statement (v. 1). The absurd stone-slinger images the prosaic "not fitting" of the summarization (v. 1). Instead of hurling the stone (i.e., the fool) far from him, the ludicrous slinger (i.e., the one giving the fool honor) binds up "the stone" so that it comes around and whacks him a good one on his own head. The syntax of verse 8 — *k* "like" + *ken* "so" — increases the decibel volume still further. Finally in addition to these lexical, syntactical, and thematic links, the assonance, a form of paronomasia, of *ṣippôr* ("sparrow"), *d^{e}rôr* ("swallow"), and *s^{e}rôr* ("binding"), turns up the volume of the restatement full blast.

In addition to focusing the composition's theme, the B versets around the pivot illuminate how one honors fools. Their inner core points to putting proverbs in their mouths (vv. 7, 9) and their outer frame to commissioning or hiring them (vv. 6, 10).[12] Turning first to the motif of "proverb" [*māshāl*], note this is the most honorific term for a wise saying; it is used otherwise only of Solomon's proverbs (1:1; 10:1; 25:1). Other wise sayings are called "the sayings of the wise" (cf. 1:6; 22:17; 24:23; 30:1; 31:1). Turning to the commissioning motif, one should note that in the ancient Near East to receive a commission to represent a dignitary was a high honor indeed. In that world, the messenger was in fact the sender's plenipotentiary (i.e., vested with his

---

12. The image of a thorn bush growing up in the drunkard's hand is an incomplete metaphor. A thorn bush does not grow in any hand. However, the image forces one to realize that as it took time for the vegetation to grow up there, so also it took time for the fool to memorize the proverbs. How else did they get in his mouth?

full authority). However, honoring the fool with any kind of service is dangerous. In sum, one can glorify a fool by giving him an education in proverbs or by hiring him.

Finally, the A versets of the saying around the pivot elaborate why it is unfitting to honor fools. These images escalate the danger of honoring fools from hurting oneself (vv. 6-7) to hurting society at large (vv. 9-10).

The images of chopping off one's feet (v. 6) and of dangling legs (v. 7) signify respectively that giving a fool honor hurts the giver and makes the educated fool look ridiculous. Sending messages by the hand of a fool is as bizarre as chopping off one's feet and as deadly as drinking poison. By infuriating the recipient of the messages, rather than gaining a pair of feet to add to one's own, the effect is precisely the opposite, tantamount to rendering one lame.

Moreover, a proverb in the fool's mouth (v. 7), which probably got there through his improper education, is absurd and worthless. As a lame person still has legs, but cannot use them for locomotion because they hang loosely and uncertainly from his body, so proverbs in the mouths of fools carry no weight and get them nowhere. A proverb aims to involve the audience to exercise their imagination to forge a connection between the proverb's moral truth and their own situation and by so doing to change their behavior. The otherwise excellent proverb, which the fool inappropriately acquired (17:16),[13] is impotent in the mouth of fools. Fools are either morally too dull to utter it seasonably, or "they invalidate its effect by their character."[14]

However, worse than being absurd and worthless (vv. 6-7), the wrongly honored fool is dangerous, even *deadly* dangerous, to society at large (vv. 9-10). He is like a drunkard[15] with a thorn bush and a mad archer. In Proverbs 20:1, intoxicants are personified as a mocker and a brawler. A thorn bush in a drunkard's hands is like the proverbial firearm in the hand of a child.[16] Today, we say, "If you drink, don't drive."[17] A proverb in the mouth

---

13. Meinhold, *Die Sprüche*, p. 439.

14. Garrett, *Proverbs, Ecclesiastes, Song of Songs*, p. 212.

15. A drunkard in the Old Testament is no down-and-out bum. Many of its thirteen references to drunkenness explicitly or inferentially refer to kings (1 Kings 16:9; 20:16; Isa. 28:1, 3) and the wealthy (1 Sam. 25:36), who could afford the quantities required.

16. So W. Gunther Plaut, *Book of Proverbs*, The Jewish Commentary for Bible Readers (New York: Union of American Hebrew Congregations, 1961), p. 268.

17. So Raymond C. Van Leeuwen, *The Book of Proverbs*, The New Interpreter's Bible 5 (Nashville: Abingdon, 1997), p. 225.

of the wise brings healing, but in the mouth of a fool, it wounds and lacerates. The utterances of fools or of wicked people are dangerous (10:32; 11:9, 11; 12:18; 13:16b; 14:3 passim), but even worse, fools use the otherwise wise and excellent proverbs they learned for destructive ends.[18]

To suggest the deadly danger of educating or hiring a fool, the compiler now heightens the image from the brawling drunkard waving his thorn bush to a berserk archer shooting arrows. This dangerous character, like a modern terrorist, randomly kills all within his sight and range. Giving honor to a fool is "unfitting," to say the least!

Conclusion (vv. 11-12)

Hebrew syntax may mark off the new section. Initial *k* occurs only in verse 11, the introduction (vv. 1-2), and the pivot (v. 8) (*pace* NIV). Be that as it may, the last two sayings, verses 11-12, draw to conclusion "A Mirror of Fools." An inclusio connects the first of them (v. 11) with the introduction. Like verses 1-2, this saying derives its negative image from the realm of animals (sparrow/swallow [v. 2], horse/donkey [v. 3], and dog [v. 11]), not from the human sphere (vv. 6-10). The second (v. 12) is connected with the body by the catchwords "wise in his own eyes" (v. 5). That connection suggests the conclusion, like the admonitions, elaborates the composition's positive countertheme that discipline is fitting for a fool.

Verse 11 asserts that the fool cannot save himself. Using an alternate pattern (ABC::A'B'C'), the saying juxtaposes a fool with the contemptible dog; his destructive folly with the dog's vomit; and the fool's obduracy with the dog's repulsive nature to return to vomit, to sniff at it, to lick it, and finally to devour it. In both the image (i.e., the dog) and the topic (i.e., the fool), the body rejects the repulsive objects (i.e., vomit and folly, respectively), but the debased spirit of the dog and fool crave them. Food poison does not affect their appetites (15:14; 17:10; 27:22).

Verse 11 pilloried the fool as incapable of saving himself because he so craves his folly that he cannot learn from his mistakes. Verse 12 opens wider a door of hope for his salvation through physical punishment and wise answers. The sages cracked that door open by suggesting a rod is fitting for a fool (v. 3). They cracked the door farther ajar by the admonition to rebut the fool wisely, before he becomes "wise in his own eyes." In this conclusion,

18. So Meinhold, *Die Sprüche*, p. 440.

they open the door of hope as wide as they dare. The "run-of-the-mill fool" (Garrett) has one hindrance — his ethical folly; the deluded fool has two — his folly and his conceit. The final saying offers more hope of salvation for the former than for the latter. The combined sayings (vv. 3, 4-5, 11-12) suggest that although the fool cannot learn from his mistakes, possibly he can be saved by timely, wise correction.

Verse 12 also functions as a janus to the next composition. The sages signal they are about to leave the fool behind for a new topic by dropping the structure of the preceding sayings. Instead of using negative images drawn from the created order as standards for evaluating the fool, they now use the fool as a standard of comparison for one who is wise in his own eyes. The saying shifts the son's gaze away from the fool to the sluggard who has castled himself in his own conceit.

Conclusion

The passage's big idea can now be stated. It is unfitting, downright dangerous, for the sake of everyone to honor a fool by educating him with proverbs and entrusting him with responsible service, but fitting to punish and rebuke him.

I deliberately chose a text from the book of Proverbs because it is most difficult to apply Haddon Robinson's method of preaching to this obvious anthology. If poetics can serve as a handmaid to his thesis in this anthology that lacks syndetic markers (e.g., "and," "because," "therefore," etc.), the logic of a fortiori suggests it can, and possibly does, serve anywhere in the Old Testament. However, poetics works best with the Hebrew text. Unfortunately, the translators of the English versions of the Bible — of whom I confess to be one — are not as literate as the original audiences were. The authors of the Old Testament presumed an audience that could identify their subtle clues to meaning and rightly interpret their texts, but translators only now are beginning to pick them up.

There is a flip side to the big idea of our sample text vis-à-vis it is fitting to honor the wise, and blessings pronounced upon him find a landing place. This flip side is another reason I chose this text. This essay aims to honor my esteemed friend, Haddon Robinson, whose name has become synonymous with the theory of combining propositional preaching with exposition. However, one has to read this small contribution in light of the whole book to see the point.

Recommended Reading

Alter, Robert. *The Art of Biblical Narrative.* New York: Basic Books, 1981.

Alter, Robert, and Frank Kermode, eds. *The Literary Guide to the Bible.* Cambridge, MA: Belknap, 1987.

Berlin, Adele. *Poetics and Interpretation of Biblical Literature.* JSOT, Supplements Series; Bible and Literature Series, no. 9. Sheffield, UK: Almond, 1983.

Greidanus, Sidney. *The Modern Preacher and the Ancient Text: Interpreting and Preaching Biblical Literature.* Grand Rapids: Eerdmans, 1988.

Long, Thomas. *Preaching and the Literary Forms of the Bible.* Philadelphia: Fortress, 1989.

Longman, Tremper, III. *Literary Approaches to Biblical Interpretation.* Grand Rapids: Zondervan, 1987.

PART II

Biblical Theological Themes

Atonement in Psalm 51

"My sacrifice, O God, is a broken spirit"

The removal of sin in the Old Testament has two aspects, the external liturgical sacrifices such as the sin and guilt offerings that through the shedding
of blood (i.e., the giving of life) make payment in expiation for a life that is
forfeit, and the internal spiritual factors involved in forgiveness.[1] The latter
involves the personal willingness of God to forgive sin and the offender's
willingness to renounce his wrongdoing. The liturgical laws of the Mosaic
law featured the former aspect; the Prophets and the Psalter, the latter.
Higher critics commonly allege that the external procedures for the removal
of sin represent an older, more primitive stage of Israel's religion, and the
personal aspects a later stage. Those who contend for the integrity of Scripture because of its plenary inspiration contend that this difference between
the Law and the Prophets and Psalter is due to their different literary genres,
not to progressive religious thinking in Israel that denied and corrected its
earlier religious reflections.

When we turn to the Psalter, it seems to support the common higher
critical view. The penitential psalms in particular appear to ignore or even

---

1. Cf. Leviticus 4:1–6:7; 14:5; 16:20-22; 17:11; cf. Hebrews 2:17; 9:5, 7; Numbers 8:7-10;
19:9. For special circumstances, other rituals such as trial by fire and washing by water were
required (cf. Num. 31:22-24).

Previously published in *The Glory of the Atonement: Biblical, Historical, and Practical Perspectives; Essays in Honor of Roger Nicole,* ed. Charles E. Hill and Frank A. James III
(Downers Grove, IL: InterVarsity, 2004). Used with permission.

repudiate blood sacrifice as a means of removing sin. A liturgical tradition that reaches back into the Middle Ages placed seven psalms under the rubric of penitential psalms.[2] In these psalms the penitent sinner pleads with God for deliverance from his deep sense of guilt, yet none of them, aside from Psalm 51, mentions atonement. But Psalm 51, the so-called "Great Penitential Psalm," is in fact the most problematic because it seems both to affirm and to deny the sacrificial system. On the one hand, it mentions ritual washing in Psalm 51:2 and makes mention of the purgation by hyssop in Psalm 51:7 and of offering sacrifices in Psalm 51:19. On the other hand, the psalmist claims in Psalm 51:16-17 that God does not want sacrifices and that the only appropriate and acceptable sacrifice is "a broken and contrite heart." Some interpret this last statement to mean an absolute rejection of the sacrificial system.[3] W. O. E. Oesterley comments: "Wholly in opposition to the belief and practice of his times, [the psalmist] repudiates the idea of material sacrifices."[4] Elmer Leslie agrees: "The psalmist is at one with Amos (5:21-22), Hosea (6:6), Isaiah (1:10-17), Micah (6:6-8), and Jeremiah (7:21-23) in his rejection of animal sacrifice as a rite that is pleasing to God. He has achieved a deeply spiritual conception of religion. It is not sacrifice that God desires, but a heart free from pride and rebellion."[5] A. A. Anderson thinks varying circumstances, not an absolute rejection, "occasioned such a radical reconsideration of the meaning of the sacrificial system."[6] Exegetes of this school of thought usually claim that Psalm 51:18-19 is a later addition from "a less spiritually minded poet."[7] Bernhard Anderson comments: "The psalm's language, in fact, was so sharply critical that a later revisionist added a qualification at the end of the psalm (Ps 51:18-19), thereby justifying the use of the psalm in Temple services."[8] These exegetes, however, do not adequately answer the liturgical references in Psalm 51:2, 7. For example, Leslie inconsis-

---

2. Psalms 6, 32, 38, 51, 102, 130, 143.

3. For scholars who hold this view, see H. H. Rowley, "The Unity of the Old Testament," *Bulletin of the John Rylands Library* 29 (1946): 5-7.

4. W. O. E. Oesterley, *The Psalms: Translated with Text-critical and Exegetical Notes* (London: SPCK; New York: Macmillan, 1939), 1:274.

5. Elmer A. Leslie, *Psalms: Translated and Interpreted in Light of Hebrew Life and Worship* (New York: Abingdon, 1939), p. 401.

6. A. A. Anderson, *The Book of Psalms*, The New Century Bible (Greenwood, SC: Attic Press; London: Marshall, Morgan & Scott, 1972), p. 401.

7. Leslie, *Psalms*, p. 402.

8. Bernhard Anderson, *Out of the Depths: The Psalms Speak for Us Today* (Philadelphia: Westminster, 1983), p. 95.

tently comments on Psalm 51:7: "We are to think here of ritual acts . . . being performed by the priest, in which hyssop . . . will be dipped in water ritually prepared for ceremonial cleansing." A. A. Anderson, with more consistency, denies that hyssop refers to a ritual act that accompanied the recitation of the psalm. According to him the hyssop is a figure, derived from the cultic life, of inward cleansing.

These explanations, which pit the psalm's teaching about the removal of sin and guilt against the Mosaic covenant, and at least to some extent against itself, are based on the common error of prooftexting. In the case cited, representative exegetes have failed to give due consideration to its form as a specific kind of lament psalm, a lament for sin. In this essay, I aim to exegete Psalm 51 in the light of its form with a focus on its teaching about atonement, the removal of sin and guilt and forgiveness.

Exegesis of Psalm 51

As is well known, lament or petition psalms typically include the motifs of an address, lament, confession of trust, petition, and praise. Psalm 51, adopting this form to lament sin and petition God for forgiveness, includes an introductory petition in connection with the address (Ps. 51:1-2, 2 lines), a lament in the form of a confession for sin (Ps. 51:3-6, four lines), a petition corresponding to his confession (Ps. 51:7-12, six lines), and praise (Ps. 51:13-19, seven lines).

Superscription

Before turning to the psalm itself, the superscription provides a helpful background to elucidating its contribution toward the doctrine of the atonement. To be sure, for more than a century most critics denied the historicity of these superscriptions, but careful exegesis refutes their objections, and recent studies in the light of Ancient Near Eastern parallels support the credibility of these superscripts and postscripts. My own research has led me to the conclusion that the superscript pertains to the psalm's composition and that its postscript, which has become confounded within the textual tradition with the following superscript, pertains to its performance.[9] The super-

9. See Bruce K. Waltke, "Superscripts, Postscripts, or Both," *JBL* 110 (1991): 583-96.

script of Psalm 51 mentions its genre, "a psalm," its author, "by David," and the historical circumstance prompting its composition, "when the prophet Nathan came to him after David had committed adultery with Bathsheba."[10] In that connection, David committed a blatantly defiant (*b^eyād rāmâ*, "with a high hand"), not an inadvertent (*bišgāgâ*, "with inadvertence"), transgression. To cover up his adultery with Bathsheba, the king coldly calculated her husband's murder over a period of at least two weeks, reckoning four days for the messenger to fetch Uriah from the battlefront and another eight days for Uriah to journey to and from Jerusalem, and counting his three days in Jerusalem. The sin offering made atonement for inadvertent sin (Lev. 4:1-35), but not for open-eyed sin of the high hand.[11] Moreover, both the sins of adultery and of murder carried a death penalty for the culprits.[12] Third, let it be noted that David could not make restitution to either Bathsheba or her husband. He could restore neither her purity nor his life. Yet in spite of these awesome deficits, David found God's forgiveness. The superscription infers the reason. He sinned and confronted death because, as Nathan accused him, he despised the word of the Lord (2 Sam. 12:9), but now he submitted himself to the prophetic word "when Nathan the prophet came to him" and through a parable brought out David's true nature, enabling the king to experience forgiveness and life.

Address and Introductory Petition — Psalm 51:1-2

David addresses Israel's covenant-keeping God by his generic title, the one and only "God," not by his personal name "the LORD" (YHWH), presumably because the so-called Elohistic Psalter (Psalms 42–83) for an unknown reason demanded it. In his introduction, David lays hold of three of the sublime attributes that manifest God's glory.[13] Standing in the deep hole of sin and death, he looked up and saw stars of God's grace that those who stand in the

---

10. See 2 Samuel 11:1–12:25. For a careful literary analysis of the Story of David and Bathsheba, see Meir Sternberg, *The Poetics of Biblical Narrative: Ideological Literature and the Drama of Reading* (Bloomington: University of Indiana Press, 1987), pp. 190-229.

11. Numbers 15:27-31. The Yom Kippur rite (Lev. 16:16, 21) provided for the high priest to represent the sinning people who were barred from the sanctuary. See Jacob Milgrom, *Leviticus 1–16: A New Translation with Introduction and Commentary*, Anchor Bible (New York: Doubleday, 1991), p. 228.

12. Leviticus 20:10; Deuteronomy 22:22; and Numbers 35:30-31 respectively.

13. See Exodus 34:6.

noonday brightness of their own righteousness never discern.[14] He petitioned God on the basis of his character to be gracious (*ḥānan*, bestowal of an undeserved favor), kind (*ḥesed*, help to the helpless because of a covenant relationship) and merciful (*raḥam*, pity for the helpless).

In the Mosaic law as well, the whole paraphernalia of worship, including sacrifice, is rooted in God's sublime, forgiving character. While God is instructing Moses on the mountain on how to worship him (Exodus 25–Leviticus 9), the people sin by erecting the infamous golden calf (Exod. 32:1-8). The omniscient God responds to their rebellion by commanding Moses to get down from the mountain. He thereupon proposes two alternative plans for dealing with their sinfulness and responds to one by Moses in order to expose the spiritual mettle of the human founder of Israel's religion. Moses rejects God's first plan of starting over again with him because it would tarnish God's reputation, making him known as an angry God, and would violate his covenant promises to Abraham, Isaac, and Jacob (Exod. 32:8-14). God rejects Moses' plan of offering himself as a sin offering because his justice demands that the people who sinned be blotted out (Exod. 32:31–33:3). Moses and his repentant people in turn reject God's plan of sending his angel before them so as not to consume them by being in the midst of sinful people because it would signal that the Lord had rejected them and that he was not pleased with Moses (Exod. 33:1-17). In that dialogue, Moses asks God for assurance of his presence by asking him to show him his glory. In the closing scene God proclaims his glory, adding to the three attributes David appeals to, his patience and his reliability (Exod. 34:1-9).[15] The holy God can dwell in Israel's unholy camp because he is willing to forgive the repentant. In other words, the priestly section of the Law combines the sacrificial system of atonement with the personal dimension of God's willingness to forgive conditioned on Israel's willingness to repent.

On the basis of God's forgiving character, David boldly makes his double petition. First, he asks God to blot out (*māḥâ*, i.e., wipe the slate clean and remove God's wrath) his transgressions, one of several metaphors for forensic forgiveness in the Old Testament. And second, he requests that God "launder" him *(kābas)* so as to "cleanse" him (*ḥāṭṭā'*, i.e., "de-sin") and purify him (*ṭāhēr*, i.e., make him fit for temple worship). God's forgiveness is required because David has violated God's standard of holiness. David's three

---

14. Cf. Alexander Maclaren, *Psalms LI to CXIV* (London: Hodder & Stoughton, 1908), p. 12.

15. See R. W. L. Moberly, *At the Mountain of God: Story and Theology in Exodus 32–34,* JSOTSup 32 (Sheffield, UK: JSOT Press, 1983).

words in the semantic domain of sin assume this standard: he fell short of it (*ḥāṭṭâ'*, "sin"), rebelled against it (*peša'*, "transgression") and deviated from it or perverted it and so incurred guilt (*'āwôn*, "iniquity").

Lament and Confession — Psalm 51:3-6

Having laid the foundation for his appeal in God's glorious character to forgive, David gives the reason for his petitions ("for I know"), and in so doing, he meets the human spiritual requirement of his recognition and confession of his sin, a feature Psalm 32 also emphasizes. In Psalm 51:3-4 (2 lines), he confesses his overt sin, and in Psalm 51:5-6 (2 lines), his moral impotence. Without excusing himself, he emphatically confesses by a synonymous parallelism his culpability and, inferentially, his renunciation of his wrongdoing: "I know *my* transgression, *my* sin is always before *me*." The proverbial truth that "he who conceals his sins does not prosper, but whoever confesses and renounces them finds mercy" (Prov. 28:13) entails naming the sin. David specifies his sin in Psalm 51:14: "Save me from blood guilt." Psalm 51:4, however, employs abstract terms so that other penitent sinners may use the psalm in connection with their specific sins.

As noted, by strict definition sin is against God, so David confesses in Psalm 51:4: "Against you, you only, I have sinned," and quickly adds the reason for his theological assertion: "so that you are proved right when you speak and justified when you judge." Because sin violates God's standard, only God can forgive sin. The keen theological minds of the teachers of the law recognized Jesus' claim to deity and authorship of the Law when he said to the paralyzed man: "Son, your sins are forgiven." They thought to themselves: "He's blaspheming! Who can forgive sins but God alone?" (Mark 2:1-12). What matters on the eternal vertical axis between God and human beings is not whether people forgive sins, but whether the Lawgiver forgives them. On the horizontal axis, however, people also need to forgive one another of their wrongdoing to also restore their relationship. Sins against people and against God are inseparable.[16] Probably not everybody, including Ahithophel — perhaps Bathsheba's grandfather — forgave David.[17] In sum, in the first part of his confession, he reveals his consciousness of sin, his confession of it, and his acceptance of God's judgment.

16. Leviticus 6:1-7 [5:20-26].
17. Cf. 2 Samuel 11:3; 15:12; 23:34.

In the second part of his confession, David traces the root of his spiritual problem to his depravity, not to excuse himself but to seek a solution. He confesses his moral impotence by contrasting his inherited sin nature with his congenital conscience against it. He inherited both during his gestation. Concerning his original sin he laments: "See, I was sinful at birth, sinful from the time my mother conceived me" (Ps. 51:5).[18] Of his embryologic conscience he says: "See, you desired truth[19] in the covered over place; you taught me wisdom in the closed [chamber of the womb]" (Ps. 51:6). Dalglish argues the organic unity of these verses by noting the parallel structure: "see [*hinnēh*] . . . see [*hinnēh*]" and the expressions pertaining to the semantic domain of gestation: "at birth" and "conceived" and "in the concealed place" (i.e., the womb, *baṭṭuḥôt*, lit. "covered over place"[20]) and "closed" (chamber of the womb, *sātum*, lit. "stopped up, bottled up").[21] What the LORD desires is moral "truth" (*'emet*, i.e., faithfulness) and "wisdom" (*ḥokmâ*), i.e., "spiritual discernment or the actualizing principle of right conduct, which is to be equated with the fear of Yahweh (Ps cxi.10; Prov ix.10; Job xxviii.28)."[22]

Petitions — Psalm 51:7-12

His petitions can also be analyzed into two broad divisions corresponding to his confession. For his overt acts of sin, he repeats his introductory petitions for forensic forgiveness and for ceremonial cleansing, using the same vocabulary, but he chiastically reverses them. "Cleanse me (*tᵉḥattᵉʾānî*, i.e., 'de-sin me') with hyssop and I will be pure *(ṭāhēr)*, launder me *(kābas)* and I will be whiter than snow" (v. 7) matches Psalm 51:2. "Hide your face from my sin" — another metaphor for forensic forgiveness — "and blot out all my iniquity" matches Psalm 51:1. The bushy and aromatic hyssop is a metonymy for the blood its ample leaves held after being dipped in blood mixed with water. The law provided a guilt offering to make atonement for, and to relieve a conscience defiled by, deceiving and wronging one's neighbor with regard to

18. Translations of Psalm 51 are mine.

19. Perfective tense, same as verse 5a.

20. Plural of extension to indicate the noun is complex (Bruce K. Waltke and M. P. O'Connor, *Introduction to Biblical Hebrew Syntax* [Winona Lake, IN: Eisenbrauns, 1990], p. 120, P.7.4.1c).

21. Edward R. Dalglish, *Psalm Fifty-One in the Light of Ancient Eastern Patternism* (Leiden: E. J. Brill, 1962), pp. 118-22.

22. Dalglish, *Psalm Fifty-One*, p. 123.

property (Lev. 6:1-7), but none for adultery and murder. David in an ad hoc way appeals to purgation by hyssop used in connection with cleansing the leper (Leviticus 14) and one defiled by death.[23] Through these rituals the one in the process of dying and the other in the realm of death were transferred to the realms of life by the atoning rituals involving blood. Of course, as the writer of Hebrews argues, the animal blood that affected the transference served as a temporary arrangement until the fulfillment in the precious blood of Christ in the new order (Heb. 9:6-10). "The blood of bulls and goats and the ashes of a heifer sprinkled on those who are ceremonially unclean sanctify them so that they are outwardly clean. How much more, then, will the blood of Christ, who through the eternal Spirit offered himself unblemished to God, cleanse our consciences from acts that lead to death, so that we may serve the living God!" (Heb. 9:13-14). In sum, the psalmist appeals to the sacrificial system with its sprinklings of blood for cleansing. Sandwiched between his petitions for cultic cleansing and forensic forgiveness based on the sprinkling of blood, he asks for a priestly oracle of absolution: "Cause me to hear joy and gladness" (Ps. 51:10) a metonymy for the word of forgiveness.

The second part of his petition (Ps. 51:10-12) addresses his moral impotence. The second half of each of these verses mentions the spirit. What he needs is a new spirit (Ps. 51:10), the Holy Spirit (Ps. 51:11), and a willing spirit (Ps. 51:12) to offset his congenital spiritual contradiction. This will require a new creation: "Create *(bārā')* for me a pure heart, O God" (Ps. 51:10). The ritual cleansing is effective only for those to whom the Spirit applies it.

Praise — Psalm 51:13-19

Instead of presuming upon God with a section on confidence and praise, he anticipates his praise in the mood of petition. "Let me teach (*'ªlammᵉdâ*, probably a cohortative of request) transgressors your ways" (i.e., his ways of grace, mercy, and covenant; kindness to the helpless, Ps. 51:1), the ways God taught Moses.[24] The praise section of lament psalms typically consists of words of praise accompanied with a sacrifice, a so-called thank offering, or (better) acknowledgment offering. "The altar and *tôdâ* (praise/ acknowledgment) go together," says Mayer.[25] The praise sacrifice *(zebah*

---

23. Numbers 19. Dalglish, *Psalm Fifty-One,* pp. 134-37.

24. See Exodus 33:13; 34:6-7.

25. G. Mayer, *Theological Dictionary of the Old Testament,* 5.436, s.v. *ydh.* Cf. Psalms 26:6-7; 40:5-8; 43:4; 107:21ff.; Jonah 2:9 [10].

tôdâ)[26] is a peace offering of sacrificial animals and sometimes cereal.[27] In Psalm 51:13-15 David anticipates his words of praise, and in Psalm 51:16-17, his sacrifice. However, in the case of a woman pregnant through adultery and a grieving family due to murder, a joyous feast is entirely inappropriate: "You do not delight in [such a] sacrifice, or I would bring it; you do not take pleasure in burnt offerings [of praise to be eaten by the celebrants]. My sacrifice,[28] O God, is a broken spirit; a broken and contrite heart [upon which all can 'feed'], O God, you will not despise." In this section of his lament/confession psalm, and on this particular occasion, David is not rejecting the sacrificial system or animal sacrifices for ritual cleansing but is presenting a joyous celebration of praise through feasting.

Whether or not Psalm 51:18-19 is a later liturgical addition is uncertain, but it is certainly not by a less spiritually minded person. In the future, when God's good hand of blessing again rests on the nation and builds the walls of Zion, perhaps under Solomon, he anticipates: "Then there will be righteous sacrifices, whole burnt offerings to delight you; then bulls will be offered on your altar."

Conclusion

Although the liturgical portion of the Mosaic covenant features the ritual atonement, the spiritual element, as we have seen, is very prominent as well. In addition, note the call for Israel's confession of sin before sacrifice in other liturgical instructions: Leviticus 5:1-6;[29] Numbers 5:5-10. Psalm 51 is totally consistent with this pattern of combining ritual efficacy with spiritual requirements. Moreover, as Dalglish has shown, Ancient Near Eastern hymnody also combines them. Besides, three other psalms mention making atonement (*kpr*, usually translated "forgive"): Psalms 65:3 [4]; 78:38; 79:9. Commenting on the translation "forgave our transgression" (NIV) the *NIV Study Bible* says: "Accepted the atonement sacrifices you appointed and so forgave our sins."[30]

---

26. Psalm 116:17.

27. Leviticus 7:11-15; Psalm 69:30-31 [31-32].

28. Reading *zibḥî*, not *zibḥê*.

29. Cf. Leviticus 26:40; 1 Kings 8:33.

30. *The NIV Study Bible*, gen. ed. Kenneth Barker (Grand Rapids: Zondervan, 1995), p. 843.

Biblical Authority: How Firm a Foundation?

Introduction

Before addressing the topic of biblical authority, we need first to lay a foundation by considering the Bible's own claim to divine authority. As an exegetical theologian I aim to lay more firmly three stones of that foundation, namely, the law, the prophets, and the writings, especially the book of Proverbs, because most scholars think it was quarried from humanism.

Changing the metaphor, I hope to steady the plumb line by which we can evaluate theological statements about biblical authority. Carl Henry, utilizing the support of David Kelsey,[1] notes that during the past half-century virtually every contemporary Protestant theologian

> along the entire spectrum of opinion from the neo-evangelicals through Karl Barth, Emil Brunner, to Anders Nygren, Rudolf Bultmann, Paul Tillich and even Fritz Buri, has acknowledged that any Christian theology worthy of the name "Christian" must, in *some* sense of the phrase, be done "in accord" with scripture.[2]

This essay aims to have the heuristic value of enabling one to evaluate better whether a theologian's understanding of Scripture's authority conforms to the Bible's own self-understanding.

1. David H. Kelsey, *The Uses of Scripture in Recent Theology* (Philadelphia: Fortress Press, 1967), p. 1.
2. Carl F. H. Henry, *God, Revelation and Authority,* vol. 4 (Waco, TX: Word, 1979), p. 44.

Previously published in *Evangelicalism: Surviving Its Success,* ed. Charles E. Hill and Frank A. James III (St. Davids, PA: Eastern University Press, 1986). Used with permission.

The Law

According to Hebrews 1:1, God communicated divine matters through varying human psychologies. To Moses he appeared in a theophany and spoke face to face. Repeatedly in the Torah, Yahweh is depicted not only as the God who acts but also as the God who spoke through Moses to his people. Again and again one finds the expression "the Lord spake unto Moses, saying . . ." (Exod. 14:1; Lev. 4:1; Num. 13:1). By speaking with Moses face to face, God gave Moses greater value and his messages more clarity than an ordinary prophet with whom he spoke in dreams and visions. When Miriam and Aaron claimed equality with Moses on the basis of their common gift of prophecy, Yahweh reprimanded them, saying:

> When a prophet of the LORD is among you,
>   I reveal myself to him in visions,
>   I speak to him in dreams.
> But this is not true of my servant Moses;
>   he is faithful in all my house.
> With him I speak face to face,
>   clearly and not in riddles;
> Why then were you not afraid
>   to speak against my servant Moses?
>
> Numbers 12:6-8; cf. Deuteronomy 5:23-31

After Moses no prophet arose in Israel like him, "whom Yahweh knew face to face" (Deut. 34:10).

The foundation stone of Torah for biblical authority is most steady not only because of the mode in which God revealed it but also because it was written down. Gottlob Schrenk emphasizes that "writing down is an important mark of revelation" in the Old Testament.[3] The Tables of Law are said to be written by the finger of God (Exod. 31:18; Deut. 9:10); God himself writes down the commands of the Lord (Exod. 24:4; 34:27); the king causes it to be written down (Deut. 17:18); and Hosea 8:12 accuses the people for regarding as alien the law written for them.

---

3. Gottlob Schrenk, *Theological Dictionary of the New Testament*, ed. Gerhard Kittel, vol. 1 (Grand Rapids: Eerdmans, 1964), p. 744.

The Prophets

The prophets give us the $n^e um$ *'ădōnāy,* the "utterance" or "declaration of Yahweh." The superscription to the book of Micah typifies this kind of revelation:

> The word of the LORD that came to Micah of Moresheth during the reigns of Jotham, Ahaz and Hezekiah, kings of Judah — the vision he saw concerning Samaria and Jerusalem. (Micah 1:1 NIV)

This introduction sets forth five essentials: the divine author: "the word of the LORD"; the human author: "Micah of Moresheth"; the time of the revelation: "during the reigns of NN kings of Judah"; the nature of the communication between the divine author and the human author: "the vision he saw"; and the addressees: "Samaria and Jerusalem." Here we comment briefly on the divine author, the human author, the nature of the communication, and its historical character.

The Divine Author

A syntactic analysis of the original text discloses that in fact there is only one topic, "the word of the LORD," which is modified by two relative clauses, "that came to Micah . . ." and "that he 'saw'. . . ." A logical correlative of divine authorship is divine authority.

The Human Author

Micah, who may be regarded as representative of the prophets bequeathing us with books bearing their names, is clearly not a mystic but a messenger. This understanding of the prophets is underscored among other factors by their own autobiographic descriptions of their calls (cf. Isa. 6:1-13), and by the expression *kô 'āmar yhwh,* "thus says the LORD." Statements on this order, notes Henry C. Thiessen, occur more than 3,800 times in the Old Testament.[4] Lindblom's investigation of this important formula showed that it

---

4. Henry C. Thiessen, *Introductory Lectures in Systematic Theology* (Grand Rapids: Eerdmans, 1967), p. 110.

goes back to the proclamation formula of old Oriental declarations and decrees; that it is unique to prophetic literature in the Bible; and that it came to serve as a self-evident signature of a prophetic statement.[5] Koehler noted that it places a radical distinction between the word of the prophet and other human speech: "When the prophet prefaces his speech with, 'Thus says the LORD,' it is then a matter of the speech of a messenger which is distinctly separated from and contrasted with human speech."[6]

The Nature of the Communication between the Divine and Human Authors

The prophets signified the reception of their divine messages by the verb *ḥāzâ* and its nominal derivative, *ḥāzôn*. Although these words are normally translated by "saw" and "vision," they designate not a visual image, though that can be included, but an auricular revelation — a word from God. The object of the verb, "saw," is normally a *dābār*, a "word." In the Balaam oracle the expressions "God opened the mouth" or "put words in the mouth" are semantic equivalents of the root *ḥzh*. For lack of time I must forgo more demonstration and appeal instead to authorities. Jepsen defines the *ḥāzôn* as:

> Not a visual image but a word from God. . . . *Ḥāzôn* is . . . an event in which words are received. . . . A theophany or visual image to be interpreted is never mentioned in connection with *ḥāzôn*.[7]

Van der Woude agrees: "*ḥzh* refers rather to auditions than to visions."[8] Occasionally, as in 1 Kings 22:17, Isaiah 6:1-13, 21:1-10, Jeremiah 46:2-6, and Ezekiel 1, the messenger's speech is based on a vision.

The conceptualization of the prophet as God's messenger through au-

5. J. Lindblom, "Die prophetische Orakelformel," *Die literarische Gattung der prophetischen Literatur* (Uppsala: Universitets Arsskrift, 1924), appendix.

6. L. Koehler, "Formen und Stoffe," *Deuterojesaja, stilkritisch untersucht* (Giessen: Töpelmann, 1923), pp. 102-5; "Der Botenspruch," *Kleine Lichter* (Zurich: Zwingli-Verlag, 1945), pp. 13-17.

7. Alfred Jepsen, *Theological Dictionary of the Old Testament*, ed. G. J. Botterweck and Helmer Ringgren, vol. 4 (Grand Rapids: Eerdmans, 1980), p. 283.

8. A. S. van der Woude, *Theologisches Handwörterbuch zum Alten Testament*, ed. E. Jenni and C. Westermann, vol. 1 (Stuttgart: Chr. Kaiser Verlag, 1971), p. 536; cf. A. R. Johnson, *The Cultic Prophet in Ancient Israel* (Cardiff: University of Wales Press, 1962), pp. 11ff.

ditions has several important consequences with respect to the authority of Scripture. First of all, no separation affecting divine authority can be made between the Word of God and the human word. If the prophet merely described "what he saw" it would still be a human word, but since he spoke "what he heard," neo-Protestant reductions of biblical authority contrasting words of the text and the Word of God are contrary to Scripture. The relationship between the Word of God and the Scriptures is not indirect, as Emil Brunner asserts, but direct.[9]

Secondly, no separation regarding authority can be made between the reception of God's Word and its delivery. Scholars in the eighteenth and nineteenth centuries tended to distinguish between the stages of the prophet's "private experience" in receiving the Word of God and the "speeches" he gave at a later time based on that experience. The Word of God came to the prophet's mind and lips at the same time. Balaam described the seer's experience and delivery thus: "The oracle of one whose eye sees clearly, the oracle of one who hears the words of God, who $\hbar \bar{a} z \hat{a}$ a $\hbar \bar{a} z \hat{o} n$ from Shaddai" (Num. 24:3-4, 15-16).

Finally, the focus is on the message, not on the experience. The gnostics, it will be recalled, and some recent critics thought of the prophets, not as thinkers, but principally as ecstatics who pronounced their incantations out of a spiritual fervor that bypassed their own reasoning. For the gnostics this entailed that the interpreter must bypass the prophet and look for the hidden divine meaning. Critics, such as Hölscher, who sought the prophetic "incantations" in pagan soothsaying, tended to define prophecy in terms of prophetic experience and the phenomena, such as ecstasy, that accompanied it.[10] The prophets, however, are not mystics but messengers. Habakkuk, in full possession of his rational faculties, alertly took his stand upon a rampart and prepared himself to see how God would answer his perceptive and critical question, "Why are you silent when the wicked swallow up those more righteous than themselves?" (Hab. 1:13; 2:1). Westermann, following H. W. Wolff,[11] made the point:

Not a trace of ecstasy can be found among the prophets in the Mari texts, as W. von Soden has noted. . . . It must be plainly stated that it is impossi-

9. Emil Brunner, *Revelation and Reason*, trans. Olive Wyon (Philadelphia: Westminster, 1946), p. 129.

10. G. Hölscher, *Die Propheten* (Leipzig: Quelle & Meyer, 1914).

11. H. W. Wolff, "Hauptprobleme alttestamentlicher Prophetie," *Evangelische Theologie* (1955): 446-68.

ble for a message to be received in a state of ecstasy. . . . An alert and sensible ability to hear is the necessary presupposition at the moment the message . . . is received. Under certain circumstances ecstasy can precede it, or it can be found in the vicinity, but in no case may one assume that the reception of the messenger's speech occurred in ecstasy.[12]

Its Historical Character

Finally, note the historical nature of the revelation. The text says literally, "the word of Yahweh *happened* [Heb. *hāyâ*] to Micah" and goes on to give the historical situation and addressees. That data may stabilize or destabilize the foundation stone of prophecy. On the one hand, it can reinforce the prophet's claim that he was dispatched as God's messenger by locating his experience in history. On the other hand, it may erode the prophet's authority for future audiences by culturally relativizing it.

Some modern scholars opt for the latter interpretation of the data. They like to speak of a "prophetic understanding," superseded by an "apostolic understanding," versus a "medieval understanding," etc. Gilkey asked: "If . . . all faiths . . . are relative to their stage and place in general history, how can any one of them claim our ultimate allegiance or promise an ultimate truth or an ultimate salvation?"[13] If the cultural relativists are right, then, as Harvey Cox said, the biblical books cease to be values and become valuations.[14] James Barr rightly commented: "there is an important distinction between the 'authority' of a historical source and the 'authority' of a theological norm or criterion. . . . Priority as a historical source is something different from theological normativeness."[15]

The editors of the prophetic books and the New Testament, however, contravene those that detract from the eternal authority and theological normativeness of the prophets. Although critical research that began in the eighteenth century, and that came to flower in the nineteenth, had a faulty view of both inspiration and the development of Israel's religion, it had the heuristic value of discovering a living person behind the prophetic books

12. Claus Westermann, *Basic Forms of Prophetic Speech*, trans. Hugh Clayton White (Philadelphia: Westminster, 1967), p. 63.

13. Langdon Gilkey, *Naming the Whirlwind: The Renewal of God Language* (Indianapolis: Bobbs-Merrill, 1969), p. 51.

14. Harvey Cox, *The Secular City* (New York: Macmillan, 1965), p. 31.

15. James Barr, *The Bible in the Modern World* (London: SCM Press, 1973), p. 80.

and forcing scholars in the twentieth century to recognize beyond the divine and human authors a third factor in the composition of the prophetic books, the redactor who edited them.[16] The redactor, in the case of Micah probably Micah himself but in other cases, such as Jeremiah, presumably someone after the prophet, regarded not only the preliterary oracles as the messages of God to their original audiences but the edited form of the book as a whole the continuing "Word of God" to a new audience, the readers of future generations. Instructively, *dābār*, "word," and *ḥāzôn*, "audition," are singular, showing that the editor thought of the entire book bearing the prophet's name as the Word of God. Commenting on Micah 1:1, Renaud observed: "One does not speak . . . of words in plural . . . but of the Word of YHWH, which almost takes the figure of hypostasis."[17]

Also instructively, the first oracle in Micah 1:2-7, although accusing Samaria of idolatry and judicially sentencing Israel's capital to destruction, is addressed to *all* people.

> Hear, O peoples, all of you,
> listen, O earth, and all who are in it,
> that the Sovereign LORD may witness against you,
> the Lord from his holy temple.
>
> Micah 1:2

The Lord Jesus and his apostles in the New Testament reflect the traditional Jewish recognition of the abiding authority of the Old Testament. The New Testament fully endorses the authoritative significance of the Old as mediating the declaration of God's revealed will. The use of *gegraptai*, "it stands written" (Matt. 4:4-10; Luke 4:8; 19:46; 1 Cor. 9:9; 14:21), reflects the New Testament view of the Old Testament as a continuing normative record. Pierre Marcel commented: "From the manner in which Christ quotes Scriptures we find that he recognizes and accepts the Old Testament in its entirety as possessing a normative authority, as the true Word of God."[18]

Jesus upbraids Jewish religious leaders for ignorance and neglect of sacred Scriptures (Matt. 12:3; 9:13) and contends that Scripture cannot be bro-

---

16. Westermann, *Basic Forms of Prophetic Speech,* p. 13.

17. B. Renaud, *La formation du livre de Michée. Traduction et actualisation* (Paris: J. Gabalda et Cie., éditeurs, 1977), p. 5.

18. Pierre Marcel, in *Revelation and the Bible,* ed. Carl F. H. Henry (Grand Rapids: Baker, 1958), p. 133.

ken (John 10:35). The theme of Scriptures, David R. Jackson notes, is as prominent in the Acts missionary message as are the resurrection of the crucified Jesus and the new life available through faith in the risen Lord (cf. Acts 2:17-21, 25-28, 34-35; 3:18, 21-25; 4:11; 5:30-31; 10:43; 13:16-23, 27, 29, 33-36, 40-41; cf. 26:22).[19] Paul formulates the gospel in 1 Corinthians 15:3-4 according to the Scriptures.

Roger Nicole established the eternal contemporaneity of Scripture by noting:

> Another interesting feature of the formulae of quotations [of the Old Testament in the New] is the frequent use of the present for the introductory words "He says" rather than "He said." This is reinforced by the use of the pronouns "we" and "you" in relation to ancient sayings, "That which was spoken unto you by God" (Matt. 22:31); "The Holy Spirit also beareth witness to us" (Heb. 10:15; cf. Matt. 15:7; Mark 7:6; 12:19; Acts 4:11; 13:47; Heb. 12:5). In this wise the eternal contemporaneity of the Scripture is emphasized, a truth of which explicit expression is found in Romans 15:4, "For whatsoever things were written aforetime were written for our learning." (Note also Rom. 4:23, 24; 1 Cor. 9:10; 10:11.)[20]

The Sage

The psychology of the sage in his experience of revelation can be deduced from the autobiographical account of one sage as to how he came to coin a proverb:

> I went past the field of the sluggard,
>   past the vineyard of the man who lacks judgment;
> thorns had come up everywhere,
>   the ground was covered with weeds,
>   and the stone was in ruins.
> I applied my heart to what I observed
>   and learned a lesson from what I saw:

---

19. David R. Jackson, "Gospel [Message]," 2:782, cited by Henry, *God, Revelation and Authority,* 4:34.

20. Roger Nicole, "Old Testament Quotations in the New Testament," in *Hermeneutics,* ed. Bernard L. Ramm (Grand Rapids: Baker, 1980), p. 46.

> A little sleep, a little slumber,
>   a little folding of the hands to rest —
> and poverty will come on you like a bandit
>   and scarcity like an armed man.
>
> Proverbs 24:30-34

In contrast to Moses, who went to the Tent of Meeting and spoke with God face to face, and to Isaiah, who, while in the temple, was caught up into the divine assembly where he saw and heard God, the sage has no direct Word from God but learns by observation and reflection while passing by a field. He does not directly rest his ladder, on which humans may ascend, on the bar of heaven, but on his own reflections, and therefore, along with the rest of humanism, it threatens eventually to come crashing down again on the earth.[21]

Critics commonly assume that Proverbs is grounded in humanism. Rankin, for example, calls the Wisdom literature "the documents of Hebrew humanism."[22] Fichtner contrasts the authority of the sage with that of the prophet:

> The prophet speaks in large measure on the basis of the authority conferred with his commission and tells his hearers "God's Word"; while the wise man — especially the earlier period! — gives advice and instruction from tradition and his own insight without explicitly or implicitly assumed divine authorization.[23]

Rylaarsdam said that the wisdom seeker must rely entirely on his natural human equipment. Gazelle similarly wrote: "Wisdom is the art of succeeding in life, both private and collective. It is grounded in humanism, in reflexion on and observation of the course of things and the conduct of man."[24]

Correlative to this point of view is a denial of the sages' categorical authority. Zimmerli, defining the crucial wisdom-term 'ēṣâ (traditionally rendered "counsel"), drew the conclusion:

21. Cf. H. Dermot McDonald, *The Concept of Authority*, p. 36, cited by Henry, *God, Revelation and Authority*, 4:8.

22. O. S. Rankin, *Israel's Wisdom Literature: Its Bearing on Theology and the History of Religion* (Edinburgh: T. & T. Clark, 1936), p. 3.

23. Johannes Fichtner, "Isaiah Among the Wise," in *Studies in Ancient Israelite Wisdom*, ed. James Crenshaw [hereafter *SAIW*] (New York: Ktav, 1976), p. 430.

24. Cited by Crenshaw in *SAIW*, p. 4.

'*ēṣâ* offers deliberative, debatable counsel; instead of appealing to the Creator's authority, sages appealed to what is in man's best interest as the justification for their validity; instead of issuing commands, they sought to compel assent.[25]

Crenshaw censured Zimmerli for eroding wisdom's authority. Lexical study showed that '*ēṣâ*, "counsel," carried the same authoritative weight as the prophet's *dābār*, "word."

Most scholars ground wisdom in both experience and tradition. Couturier described the sage's teaching this way: "the totality of life experiences transmitted by a father to his son, as a spiritual testament."[26] Many emphatically ground wisdom in tradition. R. B. Y. Scott, for example, divided the proverbs into two classes, folk proverbs and proverbs of the wisdom teacher.[27] The folk saying, according to Scott, derives its authority from "the social authority of general consent or of the obvious truism," and the wisdom saying rests its authority on "the learning of the religious teacher."

Proverbs itself, however, contradicts in several ways the grounding of its teachings in humanism. First, the proverbs in the strict sense (that is, the two collections in 10:1–22:16 and 25:1–29:27) are represented as the teachings of Solomon, king of Israel (Prov. 1:1). The king is recognized as son of God through prophetic anointing and by so much, as the proverbs themselves assert, his lips speak as a *qesem* (Prov. 16:10), rendered "oracle" in Jerusalem Bible, New English Bible, New American Bible, New International Version, "divine sentence" in King James Version, and "inspired decision" in Revised Standard Version. Israel's inspired historian traced Solomon's wisdom back to God, conferring divine authority to his proverbs (1 Kings 4:29).

Second, the sage presents his teaching under the persona of a prophet in 1:20-33. W. Baumgartner[28] and B. Gemser[29] speak of pressing the pro-

---

25. Walter Zimmerli, "Concerning the Structure of Old Testament Wisdom," in *SAIW*, pp. 176-99.

26. Guy P. Couturier, "Sagesse babylonienne et sagesse israelite," *Sciences Ecclésiastiques* 14 (1962): 309.

27. R. B. Y. Scott, "Folk," in *SAIW*, p. 418; Scott, *The Way of Wisdom* (New York: Macmillan, 1965), p. 63; Scott, "Wise and Foolish, Righteous and Wicked," in *SAIW*, p. 155.

28. Walter Baumgartner, *Israelitische und altorientalische Weisheit* (Tübingen: J. C. B. Mohr, 1933), p. 9.

29. B. Gemser, "Sprueche Salomos," in *Handbuch zum Alten Testament*, 2nd ed. (1963), pp. 5, 16.

phetic speech form into this poem, and Bauer-Kayatz[30] underscores that, although Proverbs 1–9 depend on Egyptian sapiential forms and motifs, nothing comparable to this prophetic address can be found in the Egyptian instruction literature.

Third, Bauer-Kayatz[31] also noted that the sage sometimes represents his teaching in the "I style," a form reserved exclusively elsewhere in the Old Testament and in Egyptian literature for divine speeches. Wisdom's address, "To you, O men, I call out; I raise my voice to all mankind," and her claim "I wisdom dwell together with prudence; I possess knowledge and discretion. . . . I love those who love me, and those who seek me find me" (Prov. 8:4ff.) are language elsewhere kept only for deity. Maat, the Egyptian equivalent of Hebrew *ḥokmâh*, "wisdom," was hypostatized as a goddess in contrast to *ḥokmâh*, but paradoxically never spoke with the authority of *ḥokmâh*.

Fourth, the sage explicitly attributes his wisdom as coming from God. Regarding his collected words he says: "For Yahweh gives wisdom, and from his mouth come knowledge and understanding" (Prov. 2:6). The sage assumes that behind his teaching stands God's authority; consequently, he never exhorts the son to trust his teaching but to trust Yahweh (Prov. 3:5). The close connection between God's authority and the sage's teaching is clearly implied in the prologue to the thirty sayings of the wise: "So that your trust may be in the LORD, I teach you today, even you" (Prov. 22:19).

Finally, note once again von Rad's argument that "wisdom" designates the fixed cosmic and social order of life. What von Rad failed to note properly is that the book's teachings reveal that fixed substance.[32] Wisdom's substance and its expressions are connected in the opening statement of the book's purpose: "to attain wisdom (the substance) . . . and to understand words of insight" (the expression) (Prov. 1:2). (In Egypt both substance and its expression were hypostatized as gods.) Since the sage's teachings are the semiotic signs for the fixed cosmic order, the sage designates his teachings by the same words Moses used for his revelations, namely torah (1:8; 3:1; 13:14; 28:4, 7 et passim), the authoritative admonition *kata exochēn*, and "command" [Heb. *mṣwt*] (2:1; 3:1; 4:4; 6:23 et passim).

In sum, one can say that although the psychology of the sage's reception of revelation differed radically from that of Moses, the founder of the

---

30. Christa Bauer-Kayatz, *Studien zu Proverbien 1–9* (Neukirchen: Neukirchener Verlag, 1966), pp. 119ff.

31. Bauer-Kayatz, *Studien zu Proverbien 1–9*, pp. 86ff.

32. Gerhard von Rad, *Wisdom in Israel* (Nashville: Abingdon, 1972).

theocratic state, and from that of the prophets, who called Israel back to Moses' law, he nevertheless understood his lessons, drawn from observation and reflection, as a divine self-disclosure with its inseparable correlative that it possessed divine authority. If his instruction is heeded, he promises life; if ignored, he threatens death.

McKane,[33] Whybray,[34] and others try to loosen Proverbs from being a firm foundation stone for biblical authority by distinguishing both in the Egyptian instruction and in Proverbs an older profane and secular wisdom and a younger religious and theological wisdom. The older strata were quarried from a humanistic, this-worldly wisdom, and were glazed over later with a divine, other-worldly wisdom.

This understanding, however, arises from the preunderstanding of a modern scholar; it would not have been so understood by the ancients. Egyptologists disallow the distinction. Noting that Egyptian sapiential texts span more than two millennia, from about 2500 BC to 500 BC, Henri Frankfort wrote:

> It would seem that we have here material for a history of ideas, and modern scholars have sometimes used these texts to describe a development of social and ethical thought in Egypt. I do not think that such an interpretation is tenable if we study the evidence without prejudice — that is, without an evolutionary bias. The differences between the earlier and the later texts seem largely to have been caused by accidents of preservation, while their resemblance consists, on the contrary, in a significant uniformity of tenor.[35]

A. Erman concurred.[36] Toronto University Egyptologist R. J. Williams wrote in 1981: "The old view that Egyptian wisdom-literature was almost totally utilitarian in its attitude has happily been laid to rest for many years now."[37]

---

33. William McKane, *Proverbs: A New Approach* (Philadelphia: Westminster, 1970).

34. R. N. Whybray, *Wisdom in Proverbs* (Naperville, IL: Allenson, 1965).

35. Henri Frankfort, *Ancient Egyptian Religion,* 2nd ed. (New York: Columbia University Press, 1961), p. 59. Fr. R. W. von Bissing finds a constant spiritual and moral stance throughout the history of the sapiential genre. *Altaegyptische Lebensweisheit* (Zurich: Artemis-Verlag, 1955).

36. William Kelly Simpson, ed., *The Literature of Egypt* (New Haven: Yale University Press, 1972), p. xxi.

37. Ronald J. Williams, "The Sages of Ancient Egypt in the Light of Recent Scholarship," *Journal of the American Oriental Society* 101 (1981): 11.

Correspondingly, the book of Proverbs shows much stronger similarity in basic concepts and lines of connection between its parts than a straight-line developmental process and discrepancy. Von Rad and H. Gese showed that Old Testament wisdom literature rests on the assumed basis that there is a wholesome, all-pervading divine ordering, linking deed and consequence. The overwhelming majority of proverbs express this connection. In the final analysis the true Israelite will derive this connection from Yahweh, whether Yahweh is referred to or not. J. Whedbee rightly argued:

> McKane does not deal with the basic concept of an order in the world, which seems to have formed a crucially important presupposition in the wise man's approach to reality. The wise man took this order [to be] created and guaranteed by God. . . . To say that the wise man was completely an independent, empirical operator, as McKane does, is to misread the data of the ancient wisdom and view it through the lens of a modern construct. The wise man always reckoned with God. . . .[38]

R. Murphy similarly wrote: "No distinction of 'profane' or 'sacred' is applicable here; God was considered the guardian of the social order. . . ."[39] R. Priest observed that the same two kinds of proverbs are also found in the postexilic book *The Wisdom of Sirach*.[40]

Conclusion

From our study we draw the following conclusions: "The first claim to be made for Scripture," wrote Carl Henry, "is not its inerrancy nor even its inspiration, but its authority."[41] The New Testament extends this authority to the entire Old Testament. The Scriptures, as Jesus said, "cannot be broken" (John 10:35), an axiom of both Judaism and of the primitive church. The Bible presents humans with unalterable absolutes, changeless commands, deathless doctrines, and timeless truths.

Second, Scripture's own claim to be the direct Word of God is so abun-

38. J. William Whebee, *Isaiah and Wisdom* (Nashville: Abingdon, 1971), pp. 118f.

39. R. E. Murphy, "Assumptions and Problems in Old Testament Research," *Catholic Biblical Quarterly* 29 (1967): 103; cf. David A. Hubbard, "The Wisdom Movement and Israel's Covenant Faith," *TynBul* 17 (1966): 18.

40. John F. Priest, "Where Is Wisdom to Be Placed?" in *SAIW*, p. 281.

41. Henry, *God, Revelation and Authority*, 4:27.

dant and clear that its centrality as the stable and objective expression of what God demands for faith and practice cannot be replaced by unstable and subjective human experience.

Third, the writer of Hebrews links the authoritative words of Jesus with the authoritative Hebrew Scriptures. He wrote:

> In the past God spoke to our forefathers through the prophets at many times and in various ways, but in these last days he has spoken to us by his Son. (Hebrews 1:1-2)

If the authority of the Old Testament falters, then the authority of the Christian faith also is shaken. James Boice noted a similar connection in the Gospel of John. The beloved apostle, he observed, used the word *logos* even "of the OT Scriptures in the phrases 'the word of God' or 'his word' (5:38; 8:55; 10:35; cf. also 12:38)." "In this perception," Boice continued, "John is not far from the opening verses of the epistle to the Hebrews in which the revelation of God through His Son is intimately connected with the speaking of God in OT times through the prophets. . . ."[42]

Fourth, the neo-Protestant distinction between Word of God and Scripture, inflating the authority of the former and reducing the latter's, violates the Bible's balanced linking of substance with expression.

Fifth, although the incarnate expression of the divine word takes the shape of the historical moment in which it is given, its substance as the Word of God is eternally authoritative. Besides endorsing the claim of the Old Testament as authoritative over the lives of others, Jesus himself submitted himself to it. Even after his resurrection he reminded his disciples that the words and events "must be fulfilled, which were written in the law of Moses, and in the prophets, and in the psalms" concerning him (Luke 24:44). Jesus instructed his followers not to evaluate his life and teaching apart from Old Testament teaching, but to hold them together as a unit.[43]

Finally, although all Scripture is authoritative, it is not of equal value. John Bright cleverly noted: "(Let the reader who is inclined to deny this look at his own Bible and see which pages are the most worn, and let him understand that as evidence that he has himself made value judgments.)"[44]

---

42. James Boice, *Witness and Revelation in the Gospel of John* (Grand Rapids: Zondervan, 1970), p. 70.

43. Henry, *God, Revelation and Authority*, 4:36.

44. John Bright, *The Authority of the Old Testament* (Nashville: Abingdon, 1967), p. 106.

Though a twenty-dollar bill and a one-dollar note carry equal authority with the U.S. Treasury, they do not carry equal value. So also the words of Moses carry more weight than the words of the prophets and of the sages. Solomon, the greatest of the sages, reflected upon the creation with the preunderstanding of an Israelite, that is, a member of the theocracy founded by Moses. Note Proverbs 1:1: "The proverbs of Solomon son of David, king of Israel." The words of Jesus are heavier than both. Moses was faithful as a servant in all God's house, but Christ is faithful as a son over God's house and has been found worthy of greater honor than Moses (Heb. 3:1-5). Instructively, Jesus is called in this text "the Apostle and High Priest" (Heb. 3:1), a correlation of terms that indirectly emphasizes his superiority to the Old Testament "prophet." That title is never applied to Jesus in the Book of Hebrews but contrasted rather with "son" in Hebrews 1:2. As Rengstorf observed, the terms *Apostle* and *High Priest* "herald Jesus as the final and complete revelation of God who absolutely authorizes his word (Apostle) and his work (High Priest)."[45] Jesus himself said that he was greater than Solomon (Matt. 12:42). Bernard Ramm drew the pragmatic conclusion: "If there is any tension between the older revelation and the newer, the older must give way to the newer."[46]

Hopefully we have contributed toward laying three foundation stones for biblical authority and have pointed to Jesus as the chief cornerstone.

---

45. Cited by Henry, *God, Revelation and Authority,* 4:28.
46. Bernard Ramm, "Biblical Interpretation," in Ramm, ed., *Hermeneutics,* p. 22.

Cain and His Offering

Introduction

Partially because of the laconic style in which the Cain and Abel story[1] is told and partially because of prejudgments, scholars are divided in their opinions as to why God rejected Cain's offering. This essay aims to answer that question.[2]

Prejudging that our story reflects the development of Israelite religion, Skinner proposed that the story represents an early stage of Israelite religion in which animal sacrifice alone was acceptable to Yahweh. He explained: "It is quite conceivable that in the early days of the settlement in Canaan the view was maintained among the Israelites that the animal offerings of their nomadic religion were superior to the vegetable offerings made to the Canaanite Baals."[3] Disregarding the unity of Genesis and ignoring God's mandate that Adam, the representative man, till the ground (2:5; 3:23), Gunkel claimed: "This myth indicates that God loves the shepherd and the offering of flesh, but as far as the farmer and the fruits of the field are con-

---

1. For an excellent commentary on the Cain and Abel story see "Cain and Abel" in *The New Media Bible Times* 1, no. 3 (published by the Genesis Project, 1976).

2. For the function of offerings see Claus Westermann, *Genesis* (3 vols.; BKAT 1; Neukirchen-Vluyn: Neukirchener Verlag, 1974-82), 1:401f.

3. John Skinner, *A Critical and Exegetical Commentary on Genesis* (ICC; Edinburgh: T. & T. Clark, 1910), p. 106.

Previously published in *Westminster Theological Journal* 48 (1986): 363-72. Used with permission.

cerned, He will have none of them."[4] Cassuto, by contrast, perceptively compared this story with the Creation story and the Garden of Eden story.

> There is a kind of parallel here to what was stated in the previous chapters: the raising of sheep corresponds to the dominion over the living creatures referred to in the story of Creation (i 26, 28), and the tilling of the ground is analogous to what we are told at the beginning and the end of the story of the Garden of Eden (ii 5, iii 23).[5]

Some orthodox commentators, coming to the text with the prejudgment that fallen man may approach offended God only through blood, think that God rejected Cain's sacrifice because it was bloodless. Candlish, for example, wrote: "To appear before God, with whatever gifts, without atoning blood, as Cain did — was infidelity."[6]

This writer comes to the text with the prejudgments that the storyteller drops clues in his text demanding the audience's close attention to details in the text, Genesis 4:1-16. Leupold underscored that in the lapidary style of Scripture "significant individual instances are made to display graphically what course was being pursued."[7] The second presupposition entails that the interpreter also listen to the rest of Scripture in order to determine the text's meaning and/or to validate his or her interpretation of the narrative.[8] Although the Cain and Abel story probably enjoyed preliterary independence, it must now be read as part of the Pentateuch. Skinner[9] rightly noted that the exegete must pay attention to the audience to whom a story is addressed. Unfortunately, he reconstructed the wrong audience! Shackled by his presuppositions of source criticism and lacking the modern tools of literary criticism (sometimes called "rhetorical criticism"), he interpreted the story in the light of hypothetical "first hearers" instead of the readers of the Pentateuch to

4. Hermann Gunkel, *Genesis übersetzt and erklärt* (Göttingen: Vandenhoeck & Ruprecht, 1922), p. 43.

5. U. Cassuto, *A Commentary on the Book of Genesis* (Jerusalem: Magnes, 1961), 1:203. Victor Hamilton, *Handbook on the Pentateuch* (Grand Rapids: Baker, 1982), also demonstrated the unity of Genesis 3 and 4.

6. Robert S. Candlish, *Studies in Genesis* (Edinburgh: A. and C. Black; reprinted, Grand Rapids: Kregel, 1979), p. 94.

7. H. C. Leupold, *Exposition of Genesis* (Grand Rapids: Baker, 1965; orig. 1942), 1:187.

8. Bruce K. Waltke, "Is It Right to Read the New Testament into the Old?" *Christianity Today* 27, no. 13 (September 2, 1983): 77.

9. Skinner, *Genesis*, p. 105. For this common error see also S. R. Driver, *The Book of Genesis* (London: Methuen & Co., 1904), p. 64.

whom the text in hand was addressed. (Prior to and/or apart from the modern emphasis to hear a text wholistically, studies by William Henry Green,[10] H. Segal,[11] and D. J. A. Clines,[12] each in his own way, put the unity of the Pentateuch beyond doubt.)

We commence our study with the observation that the text syntactically distinguishes between the offerer and his offering: "The LORD looked with favor on [*'el*] Abel and on [*'el*] his offering, but on [*'el*] Cain and on [*'el*] his offering he did not look with favor" (Gen. 4:4b-5a).

Cain's Offering

Offerings in the Pentateuch

The Torah, especially the priestly legislation (the so-called "P document"), has a rich and precise vocabulary to represent the sacraments offered to the LORD on an altar; each term denotes a physical object representing a spiritual truth upon which the worshiper could feed spiritually in his approach to and communion with God.[13]

The most inclusive term for presentations to God on the altar is *qorban*, "offering," from a root signifying "to bring near." This term is not used in the Cain and Abel story.

Offerings can be analyzed broadly into two classes: voluntary and involuntary. Involuntary offerings include the "sin offering" *(ḥaṭṭa't)* and the "guilt offering" *('āšām).*[14] These sacrifices make "atonement" *(kpr)*[15] and involve shedding blood for removal of sin. Were Cain presenting an involun-

---

10. William Henry Green, *The Higher Criticism of the Pentateuch* (1896; reprinted, Grand Rapids: Baker, 1978).

11. M. H. Segal, *The Pentateuch* (Jerusalem: Magnes, 1967).

12. D. J. A. Clines, *The Theme of the Pentateuch* (JSOTSup 10; Sheffield, UK: University of Sheffield, 1978).

13. G. Lloyd Carr, "*mnh*" in *Theological Wordbook of the Old Testament*, ed. R. Laird Harris, Gleason L. Archer Jr., Bruce K. Waltke (Chicago: Moody Press, 1980), 1:515; C. Brown, "Sacrifice," in *The New International Dictionary of New Testament Theology*, ed. Colin Brown (Grand Rapids: Zondervan, 1979), 3:437f.; Aaron Rothkoff, "Sacrifice," in *EncJud* 15:605f.

14. Jacob Milgrom, *Cult and Conscience: The Asham and the Priestly Doctrine of Repentance* (Leiden: E. J. Brill, 1976). Other involuntary presentations include the substitute animal for the firstborn (Exod. 34:19-20), the ritual for cleansing from leprosy (Leviticus 14), and defilement by contact with a carcass (Numbers 19).

15. Leon Morris, *The Apostolic Preaching of the Cross* (Grand Rapids: Eerdmans, 1965).

tary offering, he would have been rejected for failure to offer blood. In fact, however, in the Cain and Abel story, a part of the Books of Moses, neither "sin offering" nor "guilt offering" is used.

The voluntary offerings included the "burnt offering" (ʿōlâ), "meal offering" (minḥâ), and "fellowship offering" (šelem), including "acknowledgment offering" (tôdâ), "votive offering" (neder), and "freewill offering" (neᵈābâ). These dedicatory offerings could be either animal, as in the case of the burnt-offering (Leviticus 1), or grain, as in the case of the "meal offering" (Leviticus 2). The fellowship offering could be either (Leviticus 3). A libation offering (nešek) accompanied burnt and fellowship offerings. The priest's portion of the fellowship offering was symbolically "waved" before the LORD as his portion and called the "wave offering" (tenupa). Certain portions of it (namely, one of the cakes and the right thigh) were given as a "contribution" from the offerer to the priests, the so-called "heave offering" (terûmâ).

The term "sacrifice" (zebaḥ) may be a generic term for presentations on the altar (mizbeaḥ) or a more technical term for representing rituals in making a covenant. The slaughtering of an animal in the latter case symbolized a self-curse (that is, the one making covenant would say words to the effect, "may it happen to me as it is happening to this animal I am killing") and effected a sacrifice.[16] We need not pursue the word further because it is not used in Genesis 4.

Our narrator designates three times (vv. 3, 4, 5) the brothers' offerings by minḥâ, a grain offering, it will be recalled, in the so-called "P document." The unusual element in the story from a lexical viewpoint is not that Cain's offering is bloodless but that Abel's is bloody! In any case, by using minḥâ, Moses virtually excludes the possibility that God did not look on Cain's offering because it was bloodless. Rothkoff said:

> The terminology used with regard to the patriarchal age is that of the Torah as a whole; it is unlikely that the same words in Genesis mean something different in the other Books of Moses. Thus, Cain and Abel each brought a "gift" (minḥâ; Gen. 4:4f.), which was usually of a cereal nature as brought by Cain (Lev. 2, et al.) but could also refer to an animal offering (1 Sam. 2:17; 26:19). Noah offered up a burnt offering (ʿōlâ; Gen. 8:20ff.) and the pleasing odor of the sacrifice is stressed.[17]

16. M. Weinfeld, "The Covenant of Grant in the Old Testament and in the Ancient Near East," JAOS 90 (1970): 197f.

17. Rothkoff, "Sacrifice," p. 605.

He could have added that Noah in conformity with the later priestly and Deuteronomistic legislation distinguished between "clean and unclean" animals (Gen. 7:2, the so-called "J document"! cf. Leviticus 11 and Deuteronomy 14).

The Meaning of Minḥâ outside the Pentateuch

Most scholars trace *minḥâ* back to an Arabic root meaning "to lend someone something" for a period of time so that the borrower can have free use of the loan. In Hebrew, however, the idea of lending is lost, and it comes to mean "gift," "tribute."

In nontheological texts it designates a "gift" from an inferior to a superior person, particularly from a subject to a king, to convey the idea of homage. The Israelites, for example, who despised Saul "brought him no present" *(minḥâ)* (1 Sam. 10:27), that is, as Carr explained: "did not acknowledge the new king."[18] The kings submissive to Solomon brought "tribute" *(minḥâ)* (1 Kings 4:21 [Heb. 5:1]; cf. Judg. 3:15-18; 2 Sam. 8:2, 6). "Gifts" to Solomon included articles of silver and gold, robes, weapons and spices, and horses and mules (1 Kings 10:25).

A person brought a gift appropriate to his social standing and vocation (cf. Gen. 32:13ff. [Heb. vv. 14ff.]). Appropriately, Abel, a shepherd, brought some of his flock (that is, from the fruit of the womb of sheep and/or goats), and Cain, a farmer, brought from the fruit of the ground. Furthermore, would God reject the elder son's tribute because it came from the ground that he himself had commanded Adam to work? If *minḥâ* were translated by either "gift" or "tribute" in Genesis 4:3-5, it would be clearer that the absence of blood from Cain's presentation on his altar did not disqualify him (cf. Deut. 26:1-11).

The theological uses of *minha* comport with its nontheological uses (cf. Num. 16:15; Judg. 6:18; 1 Sam. 2:17; Ps. 96:8; Zeph. 3:10). Snaith said that *minha* could loosely be used in the sense of "gift" or "tribute" even in specific cultic contexts. Carr likewise observed: "Of particular interest in this connection is the distinction between *zebaḥ* and *minḥâ* in 1 Sam. 2:29; 3:14; and Isa. 19:21; between *'olâ* and *minḥâ* in Jer. 14:12 and Ps. 20:3 [H 4]; and between *shelem* and *minḥâ* in Amos 5:22."[19]

18. Carr, "*mnh,*" p. 514.
19. Carr, "*mnh,*" p. 514.

Our lexical study for the term designating Cain's offering gives no basis for thinking it was rejected because it was bloodless. In fact, of the many expressions for presentations to God that were available to Moses, he could not have used a more misleading term if this were his intended meaning.

Descriptions of the Offerings within the Text

The storyteller intends to contrast Abel's offering with Cain's by paralleling "Cain brought some" with "Abel brought some," by adding with Abel, "even he" *(gam hû')* (v. 4), and by juxtaposing in a chiastic construction the LORD's acceptance of Abel and his gift with his rejection of Cain and his gift (vv. 4b-5a).

He characterizes Abel's offerings from the flocks as "from the firstborn" and "from their fat." By offering the firstborn Abel signified that he recognized God as the Author and Owner of Life. In common with the rest of the Ancient Near East, the Hebrews believed that the deity, as lord of the manor, was entitled to the *first share* of all produce. The *first*fruits of plants and the *first*born of animals and man were his. The LORD demonstrated that he gave Egypt its life and owned it by taking its firstborn. Israel's gifts from the animals involved those that open the womb (Exod. 13:2, 12; 34:19) and gifts from the ground had to be the "firstfruits" *(bikkûrîm)* (Deut. 26:1-11).[20]

Abel's offering conformed with this theology; Cain's did not. In such a laconic story the interpreter may not ignore that whereas Abel's gift is qualified by "firstborn," the parallel "firstfruits" does not modify Cain's. Skinner cavalierly rewrote the story and misinterpreted the data thus: "Cain's offering is thus analogous to the firstfruits *(bikkûrîm* Ex 23:16, 19; 34:22, 26; Nu 13:20 etc.) of Heb ritual; and it is arbitrary to suppose that his fault lay in not selecting the best of what he had for God."[21]

Abel also offered the "fat," which in the so-called "P" material belonged to the LORD and was burned symbolically by the priests. This tastiest and best-burning part of the offering represented the best. Abel's sacrifice, the interlocutor aims to say, passed that test with flying colors. Cain's sacrifice,

---

20. Sometimes the principle of redemption by substitution came into play here. In the case of children, the LORD provided a substitute animal (cf. Gen. 22:1-19; Exod. 13:1-13; Deut. 15:19), and the Levitical family was consecrated to God in place of the firstborn (Num. 3:1-4; cf. 18:15-16).

21. Skinner, *Genesis,* p. 104; Gunkel, *Genesis,* p. 42, held the same view.

however, lacks a parallel to "fat." In this light Plaut's comment, "God's rejection of Cain's offering is inexplicable in human terms,"[22] appears obtuse.

Finally, is it not strange that if the narrator intended that Cain's sacrifice was disqualified for lack of blood, he does not mention blood with Abel's gift? Admittedly it is a negative clue, but when combined with the two positive clues, the mention of "firstborn" and "fat," it shouts out against von Rad's baseless claim: "The only clue one can find in the narrative is that the sacrifice of blood was more pleasing to Yahweh."[23]

Rabbinic exegesis also picked up these clues ("two expressions to emphasize that the oblation was the best of its kind . . ."[24] without mentioning "blood") and then exaggerated them, maintaining that Cain brought produce of the poorest quality. We cannot agree with Westermann, who negates these clues and draws the conclusion instead that the text merely speaks of God's immutability:

> Gott hat das Opfer des einen angesehen, das des anderen nicht. Das Gott das Opfer Kains nicht ansah, ist also weder auf seine Gesinnung noch auf ein falsches Opfer noch auf eine falsche Art des Opferns zurückzuführen. Es ist vielmehr das Unabänderliche damit ausgesagt, dass so etwas geschieht.[25]

Westermann's view represents God as capricious. Rather, Abel's sacrifice represents acceptable, heartfelt worship; Cain's represents unacceptable tokenism.

Witness of the NT

The writer of Hebrews says that by faith Abel offered a better sacrifice than Cain did (Heb. 11:4), a statement that tends to support the rabbinic interpretation. No text in the NT faults Cain for a bloodless sacrifice. To be sure, Hebrews mentions "the blood of Abel," but he has in mind Abel's blood, not that of his sacrifice (Heb. 12:24). Jesus' cleansing blood, he says, is better than Abel's blood because Abel's cried for vengeance, whereas the blood of Christ,

22. W. Gunther Plaut, *The Torah: A Modern Commentary* (New York: Union of American Hebrew Congregations, 1974), 1:46.

23. Gerhard von Rad, *Genesis: A Commentary* (Philadelphia: Westminster, 1972), p. 104.

24. Cassuto, *Genesis*, 1:205.

25. Westermann, *Genesis*, p. 403.

typified in God's sacrifice to clothe the nakedness of Adam and Eve (Gen. 3:21), cried out for forgiveness and provided salvation.

The Characterization of Cain

The Character of the Priest in the Pentateuch

The unity of the Pentateuch also enables us to discover, interpret, and validate clues regarding the brothers as priests. Leviticus 8–9, 26 teaches that the priest's character qualified him or disqualified him from the altar. An encroacher, be he Israelite or non-Israelite, must be put to death.[26] In this light, the statement in verses 4-5 that the LORD accepted one priest, Abel, and rejected the other, Cain, takes on new significance. Whereas the text explicitly characterizes Abel's offering, and more or less infers Cain's, it dwells on Cain's character, and more or less infers Abel's.

Cain's Characterization in the Text

Robert Alter[27] refined our interpretation of narrative by analyzing and classifying the following techniques used by a storyteller for communicating his meaning: statements by the narrator himself, by God, by heroes or heroines; verbal clues; juxtaposition of material; characterization; and consequences of actions. We employed the techniques of verbal clues and juxtaposition of material to discover the blemish in Cain's gift. The other techniques expose the deformity in his character.

The LORD said he is unacceptable: "If you [Cain] do what is right, will you not be accepted?" (v. 7). To this he added: "Sin is crouching at your door." After sin so dominated Cain that he killed Abel, the LORD cursed Cain even as he had earlier cursed his spiritual father, the serpent: "You are under a curse" (v. 11; cf. 3:14).

Note too how the narrator characterizes the sulking Cain as a sinner unworthy to worship. Cain's visible behavior confirms the LORD's privileged assessment of his heart. Cain's anger against God is written large on his face

---

26. J. Milgrom, *Studies in Levitical Terminology*, vol. 1 (Berkeley: University of California Press, 1970).

27. Robert Alter, *The Art of Biblical Narrative* (New York: Basic Books, 1981), p. 14.

(vv. 5-6; contrast Hab. 2:4), and he progresses in sin from deficient worship to fratricide (v. 8).

Cain's speech, disclosing his unregenerate heart, condemns him. His sarcastic question, "Am I my brother's keeper?" betrays both his callousness against God and his hate of his brother made in God's image (v. 9). He calls into question God's wisdom, justice, and love and attempts to justify himself, claiming: "My punishment is more than I can bear. Today you are driving me from the land, and I will be hidden from your presence" (vv. 13-14). Even after God mitigates his sentence (v. 15), he fails to respond to God's grace (v. 16).

As a *consequence* of his action Cain became a man without a place, an outcast from God's presence, from the ground, and from his fellowman (vv. 14-16).

Witness of the NT

The NT validates our conclusions drawn from the text. Jesus characterized Abel as righteous (Matt. 23:35), and Hebrews added that Abel, in contrast to Cain, offered his gift in faith: "By faith Abel offered God a better sacrifice than Cain did. By faith he was commended as a righteous man, when God spoke well of his offerings" (Heb. 11:4). According to John, Cain belonged to the evil one and was himself evil: "Do not be like Cain, who belonged to the evil one and murdered his brother. And why did he murder him? Because his own actions were evil and his brother's were righteous" (1 John 3:12). According to Jude, Cain spoke abusively and thought like an unreasoning animal: "Yet these men speak abusively against whatever they do not understand; . . . like unreasoning animals . . . woe to them! They have taken the way of Cain" (Jude 11f.).

Conclusion

Although the narrative by repeating the preposition '*el* with both the proper names, Abel and Cain, and with *minḥâ* syntactically distinguishes the brothers and their offerings, yet theologically, as suggested above, the two are inseparable. Elsewhere Yahweh rejected the gifts of Korah (Num. 16:15), Saul's men (1 Sam. 26:19), and apostate Israel (Isa. 1:13), not because of some blemish in their offering, but because of their deformed characters. Cain's flawed character led to his feigned worship. Had his mind been enlightened to understand his dependence upon the Creator, who fructified the ground, and the Redeemer, who atoned man's sin through Christ's blood, providing a basis for man's reconciliation to God, he would have offered not a token gift, but one from the heart, and along with Abel both he and his gift would have been pleasing to God.

The Dance between God and Humanity

It seemed fitting in this tribute to Professor J. I. Packer to write an article pertaining to "knowing God." More specifically this article aims to help Christians to know God in addressing wrongs through an analysis of the dance between God and humanity as presented in Proverbs 15:30–16:15, with a special focus on 15:30–16:3.

This essay will first present a translation of the text with a focus on isolated exegetical details, then develop its argument within a clearly defined literary unit, and finally offer an exposition of 15:30–16:3 involving theological reflections.

Introduction

Accredited theological reflection on Proverbs depends on an accurate exegesis of every detail of isolated proverbs and, if they are deliberately arranged into meaning-rich contexts of larger, unified blocks of proverbial material, on their literary contexts. If, however, the proverbs are only a random, haphazard accretion of isolated sayings, then each is an entity in itself and has no other richer meaning gained from its surrounding literary context.

Historically most commentators have occasionally noted groupings in the proverbs literature of chapters 10-29, but for the most part the larger

Previously published in *Doing Theology for the People of God: Essays in Honor of J. I. Packer,* ed. Donald M. Lewis and Alister E. McGrath (Downers Grove, IL: InterVarsity, 1996). Used with permission.

context created by such groupings has been ignored in the interpretation of the isolated proverb. In 1962 U. Skladny[1] set the stage for most subsequent discussion regarding the question of the arrangement of the proverbs into contexts. Skladny, by using analyses of form, content, and style and employing statistics to quantify his findings, further delineated smaller subcollections: A (Prov. 10–15), B (Prov. 16:1–22:16), C (Prov. 25–27), and D (Prov. 28–29). This analysis conformed in part with the obvious editorial notices of the book's structure in 10:1; 22:17; 25:1; 30:1. William McKane,[2] R. B. Y. Scott,[3] and C. Westermann[4] deny there is a context in the defined literary units literature. However, in 1968 H. J. Hermisson[5] carried Skladny's analysis a step further by trying to discern thematic and poetic unities in Collection A. In 1972 G. E. Bryce,[6] by using certain methods of French structuralism, showed that Proverbs 25:2-27 constitutes a literary unit. In 1978 B. W. Kovacs found Collection B, which he begins at 15:28, as the embodiment of a consistent worldview.[7] In 1979 R. N. Whybray showed that an editor deliberately chose the place of the Yahweh ("LORD") sayings in 10:1–22:16.[8] In 1984 R. C. Van Leeuwen[9] by structuralism, poetics, and semantics convincingly demonstrated that the proverbs in Collection C are arranged into larger literary compositions. In 1985 B. V. Malchow[10] pro-

1. Udo Skladny, *Die ältesten Spruchsammlungen in Israel* (Göttingen: Vandenhoeck & Ruprecht, 1962).

2. William McKane, *Proverbs: A New Approach* (Philadelphia: Westminster, 1970).

3. R. B. Y. Scott, "Proverbs, Ecclesiastes: Introduction, Translation and Notes," *Anchor Bible* (Garden City, NY: Doubleday, 1965).

4. Claus Westermann, "Weisheit im Sprichwort," in *Schalom: Studien zu Glaube und Geschichte Israels, A. Jepsen Festschrift,* ed. K. H. Bernhardt, Arbeiten zur Theologie 1, no. 46 (Stuttgart: Calwer, 1971), pp. 73-85.

5. H. J. Hermisson, *Studien zur israelitischen Spruchweisheit* (WMANT 28; Neukirchen-Vluyn: Neukirchener Verlag, 1968).

6. G. E. Bryce, "Another Wisdom 'Book' in Proverbs," *JBL* 91 (1972): 145-57.

7. B. Kovacs, "Sociological-Structural Constraints upon Wisdom: The Spatial and Temporal Matrix of Proverbs 15:28–22:16" (Ph.D. diss., Vanderbilt; Ann Arbor, MI: University Microfilms International, 1978).

8. R. N. Whybray, "Yahweh-Sayings and Their Contexts in Proverbs, 10:1-22, 16," in *La Sagesse de l'Ancien Testament: [travaux présentés au Colloquium Biblicum Lovaniense XXIX],* ed. Maurice Gilbert et al. (Louvain: Louvain University Press, 1979), pp. 153-65.

9. R. C. Van Leeuwen, *Context and Meaning in Proverbs 25–27,* SBL Dissertation Series 96 (Atlanta: Scholars Press, 1988; Ph.D. dissertation, University of St. Michael's College, 1984).

10. Bruce V. Malchow, "A Manual for Future Monarchs," *Catholic Biblical Quarterly* 47 (1985): 238-45.

posed that Collection D is an intricately arranged collection serving as "A Manual for Future Monarchs." The recent commentaries by O. Plöger,[11] A. Meinhold,[12] and D. A. Garrett[13] have attempted to interpret individual proverbs within larger literary units. Meinhold succeeds best in this enterprise, but there is still much work to be done.

Since 1968 rhetorical critics have developed the discipline of poetics. Their indefatigable efforts and numerous publications have shown that biblical writers, by which is meant also collectors, editors, and/or redactors, artistically gave unity to their work through such techniques as inclusio (i.e., marking off a literary unity by matching the end with the beginning), janus (i.e., linking sections together with a piece of literature that looks both back and forward), key words that stitch the work together, synonyms, paronomasia (i.e., all sorts of sound plays often connected with sense), repetition of grammatical forms, structural patterns often in connection with form criticism, chiasms (i.e., reversing the structure), acrostics, etc.

"The Argument" portion of this essay attempts to show that Solomon[14] used these techniques to give 15:30–16:15 unity.

A Translation

15:30 The light of the eyes[15] makes the heart glad, good news revives the whole person.[16]

---

11. Otto Plöger, *Sprüche Salomos (Proverbia)* (*Biblischer Kommentar Altes Testament* 17, no. 5; Neukirchen-Vluyn: Neukirchener Verlag, 1984).

12. Arndt Meinhold, *Die Sprüche: Teil 1, Sprüche Kapitel, 1-15*, Zürcher Bibelkommentare, ed. Hans Heinrich Schmid, Siegfried Schulz, and Hans Weder (Zürich: Theologischer Verlag, 1991).

13. Duane A. Garrett, *Proverbs, Ecclesiastes, Song of Songs*, New American Commentary 14, compiled by E. Ray Clendenen et al. (Nashville: Broadman, 1993).

14. For an accredited defense and definition of Solomonic authorship of Proverbs 1:1–24:34 see K. A. Kitchen, "Proverbs and Wisdom Books of the Ancient Near East: The Factual History of a Literary Form," *TynBul* 28 (1977): 69-114.

15. The reading of the Septuagint (LXX), *theōrōn ophthalmos kala*, "the eye that sees well," suggests to D. Winton Thomas the reading *mar'eh-'enayim*, not *mᵉ'or 'enayim* of the MT ("Textual and Philological Notes on Some Passages in the Book of Proverbs," in *Wisdom in Israel and in the Ancient Near East: Presented to Harold Henry Rowley*, Supplements to *Vetus Testamentum* [Leiden: E. J. Brill, 1969], pp. 286-87). He interprets the retroverted reading to mean "the pleasure of looking at" (see Eccles. 6:9). Since the parallel "good tidings" requires something seen and enjoyed, not the looking at something with pleasure, he repoints

^{15:31} The ear that listens to life-giving correction[17] dwells among the wise.

^{15:32} The one who flouts instruction is one who despises his life,[18] but the one who hears correction is one who acquires sense.[19]

^{15:33} The instruction[20] of wisdom[21] is the fear of the LORD, and humility [comes][22] before honor.[23]

^{16:1} [24]To a human being belong[25] the plans of the heart,[26] but[27] from the LORD [comes][28] the answer of the tongue.[29]

---

the form as a *hophal* participle, *mor'eh*, obtaining the rendering of the whole verse: "a fine sight cheers the mind as good tidings make the bones fat." Thomas, however, neither evaluates the paraphrastic nature of the LXX nor explains from a text-critical viewpoint how the MT reading arose. The LXX may be yet another interpretation of the unique MT.

16. Literally, "makes the bone fat."

17. Literally, "correction of life," a genitive of effect (Bruce K. Waltke and M. O'Connor, *An Introduction to Biblical Hebrew Syntax* [Winona Lake, IN: Eisenbrauns, 1990] [hereafter WOC], paragraph [hereafter not noted] 9.5.2c).

18. Or "himself." Traditionally, "his soul." *Nepheš* essentially means "passionate vitality" (see Bruce Waltke, *Theological Wordbook of the Old Testament*, ed. R. Laird Harris, Gleason L. Archer Jr., and Bruce K. Waltke [hereafter *TWOT*] [Chicago: Moody Press, 1980], 2:587-91).

19. Literally, "heart." The daghesh in *leb* shows the close connection with the preceding word (cf. WOC 1.5.4e). The LXX reads *agapai psychēn autou*, "loves himself," to create a suitable antithesis to "hate himself" (see 19:8).

20. The emendation of Perles (cited by Plöger, *Sprüche*, p. 179) and of Humbert (cited by Berend Gemser, *Sprüche Salomos in Handbuch zu Alten Testament* [Tübingen, Germany: J. C. B. Mohr/Paul Siebeck, 1963], p. 69) and accepted by J. Fichtner in *Biblia Hebraica Stuttgartensia* (Stuttgart: Deutsche Bibelgesellschaft, 1984; hereafter *BHS*), that *mûsād* "is the foundation [of wisdom]" should be rejected because it destroys the catchword connection with verse 32 (see exposition).

21. *Ḥochmâ* is probably a genitive of inalienable possession (i.e., something intrinsically proper to it) (WOC 9.5.1h).

22. The preposition entails a verb of motion (WOC 11.4.3d).

23. The LXX *kai archē doxēs apokrithēsetai autei*, "and the highest honor will correspond with it," may have pointed *'nwh* as *'ānûhā* (Ant. J. Baumgartner, *Étude critique sur l'état du texte du Livre des Proverbes* (Leipzig: Imprimerie Orientale W. Drugulin, 1890), p. 151.

24. The original LXX lacks the first three verses, perhaps because of the poor state of its Vorlage.

25. Literally, "belonging to a human being are."

26. A genitive of instrument (WOC 9.5.1b, d).

27. Or, "and" (cf. KJV).

28. See note 8.

29. Also, a genitive of instrument, a metonymy for agent.

^{16:2} All the ways of a person[30] [are] pure[31] in his own eyes, but the LORD is the one who weighs motives.[32]

^{16:3} Commit[33] to the LORD your works, and[34] your thoughts will be established.

^{16:4} The LORD works[35] all things to their counterparts,[36] even the wicked for[37] an evil[38] day.[39]

^{16:5} Everyone who is haughty[40] is an abomination to the LORD; be sure of this,[41] he will not go unpunished.

---

30. Genitive of authorship (WOC 9.5.1c).

31. *Zak* is singular to agree with collective *kol.* The adjective is derived from the root *zkk*, a bi-form of *zkh* (see KBL³ 258).

32. Literally "spirits/winds." Targum (Tg.) and Syriac (Syr.) probably read *'orhôt* (*'wrhyh*) and interpreted *tkn* to mean "direct," "order," "establish."

33. Syr., Tg., Vulgate (Vg.) *gal*, "reveal/disclose," imperative *qal* of *glh*, not *gol*, imperative *qal* of *gll.* Against the versions note *glh* in *qal* never occurs with *'el.* Moreover, "a fatal objection to this emendation is the *scriptio plena* in Ps. 37:5 (*gwl*) . . . ; also the sense of Ps. 22:9" (William McKane, *Proverbs: A New Approach* [Philadelphia: Westminster, 1970], p. 497). Although McKane has many excellent comments, his new approach to Proverbs is essentially wrong.

34. The *waw* with the nonperfective after the imperative signifies purpose or result (WOC 39.2.2a).

35. Gnomic perfective (WOC 30.5.1c) in this gnomic literature, probably not "made" or "has made."

36. G. R. Driver (review of M. Dahood's *Proverbs and Northwest Semitic Philology,* in *Journal of Semitic Studies* 10 [1965]: 113) argues *lammaʿⁿēhû* is a mixed form, consisting of *lammaʿⁿēhû* (preposition *lᵉmaʿan* + pronominal suffix), "for his own sake," and *lammaʿⁿeh* (preposition *l* + the noun *maʿⁿeh*), "for a purpose/answer." This is unlikely because *lemaʿaneh* is otherwise unattested, the antecedent *kōl* calls for a suffix (cf. McKane, *Proverbs,* p. 497), and the double determination (i.e., an article with a determined genitive [here a suffixed pronoun]) is unexceptional in West Semitic (Dahood, *Proverbs and Northwest Semitic Philology* [Rome: Pontificium Institutum Biblicum, 1963], p. 36; WOC 13.6b, p. 157, n. 40; cf. *Gesenius' Hebrew Grammar,* as edited and enlarged by E. Kautsch and A. E. Cowley [Oxford: Clarendon, 1910], p. 127i). The article probably protects the term against the unique reading *lᵉmaʿnēhû* (so Vg. *propter semet ipsum;* "for himself" [KJV], see 15:24; i.e., for the LORD's own glory; to vindicate his name [2 Kings 19:34; 20:6; Isa. 43:25; 48:11]). Tg. and Syr. understood the expression to mean "to those who respond to [i.e., obey] him."

37. Or, "to," parallel to "to its counterpart."

38. Attributive genitive.

39. With this verse the LXX closes its own series of proverbs.

40. Literally, "high of heart." The absolute form is *gabēah.*

41. Literally, "hand to hand"; the idiom thoroughly perplexed the ancient translators.

16:6 [42] Through[43] love and faithfulness sin is atoned for,[44] and through the fear of the LORD is the turning aside from evil.

16:7 When[45] the LORD[46] takes pleasure in[47] a person's ways, he compels his enemies to surrender to him.

16:8 Better a little with[48] righteousness than[49] a large income through injustice.

16:9 The heart of a human being plans[50] his way, but the LORD directs[51] his[52] step.

16:10 An inspired verdict is on the king's lips, in giving a judgment[53] his mouth is not unfaithful.

16:11 A just[54] balance and hand-scale[55] belong to the LORD,[56] all the weights in a pouch[57] are his work.

16:12 To do[58] wickedness is an abomination to the king, because a throne is established through righteousness.

42. LXX may have this verse after 15:27.

43. Causal *b* (WOC 11.2.5e).

44. *y^ekuppar* is *pual* and perhaps resultative, "to make atoned," though a denominative function cannot be excluded, "to make a ransom" (WOC 24.4a). The verb in all its uses is never used for picturing an actual process but always with regard to the result attained (Ernst Jenni, *Das hebräische Pi'el* [Zürich, 1968], p. 240).

45. Temporal *b* with the infinitive construct.

46. Genitive of agency.

47. The Hebrew verb, "to accept favorably," can take a direct object or be transitive via *b*. The English idiom requires the preposition (WOC 10.2.1c).

48. *Beth* of conmitantiae (WOC 11.2.5d).

49. A positive comparative *min* (WOC 14.4d).

50. Resultative *piel* (WOC 24.3).

51. Two-place *hiphil* (WOC 27.2a, b).

52. Genitive of inalienable possession.

53. And, "against justice."

54. An attributive genitive.

55. A construct override construction with these two closely related nouns (WOC 9.3b). In that light there is no need to emend the text as in *BHS* or with Toy to omit "just" in verset a (i.e., first half of bi-cola). The unusual grammar, though not singular (*pace* Toy), misled Jerome: "Weight and balances are judgments of the LORD," which ill-suits the parallel (Crawford H. Toy, *Critical and Exegetical Commentary on the Book of Proverbs* [Edinburgh: T. & T. Clark, 1977]).

56. Against Toy, who emends "LORD" to "king," Oesterley cites Amenemope 17: "The Ape sits by the balance, his heart is in the plummet; where is a god as great as Thoth, who invented these things and made them?"

57. Genitive of location.

58. The infinitive construct functions as subject of the clause and takes "wickedness"

¹⁶:¹³ Righteous⁵⁹ lips find the favor of kings,⁶⁰ and he⁶¹ loves whoever speaks⁶² upright things.⁶³

¹⁶:¹⁴ The wrath of the king⁶⁴ is the messengers⁶⁵ *(sic)* of death, but a wise person pacifies it.

¹⁶:¹⁵ In⁶⁶ the light of a king's face⁶⁷ is life, and his favor is like a cloud⁶⁸ of spring-rain.⁶⁹

The Argument

The pericope consists of three parts or sections: an introduction (15:30-33), the main body of YHWH ("LORD") proverbs (16:1-9), and a conclusion of royal proverbs (16:10-15).

Introductions to literary units in 10:1–22:16, as obviously in 1:8–9:18 (see 1:8, 2:1; 3:1, etc.), pertain to the wise who accept wisdom and/or honor their parents, which entails accepting wisdom (cf., e.g., 10:1; 12:1; 13:1; 16:16). Although each of the four gnomic sayings of the introduction in 15:30-33 can

---

as its object. The LXX, Tg. (see Healey), and Vg. agree in reading *'ōśeh* "the one who does wickedly," making clear that the wickedness of others, not the king himself, is in view. The Syr., however, reads "The kings who do wickedness are abominable," and the Zamora text of the Targum also independently interprets it as the king's own wickedness.

59. Attributive genitive. There is no difference in meaning between feminine *ṣ⁽ᵉ⁾dāqâ* (v. 12) and masculine *ṣedeq*.

60. Two MSS, LXX, Syr., and Tg. read "king," probably to harmonize with singular subject of verset b (i.e., second half of bi-cola). Vg. rightly retains plural, which links verses 12 and 13.

61. The syntactic disagreement between the plural subject and singular verb is common in Hebrew poetry.

62. For *qal* participle of *dbr* see WOC, p. 410, n. 39. The LXX *logous de* (Heb. *d⁽ᵉ⁾bārîm*) and Syr. *wmlt' (ūd⁽ᵉ⁾bār)* pointed the form as a noun, not a participle. This facilitating reading conforms better with *y⁽ᵉ⁾sārîm*, which normally means "upright people" (so Tg. and Syr., not LXX). Vg. reads with MT.

63. The adjective used as a substantive (8:6; Dan. 11:10; see BDE, p. 449 entry 3c). The substantive form *mêphārîm* is found in four medieval codices, probably to prevent the normal meaning "upright people."

64. Genitive of inalienable possession.

65. Form is dual.

66. Spatial *b* (WOC 11.2.5b).

67. The LXX reads *huios* for Heb. *ben*.

68. An alternative construct form (KBL³ 730).

69. Genitive of species (WOC 9.5.3g). Tg. uniquely reads "in a clear sky."

apply in isolation to many different situations, together they also function as an introduction to the carefully arranged proverbs that follow in 16:1-15. Though written in the form of maxims, these introductions praising wisdom aim to encourage the son/disciple to embrace the teaching and to adjust his life by them. These four proverbs are knit tightly together into a coherent unit by a series of "catchwords": the anatomical features, "eyes" (v. 30a), "bones" (v. 30b), and "ear" (v. 31); the root *šmᶜ* "to hear," represented by the noun *šᵉmûᶜâ* ("news/report") (v. 30a) and the participle *šomaᶜat* ("the ear that hears") (v. 31a); its compounds, *šomaᶜat/šomēᶜa tôkaḥat* ("hears correction") (vv. 31a, 32b); the noun *mûsār* ("instruction") (vv. 32a, 33a); and *ḥᵃkāmîm/ḥokmâ* ("wise/wisdom") (vv. 31b, 33a). The introduction and main body are linked by the catchword "Lord" (15:33a; 16:1b).

The main body (vv. 1-9), which is treated more fully below, coheres by the catchword "Lord" in either verset *a* or *b* of every verse, apart from verse 8. The other half of each of its verses pertains to humanity, though expressed variously as a "human being" (vv. 1a, 9a), "a person" (vv. 2a, 7a), "you" (v. 3), "wicked" (v. 4b), "everyone" (v. 5), and implicitly (v. 6). Other rhetorical features unifying verses 1-9 are treated below.

The conclusion (vv. 10-15) coheres by the catchword "king," which occurs in every verse except 11, and by the topic of living within the wise king's rule. These six verses in turn consist of three couplets. The first, verses 10-11, coheres by the catchword "justice," *mišpaṭ*, by the assonances of their initial words, *qesem* ("inspired verdict") and *peles* ("balance") and of their final words, *pîw* ("his mouth") and *kîs* ("pouch"), and by their theme (i.e., the Lord administers his just kingdom through his wise king). The second, the complementary antithetical pair, verses 12 and 13, is linked by "kings" (plural) in their versets *a,* which stand out against the singular form, "king," in verses 10 and 14, and by the stock-in-trade antonyms "abomination" and "find favor" (vv. 5 and 7) and "wickedness" and "righteousness." Both proverbs illustrate the practice of justice (cf. vv. 10-11) by the wise king's evaluations: negatively with reference to the actions of the wicked (v. 12), and positively with reference to the speech of the righteous (v. 13). Chiastically the verses begin and end with his moral tastes: "abhors" and "loves." The third, the antithetical pair, verses 14-15, brings the unit to a climactic conclusion by contrasting the king's wrath, which heralds death, with his favor, which heralds life. The same contrast is found within one proverb in 19:12. The last two couplets are linked by the catchword "favor" (the first word in v. 13a and in v. 15b).

Verses 1-9 present the Lord and humanity as engaged in a dance. Humanity forms and God performs. The inclusio, verses 1 and 9, binds this part into a whole through synonyms and clearly sounds its theme: the LORD's sovereignty over human activity. The hearts of human beings arrange their thoughts, the LORD effects their answers (v. 1); the hearts of human beings plan their course, the LORD fixes their steps (v. 9). Note the catchwords "heart" *(lēḇ)* and "human being" *('āḏām)* in their versets *a*, and "the LORD" in their versets *b*.

Verses 1-7 consist of two units (vv. 1-3 and 5-7), connected by verse 4, a janus verse. The first unit presents the LORD's sovereignty over human initiative, and the second, the LORD's sovereign justice over human morality. The term "janus" derives from the double-headed Roman god of doorways, who looks both back and ahead. The month of January, which looks back to the old year and ahead to the new, also derives from this name. Verse 4a presents the LORD's sovereignty over human activity, matching verses 1-3, and verse 4b his justice regarding the wicked, matching verses 5-7.

In this essay, we can only exegete and reflect theologically in more detail upon verses 1-3. Suffice it to note here that verse 5 asserts in the most positive terms that the arrogant are an abomination to the LORD and will be punished. Because the proud fail by their impiety in their relation to God, they also fail by their unethical activity in their relation to humanity. As the biography of Cain shows, when humanity fails at the altar, it fails in the field. By contrast, verse 7 asserts that as for those who please the LORD, the Sovereign compels their enemies to surrender to them. Sandwiched in between these two verses, verse 6 gives instruction on how both to atone for past sins and to avoid future ones: namely, by covenant fidelity for the former (v. 6a) and by fear of the LORD for the latter (v. 6b). Verse 8, "a better-than proverb," stands apart, implicitly cautioning that the LORD's justice is not effected immediately. The several "better-than proverbs" (e.g., 15:16-17; 16:8, 19; 17:1; 19:22b; 22:1; 28:6) link righteousness with poverty and wickedness with wealth and so make it perfectly plain that piety and morality do not invariably lead in experience to social and physical benefits. Moreover, many proverbs recognize the failures of justice. "There are many sayings," says Van Leeuwen, "that assert or imply that the wicked prosper . . . while the innocent suffer"[70] (e.g., 10:2; 11:16; 13:23; 14:31; 15:25; 18:23; 19:10; 21:6, 7, 13; 22:8, 22; 23:17; 28:15-16a, 27; 30:14). The very first pericope, 1:10-19, represents thugs sending an innocent person to Sheol. The calculus of the book of Proverbs

---

70. Raymond Van Leeuwen, "Wealth and Poverty: System and Contradiction in Proverbs," *HS* 33 (1992): 29.

equating virtue with life/prosperity and vice with death/impoverishment looks to a future that outlasts Sheol. Until then, "better a little with righteousness than a large income through injustice."

This interplay between humanity and God implies situations where wrongs must be righted. Humanity arranges its thoughts to address a problem, but the LORD answers (v. 1); they commit their deeds to the LORD, and he fixes them as part of his eternal plan (vv. 3, 9b). Be sure of this, the wicked will be judged (v. 5), and the righteous will triumph (v. 7). In sum, by representing the interplay between God and humanity, verses 1-9 present an "ABCDary" of addressing evil.

Exposition

Introduction (15:30-33)

The introduction consists of two quatrains (vv. 30-31 and 32-33). The first refers to "good news/report" (*šᵉmû'â*), as, for example, of the wise teacher (v. 30) and to the disciple's ear that listens (*šoma'aṯ*) (v. 31). The second pertains to "instruction" *(mûsār)*: flouted or accepted (v. 32) and elaborated upon as "the fear of the LORD" to be humbly received (v. 33). It bears repeating: these proverbs are applicable to many situations (e.g., the "good news" of verse 30 may refer to any good report), but together they also function as an introduction to the following collection. "The good news" of verse 30 refers more specifically to the wonderful report that God dances with the pure in heart!

The Good News Heard (vv. 30-31)

The favorable effects of good news: gladness and refreshment (v. 30). "The light of the eyes," literally, "the luminaries of the eyes," connotes vitality and joy.[71] The Old Testament repeatedly links light with life (Job 3:16; 33:28) and symbolizes life and good fortune by it (see Prov. 4:18; 6:23; 13:9; 16:15). These proverbs associate light and life with wisdom, suggesting that shining eyes belong to the wise (15:13a). His bright eyes "make the heart (of the one observing him [e.g., the son/disciple]) glad." Verset *b* shows that the wise messenger's joyful

---

71. Sverre Aalen, in *Theological Dictionary of the Old Testament*, ed. G. Johannes Botterweck and Helmer Ringgren (hereafter *TDOT*) (Grand Rapids: Eerdmans, 1974), 1:158.

and vital shining eyes complement his "good news." The noun glossed "news" occurs about thirty times in the Old Testament and refers to a verbal report of a recent event. Although in the historical books and prophets it is mostly used of "bad news" about battles — notable exceptions being the message the Queen of Sheba heard about Solomon (1 Kings 10:7) and glad news about the Servant's suffering to bring salvation to all (Isa. 53:1), in Proverbs it refers to the peace that good news reports have upon one. According to Y. Ratzhavi[72] the expression here and in 25:25 (cf. Isa. 52:7) reflects a blessing formula like that at the beginning of several of the Lachish letters, upon the one who hears the tidings of good (i.e., peace). If the son/disciple responds to the good news of 15:30, for example, he will experience peace indeed.

As the shining eyes of the wise gladden the heart of the observer, so the messenger's good news refreshes (literally, "makes fat") the bones (cf. 23:5). The parallels "make glad" (*yᵉśammaḥ*) and "make fat" (*tᵉḏaššen*) also occur in Sirach 26:13: "A wife's charms delight [*śimmaḥ*] her husband, and her skill puts fat on his bones."

The good effects of listening: abundant life and dwelling with the wise (v. 31). The proverb now shifts to the listening ear, implicitly admonishing the disciple to have an ear that readily permits itself to hear correction and to accept humbly its medicine in order to enter life (see 6:23) and to dwell forever within the honored company of the wise (cf. 15:12). The "good news" of v. 30 is also a corrective (v. 31) and "instruction" to make one wise (vv. 32-33). "All Scripture is God-breathed and is useful for teaching, rebuking, correcting and training in righteousness" (2 Tim. 3:16 NIV). "Teachability," says Crawford Toy, "is the key that unlocks the door of the sages."[73]

"Life" in this book refers to the abundant life in an unending relationship with God. In the book of Proverbs the noun "life" (*ḥayyîm*) occurs thirty-three times and the verb "to live" (*ḥāyâ*) four times. After analyzing its uses in wisdom literature, William Cosser draws the conclusion that "'life' in the Canonical Wisdom Literature sometimes has a technical significance, viz., the fuller, more satisfying way of living to be enjoyed by those who 'seek Wisdom and find her,' a sense which can be rendered in English by some such phrase as 'full life,' 'fullness of life,' 'life indeed.'"[74] The schools where

---

72. Yehudah Ratzhavi, "Clarification of the Blessing Formula in the Lachish Letters," *Beth Mikra* 33 (1987/1988): 454-55 (Hebrew).

73. Toy, *Critical and Exegetical Commentary on the Book of Proverbs*, p. 317.

74. William Cosser, "The Meaning of 'Life' (*Ḥayyîm*) in Proverbs, Job and Ecclesiastes," *Glasgow University Oriental Society Transactions* 15 (1955): 51-52.

wisdom was taught in Egypt were called "Schools of Life."[75] In biblical theology true life is essentially a relationship with God. According to Genesis 2:17, disruption of the proper relationship with the One who is the source of life means death. Wisdom is concerned with the proper relationship (2:5-8) and so with this life. God continues forever to be the God of the wise, delivering them from the realm of death (see Matt. 22:32). Clinical death seems to be only a shadow along the trail in that living relationship (cf. Prov. 11:7a; 12:28; 14:32; 15:24; 23:17-18; 24:15-16, 19-20). In the book of Proverbs life has the last word for the righteous, and death is the final end of the wicked.

"To dwell" glosses the poetic word "to spend the night" *(tālîn)*, connoting that one is at home among the wise and stays close to the source of life, ready to hear correction as the last thing before retiring and the first words upon awaking (cf. Isa. 50:4). The listening ear characterizes true Israel's relationship with God more than the seeing eye. In God's encounters with Israel he is always heard, but rarely seen.

Instruction Recommended and Explained (vv. 32-33)

Instruction flouted or accepted (v. 32). Verse 32 implicitly instructs the son/disciple not to rebel against instruction/correction, but to hear and receive it, because it is a matter of either loving oneself or of hating oneself, of life versus death (see 8:36; 15:6, 10). J. Gerald Janzen showed that the verb *prʿ* glossed "flout" denotes the value-laden judgment of "flouting of and rebellion against structures and constraints claimed (rightly or wrongly) to be foundational to the true and life-giving order."[76] In 4:15 the father admonished the son to flout "the false way masquerading as what is true and right,"[77] but here he cautions him not to rebel against the family's inherited wisdom (cf. 4:1-9). If the son does, he paradoxically also despises (i.e., "wants to have nothing to do with"[78]) his own life. By contrast, if he "hears

---

75. Antonin Causse, *Les disperses d'Israel* (Paris: Félix Alcan, 1928), p. 115, cited by Cosser, p. 52.

76. J. Gerald Janzen, "The Root *prʿ* in Judges v 2 and Deuteronomy xxxii 42," *VT* 39 (1989): 405. He errs in following Gerhard von Rad's identification of wisdom as the created order. This common error among academics has been refuted by Elizabeth Faith Huwiler, "Control of Reality in Israelite Wisdom" (Ph.D. diss., Duke University, 1988), especially pp. 68-69.

77. Janzen, "The Root *prʿ* in Judges v 2 and Deuteronomy xxxii 42," p. 406.

78. H. Wildberger, *Theologische Handwörter Buch zum Alten Testament* (hereafter *THAT*) (Munich: Chr. Kaiser Verlag; Zürich: Theologischer Verlag, 1971), 1:882.

correction," he "acquires sense" (literally, "heart") — that is, he gains the mental and moral capacity to live, as its parallel, "life," makes clear.

Instruction elaborated upon (v. 33). This instruction is an inalienable possession of wisdom and is equated with "the fear of the LORD," the essential religious ingredient for a relationship with God. As this writer argued elsewhere,[79] the "fear of the LORD" has a cognitive aspect (namely, the objective revelation of God) and an affective aspect (namely, the acceptance of that revelation out of awe for the Holy One). This notion constitutes a fitting transition to the main body, presenting the dance between God and people. Verset *b,* "humility," emphasizes the emotional aspect of "the fear of the LORD." Accepting this instruction has promise of eternal life (v. 31b) and of social gravitas and honor (v. 32b).

In sum, if the son/disciple accepts the good news/correction/instruction, including the truths about to be set forth, he will find gladness (15:30a), refreshment (15:30b), life (15:31a), the wholesome company of the wise (15:31b), good sense (v. 32b), the fear of the LORD, the *sine qua non* of wisdom (v. 33a), and social honor (v. 33b).

Divine Sovereignty over Human Initiative (16:1-3)

The divine sovereignty over human initiative pertains both to the disciple's speech, "the answer [*maᵃnēh*] of the tongue" (v. 1b), and to his "works" *(maᵃśēh)* (v. 3). Sandwiched in between these sayings is a proverb asserting that the LORD evaluates the motives behind them (v. 2). According to verses 1-3 human beings form, but the LORD performs; they devise, God verifies; they formulate, God validates; they propose, God disposes. They design what they will say and do, but God decrees what will endure and form a part of his eternal purposes. The time for the dance between God and human is struck in verse 1, "To humanity belongs . . . but from the LORD. . . ."

In other biblical theologies God takes the first step in the dance with humankind. According to the New Covenant, God changes the human heart of stone into a pliable heart of flesh that it may feel (Ezek. 36:26). The New Covenant superseded the Old in part because it is based upon better promises than the Old (Heb. 8:6). In the New, God takes the initiative and prom-

---

79. Bruce K. Waltke, "The Fear of the LORD: The Foundation for a Relationship with God," in *Alive to God: Studies in Spirituality Presented to James Houston,* ed. J. I. Packer and Loren Wilkinson (Downers Grove, IL: InterVarsity, 1992), pp. 17-33.

ises to open the heart and imprint the law upon it, whereas in the Old, Israel took the initiative and promised to keep law written on rock (Jer. 31:33; Acts 16:14; 2 Cor. 3:1-3). In Paul's theology God also takes the first step: "It is God who works in you to will and to act according to his good purpose" (Phil. 2:13 NIV). So also in Hebrews: "Jesus, the Pioneer and Perfecter of our faith" (Heb. 12:2 NIV).

Proverbs, however, is not concerned with this invisible first step of God. Instead, it is written for the children of the covenant, disciples, and represents them as taking the lead.

With Regard to Speech (v. 1)

The human initiative (v. 1a). The human being primarily in view is the son, for the proverbs were written for him (cf. 1:1-9) and, according to 22:21, he must give good and effective answers. He is referred to as an *'āḏām*, "human being," to differentiate him from divine beings and to connote that his potentialities and limitations are determined by God. Implicitly the son is addressing a wrong, and he needs to plan how to redress the grievance.

The noun glossed "plans" *(ma'ᵃrḵēh)* — note its alliteration with *ma'ᵃśēh* and *ma'ᵃnēh* — is unique, but its meaning, "arrangement," is not in doubt. The verb *'rk* denotes "to set things carefully in order" (like setting armies in array for battle [Gen. 14:8] or laying up wood for sacrifice [Gen. 22:9]) or "to produce a case (for justice)" (Job 13:18), or "to bring forth words" (Job 32:14). Its feminine bi-forms, *ma'ᵃrāḵâ* and *ma'ᵃreḵeṯ,* denote respectively "a row" (mostly the strategic battle line) and the carefully arranged row or stack of bread set out on the sanctuary table. Since the heart is the agent producing the careful and orderly "arrangement," appropriate glosses would be "thought-through plans" or "arguments." Every effective writer and speaker whom this writer has known, including the one to whom this volume is dedicated, carefully thinks through what he has to say before uttering it or setting it down on paper.

The sovereign response (v. 1b). The good and effective answer, however, is a gift from the LORD. Helmer Ringgren[80] rightly restricts "answer" to *"eine richtige Antwort . . . das passende Wort* [A right answer . . . the fitting word]." Unlike the English gloss, "answer," the Hebrew noun entails only a true and

---

80. Helmer Ringgren and Walther Zimmerli, *Sprüche/Prediger* (Göttingen: Vandenhoeck & Ruprecht, 1962), p. 68.

right response to a circumstance, not merely a verbal "reply" (cf. NIV). The noun occurs six times with reference to a wise "answer" that matches the situation. Job's three friends replied to him, but Elihu rightly judged "they did not find a *ma ʿᵃnēh* answer [i.e., 'refutation'] for him in their mouths" (Job 32:3, 5; cf. Prov. 15:23). An answer that hits the nail on the head is from the good and wise LORD.

In that light the son is free of ultimate responsibility in meeting the need he addresses, and all praise belongs to the Author of every good and perfect gift. The good and effective answer depends upon careful planning, weighing the arguments and arranging them, but also, above all, upon God's benediction. "These reflections," says F. Delitzsch, "seeking at one time in one direction, and at another time in another, the solution of the question, . . . are the business of men; but the answer which finally the tongue gives, and which . . . will be regarded as right, appropriate, effective, . . . is from God."[81] Disciples need to ponder their answer (15:28) and to subordinate themselves totally in faith to the LORD to make it effective in its style and substance. The many good things the wise accomplish with their tongues (12:18; 15:1, 2; 25:11-12) owe their success to God, not to themselves. Paul expressed this truth by an agricultural metaphor: "I planted the seed, Apollos watered it, but God made it grow. So neither he who plants nor he who waters is anything, but only God, who makes things grow" (1 Cor. 3:6-7 NIV).

With Regard to Motives (v. 2)

The proverb continues the theme of God's sovereignty over human activity and is linked with verse 1 by the catchword "LORD," by the synonyms for humanity in general, "human being" (*'ādām*) and "person" (*'îš*), and the human psyche in particular, "heart" (*lēb*) and "motives" (*rûḥôt*). The proverb contrasts a person's assessment of his actions with God's evaluation of his motives. The proverb does not teach that "men never condemn their own conduct" (*pace* Toy) or that there is basic conflict between the human and divine assessments, but rather, as Meinhold commented, that since people justify all their actions, conflicts of assessment will arise.[82]

The human evaluation (v. 2a). A person tends to assess "all [his] ways"

---

81. Franz Delitzsch, *Biblical Commentary on the Proverbs of Solomon*, trans. M. G. Easton (Grand Rapids: Eerdmans, 1970), 1:334.

82. Meinhold, *Sprüche*, p. 265.

(i.e., his conduct both with regard to speaking [v. 1] and to doing [v. 2]) as pure. When he becomes aware of their impurity, however, he must confess and renounce them and so obtain mercy (28:13). The word glossed "pure" in its four references to the cult refers to pure olive oil (Exod. 27:20; Lev. 24:2) and pure gold (Exod. 30:3; Lev. 24:6). In its seven occurrences in wisdom literature it refers to ethical purity. The metaphor "right" is used instead in the synoptic proverb 21:2. "In his own eyes," however, signifies that he is deluded in his evaluation of himself independently from God. The human being has an amazing facility for self-deception (cf. Jer. 17:9) and employs the poor standard of measuring his conduct by his own opinion of right and wrong,[83] rather than by the high ethical standards revealed in this book.

The divine evaluation (v. 2b). The LORD, however, weighs (i.e., gauges and evaluates) the person's motives by the standards of his own character, which are revealed in Scripture.[84] The metaphor derives from an ancient Egyptian belief that after death the human heart is weighed on a balance against Maat (Truth), represented by a feather.[85] Here, however, the evaluation takes place during the person's life. The word glossed "motives" is literally "winds," "breaths" (i.e., the dynamic vitality that moves a person [see 15:4, 15]), a synecdoche for a person's entire disposition (Ezek. 11:19; 18:31; 36:26; Eccles. 7:8, 9), the whole inner life (Job 7:7; Ps. 78:8), including his opinions or desires (cf. Ezek. 13:3), mind (Ps. 77:6), will (cf. Prov. 16:32), and motives (cf. 2 Chron. 36:22). What human being can weigh winds (cf. Job 28:25; Prov. 30:4)?

Since the final verdict as to the purity of motives belongs to the LORD, not to the doer, even though a person thinks himself pure, he must not praise himself or decide his reward beforehand but depend upon the LORD, who alone truly evaluates motives (Ps. 19:12; 139:23-24; 1 Cor. 4:5-6; Heb. 4:12-13). Furthermore, if he cannot judge his own motives, how much more should he not judge others (Matt. 7:1)? The best a person can do is to commit all he does to the LORD (Prov. 16:3) in order that his ways will be pleasing to him (cf. 16:7).

---

83. Cf. Kenneth T. Aitken, *Proverbs* (Philadelphia: Westminster, 1986), p. 247.

84. *TWOT*, 2:970.

85. Sec James B. Pritchard, *The Ancient Near East in Pictures Relating to the Old Testament,* 2nd ed. with supplement (Princeton: Princeton University Press, 1969), plate 639, p. 210.

With Regard to Deeds (v. 3)

The proverb now, using the second person of direct address, turns to "your deeds" *(maʿăśêḵā)*, admonishing the disciple to turn over the ownership of his planned righteous deeds to the LORD, that he may establish them permanently as part of his history that outlasts the temporary triumph of the wicked. Verse 2 cautions that the LORD is assessing the motives behind both our words (v. 1) and our deeds (v. 3). Verses 1 and 3 assume that the morally untarnished LORD finds them pure. Only pure words and deeds endure forever. When human motives are pure, the LORD integrates them into his fixed righteous order (cf. Prov. 10:22; Ps. 127). The faithful must not fret or worry about the effectiveness of their plans, or even about their purity, for that assessment and their achievements depend upon God, not us (Ps. 22:9[8]; 37:5; 55:23[22]; 1 Pet. 5:7). The best we can do is to resign ourselves to his assessment regarding their purity and to trust him to ratify or to veto them. Since only the LORD can bring our plans to fruition, their success can be credited only to him. The Egyptian sage Amenemope (22.7; 23.10), an approximate contemporary of Solomon, instructed: "Settle in the arms of the god." Secular man, who feels so confident in his own capability, paradoxically is plagued with fear. By contrast, pious people, who know God's sovereignty and their own limitations, live in prayer and peace.

The human commitment (v. 3a). This synthetic parallelism consists of a protasis, in the form of an imperative (3a) presenting the conditional situation, and an apodosis, presenting the consequence of satisfying the condition. The imperative glossed "commit" *(gōl)* literally means "to roll," for example, to roll a heavy stone from a well's mouth (Gen. 29:3, 8, 10). If we roll our burdens (i.e., our needs and concerns) "unto the LORD" *(ʾel YHWH),* then implicitly we roll them from upon ourselves (see Ps. 22:9[8]; 37:5). *Gōl ʾel* is onomatopoeic; one almost hears the rolling sound of the stone. Israel's sublime God can be trusted. Indeed, the proverbs were written to teach a life of faith (cf. Prov. 3:5; 22:19). "Your works," to judge from the parallel "your thoughts," refers to a person's planned deeds (cf. Mic. 2:1), not those performed (cf. Gen. 44:15). That distinction, however, may be too fine. Whatever the disciple performs he entrusts to the LORD to transform it into an eternal work.

The divine establishing (v. 3b). The root glossed "thoughts" exhibits two basic semantic elements: calculation and planning, "to think out, conceive, invent."[86] In verse 9 the personal and subjective elements are emphasized by

86. *TDOT,* 5:230.

adding "heart." "The reckoning and planning is to be interpreted subjectively as an internal thought process."[87] The verb "will be established" is also a creation term. However, whereas "thoughts" refers to inner creations, "established" (*yikkonû*) refers to the outward and overt bringing of something into existence. The meaning of *kûn*, glossed "established/fixed," can be assessed from the synonyms following it in the famous representation of creation in Proverbs 8:27-29:

> When he fixed [*bahªkînô*] the heavens, I was there,
> when he inscribed [*bᵉhûqô*] a circle upon the face of the deep.
> When he made the skies firm [*bᵉ'ammᵉṣô*] above,
> when he fixed fast [*baªzôz*] the foundations of the deep;
> when he set [*bᵉśûmô*] for the sea its limit
> — and the waters cannot go beyond his command —
> when he marked out [*bᵉhûqô*] the foundations of the earth. . . .

The creative works of human beings will come into existence as planned and be as firmly secure within history as the elements of the cosmos that the LORD planned and effected (see 8:27-29). In this way human beings participate creatively in salvation history.

Conclusion

Here then is good news: the LORD establishes forever as part of his eternal plan the creative words and deeds of the pure in heart in their overcoming of evil. When the disciple trusts the Lord to dance with him he will find gladness, peace, refreshment, life, favorable space with the wise, good judgment, a relationship with God, and social honor.

By learning the steps of this dance he also learns the "ABCDary" for correcting what is wrong:

A: Arrange your thoughts before you speak, then turn it over to him for your expression to be effective.

B: Beware of your motives; don't be so cocksure of your purity; God alone evaluates them accurately.

C: Commit your deeds to the LORD; then you will participate creatively in the salvation history that endures forever.

87. *TDOT*, 5:233.

It would take another essay to show that the LORD upholds his moral order (vv. 4-9) through his wise and just king (vv. 10-15). This ideal portrait of the king points to one who far excels failed Solomon, namely, the King of kings and Lord of lords, Jesus Christ.

Dogmatic Theology and Relative Knowledge

Dear Ian,

Congratulations on completing your Th.D. program. I thank God for your presence in the church with a depth of appreciation beyond my ability to articulate.

But now you face the option of teaching in one school that has a very detailed doctrinal statement, or another that is committed to the fundamentals but is an "evangelical open-market." Indeed, I confronted this same problem when I thought of coming to Regent. Let me share with you, then, some of my reflections regarding the philosophies of education with a more "closed" structure versus those with a more "open" one, and why I opted for the latter.

As you are well aware, theology contains many paradoxes: God is three persons, yet one. Christ is God and man, yet one person. God is absolutely sovereign, yet man is responsible. God is transcendent, yet immanent. God abounds in steadfast love and grace, yet in no way will he clear the guilty. The issue confronting us is informed by still another paradox: the faith delivered to us is eternal and unchanging, yet our understanding of that faith is relative and progressing.

The tension can be seen in Paul's admonitions to his legatee, Timothy. "Command and teach these things" (1 Tim. 4:11) balanced with "Be diligent in these matters . . . so that everyone may see your progress" (4:15). Again, "and the things you have heard me say in the presence of many witnesses entrust to reliable men who will also be qualified to teach others" (2 Tim. 2:2)

Previously published in *Crux* 15, no. 1 (March 1979). Reprinted with permission.

set against "do your best to present yourself to God as one approved, a workman who does not need to be ashamed and who correctly handles the word of truth" (2:15). The command "do your best" implies an amount of relativity and the capacity for progress in our handling of the revelation.

But the command to "teach these things" not only supposes these truths to be eternally normative but also supposes that we are able to comprehend in an absolute way some aspects of divine matters. Here we get into the thick of language and theology. Bavinck repeatedly stated that, since the Scripture is writing, it is subject to the fate of all writing. Thus the general rules of interpretation that apply to all literary work must be applied to Scripture as well. What counts here is that the message comes through. Luther, in his arguments with Erasmus, admitted problems with the words, but contended that the issues and the contents were clear. C. S. Lewis argued that there must be some knowledge that is not superseded or we would be left with change and not progress. He wrote, "If that (primary knowledge) goes, then there has been no progress, but only mere change. For change is not progress unless the core remains unchanged" ("Dogma and the Universe," in *God in the Dock* [1970], p. 45).

The crucial word, however, in this discussion regarding the relationship of absolute knowledge and relative knowledge in our understanding of an author's intention, is the word "some." Where is the line between essential, absolute knowledge of divine matters and relative knowledge within the truths challenging us to growth? The confessions of faith promulgated by the church in the course of its history show that we differ. It is amusing and instructive that the same year I left the seminary where I formerly taught, in order to find less structure, another faculty member left because he felt it was "too liberal."

Faced with this paradox, we need a philosophy of education. In short, my philosophy of education is that the confessional framework within which we teach and learn ought to be no more extensive than those truths that have been held in consensus throughout the church's history by those in the Protestant tradition who have accepted the authority and trustworthiness of Scripture. Assuming an unchanging core of theological knowledge, let me defend a more open, flexible posture for a theological institution.

In the first place this philosophy is most consistent with our *hermeneutical principles*. Our understanding of the literary forms of Scripture and the Oriental culture that gave it birth is ever expanding and being perfected. Relative knowledge is implicit within the grammatico-historical method of interpretation. All of us have had the shock of discovering that a favorite verse in the King James Version was inaccurate, and hence that we had been led into an inauthentic experience. I recall the astonishment of one of the committee members assigned to translate the book of Proverbs for the New International Version when he discovered that Proverbs 3:6 had nothing to say about guidance. He had taken as his life text: "In all your ways acknowledge him and he will direct your paths." But when confronted with the linguistic data he had to admit reluctantly that the verse more properly read ". . . and he will make your path smooth." Now let us suppose we had an article of faith pertaining to God's guidance based on this verse. We should then be left in the awkward position of having to defend an indefensible position. Furthermore, when we speak of "normative" interpretation, we generally mean "normative" in the Western view of things rather than "normative" in the Eastern way of thinking characteristic of the biblical writers. To cite a case in point: it is normative in the Ancient Near Eastern world to deliver prophecy in symbolic language rather than in literal prose. (Do not misunderstand me. I'm not advocating a "spiritual" interpretation of prophecy. But I am advocating greater awareness of figures of speech.) Because our knowledge of biblical literature and culture is ever progressing, sometimes even changing, we need a structure flexible enough to adjust to this new information.

In the second place, the *theological discipline as a scientific enterprise* commends this philosophy of education. It is important to remind ourselves that there is a difference between what God says and what we say about him. When we move beyond the core of essential truths, dogmatics is a lofty and difficult science, as a well-known theologian once said:

> That is so, in the first place, because of its purpose. It reflects upon the last things; it asks wherein lies the truth about our temporal and eternal destiny. And the arc of this question reaches from the morning of the creation of the world to the evening of the world at the last judgment; it reaches from the least, the prayer for daily bread, to the greatest, the prayer for the coming of the kingdom. (Helmut Thielicke, *A Little Exercise for Young Theologians* [1962], p. 27)

As in all science, we construct our models by which to understand the revelation and then seek to validate our understanding by testing it against all the verses of Scripture. Where the community of faith cannot agree that the model constructed satisfies all of Scripture, I think it best not to absolutize our understanding. Of course, we must always walk humbly.

A more open mind toward theological truth is also a *philosophical ad-*

vantage. We are well aware that the finite mind can never come to infinite truth. All of us are limited in our information of facts and in our ability to think logically. Therefore, we can arrive at conclusive theological statements only with difficulty. There was a time when I accepted as absolute truth every footnote in the *Scofield Bible*. Today I cannot accept over half of the notes on the first page of *The New Scofield Reference Bible*. I find the notes in the *Scofield Bible* extremely helpful, but we ought not to canonize those thoughts that have not been universally adopted. We all still see through a glass darkly. No one man or segment of the church knows as much as the church universal. This philosophy of education also has *pedagogic value.* We learn best when conclusions have not already been formulated. This is so in part because we are not as likely to run roughshod over the data in order to make them fit into our presuppositions. Recently I read a dissertation written at an esteemed conservative seminary (with a rigid and detailed doctrinal statement) in which the student only pretended to be inductive. In fact he was thoroughly deductive. He already knew from his doctrine of inerrancy how the New Testament writers had to use the Old Testament. He quoted as authoritative those that agreed with his opinion and disallowed those that disagreed; he cited data that supported his position but conveniently overlooked data that did not validate his hypothesis. The paper impressed me as a façade for scientific inquiry. His rigid mindset impeded real learning. Moreover, with a more open stance we can more objectively hear what others are saying and not be threatened by them. When confronted with options in the context I am advocating, the student can take each position seriously. I have not found the common caricature of learning "cafeteria-style," i.e., taking what you like, an accurate description of a more "open" type of school. Rather, I have found the students very earnest in their attempt to prove what is right and through honest interaction truth is internalized and becomes one's own, as Jack Rogers argued in *Confessions of an Evangelical,* p. 47. (By the way, I am not endorsing all that is said in this book.)

There is also a *spiritual advantage.* When men of faith who differ with one another have opportunity to minister freely and openly to each other, they are less likely to quench the Spirit. If we place ourselves in "closed" structures, we might feel compelled to defend a debatable position and thereby limit the work of the Spirit in ministering to us through other members of the same body. In a nonthreatening context we are more apt to be quick to hear and slow to speak. Recently in our faculty seminar on the history of hermeneutics a student read a paper on Pilgram Marpeck's hermeneutical principles. This original thinker in the Anabaptist movement contended for a community hermeneutic. John Howard Yoder, in "The Hermeneutics of the Anabaptists," *Mennonite Quarterly Review* 41:291-308, summarized the position thus:

> A basic novelty in the discussion of hermeneutics is to say that a text is best understood in a congregation. This means that the tools of literary analysis do not suffice; that the Spirit is an interpreter of what a test is about only when Christians are gathered in readiness to hear it speak to their current needs and concerns.

I am prepared to argue that theology is best done in a context of an open community, for there the Spirit of God has liberty to minister through each member. (I am not denying the centrality of the grammatico-historical method of understanding the text.)

This in turn leads me to say that such a context contributes better to the *development of one's character and personality*. A more private system of theology not exposed to critical appraisal from within may create a threatened personality. One must not generalize here. In my experience most theologians rightly hold their private interpretations with the deep conviction that they bear witness to the truth. But sometimes we subscribe to confessions before we have opportunity to think our way through the issues or before we have requisite knowledge. When caught in this dilemma, the theologian is more likely to feel threatened by opposing views and to be less capable of hearing another man's witness. I found the context to be potentially psychologically unhealthy.

Rigidity in matters that call for flexibility may lead a man into the temptation of becoming hypocritical, expedient, or behaving politically. Lest I be misunderstood here, let me underscore that some of the most noble and spiritual men I have known teach in institutions other than the more "open" context that I am commending to you for your teaching ministry. But I have experienced the temptation in a more "closed" context to feel threatened and to behave in a way that lacked Christian integrity.

This posture to theological education not only furthers the development of the Christian spirit, but it also furthers the development of the Christian mind. Academic freedom is necessary to the development of the critical capacity essential for the development of a creative theologian. If we want to develop relevant theologians we must not coerce others into our views or indoctrinate them. How can we hope to teach students to think critically in a context where the conclusions are already drawn for them?

Perhaps I can make my point best here by asking the question: Which context is most likely to publish this letter as an open letter for its students to read?

Finally, where we do not define our confession of faith beyond that which has enjoyed a common consensus we have the practical advantage of being less likely to expend our theological energies on less important matters such as modes of baptism, the state of believers and unbelievers in the millennium, etc. Hopefully we will spend more time confessing our faith in a relevant way to our hurting world.

I would be most pleased to hear from you and learn from your response to these reflections on a philosophy of education for teaching dogmatic theology with relative knowledge.

Your brother in Christ,
Bruce K. Waltke

Evangelical Spirituality:
A Biblical Scholar's Perspective

Christians define spirituality differently. For many Roman Catholics spirituality means the veneration of saints, the worship of relics, pilgrimages to shrines, the mediating and propitiatory function of the priest in celebrating the mass, and the propitiatory function of prayer. In some monastic orders the spiritual person is equated with the ascetic, one who dedicates his life to a pursuit of contemplative ideals and who, for religious reasons, practices extreme self-denial or self-mortification. For Pannenberg spirituality is the quest for self-identity, for human meaning through the Christian message. For some evangelicals spirituality is equated with exercising spiritual gifts, for others it is measured by souls won to Christ, and for still others it is the quest for self-improvement through sound doctrine.

Most evangelicals will agree with Augustine and Calvin that spirituality is best defined as love of God and love of man. Richard Lovelace wrote: "But the goal of authentic spirituality is a life which escapes from the closed circle of spiritual self-indulgence, or even self-improvement, to become absorbed in the love of God and other persons."[1]

This definition of spirituality is grounded in both Testaments. J. Gerald Janzen notes:

> It can hardly be doubted that the Shema constitutes the theological center of the Book of Deuteronomy: "Hear, O Israel: Yahweh our God,

---

1. R. F. Lovelace, *Renewal as a Way of Life* (Downers Grove, IL: InterVarsity, 1985), p. 18.

Previously published in *Journal of the Evangelical Theological Society* 31, no. 1 (March 1988): 9-24.

Yahweh is one; and you shall love Yahweh your God with all your heart, and with all your soul, and with all your strength" (6:4-5). . . . Every act of Torah-obedience finds its motivation, its purpose, and its criterion of appropriateness in Israel's love for Yahweh.[2]

"Love" in this treaty context, as William Moran has convincingly argued on the basis of relatively similar political documents in the Ancient Near East, means steadfast commitment, undivided allegiance.[3] It is an act of the will that cannot be coerced. Synonyms of love are "trust" (Deut. 1:32), "hold fast to" (4:4; 11:22), "serve" (10:12), and various expressions for obedience (11:1, 13, 22). Once allegiance is sworn, instruction is appropriate.

Note too that love involves the whole person. Commenting on the phrase "with all your heart (Hebrew *lēbāb*), soul *(nepeš)*, and strength *(mĕʾōd)*," S. Dean McBride writes:

> They were not meant to specify distinct acts, spheres of life, attributes, or the like, but were chosen to reinforce the absolute singularity of personal devotion to God. While syntactically the three phrases are coordinate, semantically they are concentric, forming a sort of (prosaic) climactic parallelism. Thus . . . *lēbāb* alone designates the intentionality of the whole man; *nepheš* similarly means the whole "self," a unity of flesh, will, and vitality. Most difficult is *mĕʾōd* since its use here as a substantive noun is a *hapax.* . . . Usually *mĕʾōd* connotes "excess, muchness" and it hence appears to function in 6:5 to accent the superlative degree of total commitment to Yahweh already expressed through the use of the preceding terms. Rather than a particular faculty, "strength" or the like, *mĕʾōd* evokes the fullest "capacity" of loving obedience to Yahweh which the whole person can muster.[4]

Jesus in Mark 12:29-30 reaffirms this basic command from Deuteronomy 6:4-5 and links with it the command of Leviticus 19:18 to love one's neighbor as oneself. This understanding of true spirituality also finds confirmation in the apostle to the Gentiles. Commenting on 1 Corinthians 13,

---

2. J. G. Janzen, "The Yoke That Gives Rest," *Int* 41 (1987): 256.

3. W. L. Moran, "The Ancient Near Eastern Background of the Love of God in Deuteronomy," *CBQ* 25 (1963): 78-84.

4. S. D. McBride, "The Yoke of the Kingdom: An Exposition of Deuteronomy 6:4-5," *Int* 27 (1973): 304.

Lovelace says, "Paul tells us that love is a far more reliable measure of spirituality than our gifts or works or theological acuity, and that it is one of the few things that last forever."[5]

Having defined spirituality as love of God and man, I will now develop these notions under the headings of "A God-Centered Life," "A Kingdom-Centered Life," and "The Dynamics of a Spiritual Life." The similarity of this outline with the one in *Renewal as a Way of Life* by Lovelace is not coincidental.

By "Biblical Scholar" and "Evangelical" in the title of my paper I understand my assignment to entail noting respectively continuities and discontinuities between the Testaments and continuities and discontinuities among evangelicals regarding these matters.

A God-Centered Life

Evangelicals will agree, I suggest, that foundational to loving God is faith in him, fear of him, and repentance before him. In this conviction they stand in marked contrast to the contemporary world.

Pannenberg notes that since the time of the literary figure Jean Paul (1763-1825) and the philosopher G. W. F. Hegel (1770-1831) people have talked about the absence or death of God.[6] In 1957, Pannenberg continues, Gabriel Vahanian used the phrase "the death of God" for his analysis of contemporary culture. What is meant by this talk is not a metaphysical thesis about the nonexistence of God but the irrelevance of God, the lack of experiencing God, in concrete experience. Modern secular culture, at least as it is represented by the news media, thinks it gets along quite well without God. Armed with technology based on scientific descriptions of the material and social universes, modern society aims to affect life and control the environment against the risk and contingencies of death and chaos. Modern man, who has expelled God from his universe, thinks he has achieved a relatively high measure of security in individual life through science, technology, and social engineering.

Contemporary theologians reinforce the contemporary *vox populi*. Pannenberg also notes that dialectical theology by its emphasis on the absolute transcendence of God, existential theology by its denial that God is approachable as a being in himself, and Paul Tillich by his theory that God is

---

5. Lovelace, *Renewal*, p. 18.

6. W. Pannenberg, *Christian Spirituality* (Philadelphia: Westminster, 1983).

absorbed into the world by disappearing into its "depth" — as well as other contemporary notions about God — all deny the possibility of a personal relationship with the God of Scripture.[7]

As a result modern culture and secular man have lost both God and meaning, sure values, and stable communities. Modern man, emancipated from God's revelation and traditional institutions, including the church and family, is profoundly afraid of the future and lonely in the present. Pannenberg elaborates upon the consequences of loneliness.

> As a consequence of this increasing experience of loneliness, fewer persons are able to develop a sense of personal identity in the course of their individual lives, and that entails the spread of neurosis. At the end of such a journey into loneliness there emerge the recourse to violence and error on the one hand, and the resort to suicide on the other.[8]

In sum, the world apart from faith in God is spiritually dead. By contrast evangelicals find spiritual life through faith in God. Although many evangelicals are not Calvinist, they will applaud Calvin's decision to root in faith the way in which saints receive the grace of Christ.[9]

All evangelicals believe in a personal God who enters into a personal "I-thou" relationship with those who trust him. In the Bible, and consequently for the evangelical who finds his knowledge of God in Scripture, God is not merely an inferred First Cause, or the hearsay of the saints met in Scripture and in church history, or an ideal of all that is beautiful, or even a system of divine matters, but a Person. Any other way of knowing God than in a personal relationship is idolatry. God walked with Adam, called the patriarchs, offered Israel at Sinai not an impersonal contract but a very personal covenant, and promises in the new covenant that the elect will know him. Jesus taught his disciples to address him as Father.

Evangelicals also agree that in both Testaments God is known by faith (cf. Hebrews 11). Evangelicals will agree with Calvin that faith arises from the promises of God:

> But since man's heart is not aroused to faith at every word of God, we must find out at this point what, strictly speaking, faith looks to in the

---

7. Pannenberg, *Christian Spirituality.*
8. Pannenberg, *Christian Spirituality,* p. 89.
9. J. Calvin, *Institutes of the Christian Religion* 3.2.7.

Word. God's word to Adam was, "You shall surely die" [Gen. 2:17]. God's word to Cain was, "The blood of your brother cries out to me from the earth" [Gen. 4:10]. But these words are so far from being capable of establishing faith that they can of themselves do nothing but shake it. In the meantime, we do not deny that it is the function of faith to subscribe to God's truth whenever and whatever and however it speaks. But we ask only what faith finds in the Word of the Lord upon which to lean and rest.[10]

Calvin finds his answer in God's promise of salvation:

It is after we have learned that our salvation rests with God that we are attracted to seek him. This fact is confirmed for us when he declares that our salvation is his care and concern.[11]

The Psalms, the supreme expression of spirituality in the OT, support Calvin's notion. These saints time and again latch on to God's sublime, merciful attributes revealed to Moses at Sinai (Exod. 34:6).

Evangelicals disagree, however, in their understanding of the object of faith. Dispensationalists contend that OT saints believed the Word of God relative to their dispensation, without specific reference to Jesus Christ. Reformed theologians believe that the elect in all dispensations, participating in a covenant of grace that transcends dispensations, have always had Christ as the object of their faith. Walter Kaiser seeks a mediating position: arguing that OT saints believed God's promise about Israel's becoming the national mediator of blessing, he disallows specifying that promise as Jesus Christ. Suffer me, if you will, to argue the Reformed position briefly here.

Adam and Eve believed in the Lord who promised the woman a seed that would destroy the serpent. Implicitly they must have looked for a second Adam, a heavenly man, to destroy this adversary whose origins are outside of the earth. Moses the lawgiver said that Abraham was counted by God as having met the righteous requirements of the law when he believed God with reference to the promised seed (Gen. 15:6), and Paul explains that that seed is one person, who is Christ (Gal. 3:16). Indeed *zera˓*, "seed," is a collective singular so that it includes all that believe in the seed who is Christ. As a result of this identification of the body with its head, Paul can

10. Calvin, *Institutes* 3.2.7.
11. Calvin, *Institutes* 3.2.7.

say, "If you belong to Christ, then you are Abraham's seed, and heirs according to the promise" (Gal. 3:29). Elsewhere Paul identifies the seed promised in the Garden of Eden with the church, presumably because of its identification with the seed: "The God of peace will soon crush Satan under your feet" (Rom. 16:20). Jesus said, "Your father Abraham rejoiced at the thought of seeing my day; he saw it and was glad" (John 8:56). The Spirit of Christ was in the prophets as they foretold his death for sin, his burial, and his resurrection. Peter wrote: "Concerning this salvation the prophets, who spoke of the grace that was to come to you, searched intently and with the greatest care, trying to find out the time and circumstances to which the Spirit of Christ in them was pointing when he predicted the sufferings of Christ and the glories that would follow" (1 Pet. 1:10-11). The gospel, says Paul, was announced in advance to Abraham (Gal. 3:8) and is according to the OT Scriptures (1 Cor. 15:3). Though not an evangelical, Gerhard von Rad as a biblical theologian expressed the truth in a classic statement: "Christ is given to us . . . through the double witness of the choir of those who await and those who remember."[12]

Old and New Testament saints differ only in the clarity with which they saw Jesus Christ. For example, while the OT saints knew he would be born of a virgin and would suffer and die for sin, they could not confess that he was born of the virgin Mary and suffered under Pontius Pilate.

Evangelicals also disagree about the author of faith. Arminian evangelicals locate the first cause of faith in the will of man; Calvinists locate it in the will of God. Again, suffer me to argue briefly the Reformed position. Christ, according to the writer of Hebrews, is the author and perfecter of our faith (Heb. 12:2). In sovereign grace God put enmity against the serpent in the heart of the woman who, left on her own, had sided with the devil against God (Gen. 3:15). Paul notes: "Rebekah's children had one and the same father, our father Isaac. Yet before the twins were born or had done anything good or bad — in order that God's purpose in election might stand: not by works but by him who calls — she was told, 'The older will serve the younger'" (Gen. 25:23; Rom. 9:10-12). He continues the argument, noting that God says to Moses,

> "I will have mercy on whom I have mercy, and I will have compassion on whom I have compassion" [Exod. 33:19]. It does not, therefore, depend

12. G. von Rad, "Typological Interpretation of the Old Testament," in *Essays on Old Testament Hermeneutics,* ed. C. Westermann (Richmond, VA: John Knox, 1963), p. 39.

on man's desire or effort, but on God's mercy. For the Scripture says to Pharaoh: "I raised you up for this very purpose, that I might display my power in you and that my name might be proclaimed in all the earth" [9:16]. Therefore God has mercy on whom he wants to have mercy, and he hardens whom he wants to harden. (Rom. 9:15-18)

Paul says that salvation is a gift, and he defines that gift as having the two faces of God's grace and man's faith (Eph. 2:8). Jesus says to the unbelieving mob, "No one can come to me unless the Father who sent me draws him" (John 6:44). And to the Father he prays: "You granted the Son authority over all people that he might give eternal life to all those you have given him" (17:2). Luke says that "all who were appointed for eternal life believed" (Acts 13:48), and Peter addresses his first letter "to God's elect . . . , who have been chosen according to the foreknowledge of God the Father" (1 Pet. 1:1-2).

Through faith all evangelicals find an inner assurance that they are the adopted children of God and call God "Abba/Father." Those who believe that faith is a gift are convinced that he "who began a good work in them will carry it on to completion until the day of Christ Jesus" (Phil. 1:6).

Evangelicals of the Augustinian and Reformed persuasion find justification and sanctification not as chronologically separate spiritual experiences but as synchronic and unified ministries of the Spirit that accompany his gift of faith. Arminian evangelicals, on the other hand, regard the Spirit's sanctifying ministry as subsequent to a person's exercise of faith. Evangelicals of the holiness movements go one step further and look for a second blessing as the *sine qua non* of spirituality.

Finally, in conclusion on this section of faith, let me return to secularism. While the evangelical radically distinguishes himself from his age by faith in Christ, secularism is having a very deleterious effect, especially on evangelical practical theologians. They are especially prone toward attempting to build the church through science and technology rather than through the Spirit and prayer.

The God-centered life also includes the fear of God. The necessity of fearing God in the OT is too well known to require much elaboration here. All know that "the fear of the Lord is the beginning of wisdom." According to Henri Blocher, "beginning" does not mean *initium* but *principium*.[13] Von Rad comments on Wisdom's slogan:

13. H. Blocher, "The Fear of the Lord as the 'Principle' of Wisdom," *TynBul* 28 (1977): 15.

There lies behind the statement an awareness of the fact that the search for knowledge can go wrong, not as a result of individual, erroneous judgments or of mistakes creeping in at different points, but because of one single mistake at the beginning.[14]

In sum, what the alphabet is to reading, and what numerals are to mathematics, and what notes are to music, the fear of the Lord is to wisdom — that is, it is fundamental to living life well.

But what exactly is the fear of the Lord, and what is its function in the life of the NT saint?

The fear of the Lord entails three ideas: (1) God's objective standard of ethics (2) accepted by saints (3) motivated by a healthy fear that God will keep his threat to punish sin. For example, in Psalm 19:7-9 "the fear of the Lord" is a synonym for the "law of the Lord" along with "the statutes of the Lord," "the precepts of the Lord" and "the commands of the Lord." In Proverbs 15:33 it is parallel to "humility." The saint, as it were, waves a flag of white surrender before God's high standards. He does so out of the healthy realization that the Avenger will right all wrongs. This fear is not contrary to faith in God's promises. Quite the contrary, it is part and parcel with it. Love, springing from faith in God's promises, and fear, arising from faith in God's threats, are two sides of the same coin: faith in the God who has spoken in Scripture. The unity of this faith keeps the evangelical from slipping into a cavalier servility and decadent self-surrender. The covenant-keeping God reveals himself in such a way as to combine fear of himself with promise of salvation. Walther Eichrodt helpfully writes: "The terrifying unapproachable God reveals himself as at the same time a leader and protector of his people, one who has bound up his gift of life with fixed ordinances governing the way that life is to be lived by the nation."[15]

Some evangelicals — citing 1 John 4:18, "There is no fear in love. But perfect love drives out fear, because fear has to do with punishment" — think that fear has no place in the Christian's spiritual life. Those who know better recognize that fear of God plays a vital role in spiritual life. According to the NT the believer must serve God "with fear and trembling" (2 Cor. 7:15; Eph. 6:5; Phil. 2:12). What John means by perfect love is perfect obedience. When we obey perfectly, obviously we have no fear of judgment. But, as I. Howard Marshall notes:

14. G. von Rad, *Wisdom in Israel* (London: SCM, 1970), p. 67.

15. W. Eichrodt, *Theology of the Old Testament* (Philadelphia: Westminster, 1961), 2:271.

It is sadly the case, however, that our relationship to God can sometimes fall away from perfect love, and then we need to be reminded of his judgment to prevent us from falling further into sin. As long as I love my fellow-men, I have no fear of the law which forbids murder. It is only when I slip away from love and begin to hate them that I need the fear of the law to warn me against letting my hate turn into murderous action and to exhort me to return to love.[16]

The Testaments, however, accent God's wrath and God's grace differently. Although the writer of Hebrews warns that it is a dreadful thing to fall into the hands of the living God (Heb. 10:31), he contrasts the age of law, which motivated conformity to God's standard by stressing fear of his wrath, with the age of grace, which motivates obedience by accenting God's love (cf. 12:18-24).

Scripture consistently links the saint's fear of God's wrath against sin with his or her flight to God's grace for salvation from his wrath. David's consciousness of his guilt in taking away Bathsheba's purity and Uriah's life prompted him to pray: "Be merciful to me, O God" (Ps. 51:1). Standing in the deep, black well of his guilt David looked up and saw stars of God's grace that those who stand in the noonday sunlight of self-righteousness never see. Jesus denied salvation to the Pharisees because they were confident of their own righteousness, but he offered it to the tax collector because he said, "God, have mercy on me, a sinner." The gospel cannot be understood apart from its promise of forgiveness of sins and redemption from the power of sin by the death of Jesus Christ. For Paul the preaching of the law must first precede the gospel. Otherwise a guilt consciousness would not arise (cf. Romans 7). The Reformers found spiritual energy in the doctrine of justification because of their experiences in the medieval cathedrals. Upon entering those cathedrals, Pannenberg notes, they passed between the wise and the foolish virgins at the portal and beneath the representation of the last judgment. Inside, they were often faced by Christ at the last judgment looking down upon them from the apse. Their agitated consciousness found liberation from sin, anxiety, and guilt through the gospel. Evangelical spirituality is rooted in the grace that teaches the heart to fear and its fears relieves.

Today, however, traditional evangelical spiritual energy is being vitiated through the critical dissolution of a guilt consciousness brought about by osmosis from the world. The effect of Nietzsche's and Freud's criticism on

16. I. H. Marshall, *The Epistles of John* (Grand Rapids: Eerdmans, 1978), p. 225.

the credibility of traditional Christian piety has been almost fatal. Allan Bloom says unequivocally that "psychologists are the sworn enemies of guilt."[17] Christian counseling may deflect itself to the false goal of trying to make people feel happy rather than to make them holy.

As faith in God leads to fear of him, so godly fear leads to repentance before him. "Before the mind of the sinner inclines to repentance, it must be aroused by thinking upon the divine judgment."[18] Typical of biblical thinking, Paul preached to the Athenians: "In the past God overlooked such ignorance, but now he commands all people everywhere to repent. For he has set a day when he will judge the world with justice by the man he has appointed. He has given proof of this to all men by raising him from the dead" (Acts 17:30-31). For some evangelicals, whose spiritual life is brain deep rather than life deep, repentance is nothing more than changing of the mind about Jesus Christ and is unrelated to fear of judgment and cleansing of the heart from sin. It is true that the Hebrew verb rendered "repent" means "return" and the Greek verb means "change the mind or the intention." But biblical repentance is more than this. Calvin defines true repentance thus:

> It is the true turning of our life to God, a turning that arises from a pure and earnest fear of him; and it consists in the mortification of our flesh and of the old man, and the vivification of the Spirit.[19]

He defends his understanding from Jeremiah 4:1, 3-4:

> "If you will return, O Israel,
>   return to me," declares the Lord. . . .
> "Break up your unplowed ground
>   and do not sow among thorns.
> Circumcise yourselves to the Lord,
>   circumcise your hearts, . . .
> or my wrath will break out and burn like fire
>   because of the evil you have done —
>   burn with no one to quench it."

17. A. Bloom, *The Closing of the American Mind* (New York: Simon & Schuster, 1987), p. 121.

18. Calvin, *Institutes* 3.3.7.

19. Calvin, *Institutes* 3.3.5.

Calvin comments: "See how Jeremiah declares that they will achieve nothing in taking up the pursuit of righteousness unless wickedness be first of all cast out from their inmost heart."[20]

Faith in God, fear of God, and repentance before him are all foundational to love of God because they lead to gratitude for his forgiveness. Ronald Clements writes:

> Throughout Deuteronomy there is a constant emphasis on the debt which Israel owes to God. All its life, both political and religious, is seen to depend upon what God has given to Israel. Consequently there is no part of this life which is not a cause for Israel to show gratitude to Yahweh, and it is this gratitude which the Deuteronomist regards as the true basis of worship.[21]

To ground Israel's allegiance in God's grace the lawgiver changes the reason for observing the sabbath from "Remember the Sabbath to keep it holy" (Exod. 20:8) to "Observe the Sabbath by keeping it holy. . . . Remember that you were slaves in Egypt, and the Lord your God brought you out of there with a mighty hand and an outstretched arm" (Deut. 5:12-15). The difference between the rationale for keeping sabbath in the two Decalogues is striking. The Decalogue given at Sinai commanded Israel to remember in order to sanctify the day. The one given on the plains of Moab expands on that command to advance Sabbath theology: Observe the sabbath in order to remember God's grace in redeeming Israel from Egypt.

The truth that love is based on gratitude entails two other truths. First, it entails that the elect love God because he first loved them (1 John 4:19). Lovelace states it well:

> The substance of spirituality is love. It is not our love but God's that moves into our consciousness, warmly affirming that he values and cares for us with infinite concern. But his love also sweeps us away from self-preoccupation into a delight in his unlimited beauty and transcendent glory. It moves us to obey him and leads us to cherish the gifts and graces of others.[22]

---

20. Calvin, *Institutes* 3.3.5.
21. R. E. Clements, *God's Chosen People* (Valley Forge, PA: Judson, 1969), p. 69.
22. Lovelace, *Renewal,* p. 18.

Second, it also entails that NT saints should love more than OT saints. They have more reason to be grateful. Recall Jesus' teaching to Simon: Of two forgiven debtors, the greater debtor will love more than the lesser (Luke 7:41-43). Whereas OT saints were vague about heaven and hell, Jesus plainly revealed the eternal destinies of saints and sinners. NT saints now know the full extent of both the canceled debt and the gift of eternal life. Commenting on imprecatory psalms Derek Kidner writes:

> There is "sorer punishment" revealed in the New Testament than in the psalms, simply because the whole scale of human destiny has come into sight. This is very clear from a comparison of Psalm 6:8 with Matthew 7:23, where the words "Depart from me, all you workers of evil" are transformed from a cry of relief by David into a sentence of death by Christ. The principle is the same: truth and lies cannot live together. "Outside" will be "every one who loves and practises falsehood." But it is one thing to be driven off by David; quite another by Christ, to the final exclusion which is also the climax of almost every parable in the Gospels.[23]

NT saints love more not only because they are aware they have been saved from sorer punishment but because they have a greater display of God's grace. God humbled himself in the OT, but never to the extent of dying for sinners. Finally, the full revelation of the doctrine of the Trinity in the NT exhibits and correlatively offers a model for love in a way unknown in the OT. Here the believer observes the Father honoring the Son and the Son honoring the Father, with the Spirit subservient to and honoring both.

A Kingdom-Centered Life

We turn now to the other quintessential aspect of true spirituality: love of fellow men. Evangelicals do not dispute the need to love the image of God (Gen. 9:6; James 3:9). Love of God and love of his image are inseparable. "If any says, 'I love God,' and yet hates his fellow man, he is a liar" (1 John 4:20). Christ says that all the specific teachings found in the law and the prophets hang on the two abstract commands to love God and to love one's neighbor as oneself. Many, I suspect, are not aware that according to the sages the wise man is very socially minded. The sages hone love for one's fellow to a fine

23. D. Kidner, *Psalms 1-72* (Downers Grove, IL: InterVarsity, 1972), p. 30.

edge. Love draws a veil over others' faults (Prov. 10:12), refuses to use one's advantage to disadvantage others (11:26), does not sing songs to one whose heart is weighed down with sorrow (25:20). The wise man knows that open rebuke is bad but that hidden love avails less (27:5). God will judge a man according to the way he responds to those staggering toward slaughter (24:11-12). Love directed to one's enemies reaps greater dividends than retaliation for wrong (25:21-22). The NT goes beyond even this with our Lord's teaching that we should wash each other's feet and, if necessary, die for one another, as Christ willingly died for sinners. He holds up the despised Samaritan as the example par excellence of a good neighbor.

Evangelicals do not agree, however, about the political structures within which this love should be exercised. Pietists give little thought to politics, but Lovelace points to the importance of community both in biblical theology and practical theology:

> Yet when we read the Bible, the kingdom of God is the central theme which ties together everything, both in the Old Testament and in the New. There is a reason for this. One of the ruling passions of humanity is the search for a righteous government. The poor and the disadvantaged contend against "the system" with the conviction that another economic order will make the world liveable. . . . This search is the "plot" of the Old and New Testaments.[24]

But what exactly is the kingdom? Baptists and Lutherans radically divorce the kingdom of God from the kingdom of the world. Calvin also clearly distinguished between the sanctifying activity of the Spirit in the church and in the secular realm of civil government. The process of regeneration occurs only in the individual, not in the community. Nevertheless in Calvin's view secular government is the expression of a general divine concern for the preservation of human society. Furthermore he recognized that it needed charismatic leaders endowed by the Spirit to guide it. Finally he calls upon all secular administrators to submit themselves humbly to the great king Jesus Christ and to his spiritual scepter and to effect universally the demands of the law. Puritans aimed not only at a social commitment to the Christian community but also at a theocratic reconstruction of the entire political order to enhance the glory of God. The theocratic thrust of the OT undoubtedly influences this aspect of Reformed theology.

24. Lovelace, *Renewal,* p. 40.

The Dynamics of a Spiritual Life

We now turn to consider the dynamics of spirituality both in its defensive posture against the kingdom of Satan and in its offensive posture within the kingdom of Christ. Augustine, with good biblical authority, divided mankind into two cities "formed by two loves: the earthly by love of self, even to the contempt of God; the heavenly by the love of God, even to the contempt of self."[25]

The saint must live within the earthly city and at the same time resist its three depraved spiritual dynamics: the devil, the world, the flesh (John 17:14-16). Since most evangelicals have more familiarity with these three deadly spiritual forces from the NT, the writer will highlight some of the rich teaching of the OT about them.

Genesis, after its accounts of creation in Genesis 1–2, exposes Satan as the source of evil in this world. The fast-talking serpent, met in Genesis 3, incarnates that diabolical spirit whose origins are not of this earth but in heaven. God pronounced all the creatures of this earth very good, but the archenemy of God and man is the epitome of evil. Moreover he knows the counsel of heaven itself. "You will become as divine beings," he cajoles the woman, "knowers of good and evil" (Gen. 3:5). After the representative pair had been blinded by this angel of light and had eaten the forbidden fruit, God announces to his divine assembly: "They have become like one of us, knowers of good and evil" (3:22). The heavenly deceiver of the whole world (Rev. 12:9) appears as a perfectly serious theologian attacking the mind. He does not dispute the existence of God but distorts his command and reduces it to a question (Gen. 3:1). This deceptive tempter slanders the goodness of God by alleging that God's commands are intended to keep humans from their full potential (3:5). According to him, God's commands are like bits in a horse's mouth, like barricades along the path. His hiss can still be heard in those who try to liberate humans from God's authoritative Word so that they become their own gods. Finally, our liberal theologian denies the threats of God's word: "You will not die" (3:4), he boldly asserts in direct contradiction to God's holy word.

OT saints conquered Satan by counting on his damnation. Every time they saw a serpent eating dust, the symbol of abject humiliation and utter defeat, they were reminded that God judged Satan and looked by faith to the seed that would destroy him (Gen. 3:14-15). That judgment found fulfillment

25. Augustine, *City of God* 14.28.

in the death and resurrection of Christ (John 16:11; Col. 2:15; 1 John 3:8). Like our Lord, his followers too prevailed over his temptations by authoritative Scripture (cf. Matt. 4:1-11 and Deut. 6:13, 16; 8:3).

We now turn to consider Satan's seed, the world allied against the kingdom of God. Israel encountered the world in the specific form of the inhabitants within the sworn land, known by the shorthand name "Canaanites." The "final solution" was the extermination of these depraved people. God allowed no peaceful coexistence with them because their corrupting influence was too powerful (Deut. 7:1-7). On the principle that a little yeast works through the whole batch of dough (1 Cor. 5:6), Israel was also commanded to put to death false prophets and even apostate relatives (Deuteronomy 13). The NT parallel to these commands is the doctrine that the holy catholic church must excommunicate "anyone who calls himself a brother but is sexually immoral or greedy, an idolater or a slanderer, a drunkard or a swindler" (1 Cor. 5:11; cf. 2 John 10-11).

With regard to the flesh — namely, the egocentricity of fallen human nature — the law clearly taught mankind's total depravity and warned Israel against self-confidence. Humility, the Augustinian virtue, is a constant spiritual requirement according to both Testaments. Shortly after declaring in unwarranted self-confidence that they would keep the law (Exod. 19:8), the Israelites demanded an idol and participated in a pagan orgy. Though they professed allegiance to God through outward circumcision, Moses said that their hearts were uncircumcised (Deut. 10:16). The very people to whom the law was given Moses accused of being stiff-necked (9:6), and he demonstrated their depravity by recalling their seditious unbelief in the wilderness, at Sinai, Taberah, Massah, and Kibroth Hattaavah (9:7-29). Likewise Paul warns the churches against self-improvement. Only participation in the covenant of grace avails. According to this covenant arrangement, God out of unmerited love to sinners grants the elect regeneration, defined by J. I. Packer as "that irrevocable work of grace whereby through union with Christ one's heart is changed and faith is born, never to die."[26] Out of hearts born from above the elect know God, know the forgiveness of sins, and have the law written on their hearts (Jer. 31:31-33). The patriarchs and true Israel must have participated in that covenant, for apart from God's grace all are sinners. None are declared righteous by keeping the law (Rom. 3:9-20).

I now turn to consider the positive spiritual dynamics operative within the kingdom of God. I have already mentioned justification and sanctifica-

---

26. J. I. Packer, *Keeping in Step with the Spirit* (Old Tappan, NJ: Revell, 1984), p. 123.

tion, which Lovelace lists among "primary elements of continuous re-newal."[27] Here I wish to treat briefly the law, the Spirit, and the sacraments. Had I more time and space I would certainly go on to missions and prayer.

Jonathan Edwards said of the law, "There is perhaps no part of divinity attended with so much intricacy, and wherein orthodox divines do so much differ as stating the precise agreement and difference between the two dis-pensations of Moses and Christ."[28]

How can it be, for example, that the psalmist found the law to be a tree of life (cf. Psalm 1) whereas Paul found it a sword of death (cf. Romans 7)? The difference is partially due to the fact that the pious psalmist was an elect saint already participating in the provisions of the everlasting covenant (cf. Jer. 31:31-34): He knew God (Ps. 9:10), had a regenerate heart (119:11), and knew the forgiveness of sin (32:1). Paul, on the other hand, was part of that elect nation that was circumcised in the flesh but not in heart, that was striv-ing to justify and sanctify itself through the law apart from the Spirit and faith. For sinners the hammer-blows of the law forge them into saints by driving them to the gospel of redemption. For saints, by contrast, the law is more therapeutic and sweeter than honey, than honey from the comb (19:10). For unregenerate sinners, gospel follows law; for regenerate saints, law and gospel are inseparable as they fulfill the law both in their justifica-tion and sanctification through faith in Christ.

The dynamics of the spiritual life of OT saints can be encapsulated as "Torah piety." They knew God through the law. A recent study by Gerald H. Wilson argues convincingly that the Psalter has been edited to set forth Da-vid as an exemplar, a model, for the saint's response to life's conflicts, crises, and victories.[29] In this light Leslie Allen calls attention to numerous and striking parallels between Psalm 18, where David serves as a role model in relying on God in distress, and Psalm 19, where David finds the dynamics of spirituality in the law:

> What is postulated of Yahweh in Ps 18 is in three cases applied to his To-rah in Ps 19, in a chiastic order. Yahweh shows himself pure (18:27[26]), and the Torah is pure (19:9[8]). Yahweh gives light (18:29[28]) and so

27. R. F. Lovelace, *Dynamics of Spiritual Life* (Downers Grove, IL: InterVarsity, 1979).

28. Cited in D. P. Fuller, *Gospel and Law: Contrast or Continuum?* (Grand Rapids: Eerdmans, 1980), pp. 5-6, and in M. W. Karlberg, "Legitimate Discontinuities Between the Testaments," *JETS* 28 (1985): 10.

29. G. H. Wilson, *The Editing of the Hebrew Psalter* (SBLDS 76; Chico, CA: Scholars, 1985).

does his Torah in turn (19:9[8]). Yahweh's way is perfect (18:31[30]) and so is the Torah (19:8[7]).[30]

More specifically the sage in Proverbs 2 spells out the psychological dynamics for mediating the wisdom of God into the heart of the saint (see vv. 6, 10). The dynamics are both passive (acceptance of the word in the heart, storing it up with delight through memorization, and attentiveness to its reading, vv. 1-2), and aggressive (crying out for it with the voice and searching for it as for hidden treasure with the eye, vv. 3-4).

The spiritual reception of authoritative, canonical Scripture also operates powerfully in developing the spiritual life of the NT saint. Jesus prayed: "Sanctify them by the truth; your word is truth" (John 17:17). Paul equated being full of the Spirit with being full of the Word of Christ (cf. Eph. 5:18 with Col. 3:16), and Peter, after noting that the living and enduring word of God birthed the young church, admonished it to crave pure spiritual milk that thereby it may grow up in salvation (1 Pet. 1:23–2:2).

As noted above, salvation occurs only as the saint receives Christ clothed in the gospel. Though the law is holy, just, and good, it cannot deliver sinners from the grip of sin. In fact, apart from gospel it tightens its stranglehold on them by condemning their consciences and deluding them into a sense of self-improvement.

The Spirit's ministry must accompany the gospel. God's kingdom has always been formed by preaching the gospel in the Spirit. But just as the gospel came in shadows and types to the OT saint and not in the full revelation in Christ Jesus, so also the ministry of the Spirit is in a penumbra in the OT in contrast to the full knowledge of his ministry in the NT. In the OT the Spirit is mentioned seventy-eight times and about half of those with reference to the new age. In the NT he is mentioned 244 times. In sum, the Spirit is mentioned about 15 percent of the time with reference to the old dispensation and 85 percent of the time with reference to the new. Nevertheless, though the Spirit's ministries are concealed, Leon Wood is certainly correct in arguing that the Spirit must have regenerated and sanctified OT saints.[31]

But the ministry of the Spirit in the two dispensations differs more than epistemologically; it also differs ontologically. In his upper-room discourse (John 14–16) Christ fortified his incipient church with the promise

30. L. C. Allen, "David as Exemplar of Spirituality: The Redactional Function of Psalm 19," *Bib* 67 (1986): 546.

31. L. Wood, *The Holy Spirit in the Old Testament* (Grand Rapids: Zondervan, 1976).

that he would continue with them in the form of the Spirit and correlatively with greater power than they or any saint had theretofore known. That promise was fulfilled when the ascended Christ gave his church the Holy Spirit, also called the Spirit of Christ because Christ administers the Spirit to the church. Prior to Pentecost saints were like children governed by law; after Pentecost they attain full maturity in the freedom of the Spirit (Gal. 3:25–4:7). NT saints, in contrast to the OT, count on the indwelling Holy Spirit to become like Christ and to continue his ministry that ushered in the new age. Christ promised that when the Spirit was given they would have power to establish the kingdom of God universally (Acts 1:8). History has validated his promise.

The insistence on a subsequent "baptism of the Holy Spirit" after regeneration was developed on the basis of experience and isolated texts (e.g., Acts 8:14-17) and not on biblical theology. J. I. Packer argues convincingly against the Wesleyan doctrine of Christian perfection, the belief that the Spirit subsequent to regeneration eradicates in one single moment every motive from the Christian's heart except love. That doctrine lacks conclusive biblical proof, has an unrealistic theological rationale, leads to unedifying practical implications, and contradicts Romans 7:14-25.[32] Packer also effectively critiques the halfway house of Wesleyan perfection, the Keswick teaching that from the inner passivity of looking to Christ to do everything will issue a perfection of performance. His criticism includes among other arguments (1) its Arminian distinction that parceled out salvation in two distinct gift packages (Christ's work as justifier from sin's guilt, and his work as sanctifier from sin's power) and (2) its inadequate exegesis of Romans 6.[33] Though pentecostalism, Wesleyanism, and Keswick teaching were intended to enhance spirituality, they impede it for many by creating false expectations, false guilt, and inauthenticity. On the other hand, the Reformed doctrine that the extraordinary gifts of the Spirit ceased in the final period of canonical revelation, a doctrine that I confess, must be validated by an appeal to history (e.g., the dead are not raised now) and may lead to spiritual deadness by reducing Christianity to a rational system of thought rather than maximizing and realizing the essential ministry of the Holy Spirit in life.

In sum, ideally the saint ever grows in sanctification and power through Spirit and Scripture. It is mischievous to pit them against one another. In this way the humble and believing saint is ever pressing toward the

---

32. Packer, *Keeping in Step*, pp. 145-63.
33. Packer, *Keeping in Step*, pp. 145-63.

mark of his high calling in Christ Jesus, but never attaining it before the redemption of his body in the final resurrection.

Finally, I turn to the sacraments. Pagans sought to re-create life through myth and ritual magically enacted. By contrast OT saints in a partial manner and measure had access to and communion with the enjoyment of the higher world through sacred personnel such as the high priest, sacred seasons such as Passover, sacred sites such as Mount Zion, and sacred actions and institutions such as sacrifice. Paul says that Israel drank from the spiritual rock that accompanied them, and that rock was Christ (1 Cor. 10:4). These symbols not only assisted mightily in the love and worship of God but also formed a community in fellowship with God and with one another. As a flag, national holidays, and national anthem bind a nation together, these symbols bound Israel together as a community of love and justice under God.

But the symbols in the OT, which on the vertical axis gave partial access to Christ and the higher world, also veiled the heavenly reality. F. F. Bruce states:

> For all the impressive solemnity of the sacrificial ritual and the sacerdotal ministry, no real peace of conscience was procured thereby, no immediate access to God. . . . The whole apparatus of worship associated with that ritual and priesthood was calculated rather to keep at a distance from God than to bring them near.[34]

On a synchronic, vertical axis these earthly symbols partially mediated heavenly realities to OT saints, but on the diachronic, horizontal axis they functioned as types pointing to the higher world that, as Geerhardus Vos expresses it, "has now been let down and thrown open to our full knowledge and possession."[35] They assist NT saints in understanding Christ and their heavenly orientation and intensify their awareness of the greatness of the present age, filling them with joyful exuberance and gratitude.

In place of the OT types Christ instituted the sacraments — baptism and the Lord's supper — enabling the church in *signum efficax* to experience and feed upon the foundational reality, the death and resurrection of Christ, that constitutes them as a community in Christ, serving God, one another,

---

34. F. F. Bruce, *Epistle to the Hebrews* (Grand Rapids: Eerdmans, 1964), pp. 148-49.

35. G. Vos, *Redemptive History and Biblical Interpretation* (Phillipsburg: Presbyterian and Reformed, 1980), p. 199.

and the nations. Regrettably, since the holy sacraments have been seen as divisive, evangelicals have tended to minimize their efficacy.

Through baptism the church recognizes that it has been saved from the condemned world even as Noah was saved from his world through the flood and that, having died to that world, it now lives in newness of resurrected life with its living Head who died for sinners.

In his "Sermon on the Sacrament of the Holy and True Body of Christ," Luther noted that the meaning of this sacrament is a twofold communion: (1) the communion of believers with Christ, and (2) the communion among all those who enjoy such unity with Christ, thus forming the one body of Christ. Luther even reapplied a powerful image from the *Didachē* (9:4): As many grains of wheat come together to form the single loaf of bread that is being broken and distributed in the sacrament, so the faithful are joined together in the sacrament to form one bread, one cup, one body in communion with Christ.[36] The power of that symbol is not only communal, it is also eschatological: It confirms the social destiny of the Church. Pannenberg writes:

> The human predicament of social life is not ultimately realized in the present political order of society, but is celebrated in the worship of the church, if only in the form of the symbolic presence of the kingdom to come. The awareness that in the liturgy of the church there is symbolically present what all social and political struggle is about without its definite achievement, is absolutely crucial to the significance of the eucharistic liturgy. Without this dimension, the eucharistic liturgy degenerates into a self-contained, ecclesiocentric ritual, if not into a self-delusive reassurance of private participating in the salvation acquired by Jesus Christ.[37]

That note about the eschatological social destiny of the church, when the kingdom of God is coextensive with creation and wherein the Lamb is the glory, is a good note on which to conclude this essay.

---

36. Cited by Pannenberg, *Spirituality*, p. 39.
37. Pannenberg, *Spirituality*, p. 47.

The Fear of the Lord: The Foundation for a Relationship with God

Dr. James Houston, Regent College's distinguished founder and professor of spiritual theology, succinctly defined "the fear of the Lord" as a combination of a person's spiritual and rational responses to God's revealed will. He wrote: "'Fear of the Lord' expresses the knowledge of the will of God in that it entails both awareness of it and whole-hearted response to it."[1] He further noted in the same discussion on "living wisely before the Creator" that "fear, or reverence for God, is also associated with both distance as awe, even a holy terror, and with proximity and communion."[2] In this essay I aim to honor my dear friend and edify the church by honing the definition of the syntagms (a syntagm is a series of linguistic elements forming distinctive syntactic units)[3] that involve the Hebrew root *yr'*, "fear," + the direct objects "Lord" and "God," or their surrogates such as "Name," pronouns for the Deity, etc. For economy I will sometimes lump together these syntagms under the rubric "fear of the Lord." Though I did not set out to validate Dr. Houston's succinct statements about this linguistic formula, my essay in fact does so.

---

1. James M. Houston, *I Believe in the Creator* (Grand Rapids: Eerdmans, 1980), p. 188.
2. Houston, *I Believe in the Creator*, p. 189.
3. Bruce K. Waltke and M. O'Connor, *Introduction to Biblical Hebrew Syntax* (Winona Lake, IN: Eisenbrauns, 1990), p. 52.

Previously published in *Alive to God: Studies in Spirituality*, ed. J. I. Packer and Loren Wilkinson (Vancouver: Regent College Publishing, 1992). Reprinted with permission.

Expressions Involving "Fear of the Lord"

One important syntagm is *yir'at yhwh*, "the fear of the Lord,"[4] consisting of the feminine verbal noun *yir'at* bound together with its objective genitive, *yhwh*.[5] It occurs twenty-one or twenty-two times, mostly in wisdom literature: fourteen times in Proverbs,[6] thrice in Isaiah in parallel with other terms for wisdom,[7] three times in the hymns,[8] once in Chronicles in connection with Jehoshaphat's instructions to Israel's administrators,[9] and possibly, though not probably, once in Job 28:28 where many, but not the majority, of manuscripts attest it.

The Deuteronomic and Deuteronomistic literature uniformly uses a verbal form of *yir'*, typically the infinitive construct in Deuteronomy, with the direct object Yahweh or its surrogates, such as a pronoun or Name. This syntagm occurs thirty-three times in this literature,[10] and twenty-nine times outside of it.[11]

The so-called Holiness Code contains five occurrences of the syntagm "You will fear your God; I am Yahweh."[12]

The singular or plural verbal adjective, *yārē'*, in construct with Yahweh or its equivalents (i.e., "who fear Yahweh") occurs eighteen times.[13] H. F. Fuhs[14] arbitrarily takes the genitive in this construction as a possessive genitive (i.e., "the worshipers who belong to Yahweh," not "those who worship

---

4. All Scriptural citations in this essay refer to the Hebrew text. The English reference may differ by one verse.

5. Waltke and O'Connor, *Introduction to Biblical Hebrew Syntax*, p. 146.

6. Prov. 1:7, 29; 2:5; 8:13; 9:10; 10:27; 14:26, 27; 15:16, 33; 16:6; 19:23; 22:4; 23:17.

7. Isa. 11:2, 3; 33:6.

8. Ps. 19:10; 111:10; 34:11, a thanksgiving song with wisdom instruction.

9. 2 Chron. 19:9.

10. Deut. 4:10; 5:29 (26); 6:2, 13, 24; 8:6; 10:12, 20; 13:5; 14:23; 17:19; 28:58; 31:12, 13; Josh. 4:24; 24:14; Judg. 6:10; 1 Sam. 12:14, 24; 1 Kings 8:40, 43 parallel 2 Chron. 6:31, 33; 2 Kings 17:7, 25, 28, 32, 33, 34, 36, 39, 41 (cf. vv. 35, 37, 38 where the syntagm refers to other gods); Neh. 1:11 is an echo of Deuteronomistic literature.

11. 1 Sam. 12:18, 24; 2 Sam. 6:9 parallel to 1 Chron. 13:12; 1 Kings 18:3, 12; 2 Kings 4:1; Isa. 25:3; 57:11; 59:19; Jer. 5:24; 10:7; 26:19; 32:39; Hos. 10:3; Zeph. 3:7; Mal. 2:5; 3:5 (with reference to *yhwh ṣᵉbā'ot*); Ps. 34:10; 67:8; 72:5 (text?); 86:11; 112:1; 119:63; Job 1:9; Prov. 3:7; 14:27; Neh. 1:11; 2 Chron. 6:31.

12. Lev. 19:14, 32: 25:17, 36, 43.

13. Isa. 50:10; Ps. 15:4; 22:24; 25:10, 12; 61:6; 115:11, 13; 118:4; 128:1, 4; 135:20; 145:19; Mal. 3:16, 20; Prov. 14:2; 31:30.

14. H. F. Fuhs, "*yr'*," *TDOT* 6:308-9.

Yahweh"), but this is unlikely in light of the consistent use of Yahweh in the other expressions as an object of the verbal action "to fear." Also, construing it as an objective genitive is consistent with the use of the verb *yr'* with Yahweh as object in Psalms 34:10, 86:11, and 130:4 and in other contexts pertaining to worship (e.g., Isa. 63:17; Hos. 10:3).

yir'at 'ᵉlōhîm, "fear of God," or its surrogates, occurs seven times;[15] the verb *yr'* + *'lhym* as direct object, "to fear God," twelve times;[16] and the verbal adjective of *yārē'* in construct with *'ᵉlōhîm*, "who fear God," seven times.[17]

These data show that this quintessential rubric, which expresses in a nutshell the basic grammar that holds the covenant community together, persists with remarkable regularity from the earliest to latest times. The English gloss, "fear the Lord," is really an inadequate rendering for this rubric because, while it denotes real fear, it fails to connote other essential nuances in the Hebrew phrase.

From Rudolf Otto's[18] description of the "holy," drawn from the history of religion, a model can be constructed that enables one both to understand and to explain the meaning of "fear of the Lord." To be sure, working as a comparative religionist, and not as an exegetical theologian, Otto misconstrued the linguistic formula in the Old Testament to mean only numinous dread.[19] Nevertheless, his descriptive study of the holy, as distinct from his dubious, conjectured history of its development, supplies insightful data from the broad field of religion for understanding the biblical expression "fear the Lord." Points of continuity between the history of religion and the religion of the Old Testament are to be expected, but the remarkably close correlation between essential concepts in Otto's "idea of the holy" and the Old Testament "fear of the Lord" is unexpected and remarkable. Of course, "fear of the Lord" in the Old Testament also exhibits strong discontinuities with the pagan religions, because of Israel's distinctive faith. Otto's model contains three essential parts.

---

15. Gen. 20:11; Exod. 20:20; 2 Sam. 23:3; Neh. 5:9, 15; *yir'at šadday*, "fear of Shaddai," in Job 6:14; *yir'at 'ᵃdōnay*, "fear of the Lord" (not Yahweh), in Job 28:28.

16. Gen. 42:18; Exod. 1:17, 21; Deut. 25:18; Jonah 1:9 ("the God of heaven"); Ps. 55:20; Job 9:35; 37:24; Eccles. 5:6; 12:13; 8:12; Neh. 7:2.

17. Gen. 22:12; Exod. 18:21; Ps. 66:16; Job 1:1, 8; Eccles. 7:18; 8:12.

18. Rudolf Otto, *The Idea of the Holy*, trans. John W. Harvey (Oxford: Oxford University Press, 1923; paperback 1958).

19. Otto, *The Idea of the Holy*, pp. 109-10.

Rudolf Otto and the Idea of the Holy

The Distinction Between the Rational and the Nonrational

Otto commences his study by distinguishing between the rational, that which can be grasped by the mind, and the nonrational, the experience of God. The former pertains to belief, the latter to feeling; the former to universals, the latter to the moment; the former can be clearly grasped, the latter is inaccessible to our conceptual thought; the former is definable, the latter is not, though it is expressible. God in himself cannot be comprehended in merely logical statements about him; he must be experienced. Otto summarized his distinction thus:

> We began with the "rational" in the idea of God and the divine, meaning by that term that in it which is clearly to be grasped by our power of conceiving, and enters the domain of familiar and definable conceptions. We went on to maintain that beneath this sphere of clarity and lucidity lies a hidden depth, inaccessible to our conceptual thought, which we in so far call the "non-rational."[20]

The Hebrew term for the ineffable is *qādôš*, "holy," but that term does not serve Otto well because it may ambiguously also pertain to the rational, viz., to ethics, to moral purity. Therefore to express clearly the category he has in mind, Otto coins the word "numen," a term that means "holy" reality minus its rational and moral factors. This numen in connection with the human psyche can be said to be numinous. The numinous is felt as objective and outside the self. In the numinous Otto principally has in view "the creature feeling" of fear produced by the encounter with the mysterious, "the wholly other."

Although Otto merely pontificates the conjunction of "the holy" with "fear," it can be validated from the Old Testament. Fuhs noted:

> An internal association between holiness and numinous fear is documented in several passages: comparison of Ge 28:17 and Ex 3:5 [see also v. 6] shows that *qādôš* and *nôrā'* [glossed in English by "fearful," "terrible," "awesome"] are synonyms; *yr'* occurs in both contexts as an expression of numinous fear. Both appear in parallel in Ps 99:3; 111:9; cf. Ex 15:11; Ps 96:9; Is 8:13; 29:23. . . .[21]

20. Otto, *The Idea of the Holy*, p. 58.
21. Fuhs, "*yr'*," *TDOT* 6:300.

The Dual Quality of the Numinous: Tremendum and Fascinans

Although the numinous is usually associated with that which is daunting, it strangely combines with it a pull of fascination. In Otto's analysis of the *mysterium tremendum* he finds the elements of "awfulness," i.e., "absolute unapproachability"; of "majesty," i.e., "absolute over-poweringness"; and of "energy" or "urgency." Concerning the first he wrote:

> It has become a mystical awe, and set free as its accompaniment, reflected in self-consciousness, that "creature-feeling" that has already been described as the feeling of personal nothingness and submergence before the awe-inspiring object directly experienced.[22]

Concerning the last two, he said:

> Luther's *omnipotentia Dei* in his *De Servo Arbitrio* is nothing but the union of "majesty" — in the sense of absolute supremacy — with this "energy," in the sense of a force that knows not stint nor stay, which is urgent, active, compelling, and alive.[23]

But if the numinous repulses, inciting terror and dread on the one hand, it also attracts, inciting love and trust on the other. Otto wrote:

> These two qualities, the daunting and the fascinating, now combine in a strange harmony of contrasts, and the resultant dual character of the numinous consciousness, to which the entire religious development bears witness . . . is at once the strangest and most noteworthy phenomenon in the whole history of religion.[24]

The numinous at one and the same time is not only something wondered at but something that entrances, captivates, and transports with a strange ravishment. According to Otto: "Possession of and by the numen becomes an end in itself; it begins to be sought for its own sake; and the wildest and most artificial methods of asceticism are put into practice to attain it."[25]

---

22. Otto, *The Idea of the Holy,* p. 17.
23. Otto, *The Idea of the Holy,* pp. 23-24.
24. Otto, *The Idea of the Holy,* p. 31.
25. Otto, *The Idea of the Holy,* p. 33.

The Schematization of the Numen, the Nonrational, by Ethos and by Telos, the Rational

As some ideas are inseparable, argued Otto, so also bipolar religious feelings have an inherent connection with the ethical. Faith seeks understanding, Anselm said. Otto observed in the history of religion:

> Almost everywhere we find the numinous attracting and appropriating meanings derived from social and individual ideals of obligation, justice, and goodness. These become the "will" of the numen, and the numen their guardian, ordainer, and author.[26]

Otto calls this essential interconnectedness "schematization."[27] He illustrates the notion by the essential connection of the category of causality with its temporal "schema," the temporal sequence of two successive events, which by being brought into connection with the category of causality is *known* and recognized as a causal relation of the two. He wrote:

> Now the relation of the rational to the non-rational element in the idea of the holy or sacred is just such a one of "schematization," and the non-rational numinous fact, schematized by the rational concepts . . . yields us the complex category of "holy" itself, richly charged and complete and in its fullest meaning.[28]

The nonrational provides the warp of the holy, and the rational its weft. "We must always understand by it [the holy] the numinous completely permeated and saturated with elements signifying rationality, purpose, personality, morality," Otto summarized.[29] The sex instinct may be schematized by poetic expression, and the feelings of music by song; but these analogies fail because they are not necessary connections. "In every highly-developed religion," Otto wrote, "the appreciation of the moral obligation and duty, ranking as a claim of the deity upon man, has been developed side by side with the religious feeling itself."[30] The ethical schematizes the fearful aspect

26. Otto, *The Idea of the Holy,* p. 110.
27. Otto, *The Idea of the Holy,* pp. 45-49.
28. Otto, *The Idea of the Holy,* p. 45.
29. Otto, *The Idea of the Holy,* p. 109.
30. Otto, *The Idea of the Holy,* p. 51.

of the numinous, on the one hand, by the category of God's wrath against sin; and its attractive aspect, on the other hand, by the category of God's grace, including his goodness and love, promoting trust. According to Otto:

> The *tremendum,* the daunting and repelling moment of the numinous, is schematized by means of the rational ideas of justice, moral will, and the exclusion of what is opposed to morality; and schematized thus, it becomes the holy "wrath of God," which Scripture and Christian preaching alike proclaim. The *fascinans,* the attracting and alluring ideas of goodness, mercy and love, so schematized, becomes all that we mean by Grace.[31]

All three elements, the nonrational, the rational, and their interpenetration, make the weft of religion. They derive *a priori* from the human experience and are not *a posteriori* to it, though stimuli incite them. The rational and nonrational elements, however, though always present do not always carry the same weight. Sometimes the affectional, with its gradations of fear and trust, is dominant; sometimes, the cognitive.

With this paradigm from the history of religion in hand, we now turn to the biblical expression of our theme.

Fear of the Lord in the Old Testament

The fear of the Lord involves both the nonrational and the rational: the former, fear, love, and trust; the latter, ethics, justice, and uprightness. All these elements cohere, as the following data show.

The Distinction Between Nonrational and Rational

Syntagms pertaining to "fear of the Lord" rarely refer exclusively to numinous dread, but always include it.

A veritable classroom example distinguishing between "fear" alone, signifying the inward agitation in the presence of God produced by the *mysterium tremendum,* and the syntagm "fear of the Lord," signifying also the moral dimension, is clearly seen in Exodus 20:18-20:

31. Otto, *The Idea of the Holy,* p. 140.

When the people saw the thunder and lightning and heard the trumpet and saw the mountain in smoke, *they trembled with fear* [*wayyar'... wayyārū'û*]. They stayed at a distance and said to Moses, "Speak to us yourself and we will listen. But do not have God speak to us or we will die." Moses said to the people, "*Do not fear* [*'al-tîrā'û*]. God has come to test you, so that *the fear of God* [*yir'ātô*] will be with you to keep you from sinning."

Here *yr'* by itself and its synonym, *nû'*, denotes the momentary panic before the numinous presence of God, while the syntagm, "fear of God," links the numinous feeling with the ethical and enduring quality that keeps the people from sinning.

The numinous nature of Yahweh is represented by *nôrā'*, "terrible," and a wealth of verbs expressing dread.[32] To express merely the numinous with the verb *yr'*, Hebrew sometimes uses the preposition *mir*, designating movement "from" (Ps. 33:8), or a compound with it, either *millipnê* (Eccles. 3:14; 8:12) or *mippᵉnê* (Exod. 9:30). The preposition indicates that Yahweh is the cause or agent of the fear.[33] For example:

Let all the earth fear [on account of] the LORD [*yîrᵉ'û mēyhwh*];
 let all the people of the world revere [on account of] him
 [*mimmennû yāgûrû*]. (Ps. 33:8)

Several passages (1 Sam. 12:18; Jonah 1:16; Zeph. 3:7; Isa. 57:11; 59:19; Job 37:24) superficially may seem to employ "fear of the Lord" for only numinous dread. In 1 Samuel 12:18, however, Samuel is added to Yahweh, throwing this verse somewhat outside of the limits of this study. Jonah 1:16 reads: *wayyîrᵉ'û hā'ᵃnāšîm yir'ā' gᵉdôlâ 't-yhwh*, "and the men feared Yahweh exceedingly" (cf. v. 10), with reference to only the numinous. The addition of the cognate accusative construction,[34] however, breaks up the syntagm, throwing this instance also outside of this essay's frame of reference. In Zephaniah 3:7 the aspect of real fear is prominent, but its parallel, "accept correction," shows that the rational, the moral aspect, is also present. Isaiah 57:11 reads:

Whom have you so dreaded and feared [*wattîr'î*]. . .
Is it not because I have long been silent
 that you do not fear me [*wᵉ'ôtî lō' tīrā'î*]?

---

32. Fuhs, "*yr'*," *TDOT* 6:239-94.
33. Waltke and O'Connor, *Introduction to Biblical Hebrew Syntax*, p. 213.
34. Waltke and O'Connor, *Introduction to Biblical Hebrew Syntax*, p. 167.

The rest of the context, however, suggests that the moral element is also present with the numinous, however weakly. The next verse reads: "I will expose your righteousness and your works, and they will not benefit you." In Isaiah 59:19 "men will fear the name of the LORD" as he comes in awesome judgment, but he comes dressed as the righteous warrior on behalf of justice (Isa. 59:11-17), suggesting that here too the formula includes a moral dimension. Job 37:24 is ambiguous in light of verse 23.

Religious emotions alone, however, seem to be in view in Exodus 14:31, to be looked at below, and in Job 9:35. The fuller context of the latter reads:

> If only there were someone . . . to remove God's rod from me,
>   so that his terror would frighten me no more.
> Then I would speak up without fear of him [*wᵉlō' 'îrā'ennû*],
>   but as it now stands with me, I cannot. (Job 9:34-35)

Exodus 14:31; 1 Samuel 12:18; Jonah 1:16; and Job 9:35 are exceptional in not clearly suggesting the rational, moral element. In light of the clear example in Exodus 20:18-20 coupling the rational and nonrational in contrast to only the latter, perhaps the moral dimension ought not be eliminated in even these exceptional instances.

Some scholars wrongly contend that in the wisdom formula "fear of the Lord," the syntagm loses its emotional character.[35] This is true in Isaiah 29:13, an exception that in fact proves the rule. In Isaiah's apostate age "the fear of the Lord" had indeed degenerated into the purely rational, excluding the religious feeling:

> These people come near to me with their mouth
>   and honor me with their lips,
>   but their hearts are far from me.
> Their worship of me [*yir'ātān 'ōtî* = "their fearing me"]
>   is made up only of rules taught by men.

The Lord condemns these rationalists for excluding the ineffable, the nonrational religious experience, from their theology. One may infer, therefore, that the sages who claimed divine inspiration (cf. Prov. 2:6) and whose teachings providence approved by preserving them in Holy Scripture did not exclude this required element in true religion from their key religious formula.

35. Gunther Wanke, *"phobeō,"* TDNT 9:201-202.

The nonrational is also present in the syntagm "who fear the Lord." In Psalm 22:24 the syntagm finds its parallel in a word signifying real fear:

You who fear the LORD [*yir'ê yhwh*], praise him! . . .
Revere him [*w^egûrû mimmennû*], all you descendants of Israel.

Joüon[36] and Derousseaux[37] agree that the parallel verb *gûr* (= "stand in awe") means "retreat out of fear." On the other hand, the worshiping community encountered in the psalms is also characterized by its commitment to Yahweh's covenant:

The LORD confides in those who fear him [*lîrê'āyw*],
    he makes his covenant known to them. (Ps 25:14)

In true religion this awe felt in God's holy presence is just as essential as is its rational definition. Without the felt awareness of God's holiness, humans would not throw themselves through the veil of God's wrath against sin upon his merciful heart. As John Newton taught us to sing: "'Twas grace that taught my heart to fear, and grace my fears relieved."

In sum, fear of the Lord, apart from a few instances, never signifies what the English gloss might suggest, "terror" and "dread" of God alone. Rather it combines both the rational and nonrational, the ethical and the numinous, in an inseparable unity. Becker rightly asserts that numinous fear is the abiding and basic characteristic of "fear of the Lord."[38] To maintain the balance between the rational and nonrational one might employ the glosses "stand in awe" or "revere" (i.e., "awe tinged with fear"), depending on the felt degree of numinous fear and of perceived moral uprightness.

Before I conclude this section, it should be noted that this psychological attitude is intensified in Israel beyond what is found in pagan religions. Eichrodt notes two reasons for this. First, instead of yielding to the claims of the mysterious wholly other, paganisms seek to exert pressure upon it by magic. Second, instead of yielding to the one true God, they transfer and disperse their psychological energies to many deities and demons. Eichrodt said of the psychology of Old Testament believers:

36. Paul Joüon, "Crainte et peur en hebreu biblique," *Bib* 6 (1925): 176.
37. Louis Derousseaux, *La crainte de Dieu dans l'Ancien Testament. Lectio divina* 63 (Paris: Cerf), p. 74.
38. Joachim Becker, *Gottsfurcht im Alten Testament, Analecta Biblica* (Rome: Pontifical Biblical Institute, 1965), pp. 80-82.

Consequently *the encounter with the one Lord of the divine realm,* in whom all the saving and destructive effects of higher powers were combined, *constituted an absolute imperilling of human existence,* against which there was no protection. The fear of God is here deepened to a basic attitude affecting the whole man.[39]

The Dual Quality of the Numinous: Tremendum and Fascinans

The religion of Israel, along with other religions, inherently unites the unlikely psychological bedfellows of the daunting and the attractive, of fear and love, of flight and trust, or, to paraphrase Professor Houston, of emotional distance and proximity. Israel's experience at the wondrous crossing of the Red Sea provides a textbook example:

And when the Israelites saw the great power the LORD displayed against the Egyptians, the people *feared the LORD [wayyîrᵉʾû . . . ʾet-yhwh] and put their trust in him* and in Moses his servant. (Exod. 14:31)

"The shrinking, awe and alarm of the elders of the people in the face of the wonder-working God," says Eichrodt, "leads them to recognize Moses as his messenger and to accept in faith the liberation promised by him."[40] Their raw religious energy at the Red Sea will shortly be channeled through the Mosaic covenant given to them at Sinai (Exod. 19:4-6).

The unified psychological poles come prominently to the fore in the surprisingly uniform Deuteronomic and Deuteronomistic expressions involving "fear of the Lord." Deuteronomy 10:12 represents the data:

And now, O Israel, what does the LORD your God ask of you but *to fear the LORD your God, . . . to love him, to serve the LORD your God [lîrᵉʾâ ʾet-yhwh ᵉlōheykā . . . ûlᵉʾahᵃbâ ʾōtô wᵉlᵃᵃbōd ʾet-yhwh ᵉlōheykâ]* with all your heart and with all your soul.

Instructively, the heart that both fears and loves God at one and the same time is not divided but unified in a single religious response to God.

---

39. Walter Eichrodt, *Theology of the Old Testament,* trans. J. A. Baker II (Philadelphia: Westminster, 1967), p. 270.

40. Eichrodt, *Theology of the Old Testament,* p. 274.

Elsewhere I tried to explain this curious emotional unity by claiming that both emotions are rooted in trust: faith in his threats, causing one to fear, and faith in his promises, causing one to love.[41] My rationalization, however, is debunked by Otto's study of comparative religion and such texts as Exodus 14:31.

Fuhs establishes that the linguistic antonyms "fear" and "love" are in fact religious synonyms by connecting Deuteronomy 5:29 with 6:2:

> According to 5:29, the people should "fear" Yahweh with their heart; according to 6:2 they should "love" him. In other words, *yr'* ["fear"] and *'hb* ["love"] belong to the terminology of the general clause in the covenant treaty and are to this extent synonymous.[42]

G. Wanke agrees that the terms are interchangeable:

> The combining of two other words with *yr'*, namely, *'hb* "to love" and *dbg* "to cleave to," Dt 10:12, 20; 13:5, makes possible a broader understanding of the content of fearing God, esp. since what is said about *yr'* ["fear"] . . . applies to *'hb* ["love"] and *dbg* ["cling to"], and the terms are thus more or less interchangeable.[43]

Other data confirm these assessments. Deuteronomy 6:1 speaks of "this command" (singular, *contra* "These are the commands" [NIV], presumably consisting of "statutes and judgments"). The "command" is explicated in the rest of the chapter as consisting of "Love the LORD your God with all your heart, with all your soul and with all your strength" (Deut. 6:5), and "Fear the LORD your God, serve him only and take your oaths in his name." According to Deuteronomy 6:2 this command (v. 1) is given so that Israel "might fear the LORD your God." The disconcerting oscillation between the psychological poles, "fear the Lord" and "love the Lord," suggests that they are interchangeable for expressing the true religious experience.

Klaus Baltzer,[44] on whose study Fuhs based his remarks on Deuteronomy 5:29 and 6:2, has shown from his comparison of the covenants in the

---

41. Bruce K. Waltke, "Evangelical Spirituality: A Biblical Scholar's Perspective," *JETS* 31 (1988): 14.

42. Fuhs, "*yr'*," *TDOT* 6:307.

43. Wanke, "*phobeō*," *TDNT* 9:201.

44. Klaus Baltzer, *The Covenant Formulary in Old Testament, Jewish, and Early Christian Writings*, trans. David E. Green (Oxford: Blackwell, 1971).

Old Testament with Ancient Near East vassal treaties that the command "to love God" is the central command, the substance, of the covenant (cf. Deut. 6:5). In Joshua 24, however, "fear the Lord" expresses its substance. In this account Joshua renews in Canaan the covenant between Yahweh and Israel that Moses mediated in Sinai and renewed at Moab. The substance of the covenant in its finally renewed form is "fear the Lord," not "love the Lord." The substance begins with "And now" [$w^{e'}att\hat{a}$] (v. 14):

> Now fear the LORD and serve him with all faithfulness. Throw away the gods your forefathers worshiped beyond the River and in Egypt, and serve the LORD.

The positive aspect of the covenant formula is "fear the Lord" and its negative aspect "throw away the gods." Baltzer wrote:

> This relationship is defined both positively and negatively in a series of imperatives:
>
> וְעַתָּה יְראוּ אֶת-יהוה
>
> וְעִבְדוּ אֹתוֹ   בְּתָמִים וּבֶאֱמֶת
>
> וְהָסִירוּ אֶת-אֱלֹהִים   אֲשֶׁר עָבְדוּ אֲבוֹתֵיכֶם
>
> וְעִבְדוּ אֶת-יהוה
>
> The point is absolute loyalty toward Yahweh. This loyalty presupposes the rejection of the service (i.e., the cult) of "foreign gods."[45]

"Fear of the Lord" here encapsulates Israel's religion and as such entails the emotional opposites of fear, namely, "love" and "trust." Actually, as Derousseaux noted, yr', "fear," goes beyond $'bd$, "serve," and $'hb$, "love," which may express merely earthly loyalty, by incorporating also acknowledgment of Yahweh's absolute sovereignty.[46]

In that light the syntagm "who fear Yahweh" in the Psalter and in other contexts of worship such as Malachi 3:20 [Eng. 4:2] designates true worshipers who loyally love God and fear him.

In Israel this religious experience, call it "worship" if you will, surpassed the pagan religious experience because it was focused on the one, true, living, and holy God, not on a pantheon of warring deities displaying the same vices as depraved humans.

45. Baltzer, *The Covenant Formulary*, p. 21.
46. Derousseaux, *La crainte*, pp. 220, 256.

The religious experience involving both fear and love of God, which is at the heart of the covenant relationship, cannot be taught through the sheer dint of a teacher's will, any more than any other spiritual response can be communicated through human willpower. It must be awakened by the Spirit in the heart of the elect people (cf. 1 Cor. 2:9-16). It can be commanded, however, for this affective aspect in religion depends on the will of the audience. Humans suppress the fear of the Lord, whose awesome majesty is clearly displayed in creation. The Lord chided Israel for quenching this instinct:

> "Should you not fear me?" declares the LORD.
> "Should you not tremble in my presence?
> I made the sand a boundary for the sea,
> an everlasting barrier it cannot cross.
> The waves may roll, but they cannot prevail;
> they may roar, but they cannot cross it.
> But these people have stubborn and rebellious hearts;
> they have turned aside and gone away.
> They do not say to themselves,
> 'Let us fear the LORD our God [*nîrā' na' 'et-yhwh 'ĕlōhênû*]. . . .'"
>
> (Jer. 5:22-24a)

Humans need to contemplate God's revelations of himself, not hide themselves among the trees so as not to encounter him and hear his voice.

Before leaving this section, note that through the rational, moral dimension the emotions of love and trust are intensified in Israel's religion beyond anything found in pagan religions. Yahweh graciously committed himself to his people as the sovereign, covenant-keeping God. The pagan deities, by contrast, were capricious and themselves subordinate to chance. Eichrodt says:

> The confident trust which constantly prevails as the basic note in Israel's fear of God has no parallel in the other religions of the ancient Near East. The will of these nature gods is too little reliable and too ambiguous for men to be able to credit them with a coherent total purpose; and they are themselves too strongly exposed to the evil power of the demons for their promises to be able to banish anxiety.[47]

---

47. Eichrodt, *Theology of the Old Testament*, p. 272.

The Schematization of the Numen, the Nonrational, by Ethos and by Telos, the Rational

God's will, his law if you please, schematizes Israel's religious, non-natural emotions of fearing and loving God. This revealed schematization gave Israel's religion its distinctive character and set it above all paganism: "See," says Moses, "I have taught you decrees and laws as the LORD my God commanded me. . . . Observe them carefully, for this will show your wisdom and understanding to the nations, who will hear about all these decrees and say, 'Surely this great nation is a wise and understanding people'" (Deut. 4:5-6). Whereas pagans responded with myth and ritual, magical words accompanying voodoo rites, to manipulate their deities to perform their will, God's covenant demanded that Israel submit to his will. Any attempt to manipulate God and human destiny by observing superstitious practices and/or the occult repulses God. Instead, he demands ethical behavior: "Do my will and you will live, and not die."

God revealed his will in two ways: to all humans through conscience, and to his covenant people in particular through special revelations (e.g., the Mosaic law, the teaching of the sages, the prophetic oracles, and meditation upon inspired hymns). "Fear of *ᵉlōhîm* ['God']," the name associated with his transcendence, is often connected with general revelation, and "fear of *yhwh* ['the Lord']," his covenantal name, with particular revelation. No ironclad distinction, however, can be made between "fear of God" and "fear of the Lord" because some literary strata prefer one name over the other and because the line between them, consisting of the emotional, the rational, and their interpretation of one another, becomes attenuated. Both expressions entail the avoidance of evil (cf. Job 1:1; 8:2-3; 28:28 with Ps. 34:12-15; Prov. 3:7; 16:6). These elements are, as Eichrodt said, "an indispensable virtue of the judge [Exod. 18:21], and part of the necessary equipment of the king [2 Sam. 23:3; Isa. 11:2]."[48] Nevertheless, sometimes there is some difference. "Fear of God," in contrast to "fear of the Lord," may refer, as Whybray put it, "to a standard of moral conduct known and accepted by men in general."[49]

Let us look first then at "fear of God" used in this distinctive sense, and then at "fear of the Lord."

As is well known, two rival explanations are given on how finite hu-

48. Eichrodt, *Theology of the Old Testament*, p. 273.
49. R. N. Whybray, *Wisdom in Proverbs: The Concept of Wisdom in Proverbs 1–9* (London: SCM, 1965), p. 96.

mans know as much as they do and how they acquire knowledge so quickly. Most continental European philosophers take the view that some knowledge is innate, but English scholars in the tradition of Locke, Berkeley, and Hume hold that the mind is *tabula rasa* at birth and knowledge is acquired only empirically. Studies in linguistics during the past several decades, most notably those by Noam Chomsky,[50] have broken the impasse by showing that knowledge of linguistic universals is so deeply ingrained in the human consciousness that they can only be explained as inherited, not as learned. Chomsky wrote:

> In short, the structure of particular languages may very well be largely determined by factors over which the individual has no conscious control and concerning which society may have little choice or freedom. On the basis of the best information now available, it seems reasonable to suppose that a child cannot help constructing a particular sort of transformational grammar to account for the data presented to him. . . . Thus it may well be that the general features of language structure reflect, not so much the course of one's experience, but rather the general character of one's capacity to acquire knowledge — in the traditional sense, one's innate ideas and innate principles.[51]

So also humans inherently share unvarying rules of moral intuition, but in their spiritually fallen condition they more or less suppress this critical faculty (Rom. 1:18; 2:12-16). Alister McGrath, in his recent article on "Doctrine and Ethics," seems to contradict himself. On the one hand, he says: "Works such as Jeffrey Stout's *Ethics after Babel* destroyed the credibility of the idea of a 'universal morality.'"[52] Later, however, he writes: "[The doctrine of original sin] allows us to understand that human beings are fallen, with an alarming degree of ability to do evil while knowing that it is evil." Western culture today is in a state of moral chaos because it has self-consciously rejected its innate "fear of God" and its inherited "fear of the Lord" and chosen instead spiritual darkness, including the so-called New Age movement which distorts the distinction between truth and error.

---

50. Noam Chomsky, *Aspects of Theory of Syntax* (Cambridge, MA: MIT Press, 1965), pp. 33-59. See now Paul Johnson, *The Intellectuals* (London: Weidenfeld & Nicolson, 1989), p. 338. Johnson mistakenly cites Chomsky's *Syntactic Structures*.

51. Chomsky, *Aspects of Theory of Syntax*, p. 59.

52. Alister McGrath, "Doctrine and Ethics," *JETS* 34 (1991): 147.

Abraham distrusted the moral atmosphere of Abimelech's court because he thought it suppressed this innate moral sense. In his apology to Abimelech, the pagan king of Gerar, who confessed to God that he had "a clear conscience" [*b*ᵉ*tom-l*ᵉ*bābî*] (Gen. 20:5), the patriarch explained his distrust: "I said to myself, 'There is surely no fear of God [*'ên-yir'at* *'*ᵉ*lōhîm*] in this place, and they will kill me because of my wife'" (Gen. 20:11). The Hebrew midwives, in contrast to the Pharaoh, also did not suppress their intuitive sense of right and wrong. When the Pharaoh commanded them to kill the Israelite male babies they refused, "because they [the midwives] feared God [*wattîr*ᵉ*'nā . . . 'et-*ᵉ*lōhîm*]" (Exod. 1:17).

"Fear of the Lord" includes this general knowledge and more. In much of the Old Testament, especially Deuteronomy and the Deuteronomistic literature, it refers to the covenant the Lord made with Israel through his mediator Moses. The stipulations of this covenant include both moral and cultic regulations. The use of the formula in 2 Kings 17:32-39 shows that the latter is in view; its use in Deuteronomy 4:10, 17:19, and 31:12-13 points to the former.

Becker distinguished three main meanings for what he summarized as "fear of God": *cultic* (fear of God as worship), *moral* (fear of God as upright behavior), and *legal* (fear of God as observance of the law). He assigned to the first the bulk of the Old Testament passages, including Deuteronomic and Deuteronomistic literature; to the second, such passages as Genesis 20:11 and Exodus 1:17, 21 discussed above, along with references in the wisdom literature and elsewhere; and to the third, passages in the Psalms where "fear of the Lord" becomes a synonym for the law (Ps. 19:10; 111:10; 112:1; 119:38, 63; 128:1, 4). But these distinctions are too rigid and often debatable. Blocher is certainly right when he criticizes this rigid categorization: "Becker's distinctions may be too clear-cut, especially as they are based on current, but questionable, source-criticism hypotheses."[53] Derousseaux[54] rightly replaces "cultic fear" with "covenant-fear" *(crainte d'alliance)* mostly in Deuteronomy, for he too thinks Becker's distinctions too clear-cut. In the wisdom literature, especially in Ecclesiastes and Job, "fear of God" may refer to the moral laws of general revelation, but in Proverbs, especially in chapters 1-9, "the fear of the Lord" denotes the sage's "teachings." "My son," he says, "if you accept my words . . . you will find the fear of the

---

53. Henri Blocher, "The Fear of the Lord as the 'Principle' of Wisdom," *TynBul* 28 (1977): 8.

54. Derousseaux, *La crainte*, p. 10 n. 23, pp. 100-101.

LORD" (Prov. 2:1-5). In these chapters he labels his teachings as "laws" and "commandments" (cf. 1:8; 3:1; etc.).

Before concluding this section we need to remind ourselves that here numinous fear and law combine themselves. Psalm 119:120 and 119:161 clearly exhibit this phenomenon, using a different Hebrew verb or *yr'* with the preposition *min*.[55] Deuteronomy 28:58-59, however, does weave fear of the Lord together with the law:

> If you do not carefully follow all the words of this law, which are written in this book, and do not revere this glorious and awesome name — the LORD your God — the LORD will send fearful plagues on you and your descendants, harsh and prolonged disasters, and severe and lingering illnesses.

The rational element can be taught and learned, and so commanded: "Come, my children, listen to me; I will teach you the fear of the LORD" (Ps. 34:10), whereupon the sage-king gives his own moral instructions. Before the instruction, however, he impressed upon his audience God's greatness in saving him. Indeed, both the emotional and rational aspects of the fear of the Lord can be demanded: the former, as noted above, because humans can repent, stop quenching their innate religious instincts, and contemplate God's revelations of himself; the latter, because they can direct their wills to cognitively grasp the revealed content.

Conclusion

Syntagms involving the verbal root *yr'*, "to fear," with God or equivalents as its direct object, denote a rich and complex thought that epitomizes Israel's religion. At one and the same time it signifies nonrational, numinous fear combined with love and trust, both of which are schematized by moral uprightness. In some texts the nonrational predominates, in others the rational; but "awe" of God characterizes its core. This root of religious experience is organized by God's will, revealed through conscience, and usually overlaid with special revelation.

In sum, "fear of the Lord/God" entails two axes, each with its own poles. We can depict the rich and complex nature of "fear of the Lord" by this diagram:

55. Derousseaux, *La crainte*, p. 9.

General Revelation

rational axis

Fear ———————————————————— Love

nonrational axis

Special Revelation

On the nonrational axis the poles are "fear" and "love," and on the rational axis, general revelation and special revelation. Both elements are normally present on the horizontal axis, but in varying degrees. The vertical axis may become attenuated with little difference between its poles,[56] though sometimes general revelation is clearly in view with "fear of God" and special revelation with "fear of the Lord." Both axes are normally present in varying degrees, though in a few texts the rational axis is not apparent. Specific nuances of the syntagms involving "fear of the Lord" in the biblical texts must be plotted in relation to these poles. Sometimes fear is subordinated to love and vice versa; sometimes the affective emotions are subordinated to cognitive understanding and vice versa.

Stimuli inciting "fear of the Lord" have not been investigated here. Suffice it to note that God's marvelous revelations in creation, in sacred history, and in Scripture are sufficient reasons "to fear him" in the fullest sense of that word. The problem is not the lack of the numinous — it is everywhere; nor the lack of moral consciousness — it is inherent in human nature. Rather, people make their hearts stubborn and rebellious against God (cf. Jer. 5:20-25). In short, God demands both the affective and the cognitive aspects of fear, for both depend on the human will. One cannot be indifferent to "fear of the Lord"; it is a matter of life and death. "Such fear," says Professor Houston, "brings blessing in every sphere of life."[57]

56. H. A. Brongers, "La crainte du Seigneur (Jir at Jhwh, Jir at 'Elohim)," *Oudtestamentische Studiën* 5 (1948): 163.

57. Houston, *I Believe in the Creator*, p. 189.

Hermeneutics and the Spiritual Life

Most textbooks on hermeneutics and exegesis written by evangelicals during the past decade [the 1980s] emphasize and refine the grammatico-historical method and neglect the role of the Holy Spirit and the spiritual qualification of the interpreter.[1] None of the ten books listed in the first footnote devote a

---

1. Cf. D. A. Carson, *Exegetical Fallacies* (Grand Rapids: Baker, 1984). Carson deliberately refrains from a sustained discussion of the Holy Spirit's role in the exegetical task because it "involves a shift to a hermeneutical focus that would detract from the usefulness of this book as a practitioner's manual." In my opinion, however, the "scholarly fallacy" is lethal and cannot be sidestepped as impractical.

- Dunnett, W. M. *The Interpretation of Holy Scripture.* Nashville: Thomas Nelson, 1984.
- Fee, G. D., and D. Stuart. *How to Read the Bible for All Its Worth.* Grand Rapids: Zondervan, 1981.
- Green, J. B. *How to Read Prophecy.* Downers Grove, IL: InterVarsity, 1984.
- Kaiser, W. *Toward an Exegetical Theology.* Grand Rapids: Baker, 1981.
- Liefeld, W. L. *New Testament Exposition: From Text to Sermon.* Grand Rapids: Zondervan, 1984.
- Osborne, G. R. *Handbook for Bible Study.* Grand Rapids: Baker, 1979.
- Stuart, Douglas. *Old Testament Exegesis: Primer for Students and Pastors.* Philadelphia: Westminster, 1984.
- Vandergoot, H. *Interpreting the Bible in Theology and the Church.* Lewiston, NY: Edwin Mellen, 1985.
- Yoder, P. *Toward Understanding the Bible.* Newton, KS: Faith and Life Press, 1978.

Helpful essays on the subject have appeared; e.g., R. L. Saucy, *The Bible: Breathed from God* (Wheaton, IL: Victor Books, 1978), pp. 103-12; Fred K. Klooster, "The Role of the Holy Spirit," in *Hermeneutics, Inerrancy, and the Bible*, ed. E. D. Radmacher and R. D. Preus (Grand Rapids: Academie, 1984), pp. 451-72.

Previously published in *Crux* 23, no. 1 (March 1987).

chapter or even a section to the doctrine of illumination and the personal dimension in exegetical labors. The Spirit, if mentioned, is demoted to the secondary role of applying the text. It should be clearly understood that I do not name these works by dedicated servants to condemn them; they are too well written, too brilliant, and too full of an excellent spirit for that. I reluctantly mention them only to document the widespread neglect of the most important factor in exegesis. My own teaching too is flawed by the same imbalance. Virkler[2] devotes two pages to "spiritual factors" in the perceptional process but does not do justice to the biblical texts (Rom. 1:18-22; 1 Cor. 2:6-14; Eph. 4:17-24; 1 John 2:11; cited by Virkler) teaching that spiritual commitment, or lack of it, influences the ability to perceive spiritual truth. According to him, "Unbelievers do not know the full meaning of scriptural teaching, not because that meaning is unavailable to them in the words of the text, but because they refuse to act on and appropriate spiritual truths for their own lives."[3] Although these authors would undoubtedly balk at Ernesti's claim that prayer and a pious simplicity of mind are useless in the investigation of Scriptural truth,[4] by their silence they tacitly support him.

The neglect of the spiritual dimension has robbed seminarians of the most important aspect in theological education. My superb teaching assistant at Regent College, John Marcott, called to my attention this complaint by Diane Karay of the Presbyterian Church, Rantoul, Illinois, in an article titled, "What I Wish I'd Learned in Seminary":

> Each Thursday afternoon I sit at my desk and do the hardest work in composing a sermon. It is not choosing a text or topic, nor the background research, nor even the composition of the sermon itself. The struggle is opening my heart to a deeper realm where God still whispers to Samuel, and Jesus eternally feeds the thousands.
>
> In seminary I was taught to scrutinize a text but not to let it speak. I was taught the sociology of ancient peoples, the theology of biblical authors, the mechanics of preaching, and how to decipher Greek and Hebrew. But nowhere did anyone suggest, much less teach, that the true work of preaching is engaging the hidden and mysterious God who alone teaches, inspires, and gives us the Word that needs to be heard.[5]

2. H. A. Virkler, *Hermeneutics: Principles and Processes of Biblical Interpretation* (Grand Rapids: Baker, 1981), pp. 29-31.

3. Virkler, *Hermeneutics*, p. 30.

4. J. A. Ernesti, *Principles of Biblical Interpretation*, vol. 1 (Edinburgh, 1882), p. 5.

5. *Leadership*, 6, no. 4 (1985): 124.

Earlier I used the word "trend" self-consciously. One notes a diminishing appreciation of spiritual factors from the Reformers to their present sons. The Reformers finely balanced the "scholarly" and "spiritual" factors in hermeneutics. Herbert Jacobsen, in an article titled "On the Limitations of Hermeneutics," wrote:

> It puzzles me at times that the literature on hermeneutics, at least in the Protestant tradition, does not deal more extensively and seriously with this personal dimension. When the Reformation began, there seemed to be a much more balanced approach to hermeneutics than there is today.[6]

The Puritan divine John Owen[7] in 1678 wrote a masterful treatise on the necessity of the Spirit for illumination and the means for understanding the mind of God. Wesleyan scholars W. McCown and C. Michalson in *Interpreting God's Word for Today*[8] set a model for evangelicals to emulate by reasserting Wesley's emphasis that Bible study is more a devotional exercise undergirded by spiritual illumination than a scholarly procedure. About a century ago Patrick Fairbairn in the *Hermeneutical Manual*[9] and Milton Terry in his classic, *Biblical Hermeneutics*,[10] gave insightful, though more limited, treatment of the spiritual qualifications required of the biblical exegete. By contrast, evangelical books on hermeneutics and/or exegesis published during the past twenty-five years begin to show signs of depreciating the necessity of a healthy spiritual life in the exegetical task. One still finds forthright treatments of the devotional dimension in Daniel Fuller's *Hermeneutics*[11] and Arthur W. Pink's *Interpretation of the Scriptures*.[12] Ber-

---

6. Herbert Jacobsen, "On the Limitations of Hermeneutics," in *Interpreting the Word of God*, ed. S. J. Schultz and M. A. Inch (Chicago: Moody Press, 1976).

7. John Owen, *Works* (Edinburgh: T. & T. Clark, 1862), 4:118-234.

8. W. McCown and J. E. Massey, eds., *Interpreting God's Word for Today* (Anderson, IN: Warner, 1982), esp. pp. 4f., 31-43.

9. P. Fairbairn, *Hermeneutical Manual: or, Introduction to the Exegetical Study of the Scriptures of the New Testament* (Edinburgh: T. & T. Clark, 1888), pp. 63-67.

10. Milton S. Terry, *Biblical Hermeneutics* (New York: Eaton & Mains, 1890; republished by Zondervan, 1968), pp. 28-30.

11. Daniel P. Fuller, *Hermeneutics* (Pasadena, CA: Fuller Theological Seminary, 1974), 9:1-8.

12. Arthur W. Pink, *Interpretation of the Scriptures* (Grand Rapids: Baker, 1972), pp. 13-19.

nard Ramm,[13] Henrichsen,[14] and McQuilkin[15] do not lose sight of the spiritual dimension, but their discussions are not as extensive and penetrating as earlier works. Other evangelical works published during the same quarter of a century bypass the topic.[16]

This trend is puzzling not only in the light of the Protestant tradition, but also in light of the clear teachings of Scripture and the recent focus in philosophical hermeneutics on the role of the interpreter. In this essay I hope to make a contribution toward reversing the recent trend by arguing that one's spiritual life is more important than one's educational qualifications. The personal nature of Scripture, its impersonal nature, and the nature of God's revelation, especially his revelation in Christ Jesus, validate my thesis. Bultmann's thesis that contemporary readers and biblical authors share a consanguinity of preunderstanding — which prompts similar questions about the structure and meaning of human existence (to which faith is an answer) — also supports my thesis.[17] This philosophical argument, however, demands a separate study.

The Personal Nature of Scripture

The nature of any object dictates the method of approach appropriate for understanding it.

Dr. James Houston makes the clever pun: one must stand under an object to understand it.[18] If one wishes to study the moon, for example, one had better view it through the lens of a telescope, not a microscope. On the other hand, to study a microorganism, the opposite applies. If we were to use the wrong apparatus with either object, we could see nothing. Elaine Botha

13. B. Ramm, *Protestant Biblical Interpretation,* 7th ed. (Boston: Wilde, 1975), p. 7.

14. W. A. Henrichsen, *A Layman's Guide to Interpreting the Bible* (Grand Rapids: Zondervan, 1978), pp. 25-27.

15. J. R. McQuilkin, *Understanding and Applying the Bible* (Chicago: Moody Press, 1983), pp. 55-57.

16. L. Berkhof, *Principles of Biblical Interpretation* (Grand Rapids: Baker, 1952); A. B. Mickelsen, *Interpreting the Bible* (Grand Rapids: Eerdmans, 1963). Mickelsen has a helpful chapter on "Devotion and Conduct" (pp. 352-64), but he has in mind the proper use of the Bible in devotion and conduct and not the role of these spiritual virtues in the interpretation of the Bible.

17. Rudolf Bultmann, "The Problem in Hermeneutics," in *Essays,* trans. James C. G. Greig (London: SCM Press, 1955), pp. 239-43.

18. In personal communication.

in a lecture given at Regent College illustrated the point with an orange. She suggested that if we came at an orange with a hatchet instead of a paring knife, we would discover little more than the fact that an orange has juice that sticks to our fingers. These illustrations also imply that one must spend some time with an object to generate a preunderstanding of its nature before scientifically examining it.

The Bible in its own self-conscious statements about itself informs us that it has a dual nature: it is both personal and impersonal. Paul's well-known doctrine "all Scripture is inspired by God" (2 Tim. 3:16) entails that Bible study involves three objects at one and the same time: the Author ("God"), the human agent (the "inspired" person), and the text ("Scripture"). The first two are personal; the last is impersonal.

Immanuel Kant, it will be recalled, radically differentiated ways of knowing personal objects (that is, those possessing volition) from impersonal ones (that is, those lacking volition). For knowing the latter, he used the German word *Erklärung;* for the former, he used *Verstehen.* He cogently argued that we "explain" impersonal objects, but we "know" personal objects. For the former, the scientific method is appropriate; for the latter, it is inappropriate. To understand objects that lack volition, one distances oneself from them and attempts to be detached and as dispassionate as possible. On the other hand, to know a person involves passion; one must commit oneself to him or her.

I was once asked to teach a course on the Psalms at a state university. As I reflected on my assignment I contemplated how I could communicate the Psalter's highly devotional content to students schooled in the scientific method. In the first lecture I introduced the course by noting Kant's distinction. To get my point across, I asked one of the students to stand in a corner of the room. While he stood there we observed him, analyzed him, and systematically classified our information without talking to him or allowing him to talk to us. The point became quickly apparent to the students that by our method we had actually positioned ourselves not to know him. I drew the obvious conclusion that were I to teach the Psalms without commitment to God, we could never understand the object of their content.

The scientific method, which we traditionally call the grammatico-historical method, is appropriate for understanding the text, but it is inappropriate for the principal aim of Christian understanding of Scripture, the knowledge of God. John Calvin, in the opening sentence of his *Institutes of the Christian Religion,* wrote:

Nearly all the wisdom we possess, that is to say, true and sound wisdom, consists of two parts: the knowledge of God and of ourselves.[19]

Knowing God demands passionate commitment to the Author of Scripture. God is Spirit; to know him demands a spiritual lens. The inspired sage developed the spiritual dimension in exegetical labors this way:

My son, if you accept my words and store up my commands within you, turning your ear to wisdom and applying your heart to understanding, and if you call out for insight and cry aloud for understanding, and if you look for it as for silver and search for it as for hidden treasure, then you will understand the fear of the LORD and find the knowledge of God. For the LORD gives wisdom, and from his mouth come knowledge and understanding. (Prov. 2:1-6)

Perhaps evangelicals have tended to downplay spiritual understanding because they have forgotten that the aim of Christian hermeneutics is the knowledge of God. Defending this thesis, Charles M. Wood wrote:

In an earlier age, the claim which this thesis advances might simply have been taken for granted, so that the statement of it would have been superfluous. Today . . . it would not occur to many interpreters to describe the goal of their efforts in this way. Not that they would necessarily deny the claim if it were proposed to them. They might well assent to it then as a proper theological statement of the eventual telos of exegetical labours from a Christian standpoint. . . . But to grant the truth of the claim at some level of abstraction or at some stage of eschatological remoteness is one thing; to give it a place in one's ongoing reflections upon the practice of interpretation is another.[20]

A textbook on hermeneutics and/or exegesis should at a minimum include a chapter on how to read the Bible devotionally. I have never received or given formal instruction on this topic.

19. John Calvin, *Institutes of the Christian Religion,* ed. John T. McNeill, trans. Ford Lewis Battles, The Library of Christian Classics, 20 vols. (Philadelphia: Westminster, 1960), 3.35.

20. Charles M. Wood, *The Formation of Christian Understanding: An Essay in Theological Hermeneutics* (Philadelphia: Westminster, 1981), p. 30.

Besides the personal dimension of the Divine Author there is that of the human author as well. Superior intellectual talent and superb educations, though not to be despised, do not render one fit to interpret Scripture. Fairbairn lays down as his first general rule to be followed in the interpretation of particular words and passages: the interpreter "must endeavour to attain to a sympathy in thought and feeling with the sacred writers, whose meaning he seeks to unfold."[21] Occasionally scholars who make no claim to being led by the Spirit read the text with more perspicacity than those who claim such leading because in fact they read it more empathetically. Frequently, however, they miss its meaning through their lack of affinity. One time I was in attendance at the lecture of a professor who taught me much about the text of Scripture. In the question period that followed his discourse a student asked him the identities of the seed of the serpent and the seed of the woman in Genesis 3:15 and the meaning of the text. To my astonishment he interpreted the text with crass literalness: according to him it presented in mythical form the eternal antipathy between humans and snakes. The same pens that give brilliant textual analyses other times give jejune and superficial interpretations to the taste of a spiritual man. We need not develop the thought here because the principle that the exegete must share the same "inscape" to see the same landscape is equally necessary in respect to any author.[22] Modern hermeneutics would express the attempt to bring the interpreter's thoughts and feelings into those of the author as the merging of two horizons. The importance of shared preunderstanding was not unknown to earlier generations. Says Carl Michalson:

> Preunderstanding (*Vorverstaendnis*) was not unknown to Wesley. Probably it was known to him, technically, in German before it was in English, even though Locke and Shaftesbury gave the notion its earliest philosophical development. It was Oetinger, however, who gave to the experience of "presentiment" and "taste" the German translation *Vorempfindungen*.[23]

---

21. Fairbairn, *Hermeneutical Manual*, p. 63.

22. Cf. James M. Houston, *I Believe in the Creator* (Grand Rapids: Eerdmans, 1980), p. 15.

23. C. Michalson, in McCown and Massey, eds., *Interpreting God's Word for Today*, p. 26.

The Impersonal Nature of the Text

Let us now look at the impersonal text and the spiritual conditions for its comprehension. First, however, let it be emphasized that the two kinds of study take place at one and the same time. David Steinmetz informs us that Luther compared Scripture to the spiritual and material nature of the eucharist.[24] Both the spiritual presence of Christ and the material bread are necessarily ingested at the same time. Nevertheless, they are ingested differently. The worshiper eats the spiritual presence of Christ in Spirit; he eats the bread physically. So also the exegete, who should always be a worshiper, receives the spiritual presence of God in his Spirit as he employs the scientific method, which I prefer to describe as the grammatico-historical-canonical method, to digest it.

Now the scientific method also requires a right spirit. Ramm notes:

No matter how accurately a lens may be ground, unless the glass is crystal-pure the image passing through the lens will suffer distortion.[25]

The scientific method operates best when it is free from "prejudices, preconceived opinions, engagements by secular advantages, false confidences, authority of men, influences from parties and societies."[26] Through God's common grace scholars without special, sovereign grace relatively attain this ideal. By walking in the Spirit, however, the exegete has a special enablement to achieve it even more perfectly, though always imperfectly.[27] I need not develop the point further, for what I have to say here also applies to all scholarship, not just the study of the Bible.

24. David C. Steinmetz, "Luther as an Interpreter of the Psalms," *Archiv für Reformationsgeschichte* 70 (1979): 71.

25. Ramm, *Protestant Biblical Interpretation*, p. 7.

26. Terry, *Biblical Hermeneutics*, p. 202.

27. A sense of proportion is needed here. J. D. Smart, *The Interpretation of Scripture* (London: SCM Press, 1960), p. 29, lacks it when he says without qualification: "The claim of absolute scientific objectivity in interpreting Scripture involves the interpreter in an illusion about himself that inhibits objectivity and makes eisegesis inevitable." A distinction is necessary between perfect understanding and adequate understanding. The latter occurs when the audience responds in a way the speaker anticipated or should have anticipated.

The Nature of Revelation

The Nature of Revelation in General

Finally, the nature of revelation demands that the exegete be led by the Spirit of God. The Bible is God's gracious revelation to humans of matters necessary for their salvation. He begins the process by revelation, effects it by inspiration, and completes it by illumination. Man cannot manipulate the revelation; God through his Spirit must graciously give it. Permit me to return to Steinmetz's presentation of Luther's thought here:

> Scripture is not in our power. It is not at the disposal of our intellect and is not obliged to render up its secrets to those who have theological training, merely because they are learned. Scripture imposes its own meaning; it binds the soul to God through faith. Because the initiative in the interpretation of Scripture remains in the hands of God, we must humble ourselves in his presence and pray that he will give understanding and wisdom to us as we meditate on the sacred text. While we may take courage from the thought that God gives understanding of Scripture to the humble, we should also heed the warning that the truth of God can never coexist with human pride. Humility is the hermeneutical precondition for authentic exegesis.[28]

Consider, if you will, two biblical illustrations. When Balaam went to God honestly desiring to know whether or not he should go with the Midianites to put a curse on Israel, God said: "Do not go with them." But when enticed by the lure of more silver and gold and pressured by men more numerous and of higher station, he returned to see what else God would tell him. This time God deluded him. After telling him to go with them, God was so angry with the seer he nearly killed him (cf. Num. 22:2-35). Consider also the case of Ahab. Acceding to Jehoshaphat's request that they seek a prophet of the LORD besides others to determine whether to go to war or to refrain, Ahab sent a messenger to fetch Micaiah son of Imlah. The messenger instructed Micaiah to let his words agree with the others. When he arrived in Ahab's presence and was asked by him the LORD's mind, God deluded Ahab once again even as he had through the false prophets. "Attack and be victorious," Micaiah said, "for the LORD will give it into the king's hand." But when

---

28. Steinmetz, "Luther as an Interpreter of the Psalms," p. 28.

the king said to him, "How many times must I make you swear to tell me nothing but the truth in the name of the LORD?" Micaiah answered, "I saw all Israel scattered on the hills like sheep." And even then the Word of God failed to enlighten Ahab's darkened understanding. Trusting in his own techniques, he marched off to his death, his chariot was washed at the pool where prostitutes bathed, and the dogs licked up his blood (1 Kings 22:1-38). To be sure, men can mouth the gospel when they want to know cognitively what the Bible says, but without the Spirit's gracious and efficacious ministry to bring faith and repentance they hear without understanding. Apostates, like Balaam and Ahab, think they have the mind of God in Scripture, but God has hidden himself from them and deluded them. The Apostle Paul said: "They perish because they refused to love the truth and so be saved. For this reason God sends them a powerful delusion so that they will believe the lie and so that all will be condemned who have not believed the truth but have delighted in wickedness" (2 Thess. 2:10b-12).

Ahab's experience instructs us that a man who desires honestly to know what the Bible says can rehearse its content, but without the Spirit's gracious efficacious ministry that brings faith and repentance, he hears without understanding. In the classic text on this subject, Paul wrote: "The Spirit searches all things, even the deep things of God. For who among men knows the thoughts of a man except the man's spirit within him? In the same way no one knows the thoughts of God except the Spirit of God. We have not received the spirit of the world but the Spirit who is from God, that we may understand what God has freely given us. This is what we speak, not in words taught us by human wisdom but in words taught by the Spirit, expressing spiritual truths in spiritual words. The man without the Spirit does not accept the things that come from the Spirit of God, for they are foolishness to him, and he cannot understand them because they are spiritually discerned" (1 Cor. 2:10b-14).

Did not God commission Isaiah to preach to the unrepentant to make their hearts calloused, to make their ears dull, and to close their eyes (Isa. 6:10)? And did not our Lord tell parables to be enigmatic, to be understood by believers and misunderstood by unbelievers (Matt. 13:10-11)?

The Nature of Revelation in Jesus Christ

Most particularly, God has hidden the revelation of himself in Jesus Christ both in his physical presence at his advent and in his textual presence in

Scripture. While he walked among men, most thought he was a great prophet. When Peter, however, confessed him to be the Son of the living God, Jesus said: "This was not revealed to you by man, but by my Father in heaven." Earlier in his ministry the Lord Jesus praised his Father for having hid divine matters, including his identity, from the wise and learned and revealing it to little children (Matt. 11:25).

Regarding his teaching, known today in the text of Scripture, Jesus Christ said:

> My teaching is not my own. It comes from him who sent me. If anyone chooses to do God's will, he will find out whether my teaching is from God or whether I speak on my own. (John 7:16-17)

Saul the Pharisee with the rest of his brothers had a veil over his heart when he read the text of the old covenant until Christ took it away in his turning to the Lord (2 Cor. 3:14-16). After his conversion and call to become an apostle, if we may generalize his behavior at Corinth, he reasoned in the synagogues relatively unsuccessfully in terms of numbers, trying to persuade both Jews and Greeks that Jesus was the Christ (cf. Acts 18:4). Salvation belongs to the Lord; it entails the Spirit's illumination of the text.

Conclusion

Spiritual exercises that grind the exegete's spiritual lenses deserve separate treatment. I mentioned Luther's *oratio* (by prayer), *meditatio* (by prayer and contemplation), and *tentatio* (by personal experience) elsewhere.[29] Owen argues persuasively for a "fervent and earnest prayer for the assistance of the Spirit of God revealing the mind of God," "readiness to receive impressions from divine truths as revealed unto us," "practical obedience in the course of walking before God," etc.[30] We ought not to consign these concerns to Pneumatology or relegate them to devotional books on the spiritual life. They are at the heart of the exegetical process. What I am contending for in this paper is that the Bible is not like ordinary literature any more than the eucharist is like ordinary food. To make my point memorable, let me state it

29. B. K. Waltke, "On How to Study the Psalms Devotionally," *Crux* (June 1980). See *Luther's Works* 34:285-87.

30. Owen, *Works*, 4:118-234.

311

absurdly: exegetical theologians who dedicate themselves to instructing the expositor on how to exegete the text by the grammatico-historical method alone are like systematic theologians who, in explaining the eucharist, dedicate themselves to instructing the worshiper on how to chew the bread and digest it.

How I Changed My Mind about Teaching Hebrew (or Retained It)

Introduction

Let me take this opportunity to thank the president of the National Association of Hebrew Professors for inviting me to be one of the four participants on this panel assigned the topic "How I Changed My Mind about Teaching Hebrew." As the title suggests, my presentation is a personal, descriptive statement of my pilgrimage in teaching Hebrew, not a prescription for others to follow. Nevertheless, it would gratify me if this exercise proves profitable to you in our common task. Because of time restraints, I must address the topic selectively, not exhaustively. I have divided my presentation into two parts: What I retained in teaching biblical Hebrew, and what I changed or intend to change.

What I Retained in Teaching Hebrew

Theological motivation. First and most importantly, I have not changed my mind about the importance of motivation in teaching and learning Hebrew. The primary work of a teacher is to motivate students to love, not hate, to be attracted to, not repulsed by, to be enthusiastic for, not bored by, his subject. If the student is motivated to learn the course of study, no matter how poorly it may otherwise be taught, the student will eventually master it. A teacher

---

Paper presented at a gathering of the National Association of Hebrew Professors meeting in Washington, D.C., in November 1993. Previously published in *Crux* 29, no. 2 (June 1993).

who bores students should have a millstone tied around his neck and be cast into the sea.

Shortly after I began the study of Hebrew, over forty years ago now, I became motivated to comprehend the biblical languages when I realized that most of my knowledge of God was derived from Holy Scripture, and the accuracy of that knowledge was contingent upon the correctness with which I handled its languages. God incarnated himself in those languages, not only in the body of Jesus Christ to whom they point. Instructively, in the closing letters of Paul, the apostle to the Gentiles, and of Peter, the apostle to the Jews, just prior to their deaths, they both wed their Christian teachings with the God-breathed Old Testament. In his letter with the famous closing line, "I have fought the good fight, I have finished the race, I have kept the faith" (2 Tim. 4:7), Paul wrote:

> But as for you, continue in what you have learned and have become convinced of, because you know those from whom you learned it, and how from infancy you have known the holy Scriptures, which are able to make you wise for salvation through faith in Christ Jesus. All Scripture is God-breathed and is useful for teaching, rebuking, correcting and training in righteousness, so that the man of God may be thoroughly equipped for every good work. (2 Tim. 3:14-17)

Likewise Peter, immediately after writing "I think it is right to refresh your memory as long as I live in the tent of this body, because I know that I will soon put it aside, as our Lord Jesus Christ has made clear to me," added:

> And I will make every effort to see that after my departure you will always be able to remember these things. We did not follow cleverly invented stories when we told you about the power and coming of our Lord Jesus Christ, but we were eyewitnesses of his majesty. . . . And we have the word of the prophets made more certain, and you will do well to pay attention to it, as to a light, shining in a dark place, until the day dawns and the morning star rises in your hearts. Above all, you must understand no prophecy of Scripture came about by the prophet's own interpretation. For prophecy never had its origin in the will of man, but men spoke from God, as they were carried along by the Holy Spirit. (2 Pet. 1:13-21)

The logic of this Christian theology, that God revealed himself through the Scripture, inescapably led me to the conclusion that the authenticity of that knowledge rested on a precise understanding of the biblical languages. That conviction led me to earn my first doctorate in Greek and New Testament and the second in the Ancient Near Eastern languages and literatures with a major in Old Testament. From the beginning of my formal theological education it remained my purpose, by God's grace, to be in God's house an article of gold and silver, not of wood and clay, for noble purposes, not ignoble, so as to be "an instrument for noble purposes, made holy, useful to the Master and prepared to do any good work" (2 Tim. 2:20-21). I must confess that I find it difficult to engage theological presentations that have not been purged through the fire of careful exegesis.

This theological motivation also led scholarly Jews such as Saadia Gaon (882-942 CE), Menahem ben Saruq (c. 910-c. 970), Dunash ben Labrat (c. 929-990), Yehuda Hayyuj (c. 940-c. 1010) and Jonah ben Janah (990-1050) to write the first Hebrew grammars. The first Jewish grammarians defended their activity with the philosophical and theological argument that proper knowledge of the Hebrew Scriptures depends on grammar. David Tene noted:

> Around the end of the first millennium C.E. writing about linguistic issues was a new phenomenon in Jewish literature, considered by many important people as a vain, senseless activity. Therefore in their introductions, the authors [of grammatical works] discuss the motivating fact which stimulated them to write their linguistic works. They seek to prove to their readers that it is incumbent upon Jews to take up the investigation of their language, and their arguments include the following points: (1) language is the means for all discernment and linguistics is the means for all investigation and wisdom; (2) the fulfillment of the commandments depends upon the understanding of the written word, and in turn, the proper knowledge of the language is impossible without the aid of linguistics.[1]

These arguments are still cogent and inescapable for any community that builds its faith on Holy Scripture. That rationale motivated the several Christian schools that have hired me to teach Hebrew over these past forty years to include courses on Hebrew in their curricula. I have not dared to betray their trust.

---

1. Cited by Bruce K. Waltke and M. O'Connor, *An Introduction to Biblical Hebrew Syntax* (Winona Lake, IN: Eisenbrauns, 1990), p. 32.

True theology and precise exegesis are, to use modern jargon, systemically dependent upon one another. Without a right relationship to the Spirit who inspired Scriptures, good exegesis is impossible, and without grammatico-historical exegesis, good theology is impossible. Jacques B. Doukhan, in the Old Testament Department at Andrews University Theological Seminary, recently wrote:

> Who would question the pertinence of learning the English language in order to understand the world of Shakespeare? Or, to be more up-to-date, who would ignore the need for learning English to be able to understand and handle the current intricacies of the political and economical life in America? Yet, when it comes to the Bible, it seems that ignorance is allowed and even recommended. The reason for this paradox lies especially in our "religious" sympathy with the Israel of the Bible, because we identify the God of Ancient Israel with our God. In more simple terms, this means that the claim for a present relationship with the God of Israel makes the study of the antique language irrelevant. This subjective approach overlooks the importance of God's revelation in history.[2]

Once students grasp how essential precise exegesis is to sound theology, they tune in. In fact, many informed students begin their study of Hebrew highly motivated for theological reasons. I have aimed throughout my career to inculcate, foster, nurture, and capitalize on this motivation. Doukhan, citing Frank Michaeli,[3] rightly noted that a nontheological approach to teaching Hebrew will kill the language a second time. Doukhan says: "Rules which have been taught apart from the biblical text and apart from a reference to the religious dimension, hence apart from what essentially motivates students of biblical Hebrew, will hardly be grasped and memorized."[4]

Let me validate my point by an anecdote. When I became head of the department of Old Testament at Dallas Theological Seminary in 1968, I held a daylong retreat at a local Ramada Inn for the approximately twenty-

2. Jacques B. Doukhan, *Hebrew for Theologians: A Textbook for the Study of Biblical Hebrew in Relation to Hebrew Thinking* (Lanham, MD: University Press of America, 1993), pp. ix, x.

3. Cf. Frank Michaeli, "Grammaire hébraïque et théologie biblique," in *Hommage à Wilhelm Vischer* (Montpellier: Causse-Graille-Castehiau, 1960), p. 145.

4. Doukhan, *Hebrew for Theologians*, pp. xxiv, xxv.

five students majoring in Old Testament. The topic of the day was: "What is wrong with the Old Testament Department at the seminary?" I wanted frank and candid answers. Though I think of myself as making myself vulnerable to students, I was surprised by my reaction. When I came home that night I literally threw up; I had so internalized their criticisms. Their main complaint was that the department taught the nuts and bolts of Hebrew but without an adequate theological dimension. From that point on, I determined to integrate all my teaching with theology. Within two years we became the largest department in the school, an amazing phenomenon when one considers that Dallas holds the theological distinctive and, as I now realize, aberrant theology that the Old Testament is meant for Jews, not for Christians!

Let me now illustrate how I do this from how I teach the alphabet, normally the first lesson in Hebrew grammar. The alphabet is obviously foundational to all exegesis of the Hebrew Scriptures, but its own exegetical relevance can be discerned in the acrostic poems, Psalms 9, 10, 25, 34, 37, 111, 112, 119; Lamentations 1–4; and Proverbs 31:1-31. In particular I show on an overhead Psalm 34. Here the student readily sees that each verse begins with a successive letter of the Hebrew alphabet. Something is wrong, however, because its last verse begins with peh after verse 22, instead of taw, the last letter of the Hebrew alphabet. To complicate the matter, verse 17 also begins with peh, as expected. Is verse 23 a later scribal addition? That unlikely hypothesis is falsified by the same phenomenon in Psalm 25. More probably, this didactic psalm intentionally employed on its vertical axis in initial position aleph ('), as its first letter, lamed (l) as its medial letter, and peh (p) as its final letter, because *'lp* means "teach." Our suspicion is confirmed when one finds on the horizontal axis of the first verse the same sequence: ' being its first letter, l its medial, and p its final consonant.[5] Moreover, its synonym, *lmd*, "to teach," is the last word of the middle verse, the lamed line in verse 12. The next period, by way of review, I show students that Jeremiah, so as not to offend the Babylonians, used the code known as Atbash. In this code aleph equals tav; beth, the second letter of the Hebrew alphabet, matches shin, the second letter from the end of that alphabet; and so forth. With this code in hand, it becomes apparent that the anomalous "Sheshak" in Jeremiah 25:26; 51:41 is "Babel." Perhaps Ezekiel, his contemporary, used a similar code with "Magog." That enigmatic name, unfortunately providing great sport for amateur prophecy buffs, is unique in all of the thousands of An-

5. The final yodh is a *mater lectionis,* not a consonant.

cient Near Eastern texts apart from the Bible.[6] When read backwards, however, and each letter reduced by one, it also means "Babel."[7]

Deductive and inductive method. Second, I have not changed my mind about mixing a deductive approach to teaching Hebrew with an inductive approach. The former is necessary to give students an understanding of the whole, for the parts of anything are learned best when their function within the whole system is understood. Furthermore, since grammatical forms only have meaning in opposition to other grammatical forms, the meaning of any given form can only be demonstrated in light of the overall opposing structures within the language. One Hebrew teacher confessed to me that during her first year of studying Hebrew her professor employed exclusively the inductive approach. She found what she had comprehended to be so meager that it was practically worthless, and that she had to start all over again to grasp the language more comprehensively and clearly through a deductive approach. On the other hand, a hands-on experience with the text itself, which positively affects the psychology of the student, cannot be replaced by a secondhand discussion of it.

Exegesis, not speaking. Third, I have not changed my mind that within Christian schools Hebrew must be taught to enable students to use effectively exegetical tools, not to speak the language. We learn our native language inductively by speaking it, and this probably remains the ideal way to learn a second language. Unfortunately, that method is impossible in our Christian theological schools. The United States Army determined scientifically that its takes ten months (= 5,000 hours) of saturated study (i.e., hearing exclusively the one being studied) to speak adequately any language. By contrast, the Hebrew teacher typically has a student in class three hours a week for thirty weeks during the school year, for a total of ninety hours a year. Moreover, most deans insist that a teacher not exact more than two hours of study outside of class for each hour spent in class, allowing the stu-

---

6. A popular and sober etymology derives the name from Akkadian (*ma[t] gugu,* "land of Gyges [king of Lydia])." If that derivation is correct, then Ezekiel, an approximate contemporary, failed to understand it, for he uses the Hebrew word for "land" alongside *Mago,* an unlikely redundancy if the popular etymology is correct. Others derive it from the prefix *ma-,* indicating place (*Introduction to Biblical Hebrew Syntax,* 5.6b, p. 90). Therefore it means Gog's place. The prefix, however, is normally used with verbal roots, not proper names. Moreover, the fact remains that the name is unexpectedly unattested outside of the Bible (Gen. 10:2; 1 Chron. 1:5; Ezek. 38:1-6; 39:6; Rev. 20:8).

7. I am indebted to the late Raymond Dillard, professor of Old Testament at Westminster Theological Seminary, for this suggestion.

dent the leisure of another 180 hours, for a sum total of 270 hours per year, less than one-sixth the required time required to speak it. Furthermore, the study of Hebrew in our Christian schools is not saturated study, because students must learn the other subjects in their native language. In short, the quantity and quality of time of theological education do not allow any other approach than a shortcut that empowers students to interpret accurately the Hebrew text by employing the exegetical tools, such as the dictionaries and concordances available to them.

Primary sources. Finally, I have learned over the years to use primary sources as much as possible. For example, instead of having students merely read the introduction to *Biblia Hebraica Stuttgartensia,* which is based on the oldest complete Hebrew codex, Leningrad (1009 CE), and universally accepted by scholars as the diplomatic text of Hebrew Scriptures, I now show students overheads of the Leningrad Codex itself. In this light Samuel ben Jacob, who, according to the front piece of his now famous codex, "copied, vowel-pointed and Masoretically annotated [his exemplar]," becomes a living person with whom they identify. By seeing photographs of his codex they enjoy his creativity in forming the Masorah in connection with Exodus 15, "The Song of the Sea," in the shape of waves; his method of adjusting the left margin of the column by adding nonmeaningful signs as his linotype; and his ' mistakes, such as scratching out text either to change, add, or delete it.

How I Have Changed My Mind about Teaching Hebrew

One year of required study. I have changed my mind about the amount of time a theological student should be required to take Hebrew. I have taught in situations where students were required to take one, two, and three years of Hebrew. My experience has taught me that students who take it for more than a year against their will do not retain or use the language any more effectively than those who studied it for one year only. Moreover, I have found that students who elect second-year Hebrew come highly motivated, learn more and better, and enjoy a contagious esprit de corps.

On the other hand, I still argue that a student should be required to take at least one year of Hebrew for several reasons. First, only then can a student make an intelligent decision whether or not to continue the study. Second, it takes that amount of time to develop minimal competency in using the language. To be sure, all learning is relative, and one lecture on exegesis is better than none, but to develop adequate exegetical competence —

the foundation for authentic theology — takes at least a year of study. Nevertheless, a course in exegesis that uses only the English Bible has the marked advantage of subverting a simplistic reading of the Bible and creating a hermeneutics of suspicion. The church, however, is in desperate need of leaders who can critically appraise the various theological winds that blow every which way. Without that critical ability, the liberal position usually wins out. The church's uneducated members, and sadly, even its leaders, are incompetent to evaluate learned debate. They typically throw up their hands in despair, lamely crying, "If the authorities can't agree, how can we decide?" Whereupon, the debated doctrine and practice that best comply with the latest cultural fad are adopted and the true biblical doctrine and practice are rejected. To be sure, we have good translations, but as the Italian proverb goes, "Traduttore traditore," "translations are treacherous." Moreover, due to the many translations that currently surfeit the market, some Christians run down the fire escape of calling the translation they dislike into question and fleeing to one more to their liking. It amazes me how arrogantly some uneducated Christians pronounce a translation good on this basis. A year of study in the original languages by Christian leaders would help stamp out this nonsense.

Vocabulary. Second, I have changed my mind on the importance of learning vocabulary; I need to spend more time focusing on word-stock and on teaching students how to memorize. M. Brown Azarowicz et al. noted that words are best learned:

1) by memorizing words groups according to related meaning (e.g., *'alah,* "to go up," *'al,* "upon," *'ola,* "burnt offering," *ma'la,* "ascent," etc.); 2) by review ten minutes after initial learning; 3) by review sixty minutes after that; 4) by review again twenty-four hours later; 5) by review every two days until automatic recall is attained.[8]

Mechanical parsing. Finally, were I teaching first-year Hebrew, I would spend more time on teaching students by means of a mechanical method of parsing. In addition to learning paradigms, students will be greatly assisted to parse grammatical forms, especially the many dialectical variants that must be confronted in the Hebrew text. By learning to think in terms of vowel classes, a higher abstraction of structure, these morphological differ-

8. M. Brown Azarowicz et al., *Yes! You Can Learn a Foreign Language* (Lincolnwood, IL: Passport Books).

ences can be transcended. For example, in prefix conjugation forms, the performative i class of vowels is found in the Qal and Niphal stems, indistinct vowels in D stem forms, and a class of vowels in the Qal and Hiphil stems.

Conclusion

In conclusion I want to thank God for allowing me the privilege of teaching Hebrew, the Bible, and theology to more than seven thousand students over these past thirty-five years. When I was a resident at Harvard, I read many times on the Johnson Gate leading into the Yard the reason why the Puritans founded the college. Their dedication begins: "Dreading to leave an illiterate clergy. . . ." Though I would change the word "clergy" to "church," their words articulate my motivation for teaching Hebrew. Consistent with their stated purpose, the second chair the Puritans established at Harvard was the chair of Old Testament.

Kingdom Promises as Spiritual*

Introduction

By "kingdom promises as spiritual" is meant God's OT promises in covenants, types, and prophecy to come into the world in the person of his king and establish his righteous, universal, everlasting, beneficent reign as fulfilled, according to the NT witness, in the advent of the Lord Jesus Christ. His advent occurred in two phases: first in the flesh, and then, after his ascension to his heavenly throne, in the Holy Spirit, by whom he forms his body, the church, in the world.

This essay aims to interpret the covenantal promises in the light of salvation history, and on that basis to lay out accredited rules for the interpretation of types and prophecy. It will be concluded that the kingdom promises are comprehensively fulfilled in the church, not in restored national Israel.

Before sketching salvation history with a focus on God's covenants, here are some rules for the interpretation of Scripture that the writer holds as self-evident beyond the widely accredited grammatico-historical approach.[1]

The rule *sola scriptura* (the Bible alone is authoritative for faith and practice), as opposed to the authority of tradition, is too well known to re-

---

*This essay is dedicated in honor of Professor S. Lewis Johnson, through whom — more than anyone else — God influenced me to think and live biblically.

1. See Bruce K. Waltke, "Historical Grammatical Problems," in *Hermeneutics, Inerrancy, and the Bible*, ed. Earl D. Radmacher and Robert D. Preus (Grand Rapids: Zondervan, 1984).

Previously published in *Continuity and Discontinuity, Perspectives on the Relationship between the Old and New Testaments: Essays in Honor of Lewis S. Johnson Jr.*, ed. John S. Feinberg (Westchester, IL: Crossway, 1988).

quire comment here. Contemporary theologians of varying positions, however, are looking to the state of Israel for their interpretation of Scripture. Some modern ecumenicists are reasserting an abiding link between the Jewish people, the Bible, and the land of Palestine, and claim that national Israel retains in the purpose of God's grace an essential role in the mediation of reconciliation.[2] Some Dutch theologians are calling both for a new understanding of the place of the Jewish people and their state in God's program for history and for a reevaluation of Reformed theology and hermeneutics.[3] Premillennialists plausibly appeal to the restoration of national Israel as confirmation of their cherished belief that Christ's consummate glory in history will be displayed in his reign with the church over restored national Israel.[4]

Ancient Israel made a similar error during its last century of existence when, instead of looking solely to Scripture to understand its history, the religious establishment looked to God's remarkable deliverance of Jerusalem in 701 BC as confirmation of their tragic delusion that the temple could not fall.[5] Superficial judgments often lead to mistaken conclusions.[6]

Priority of New Testament Interpretation over the Interpretation of Theologians

Second, the classical rule *sacra scriptura sui ipsius interpres* (the Bible interprets itself) — more specifically, the New interprets the Old — should be accepted by all Christian theologians. Is it not self-evident that the author of Scripture is the final exponent of his own thoughts? Should not the rule so often used by dispensationalists, who traditionally saw no connection between the OT promises and the church, that the NT cannot contradict the OT, be reversed to say that the OT cannot contradict the NT? Should not

2. T. F. Torrance, *The Mediation of Christ* (Grand Rapids: Eerdmans, 1983), pp. 25-26, 55-56. For a critique of similar views of Paul Van Buren, see Mark Karlberg, "Israel as Light to the Nations: A Review Article," *JETS* 28 (1985): 205-11.

3. See, for example, Hendrikus Berkhof, *Christ the Meaning of History* (Richmond, VA: John Knox, 1966); A. A. van Ruler, *The Christian Church and the Old Testament* (Grand Rapids: Eerdmans, 1971); and more recently Willem A. VanGemeren, "Israel as the Hermeneutical Crux in the Interpretation of Prophecy," *WTJ* 45 (1983): 132-44 and *WTJ* 46 (1984): 254-97. Some of these writers deny even more fundamental doctrines of Reformed theology.

4. Hal Lindsey, *The Late Great Planet Earth* (Grand Rapids: Zondervan, 1970).

5. John Bright, *A History of Israel*, 3rd ed. (Philadelphia: Westminster, 1981), p. 335.

6. See Mark Noll, "Misreading the Signs of the Times," *Christianity Today*, February 6, 1987, pp. 10-11.

theologians who put the enigmatic visions of prophets on a par with the most direct revelation in Christ fear? Recall how God judged the prophet and prophetess, Aaron and Miriam, for putting themselves on a par with Moses, to whom he gave more direct revelation (cf. Numbers 12). Does not the posture that begins first with the theologian's interpretation of the OT instead of with the NT beg the issue by presuming a hermeneutic for interpreting the promises before looking to the Scriptures themselves? Are not dispensationalists inconsistent with their own theology, which looks to the teachings of our Lord after his moral rejection by Israel and to the apostles as normative for the faith and practice of the church, when they start not with the literature they find normative, but with their own autonomous rules for interpreting the OT? Lewis Johnson Jr. wrote:

> The use of the Old Testament in the New is the key to the solution of the problem of hermeneutics. Unfortunately that has been overlooked, but surely, if the apostles are reliable teachers of biblical doctrine, then they are reliable instructors in the science of hermeneutics.[7]

If someone objects that the rule is too broad because NT writers use the OT in various ways, most will at least agree with C. H. Dodd:

> The employment of these scriptures [Old Testament prophecy] as testimonies to the *kerygma* indicates that the crisis out of which the Christian movement arose is regarded as the realization of the prophetic vision of judgment and redemption.[8]

Priority of Clear Texts over Obscure Ones

The Westminster divines recognized that "all things in Scripture are not alike plain in themselves, nor alike clear unto all. . . ."[9] Is it not self-evident

7. S. Lewis Johnson Jr., *The Old Testament in the New* (Grand Rapids: Zondervan, 1980), p. 23.

8. C. H. Dodd, *According to the Scriptures* (London: Collins, 1952), p. 72; cf. Roger R. Nicole, "Patrick Fairbairn and Biblical Hermeneutics as Related to the Quotations of the Old Testament in the New," in *Hermeneutics, Inerrancy and the Bible*, ed. Earl D. Radmacher and Robert Preus (Grand Rapids: Zondervan, 1984), pp. 756-78; G. Ernest Wright, "The Problem of Archaizing Ourselves," *Int* 3 (1979): 457ff.

9. Westminster Confession, 1.7.

that unclear texts should be interpreted in the light of clear ones and not vice versa? As the law of Moses is clearer than the dreams and visions of prophets (Num. 12:6-8), so also the apostolic letters and epistles in plain speech, though admittedly containing "some things that are hard to understand" (2 Pet. 3:16), are clearer than prophetic visions and the symbolic visions of apocalyptic literature that need angels to interpret them. Should the Christian theologian construct his theological model from symbolic texts and distort and cut up clear ones to fit his dubious mold? Theological models should be built from the clear teachings of our Lord and his apostles and then, and only then, adorned with symbolic texts.

Priority of Spiritual Illumination over Scientific Exegesis

As the saint imbibes the spiritual presence of Christ while eating the bread and drinking the cup at the Lord's Table, so also in the reading of the Scriptures one participates in the life and thought of God through Christ Jesus in the Spirit (Eph. 2:18).

Moreover, the Holy Spirit, Scripture's divine author, both authenticates it to the saint by his inward witness and opens his mind to understand its meaning.[10] Without God's supernatural enlightenment, which is granted only to the childlike, his truths about Christ and his kingdom are hidden from the wise and the learned (Matt. 11:25-27). Even the apostles, whose eyes saw and whose hands touched the blessed Son of God (1 John 1:1), needed supernatural enlightenment to know his true identity (Matt. 16:17). The orthodox Jews, who confessed the infallible authority of Scripture, did not know him (John 5:45-47), because God had drawn a veil over their unbelieving hearts (2 Corinthians 3).

The rule that one must first establish what the revelation meant to the original audience is problematic, because to unbelievers it meant one thing and to believers it meant another. All too often evangelicals have interpreted the text wherein God has hidden himself according to its meaning to unenlightened minds. One must look to the Spirit's interpretation of God's thoughts (1 Cor. 2:9-16). Furthermore, evangelical teachers of every persuasion, including this writer, need to repent for their brash attempts to find God, who veils himself in Scripture from the proud, through merely scien-

---

10. "The Chicago Statement on Biblical Inerrancy," in *Inerrancy,* ed. Norman Geisler (Grand Rapids: Zondervan, 1979), pp. 493-502.

tific exegesis which they control. Furthermore, he will delude any evangelical, including this writer, if he or she comes to the Scripture with a closed mind, feigning to hear his word, even as he deluded Balaam (contrast Num. 22:20 and 22) and Ahab (cf. 1 Kings 22:15-17).

Let us now consider the covenantal promises within the frame of salvation history.

Salvation History

By "salvation history" is meant the particular and unified history of God's mediatorial kingdom, in contrast to his universal kingdom, as it is revealed and interpreted in Scripture and through which he is effecting his moral will on earth. It does not mean here, as German theologians use the term, that this history is the ultimate datum of revelation, nor is it used as an excuse to exercise a measure of criticism upon Scripture or to pit it against actual history.

Throughout sacred history God has elected saints to enjoy what Jeremiah later proclaimed as the provisions of the "new covenant" — namely, regeneration, the forgiveness of sin, and intimate knowledge and communion with God (Jer. 31:31-34). More specifically, God forms and sustains this mediatorial kingdom by his word of promise about the Christ in the OT and through the gospel proclamation, the kerygma of Jesus Christ, in the NT. To use the classic statement of Gerhard von Rad, "Christ is given to us only through the double witness of the choir of those who await and those who remember."[11] He who alone authors virtue gives his elect the gift of faith, attended with writing his law on their hearts and cleansing them from sin through the blood of Christ (Rom. 3:21-26).

This mediatorial kingdom began with Adam and Eve in the Garden of Eden, where God in sovereign grace put enmity in their hearts against Satan (Gen. 3:15), an enmity that carries as its correlative a love of God (cf. Deut. 6:5; Matt. 22:37ff.; Mark 9:40). To the formerly wretched couple he promised a "seed" that would destroy the serpent. No sensitive reader can construe the story as an etiology explaining the antagonism between humans and snakes, as the professor who, second to Lewis Johnson, was most influential in developing the scholarship of this writer, insisted was the "plain sense" of the

11. Gerhard von Rad, "Typological Interpretation of the Old Testament," in *Essays on Old Testament Hermeneutics*, ed. Claus Westermann (Richmond, VA: John Knox, 1963), p. 39.

passage. The serpent, a diabolic personality, more intelligent than humans, filled with a spirit of unbelief, and venomously opposed to God and man, *obviously* originated outside of the creation described in Genesis 1–2. John unmasks him as Satan in Revelation 20:2, the only interpreted symbol in that debated text, and our Lord counts the unbelieving Pharisees among his seed (John 8:44).

Even as Satan's seed is "spiritual," so is the woman's. That seed, according to normative Christology, is Christ and the church in him (Rom. 16:20). Adam, seizing by faith this one promise in the midst of curses, named his wife Eve, "Life," and she became the mother of the living, presumably of the spiritual seed. God provided a sacrifice for the formerly spiritually divorced couple, restoring them in love to one another. The mediatorial kingdom that destroys the Devil is also soteriological, having been saved from his domain.

Noah prophesied both that the Lord committed himself (and implicitly his soteriological kingdom) to Shem and that Japheth would come to "dwell in his tent." That is, according to Vos,[12] the Japhethites would overrun Shemitic lands, entailing a coming religious blessing to Japheth.

God so delighted in his friend, the Semite Abraham, that he purposed to concentrate his mediatorial realm in his physical seed and carefully marked it out by circumcision. To Abraham and his seed (Gal. 3:16) God promised, "I will bless those who bless you . . . and all peoples on earth will be blessed through you" (Gen. 12:3). Note first the "seed," and then the "peoples."

Peter in Acts 3:25-26 identifies Abraham's offspring mediating blessing not with the nation of Israel, who themselves needed to be blessed, but with the servant, Jesus Christ. Commenting on this text, McComiskey wrote:

> Peter understood Christ to be the mediator of the blessings of the promise. This is clear from his ascription of the blessing cited in Acts 3:25 to the work of the servant (v. 26).[13]

Paul emphatically equated the promised mediatorial seed with Christ: ". . . Abraham and to his seed . . . who is Christ" (Gal. 3:16).

By the Spirit's baptism (1 Cor. 12:13) the whole church, both Jew and Gentile, becomes Christ's body, so that it too is the seed of Abraham (Gal. 3:29) and may be designated a "spiritual kingdom." Paul elsewhere says: "If

---

12. Geerhardus Vos, *Biblical Theology* (Grand Rapids: Eerdmans, 1948), pp. 70ff.

13. Thomas Edward McComiskey, *The Covenants of Promise* (Grand Rapids: Baker, 1985), p. 31.

you belong to Christ, then you are Abraham's seed, and heirs according to the promise" (Gal. 3:29; cf. Eph. 2:19). Moreover, Christ, who never married, begets his "offspring" after his death (Isa. 53:10). The exalted Christ, the head of the mediatorial kingdom called "the church" in the NT, uniquely mediates blessing through his death and resurrection, and his body on earth now fills up his sufferings by faithfully mediating his work in word and life to a hostile world (Col. 1:24). "Understand, then, that those who believe are children of Abraham" (Gal. 3:7).

The stories about Abraham underscore that the seed is essentially spiritual, not carnal. On the one hand, not all of Abraham's offspring participated in this mediatorial role of blessing. Ishmael of Hagar and the half-dozen sons of Keturah were all excluded from mediating blessing (that is, life and prosperity and victory over their enemies), so that the seed would come through Isaac out of Sarah's dead womb in response to the godly couple's faith in God's promise (Rom. 4:18-21). On the other hand, the mediatorial kingdom included circumcised persons who were not Abraham's offspring (Gen. 17:12).

Circumcision, the sign of this everlasting covenant (Gen. 17:13), symbolized the circumcision of the heart (Deut. 10:16; 30:6). With the advent of Christ and the establishing of the church, the doors of the temple of the living God were flung wide open to Gentiles, and the fleshly sign, so appropriate when God concentrated the mediatorial kingdom in Abraham's physical seed, was done away and probably replaced by baptism (Col. 2:11-12).

God also promised that the soteriological kingdom, now identified with Abraham's offspring, would enjoy intimate fellowship with God (Gen. 17:7-8), an essential provision of the New Covenant. The promise of knowing the holy God entails redemption, the forgiveness of sin through the blood of Christ.

As the mediatorial seed is spiritual, so also the nations that God has promised to bless are essentially spiritual, not political, in character. Regarding the nations, note first Paul's inspired comment on the above text: "The Scripture . . . announced the gospel in advance to Abraham: 'All nations will be blessed through you.' So those who have faith are blessed along with Abraham, the man of faith" (Gal. 3:8-9). The promise "I have made you a father of many nations" (Gen. 17:5) does not refer to the Ishmaelites, Edomites, Asshurites, Letushites, and the Leummites, though begotten physically from Abraham, but to nations that believe in Christ — though apart from Christ they can claim no descent from Abraham (Rom. 4:17).

In connection with his promise to make Abraham the father of nations, God also promised that kings would come from Abraham (Gen. 17:6). Once again, physical kings apart from Jesus Christ are not in view, though physical kings did come from Abraham, but both Israelite and Gentile kings who are sprinkled with Christ's blood and who worship him as Lord of all (cf. Isa. 52:15).

The nations are no longer reckoned as nations but as one nation, for the promise said, "I will make you into a great nation . . . and all peoples on earth will be blessed through you."[14] That nation composed of families from all over the earth is the church (1 Pet. 2:9-10). In sum, the seed and the nations become one.

Finally, note that a person becomes a member in this righteous nation by faith (Gal. 3:9). Abraham, the father of us all, saw the day of Christ and rejoiced (John 8:56). He believed the promise of a resurrected seed, and it was counted to him for righteousness (Rom. 4:22ff.); and "the words 'it was credited to him,'" says the apostle to the Gentiles, "were written not for him alone, but also for us . . ." (v. 24ff.).

Those who read the text with an accent on the Jews, who are normally identified as not believing in Christ, and not on the church in Christ, have dull minds, according to the apostles, and need to awake from their spiritual stupor. Many well-intentioned evangelical leaders distort these promises to Abraham and dishonor Christ and his church by classifying Abraham as "Jewish" and by referring these promises to unbelievers who profess to be Abraham's physical offspring. Official expressions of Judaism deny that Jesus is the Christ, the Son of God. Furthermore, by interpreting God's threat to curse those who do not bless Abraham's seed (Gen. 12:3a) as referring to the failure to support his unbelieving physical seed, they lay the church under false guilt and bondage if it does not support the state of Israel. The cause of Zionism has to be championed on other grounds than God's promises to Abraham.

God also promised Abraham's spiritual seed a land. He fulfilled this promise materially to national Israel to display within history his faithfulness to his promises, but that fulfillment does not exhaust its significance, as later revelation clarifies (e.g., Ps. 95:11; Heb. 3:7–4:13; 11:39ff.). The material manifestations of the promises to Abraham — circumcision, the birth of Isaac from the dead bodies of his parents, the sacrifice of Isaac, etc. — are all types of the spiritual kingdom brought to fulfillment in Christ and, as will be argued, will be consummated in the new earth. Murray wrote: "It is a prom-

14. W. J. Dumbrell, *Covenant and Creation* (Exeter, UK: Paternoster, 1984), pp. 65-67.

ise that receives its ultimate fulfillment in the consummated order of the new heavens and the new earth."[15] The subject of "land" is taken up again under "types" and "prophecy."

The drama of sacred history took a complicating twist when God added centuries later the Mosaic Covenant to Abraham's seed. As Abraham was the father of "true Israel" (his physical seed that believed in Christ), Moses was the founder of national Israel (Abraham's natural and spiritual seed as administered under the law). God's soteriological kingdom, originally founded on the principle of promise-faith, now became united in a kingdom with the contrary principle of law-inheritance. God revealed to national Israel a law that taught them righteousness, governed their civil behavior, and prescribed how to worship him. He asked them to accept it out of gratitude for saving them from their slavery in Egypt and to trust God, but he made no provision in the law to write it upon their hearts (contrast Deut. 10:16 with 30:6). This Old Covenant, which formed the nation, promised blessings and life for obedience, and threatened curses and death for disobedience (Lev. 26:3-45; Deuteronomy 28). Both the New and Old Covenants were righteous and promised life; but whereas the former was unconditional, because it depended solely on God's sovereign grace, the latter was conditional, because it depended on fallen man to keep it (Gal. 3:10-14; Rom. 10:5-13).

Even while God drew near to walk with this nation, indicted by Moses as blind, deaf, proud, ungrateful, stiff-necked, and spiritually uncircumcised of heart (Deut. 1:26-43; 8:14ff.; 9:7ff.), at the same time he drew a veil separating it from him. Although he bore them out of Egypt on eagle's wings, he terrified them with thunder and smoke at Sinai (Exodus 19; Heb. 12:18-21). Space is lacking to discuss the relationship of believing Israel to the law, but one observes its faith and practices in the Psalms (e.g., Psalms 1; 19; 119).

As the drama of salvation unfolded, God placed David over his kingdom and promised him an eternal seed, an eternal throne, and an eternal kingdom (2 Sam. 7:12-16). The seed, as most will agree, is the same seed promised to Eve and Adam and to Abraham (cf. Gen. 17:6) — that is, Christ. The kingdom also is the one promised to Abraham, a spiritual nation composed of families of varying ethnic backgrounds, be it recalled. The eternal nature of this kingdom cannot be material, because David's political throne and dominion perished, but his spiritual kingdom is and will be forever on earth.

As the material aspects of the promises to Abraham typify Christ and his

---

15. John Murray, *The Epistle to the Romans,* 2 vols., The New International Commentary on the New Testament (Grand Rapids: Eerdmans, 1960), 1:142.

church, so also with the promises to David; e.g., Mount Zion typifies and finds its fulfillment in heavenly Mount Zion (Heb. 12:22). Scripture itself must clarify what is fulfilled materially (e.g., both the seed of Abraham and of David have a material fulfillment in the lineage of our Lord) and what aspects of the type became obsolete when they were replaced by their heavenly antitypes.

The Assyrian and Babylonian invasions, conquests, and annexations of the land sworn to Abraham triggered the prophetic movement in Israel, which under inspiration of the Spirit saw that God was now fulfilling his threat to destroy national Israel for the failure to obey the law. As will be seen, the prophets threatened the unbelieving nation's doom, but beyond that judgment they foresaw in harmony with God's covenantal promises that God would reestablish them in the mediatorial kingdom, administered exclusively under the New Covenant (Jer. 31:31-34) and ruled by Messiah, the ideal king.

As is well known, John the Baptist and Christ announced that the kingdom of God was at hand — that is, the kingdom anticipated in the prophetic and apocalyptic literature, wherein Messiah would come to restore Israel and judge the nations. Note first that in the NT, in contrast to the expectation of Judaism, the kingdom's character is "heavenly" and "spiritual," not "earthly" and "political"; and second, that instead of coming in one stage, as Judaism expected, it is consummated in two.[16]

Christ never presented himself as an earthly king ruling over a restored political state. George Ladd rightly affirmed:

> Jesus did not offer to the Jews the earthly kingdom anymore than he offered himself to them as their glorious earthly king. Here we may take our stand on firm ground.[17]

Philip Mauro validated the point:

> Did your Lord, during His earthly ministry . . . ever present or announce Himself as an earthly King. . . ? Did He ever offer to the oppressed people of Judea, either in person or through the lips of His disciples, the earthly kingdom they had been taught to expect? Had He ever, by word or act, sought to incite insurrection against the rule of Caesar, or given

---

16. Mark W. Karlberg, "Legitimate Discontinuities Between the Testaments," *JETS* 28, no. 1 (March 1985): 9-20.

17. G. E. Ladd, *Crucial Questions about the Kingdom of God* (Grand Rapids: Eerdmans, 1952), p. 113.

any countenance whatever to the political ambitions of the Jews?[18] . . .
Manifestly, had the Lord uttered a single word that could have been con-
strued as a proclamation or suggestion that He was about to claim the
throne, or would accept it, there would have been thousands of witnesses to prove the accusation. But there was no proof forthcoming.[19]

This truth negates both Johannes Weiss's[20] and Albert Schweitzer's[21]
"consistent eschatology theory" (namely, that Christ's kingdom was not a
spiritual kingdom but entirely a future apocalyptic reality) and Scofield's[22]
and Chafer's[23] "postponement theory" (namely, that when Israel rejected
Christ, he withdrew the earthly kingdom, postponing its coming until after
his second advent and in the interim intercalated a spiritual kingdom, the
church, which was unforeseen by the prophets).

The arrival of the messianic kingdom in the advent of our Lord inaugurated a kingdom at the end of the ages that has both a present and a future
fulfillment. This "semi-eschatological kingdom" (Vos's term) is already present in his person, who redeems believers from their sin and judges Satan; but
final deliverance and judgment await his second, glorious appearing. Earle
Ellis[24] diagrams this perspective in contrast to Platonism and apocalyptic
Judaism as follows:

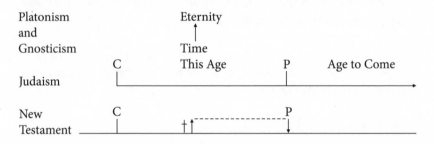

18. Philip Mauro, *God's Present Kingdom*. The relevant portion was reissued as
Dispensationalism Justifies the Crucifixion (Swengal, PA: Reiner, 1966), p. 6.

19. Mauro, *Dispensationalism Justifies the Crucifixion*, p. 20.

20. Cited by Ladd, *Crucial Questions*, p. 29.

21. Ladd, *Crucial Questions*, p. 29.

22. *The Scofield Reference Bible* (1917), p. 1011, n. 1; *The New Scofield Reference Bible*
(1967), p. 996, n. 4, *passim*.

23. L. S. Chafer, *Systematic Theology*, vol. 5 (Dallas: Dallas Theological Seminary,
1948), p. 343.

24. E. Earle Ellis, *Prophecy and Hermeneutic in Early Christianity* (Tübingen: Mohr,
1978), p. 164. "C" = creation; "P" = coming of the Messiah.

The increasing acceptance of understanding the kingdom of God as "already but not yet" is tending both to solidify premillennialism into what Ladd called "historic premillennialism"[25] (i.e., OT kingdom promises are being spiritually realized in the church age and will be materially fulfilled in a millennium when national Israel will be restored), and to bridge partially the gap between premillennialism and amillennialism. Whereas historically dispensational premillennialism radically divorced in interpretation, though not necessarily in application, the OT promises of a restored Israel under an earthly Messiah from the advent of Christ to his church in the Holy Spirit, "modified dispensationalists" are granting in varying degrees that the NT regards the church as a partial fulfillment of those promises.[26] At the same time, amillennialists are accenting more and more the future aspect of the kingdom, which they identify not with a supposed "Israelite" millennium but with the new cosmos (Revelation 21–22).

Nevertheless, there are profound differences between premillennialism in all its forms and amillennialism: in their hermeneutics, in their understanding of history, in their evaluation of national Israel and the church, and in their eschatological systems. Amillennialists emphasize that the present age is the last stretch of historical time with the correlative truths that there is no second chance for anyone, that Christ's consummate glory is in his church, that Christ authoritatively rules the nations today, and that social change must come now. As the liberal doctrine of salvation apart from Christ depre-

---

25. George Eldon Ladd, "Historic Premillennialism," in *The Meaning of the Millennium,* ed. Robert Clouse (Downers Grove, IL: InterVarsity, 1977), pp. 17-40.

26. Kenneth L. Barker, "False Dichotomies Between the Testaments," *JETS* 25, no. 1 (March 1982): 3-6, lists the view that the "OT is concerned with Israel and the NT is concerned with the Church" as a false dichotomy (see pp. 10-14). Robert Saucy, "Contemporary Dispensational Thought," *TSF Bul* 7, no. 4 (March-April 1984) says sympathetically that some dispensationalists agree with nondispensational premillennialism "that it is preferable to interpret this age as the first phase of the fulfillment of the one promised Messianic kingdom" (p. 11). Saucy separates the two by affirming that historic premillennialism merges the identity of Israel and the church in the present age, whereas this form of dispensationalism keeps them distinct while sharing the common messianic salvation. Since he does not intend by this to deny the unity of the body of Christ as taught in Ephesians 2:11–3:7, the distinction is so slight that to label one as "dispensational" only further tangles the briar patch. (Some amillennialists, such as Murray, also see a future spiritual restoration of Abraham's physical seed.) David L. Turner, "The Continuity of Scripture and Eschatology: Key Hermeneutical Issues," *GTJ* 6, no. 2 (1985): 275-87, while defending dispensational premillennialism, asks dispensationalists to be "more open to the legitimate exegetical insights of Ladd and others concerning the present aspect of God's rule" (p. 287).

ciates the value of Christ's work on the cross, as the Roman Catholic doctrine of purgatory depreciates the value and dignity of this life, so also premillennialism, the writer suggests, with its doctrine that Christ will prevail over evil through restored Israel after the rapture of the church, depreciates the dignity, value, and authority of the church in its mediatorial mission.

Amillennialists differ from dispensational premillennialists in their hermeneutics by calling for a spiritual interpretation of kingdom promises over against a "literalistic" (J. I. Packer's term) interpretation of them.[27] Amillennialists emphasize with Augustine that "the New is in the Old concealed and the Old is in the New revealed," while dispensationalists complain that in the amillennial system "the Old is by the New restricted and the New is on the Old inflicted."[28]

Amillennialism and historic premillennialism both recognize that kingdom promises must be interpreted both materially and spiritually, but they differ in their application of the principles. They also differ in their interpretation of types, for whereas the former regards them as comprehensively fulfilled in the church, the latter sees the type as being materially restored in the millennium, a strange type to say the least.

Returning to the progress of revelation and salvation history, one discovers that after Pentecost, when the Spirit was given to "guide you [the apostles] into all truth . . . and . . . tell you what is yet to come" (John 16:13), and to "bring glory to me [Christ] by taking from what is mine and making it known to you" (v. 14), *not one* clear NT passage mentions the restoration of Israel as a political nation or predicts an earthly reign of Christ before his final appearing. *None* depicts the consummate glory of Christ as an earthly king ruling over the restored nation of Israel. The Spirit's silence is deafening.

To be sure, prior to Pentecost the unenlightened apostles were still asking when the Lord would restore the national kingdom to Israel (Acts 1:6). The church, however, must not be guided by ignorance. If one argues that had our Lord disagreed with their false assumption, as a good teacher he would have corrected them, let it be noted that he did not correct the false assumption of the early church that the Apostle John would not die. Because our Lord had said in answer to Peter's question about John's death, "If I want him to remain alive until I return, what is that to you?" the rumor spread

27. Earl D. Radmacher, "The Current Status of Dispensationalism and Its Eschatology," in *Perspectives on Evangelical Theology,* ed. K. S. Kantzer and S. N. Gundry (Grand Rapids: Baker, 1979), pp. 163-76.

28. Cited by Turner, "The Continuity of Scripture and Eschatology," p. 282, n. 24.

among the primitive church that John would not die. As John has to correct their faulty inference based on ambiguity, saying, "But Jesus did not say that he would not die" (John 21:22ff.), so also with Acts 1:7-8 the theologian should teach: "But our Lord did not say, 'I will restore the kingdom to Israel.'" Let Christians focus not on a faulty inference, but on the explicit answer: be my authoritative witnesses now. Christ's answer is consistent with the Lukan emphasis that Christ must pass through earthly Jerusalem and its cross on his way to inheriting in heaven David's throne, from which he builds his church through the Spirit while dismantling earthly Jerusalem.

Ladd, in contradiction to dispensational premillennialists, properly started with the NT, but improperly, the writer suggests, built his case almost exclusively on one text, Revelation 20:1-6. His approach is problematic for several reasons.[29] First, elsewhere Ladd granted that some promises and prophecies should be interpreted spiritually, but in this one passage in apocalyptic literature he insisted on a wooden literalism, causing him to introduce "millennial" as a qualifying adjective in many texts regarding the kingdom. Second, he thought that one could interpret the text strictly inductively. This just is not so. One's theology influences one's interpretation of particular passages, especially in the case of apocalyptic literature.[30] Third, note the many symbols in verse 1: "key," "Abyss," "chain," and then in verse 2 "dragon," the only interpreted symbol. If "key," "chain," "dragon," "Abyss," etc. are symbolic, why should the number 1000 be literal, especially when numbers are notoriously symbolic in apocalyptic literature? The potential danger of interpreting numbers in apocalyptic literature literalistically can be seen in the aberrant eschatology of Seventh-Day Adventists and Jehovah's Witnesses, who derive their theology in part by applying that method to Daniel 8:14 and Revelation 14:1-4.

Fourth, none of the characteristics of this "millennium" — resurrected martyrs judging, living, and reigning with Christ in heaven — link it with the OT kingdom promises, a remarkable absence in the NT book that shows more links with the OT than any other book. Fifth, this millennium terminates in a revolt against Christ, making it "the most wicked dispensation." Yet the OT kingdom promises envision a golden age of endless peace. A poetic hyperbole for eternal life marks its only blemish: "he who dies at a hundred will be thought a mere youth" (Isa. 65:20). Sixth, the text can be interpreted satisfactorily within the amillennial system.[31]

---

29. Turner, "The Continuity of Scripture and Eschatology," pp. 279-82.
30. J. I. Packer, "Hermeneutics and Biblical Authority," *Them* 1 (1975): 3-12.
31. William Hendriksen, *More Than Conquerors* (Grand Rapids: Baker, 1940), pp. 184-93.

Premillennialists sometimes appeal to Romans 11, especially verses 16-24, to validate their belief that national Israel will be restored. The cultivated olive tree, however, in this text represents not national Israel but God's mediatorial kingdom, for branches live in this tree by faith, and dead branches are broken off for unbelief according to the sovereign grace and power of God. Its roots represent the patriarchs; its live branches stand for "true Israel" and its dead ones, which are broken off, unbelieving Israel. The wild olive tree stands for unbelieving Gentiles, and its branches grafted into the cultivated olive tree represent believing Gentiles, who participate in "true Israel's" covenants (see Eph. 2:19; Gal. 3:13-29). The natural branches that implicitly are grafted back in at the end of history — the "all Israel" of verse 26 — no more represent national Israel than the wild branches or any other part of the trees represent political states. Rather, they represent a conversion of Israel, Abraham's physical offspring, to faith in Jesus Christ, the promised seed, at the end of history. F. F. Bruce observed that Paul is saying "nothing about the restoration of an earthly Davidic kingdom. What he envisaged for his people was something infinitely better."[32] In sum, the apostle to the Gentiles predicts Israel will be restored to the mediatorial kingdom, rather than the earthly kingdom being restored to Israel.

Acts 3:19-21 is more ambiguous and cannot be discussed adequately here. F. F. Bruce wrote:

> The exact meaning of these words of Peter has been debated from various points of view. This at least may be said with assurance: the whole house of Israel, now as on the day of Pentecost, received a call to reverse the verdict of Passover Eve and to accord Jesus united acknowledgment as Messiah. Had Israel as a whole done this during these Pentecostal days, how different the course of world history and world evangelization would have been! How much more swiftly (we may imagine} would the consummation of Christ's kingdom have come! But it is pointless to pursue the "might-have-beens" of history.[33]

As the obverse side of the NT coin bears the hard imprint that no clear passage teaches the restoration of national Israel, its reverse side is imprinted

32. F. F. Bruce, *The Epistle of Paul to the Romans*, Tyndale New Testament Commentary (Grand Rapids: Eerdmans, 1971), p. 221. See also John Murray, *The Epistle to the Romans*, 2:75-103; C. E. B. Cranfield, *The Epistle of Romans*, ICC 2 (Edinburgh: T. & T. Clark, 1979), p. 579.

33. F. F. Bruce, *Commentary on the Book of the Acts* (Grand Rapids: Eerdmans, 1979), pp. 91ff.

with the hard fact that national Israel and its law have been permanently replaced by the church and the New Covenant. Without wresting Matthew 15:13 and Mark 12:1-9, our Lord announced in these passages that the Jewish *nation* no longer has a place as the special people of God; that place has been taken by the Christian community which fulfills God's purpose for Israel. The writer of Hebrews, after establishing that the New Covenant administration has superseded the Old, writes: "By calling this covenant 'new,' he has made the first one obsolete; and what is obsolete and aging will soon disappear" (Heb. 8:13). Other NT texts designate the church age as the "last days" — that is, the last stretch of historical time. "The expressions," says Charles Hodge, "'ends of the ages' (1 Cor 10:11), 'end of days' (Heb 1:2), 'fulness of time' (Gal 4:4), and 'fulness of times' (Eph 1:10), are all used to designate the time of Christ's advent."[34]

But what about the other expression "the age to come" (e.g., Eph. 1:21) in contradistinction to "this age"? Space limitation forbids rehearsing the erudite research and sustained argument of Geerhardus Vos. Suffice it to note that he defines the term almost as an equivalent of the "kingdom of God" — that is, as a semi-eschatological expression incorporating the heavenly realm both in the present and future. Independently from Ellis, Vos diagrams his conclusion about the meaning of this Pauline phrase in the same way Ellis diagrammed the Synoptic meaning of "kingdom of God."[35]

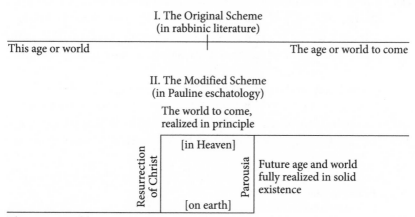

I. The Original Scheme
(in rabbinic literature)

This age or world   The age or world to come

II. The Modified Scheme
(in Pauline eschatology)

The world to come,
realized in principle

[in Heaven]

Resurrection of Christ   Parousia   Future age and world fully realized in solid existence

[on earth]

This age or world

34. Cited by John Wilmot, *Inspired Principles of Prophetic Interpretation* (Swengel, PA: Reiner, 1975), p. 35.

35. Geerhardus Vos, *The Pauline Eschatology* (Princeton: Princeton University Press, 1930), p. 38.

Regarding the coming of the Lord, Peter, who agrees with Paul on this subject (2 Pet. 3:15), in rebuking scoffers regarding the promise of Christ's coming (v. 3), affirms that the fulfillment of that promise will be catastrophic, simultaneous with the "day of judgment" and the creation of "a new heaven and a new earth" (vv. 7, 13).

The interpretations of the expression "then the end will come" in 1 Corinthians 15:24 are too numerous to be entertained here. The most common and natural identification of the "end" is "the end of the world" (i.e., the close of the present order of things, the consummation of the work of redemption).[36] This interpretation is adequately defended by Hodge.[37]

Typology

Although the NT writers never use the term *salvation history,* the concept is evident in their use of types. Goppelt drew the conclusion that "under Paul's influence *typos* became a hermeneutical term in the whole Church."[38] "Typology," says Lewis Johnson, "is the study of the spiritual correspondences between persons, events and things within the historical framework of God's special revelation."[39] Others restrict the term to the prefigurements in the OT of truths fully revealed in the NT.[40] In this essay the more narrow definition is followed.

First of all, then, both the type and antitype are *historical.* Unlike allegory that bypasses the original historical event, typology first considers the historical purpose of the type in the drama of salvation history within its own historical horizon.

Second, it is *analogical and progressive.* "Typology," says David Baker, "is not an exegesis or interpretation of a text but the study of relationships between events, persons and institutions recorded in biblical texts."[41] Note, however, that typology is analogical on both its vertical, cosmological axis

---

36. Charles Hodge, *A Commentary on 1 and 2 Corinthians* (Edinburgh: The Banner of Truth Trust, 1854; repr. 1974), pp. 326-31.

37. Hodge, *A Commentary on 1 and 2 Corinthians,* p. 328.

38. L. Goppelt, *Typos. Die Typologische Deutung des Alten Testaments im Neuen* (Darmstadt: Wissenschaftliche Buchhandlung, 1969; repr. of 1936 ed.), pp. 286, 240.

39. S. Lewis Johnson Jr., *The Old Testament in the New* (Grand Rapids: Zondervan, 1980), p. 55.

40. C. T. Fritsch, "Principles of Biblical Typology," *BSac* 104 (1947): 214.

41. D. L. Baker, "Typology and the Christian Use of the OT," *SJT* 29 (1976): 41.

and on its horizontal, temporal axis. The contrast between the heavenly original and the earthly shadow creates discontinuities as great as the heavens are higher than the earth. As the heavenly original ("truth") breaks into history, the antitype supersedes the type. If the analogies did not contain this contrast, with the heavenly replacing the earthly, history would be cyclical and not progressive. Israel's cultus — its sacred site (Mount Zion), seasons (sabbaths, holy days, and festivals), persons (priests, Levites, king), institutions (sacrifices, ceremonial cleansings, and blowing of horns) — although symbolizing the heavenly originals (Exod. 25:9, 40; 26:30; 1 Chron. 28:11-12; Heb. 8:5), also contains earthly dross that has been done away. Hebrews 8:1–10:18 aims to show that Christ's present reign as king-priest at the right hand of God eschatologically fulfills the inferior types of the old age that are passing away as stars fade before the rising sun. Commenting on Hebrews 7:19-20, Bruce wrote:

> It was inevitable that the earlier law should be abrogated sooner or later; for all the impressive solemnity of the sacrificial ritual and the sacerdotal ministry, no real peace of conscience was procured thereby, no immediate access to God. . . . The whole apparatus of worship associated with that ritual and priesthood was calculated rather to keep men at a distance from God than to bring them near. But the "hope set before us" in the gospel is better because it accomplishes this very thing which was impossible under the old ceremonial; it enables Christians to "draw nigh unto God." . . . The fact that the gospel, unlike the law, has opened up a way of free access to God is our author's ground for claiming that the gospel has achieved that perfection which the law could never bring about.[42]

Third, both the type, apart from the dross of the Old Covenant, and antitype are *spiritual*. The type, the earlier earthly reality, was a shadow, a symbol, of the spiritual reality, the "truth" (John 1:17; cf. Col. 2:17) brought to light in the revelation of Jesus Christ. By definition there can be no figure without a reality. The Lord Jesus, though he came into the world late in time, is the alpha and the omega. Vos wrote:

> The same world of heavenly spiritual realities, which has now come to light in the Person and work of Christ, already existed during the course

42. F. F. Bruce, *Epistle to the Hebrews* (Grand Rapids: Eerdmans, 1964), pp. 148ff.

of the Old Covenant, and in a provisional typical way through revelation reflected itself in[,] and through redemption projected itself into[,] the religious experience of the ancient people of God, so that they in their own partial manner and measure had access to and communion with and enjoyment of the higher world, which has now been let down and thrown open to our full knowledge and possession.[43]

Israel in the wilderness spiritually participated in Christ through symbol and type when they received in the manna "spiritual food" and in the water "spiritual drink" from "the spiritual rock" and "that rock was Christ" (1 Cor. 10:1-5). On entering into the sworn-land, they looked higher than that land. God gave them that land as a gift of life, as Moses emphasized over thirty times in Deuteronomy, a gift that Israel learned at both Kadesh-Barnea and Ai could be obtained only by faith. In contrast to Egypt, which symbolized Satan's realm of sin, tyranny, and death, God uniquely offered the blessings of his presence to his elect in the sworn-land.[44]

These striking correspondences between the land and Christ suggest the sworn-land is a type of the kingdom of God embodied in Christ. W. D. Davies drew the conclusion:

> In sum, for the holiness of place, Christianity has fundamentally, though not consistently, substituted [for the Old Testament teaching about the land] the holiness of the Person; it has Christified holy space.[45]

Fourth, typology entails *divine determination*. Johnson assumes this element in his definition because he later commented:

> The fundamental basis of typology is theological. Biblical typology is built squarely on *the sovereignty of God*. It is He who controls history and, therefore, guides events in such a way that types find their correspondence in antitypes.[46]

Ellis further validated the point:

43. Geerhardus Vos, *Redemptive History and Biblical Interpretation* (Grand Rapids: Baker, 1981), p. 199.

44. Elmer Martens, *God's Design* (Grand Rapids: Baker, 1981), pp. 97-116.

45. W. D. Davies, *The Gospel of Land* (Berkeley: University of California Press, 1974), p. 368.

46. Johnson, *The Old Testament in the New*, pp. 124ff.

For the NT writers a type has not merely the property of "typicalness" or similarity; they view Israel's history as *Heilsgeschichte,* and the significance of an Old Testament type lies in its particular *locus* in the Divine plan of redemption. When Paul speaks of the Exodus events happening *typikōs* and written "for our admonition," there can be no doubt that, in the apostle's mind, Divine intent is of the essence both in the occurrence and in their inscripturation. The rationale of NT typological exegesis is not only "the continuity of God's purpose throughout the history of his Covenant," but also His Lordship in moulding and using history to reveal and illumine His purpose. God writes His parables in the sands of time.[47]

Since God divinely determined the type, it follows that the type is a divine *prediction.* Johnson takes France to task for denying the predictive element, because, according to France, the human author did not intend it as a prediction. Johnson grants his point but gives priority to the divine authorship of the type. He writes:

> But Scripture is a divine as well as a human product; God is the source and man only the agent in its communication. In the sense that Scripture ultimately comes from God, His intention that the Old Testament revelation should look forward to the New must be acknowledged. . . . In this sense, then, we assert that predictiveness is an essential feature of a type.[48]

While Johnson finds firm footing in the divine author, the human authors may have understood more than is granted. Abraham, we are authoritatively told, "was looking forward to the city with foundations, whose architect and builder is God" (Heb. 11:10), and Jesus said: Abraham "saw it [my day] and was glad" (John 8:56). The message of Christ is not something tacked on to the OT; he is at its heart, for the Spirit of Christ was in its prophets predicting "the sufferings of Christ and the glories that would follow" (1 Pet. 1:11).

Having established the predictive nature of typology on theological grounds, Johnson validates it textually:

47. E. Earle Ellis, *Paul's Use of the Old Testament* (Grand Rapids: Baker, 1957), pp. 127ff.

48. Johnson, *The Old Testament in the New,* p. 56.

Further, the very use of the term "fulfilled," so common in the introduction of the antitypical in the New Testament, justifies our conclusion about the predictiveness of types.[49]

Finally, and correlatively, typology is *comprehensive*. Some types continue even after their fulfillment in the NT. For example, the historical story about God's gift of the bride to the husband continues to exist after its fulfillment in its antitype of God's gift of Christ to the church (Eph. 5:22-32), because the creation institution of marriage continues throughout the epochs of salvation history. On the other hand, the apostles taught that the type of national Israel and its law as a means of governing the nation were done away finally and permanently. The typological approach of the NT is grounded in an understanding that the new age in Christ fulfills the salvation toward which the old is reaching. Retrogression from the surpassing antitype to the shadows at the end of history would have God walk backward and would draw an abhorrent veil over the glory of Christ and his church now revealed.

Jesus taught in several places that the true people of God are not to be found in national Israel but in the Christian community that replaced it (cf. Mark 12:1-9; Matt. 15:13). His apostles continued his teachings. They emphatically taught that the Old Covenant with its types has been done away forever in favor of the superior and eternal New Covenant that governs the church (Jer. 32:40; 50:5; Ezek. 16:60; 37:26; Heb. 8:1-13). They warn the church not to go back to them (Rom. 10:4; Gal. 2:15–4:7; Eph. 2:14-18; argument of Hebrews). Wilmot makes the case with regard to the covenants:

> Very generally in Scripture we come upon this balancing or placement of opposites, such as the First and the Last; the Beginning and the End . . . the old covenant and the new covenant; take away the first and establish the second; glory done away and glory that excelleth; the law of works and the law of faith; the curse incurred and the curse removed; the law by Moses and grace and truth by Jesus Christ. . . .[50]

France makes the point with regard to the nation:

> The implication is that the Jewish nation has no longer a place as the special people of God; that place has been taken by the Christian community, and in them God's purposes for Israel are to be fulfilled.[51]

49. Johnson, *The Old Testament in the New*, p. 56.
50. Wilmot, *Inspired Principles*, pp. 25ff.
51. R. T. France, *Jesus and the Old Testament* (London: Tyndale, 1971), p. 67.

In John's term, Christ is the "true [i.e., the superior and eternal reality in contrast to the inferior and temporary] vine," and his church is its branches. Biblical typology as taught by Christ's apostles disallows the notion that the material types of the Old Covenant will be reintroduced into this history after the church upon whom the end of the ages has come (cf. Heb. 7:18).

Finally, although the semi-eschatological nature of the kingdom of God and of "the world to come" entails a more solid form of the kingdom in the new earth (cf. Heb. 2:5; 11:10; 13:14), typology in the NT focuses on its comprehensive fulfillment in the Christ and his church.

Prophecy

Lewis Johnson called for a "well thought out and formulated structure for the interpretation of messianic prophecy."[52] His student aims here to take one baby step in that direction. To interpret the prophets correctly one must be aware of the forms of their oracles, their need to intensify the types of the OT, the generic nature of some oracles, and their clarification through progressive history as represented in the expanding canon giving them more and more specificity.

Forms of Oracles

Luther complained about the prophets:

> They have a queer way of talking, like people who, instead of proceeding in an orderly manner, ramble off from one thing to the next, so that you cannot make head or tail of them or see what they are getting at.[53]

These abrupt transitions that Luther describes reflect the manner in which various kinds of oracles, originally independent, were edited.

---

52. S. Lewis Johnson, "A Response to Patrick Fairbairn and Biblical Hermeneutics as Related to the Quotations of the Old Testament in the New," in *Hermeneutics, Inerrancy, and the Bible*, ed. E. Radmacher and R. Preus (Grand Rapids: Zondervan, 1984), p. 798.

53. Cited by Leslie C. Allen, *Joel, Obadiah, Jonah and Micah*, NICOT (Grand Rapids: Eerdmans, 1976), p. 257, n. 56, from von Rad, *Old Testament Theology*, vol. 2, p. 33, n. 1.

Form critics have analyzed prophetic oracles into two basic types among others: oracles threatening judgment *(Unheilseschatologie)* and oracles promising salvation beyond the judgment *(Heilseschatologie)*.[54] More specifically, the oracles of woe were hurled against national Israel, and the oracles of weal were intended for the restoration of Israel's remnant into the spiritual kingdom. Initially the restored community was a remnant of national Israel that outlasted the Babylonian exile (Ezek. 11:14-21; cf. Jer. 24:4-10; Hos. 5:15–6:3; Jer. 3:12-14). Moses had earlier looked beyond the judgment of the exile and had prophesied Israel's restoration back to the land after their spiritual circumcision, and not vice versa (Deut. 30:1-10).

Heils- and *Unheilseschatologie* are two sides of the expected day of the Lord, wherein he comes first in judgment and then in blessing. The prophets hurled their spiritually charged oracles (cf. Jer. 1:9-10) against national Israel, because it had come under the curse of the law-inheritance principle. God dismantled it first by deposing the earthly monarchs of David's house in 586 BC, and finally and permanently by the razing of Jerusalem in AD 70.

The potent oracles of salvation effect a kaleidoscope of blessing. Central to them is the dynamic breaking in of God himself into the world.[55] The holy and righteous rule of the Lord Almighty triumphs universally in time and space over all unrighteousness and injustice. God himself will not ascend Israel's throne, but instead of its former worthless kings, he will appoint the ideal king, the Messiah, in Zion. He enacts his will through the New Covenant effected by Messiah (Isa. 42:6; 49:8; 54:10; 55:3; 59:21; 61:8; Jer. 31:31-33; 32:40; Ezek. 34:25; 37:26). This administration issues into a total transformation of humanity, of nature, and of the sworn-land that had been devastated. The kingdom is consummated in the regaining of paradise itself. This predicted kingdom cannot fail because it is based on sovereign grace, and so it is a promise received by faith.

Edelkoort called the OT "the book of the expectation," likening it to "the unfinished symphony, waiting for the master's hand to add to it the fitting conclusion."[56] For Christ and his apostles the prophetic expectation, based on the earlier covenants and toward which the OT is pressing, is fulfilled in him and his body which is living in the last days. They saw the pro-

54. Claus Westermann, *Basic Forms of Prophetic Speech,* trans. Hugh Clayton White (Philadelphia: Westminster, 1967).

55. For a review of scholarly thought on this subject see Dirk H. Odendaal, *The Eschatological Expectation of Isaiah 40–66 with Special Reference to Israel and the Nations* (Phillipsburg, NJ: Presbyterian & Reformed, 1970), pp. 1-33.

56. Cited by Odendaal, *The Eschatological Expectation of Isaiah 40–66,* p. 14.

gressive unfolding of God's unified history in Abraham's seed (he does not say "seeds"), and brought to fulfillment in Christ and his church.

Again and again Matthew uses "fulfilled" to show the correspondence between the OT expectation and its realization in Christ. Jesus said, "'Everything must be fulfilled that is written about me in the Law of Moses, the Prophets and the Psalms.' Then he opened their minds so they could understand the Scriptures" (Luke 24:44ff.). Peter wrote to the church, or at least to true Israel which became united with Gentiles in the unified church: "the prophets . . . spoke of the grace that was to come to you" (1 Pet. 1:10). This matched his earlier sermon: "Indeed, all the prophets from Samuel on, as many as have spoken, have foretold these days" (Acts 3:24). He applied this principle of hermeneutics to Joel 2:28-32, stating in the first post-Pentecostal interpretation of the OT that what happened at Pentecost is what Joel had predicted (Acts 2:16). James, addressing the first church council, convened to consider the fate of the Gentiles in the church, drew the conclusion with apostolic approval that the salvation of the Gentiles agreed with the prophetic expectation (Acts 15:14ff.). Paul, with reference to the joy of the Gentiles in finding this salvation, cites Isaiah 11:10 — "The root of Jesse will stand as a banner for the peoples; the nations [Gentiles] will rally to him, and his place of rest will be glorious" (Rom. 15:12). The writer of Hebrews interprets the New Covenant, originally addressed to the house of Israel and Judah, as fulfilled in the church age (Heb. 8:7-13).

Unless one resorts to the desperate argument that there are two New Covenants, one for Israel and one for the church, one must draw the inescapable conclusion from Hebrews 8:7ff. that the church in Christ fulfills promises given to "Israel" and "Judah" (Jer. 31:31 and by implication the other sixteen references to the New Covenant in the OT).

Symbolic Language

As these references suggest, the prophets represented the new under the imagery of the old. To represent invisible things writers and speakers must use figures. For example, to represent the molecule, which no eye has seen, scientists employ billiard balls; biblical writers use anthropomorphisms to represent God. Likewise, God used the tabernacle and its parts to symbolize the heavenly reality (e.g., Exod. 25:9). Similarly, the prophets employed these same symbols to represent the heavenly kingdom that was lowered from heaven first into the manger at Bethlehem and then in flaming tongues of fire at the temple about to be left desolate. On the other hand, their prophecies about events prior to Pentecost find a material fulfillment; for example, in Israel's return from exile and in the life of our Lord, his birth, ministry, death, and resurrection. With the transformation of Christ's body from an earthly physical body to a heavenly spiritual body, and with his ascension from the earthly realism to the heavenly Jerusalem with its heavenly throne and the outpouring of his Holy Spirit, the earthly material symbols were done away and the spiritual reality portrayed by the symbols superseded the shadows. Consequently, OT prophecies about Israel's future kingdom that pertain to the church age, which began with Pentecost, find a spiritual fulfillment.

Through the symbols of the old dispensation (e.g., feast days, cooking pots, Jerusalem, etc.; cf. Zech. 14:16ff.), the prophets represented the final dispensation before the new earth. Mickelsen wrote regarding Ezekiel 40–48:

> To suppose that the ancient ritual will be restored should be abhorrent to everyone who takes seriously the message of the book of Hebrews. . . . With Christ as a priest coming out of the tribe of Judah (not Levi), there is a change of both priesthood and law (Heb 7:12-14). This change is dramatic and far-reaching.[57]

Our Lord contrasts his figurative use of language before Pentecost with his plain speech after it (cf. John 16:25). He too used the symbolic language of the old to depict the new. In contrast to his often-offended audiences who insisted on a material meaning to his words, he consistently meant a deeper spiritual meaning that they should have understood. For example, the "temple" is not the one in Jerusalem but his body (John 2:21); the new birth is not from flesh but from Spirit (3:6); the water in Jacob's well quenches temporarily the thirst of the body, but the "water" he gives quenches eternally the thirst of man's spirit (4:13-14); he is the true bread from heaven (6:41-42); the "streams of living water [that] flow from within" is the Spirit that flows from the human temple (John 7:37-39), "as the Scripture has said" (cf. Ezek. 41:1ff.).

Regarding the last reference, Hodges argued persuasively that the Scripture in view is Ezekiel 47:1ff., but unconvincingly argued that because Jesus uttered these words on the last day of the Feast of Tabernacles, the be-

---

57. A. Berkeley Mickelsen, *Interpreting the Bible* (Grand Rapids: Eerdmans, 1963), p. 298.

lievers would not become "this source of living water in the world that God was remaking and would fill with His own supernatural blessing" until their resurrection and glorification.[58] If a connection be made with that "last day," it seems more plausible to suppose that the believer living now in the last days embodies Ezekiel's vision.

This likening of the believer in the new dispensation to Ezekiel's temple and its life-giving waters to a stream that grows ever deeper and wider until it transforms the brackish Dead Sea into fresh water whose banks are lined with trees, and in which living creatures swarm, illustrates the additional point that the prophets, to show the surpassing greatness of the New Covenant to the Old, supercharged their figures. Mount Zion becomes the highest mountain (Mic. 4:1); Jerusalem will become so holy that the inscription on the high priest's diadem, "Holy to the LORD," will be found on the bells of the horses, and even the city's slop bucket will be usable for sacrifice in the sacred temple's precincts (Zech. 14:20). After citing these examples among others, Edmund Clowney wrote: "In the eschatological newness of the worship of 'that day,' the ceremonial is sublimated in absolute glory."[59]

These symbols from the old should not be interpreted as opposed to the new; but the new should be interpreted as a gradation of these intensified symbols.

Return, if you will, to the earlier discussion about Christ's announcement, "the kingdom of God is at hand." Dispensationalists correctly note that Jesus never interpreted the expression but assumed its meaning. But instead of looking to the author of our faith for its interpretation, they incorrectly, this writer suggests, look to his unbelieving audience, who loved money, to whom the cross was an offense (Matt. 16:21-23; 1 Cor. 1:23), and whose minds were made dull because a veil remains over them when the Old Covenant is read (2 Cor. 3:14). Above, it was argued that Jesus never once offered a material kingdom; in fact, he rebuked the people for seeking material bread (John 6:26-27). Since he was offering a spiritual, heavenly kingdom as a fulfillment of the OT expectation, it follows that the promises of that kingdom in the prophetic and apocalyptic literature should be interpreted not literalistically with reference to the earth, but spiritually with reference to the heavenly kingdom.

---

58. Zane Hodges, "Rivers of Living Water — John 7:37-39," *BSac* 136 (1979): 239-48.

59. Edmund P. Clowney, "Israel and the Church," in *Dreams, Visions and Oracles*, ed. Carl Edwin Armerding and W. Ward Gasque (Grand Rapids: Baker, 1977), p. 214.

Generic Prophecy

Scholars generally agree that prophets saw the future on an essentially flat tableau, where at best they saw that the glories of Christ followed his sufferings (1 Pet. 1:10-12). The birth of Immanuel, for example, is brought into relation with the threat of the Syrian invasion in the days of Ahaz (Isa. 7:1-14). Exegetes must distinguish carefully between the *Zeitgeschichtliche* ("present historical") and *Endgeschichtliche* ("final historical").

Beyond this, however, note that one and the same oracle sometimes has a certain "thickness," containing within itself both the present and final. A prophetic oracle may portray as a final event what in fact has several events separated by intervals of time. Beecher described this phenomenon that resembles typology in that it also combines the material and spiritual into one event as "generic prophecy."[60] Kaiser profitably has popularized this principle and applied it to a number of prophecies.[61] Odendaal independently came to a similar conclusion from his investigation of Isaiah 40–66. He concluded that Isaiah predicts the return from the exile as part of the eschaton. He wrote:

> They are . . . to such an extent portrayed according to their ideal character, that they must in reality be regarded as the beginning of the final realities of the consummation.[62]

Earlier he wrote:

> Every historical coming of this day [of the Lord] is always type and promise of its final coming and forms an intrusion of the consummation.[63]

It follows that prophecies about the restoration, both in respect to the prediction and fulfillment, contain a material aspect.

---

60. Willis Judson Beecher, *The Prophets and the Promise* (Grand Rapids: Baker, repr. 1963), p. 130.

61. Walter C. Kaiser, *The Uses of the Old Testament in the New* (Chicago: Moody Press, 1985).

62. Odendaal, *The Eschatological Expectation of Isaiah 40–66*, p. 32.

63. Odendaal, *The Eschatological Expectation of Isaiah 40–66*, p. 32.

Canonical Process

But how shall these parts be isolated and fitted into the drama of salvation history? In another article this writer contended for a "canonical process approach" in the interpretation of the Psalms. He defined his approach thus:

> . . . the recognition that the text's intention became deeper and clearer as the parameters of the canon were expanded. Just as redemption itself has a progressive history, so also older texts in the canon underwent a correlative progressive perception of meaning as they became part of a growing canonical literature.[64]

The same approach is applicable to prophecy. The divine author's intention comes into ever-sharper focus through the magnifying glass of progressive revelation until it reaches a flashpoint in the coming of Jesus Christ. This approach is similar to *sensus plenior* in that both methods depend on further revelation to find the full meaning of an earlier text. But the distinction from it lies in this: whereas the supposed *sensus plenior* depends exclusively on further revelation and may allow a reinterpretation of the prophecy, the canonical process approach combines further revelation with the sharpening focus of history itself and disallows the possibility of reinterpretation.[65]

For the preexilic and exilic prophets the new age began with the restoration of the exile. Both Micah and Isaiah refer to the new age as beginning "now"[66] — that is, with the return from Babylon. One stands here at the intersection of two ages: the old is passing away and the new is breaking in, pressing forward for fulfillment and realization. With reference to the remnant's return, prophecy is fulfilled materially.

But in that return there is a deeper meaning, as Zimmerli perceived.[67]

---

64. Bruce K. Waltke, "A Canonical Process Approach to the Psalms," in *Tradition and Testament: Essays in Honor of Charles Lee Feinberg,* ed. John S. and Paul D. Feinberg (Chicago: Moody Press, 1981), p. 7.

65. Cf. Vern Poythress, "Divine Meaning of Scripture," *WTJ* 48 (Fall 1986): 241-79. Poythress establishes the same approach on the basis of communication theory.

66. Cf. Micah 4:8, 10; 5:1 (EV). See Odendaal, *The Eschatological Expectation of Isaiah 40–66,* pp. 108-16, and Bernard Renaud, *La Formation du Livre de Michée. Tradition et Actualisation* (Paris: Gabalda, 1977), p. 203.

67. W. Zimmerli, "Das Wort des göttlichen Selbsterweises (Erweiswort). Eine prophetische Gattung," *Gottes Offenbarung,* Theologische Bücherei, 19 (Munich: Chr. Kaiser Verlag, 1963), p. 201.

The outward restoration of the remnant from national Israel also very definitely involves the spiritual renewal of the people. Odendaal wrote:

> But even the outward restoration does not lead us to an Israel-centered nationalistic type of eschatology. The restoration is typical of and woven into the final coming of the kingdom of Yahweh, bringing full and everlasting salvation to his people. The return from exile, the repopulation of the country, and the rebuilding of the temple are seen ideally in their relationship to and significance for the final triumph of the kingdom of God; and thus something of that eternal glory already pervades the description of the earthly realities.[68]

On these data he drew the hermeneutical rule:

> Therefore it is evident that neither a purely spiritual nor a purely literal explanation can fathom the fulness of the prophetic proclamation.[69]

That spiritual renewal was not realized in the postexilic community and so was projected by the postexilic prophets into a future that outlasts the OT and awaits the NT revelation.

Finally, recall that in our Lord's teaching about "the kingdom of God" and in Paul's about "the age to come" an aspect of promise remained beyond the present fulfillment — a time when all things will be made new, when the church will no longer see through a poor reflection but face to face (1 Cor. 13:12), when Christ will once again drink wine with his resurrected disciples (even as he in his resurrected body ate fish with them), when the earth will be regenerated (Rom. 8:21), when mortality will put on immortality. If the study of salvation history be persuasive, then this "more than" element awaits its consummate realization in the new earth, as Hoekema argued so persuasively.[70]

The apostles connected the new earth with this earth, even as they linked the believer's earthly and resurrected bodies. The heavens and the new earth and the bodies of believers arise from the old, though purged by judgment from all the results of sin. Vos wrote:

---

68. Odendaal, *The Eschatological Expectation of Isaiah 40-66*, p. 126.
69. Odendaal, *The Eschatological Expectation of Isaiah 40-66*, p. 178.
70. Anthony A. Hoekema, *The Bible and the Future* (Grand Rapids: Eerdmans, 1979).

Paradoxical though it may seem, revelation has not shunned here to wed the eternal in point of duration to the temporal in point of make up.[71]

The approach is here applied to the prophetic promise that Israel will return to the land (e.g., Jer. 30:3). Jeremiah was so confident that Israel would return in keeping with the Lord's covenantal promises that he even bought land while the Babylonians were razing Jerusalem (Jer. 32:1-15). He then links that return with Israel's spiritual restoration (vv. 36-44). This spiritual restoration, however, was not realized in the return from Babylon, and so gave promise of its fulfillment in a more remote future. It finds fulfillment in spiritual Israel today, those who have had their hearts circumcised by Christ's Spirit; but it awaits its full consummation in the new earth (Heb. 11:39ff.). The present salvation in the Spirit is an earnest of the believer's final redemption (Eph. 1:13-14).

Conclusion

Regarding the interpretation of prophecy, Delbert Killers, professor of Near Eastern Studies at Johns Hopkins University, wrote:

> The books of Israel's prophets are among the most difficult in the Old Testament, and probably among the most difficult books ever written.[72]

And regarding the relationship of the Mosaic law to the church, Jonathan Edwards wrote:

> There is perhaps no part of divinity attended with so much intricacy and wherein orthodox divines do so much differ as stating the precise agreement and difference between the two dispensations of Moses and Christ.[73]

---

71. Vos, *Redemptive History and Biblical Interpretation*, p. 331.

72. Delbert R. Hillers, *Covenant: The History of a Biblical Idea* (Baltimore: Johns Hopkins University Press, 1982), p. 124.

73. Cited in D. P. Fuller, *Gospel and Law: Contrast or Continuum? The Hermeneutics of Dispensationalism and Covenant Theology* (Grand Rapids: Eerdmans, 1980), pp. 5-6, and by Mark W. Karlberg, "Legitimate Discontinuities Between the Testaments," *JETS* 28, no. 1 (March 1985): 10.

Regrettably, well-meaning men have solidified in sacrosanct confessions positions on such complex and difficult issues as the relationship between the church and Israel and the interpretation of prophecy, tending to force later leaders to become custodians of these confessions endowed with supreme authority and impeding research. Perhaps a first step toward maturity could be taken by adding an article to all confessions similar to that in the Westminster Confession:

> All synods or councils, since the Apostles' times, whether general or particular, may err; and many have erred. Therefore they are not to be made the rule of faith or practice. . . .[74]

Likewise, Walvoord recently made a helpful distinction in degrees of certitude within the Christian faith:

> I'm firmly committed to a certain eschatological view, but not with the certitude that I have of the deity of Christ and the Virgin Birth, and other doctrines. So I have to hold the theoretical possibility that I could be wrong there.[75]

These statements by earlier and more recent theologians open the door for prudent change.

As we wait for the more solid form of the church when it is united with its Lord in the new earth and his kingdom is coextensive with the new creation, let believers now in faith and meditation reflect upon the beloved and all things heavenly and be transmuted into his likeness.[76] This is not a bromide with which to conclude an essay; it is the apostolic exhortation based on their eschatology.

74. Westminster Confession, 31.3.

75. John F. Walvoord, "Our Future Hope: Eschatology and Its Role in the Church," *Christianity Today*, February 6, 1987, pp. 1-12.

76. Cf. David C. Steinmetz, "Luther as an Interpreter of the Psalms," *ARG* 70 (1979): 41.

Old Testament Texts Bearing on the Problem of the Control of Human Reproduction

Introduction

Before turning to the passages in the Old Testament pertaining to the problem of the control of human reproduction, it is first necessary to resolve some of the tensions that Christians normally experience when seeking to apply the Old Testament to their lives.

First, we must resolve the theological tension concerning the applicability of instructions in the Old Testament today. One rightfully asks: "In what sense is the Old Testament authoritative for the church?" This same tension can be felt within the New Testament itself. On the one hand the Apostle Paul says, "We are discharged from the law" (Rom. 7:6), but on the other hand he writes: "All Scripture is inspired by God and profitable for teaching, for reproof, for correction, and for training in righteousness, that the man of God may be complete, equipped for every good work" (2 Tim. 3:16-17). A valid working hypothesis to relieve this tension is suggested by John Bright: Old Testament passages must be referred to the New for its verdict, whether it be ratification, modification, or abrogation.[1]

Second, we face a sociological tension. In contrast to our society, someone living in the Old Testament world valued a large family because it provided both economic and national security. Survival demanded growth

---

1. John Bright, *The Authority of the Old Testament* (New York: Abingdon, 1967), p. 200.

Previously published in *Birth Control and the Christian*, ed. Walter O. Spitzer and Carlyle L. Saylor (Wheaton, IL: Tyndale, 1969).

and expansion. Fagley says: "Underpopulation, rather than overpopulation, was the dominant reality."[2] In addition, people in the ancient society differed from Christians today in that they sought "social immortality"; i.e., preservation of their memory upon earth through their offspring. Christians, on the other hand, seek "individual immortality"; i.e., the hope of life after death. In a word, Old Testament saints living in the structure of a rural society were much more favorably disposed toward large families than many Christian couples today living in overcrowded cities. For us, children tend to be a financial hindrance rather than help. In the light of these changed conditions we must raise the question: How relevant for us is the obviously favorable attitude toward large families in the Old Testament? In order to relieve this second tension, we must select only those texts that indicate the eternal purposes and attitudes of the Creator.

A third tension is a logical one growing out of the apparently recent technology for the prevention and control of life. Were the authors of the Old Testament conscious of techniques for such things as birth control and abortion? If not, we may be asking the Old Testament writers questions they had never faced and thus be in danger of inferring wrong answers from the Scriptures. In the course of this essay, therefore, we will attempt to determine whether they were aware of such means by studying the Old Testament itself and the extrabiblical literature of the Ancient Near East.

Let us now consider texts pertaining to the means of limiting human reproduction. In each case we will seek to determine whether or not God prohibits it. After this, we will look at the texts that advance reasons for the institution of marriage, in order to determine the ends that any nonprohibited method of birth control should serve.

Texts Bearing on the Means of Limiting Human Reproduction

A married man and woman in the world of the Old Testament had five means by which they could limit their reproductive capacity: abortion, sterilization, infanticide, continence, and contraception by withdrawal (often referred to as *coitus interruptus* in the older literature). We shall consider these respectively.

---

2. Richard Martin Fagley, *The Population Explosion and Christian Responsibility* (New York: Oxford University Press, 1960), p. 110.

Texts Bearing on Abortion

Under this heading we will advance from the Scriptures two arguments that allow procured abortion and then three arguments that protect the fetus.

The first argument in favor of permitting induced abortion is the absence of any biblical text forbidding such an act. Here we must appeal to the literature of the Ancient Near East to weigh this negative evidence. In this case the silence of the Bible is significant because an Assyrian law dated between 1450 BC and 1250 BC prescribed death by torture in cases of induced abortion. The text reads: "If a woman by her own deed has cast that which is within her womb, and a charge has been brought and proved against her, they shall impale her and not bury her. If she dies from casting that which is in her womb, they shall impale her and not bury her."[3] Against this background the silence of the Old Testament appears to be both deliberate and instructive. The failure of God to set forth a similar law becomes even more profound when one realizes that the Mosaic code is normally more extensive and more severe than these other codes in sexual matters.[4] Kaufmann says: "The sexual prohibitions of the Torah are more comprehensive and their violations more severely punished [than in these other codes]."[5] From this negative evidence we may infer that God does not invariably prohibit abortion.

A second argument in favor of permitting induced abortion is that God does not regard the fetus as a soul (Hebrew *nephesh*), no matter how far gestation has progressed. Therefore, the fetus does not come under the protection of the fifth commandment. That he does not so regard the fetus can be demonstrated by noting that God does not impose a death penalty for the destruction of a fetus. A basic feature of the Mosaic code is the *lex talionis,* or

3. H. W. F. Saggs, *The Greatness That Was Babylon* (New York: Hawthorn Books, 1962), p. 215.

4. It should be noted in this connection that abortion was known in antiquity. The classical Greek philosophers advised abortion under certain circumstances. Plato (*Republic* V, 46off.) recommended that when parents have passed the age assigned for procreation the child should not be allowed to be born. Aristotle (*Politics* VII, 16, 1335) objected to the birth of imperfect or deformed children and recommended abortion in certain circumstances. In Rome abortion was practiced for reasons of poverty, sensuality, or luxury (Seneca, *Digesta* 25, 3, 4), In the light of this evidence Neufeld concludes: "Foeticide, throughout the course of history, has never become a recognized social practice, but has been, in the main sporadic" (E. Neufeld, *Ancient Hebrew Marriage Laws* [New York: Longmans, Green & Co., 1944], p. 252, n. 3).

5. Yehezkel Kaufmann, *The Religion of Israel,* trans. Moshe Greenberg (Chicago: University of Chicago Press, 1960), p. 318.

principle of "an eye for an eye, life for life" (*e.g.,* Lev. 24:18). The law plainly exacts: "If a man kills any human life [Hebrew *nephesh adam*] he will be put to death." But according to Exodus 21:22ff. the destruction of a fetus is not a capital offense. The divine law reads: "When men struggle together and one of them pushes a pregnant woman and she suffers a miscarriage but no other harm happens, he shall be fined according as the woman's husband may exact from him. . . . But if harm does ensue, then you shall impose soul [*nephesh*] for soul [*nephesh*] . . ." (Exod. 21:22-24). Clearly, then, in contrast to the mother, the fetus is not reckoned as a soul *(nephesh)*. The money compensation does not seem to have been imposed in order to protect the fetus but to indemnify the father for his loss. Mace concludes: ". . . but the fixing of the indemnity is left to the husband, on the principle that he has suffered the loss of a potential child."[6]

With respect to an accidental miscarriage the contrast between the Mosaic law and the Assyrian law is once again instructive. In a similar context the Assyrian law reads: "[If a seignior] struck a(nother) seignior's [wife] and caused her to have [a miscarriage], they shall treat [the wife of the seignior], who caused the (other) seignior's wife to [have a miscarriage], as he treated her; he shall compensate for her fetus with a life. However, if that woman died, they shall put the seignior to death; he shall compensate for her fetus with a life. But when that woman's husband has no son, if someone struck her so that she had a miscarriage, they shall put the striker to death; even if her fetus is a girl he shall compensate with a life."[7] We should note this contrast between the Assyrian law and the Mosaic law: the Old Testament, in contrast to the Assyrian code, never reckons the fetus as equivalent to a life.

As indicated, we will now advance three arguments that protect the fetus.

In the first place, in contrast to the Assyrian code quoted above, the Old Testament never exacts "a fetus for a fetus," apparently protecting the fetus.

Second, the conception is a gift of God. Mace observes: "It is an essential feature of the Hebrew belief about children that they are not simply the result of a sexual union, but a direct gift from God. . . . The Bible does not contest the fact that there is a causal connection between sexual intercourse

6. David R. Mace, *Hebrew Marriage: A Sociological Study* (London: Epworth, 1953), p. 207.

7. James B. Pritchard, *Ancient Near Eastern Texts Relating to the Old Testament* (Princeton: Princeton University Press, 1950), p. 184. Hereafter *ANET.*

and conception, but it denies that the effect is inevitable, or that parents possess the power to ensure it."[8] Eve at the birth of Cain declares that she has received him from the Lord (Gen. 4:1). Sarah believes that the Lord has restrained her from bearing (16:2), which is confirmed when Abraham later receives the divine assurance that she will now have a son (17:19). Taking pity on Leah, the Lord "opened her womb" (29:31), as he did also afterwards in the case of Rachel (30:22). Of Ruth it is recorded that "the Lord gave her conception" (Ruth 4:13). Babbage succinctly states: "God permits man to share in the joyous task of creation."[9] The Christian, therefore, will seek to protect the fetus because he ought not destroy what God has put together.

Third, God is actively involved in the process of fashioning the fetus. Of himself David said: "You created my kidneys; you skillfully wove me in my mother's womb. . . . My skeleton was not hidden from you when I was carefully formed in the darkness; when I was embroidered with variegated colors in the innermost part of the earth" (Ps. 139:13-18).[10]

We conclude, therefore, that while the Old Testament does not equate the fetus with a living person, it places great value upon it. The Talmud appears to reflect the biblical balance by allowing abortion when the life of the mother was in danger (*Mishna, Oholot,* 7:6).

Texts Bearing on Sterilization

Apparently the early Hebrews realized that the male as well as the female could be the cause of a childless union. We read in Deuteronomy 7:14, "There shall not be a barren male or female among you." In practice, however, only the male could be made sterile artificially.[11] We may assume that principles derived from texts pertaining to the sterilization of the man are also applicable to the woman.

The point to be made here is that God rejected the common Near Eastern practice of sterilizing males. According to Deuteronomy 23:1 [2], a eunuch

---

8. Mace, *Hebrew Marriage,* p. 202.

9. Stuart Barton Babbage, *Christianity and Sex* (Chicago: InterVarsity, 1963), p. 15.

10. Translation my own.

11. B. Landsberger, "Zu den Frauenklassen des Kodex Hammurabi," *Zeitschrift für Assyriologie* 30 (1916-17): 71, assumed that women of the Ancient Near East could be artificially made sterile. Such an operation, however, was beyond the scope of ancient surgery according to G. E. Driver and Sir John C. Miles, "The SAL.ZIKRUM 'Woman-Man' in Old Babylonian Texts," *Iraq* 6 (1939): 67. So also Saggs, *The Greatness That Was Babylon,* p. 350.

was excluded from the communal life in Israel. The law reads: "He whose testicles are crushed or whose penis is cut off may not enter the congregation of the Lord." This law is peculiar to the Mosaic code. Neufeld says: "The restrictions imposed on a eunuch under the biblical law are isolated and outstanding and no parallel can be traced to some other Semitic legislations."[12]

In addition, sterilization was also unique with respect to other types of mutilation of the body. While deformities of the body such as blindness, lameness, etc. restricted Aaron's descendants from serving as priests, only this mutilation — whether congenital, accidental, or self-willed — excommunicated a male from the covenant community. What then is the reason for this unique piece of legislation? We might tentatively suggest that God excommunicated eunuchs because they no longer mirrored his generative power. Delitzsch reasons: "The reason for the exclusion of emasculated persons from the congregation of Jehovah . . . is to be found in the mutilation of the nature of man as created by God."[13]

The least we can conclude from this text is that God looks with disfavor upon sterilization as a means of limiting human reproduction.

As stated in the introduction, however, this conclusion must be evaluated in the light of the teaching of our Lord with respect to eunuchs (Matt. 19:12).

Texts Bearing on Infanticide

Although infanticide in the Ancient Near East was normally practiced for religious reasons, it was also used to rid the parent of an unwanted child. For example, the mother of Sargon of Agade, by tradition a high-priestess expected to live in chastity, disposed of her unwanted child by exposure.[14] The fact that infanticide by exposure was known in Israel can be gathered from a reference in Ezekiel, where Jerusalem is described as though she "were cast out on the open field, for [she] was abhorred, on the day [she] was born" (Ezek. 16:5). Moreover, it is well known that the Arabs practiced female infanticide.[15]

Godly Hebrews never engaged in infanticide. The Old Testament for-

12. Neufeld, *Ancient Hebrew Marriage Laws,* p. 223.

13. F. Delitzsch, *Biblical Commentary on the Old Testament,* vol. 3: *The Pentateuch* (Grand Rapids: Eerdmans, 1951), p. 413.

14. For text see *ANET,* p. 119.

15. For female infanticide among the Arabs see Robertson Smith, *Kinship and Marriage* (London: A. & C. Black, 1903), pp. 291-96.

bade the common practice of child sacrifice, for it "profaned the name of God" (Lev. 18:21). Those who did practice it were to be stoned to death (Lev. 20:2). Undoubtedly, the life of the child also came under the protection of the fifth commandment.

Texts Bearing on Continence

We may infer that continence was also practiced as a means of limiting children, from a Sumerian proverb that mentions a proud husband boasting that his wife had borne him eight sons and was still ready to lie down to accept his nuptial embrace.[16] Evidently, some wives would not. However, there is no evidence that periodic continence was known in Israel, for the spacing or limitation of pregnancies. In fact the Mosaic law indicates that continence has no place in marriage. A salient text leading to this conclusion reads: "If [the owner] marries another woman, he must not diminish from [the female slave] her food, her clothing or her conjugal rights" (Exod. 21:10). Mielziner notes: "The Mosaic law contains no express provision concerning marital rights and duties, except the injunction made in a certain case: 'Her food, her raiment, and her conjugal rights shall he not diminish.'"[17] In addition, as Charles Ryder Smith points out: "The Old Testament has no sanction for celibacy; its priests married, and even its typical ascetic, the Nazirite, was commanded other abstinences than this" (Num. 6).[18]

Sexual intercourse was only to be forgone by women during their ritual uncleanness occasioned by menstruation (Lev. 15:19-28; 18:19; 20:18) and childbirth (Lev. 12:1-8), and by men for religious reasons (Exod. 19:15; 1 Sam. 21:4-5). Some have contended on the basis of the passages in Leviticus that continence should be practiced for birth control.[19] But this is not legitimate, for instead of limiting birth these restrictions tend to increase fertility. Herman Wouk says: "The main practical result of this [abstinence after the menses] is that they rejoin at the time when the wife is most likely to conceive. It is the exact opposite of the rhythm system of birth control."[20]

16. Saggs, *The Greatness That Was Babylon*, p. 186.

17. M. Mielziner, *The Jewish Law of Marriage and Divorce in Ancient and Modern Times* (Cincinnati: Block Publishing and Printing Co., 1884), p. 99.

18. Ryder Smith, *Bible Doctrine of Womanhood* (London: Epworth, 1923).

19. For example, Keith L. Brooks, *What Does the Bible Teach about Birth Control?* (Los Angeles: American Prophetic League), pp. 13ff.

20. Herman Wouk, *This Is My God* (Garden City, NY: Doubleday, 1959), p. 156.

The conjugal regulations in the Talmud accurately reflect the teaching of the Old Testament. Mielziner says: "The duty of conjugal cohabitation is legally, as well as ritually and ethically regulated in the Rabbinical Code. A continual refusal, on either side, regarding this duty, if not excused by sickness and circumstances, offers a ground for divorce."[21]

The Apostle Paul in the New Testament likewise enjoins intercourse as a mutual duty owed by each to the other, to be withheld only during limited periods of special religious observance (1 Cor. 7:5).

Texts Bearing on Contraception

Three lines of evidence support the common assumption that withdrawal was undoubtedly the most universal and commonly practiced method of averting conception in biblical times: (1) the terms for various kinds of temple prostitutes in Assyria and Babylonia; (2) references in the Talmud; (3) the incident of Onan recorded in Genesis 38:8-10.

The terminology applied to the female temple personnel in the Code of Hammurabi and other Babylonian documents indicates that these priestesses were sexually active, but in some way they prevented conception. No women consecrated to gods were allowed to bear children, even in marriage. Since contraceptives and sterilization of women were unknown and technically unfeasible in antiquity,[22] a priestess, or hierodule, could avoid impregnation only by using abnormal methods of intercourse. One text prescribed the extreme precaution against impregnation by intercourse per anum: "The high priestess will permit intercourse per anum in order to avoid pregnancy."[23] However, this extreme measure of precaution does not seem to have been practiced by other classes of female cult personnel. The titles and expressions used to denote these other priestesses may point to the avoidance of pregnancy by *coitus interruptus*. Astour concludes: "In the expression *Kulmašītu ša qerebša ma'd[a] 'a, kulmašītu*[24] whose womb is 'many' (who has intercourse with many men) points to a more normal way of inter-

21. Mielziner, *The Jewish Law of Marriage and Divorce*, p. 101.

22. Concerning sacral prostitution and contraception in the Old Testament world, see Michael C. Astour, "Tamar the Hierodule," *JBL* 85 (1966): 185-96.

23. *The Assyrian Dictionary of the Oriental Institute of the University of Chicago*, ed. I. G. Gelb, T. Jacobsen, B. Landsberger, and A. L. Oppenheim (Chicago: Oriental Institute, 1958), vol. 4, p. 325.

24. Possibly from Sumerian NU.BAR "to separate sexual organs."

course, and if the term *kulmašītu (m)* [means 'pure (of) semen'] . . . , it would hint to *coitus interruptus,* as in Genesis 38:9."

The Talmud also indicates that withdrawal was practiced to avoid pregnancy. According to the *Yebamot* section of the Talmud (34b), during the twenty-four months in which a child is nursed, "a man must thresh inside and winnow outside," a euphemism for withdrawal.[25]

The case of Onan (Gen. 38:8-10) provides the one clear example of withdrawal with contraceptive intent in the Old Testament. Our text reads: "Then Judah said to Onan: 'Go in to your brother's wife and perform the duty of a brother-in-law to her, and raise up offspring for your brother.' But Onan knew that the offspring would not be his; so when he went in to his brother's wife, he spilled [the semen] upon the ground, lest he should give offspring to his brother. And what he did was evil in the sight of the Lord, and he slew him also."

The context clearly indicates that Onan's sin lay in his selfish unwillingness to honor his levirate duty.[26] Roman Catholic exegetes reject this explanation, however, and insist that God killed Onan for practicing birth control. They argue that Onan paid for his deed with his life, whereas the penalty for refusing the responsibilities of the levirate marriage was far milder in the normally severe Mosaic code. Such a man, they point out, merely had his sandals removed and was spat upon the face before all the elders of the village. Ruth did not even insist upon this punishment when her nearest kinsman refused to honor his duty.

The texts can be harmonized by recognizing that the Mosaic law pertains to a man who refuses to marry his brother's widow, whereas the case of Onan pertains to a man who was willing to marry his brother's widow but then perverted the institution. The Lawgiver had the bereaved couple at heart; but Onan used levirate marriage for his personal gratification. In a word, he used his brother's wife with no respect for her personality and dignity, and without brotherly concern. We conclude, then, that this passage instructs us concerning the responsible use of sex; it does not forbid contraception *per se.*

---

25. A. van Selms, *Marriage and Family Life in Ugaritic Literature* (London: Luzac, 1954), p. 24, notes: "Comparisons between sexual intercourse and the cultivation of a field abound in ancient literature."

26. The institution of levirate (from Lat. *levir* = "brother") marriage had a wide usage in the Ancient Near East. Similar, though not identical, provisions can be found in the Assyrian laws, the Hittite code, and the Nuzi tablets. According to this institution, a man was responsible to provide for his brother's widow, and to preserve the name of his deceased, childless brother (Deut. 25:5-10).

In the light of the fact that contraception was practiced by withdrawal, one would expect to find an express prohibition of the practice somewhere in the Bible if God considered it to be a sinful act in itself. But we do not find any such prohibition.

Two passages occur where one might ordinarily expect to find such prohibition. The first reads: "And if a man has an emission of semen, he shall bathe his whole body in water and be unclean until the evening. And every garment and every skin on which the semen comes shall be washed with water, and be unclean until the evening. If a man lies with a woman and has an emission of semen they shall bathe with water and be unclean until the evening" (Lev. 15:16-18). The cogent point is that the emission of semen apart from coitus is not regarded as a sinful act. Because no sacrifice is demanded, Barclay says: "No moral fault is implied in connection with these impurities. So the laws are ceremonial."[27]

The second passage is Leviticus 20:10-21. Here the Bible lists sexual crimes punishable by death. All of these involve intercourse with a person apart from the marriage relationship. Once again we find no reference to withdrawal as a sexual abuse.

We conclude, therefore, that the Old Testament prohibits infanticide, sterilization, and continence as means of avoiding pregnancy, but that it does not prohibit contraception.

Because God has not prohibited contraception, we must now turn to passages bearing on the purposes of marriage in order to determine what use may be made of this means.

Texts Bearing on the Use of Contraception: The Purpose of Marriage

Van Selms says concerning the purpose of marriage in Ugarit: "As in most ancient societies the real purpose of marriage is the procreation of lawful sons."[28] This statement, however, would be a gross overgeneralization if applied to the Bible. Undoubtedly, some males in the Old Covenant regarded sex merely as a means for the procreation of children or as a source of sensual pleasure, but this understanding of marriage does not exhaust the divine purpose of marriage. God's reasons for giving marriage to his people are manifold:

27. R. A. Barclay, *The Law Givers* (New York: Abingdon, 1964), p. 39.
28. A. van Selms, *Marriage and Family Life in Ugaritic Literature*, p. 13.

For Companionship

God instituted marriage that man might have company: "And the Lord God said: 'It is not good that the man should be alone; I will make a helper fit for him'" (Gen. 2:18). Likewise the psalmist says: "God gives the desolate a home to dwell in" (Ps. 68:6 [7]).

For Completeness

It is within the framework of marriage that man achieves his unity; apart from marriage he is broken, incomplete. "Therefore a man leaves his father and mother and cleaves to his wife and they become one flesh." The joy of the reuniting of man and woman and the sadness of their parting are celebrated in an incomparable way in the Song of Songs.

For Enjoyment

God instituted marriage in order to give pleasure — not merely sensual pleasure — to both the man and the woman. To the woman he said ". . . your desire shall be for your husband." To men the inspired sage advises: "Enjoy life with the wife whom you love . . ." (Eccles. 9:9). Other texts that belong under this heading are: Prov. 12:4; 18:22; 19:14; 31:31; Gen. 29:20; 1 Sam. 1:8; 2 Sam. 11:11.

For Procreation

The Old Testament assumes procreation as a purpose of marriage and considers children as an evidence of God's blessing: "And God blessed them and said to them: 'Be fruitful and multiply and fill the earth and have dominion over the fish of the sea and over the fowl in the heavens and over every living thing that moves upon the earth'" (Gen. 1:28). The injunction is repeated again to Noah after the fall (Gen. 9:1, 7). When the text declares, "God blessed them," it means in part that he made them virile. On this basis he gives the command to reproduce. The Psalmist says: "Lo, sons are a heritage from the Lord, the fruit of the womb a reward. Like arrows in the hand of a warrior are the sons of one's youth. Happy is the man who has his quiver full of them!" (Ps. 127:3-5). By contrast a marriage without offspring is considered cursed: "But if you will not obey the voice of the Lord your God or be careful to do all His commandments and His statutes which I command you this day . . . cursed shall be the fruit of your body and the fruit of your ground, the increase of your cattle, and the young of your flock" (Deut. 28:15-18). The divine norm is for all of nature to be fertile. Predicting the golden age to come, Jeremiah says: "Behold the days are coming, says the Lord, when I will sow the house of Israel and the house of Judah with the seed of man and the seed of beast" (Jer. 31:27; cf. also Gen. 1:22; 8:17; 49:22; Ps. 128:3). Fagley correctly appraises the norm as follows: "It is not a static balance, however, that is sought. Rather it is one that is dynamic, rapidly expanding. The dream might be called the abundant society. . . ."[29] Clearly, in the Old Testament, God does not regard children with contempt or treat the bearing of children as a common thing.

We must leave it to the moral theologian, however, to evaluate the applicability of this ideal to our present situation where, to use Thielecke's terminology, the order of creation and history are in tension.[30]

It should be noted that with the blessed promise of offspring there is also the injunction to subdue the earth. Babbage says: "His dignity lies in 'subduing' it. . . . He has it in his hands to shape and transform it; this is his duty and responsibility."[31] This text may apply to cases of overpopulation where the balance with nature cannot be maintained. Perhaps in such cases God enjoins human beings to use their technological achievements to maintain a balance for the good life.

To Produce a Godly Seed

God instituted monogamy, says Malachi, "to seek a godly seed" (Mal. 2:15). Innumerable Old Testament passages instructing his people on raising a godly seed belong here; for example, Deuteronomy 6:4ff. We may infer from these that his people are expected to be co-laborers with God in producing a godly seed to bless the earth.

29. Fagley, *The Population Explosion and Christian Responsibility*, p. 112.
30. Helmut Thielecke, *The Ethics of Sex* (New York: Harper & Row, 1964), p. 202.
31. Babbage, *Christianity and Sex*, p. 36.

To Illustrate His Love for Israel

Finally, God used marriage to illustrate his love for Israel. The analogy of the love of a husband for his wife is repeatedly used by the prophets to illuminate God's persistent love for Israel. The analogy, however, can be used only by implication in the problem at hand.

In conclusion, God intended marriage to serve all of these purposes: enjoyment, companionship, unity, procreation, to produce a godly seed, and to illustrate his love for Israel. Protestant theologians frequently justify birth control by separating these purposes from each other. While they may have legitimate grounds for doing so, such separation is against the ethos of the Old Testament. According to the Old Testament the Creator instituted marriage to serve all these ends together. Montgomery's judgment harmonizes with this prudence derived from the Old Testament: "The burden of proof rests, then, on the couple who wish to restrict the size of their family."[32]

32. John Warwick Montgomery, "How to Decide the Birth-Control Question," *Christianity Today*, March 4, 1966, p. 10.

Note: Professor Montgomery does well in calling attention to an alternative interpretation of Exodus 21:22-24 (pp. 87f.). He errs, however, by asserting that I follow David Mace, an English sociologist, "against virtually all serious exegetes." On the contrary, measured by the weight of scholarly opinion, Montgomery's view has little support. The view advanced in this chapter follows the traditional, normative interpretation of the passage as the following evidence confirms:

1) The translation presented in this chapter has the support of the following ancient translations: LXX, Peshitta, Vulgate, Onkelos, and Targum Jonathan. Of the English translations I consulted it agrees with AV, EV (ASV), Rotherham, JPS, Moffatt, American, Basic English, ESV, Jerusalem, Berkeley, Torah (1962), Confraternity, and Amplified. To my knowledge the only translations that disagree are the Improved (1912) and Young's Literal (a noninterpretative translation).

2) Commentators with whom I concur are: Philo, Jarchi, Aben Ezra, Rashi, Maimonides, Lange (trans. Charles M. Mead), Murphy, S. E. Driver, A. H. McNeile, Dummelow, Philip C. Johnson, J. Edgar Park (in *IB*). Most recently John E. Huesman (*The Jerome Bible Commentary*, 1968) supports this view.

In addition, Montgomery is mistaken when he says: "The equality of mother and unborn child in Exodus 21 is upheld . . . by a classic Old Testament scholar such as the nineteenth-century Protestant Delitzsch." In reality, Keil (not Delitzsch) is making a different point; namely, the child in question is not a fetus but a fully developed human being. Lange calls this interpretation "strange." Obviously, Keil's interpretation has nothing to do with Montgomery's conclusion.

The Phenomenon of Conditionality within
Unconditional Covenants

E. Kutsch made an important contribution to biblical studies by defining Hebrew *bĕrît* (traditionally, and misleadingly, rendered in English "covenant") not as "relationship," "pact," or "agreement," but as "obligation" or "designation."[1] M. Weinfeld, who supported Kutsch's definition by citing terms paralleling *bĕrît* in the Ancient Near East, points out that Kutsch's definition lays to rest "a lot of misunderstandings and pseudo-ideologies." He explains:

> Thus W. Robertson Smith's notion about the covenant as "the bond of truth and life fellowship" or the idea of "community of *sacra*" hidden in the blood falls to the ground. The blood in the covenantal ceremony does not serve as a symbol of holy communion, but, as can be learned from Aeschylus quoted by Kutsch, constitutes the dramatization of the punishment which will befall the one who violates the oath: his blood will be shed. The same applies to Wellhausen for whom the covenant is some kind of *bond between God and the people* which was reinterpreted by the Prophets.[2]

Weinfeld summarizes Kutsch's specific meanings for Hebrew *bĕrît* as follows:

---

1. Ernst Kutsch, *Verheissung und Gesetz, Untersuchungen zum sogenannten "Bund" im Alten Testament* (BZAW, 131) (Berlin and New York: Walter de Gruyter, 1973).
2. Moshe Weinfeld, "Bᵉrith — Covenant vs. Obligation," *Bib* 56 (1975): 123-24; Moshe Weinfeld, "Bᵉrîth," *TDOT*, 2:255-56.

Previously published in *Israel's Apostasy and Restoration: Essays in Honor of Roland K. Harrison,* ed. Avraham Gileadi (Grand Rapids: Baker, 1988), pp. 123-39.

A. A commitment by the subject of the *bĕrît*. That is, a promise given by the subject (mostly sanctified by oath).
B. An obligation imposed by the subject of the *bĕrît* upon someone else.
C. A mutual obligation by which two parties make pledges one to another.
D. A mutual obligation sponsored by a third party.

The biblical series of covenants between YHWH and man, or Israel — the concern of this essay — belong to the first two definitions. Both may be called unilateral because YHWH either binds himself to serve his servants (class A) or binds his servants to serve him (class B). In neither case does the covenant's existence depend on pledges by both parties. Class C may be called bilateral because the covenant contains terms that indicate duties incumbent upon both parties.

D. N. Freedman conveniently calls the class A covenant "a covenant of divine commitment" and the class B covenant "a covenant of human obligation."[3] Weinfeld labels them more succinctly "grant" and "treaty" respectively. He writes:

> While the "treaty" constitutes an obligation of the vassal to his master, the suzerain, the "grant" constitutes an obligation of the master to his servant. . . . The "grant" serves mainly to protect the rights of the *servant*, while the treaty comes to protect the rights of the *master*.[4]

In this essay I also use the terms *oath* for YHWH's commitment to the beneficiary and *law* for the obligations imposed by him on Israel.

Class A may be called unconditional in the sense that no demands are made on the superior party, and class B, conditional in the sense that the superior party promises to reward or punish the inferior partner for obeying or disobeying the imposed obligations. So defined, the distinction is valid, but the terms *unconditional* and *conditional* may be misleading. Some have mistakenly thought that class A contains no conditional aspects with reference to the beneficiary, and class B no unconditional aspects. I hope this essay will correct any mistaken notions.

---

3. David Noel Freedman, "Divine Commitment and Human Obligation: The Covenant Theme," *Int* 18 (1964): 420.

4. Moshe Weinfeld, "The Covenant of Grant in the Old Testament and in the Ancient Near East," *JAOS* 90 (1970): 185.

The first kind of covenant — the grant — includes the covenants with Noah (Genesis 9), the Patriarchs (Gen. 12:1-3; 15; 17; 22:15-18; 26:3-5; 28:13-15), Phinehas (Num. 25), and David (2 Sam. 7 = 1 Chron. 17; Ps. 89:4, 29[3, 28], 34, 39; Jer. 33:21; passim). Covenants of the second type — the treaty — include those given by YHWH to Adam[5] in the Garden of Eden and to Israel at Sinai and Moab (Exodus 19, Leviticus, and Deuteronomy). The latter was renewed at Shechem by Joshua (Joshua 24) and again in the days of Jehoiada (2 Kings 11:17; 2 Chron. 29:10), Josiah (2 Kings 23:3), and Ezra-Nehemiah (Ezra 10:3).

Scholars committed to the documentary hypothesis usually refer to the covenant made at Sinai as the "Sinaitic covenant" and to the one made at Moab as the "Deuteronomic covenant," the covenant book par excellence according to J. Muilenburg.[6] For the purpose of this essay, I will group these two covenants together and call them the "Mosaic covenant." (I do not mean to imply that the two share a common form.)[7]

Covenants between men usually belong to class C, in which the situation is effectively bilateral.[8] None of the covenants involving YHWH belong to this category. Class D is not pertinent for this study either.

Instructively, YHWH's grants feature most prominently gifts of offspring and land, matching the prominent gifts of house (that is, dynasty) and land by the suzerain in the Hittite and Syro-Palestinian political reality.

The distinction between *grant* and *treaty* is essential in understanding biblical theology, but scholars often fail to understand the terms' complementary relationship. For example on one hand, J. D. Levenson accuses C. Shedl, R. de Vaux, and A. H. J. Gunneweg of improperly integrating the Davidic and Sinaitic covenants by subordinating the Davidic to the Sinaitic. On the other hand, he accuses J. Bright and G. E. Mendenhall of improperly

---

5. Although the Bible does not formally express the relationship between YHWH and Adam by the term *covenant,* yet in substance the relationship meets our definition of the word.

6. James Muilenburg, "The Form and Structure of the Covenantal Formulations," *VT* 9 (1959): 350.

7. See Dennis J. McCarthy, *Treaty and Covenant: A Study in Form in the Ancient Oriental Documents and the OT,* AnBib 21 (Rome: Pontifical Biblical Institute, 1963). Although he modified the analysis of Alt and Mendenhall, McCarthy still considers the commandments as an integral part of the covenant at Sinai, though not as an element of a treaty formula (pp. 158 n. 11, 163-64, 172-73).

8. For examples, see Dennis J. McCarthy, "*B*ᵉ*rit* and Covenant in the Deuteronomistic History," *SVT* 3 (1972): 65-85.

segregating the two covenant forms by pitting them against one another. Levenson himself, however, errs by radically divorcing them.[9]

In this essay I aim to study, primarily, the phenomenon of conditionality within irrevocable grants, a study I hope will clarify the relationship between YHWH's oaths to Abraham and David and the obligations he imposed on Israel. I will argue that YHWH's grants and treaty do not rival or exclude, but complement one another. If a more accurate biblical theology can be written as a result, then I will have achieved my purpose in this attempt to honor Professor R. K. Harrison.

A contribution of this study may be that it will help lay to rest the notion that the Deuteronomist, the redactor of Deuteronomy through the Book of Kings, reinterpreted the grants to Abraham and David by putting conditions on them.[10] This result would be especially appropriate in view of Harrison's interests.

I will begin the study with an analysis of the unconditional and conditional aspects of the grants given to Noah, Abraham, and David; I will then analyze the same features in the treaty imposed on Israel; finally, I will analyze the new covenant which successfully resolves the tension between YHWH's oaths and Israel's obligations. I will not attempt to reconstruct a hypothetical genesis of the covenant idea within Israel, a will-o'-the-wisp enterprise at best,[11] apart from noting that most scholars recognize that *covenant* was consciously applied to YHWH's relationship with Israel from the earliest times. Furthermore, the Pentateuch deserves to be interpreted as a unity.[12]

Finally, by way of introduction, I will treat my subject thematically, not lexically, even though this treatment exposes the study to the danger of subjective selection and arrangement of material.[13] The reader must judge whether I achieve objectivity.

---

9. Jon D. Levenson, "The Davidic Covenant and Its Modern Interpreters," *CBQ* 41 (1979): 215.

10. Compare Weinfeld, "Covenant of Grant," p. 195.

11. Dennis J. McCarthy, "B^erit in Old Testament History and Theology," *Bib* 53 (1972): 110-21, esp. 121.

12. See D. J. A. Clines, "The Theme of the Pentateuch," *JSOT* (1978).

13. Instructively, with reference to the Davidic covenant, the term *běrît* is found in poetic texts (Ps. 89:4, 29, 35[3, 28, 34]) but not in prose accounts (2 Sam. 7).

God's Covenant with Noah

Unconditional Aspects

D. J. McCarthy notes: "No $b^e r\hat{\imath}t$ is one-sided unless the obligation is incumbent on one party and one party makes the $b^e r\hat{\imath}t$."[14] According to this definition, God's covenant with Noah is one-sided; it is unilateral and unconditional in the sense that no demands are made on Noah.

God's covenant with Noah involves all mankind. Strictly speaking, it involves a divine commitment both to the creation and to man. Note that its prominent features are land and offspring. With respect to land, God promises never again to curse the ground or destroy all living creatures as he did in the Flood, but to give the earth its seasons and harvest as long as it endures (Gen. 8:21-22). With regard to offspring, he promises to make man fruitful and give him dominion over every living creature (9:1-4). Although God holds man accountable to exact capital punishment (9:5-6), the promises are not contingent upon it. Because of God's commitment, man can confidently multiply and increase on earth (9:7).

God's promises to both the creation and man are explicitly not contingent on man's behavior:

> Never again will I curse the ground because of man, even though every inclination of a man's heart is evil from his childhood. (Gen. 8:21)

The sign of God's commitment to all life (compare Gen. 9:12-13, 17), the rainbow, functions to remind God, not man, of God's promise. God proves his commitment by not reneging on his promise after Noah gets drunk and involves himself and Ham in sexual impropriety (9:20-24). To be sure, Canaan will be cursed with slavery, but the earth is not cursed.

Conditional Aspects

The pleasing aroma. McCarthy[15] emphasizes the important point that the making of a covenant does not initiate a relationship, but rather formalizes

---

14. McCarthy, "$B^e rit$ in Old Testament History," p. 84.

15. Dennis J. McCarthy, "Covenant-Relationships," in *Questions Disputées d'ancien Testament*, ed. C. Brekelmans (Gembloux, Belgium: J. Duclot, 1974), pp. 91-103.

and gives concrete expression to one already in existence. In every covenant of divine commitment, the beneficiary first creates a spiritual climate leading to the commitment. As in the royal grants in the Ancient Near East, God also grants gifts pertaining to land and progeny to Noah, Abraham, and David, because they excelled in loyally serving him.[16] By building an altar to YHWH and making pure sacrifices, Noah prompted YHWH to grant the covenant: YHWH smelled the pleasing aroma and said in his heart: "Never again will I curse the ground" (Gen. 8:20-21).

Earlier (6:9) we were informed that Noah was a righteous man *('îš ṣaddîq)*, blameless *(tāmîm)* in his generation. By faith he obeyed God and built the ark as instructed. Without those qualities, his sacrifice would not have pleased YHWH. In a very real sense, the covenant came about because of Noah's spiritual virtues. If a covenant does not establish a relationship, it nevertheless represents the climax of an already-existing spiritual relationship. As we will see, there are local exceptions to this covenant; however, we may assume, on the principle of spiritual reciprocity, that the promises given to mankind flourish best among creatures pleasing to God.

Unique blessings and curses. The Creator's oath to all mankind never again to *universally* "curse the ground" *(qallēl . . . hā'ădāmâ)* because of man's sin (8:21), and to give the earth "seedtime and harvest" *(zeraʿ wĕqāṣîr)* (8:22), does not exclude local exceptions. God may *locally* manipulate life within the created order. On the one hand, with respect to the elect nation, he controls the rain and harvest in the promised land so as to encourage his people to obey the law mediated through Moses (Deut. 11:13-17; 28:1-6, 15-24) — he promises to bless them exceptionally when they keep it (see the Abrahamic covenant below). On the other hand, he blesses the nonelect (that is, fills them with the potential of life) when they bless the elect (that is, pay them respect as the mediators of life) and curses *('ārar)* them when they curse *(qālal)* the elect (compare Gen. 12:2-3; 17; 20:3; 26:10).

Famines and other devastations. Finally, there exist providential local famines apart from moral considerations (see Gen. 26:1; passim), and local judgments for flagrant immorality when the elect are not involved, as in the case of Sodom and Gomorrah (see Genesis 19).

---

16. Weinfeld, "Covenant of Grant," p. 185.

Conclusion

God's grants of seasonal harvest and blessing are in space and time universally irrevocable, but locally and temporarily conditional upon moral behavior or providential acts. Both the irrevocable and conditional aspects of the covenant further man's spiritual life. The theological certainty that the stage for redemption is in place until the end of time allows man to live confidently and to follow God in hope. But the historical variations warn him to walk softly before his Creator.

God's Covenant with Abraham

Unconditional Aspects

A covenant of divine commitment is well illustrated in Genesis 15. N. M. Sarna[17] analyzes the chapter as having two parts (vv. 1-6 and 7-21) that share a common form: a divine promise (vv. 1, 7) followed by Abraham's question (vv. 2-3, 8), concluding with a divine response confirming the promise by a sign (vv. 4-6 and 9-21). The first six verses deal with the promise of patriarchal progeny, the rest with possession of the promised land.

The Creator confirms his promise regarding an innumerable offspring by visually displaying the stars in the heavens and the sand on the shore. He ratifies the covenant to give Abraham the promised land by symbolically passing as a smoking firepot and flaming torch among the three slaughtered animals, symbolizing a threefold oath, and provisionally identifying himself with the slaughtered animals' fate. To judge from Ancient Near Eastern parallels, Jer. 34:18-20 and Aeschylus, as YHWH passes among the slaughtered animals he is saying in the boldest symbolism: "May it be done to me as it has been done to these animals, if I do not fulfill my promise." Significantly, only YHWH makes promises, and only he passes between or among the butchered parts, demonstrating that this is a unilateral covenant.

The fulfillment of the covenant to Abraham and his descendants, the beneficiaries, depends on YHWH's faithfulness, which, as Freedman notes,[18] is axiomatic.

17. Nahum M. Sarna, *Understanding Genesis,* 3rd ed. (New York: Schocken, 1974), pp. 120-22.

18. Freedman, "Divine Commitment and Human Obligation," p. 425.

YHWH assumes this covenant regarding the offspring of Abraham and their land when he promises to make Abraham into a great nation that will bless others (Gen. 12:1-3). He confirms the promises in Genesis 17, adding that Abraham will become the father of a multitude of nations, that he will be their God, and that these promises are forever *(ʿôlām)* (17:8). (We need to remind ourselves that even if Genesis 15 and 17 stem from different sources, the text we have in hand is meant to be read as a unity.) YHWH swears in Genesis 22:15-18 to fulfill this covenant, adding that Israel will defeat her enemies. The divine commitment is repeated to Isaac (26:24) and Jacob (28:13-15). In sum, YHWH commits himself unilaterally to fulfill these promises to the Patriarchs, presenting them as irrevocable by promising, ratifying, swearing to, and confirming his promises in covenants (compare Heb. 6:13-17).

Conditional Aspects

The oaths presume an existing spiritual relationship. Here too we find the principle of spiritual reciprocity at work. YHWH commits himself to these promises in response to Abraham's exceptional faith. Genesis 12:1-3 shares a common form with Genesis 1: Announcement, "And God said" (Gen. 1:3, 6, etc., and 12:1), followed by imperatives, "Let there be . . ." (1:3, 6, etc.) and "Go" (12:1), followed by a report of fulfillment, "So God made . . ." (Gen. 1:7) and "and Abraham went" (12:4). The pattern, however, differs from Genesis 1 in that God adds six promises:

> I will make you into a great nation . . . bless you . . . make your name great . . . bless those who bless you, and whoever curses you . . . curse; and all peoples on earth will be blessed through you.

These promises appear between the imperative and the report of their fulfillment, so that Abraham's obedience to the command becomes a faithful response to the promises. Had he not acted on his faith, presumably the promises would not have taken effect. Moreover, were the order of promise and report reversed, the notion of contingency would have been significantly reduced.

The promise to confirm the covenant in Genesis 17:2 is preceded by the command "Walk before me and be blameless" (17:1), clearly hinting at a connection between Abraham's ethical behavior and YHWH's fulfillment of the covenant with him. The oath in 22:16-17 is explicitly grounded in Abraham's exceptional loyalty and obedience to YHWH:

> I swear by myself, declares YHWH, that because you have done this [*kî ya'an 'ăšer 'ā'sîtā 'et-haddābār*] and have not withheld your son, your beloved son, I will surely bless you.

YHWH connects his promises in Genesis 15 regarding the offspring and land with Abraham's acts of faith, by introducing them with the statement: "Your reward is very great" (15:1).

In short, the oaths do not initiate a relationship, but reciprocate Abraham's loyalty. This explicit connection between Abraham's faith and the divine commitment may imply that for his descendants to qualify for these blessings they too must create the same spiritual climate. The following contingencies connected with YHWH's promises to Abraham tend to justify this notion.

The beneficiaries are to be devoted to YHWH. The confirmation of the covenant in Genesis 17 clearly falls into two parts: "As for me . . ." (17:4-8) and "As for you . . ." (vv. 9-14), but this dialectical tension must not be resolved in such a way as to make the promises mutually dependent on one another in the sense that if one party fails, the other is relieved of responsibility. The first part unequivocally commits YHWH to fulfill his promises to give Abraham an enlarged progeny including kings (vv. 4-6), to be his and their God (v. 7), and to give his descendants the land of Canaan forever (v. 8). The second part places conditions upon the beneficiaries. Only Abraham's circumcised descendants will participate in the grant. Here we enter into the mystery of divine sovereignty and human accountability. YHWH will fulfill his promises but not apart from faith on the part of their beneficiaries. The tension can be seen, in part, in this divine promise to Abraham: "to be your God and the God of your descendants after you" (17:7). The full meaning of this addition to the covenant is "I will be your God and you will be my people," an expression suggesting the marriage of the two parties. Weinfeld says,

> The marriage contract formula known to us from the Near East, "I will be to you a husband and you will be to me a wife," stands in fact behind the statements [*wĕhāyîtî lākem lē'ĕlōhîm wĕ'attem tihyû lî lĕ'ām*] which occur in the context of *bĕrît* (Lev. 26:12; compare Exod. 6:7; Deut. 29:12-13; Jer. 31:33).[19]

19. Weinfeld, "Bᵉrith — Covenant vs. Obligation," p. 125.

The prophets exploit the metaphor and picture YHWH as putting away his wife when she proves herself unfaithful to him (Hos. 2:2-13; Jer. 3:1-3; passim). Nonetheless, because of YHWH's faithfulness to Abraham, the prophets do not envision God as divorcing Israel so that he could never take her back (compare Isa. 50:1-3; 49:14-26; Mic. 7:18-20; passim). Through YHWH's sovereign grace, a loyal remnant always exists, giving hope for a full realization of the grant.

YHWH explains that his grant extends only to those within Abraham's household who behave ethically:

> For I have chosen him, in order that he may direct his children and his household after him to keep the way of YHWH by doing what is right and just, so that YHWH will bring about for Abraham what he has promised him. (Gen. 18:19)[20]

Moses, equating the "way of YHWH" with the law mediated through him, confirms the principle:

> You are standing here in order to enter [*'ābar*] into a covenant [*běrît*] with YHWH your God and into his oath [*'ālâ*] which YHWH your God is making [*karat*] with you today in order that he may *establish* [*hāqîm*] you today as his people and that he may be your God, just as he spoke to you and he swore to your fathers, to Abraham, Isaac, and Jacob. (Deut. 29:10-13)

The author of the Pentateuch views the two kinds of unilateral covenants, oath and law, as mutual complements defining the relationship between YHWH and Israel. The oath gives theological certainty of an enduring relationship; the law gives a moral quality to it.

I will discuss the resolution of the dialectical tension between YHWH's irrevocable, and yet qualified, commitment to Israel more fully in connection with the discussion on the New Covenant. Let it suffice to note that YHWH must elect true Israel to guarantee his irrevocable promises to the Patriarchs.

The uncircumcised are to be cut off. The second half of the covenant in Genesis 17 states that YHWH's covenant with the Patriarchs extends only to those within Abraham's lineage who embrace their father's faith, and it reaches beyond them to foreigners that share in it:

---

20. I am indebted to Avraham Gileadi for calling my attention to this important text. Note that this condition put upon the grant is found not in putative D but in J.

> As for you . . . every male among you shall be circumcised . . . including those born in your household or . . . those not your offspring. . . . Any uncircumcised male, who has not been circumcised in the flesh, will be cut off from his people [that is, excommunicated from the covenantal community and exposed to death from a divine agency]. (Gen. 17:9-14)

Elsewhere the Lawgiver clarifies that the circumcision in the flesh functioned symbolically as a circumcision of the heart (Deut. 10:16; 30:6).

Conclusion

YHWH irrevocably committed himself to give Abraham an innumerable progeny and make him a father of many nations, to give him and his descendants the promised land forever, to be their God, and to bless others through them. His grant, however, extends only to Abraham's spiritual progeny. Paul's distinction between spiritual and natural Israel is firmly rooted in the Pentateuch. Paul puts it this way: "For not all who are descended from Israel are Israel" (Rom. 9:6).

Though conditional on human obligations, YHWH's grants to the Patriarchs are unilateral because they do not depend on Israel's pledge to fulfill obligations. The irrevocable oaths to the Patriarchs, qualified to extend only to a loyal progeny, logically entail that YHWH must sovereignly and graciously elect Abraham's seed. Without these attributes and activity, the promises would fail.

God's Covenant with David

Unconditional Aspects

YHWH's grant to David places no obligations on David for its enactment or perpetuation. It is unilateral, and in that sense unconditional.

R. A. Carlson[21] divides the grant into two parts — promises to be realized during David's lifetime (2 Sam. 7:8-11a) and promises to be fulfilled after his death (7:11b-16). The two halves are formally divided from one another

---

21. R. A. Carlson, *David and the Chosen King* (Uppsala: Almqvist & Wiksell, 1964), pp. 111-14.

by breaking YHWH's address delivered in first person in verses 9-11a and 12-16 with a statement in third person, "YHWH declares to you" (v. 11b), and by locating the promises given in verses 12-16 in the time "when your days are over and you rest with your fathers" (v. 12a).

YHWH promises three things to David before his death: a great name (v. 9; compare 8:13), a place for the people (v. 10; compare the catalog of David's victories within and beyond the promised land in chap. 8), and rest (v. 11; compare 1 Kings 5:4). Promises to be realized after his death include an eternal house (an everlasting dynasty, vv. 13 and 16), and an eternal throne and kingdom (vv. 13 and 16).

Perhaps no external sign, such as a rainbow (see Gen. 9:12-13), circumcision (17:11), or sabbath (Exod. 31:13, 17), is needed, because anything in addition to the promised son(s) would be superfluous.[22] David accepts the promises as certain, with no obligations imposed on him: "For the sake of your word and according to your will, you have done this great thing and made it known to your servant" (2 Sam. 7:21).

Significantly, the author of Samuel tells of David's sin with Bathsheba (2 Sam. 11–12) immediately after narrating the covenant, for the same reason that the author of Genesis juxtaposes the stories of Noah's covenant and drunkenness. By this arrangement he subtly instructs us that the beneficiaries' darkest crimes do not annul the covenants of divine commitment.

Conditional Aspect

Favor is based on the prior spiritual relationship. Like Noah and Abraham, David, through his loyalty to YHWH, had created the spiritual climate favoring this covenant. YHWH grants David an eternal house (dynasty) because David desired to build YHWH an enduring house (temple). YHWH connects David's loyalty with the promises by calling David "my servant" (2 Sam. 7:8). Once again we see the principle of historical relationship and spiritual reciprocity in effect, and we can assume from the following condition that David serves as a paradigm of the kind of individual that historically experiences the covenant's provisions.

---

22. Avraham Gileadi, in "The Davidic Covenant: A Theological Basis for Corporate Protection," in *Israel's Apostasy and Restoration: Essays in Honor of Roland K. Harrison,* ed. Avraham Gileadi (Grand Rapids: Baker, 1988), suggests that YHWH's presence in Zion constitutes the sign of the Davidic covenant. That may be, but in contrast to the other biblical covenants, YHWH does not explicitly confirm his grant to David with a sign.

Son of God. The irrevocable and conditional aspects of YHWH's grant to David are brought together under the evocative imagery of sonship:

> I will be his father, and he will be my son. When he does wrong, I will punish him with the rod of men, with floggings inflicted by men. But my love [*ḥesed*] will never be taken away from him, as I took it away from Saul, whom I removed from before you. (2 Sam. 7:14-15)

The phrase "I will be his father, and he shall be my son" forms an adoption formula[23] that provides both the judicial basis for the gift of the eternal dynasty (compare Pss. 2:7-8; 89) and the qualification that disloyal sons will lose YHWH's protection (compare 1 Kings 6:12-13; 9:4, 6-7).[24] YHWH granted both Abraham and David an eternal progeny and fief. Loyal sons (those that fulfilled the stipulations of the treaty with Israel) would fully enjoy the fief; disloyal sons would lose YHWH's protection and, if they persisted in their wrongdoing, the possession of the fief itself. The fief, however, would never be confiscated — a promise that opens up the hope that YHWH would raise up a loyal son.

David is under curse. Although the covenant is irrevocable, David himself is punished for his crime. Nathan threatened: "This is what YHWH says: 'Out of your own household I am going to bring calamity upon you'" (2 Sam. 12:11).

Conclusion

Freedman effectively summarizes the tension between unconditional commitment and conditional benefits in the Davidic covenant:

> The fate of individual kings or claimants was not guaranteed, but in the end the divine promise would be fulfilled. Historical contingency was balanced by theological certainty concerning the place of the house of David in the destiny of the nation.[25]

A. Gileadi makes the same point:

---

23. See C. Kuhl, "Neue Dokumente zum Verständnis von Hos. 2:4-15," *ZAW* 52 (1934): 102ff.; Weinfeld, "Covenant of Grant," p. 190.

24. See Gileadi, "Davidic Covenant."

25. Freedman, "Divine Commitment and Human Obligation," p. 426.

Although the conditional aspect of the Davidic covenant — the question of the king's loyalty to YHWH — could affect Israel's protection by YHWH for better or worse, the covenant's unconditional aspect — that of an enduring dynasty — left open the possibility of YHWH's appointment of a loyal Davidic monarch in the event of a disloyal monarch's default. YHWH's protection of his people, by virtue of the Davidic covenant, could thus be restored at any time.[26]

Note that the explicit condition put upon the Davidic covenant, extending the irrevocable grant only to a faithful son who keeps the obligations of the treaty, is found not only in putative D (compare 1 Kings 2:4; 6:12-13; 8:25; 9:4ff.) but also in the apparently ancient Psalm 132:

> YHWH swore an oath to David,
>   a sure oath that he will not revoke:
> One of your own descendants
>   I will place on your throne —
> if your sons keep my covenant
>   and the statutes I teach them,
> then their sons will sit
>   on your throne for ever and ever. (vv. 11-12)

The Abrahamic, Mosaic, and Davidic covenants function as complements of one another in defining true Israel. Though unilateral, these covenants are as inseparable as the strands that make up a rope.

God's Covenant with Israel at Sinai and Moab

Unconditional Aspects

The law is unilateral with reference to Israel and unconditional with reference to YHWH. YHWH's covenants with Israel, mediated through Moses at Sinai, augmented on the way from Sinai to Moab (see Num. 19), and supplemented at Moab (compare Deut. 29:1), call upon Israel to pledge herself to him without obligating him by a like pledge to Israel. The treaty is unilateral with reference to Israel and unconditional with reference to YHWH.

---

26. Gileadi, "Davidic Covenant."

The similarities between Deuteronomy and the suzerainty treaties of the Hittites in the second half of the second millennium, and to those of the Assyrians in the first half of the first millennium, are too well known to be rehearsed here. In the first essay establishing this analogue, Mendenhall notes that treaties are unilateral on the part of the vassal. Contrasting the Mosaic covenant with YHWH's grants, he writes:

> The covenant of Moses, on the other hand [sic] is almost the exact opposite. It imposes specific obligations upon the tribes or clans without binding Yahweh to specific obligations, though it goes without saying that the covenant relationship itself presupposed the protection and support of Yahweh to Israel.[27]

The rewards and penalties for obedience and disobedience, couched in the form of blessings and curses, serve as encouragement to the recipients of the covenants not to renege on their commitment. The covenant itself, however, is not bilateral — it does not consist of two parties making pledges to one another to keep mutual obligations.[28]

The law is eternal and irrevocable. The suzerainty treaties were meant to be kept into the remote future. For example, the Hittite king Mursilis, who calls himself in the preamble of his treaty "the great king," stipulates to Duppitessub, his vassal in Amurru: "But you, Duppitessub, remain loyal toward the king of the Hatti land, the Hatti land, my sons [and] my grandsons forever!" Similarly, YHWH's law is said to be eternal. For example, one reads again and again of lasting (ʿôlām) ordinances (Exod. 12:14; passim). Isaiah complains:

> The earth is defiled by its people;
> they have disobeyed the laws;
>   violated the statutes
>   and broken the everlasting [ʿôlām] covenant.

(Isa. 24:5)

27. George E. Mendenhall, "Covenant Forms in Israelite Tradition," *BA* 17 (1954): 62.

28. See George E. Mendenhall, *Law and Covenant in Israel and the Ancient Near East*, Biblical Colloquium, Pittsburgh, 1955 (= *BA*, 1954); Walter Beyerlin, *Herkunft and Geschichte der ältesten Sinaitraditionen* (Tübingen: Mohr, 1961) (English translation, Oxford: Oxford University Press, 1965); K. Baltzer, *Das Bundesformular,* WMANT 4 (1964) (English translation, Oxford: Oxford University Press, 1971); Delbert R. Hillers, *Covenant: The History of a Biblical Idea* (Baltimore and London: Johns Hopkins University Press, 1969).

Jesus said:

> I tell you the truth, until heaven and earth disappear, not the smallest
> letter, not the least stroke of a pen, will by any means disappear from the
> law until everything is accomplished. (Matt. 5:18)

In short, YHWH's law is as irrevocable as his oaths are. Its absolute and
eternal obligations do not stand or fall on Israel's loyalty or disloyalty to
them. In this sense the Mosaic covenant is also unconditional.

Conditional Aspects

Carried on eagle's wings. The Mosaic covenant also comes as the climax of a
long spiritual relationship between YHWH and Israel. Like the Noahic,
Abrahamic, and Davidic covenants, it is an expression of spiritual reciprocity. The Hittite kings encouraged vassals to reciprocate their love by rehearsing the gracious relationship between them in the historical prologues of
their treaties. The point stressed is the overlord's kindness. D. R. Hillers
shrewdly adds: "Parenthetically, if the history were to create any sense of obligation, it had to be substantially accurate."[29] E. Gerstenberger notes: "The
treaty relationship frequently was couched in kinship terms. The concepts of
'brotherhood' (*'aḫḫūtu*) played a prominent role in this regard."[30]

Likewise, YHWH aimed to move Israel to accept his treaty by remind-
ing her of his loyalty to the Patriarchs. Faithful to his promises to her, he had
made Israel into a nation by miraculously increasing her and by delivering
her from Egypt. He summarizes that history with a memorable metaphor:

> You yourselves have seen what I did to Egypt, and how I carried you on
> eagles' wings and brought you to myself. (Exod. 19:4)

In sum, the law is conditioned by a history of a gracious relationship
on the part of the overlord and rests on the principle of spiritual reciprocity.

Law is based on love of God. The ancient Hittite treaties, parallel in
form and substance to the Mosaic covenant, reveal the great king promising
his vassal protection against external and internal enemies, and guarantee-

---

29. Hillers, *Covenant*, p. 31.
30. Erhard Gerstenberger, "Covenant and Commandment," *JBL* 84 (1965): 40.

ing the succession of his dynasty. W. Eichrodt notes: "[These statements] show plainly the mutuality of the new relationship, even though it is initiated and legalized by the king alone."[31]

On the basis of the parallels between these treaties and Mosaic law, K. Baltzer[32] notes that the substance of the law consists in loving God; W. Moran[33] argues convincingly that this love meant Israel would faithfully and devotedly dedicate herself to yhwh's service. R. Clements cautions that we must not think this command is mere legal terminology, empty of spiritual sentiment:

> The value of Moran's observations and comparisons cannot be discounted, but it must be strongly urged that the deuteronomic demand for love to God is wholly consonant with the character and aim of the work as a whole. An appeal to a right attitude to God fits closely into the scheme which asserts the spiritual and moral nature of all divine service.[34]

The love mandated from Israel of necessity depends on yhwh's sublime attributes and acts, frequent themes of Deuteronomy. Regarding the language of Deuteronomy, Eichrodt, in an insightful article, writes:

> [It] is not that of law but that of the heart and conscience. . . . Those who speak to us in the pages of Deuteronomy are men who know that a national law can never attain its goal so long as it remains a system reluctantly endured and effective only by compulsion; it must be founded on the inward assent of the people.[35]

In sum, for the covenant to be effective it must be maintained; it rests on the basis of spiritual reciprocity. Eichrodt notes:

> In fact, everything depends on whether the God who founds the Covenant continues to remain for his people in overwhelming reality a pres-

31. Walter Eichrodt, "Covenant and Law," trans. Lloyd Gaston, *Int* 20 (1966): 310.

32. Baltzer, *Das Bundesformular*.

33. William Moran, "The Ancient Near Eastern Background of the Love of God in Deuteronomy," *CBQ* 23 (1963): 77-87.

34. Ronald E. Clements, *God's Chosen People: A Theological Interpretation of the Book of Deuteronomy* (Valley Forge, PA: Judson, 1969), p. 65.

35. Walter Eichrodt, *Theology of the Old Testament*, vol. 1 (London: SCM Press, 1961), p. 91.

ent, living encounter, as he was experienced at the beginning, or whether he disappears behind the mechanism of a distributive justice, dispensing reward and punishment.[36]

Conclusion

The unilateral covenant eternally committing YHWH to Abraham and his descendants, and the unilateral covenant imposing obligations on Israel are, in fact, inseparable.[37] On the one hand, YHWH's faithful discharge of his promise to Abraham provides the spiritual basis for Israel to accept and keep the covenant with commandments. On the other hand, the commandments set forth the conditions that qualify one to become a beneficiary of YHWH's grant. Both oath and law are presented unilaterally.

In this way YHWH irrevocably commits himself to fulfilling his promises, but not apart from ethical behavior on Israel's part. This connection between the two covenants explains how the two apparently incompatible kinds of covenants — oath and obligation — could be made with the same people. Under the terms of the *oath*, YHWH committed himself forever to Israel as a whole; under the terms of the *obligation*, he could discipline them individually, even to the point of putting them under curses.

Through the Davidic covenant, one man came to represent the people. Gileadi clarifies the relationship between the Mosaic and Davidic covenants: "The Davidic covenant did away with the necessity of all Israel — to a man — maintaining loyalty to YHWH in order to merit his protection."[38]

YHWH irrevocably committed himself to the house of David, but rewarded or disciplined individual kings by extending or withholding the benefits of the grant according to their loyalty or disloyalty to his treaty.

This dialectal arrangement also had distinct spiritual advantages. Israel kept YHWH's commands not on the basis of divine obligation but of divine benevolence. Israel could not put YHWH in her debt to fulfill his part of

36. Eichrodt, "Covenant and Law," p. 315.

37. Eissfeldt and Cross deny that this relationship has a historical basis (see Frank Moore Cross Jr., "Yahweh and the God of the Patriarchs," *HTR* 55 [1962]: 225-59; Frank Moore Cross Jr., *TDOT*, 1:255ff.; Frank Moore Cross Jr., *Hebrew Myth and Canaanite Epic* [Cambridge, MA: Harvard University Press, 1973]). Cross claims that the Patriarchs worshiped the Canaanite god 'El and alleges that the Pentateuch deliberately distorts the historical situation.

38. Gileadi, "Davidic Covenant."

a bargain. The curses and blessings of the covenant that obliged Israel to keep YHWH's ethical demands gave Israel incentive to keep them. By these unilateral commitments, the relationship between YHWH and Israel was not contractual but covenanted — devoted and loving toward one another.

The arrangement, however, had one flaw: it could not compel the consent of Israel because of her hard heart, forehead of bronze, and stiff neck (Exod. 32:9; passim). Because of this fundamental spiritual flaw — a flaw found in the human race as a whole (though exacerbated in Israel, according to Hebrew Scripture) — the fulfillment of the promises to Abraham remained sporadic and partial. Although the covenant with commands was first given to all Israel, over the course of Israel's history its judicial leaders proved to be, by-and-large, faithless, which left only a remnant of true Israel — those true to the spiritual nature of the covenants, be they oath or law. The threatened curses, rather than the promised blessings, were fulfilled.

The two kinds of covenants, grant and treaty, are both eternal because both are founded on eternal attributes of YHWH — the former on his faithfulness, the latter on his holiness. Anticipating Israel's fracture of the treaty (which would disqualify her from the blessing of the grant), both putative P (Lev. 26:44-45) and D (Deut. 30:1-10) resolved the tension by predicting the restoration of the nation after its judgment. After predicting maledictions, P reads:

> Yet in spite of this, when they are in the land of their enemies, I will not reject them or abhor them so as to destroy them completely, breaking my covenant with them. I am YHWH their God. But for their sake I will remember the covenant with their ancestors. (Lev. 26:44-45)

D resolves the tension between the working-out of the two covenants in a similar way but also anticipates the new covenant by promising that upon her return Israel will be given a new heart:

> When all these blessings and curses I have set before you come upon you . . . and when you and your children return to YHWH your God and obey him with all your heart. . . , then YHWH your God will restore your fortunes. . . . YHWH your God will circumcise your hearts . . . so that you may love him with all your heart. (Deut. 30:1-6)

Note that both putative P and D put conditions on the irrevocable grant and work out the historical tension in the same way. No purpose is served by arguing that Deuteronomy 30:1-10 is a later addition. The deuteronomic literature does not threaten the annihilation of the nation for failure to keep the treaty any more than does P.

As D anticipated, another arrangement had to be sought to bring the everlasting promises to the Patriarchs and to David to fruition by keeping the conditions of the treaty.

The New Covenant

As anticipated in these passages from the Pentateuch, Israel's history, always torn between what had been projected for Israel's history and what had been realized, provoked an acute tension between the two kinds of unilateral covenants. On the one hand, YHWH's oaths committed him to bless Israel irrevocably. On the other hand, Israel's inability to keep his treaty (containing his eternal law, consistent with his unchanging character) disqualified the nation from participating in these blessings. Only an elect remnant within the nation kept the treaty. As a result, contrary to YHWH's desires, the nation was cursed, not blessed. A new arrangement had to be sought.

The prophets of the exile foresaw an escape from this dilemma. In the name of YHWH, they announced that YHWH would grant Israel a new covenant in place of the old treaty. This new covenant would contain the substance of the treaty — the eternal law of YHWH — but not its form. Instead of having the form of a unilateral treaty depending on Israel's obedience, it would take the form of a grant, like the Abrahamic and Davidic covenants. YHWH would put his law in Israel's heart.

In setting forth this new covenant arrangement, Jeremiah unmistakably shows its continuity with the provisions of the old law:

> I will put my law in their minds. . . . No longer will a man teach his neighbor, or a man his brother, saying, "Know YHWH." (Jer. 31:33-34)

The "law" in view here is unquestionably the Mosaic treaty. It is summarized by the expression "Know YHWH." H. B. Huffman[39] points out that Near Eastern kings use the verb *to know*, as well as the verb *to love*, as a treaty term. The former has two technical legal senses: to recognize as legitimate a

---

39. Herbert B. Huffman, "The Treaty Background of Hebrew *Yada'*," *BASOR* 181 (February 1966): 31-37.

suzerain or vassal, and to recognize treaty stipulations as binding. For example, the Hittite king, "the Sun," in a treaty with Huqqanas stipulated: "And you, Huqqanas, know only the Sun regarding lordship. Moreover, do not know another lord! Know the Sun alone!"

In short, the new covenant assumes the content of the old Mosaic treaty. But its form is like that of YHWH's grants to Abraham and David. Unlike the Mosaic treaty that rested on Israel's willingness to keep it, YHWH will unilaterally put his law in Israel's heart:

> "The time is coming," declares YHWH, "when I will make a new covenant with the house of Israel and with the house of Judah. It will not be like the covenant I made with their forefathers when I took them by the hand to lead them out of Egypt, because they broke my covenant, though I was a husband to them," declares YHWH. "This is the covenant I will make with the house Israel after that time," declares YHWH. "I will put my law in their minds and write it on their hearts." (Jer. 31:31-33a)

As a result, the intention of the Abrahamic covenant will finally come to fruition:

> "I will be their God, and they will be my people. . . . They will all know me, from the least of them to the greatest." (vv. 33b-34)

Under this arrangement there is no possibility of curses. Rather, the covenant will be preceded by forgiveness: "For I will forgive their wickedness and remember their sins no more" (v. 34b).

The Redeemed and the Righteous: A Study in the Doctrine of Man as Found in the Psalms

The psalms divide humanity in two: the righteous and the wicked, and there is no third. Psalm 1, the gateway into the psalter, presents the enviable character and estate of the righteous (1:1-3) over against the unenviable situation of the wicked (1:4-6).

The blessed man is one who enjoys a present relationship with God and on that basis has the hope of experiencing all that the creator intended man to do before his fall. Psalm 144:12-15 presents a veritable classroom example of the blessed man's prospect: children free from congenital defects (144:12), abounding crops and fertile herds (144:13), all within secure parameters and without the threat of war (144:14). Such a person is called "blessed" by God's inspired psalmist (144:15).

But that prospect is always future, either more immediately or more remotely. Even a person like Job who is presently experiencing the Lord's chastening hand may be called blessed, if healing awaits him in the future (cf. Job 5:17). The issue is: Is he presently enjoying a relationship with God that guarantees such a future?

A relationship with God, in Psalm 1, entails renouncing the company of sinners (1:1) and choosing fellowship with God by meditating upon his word (v. 2). That man, says the psalmist, is like a tree planted, not by rivers of waters that can run wild, nor by wadis that can run dry, but by streams of water that provide a steady and ample supply of life. In due time he will bear fruit while he wears leaves of eternal life (1:3). But not so are the wicked, who are like lifeless, worthless, broken straw and husks (1:4) and headed for eter-

---

Previously published in *The Canadian Baptist,* January 1985. Used with permission.

nal death at the time of judgment (1:5). The righteous are on the road to eternal life, and the wicked are bound for an eternal death, not because of some ineluctable destiny, but because the moral governor of the universe will so intervene in history as to guarantee their appropriate destinies (1:6).

In sum, at the threshold of the psalter we find humanity divided into two classes: the righteous and the wicked, and there is no third. In this essay we focus our attention on the righteous: their hearts, their salvation, their king, their mission, and their prayers.

Their Hearts

The mark of the righteous person in the first psalm is his *delight* in the law of the Lord. You can tell a lot about a person by that which he/she delights in, observed C. S. Lewis. Sports fans delight in their goalies, musicians praise their composers, and literate folk their poets. The righteous praise God and delight in his law.

That word "delights in" is important, for it entails that righteousness is really a matter of the heart. To use the language of the Lord Jesus, it is a matter of being "born again."

We are born estranged from God, speaking lies from birth, and in need of new spiritual birth. The apostle Paul links various psalms together to prove mankind has no prospect of being blessed apart from coming into a relationship with God. "As it is written," he argued:

> There is no one righteous, not even one;
> there is no one who understands,
> no one who seeks God.
> All have turned away,
> they have together become worthless;
> there is no one who does good,
> not even one. (Ps. 14:1-3; 53:1-3)

> Their throats are open graves;
> Their tongues practice deceit. (Ps. 5:9)

> The poison of vipers is on their lips. (Ps. 140:3)

> There is no fear of God before their eyes. (Ps. 36:1; cf. Rom. 3:10-18)

Regarding his natural birth David confessed:

> Surely I have been full of sin from birth,
> sinful from the time my mother conceived me. (Ps. 51:5)

To join the righteous, one must respond to the call of God: "Call upon me in the day of trouble; I will deliver you, and you will honor me," says the Lord (Ps. 50:15).

"Delight" connotes an attitude of love. For example, to describe Shechem's love for Dinah, the omniscient narrator of Genesis says: "The young man . . . lost no time in doing what they said, because he was delighted with Jacob's daughter." He followed instructions because he was in love.

So also the righteous follow God's law not so much because they admire it or because they have to, but because they love the Lord. It is a matter of the heart. We can now understand the poet's division of men, apparently overly simplistic to us upon first reading, into saints and rascals. A person's heart is either in love with God or not. Jesus put it this way: "He who is not with me is against me" (Matt. 12:30); there is no third, "an in-between heart."

Without a new heart, one finds with the Apostle Paul that the law brings spiritual death and not life (cf. Rom. 7:10). "It is one thing to be in the law," said Augustine, "another to be *under* the law. He who is in the law, deals according to the law; he who is under the law is dealt with by the law. The one is free, the other a bondsman." The righteous delight in the law; they do not rely on keeping it as a means of pleasing God or think of themselves as slaves under it (cf. Gal. 3:1-23) or have a Pharisaical attitude of superiority toward others (cf. Luke 18:9:14).

Their Salvation

What moves the righteous to love God? Israel's love and praise flow from its gratitude toward God for saving it as a nation from foreign oppression and as individuals from sin.

The righteous never tire of praising God for saving them out of Egypt, preserving them in the wilderness, and giving them the land he swore on oath to their fathers. Let's make our way to the temple and listen to their songs of praise sung on their festivals, be it Passover in early spring, or Pentecost at the early harvest in May, or Tabernacles when the grapes and olives were crushed for their precious wine and oil in early fall:

Give thanks to the LORD, call upon his name;
make known among the nations what he has done. . . .
He is the LORD our God;
his judgments are in all the earth.
He remembers his covenant forever,
the word he commanded to a thousand generations. . . .
He sent Moses his servant,
and Aaron, whom he had chosen.
They performed his miraculous signs among them,
his wonders in the land of Ham. . . .
He brought out Israel, laden with silver and gold,
and from among their tribes no one faltered. (Ps. 105)

Pharaoh, king of Egypt, had consigned Israel to perpetual slavery. His edict to control their numbers by killing Israel's male babies left God's people without hope. Egypt is a figure of the world in which we once lived before Jesus saved us. In that world we were slaves of our pride and passions, the wages for our sin was death, and our ruler was Satan. Like Israel we too were without hope.

Eugene Peterson in his superb book *A Long Obedience in the Same Direction* (a devotional commentary on the ascent psalms [Psalms 120–134]) observed that people may be willing to stay in the world as long as they have hope — hope of a political leader that will bring righteousness and peace to our bloodstained earth, hope for some science and technology that will save us from our sin and death, hope for an economic policy that will distribute the wealth with equity and justice. When Israel realized they were without hope, they groaned and cried out to God to save them. So also we, when we come to ourselves and realize that no politician can change the human heart and thereby bring peace to the earth, that no science or technology can change humanity's sinful condition and resulting death, and no economic policy can change mankind's greed and avarice, then we too, I say, will groan in our plight and cry out to Jesus who alone can save us by changing us through his cleansing blood and giving us his Holy Spirit.

These songs in the five books of the psalter functioned in part as a libretto to the Mosaic ritual. Through Moses, God instituted the sacrificial ritual of shedding blood to cleanse his people from their sins. David gave the saints voice as they confessed their sins and experienced God's cleansing of their consciences and creating in them new hearts. Facing death because he had committed adultery with Bathsheba and had murdered her husband,

David cried out to God to cleanse him with the hyssop sprig holding the sacramental blood and water (Ps. 51:7). He handed over his confession, Psalm 51, to the chief musician, so that the believing community might join him in song for their own cleansing and learn from experience that God forgives sinners.

Their King

Psalm 1 divides humanity into saint and sinner; Psalm 2 presents them in conflict with one another and introduces us to the triumphant, righteous king. One can no more understand the psalter and the righteous humanity apart from the king than one can understand the New Testament and the Christian apart from Jesus Christ. In most of the psalms, the human subject is the king, as John Eaton so effectively argued in his well-researched book *Kingship and the Psalms* (1976) (especially pp. 20-26). Since most readers of the psalms identify the "I" of the psalms with Mr. Everyman, we had better review just a few of Eaton's many arguments:

1. About half the psalms contain in their superscriptions the notice "of David," signifying either that King David authored the psalm or that his house is the subject of it.

2. The situation in many psalms pertains only to a king. For example, in Psalm 3 he is confronted with a myriad of enemies drawn up on every side. This is no ordinary man! In Psalm 4:2 his influential inner cabinet, "the men" (Hebrew *bene 'ish*) — translated in NIV as "highborn" — are turning his glory into shame by turning away from him in favor of false gods.

3. Motifs or expressions fit only for royalty abound in the psalms. Eaton wrote: "All nations attend to the psalmist's thanksgiving (Pss. 18:50[49]; 57:10[9]; 138:1, 4; 119:46). His deliverance has vast repercussions (22:28f). He invokes a world judgment to rectify his cause (7:7, 9; 56:8; 59:6, 9[5, 8] . . .). He depicts himself as victorious over the nations through God's intervention (118:10-12, 9). He confronts armies (3:7; 27:3; 55:22; 56: 2f; 59; 62:4; 109:3; 120:7; 140:3, 8). He is like a bull raising horns in triumph (92:11[10]; 1 Sam. 2:1). He is God's son (2:7; 27:10; etc.). . . . He stands out before the vast festal congregation (22:23, 26[22, 25]; 40:10f.). His head is raised on high (89:20[19]; 91:14; 3:4[3]; 27:6). His glory receives special mention (21:2, 6). He is blessed with superabundant life (21:2-7; 61:6f.; 121:8). . . . He is called with some emphasis *saddiq*, 'the righteous one' (75:11[10]; 5:13[12]; 92:13[12]), and *hasid*, 'the faithful one' (16:10; cf. 116:15; 4:4[3]) . . ." (pp. 23f.).

4. He represents the faithful community. Throughout the psalter one finds a constant interchange between "I" and "we." For example, Psalm 44 begins with the plural pronouns "we/us":

> **We** have heard with **our** ears, O God;
> **our** fathers have told **us** . . . (v. 1)

But quite fluidly the speaker changes to the first person singular pronouns "I/me," and then back to the group:

> You are **my** king and **my** God,
> who decrees victories for Jacob.
> Through you **we** push back **our** enemies;
> through your name **we** trample **our** foes.
> **I** do not trust in **my** bow,
> **my** sword does not bring **me** victory;
> but you give **us** victory over **our** enemies,
> you put **our** adversaries to shame." (vv. 4-7)

In the psalter, the righteous and their king are inseparable. Who is this king bearing as one of his epithets "Son of God"? In one sense David and all his sons are "sons of God." For example, of David it is said: "He will call out to me, 'You are my Father' . . . I will also appoint him my firstborn" (Ps. 89:26f.), and of Solomon God said: "He will be my son, and I will be his father" (1 Chron. 22:10; cf. 28:6). Many psalms have in view all the descendants of David, a lineage that God guaranteed forever: "I will establish his line forever" (Ps. 89:29).

They find their fulfillment, however, in a Son greater than David. The inspired poets robed the king in majestic purple; they often represented him as an ideal. For example:

> Endow the king with your justice, O God,
> the royal son with your righteousness.
> He will judge your people in righteousness . . .
>
> He will defend the afflicted among the people
> and save the children of the needy;
> he will crush the oppressor.
> He will endure as long as the sun,

as long as the moon, through all generations.
He will be like rain falling on mown fields,
like showers watering the earth.
In his days the righteous will flourish;
prosperity will abound till the moon is no more.
He will rule from sea to sea
and from the river to the ends of the earth. (72:1-8)

None of David's line during the Old Testament period had shoulders broad enough to wear this magnificent purple garment and many other royal psalms that fill the wardrobe of the psalter. Solomon's shoulders became stooped in his old age and the gorgeous robes of these psalms slipped off him. At each coronation Israel draped the successor to David's throne with these kingly robes, but for generation after generation the robes did not fit. Finally, some four centuries after David, the king was dethroned by the wicked, and Israel was left with the wardrobe of magnificent royal psalms, waiting for a king worthy to wear them.

That hoped-for king is Jesus Christ, by which we mean, Jesus the anointed king. Here was the Son of God not only in the sense that he was the son of David but also as one begotten by the Holy Spirit through the virgin (Luke 1:35). In him there is no sin (Heb. 4:15) and he brings justice wherever he goes (Matt. 12:9-21). He is bringing everything, even sin and death, under his rule (cf. Ps. 8:5-8 and Heb. 2:5-9). He exalted the throne of David to heaven itself (Acts 2:24-36), and from this heavenly throne he not only reigns forever but he extends his worldwide dominion to the elect (Matt. 28:18-20; John 17:2), just as we are experiencing it.

The Lord Jesus understood himself as the subject of these psalms. For instance, facing death, he lamented: "my soul is troubled" (John 12:27 from Ps. 6:4[3]) and on the cross he cried "Why have you forsaken me?" (Matt. 27:46 from Ps. 22:1) and "into your hands I commit my spirit" (Luke 23:46 from Ps. 31:6[5]).

There are many such citations and illustrations in the New Testament relating Jesus to the "I" of the psalms. Some psalms speak only of him. Of the Pharisees Jesus asked: "Whose son is the Christ?" And when they replied the "son of David," he asked "How is it then that David . . . calls him *Lord?* For he says, 'The Lord said to my Lord: *Sit at my right hand until I put your enemies under your feet.*' If then David calls him Lord, how can he be his son?" (Matt. 22:43-45 from Ps. 110:1).

Today the king's righteous, covenantal community is the church, the heirs of ancient Israel's covenants and promises (Eph. 2:19-22). The king says that we are his brothers (Heb. 2:10-12 and Ps. 22:22).

Their Mission

Let us return to Psalm 2 and note that the righteous king, and implicitly his faithful nation, must establish his kingdom in the midst of the rebellious wicked.

Psalm 2, interpreted by the apostles and the church as referring to Jesus Christ (Acts 4:25-26; 13:33; Heb. 1:5), consists of four stanzas with three lines in each one. In verses 1-3 we hear the voice of the rebels refusing to come under God's rule represented by his anointed king: "Let us break their chains," they rage, "and throw off their fetters." Herod the Edomite tried to kill him at his birth (Matt. 2:16); his own nation attempted it at his first sermon (Luke 4:28f.); and finally, both the Jews and Romans achieved their resolve when they crucified the king on the cross (Matt. 27:37). The true kingdom of righteousness has always had to make its way through opposition. James Russell Lowell put it this way:

> Careless seems the Great Avenger;
> History's pages but record one death grapple
> in the darkness twixt old systems and the Word;
> Truth forever on the scaffold; Wrong forever on the throne;
> Yet that scaffold holds the future, and behind the dim unknown,
> Standeth God within the shadow, keeping watch above his own.

The inspired poet now lifts his audience above the sun into the heavenly throne room where God rules (vv. 4-6). There, to our astonishment, God is laughing at the rebels, who before him are as puny as Lilliputians before Gulliver. His laughter erupts from the victory of the righteous over the wicked, a triumph so lopsided that it is almost comical (see Ps. 37:13; 52:6; 59:8). God reversed the fortunes of the righteous and wicked by installing his righteous king on Mount Zion (v. 6), that is, as the New Testament explains, on his throne in the heavenly Mount Zion (Acts 2:36; Heb. 12:22). His resurrection and ascension in the past are the guarantee of the church's ultimate victory.

The king now speaks, proclaiming by what right he inherits the earth and the manner in which he will subdue it (vv. 7-9). He is a Son, he proclaims (v. 7), and as such has an inheritance — the ends of the earth. But he must ask for it:

> "Ask of me," says the Father to his Son, "and I will make the nations your inheritance, the ends of the earth your possession." (v. 8)

The Father now commissions him to subdue the wicked (v. 9). At his ascension Christ poured out upon his church the same Spirit that God had bestowed on him, and the Holy Spirit has transformed malice into love, superstition into faith, war into peace, alienation into wholeness, self-serving into self-sacrificing.

Finally, our poet, full of the Spirit, calls upon the nations to worship this God, to kiss the Son — that is, to own him as king and to replace their hostility against him with faith and thereby find God's salvation and not his wrath (vv. 10-12).

With the command to ask for the nations ringing in our ears, we leave the introduction to the psalter, and in the remainder of the psalter we find the king and his people in prayer in battle and in praise in victory. The psalter is the hymnbook of righteous missionaries!

Their Prayers

Carrying the mandate to pray that God's kingdom would come on earth as it is in heaven, the righteous king and his loyal followers fall on their knees with their petitions to God. The kingdom does not come to earth on a balmy breeze but through stormy seas threatening to capsize the righteous' ship of faith. Fifty times in the psalter they bring their petitions to the temple, the portal to the heavenly throne, and through their prayers inspired by the same Spirit that prays for us we learn how to pray (cf. Rom. 8:26-27).

These petitions consist of five elements: address, lament, confidence, petition, and praise. Let us consider Psalm 3 as a pattern for these petitions. *Lamenting* that he is surrounded by the surging foe (3:1-2), the king *addresses* God (3:1). His head is buoyed high over them by his *confidence* that God with one man is greater than the myriad of puny men against him (3:3-4). Indeed, so great is his faith that in the face of insurmountable odds he even lay down and fell asleep unafraid of the myriads drawn up against him on every side (3:5-6). Against the powers of darkness he *petitions* God: "Deliver me, O my God! Strike all my enemies on the jaw; break the teeth of the wicked" (3:7

author's translation). Finally, addressing the congregation he announces with *praise:* "From the LORD comes deliverance." This fivefold pattern gives us entrance into the heart of the righteous.

Their Lament

The righteous lament that the forces of darkness surround them on every side. Satan controls the kingdoms of this world — its governments bent on war, its educational institutions that blaspheme God, its corporations that ignore God. Their own bodies are corrupt and dying and they have ingrained, vile habits they cannot kick. Worse yet, their witness falls on deaf ears and the despairing say, "There is no deliverance."

Their Address

But as sure as the salmon returns to its spawning grounds at the time of death and birds fly south with the coming of winter, the righteous look to God for salvation. To turn anywhere else for deliverance would be sin. In Psalm 4 the king's false friends lose confidence in him because his prayers seem impotent during a devastating drought. As the crops wither in the fields and the grapes on the vines shrivel, he complains to his reckless, despairing advisers: "How long will you love delusions and seek false fertility deities?" He then assures them: "Know that the LORD has set apart the godly for himself; the LORD will hear when I call to him."

It is not that they despise means. Psalm 3, we are told, was composed during Absalom's revolt. As David is out in the wilderness depending upon God, he has also sent his friend Hushai to frustrate the counsel of Ahithophel, Absalom's brilliant but wicked intelligence man (2 Sam. 15:13-37). The saint does not despise human means; rather, he does not depend on them.

Their Confidence

What gives the righteous confidence in spiritual crises in which he can never cope on his own? First of all, he knows his own identity; "You are the one who bestowed glory on me, the one who lifts up my head" (Ps. 3:3 Beck's translation).

What affirmed David in this conviction? Two things: the prophetic word and the Spirit. The prophet Samuel proclaimed him king and the Spirit of God fell on him (1 Sam. 16:13). So also, John the Baptist affirmed Jesus as the Son of God, and the Spirit descended upon his anointed shoulders (Matt. 3:16). In the same way, the prophetic Scriptures energized by the same Holy Spirit convince us that, as John put it: "Yet to all who received Jesus, to those who believed in his name, he gave the right to become children of God" (John 1:12).

His confidence also rests on his sure knowledge of God's character. In Psalm 3, confronted by the myriad of deadly foes, he is confident that God hears and answers prayer from his holy hill even though the psalmist is removed from it by miles. In Psalm 4 in the midst of the drought, he assures the timid that God is righteous, that is, that the God who called him to be his servant will do what is right by him. The Lord does not call upon us to risk our lives to bring his will on earth as in heaven and then abandon us. Rather, says the king in Psalm 23: "He leads us in paths where he does what is right." Turning to God he adds: "Yea, though I walk through the valley of the shadow of death, I will fear no evil, for you are with me. Your rod and your staff, they comfort me" (Ps. 23:3-4). When Jesus commissioned his disciples to bring in the kingdom by making disciples of all nations, he promised: "And surely I will be with you always, to the very end of the age" (Matt. 28:17-20); could he do wrong by abandoning us? God forbid!

In Psalm 139, once again surrounded by bloodthirsty men seeking to overwhelm the light of God with Satan's darkness (139:19), the king found confidence in God's omniscience and omnipresence:

> O LORD, you have searched me and you know me.
> You know when I sit and when I rise;
> you perceive my thoughts from afar.
> You discern my going out and my lying down;
> you are familiar with all my ways. . . .
>
> Where can I go from your Spirit?
> Where can I flee from your presence?
> If I go up to the heavens, you are there;
> if I make my bed in the depths, you are there. . . ." (Ps. 139-1-12)

These invisible qualities of divinity are clearly seen in the creation of man:

For you created my inmost being;
you knit me together in my mother's womb.
I praise you because I am fearfully and wonderfully made;
your works are wonderful, I know that full well.
My frame was not hidden from you when I was made in the secret
    place. . . ." (Ps. 139:13-18)

Their Petition

Returning to Psalm 3, we find the beleaguered king, now full of faith, peti-tioning God to deliver him by striking all his enemies on the jaw and "break-ing the teeth of the wicked" (Ps. 3:7). Likewise today we pray that he will conquer the principle of death at work in our bodies by hearing us and by raising us from the dead. As we wrestle not against flesh and blood, but against rulers, against authorities, against the powers of this dark world, and against the spiritual forces of evil in the heavenly realms (Eph. 6:12-13), we pray that God will destroy the venality and corruption of government, the abuse of labor by management, and employees' bent to take advantage of those who hire them.

Their Praise

Finally, the king proclaims in praise: "From the LORD comes deliverance." *Deliverance,* the key word of this psalm (3:2, 7-8), is the Hebrew word *yasha',* from which is derived the name Jesus. It signifies that release from a crush-ing situation is one's right. The sons of light have a right not to be over-whelmed by darkness and death, for they serve the God of light and life. Death is not God; therefore it cannot have the last word.

The God of creation — the God of Abraham, Isaac, and Jacob, the God who raised Jesus from the dead — he is God, and he will have the last word. Victory belongs not to the wicked but to the righteous.

Reflections on Retirement from the Life of Isaac

Recently the Board of Governors of Regent College graciously appointed me Professor Emeritus. Although an honorific appointment, the Latin word *emeritus* means "worn out, unfit for service." When I pointed this out to a faculty wife, she commented: "You wear your laurel well!" So much for a sympathetic listener!

The appointment as Professor Emeritus signals for me a beginning of the spiritual test facing an increasing number of older Christians: How should a Christian think of retirement? The alumni media that come regularly across my desk constantly remind me of peers who have retired. What does retirement, often mandatory, mean to them? What should it mean to me?

Investment commercials on television picture retirement as a time of self-indulgent ease. Some of my peers think: "I have had my nose to the grindstone all my life; I have earned the right to enjoy the sweet fruits of my hard labors." Are they right? Wealthier folk — this is not my temptation — look forward to the prospect of wiling away their hours playing golf, pursuing their hobbies, cruising to exotic ports-of-call, and taking breaks from such strenuous activities by sitting on their back porches in rocking chairs drinking mint juleps.

Christians agree that it is wrong to think of the time before retirement as grinding years of labor with little or no time for play. Is it also wrong to think of retirement as play with little or no time for work? Having failed in

Previously published in *Crux* 32, no. 4 (December 1996). Professor Waltke delivered this talk in a Regent College chapel on 5 November 1996.

my working years to take more time for play, is it wrong to envision retirement as a time to indulge myself a little?

The other evening my wife Elaine and I attended with Gordon and Maudine Fee a marvelous rendition by the Vancouver Symphony Orchestra of four Haydn symphonies. The program notes mentioned that Haydn wrote these in his retirement. I was about to latch on to him as my model until I learned, as I continued to read, that he wrote them because he was competing against a former student!

Introduction to Isaac

If Haydn represents a tarnished model for retirement, Isaac, the subject of this message, exemplifies a negative one. This second-generation patriarch went, as we shall see, "from hero to zero" in his old age — in his retirement, if you will allow the anachronism.

Even though a person's life is normally complex and contains ambiguities, biographers seek to find their subject's defining characteristic. One thinks of Scrooge as stingy, of Sherlock Holmes as perceptive, of Abraham as a man of faith. What is the defining characteristic of Isaac? Before preparing this message I thought of him as "bland," "passive," "submissive." That appraisal, I now realize, is too sanguine. The evaluation of Alexander Whyte, the most famous biographer of biblical characters, is closer to the mark, even if expressed too harshly:

> The patriarch Isaac presents but a pale appearance as he stands planted between two so stately and so impressive personages as his father Abraham on the one hand, and his son Jacob on the other hand. . . . And indeed, as we follow out the sad declension of Isaac's character to the end, it is forced upon us that it would have been well for Isaac, and for all connected with Isaac, that Abraham's uplifted hand had not been arrested by the angel of the Lord.[1]

Although none of the patriarchs are what narrative critics call "flat figures"[2] (i.e., static and stereotypical), but "round figures" (i.e., complex and

---

1. Alexander Whyte, *Bible Characters: Adam to Achan* (Edinburgh and London: Oliphant, 1900), p. 151.

2. Adele Berlin, *Poetics and Interpretation of Biblical Narrative* (Winona Lake, IN: Eisenbrauns, 1985), p. 23.

developing), they are steadily moving toward a defining moment when their dominant characteristics come to full flower. Bar-Efrat comments: "We meet the biblical characters primarily in special and unusual circumstances, in times of crisis and stress, when they have to undergo severe tests."[3] And, we may add, when their true character emerges.

The drama of Abraham, the icon of *faith*, peaks when against all natural instincts he raises his hand to sacrifice Isaac, his unique son, trusting God somehow to provide. Jacob, the icon of *ambition*, reaches his defining moment when he wrestles with the God-man and prevails. Quintilius somewhere said: "Ambition is a vice but it can become the mother of virtue." This is true of Jacob. His ambition, theretofore a vice, became the mother of virtue when the God-man broke Jacob's hip, and the broken wrestler continued to struggle by clinging to God now in prayer, crying out: "Bless me!" whereupon God changed his name from Jacob, "overachiever," to Israel, "prevailer with God and humanity" (Gen. 32:28). In a similar way Judah, at first a cynical half-brother and calloused son willing to sell Joseph into slavery, and without compassion toward his father (37:26-35), is transformed into a caring man willing to sell himself into slavery for Benjamin, Joseph's full brother, because otherwise he could not bear to face his father (44:30-33). However, whereas these patriarchs developed into men of mature virtues, Isaac steadily declined in old age to his spiritual nadir. This comes out clearly in our text, Genesis 26:34–27:46, which deals with the episode of "Isaac blesses his twin boys." The distinguished patriarch's awful failure in old age sobers all the elect facing old age and retirement.

The narrator of Genesis implies Isaac's failure by "gapping" (i.e., deleting expected material) his narrative. The rendering "this is the account of . . . Isaac" (25:19 NIV) misleads the reader. "Account" renders *toledoth*, the crucial Hebrew term used for giving structure to Genesis. More accurately, *toledoth*, from the root *yalad*, "to bear," means "descendants," "generations."[4] The superscription "the *toledoth* of Terah" (11:27) introduces the cycle of stories about Abraham, not Terah (11:27-25:11). The next superscription, "the account [*toledoth*] of . . . Ishmael" (25:12), introduces his descendants (25:13-18). Likewise "the *toledoth* of Isaac" introduces the cycle of stories about Jacob, not Isaac. Remarkably, the narrator offers no cycle titled "this is the *toledoth* of Abraham," the most famous patriarch of all! There is a *toledoth*

---

3. Shimon Bar-Efrat, "Narrative Art in the Bible," in JSOTSup 70; Bible and Literature Series 17 (Sheffield, UK: Almond Press, 1989), p. 123.

4. So King James Version and New Revised Standard Version.

for all the patriarchs (see 11:27; 25:19; 37:2), and even for Abraham's nonelect descendants, Ishmael (25:12-18) and Esau (36:1), but strikingly there is none for Abraham. In other words, there is no distinct narrative for Isaac.

Narrative critics distinguish between "blanks," insignificant and nonmeaningful omissions, and "gaps," significant and meaningful deletions, what Meir Sternberg designates as "irrelevancies" and "relevancies" respectively.[5] The distinction between "gaps" and "blanks" is sometimes subjective and questionable from the audience's viewpoint, but less so here. Our suspicion that the omission of Isaac's narrative is intentional and significant is confirmed by the narrator's silence about him after this tragic episode. After the resolution of this climactic episode, wherein Isaac and Rebekah pack Jacob off to his uncle Laban to save him from Esau's wrath, the unhappy couple are not heard of again apart from the mention of Isaac's death and burial at the end of the Jacob narrative (35:27-29). Rebekah's life is not even brought to that closure. Her last words to the departing Jacob are: "I'll send word for you to come back from there . . ." (27:45). She never does. Instead of mentioning the death and burial of the matriarch, the narrator memorializes Deborah, her nurse from childhood and closest surrogate (35:8)! The silence is deafening. Isaac is given no memorial narrative in Holy Scripture. He is saved by only the skin of his teeth (Job 19:20; 1 Cor. 3:15).

However, although Isaac's story is "gapped," some of the elements of his rise and fall can be pieced together from the impressive narratives about his father Abraham (Gen. 11:27–25:11) and his son Jacob (25:19–35:27). In the former we find pieces of information from his birth to his marriage at forty years of age, and in the latter, from his marriage to his death at 180 years of age. Putting all these pieces together we can document the trajectory of Isaac's life more or less as follows: He ascends spiritually until his twin sons, who are born when he is sixty years old, become grown up; from then on, at about seventy-five, he descends until he hits bottom in the defining episode of our text. The chronology of Genesis places this episode when he is well beyond 100 years of age. In sum, the narrator presents pieces from which we can fit together a verbal portrait of a younger and triumphant Isaac, and an episode that defines an older and tragic Isaac.

Since faculty are asked in chapel talks to personalize their chapel messages, I ask you in advance to forgive me for personally empathizing with the first portrait and feeling antipathy toward the second.

---

5. Meir Sternberg, *The Poetics of Biblical Narrative: Ideological Literature and the Drama of Reading* (Bloomington: Indiana University Press, 1985), p. 236.

Triumphant Isaac

Five "pieces" in the triumphant Isaac's puzzle merit comment.

His miraculous birth. The Abraham narrative (11:27–25:11) features the miraculous birth of Isaac. The narrator sounds the theme of this narrative in its "exposition": "Now Sarai was barren; she had no children" (11:29-30). Bar-Efrat defines "exposition" as

> an introduction to the action described in the narrative, supplying the background information, introducing the characters, . . . and providing the other details needed for understanding the story.[6]

The tautology "barren" and "had no children" underscores Sarah's infertility. Only a miracle could change her situation. The plot of Abraham's narrative focuses on the maturing of Abraham's and Sarah's faith through their desire to have the baby God promised them. Only after Abraham's body became dried up like a sapless tree and Sarah's womb wilted like a faded flower did God quicken them with Isaac's life. Isaac's miraculous birth, however, was no guarantee that his life would not miscarry.

My own birth was something of a miracle. A year before I was conceived, my father fell from the roof of a five-story building and was given up for dead. An insurance agent broke the news to my mother by assuring her that she was insured for life along with her two children until the age of sixteen. My mother was a woman of great faith and believed my dad would live. And so he did, and I was given the miracle of life. Indeed, every life is a miracle, but the happy birthdays of youth may become wretched birthdays in old age.

His superb education. The miracle baby received the finest available theological education. The LORD chose Abraham for this very reason. In his self-talk the LORD says:

> Shall I hide from Abraham what I am about to do? Abraham will surely become a great and powerful nation, and all nations on earth will be blessed through him. For I have chosen him, so that he will direct his children and his household after him to keep the way of the LORD by doing what is right and just, so that the LORD will bring about for Abraham what he has promised him. (18:17-19)

6. Bar-Efrat, "Narrative Art in the Bible," p. 123.

Abraham both talked and modeled the faith, and Isaac was a good son, both of which are demonstrated in the episode titled by the rabbis the "Binding of Isaac" (chap. 22). A son who was strong enough to carry on his back a load of wood sufficient for a sacrifice was certainly able to resist an aged father had he been so minded. Instead Isaac freely consented to Abraham's will. Deane comments: "We scarcely know which to admire — the brave spirit of the patriarch or the meek resignation of the youth. The son exceeds in 'humble endurance.'"[7] In this episode the narrator depicts Isaac as having the habit of obedience, a trust in his father's love and care, and trust in God's provision. Although the narrator "blanks" Isaac's feelings in this episode, Josephus, as summarized by Whyte, reports a remarkable, though obviously apocryphal, dialogue that passed between Abraham and Isaac that day:

> Now, Isaac was of such a generous disposition that he at once answered that he was not worthy to be born at first, if he should now reject the determination of God and his father, and should not resign himself up readily to both their pleasures. So he went up immediately to the altar to be sacrificed.[8]

With regard to a fine theological education, I can identify with Isaac. At Dallas Theological Seminary I earned my first doctorate in Greek and New Testament. The administration there at first hired me to teach both Greek and Hebrew, and then honed me to teach only Hebrew and Old Testament, offering me a scholarship toward my second doctorate at Harvard in the department of Ancient Near East Languages and Literatures. As one of my students punned at the second graduation: "You are now a 'pair-o-docs.'" By God's grace I assumed a childlike posture before the whole counsel of God, but I confess I am an unprofitable investment. Whatever relative success I have achieved heretofore by God's grace, however, is no guarantee that my life will end a relative success. If even Solomon, the wisest of men, died a fool, how much more will I stray if I stop listening to instruction (Prov. 19:27)?

An auspicious marriage. Third, Isaac and Rebekah entered into the proverbial marriage "made in heaven." On earth Abraham arranged for the marriage by sending his shrewdest servant back to his home in Northwest

---

7. George Rawlinson, *Men of the Bible: Isaac and Jacob, Their Lives and Times* (New York, Chicago, and Toronto: Fleming H. Revell, n.d., citing Deane's "Abraham," p. 145), p. 24.

8. Whyte, *Bible Characters*, p. 153.

Mesopotamia to get a wife for his son. Upon the chief servant's arrival at the well outside of Nahor, Abraham's hometown, he prayed to the LORD to prosper his journey:

> "O LORD, God of my master Abraham, give me success today, and show kindness to my master Abraham. See, I am standing beside this spring, and the daughters of the townspeople are coming out to draw water. May it be that when I say to a girl, 'Please let down your jar that I may have a drink,' and she says, 'Drink, and [here's the stinger] I'll water your [ten] camels too' — let her be the one you have chosen for your servant Isaac. By this I will know that you have shown kindness to my master."
>
> Before he had finished praying, Rebekah came out . . . [and fulfilled his prayer]. (24:12-21)

After rehearsing this providential scene to Rebekah's family, the faithful steward drew the conclusion: "I praised the LORD, the God of my master Abraham, who had led me on the right road to get the granddaughter of my master's brother for his son" (24:48).

The beneficent providence peaked when the lovers' eyes first met simultaneously at Beer Lahai Roi (= "The Well of the Living One Who Sees"): "Isaac went out to the field one evening to meditate, and as he looked up, he saw camels approaching. Rebekah also looked up and saw Isaac" (24:62-64). The tautologous "looked up and saw," as Wenham comments, "always indicates that what is about to be seen is of great significance,"[9] and its timing and setting indicate the smile of Providence.

Nevertheless, this marriage made in heaven became dysfunctional. In connection with their conflict in the "Isaac blesses the twin boys" episode, husband and wife were no longer communicating.

I too have been blessed with a good wife; nevertheless, I can identify a little with the failed Isaac.

A godly man. Fourth, he was a godly man until his old age. We already noted in the "Binding of Isaac" episode his habits of trust and obedience to both God and his father. In the exposition to the "birth of the twin boys" episode (25:21-26), the narrator, who speaks for heaven, reveals his evaluative point of view in his comment: "Isaac prayed to the LORD on behalf of his wife, because she was barren. The LORD answered his prayer, and his wife

---

9. Gordon Wenham, *Genesis 16–50*, Word Biblical Commentary 2 (Dallas: Word, 1994), p. 151.

Rebekah became pregnant" (25:21). Indeed he persevered in this prayer for twenty years (cf. 25:20 and 25:26). The young husband with his father's faith patiently trusted the LORD to fill his barren wife with his holy seed.

Isaac's faith and prayer for his barren wife stand in marked contrast to that of his son Jacob. This is what narrative critics call a "foil."[10] Like Abraham and Isaac, Jacob was also confronted with the barrenness of his wife: "Rachel said to Jacob, 'Give me children, or I'll die!'" (30:1). The insensitive and prayerless husband "became angry with her and said, 'Am I in the place of God, who has kept you from having children?'" (30:2). The man who later prevailed through prayer (32:26-28; Hos. 12:4), early in his marriage did not even think of it! How much worse, however, to begin life's narrative with prayer and to end prayerless, as in the case of Isaac!

Here too I can identify with Isaac. I can look back upon marvelous answers to prayer as God has led me to various blessed ministries, but I also confess my propensity not to pray.

Blessed by God. Finally, until his relative old age the blessing of God shone cloudless upon him. The episode "God protects Rebekah in the Philistine's harem" (26:1-11) occurred between her marriage to Isaac and the birth of the twins. As is often the case in biblical narrative, narrative time does not coincide with chronological time. We can infer that this episode occurred before the "birth of the twin boys" episode (25:21-26) from the fact that Abimelech did not know Isaac and Rebekah were married. Had she been pregnant with the twins, or nursing them, or having them tugging at her skirt, Abimelech would have known she was married. Narrative critics call such flashbacks "analepsis," "the telling of events after the moment in which, chronologically, they took place."[11] The narrator does this in order to link together, on the one hand, the two episodes, the "birth of the twins" (25:21-26), and "Esau sells his birthright to Jacob" (25:27-34), and, on the other hand, the episodes "God protects Rebekah in the Philistine's harem" (26:1-11) and "Isaac triumphs over the Philistines at Beersheba" (26:12-33).

These last two episodes repeat the episodes that can be summarized as "God protects Sarah in the Philistine king's harem" (20:1-17) and "Abraham triumphs over the Philistines at Beersheba" (21:22-34). These incidents are so similar that source critics for over a century have held them up as parade ex-

---

10. Jean-Louis Ska, SJ, *"Our Fathers Have Told Us": Introduction to the Analysis of Hebrew Narratives,* Subsidia Biblica 13 (Rome: Edifice Pontificio Istituto Biblico, 1990), pp. 86, 87.

11. Ska, *"Our Fathers Have Told Us,"* p. 8.

amples of a crude redactor's piecing together of contradictory doublets of the same events. During the last quarter of this century, however, narrative critics have made the case that the biblical authors were careful artists. Through their lens these "doublets" represent Isaac and Rebekah, the second generation, as inheriting the same blessings as the first. The narrator himself carefully distinguishes the episodes "God protects Sarah" and "God protects Rebekah" by noting in the exposition of the second, "there was a famine in the land, besides the first famine that was in the days of Abraham" (26:1). He also notes that Isaac re-dug his father's wells (26:15-22). These echoes show that God kept his promise to bless Abraham's offspring along with him (22:15-19; 26:23-25).

As God's good hand was upon Isaac, so also it has been upon me. When I embarked on my theological education I had no idea that the LORD would bless me in teaching the Old Testament. In fact, I majored in Old Testament in my Masters of Theology program because I did not understand it. As I now look back over my life I can only draw the conclusion that God's good hand has been upon me in teaching the Old Testament. Sometimes I think of myself as Balaam's donkey; the LORD filled my mouth with his Word. Once when I spoke at First Baptist Church, Vancouver, I told the church secretary beforehand I would be speaking on Balaam's donkey. When I arrived that evening, I found written in large capitals on the church's prominent bulletin board: "The Talking Donkey: Dr. Waltke"! The early rains, however, are no guarantee of latter rains.

Tragic Isaac

If the pieces of the artful narrator's first portrait of Isaac are bright and happy, the "Isaac blesses the twin boys" episode is dark and tragic. The inspired narrator poignantly "foreshadows"[12] Isaac's climactic defeat in the exposition introducing the episode "Esau sells his birthright": "Isaac, who had a taste for wild game, loved Esau" (25:28 NIV). A more literal rendition of the Hebrew is "Isaac loved Esau because of the game in his mouth!" His desire to indulge his appetite is the fly that will spoil the ointment, the little fox that will spoil the vine.

I and all Christians facing retirement need to take heed. Rawlinson comments:

12. Cf. Sternberg, *The Poetics of Biblical Narrative*, p. 279.

The father ... "loves him because he did eat of his venison, giving evidence thereby of" a spirit, which lapped in a life of ease, had become in a certain measure tainted with sensuality, not of a gross kind, indeed, but still such to seriously weaken his character and to place him on a lower level of spiritual development than either his father Abraham or his son Jacob.[13]

Isaac's indulgent sensuality became overripe, rotten summer fruit in the episode "Isaac blesses the twin boys" (26:33–27:46). This episode has three parts: the exposition (26:33-34; 27:1a), the conflict (27:1b-41), and its resolution (27:41-46). The conflict has four scenes: Isaac and Esau (27:1b-4), Rebekah and Jacob (27:5-17), Isaac and Jacob (27:18-29), and Isaac and Esau (27:30-40).

Unfortunately the chapter division is misleading. The change of protagonists and of scenes shows that 26:34-35 belongs with 27:1-46, not with 26:1-33. The protagonists and scenes shift from the triumphant Rebekah (26:1-11) and Isaac (26:12-33) versus defeated Abimelech in his harem and fields to the heartbroken Rebekah and Isaac versus profane Esau within their family's tent (26:34-35). Moreover, the narrator encloses this tragic episode that brings the curtain down on Isaac's and Rebekah's lives within a framing inclusio by mentioning at the beginning and the end of the episode the Hittite women that repulsed them (26:34-35; 27:46), showing that 26:34-35 is part of the exposition to the episode that draws to conclusion in 27:46.

Five features merit attention in this dark portrait: one from the exposition and one from each of the four scenes.

His rebellion: rejection of God's word and his Spirit. It is instructive to connect the exposition to the "birth of the twins" episode with that of "Isaac blesses the twin boys." By coupling them it becomes clear that in his failed attempt to bless Esau, Isaac violated both God's word and the inner witness of his spirit. Instead of being led by the Word and the Spirit, he was led by the flesh, if one applies Pauline categories of thought to this ancient episode.

In the exposition to the "birth of the twin boys" the LORD revealed to Rebekah, and presumably through her to Isaac, that Jacob would rule over Esau, clearly inferring that the blessing that conferred dominion should be given to Jacob, not Esau:

The LORD said to her, "Two nations are in your womb, and two peoples from within you will be separated; one people will be stronger than the other, and the older will serve the younger." (25:23)

13. Rawlinson, *Men of the Bible*, p. 42.

Isaac, however, tried to thwart the divine purpose. In dramatic irony he countered God's word with his benedictory blessing intended for Esau: "May nations serve you and people bow down to you. Be lord over your brothers, and may the sons of your mother bow down to you" (27:29).

In his scheme to bless Esau, Isaac also transgressed his own heart. The exposition to our text provides the reader with the background information essential to interpret the narrator's intention:

> When Esau was forty years old, he married Judith daughter of Beeri the Hittite, and also Basemath daughter of Elon the Hittite. They were a source of grief to Isaac and Rebekah. (26:34-35)

"Source of grief" in NIV represents Hebrew *mar ruah,* "bitterness of spirit." Esau's wives galled them, destroying and crushing their spirits. Nevertheless, in spite of his heartache Isaac is determined to bless Esau and his offspring by these loathsome wives that negated the identity and *raison d'être* of the holy family. In short, in his old age the once righteous Isaac muddied the waters by rejecting the witnesses of God's word and Spirit (cf. Prov. 25:26).

It makes no difference whether I am facing the beginning of my narrative or its drawing to a close. I must compromise neither God's word nor my heart. My use of my retirement years must conform to Scripture, not to the world, and be lived in vital, active faith.

We now turn to the conflict and its first scene, Isaac and Esau.

His motive: self-indulgence. Understanding the significance of the patriarch's blessing gives a yardstick by which to measure the full extent of Isaac's sinful ambition to bless Esau (cf. 27:4). Roop comments: "The elder son [who traditionally received the blessing by primogeniture] became the head of the family, the one who carries the family tradition: defining the family's understanding of itself, speaking for the family, and carrying out the family's direction."[14] Is Esau worthy of this leadership?

Isaac's physical blindness symbolizes his spiritual blindness. He should have "seen" from the episode "Esau sells his birthright" why God rejected Esau from having dominion over Jacob. Esau's choice of a bowl of soup over the birthright displayed a character intent on its immediate gratification of drives and appetites without regard to the future and an unwillingness to deny itself a moment of pleasure to receive a much greater reward in the fu-

---

14. Eugene F. Roop, *Genesis,* Believers Church Bible Commentary (Scottdale, PA, and Kitchener, ON: Herald Press, 1987), p. 183.

ture. The soup's red color probably connoted passion, a color that stuck to him for life in his alias, Edom, "Red." His given name Esau means "Hairy," symbolizing his animal-ish nature. If Esau had a car, he would have displayed the godless bumper sticker, "Just do it." Whereas the godless give priority to today's gratification, not tomorrow's hope, godly people at any stage of life count their present sufferings for righteousness as "light and momentary troubles . . . achieving . . . an eternal glory that outweighs them all" (2 Cor. 4:17).

The narrator concludes this episode with the quick serial situations: "Esau ate and drank, and rose up and left" (Gen. 25:34). Bonchek says:

> When we have such uninterrupted serial actions, we realize that the acts were done without forethought. Esau's actions are automatic, unthinking, reflex-like. Such flagrant and callous disregard for the value of the birthright is certainly to "despise it." Again we see the nature of Esau's actions — they are reflexes, not reflective.[15]

Incredibly, Isaac wants to bless his brutish, unreflective son with dominion over his cultured, reflective twin brother. Why?

According to the prophetic narrator, Isaac loved Esau because the skillful hunter indulged his appetites, not because Esau was his firstborn. His taste for game jaded his spiritual "taste." Narrators often communicate meaning through repetition and especially by a *Leitwort*, a term coined by Martin Buber[16] for "a leading word" that is repeated to reveal or clarify emphatically a text's meaning. Three times in our text the narrator repeats the expression that Isaac loved tasty food. In the scene involving Isaac and Esau he himself confesses: "Prepare me the kind of tasty food I love and bring it to me to eat, so that I may give you my blessing before I die" (27:4). In the second scene Rebekah repeats the expression (27:9) and so does the narrator (27:14). Six times in this episode the "leading word" *mat'ammim* "tasty food" is used (see 27:4, 7, 9, 14, 17, 31), and eight times its synonym *ṣayid* "game" (27:3, 5, 7, 19, 25, 30, 31, 33). The narrator's evaluative point is unmistakable. Whyte comments:

15. Avigdor Bonchek, *Studying the Torah: A Guide to In-Depth Interpretation* (Northvale, NJ, and London: Jason Aronson Inc., 1996), p. 28.

16. Martin Buber, "*Leitwort* Style in Pentateuch Narrative," in *Scripture and Translation* by Martin Buber and Franz Rosenzweig, trans. Lawrence Rosenwald with Everett Fox (Bloomington and Indianapolis: Indiana University Press, 1994), pp. 114-28.

When I read Isaac's whole history over again, with my eye upon the object, it becomes as clear as a sunbeam to me that what envy was to Cain, and what wine was to Noah, and what lewdness was to Ham, and what wealth was to Lot, and what pride and impatience were to Sarah — all that, venison and savory meat were to Isaac. I cannot get past it. I have tried hard to get past it. Out of respect for the aged patriarch, and out of gratitude for the mount of the Lord. . . , I have tried to get past it; but I cannot.[17]

The "game in his mouth" has now become the dominating reality of Isaac's old age. Recall the way Robert Louis Stevenson represented the base human nature overcoming the more spiritual in his macabre novella, *Dr. Jekyll and Mr. Hyde*. At first the kindly Dr. Jekyll experimented with the potent brew he had concocted to unleash the diabolical Mr. Hyde within him. Each time he drank of it, however, he became more addicted to it until finally, without even drinking the diabolical stuff, he became the Mr. Hyde who terrorized London's streets. The good doctor's addiction took over, triumphed, and destroyed him. So also Isaac's lust to gratify his swollen appetite finally ruined him.

By seeing Isaac's whole life we see clearly the spiritual danger of regarding old age and retirement as a time of ease and self-indulgence. Though having flesh in the mouth is very tempting, I dare not rationalize the Lord's clear teaching that Christians are to deny themselves and take up their cross. My reward for years of hard labor is his to give in eternity, not a right I have to bestow upon myself now. Put in the terms of judging and rewarding myself, the notion that I have earned a life of ease in retirement seems absurd. In truth I judge my best efforts as worthless.

Facing the temptation of retirement I need to recall Jesus' parable about the tragic fool who also linked financial security with indulgent ease:

The ground of a certain rich man produced a good crop. He thought to himself, "What shall I do? I have no place to store my crops." Then he said, "This is what I'll do. I will tear down my barns and build bigger ones, and there I will store all my grain and my goods. And I'll say to myself, 'you have plenty of good things laid up for many years. Take life easy; eat, drink and be merry.'" But God said to him, "You fool! This very night your life will be demanded from you. Then who will get what

17. Whyte, *Bible Characters*, p. 158.

you have prepared for yourself?" This is how it will be with anyone who stores up things for himself but is not rich toward God. (Luke 12:16-21)

The problem with the world's idea of retirement is that it carries the liability of eternal death.

His manner: secretive. The second scene portrays Isaac's condemning heart as causing him to act covertly. If the first scene pictures Isaac putting his mouth before his heart, the second depicts him carrying out his nefarious scheme behind closed doors. The patriarch's passing on the divine blessing within the holy family should have been a joyous family celebration. Jacob blessed his offspring openly: "Gather round so that I can tell you what will happen to you in days to come. Assemble and listen, sons of Jacob; listen to your father Israel" (Gen. 49:1-2).

Likewise the dying Moses openly blessed the tribes of Israel (Deut. 33:1).

Isaac's sensual choice of Esau over Jacob, however, could not stand up to the blazing light of the family's scrutiny, and he knew it. To escape their censure, especially that of his more spiritual wife, he darkly chooses to do God's business privately: "Now Rebekah was listening as Isaac spoke to his son Esau" (Gen. 27:5). Obviously she was eavesdropping, for in the preceding scene Isaac had summoned only Esau for his audience. He intended his audience with Esau to be as private in the first scene as she intended hers to be with Jacob in the second.

I can often judge whether my actions are right or not by my willingness to lay them open to public scrutiny. If, for example, I handle my money well by generously sharing it with the truly needy, I speak well, truthfully, and openly. By contrast, if I use it selfishly, my speech is more distorted. In other words, I can discern the motive of my deceptive heart by the manner in which I effect its will. Am I an open book? Or perhaps better, is my checkbook an open book? When my conscience condemns me, I am neither an open book for all to read nor a bubbling brook from which all can drink.

His guidance: his fallible senses. The third scene, the encounter between Isaac and Jacob, reveals the sensual and secretive rebel dependent upon his fallible senses to lead him. Instead of being led by God's Word and Spirit, Isaac is misled by his fallible senses. He decided Jacob's identity by what he heard, felt, and smelled. He says to Jacob:

> "Come near so that I can touch you, my son, to know whether you really are my son Esau or not. . . . The voice is the voice of Jacob, the hands are the hands of Esau. . . . Come here, my son, and kiss me." So he went to

him and kissed him. When Isaac caught the smell of his clothes, he blessed him. (Gen. 27:21-27)

Kidner comments:

> All five senses play a conspicuous part, largely by their fallibility, in this classic attempt to handle spiritual responsibilities by the light of nature. Ironically, even the sense of taste on which Isaac prided himself gave him the wrong answer. . . . The real scandal is Isaac's frivolity: his palate had long since governed his heart (25:28) and silenced his tongue (for he was powerless to rebuke the sin that was Esau's downfall); he now proposed to make it his arbiter between peoples and nations (27:29). Unfitness for office shows in every act of this sightless man rejecting the evidence of his ears for that of his hands, following the promptings of his palate and seeking inspiration through — of all things — his nose (v. 27).[18]

As a result he becomes a joke. The scene is full of dramatic irony, which Bar-Efrat defines:

> The character [Isaac] knows less than the reader, or unknowingly does things which are not in his or her own best interest, or from the course of events leading to results which are the reverse of the character's aspirations. . . . The character speaks in all innocence, while the author, who is after all responsible for the way the character phrases the words, gives them an ironic flavour.[19]

All three elements of dramatic irony are present in this scene; Isaac thinks he is blessing Esau but in fact he is deliciously blessing Jacob, God's choice. Bar-Efrat explains the function of dramatic irony:

> Dramatic irony has a variety of functions, such as expressing criticism, stressing a shocking event or emphasizing a tragic situation. . . . Dramatic irony sometimes serves as a vehicle for the view that justice rules the world and that everyone receives just deserts, in contrast to the distorted view held by the character concerned.[20]

18. Derek Kidner, *Genesis,* Tyndale Old Testament Commentaries (Leicester, UK, and Downers Grove, IL: InterVarsity, 1967), p. 156.

19. Bar-Efrat, "Narrative Art in the Bible," p. 125.

20. Bar-Efrat, "Narrative Art in the Bible," p. 125.

In other words, Isaac and his vice are treated as a joke, but God and virtue have the last laugh.

If I listen to the television investment commercials and govern my retirement years by my senses, not by the Scriptures and the witness of God's Spirit, I will become a joke, serving decaying vice, not enduring virtue.

His faith. The fourth and last scene teaches the remarkable point that in spite of his vices, Isaac nevertheless exercised faith in God while pronouncing the blessing. He firmly believed he mediated God's irrevocable blessing. When Esau burst out with his loud and bitter cry, "Bless me — me too, my father!" Isaac answered: "Your brother came deceitfully and took your blessing. . . . I have made him lord over you and have made all his relatives his servants, and I have sustained him with grain and new wine." The writer of Hebrews in amazing grace recalls only Isaac's faith: "By faith Isaac blessed Jacob" (Heb. 11:20).

This strange mixture of vice and virtue characterizes most who minister, for "the heart is deceitful above all things and beyond cure" (Jer. 17:9). I confess that I have ministered out of wrong motives but experienced God's blessings through faith.

Conclusion

The narrator, as I have argued, aims to make his audience feel antipathy toward sensual Isaac in his old age. Isaac began well but finished poorly. His triumphant years were defined by submission, but his final, defining trait is sensuality. By sensuality I mean that in connection with rebelling against God's Word and his Spirit he is motivated by the desire to gratify his senses, not to serve his LORD; that his manner is secretive; and that he takes his guidance from his fallible senses. If I were to regard retirement as a time of self-indulgent ease and pleasure I am thinking sensually, not Christianly.

The narrator, however, also aims to point us beyond Isaac to the seed that would crush the Serpent (Gen. 3:15). As noted above, he structured his book in such a way as to trace that seed. He could track that seed only to Judah (Gen. 49:8-12). The rest of the Bible narrows that seed to the Lord Jesus Christ and his church (Gal. 3:16, 29; Rom. 16:20).

Our Lord, of course, died in the prime of life, but he never yielded to the temptation of retiring from the work the Father gave him to do. The Apostle John reveals Jesus' point of view by his last words at death: "When he had received the drink, Jesus said, 'It is finished.' With that he bowed his head and gave up his spirit" (John 19:30). As long as we live we have the task to deny ourselves and take up his cross (Matt. 16:24), and as long as it is day, Jesus said, "we must do the work of him who sent me. Night is coming, when no one can work" (John 9:4). The rabbis expressed a similar sentiment: "It is not thy duty to complete the work, but neither art thou free to desist from it."[21]

United with Christ, the Apostle Paul sets the pace for all Christians:

> Do you not know that in a race all the runners run, but one gets the prize? Run in such a way as to get the prize. Everyone who competes in the games goes into strict training. They do it to get a crown that will not last; but we do it to get a crown that will last forever. Therefore I do not run like a man running aimlessly; I do not fight like a man beating the air. No, I beat my body and make it my slave so that after I have preached to others I myself will not be disqualified for the prize. (1 Cor. 9:24-27)

At his death he too made a good confession:

> For I am already being poured out like a drink offering, and the time has come for my departure. I have fought the good fight, I have finished the race, I have kept the faith. Now there is in store for me the crown of righteousness, which the Lord, the righteous Judge, will award to me on that day — and not only to me, but also to all who have longed for his appearing. (2 Tim. 4:6-8)

Our Lord and Paul, not Isaac, exemplify for me the way to face old age: to continue the good work of being a disciple and not to retire.

21. M. Avot 2, 21, cited by Yehuda T. Radday, "Chiasm in Kings," *LB* 31 (May 1974): 62.

The Relationship of the Sexes in the Bible

Introduction

We are now in the process of taking a new look at sexual roles in Western culture. Women are standing up to be counted and are challenging both the Scriptures and/or the traditional interpretations of it, which they feel have suppressed feminine dignity. This fresh breeze, or should I say, wind, has had the heuristic value of blowing away the clouds of traditional male prejudice and enabling the exegetical theologian to see the Scriptures afresh in a new cultural context. In this contextualization we can better separate the pure ore of Scriptural teaching about the role of the sexes from the impurities of vain traditions that have become mixed with it.

Let us begin our study in Eden, before the Fall, to establish the ideal pattern for the relationship of the sexes. That paradigm stands at the beginning of the Bible as the ideal that the rest of Holy Scripture seeks to work out in practice. Confronted with the hard reality of Israel's stiff neck and its lack of the Holy Spirit's full ministries, Moses had to compromise the ideal, but our Lord, having poured out the full measure of the Spirit on his church, aims to restore it (cf. Matt. 19:3-12). In the Old Testament, Moses with the law, the prophets with their stories and oracles, the sages with their aphorisms, all seek to work out in the fallen world in practice as much as is possible the original ideal relationship; in the New Testament, our Lord with his apostles works to re-create Eden in the life of the church.

To better understand God's design for the sexes we shall first exegete

---

Previously published in *Crux* 19, no. 3 (1983). Used with permission.

the "Gift of the Bride to Adam" story and then relate its truths systematically to the rest of the Bible, in each case beginning with the Old Testament and concluding with the New. Our approach is committed to the literary and theological integrity of the canon. For too long older critics have reduced the sacred corpus to a hacked-up corpse; modern critics now tend to bring its bones together and allow the resurrected body to breathe once again its life upon our Western world, which, where it has been cut off from its spiritual source of life, is decaying.

In this essay we have time to develop only three points of doctrine from the arche-wife story. But before sifting the story for its precious theological ore, we need first to note that the story is both historical and suprahistorical. For our purposes here we do not need to defend viewing our text as history instead of fiction, a viewpoint that has gained fresh impetus from the recent book of Robert Alter, *The Art of Biblical Narrative* (New York: Basic Books, 1981). We need, however, to justify here the assumption that our story represents the ideal of every marriage. We can do this deftly, if not definitively, by noting that the judgment pronounced upon the First Pair falls upon Every Man and Every Woman. Who interprets the LORD's sentence against Adam, in which the created order is so reversed that the ground which man was given to till now works against him and finally swallows him up, as a sentence only against the historical Adam? Do we not intuitively recognize that God's sentence is against Every Man? And who interprets the LORD's sentence against the woman, in which the created order is so reversed that the woman who was created to bring children into the world now achieves her mission only through difficult labor, as a judgment only upon the first woman? Is she not the archetypal mother representing Every Woman? So also the LORD's gift of a bride to Adam represents his gift in every marriage. Our intuitive grasp of the story finds external confirmation in the way in which our Lord and his apostles use it in establishing the proper relationship between every Christian man and woman. James G. Williams in his book *Women Recounted: Narrative Thinking and the God of Israel* (Sheffield, UK: Almond Press, 1982) justly regards Eve as the arche-woman.

Marriage the Ideal Relationship

Our archetypal situation for the sexes presents marriage as God's ideal for both sexes. The Creator, who himself does not exist without friendship in his own triune Person and with his heavenly court, evaluates Adam's aloneness due to his uniqueness as "not good." He does not judge his singleness as *'ēn tôb* ("lacking in goodness") but as *lō' tôb* ("not good," i.e., "bad").

The Creator's robust affirmation of marriage in the creation stories finds reinforcement throughout the inspired canon. The sage is explicit:

> He who finds a wife finds what is good
> and receives favor from the LORD. (Prov. 18:22)

A godly couple can enter into the marriage relationship full of the faith and hope that God intends them to do so.

Moses' Torah affirms the sanctity of marriage indirectly by assuming the marriage of Israel's most holy persons. The High Priest, the quintessential representative of holiness, married. The Law, in fact, implicitly required him to marry and beget children by stipulating that he must marry only a virgin, in contrast to a widow or divorcee, to guarantee the purity of his descendants (Lev. 21:7-15). The Nazirites, the men or women who, unlike the High Priest, were denied the right of complete separation to the living God by birth, could spontaneously separate themselves to him by abstaining from the fruit of the vine, the symbol of earthly joy; by not going near a dead body, the symbol of that which is contrary to the living God; and by not allowing a razor to be used on their heads, their uncut hair serving as a symbol that they belonged to the Creator, even as the uncut fieldstones of Israel's altars, and its unpruned vines and orchards, symbolized the same identification (Num. 6:1-8; cf. Exod. 20:25; Lev. 25:5, 11). But both the High Priest and the Nazirites, the symbols of spontaneous and institutionalized holiness respectively, participate in marriage. In sum, a godly couple can enter into the marriage relationship confident that they are sharing a holy bed.

In the New Testament, marriage on the human level is elevated to symbolize the spiritual marriage between Christ and his church. In this higher spiritual relationship the Apostle teaches that if marriage is not necessary to serve as an anodyne to sexual passions, then so much the better, for in that single state they can more fully consecrate themselves in their marriage to Christ (1 Cor. 7).

Men and Women Are Equal in Their Being

Our archetypal text, in the second place, instructs us in at least four ways that men and women are equal in their being. First, the woman is said to be man's counterpart, *kᵉnegdô* (v. 18). The standard lexicographers, Brown, Driver, and Briggs, interpret "I will make a help corresponding to him" to mean that God would make for Adam one "equal and adequate to himself" in contrast to any of the animals of which the same thing could not be said (v. 20) (Brown, Driver, Briggs, p. 617). The meaning of equality finds expression in Tobiah's and Sarah's prayer on their wedding night:

> You made Adam and gave him his wife to be his helper and support; and from these two the human race descended. You said: "It is not good for the man to be alone; let us make him a partner like himself." (Tobit 8:6)

Second, her equality is suggested by her being formed from man's ribcage (v. 21). The old adage may have captured quaintly the true reason why God selected man's rib to build the woman:

> . . . Eve was not taken from Adam's head that she should rule over him, not from his feet, to be trampled under foot, but she was taken from his side that she might be his equal; from under his arm that she might be protected by him; near his heart, that he might cherish and love her. (Russell C. Prohl, *Women in the Church* [Grand Rapids: Eerdmans, 1957], p. 46)

Third, in man's only words prior to his Fall, he celebrates her full ontological equality with him. With rapture he composes the first poem:

> Now finally, she is here. Bone of my bones, flesh of my flesh; she shall be called *'iššāh* ("woman") because she was taken out of *'îsh* ("man").

Fourth, both surprisingly and instructively, our artful storyteller adds in his epilogue: "Therefore a man leaves his father and mother and clings to his wife." One would have expected, according to the badmouthing of biblical feminists, the opposite, namely, that a woman leaves her parents to cling to her husband.

Before tracing the doctrine of the sexual ontological equality in the rest of Scripture let us pause here to refute Phyllis Trible's (*God and the Rhetoric of Sexuality* [Philadelphia: Fortress Press, 1978], p. 77) attempt to demonstrate equality of the sexes in our archetypal text by interpreting *hā-ādām* in Genesis 2:4-22 as "earth-creature," i.e., a sexually undifferentiated creature until the creation of the woman. Unquestionably *'ādām* in the first Creation account has the generic sense "mankind," including both sexual modes, but this is not the meaning of *hā-ādām* in the second and complementary account found in Genesis 2:4–3:24. Here it denotes the male's personal name, Adam, for at least three reasons.

First, Adam clearly says in his poem "the woman was taken out of *'îš* ("man"), a word that unambiguously designates a male in contrast to a female. His words in verse 23, *mē'îš luqôhâ zō't* ("from man this one was taken") match verse 22, "And the LORD built the rib which he had taken from Adam *('ašer lāqah min-hā-ādām)* into woman, showing unmistakably that *hā-ādām* and *'îš* share the same semantic external reference. Second, as Trible herself concedes, *hā-ādām* must refer to the male, Adam, when, after the woman's creation, we are told: "And the LORD brought the woman to *hā-ādām*, whereupon *hā-ādām* composed his poem about her. But if *hā-ādām* means Adam in verses 22-23, then surely it is most arbitrary to invest the word with a different meaning in the preceding verses. Finally, her arbitrary interpretation runs head on against the inspired interpretation of our text that Adam was formed first, then Eve (1 Tim. 2:13).

Returning to our argument, we now aim to demonstrate the teaching of the equality of the sexes with reference to their essence in the rest of Scripture. Unfortunately this doctrine has been distorted in the secondary literature. Leonard Swidler in *Women in Judaism: The Status of Women in Formative Judaism* (Metuchen, NJ: Scarecrow Press, 1976) has shown conclusively that first-century Judaism shows evidence of strengthening its misogyny and stressing the inferiority of woman, running counter to its own heritage and the New Testament. For that reason Josephus is probably a valid spokesman for first-century Judaism when he said:

> The woman, says the Law, is in all things inferior *(cheirōn eis hapanta)* to man. (*C. Apionem* 11:201)

Ecclesiastics in the history of the church also ran counter to their biblical heritage. Aquinas in *Summae Theologica* brings out the feminist in every woman when he wrote:

> Woman was made to be a help to man. But she was not fitted to be a help to man except in generation, because another man would prove a more effective help in everything else. (cited by Sheila D. Collins, "Toward a Feminist Theology," *Christian Century*, August 2, 1972, p. 797)

On the other hand, Sheila Collins inferentially slurred and misrepresented the Old Testament when she wrote about Old Testament times:

... women were regarded as an inferior species to be owned like cattle, an unclean creature incapable of participating in the mysteries of the worship of Yahweh. For whatever historical reason ... ancient Hebrew society was blatantly misogynist and male-dominated. (p. 796)

In fact, however, the rest of the Old Testament underscores the doctrine of the sexes' equality clearly established in our foundational text. We note, in the first place, revelation came to women and proceeded from them as in the case of the matriarch Rebekah (Gen. 25:23); Manoah's wife (Judg. 13:3); the prophetesses Miriam (Exod. 15:20-21; Num. 12:2), Deborah (Judg. 4:4), and Huldah (2 Kings 22:14-20); and the anonymous prophetess (Isa. 8:3). Most amazing is God's revelation to Hagar. Nowhere else in Ancient Near Eastern literature is it recorded that deity called a woman by name, yet the angel of the LORD does just that twice in the case of Hagar (Gen. 16:8; 21:17). The conversation between the angel of the LORD and Hagar is as startling in its cultural milieu as the conversation of Jesus with the Samaritan woman in his day. In both instances God invests a woman with full dignity by solicitously caring for her and by giving her revelations, even though both of them come from outside the pure race and are sinners.

Second, women pray to the LORD for children and thereby influence the shape of sacred history, as in the case of the matriarchs Rebekah (Gen. 25:22), Rachel (Gen. 30:6, 22), and Leah (Gen. 30:17). Hannah's prayer is worthy of comment. Hannah prayed for a boy at the nadir of Israel's spiritual apostasy when the High Priest, contextualized by his era, misinterpreted a woman's fervency in prayer at the House of God as a sign of drunkenness, and when his sons, the heirs apparent to his sacred office, humbled the women who consecrated themselves to divine service at the House of God by treating them as Canaanite sacred prostitutes. Significantly, at the time she fulfilled her vow by dedicating the one "asked of the LORD," she thanked God for giving Israel a saving king, a generation before a king appeared on the stage of sacred history. Hannah by faith prayed:

> He will give strength to his king and exalt the horn of his salvation. (1 Sam. 2:10)

The LORD marvelously rewarded her faith by using her son, Samuel, to anoint Israel's first kings. This godly mother in Israel illustrates the old adage: "The hand that rocks the cradle rules the world."

Third, women in their own right offered sacrifices after purification from childbirth (Lev. 12:6) and bodily discharges (Lev. 15:29).

Fourth, women as well as men could become Nazirites (Num. 6:2). Perhaps this fact has been obscured by the point of Hebrew grammar that the masculine pronoun can also serve for women. Numbers 6:2 says plainly: "If a man or woman wants to make a special vow, a vow of separation to the LORD as a Nazirite," but the pronoun referring to both sexes in the rest of the regulation in question is masculine singular and inaccurately rendered into English by "he" rather than by "he or she."

Fifth, a woman who felt wronged by her husband could appeal to the LORD for justice. Sarah, whom Peter holds up before Christian wives as the example of beauty through submissiveness to her husband (1 Pet. 3:5-6), when wronged by Hagar and not protected by Abraham, said to him: "May the LORD judge between you and me." She issued no ultimatum, no threat of litigation; rather, in faith, she turned the matter over to God. Abraham responded by submissively acceding to Sarah's wish (Gen. 16:1-6).

Sixth, Clarence Vos, in his dissertation written for the Free University of Amsterdam in 1968, "Woman in Old Testament Worship," with a wealth of information on our subject, pointed out that the laws for the woman's ceremonial cleansing after bodily discharges are essentially the same as those for men (Lev. 15:32-33) (pp. 147-51).

Seventh, in contrast to the later Essene community, which, according to Josephus and Philo, would not tolerate women in their communities because they thought women were the source of all discord, and which has given us at Qumran a lengthy poem portraying evil in the guise of a wicked woman, the Book of Proverbs uses women to symbolize both wisdom and folly (Proverbs 9). Like Xenophon (*Oeconomicus* VII-X), perhaps centuries after him, and like Musconius, a first-century Stoic (see Luise Schottroff, "Frauen in der Nachfolge Jesu in neutestamentlicher Zeit," in *Traditionen der Befreiung,* vol. 2: *Frauen in der Bibel,* ed. Willy Schottroff and Wolfgang Stegemann [Munich: Christian Kaiser Verlag, 1980], pp. 91-133), the inspired sage wants women to take major responsibility for being superintendents of the manor and to be fully trained for it.

Finally, the mother stands on equal footing with the father before the children. Children are commanded to honor and fear both mother and father (Exod. 20:12; Lev. 19:3), the death penalty is exacted against the child that curses either one (Exod. 21:15, 17; Deut. 21:18-21), both parents are instructed in the Law (Deut. 31:12) and teach the children (Prov. 1:8; 31:26), and both name the children. According to Vos, in the forty-five cases in which the Old Testament records the naming of children, the woman names them twenty-six times, the man fourteen times, and God five times.

In the light of these facts one cannot help but wonder what law Josephus was reading. Paul's doctrine that men and women are spiritual equals (Gal. 3:26-28) is not unique to the new dispensation.

The Subordination of Women in Government

But men and women are not equal in government. Our archetypal narrative, what Karl Barth called the Magna Carta of our humanity (*Kirchliche Dogmatik* I/2, P. 45, p. 351 [291]), establishes this counterdoctrine in at least four ways: 1) woman was created for the man; more specifically 2) to help him; 3) she was created from him; and 4) God prepared man to assume leadership when he had him exercise authority over the creation by naming the animals before giving Adam his wife.

John Calvin, in an uncharacteristic exegetical blunder, took "help" in 2:18 to mean an "inferior aid." The use of the word *'ēzer* ("help") elsewhere clearly suggests quite the opposite; in fact, it could be interpreted on this basis to mean a "superior aid." The word in question appears nineteen times outside of our text: once in a question, three times of man's ineffectual help, and fifteen times of God's effectual help. The word implies that one is confronted with a situation with which one cannot cope and therefore stands in need of effectual aid. Since it is used only of God's effectual aid it could imply here woman's superiority. The text, however, guards itself against this view by modifying "help" with "corresponding to him," which, as we saw above, speaks of equality.

But the word not only implies that man cannot cope without a wife; it also implies her subordination in government. My children used to come to me to help them with their homework. At one time I could have done their assignments both better and faster, but I could not violate the school's government nor the children's responsibility by supplanting them. I could only advise, suggest, help — no more. Had I used the pragmatic argument "but I can do it better" to justify my usurpation of their position, I would nevertheless have acted illegally, and the victor is not crowned unless he competes according to the rules (cf. 2 Tim. 2:5).

Our text also teaches the hierarchical subordination of women by presenting the woman as one created from the man. On that fact the Apostle Paul built his doctrine of headship, which as Stephen Bedale ("Notes and

Studies: The Meaning of *kephalē* in the Pauline Epistles," *JTS* new series, 5 [1954]: 211-15) has shown, means that leadership, or governmental priority over another, belongs to the source from which the other party was created. Christ is the head of the church, that is, he is prior both as its source and, therefore, societally. Because the church was created out of his bleeding side, he functions as its leader. So also the husband is the head of his wife because she was formed from his bleeding side. From this viewpoint man's authority over his wife derives from a relative priority (causal and temporal) in the order of creation.

As noted, the Creator prepared the man for leadership by causing him to name the animals prior to making the woman. Cassuto (*A Commentary on the Book of Genesis* I [Jerusalem: Magnes, 1961], p. 130) commented on this part of the story:

> The naming of something or someone is a token of lordship (cf. Num. xxxii 38; ii Kings xxiii 34; xxiv 17; ii Chr. xxxvi 4). The Lord of the universe named the parts of the universe and its time-divisions (i 5, 8, 10), and He left it to man to determine the names of those creatures over which He had given him dominion.

Again, significantly, Adam exercised this lordship apart from the woman.

This doctrine of woman's subordination to her husband in government no more undercuts the doctrine of her equality in being than Jesus' statement, "the Father is greater than I," undercuts his claim: "I and my Father are one." Likewise, this complementary narrative to the first creation narrative in Genesis 1 no more contradicts the doctrine of that account that man and woman together rule the creation than the doctrine that the church is under Christ's headship contradicts the truth that Christ and his church inherit the earth as coheirs (Rom. 8:17), and that the persevering church will reign with him (2 Tim. 2:12). These truths regarding the equality and inequality of the sexes must be held in dialectical tension, by allowing them the same weight at the same time, and by not allowing one to vitiate the other by subordinating one to the other.

The rest of the Bible gives instruction to effect the Creator's design for a hierarchical government in marriage. King Lemuel's mother holds up to her son as a model wife one who contributes materially to the household and thereby gives him the leisure to sit with dignity among the elders at the city gate (Prov. 31:10-31, especially verse 23).

The Lawgiver protects the father's and/or husband's authority over his household by giving him veto power over his daughter's and/or wife's vows. The daughter or wife enjoys a direct relationship with God in the matter of making vows apart from the father's and/or mother's mediatorial role, but if the father and/or husband disapproved of the vow the LORD stood behind his authority to veto it. The regulation that a widow's or divorcee's vow was as binding on her as those of a man upon him shows that the LORD gave the male leader of the home veto-power not because women were psychologically or spiritually inferior, but because they were socially inferior. The woman's vows are conditioned by virtue of her subordination to the one placed over her. Vos made the point well:

> The intent [of Numbers 30] is to make clear that the cult may not be the means by which one escapes life's basic obligations. It was woman's duty to be subordinate to her father and/or husband, and true religion did not consist first of all in vows of abstinence, but in fulfilling the role of daughter, wife, and mother, and the obligations involved. It would be a misuse of the cult to make it a means of escaping these obligations. (p. 95)

The Lawgiver also protected the husband's leadership in his home by allowing him to write a certificate of divorce if he found some "indecency" in his wife. In the first century AD, Hillel, a rabbinic scholar, thought the phrase meant any trivial thing, such as a badly cooked dish. That interpretation runs counter to the argument of the book, whose laws serve to protect Israel's covenantal commitment to love God with all their hearts (Deut. 6:5), and to the word's only other use in Deuteronomy 23:14 where it refers to that which offends Yahweh's holiness. If we carry that notion over into the law regarding divorce it fits the book's argument well. A lewd or bawdy wife would hinder both the husband's service to God out of gratitude for his good gifts, and the propagation of the faith to the children (cf. Deut. 6:7-9). This interpretation also explains why it would be an abomination to take such a woman back into the home after she had remarried; that would be levity, an abuse of the law's spiritual intention.

The New Testament likewise protects the authority of the husband over the home for which he is responsible by commanding the wife to obey from the heart her husband in everything (Eph. 5:24) and by not allowing the woman to teach or usurp authority in the house of God (1 Tim. 2:11; cf. 3:14-16).

Conclusion: Why the Battle of the Sexes?

Why is it that instead of enjoying marital bliss wherein the husband respects his wife as his equal and she owns him as her lord, we commonly experience conflict? Homes conceived in love and brought forth through faith die in cynicism and despair. If we can identify the problem we will be halfway home to its solution. The problem stems from fallen woman's desire to rule her husband and from the fallen husband's response to rule his wife through domination, arbitrariness, and arrogance.

The LORD punished the woman for her rebellion against him by allowing her to nurse the same spirit against her husband. To the woman he said:

> Your desire will be for your husband, and he must master you. (Gen. 3:16)

The *crux interpretum* here is that of deciding the meaning of "desire." Many suggestions have been offered, but Susan Foh (*Women and the Word of God: A Response to Biblical Feminism* [Phillipsburg, NJ: Presbyterian and Reformed Publishing Co., 1980], pp. 67-69) is almost certainly right in her interpretation that the woman's desire is her desire to rule her husband. Two lines of evidence support her interpretation, though she offered only the second.

In the first place, the chiastic parallelism strongly suggests this meaning. If we lay out the parallelism as follows one can readily see that in these otherwise synonymous lines, "desire" is parallel to "rule":

Your	desire will be for	your husband
but he	will rule over	you.

This suggestion is strengthened considerably by the identical parallelism in Genesis 4:7b. Here we read:

Its [sin's]	desire will be for	you
but you [Cain]	must rule over	it.

In this grammatically and poetically identical construction it is quite clear that sin desires to rule Cain, but that he must struggle or wrestle with it. This text in the same literary document and in close proximity to it supports the same meaning for Genesis 3:16 as that suggested from its own parallelism. If Foh's interpretation is correct, and to the best of my knowledge it is, she has uncovered the root that brings forth its bitter fruit in our homes. Instead of being content to help her husband, fallen woman desires to rule him, and fallen man tries to rule her from his depraved posture.

But in the New Covenant we find our salvation. Filled with the Spirit, the Christian woman turns away from her old self-assertiveness, and giving expression to the spirit of submissiveness, she desires to serve her husband. The husband, on his part, filled with that same spirit of submissiveness, and turning away from ruling as the Gentiles do by lording it over her (Matt. 20:25), accepts her help, appreciates her as every bit his equal, and uses his position to serve her out of love.

Responding to an Unethical Society:
A Meditation on Psalm 49

Psalm 49

1 Hear this, all you peoples;
     listen, all who live in this world,
2 both low and high,
     rich and poor alike:
3 My mouth will speak words of wisdom;
     the utterance from my heart will give understanding.
4 I will turn my ear to a proverb;
     with the harp I will expound my riddle.

5 Why should I fear when evil days come,
     when wicked deceivers surround me —
6 Those who trust in their wealth and boast of their great riches?
7 No man can redeem the life of another
     or give to God a ransom for him —
8 the ransom for a life is costly,
     no payment is ever enough —
9 that he should live on forever and not see decay.

10 For all can see that wise men die;
     the foolish and the senseless alike perish
     and leave their wealth to others.

Previously published in *Stimulus* 1, no. 3 (August 1993). This article is abridged from a sermon preached at Elizabeth Street Chapel, Wellington, New Zealand, on May 3, 1992.

^{11} Their tombs will remain their houses forever,
    their dwellings for endless generations,
    though they had named lands after themselves.

^{12} But man, despite his riches, does not endure;
    he is like the beasts that perish.
^{13} This is the fate of those who trust in themselves,
    and of their followers, who approve their sayings.

Selah

^{14} Like sheep they are destined for the grave,
    and death will feed on them.
The upright will rule over them in the morning;
    their forms will decay in the grave,
    far from their princely mansions.
^{15} But God will redeem my life from the grave;
    he will surely take me to himself.

Selah

^{16} Do not be overawed when a man grows rich,
    when the splendor of his house increases;
^{17} for he will take nothing with him when he dies,
    his splendor will not descend with him.
^{18} Though while he lived he counted himself blessed —
    and men praise you when you prosper —
^{19} he will join the generation of his fathers,
    who will never see the light of life.

^{20} A man who has riches without understanding
    is like the beasts that perish.*

There is a story of a student at the University of Kentucky who was assigned a theme paper on a character in Shakespeare's *Othello*. When he got his paper back from the professor it was graded an "A" and under it was written, "Please see me." The student was delighted to have received an A.

At the appointed hour he appeared at the professor's office. The professor invited him in, had him seated, turned his back on him, lit up his pipe

*A Wisdom Psalm of the Sons of Korah. Biblical citations from the New International Version.

and began making pleasantries about the paper. Then the conversation changed somewhat and he said, "Tell me, do you belong to such and such a fraternity?" The student, perplexed by the question, why the professor should be interested in his fraternity, said "Yes sir, I do belong to that fraternity." The professor said, "Do they still have that file there of old exams and papers from former students?" The student blushed and realized he was in trouble and said, "Yes sir, we still have that file there of papers." The professor said, "Now tell me the truth, did you copy that paper out of the file?" The student realized that the professor must be on to him, gulped, confessed, and said, "Yes sir, I copied that paper out of the file."

The professor said, "When I was a student here I was a member of that fraternity and I wrote that paper." After the student got over his shock he said, "Well, sir, how come you gave me an 'A'?" The professor said, "Well my professor gave me a 'C+' but I always thought it was worth an 'A'!"

The story highlights the problem that all of us have: that we live in an unethical society. Christian students have to compete against non-Christian students. Many non-Christians don't have too many quibbles about cheating on an examination or plagiarizing work, but a Christian cannot cheat on the exam and cannot plagiarize his or her work. Yet the Christian student must achieve grades as good as the non-Christian student if he or she hopes to get into the better universities, and upon graduation to have the better job opportunities.

All of us, as Christians, have to compete against unethical competition. The Christian salesperson must represent his or her product with integrity; the non-Christian can misrepresent it and lie about it, and yet the Christian salesperson, to survive, must make the sale as well as the non-Christian.

The Christian contractor must build and work with integrity. The same workmanship and quality of goods must be used in a construction where they cannot be seen as in one where they are visible. Non-Christians may be willing to take shortcuts and under-cost the work; yet Christian contractors, to stay in business, must compete in an unethical world.

Professional people face similar circumstances. For example, a non-Christian lawyer who has no time for God or his family can make the case his or her god, and work fourteen or sixteen hours a day seven days a week. A Christian has better values and is not willing to compromise in that way. The Christian will take time to worship, to do acts of charity, and spend time with his or her family, and yet in the courtroom has to compete and win the case.

All of us face the challenge of an unethical society. It is rather like trying to play tennis against an opponent who is allowed to hit the ball anywhere but you have to return it within the guidelines of the court. It is almost an impossible game to play, and we are tempted to embrace a wrong philosophy, as the world does. We are liable to embrace the godless philosophy that you have to fight fire with fire, or when in Rome, do as the Romans.

Psalm 49 is written to encourage us as saints and Christians to not embrace these godless philosophies. It gives us another philosophy that we can carry with us back out into the marketplace. I want to share this wisdom with you so that you can carry it with you throughout your life.

You discover something of the context of the Psalm in verse 5: *Why should I fear when evil days come, when wicked deceivers surround me? . . .* The psalmist is surrounded by unethical, deceptive people who bring evil days upon him.

The Psalm falls into two parts, broadly speaking. In verses 1-4 we have the introduction and in verses 5-20 we have the main message of the Psalm. Let us look first of all at the introduction (vv. 1-4). The introduction has two parts. First of all there is a word about the audience being addressed (vv. 1, 2) and then a word about the author (vv. 3, 4).

Let us look first of all at the word to the audience: *Hear this, all you peoples; listen, all who live in this world, both low and high, rich and poor alike . . .* (vv. 1, 2). I suggest that my assignment is to be a mirror. There are two points to be made here and they are perfectly obvious.

1. This wise person is crying out to be heard. He says: *Hear this . . . listen . . .* On his behalf I ask you to put aside whatever is distracting you, wherever your mind might be wandering — on behalf of the psalmist I ask you, hear this and listen. What we are about to hear we will not read about in the *Dominion* or in the *Evening Post* or any business magazine. It is a word you will not hear in the news media, and yet the world desperately needs to hear it. So on his behalf, the first thing is, listen to what he has to say.

2. The word here is for everyone. Whatever your economic situation there is a word here for you. He says . . . *all you peoples: all who live in this world, both low and high, rich and poor alike . . .* The low are to be consoled, the high will be warned; the rich are to be sobered and the poor will be comforted. There is a word for each of us, and may God apply that word to our lives.

We now come to the author in verses 3 and 4. First we learn that the author is a sage. He is a wise person; he speaks wisdom. He says in verse 3: *My mouth will speak words of wisdom; the utterance from my heart will give un-*

derstanding . . . One of the characteristics of wisdom literature is the frequent use of words like *wisdom, discernment,* and *understanding.* The psalmist is saying: "I offer you wisdom — the skill of life. I am going to give you understanding for life." It is a precious gift he offers to us. The wisdom teachers draw their inspiration from the creation. They turn our attention to look at things we all see every day and yet they help us to see them afresh, in a new light. They help us to gain insight from things that we see all around us.

In verse 3 he said something about his substance, namely, *wisdom* and *understanding.* In verse 4 we read about the style: *I will turn my ear to a proverb; with the harp I will expound my riddle.* Here we find a Scriptural proverb outside the book of Proverbs. The fact that it is a riddle means that we will need to think about it. It will be opaque to those who don't want to have open eyes to see it, but for those who are willing to look they will find a precious truth in the proverb that the psalmist wants to give to the believing community.

That is the introduction. Now we come to the message of the Psalm. Verses 5-20 fall into two even parts. Verses 5-12 form the first stanza of the hymn (it is a song), and verses 13-20 the second. The two stanzas are divided by the common refrain at the end of verse 12 and at the end of verse 20. Here is the refrain and here is the proverb; he is like the beasts that perish. Reading verse 12: But man, despite his riches, does not endure; *he is like the beasts that perish.* Again in verse 20 we have the same refrain: *A man who has riches without understanding is like the beasts that perish.* The proverb is very simple. A rich person is like the beasts that perish.

In the Hebrew text you cannot miss that this is the proverb of the Psalm. When he said back in verse 4 *I will turn my ear to a proverb,* the Hebrew word translated "proverb" is *mashal* and the verb that is translated in verses 12 and 20, *he is like,* is the Hebrew verb *"mashal,"* but in verb form it is a denominative. You take a noun *"mashal"* and make it into a verb; for example, you might take a noun like "skin," then by saying "skin the cat" make the noun into a verb. That is what is done here. The verb translated "he is like," appearing in both verses 12 and 20 is the Hebrew word *nimshal.* There is no misunderstanding this is the proverb: *a rich man is like the beasts that perish.*

We need to develop that and think about it, so let's look at the first stanza (vv. 5-12). His major point is that the rich person gains only temporary glory from his wealth. What does he mean when he speaks of a rich person?

The answer is given in verse 6. The rich are defined as *those who trust in their wealth and boast of their great riches.*

The biblical concept of a rich person is not exactly coincidental with what we mean in the English language by a rich person. We define a rich person as anyone who has an excess of material goods in any kind of property form, chattel or material possessions. The Bible means that, but it means something other than that as well. It needs more definition. A rich person in the Bible is one who finds his or her *security* and his or her *significance* in wealth. It is a spiritual attitude toward money and possessions — rich persons look to money as their security in this world, as that which gives them a sense of success and of significance. I suspect most people pursue money for those two reasons. They are looking for security to protect them and they are looking for significance.

The wisdom literature is not, however, a diatribe against wealth. The fact of the matter is that a person who lives according to wisdom will normally accumulate wealth. It is part of the cause-and-effect relationship. If you turn to Proverbs 8 you will see that wisdom is often attended with wealth. In Proverbs 8:12 lady wisdom in her soliloquy says, *I wisdom dwell together with prudence; I possess knowledge and discretion.* Further, in verses 17-21, she says:

> I love those who love me,
> and those who seek me find me.
> With me are riches and honor,
> enduring wealth and prosperity.
> My fruit is better than fine gold;
> what I yield surpasses choice silver.
> I walk in the way of righteousness,
> along the path of justice,
> bestowing wealth on those who love me
> and making their treasuries full.

So often, to walk in the ways of wisdom is attended with wealth; and it is really better than gold, as she says in verse 19, because money can put food on the table but money cannot give fellowship around the table. Money can get us beautiful houses but it cannot give us homes. Money can put rings on a woman's finger and fur on her back but cannot give her the love she really wants. Wisdom will put food on the table but better than that; it will give fellowship around the table. Wisdom will get houses but better than that, it will create homes — in the Western world we are having bigger houses but evermore fragmented homes. It will give us what we really want — love and spiritual qualities. I think you can see that this is not a diatribe in a polemic against money as such, but the Bible is concerned that God's good gift to us can become the invidious enemy of our souls. It can destroy us when we make it our security and our significance.

What the sage means by "rich" is seen in Proverbs 18:11: *The wealth of the rich is their fortified city; they imagine it an unscalable wall.* They find their defense and security in this world and their protection against evil, in their money, which they think is like a wall that cannot be breached. But it is all a false security.

The sage defines what he means by a rich man very clearly in the last proverb dealing with riches in Proverbs 28:11. The NIV has *A rich man may be wise in his own eyes, but a poor man who has discernment sees through him.* But the Hebrew does not have the words *may be.* A clearer translation would be, and it defines what the proverb means by a rich man: *A rich man is wise in his own eyes* (so NASB and see NRSV). The person described is one who is autonomous, a person who is self-secure, who finds his or her resources in him- or herself. That is what the Bible means by a rich person. Such a person can in no wise enter into the kingdom of God because they have the wrong basis of confidence and security. Instead of finding their security in Christ and his blood and their significance in God's love, the rich seek their security apart from Christ and significance apart from his great love towards sinners, which gives us eternal life. There is then a difference between the rich person in the English language and the rich person in biblical language, and yet they overlap because it's difficult to have an abundance of wealth and not make it one's security and one's significance. Turn with me to Proverbs 30:7-9. I love Agur because he is an honest sort of a person and truthful about life. He says in verses 7-8b, *Two things I ask of you, O LORD; do not refuse me before I die. Keep falsehood and lies far from me* [i.e., may I be always able to speak the truth in life and not fake it]; *give me neither poverty nor riches, but give me only my daily bread* [In other words, he is praying, "O LORD, may I never win the lottery, it would destroy me"]. Why doesn't he want too much? Here's the reason — *Otherwise I may have too much and disown you and say, "Who is the LORD?"* I don't need God in my life, I'm secure apart from him. When we have an abundance of wealth it is very easy to transfer our trust to the bank account. But Agur also recognizes the danger of poverty — he says very honestly: *Or I may become poor and steal, and so dishonor the name of my God.*

Having clarified the way the word *rich* is to be understood, let us now return to Psalm 49. Verse 6 speaks of *those who trust in their wealth.* Paul counters this attitude with the warning, *Tell those who are rich in this world not to trust in uncertain riches* (1 Tim. 6:17). Not only do they find security but they find their significance in wealth — they *boast of their great riches.*

You can tell a lot about people by what they talk about. Sports fans talk about their sports heroes; literate people praise their authors; musicians praise their composers; rich people talk about money. You cannot be around a person who is rich, as the Bible defines it, without talking about money eventually.

The day after the stock market crashed in 1987, I was at Westminster [Theological Seminary] and I thought the greatest tribute to the faculty was that we went the whole evening and nobody even mentioned the stock market crash. Nobody could care less about the whole thing; it was clear that none of us were rich.

The Psalm goes on to say that wealth is only temporary, and a false and stupid god. *No man can redeem the life of another or give to God a ransom for him — the ransom for a life is costly; no payment is ever enough — that he should live on forever and not see decay* (vv. 7-9). In other words, money is a false god — when you most need it, it's worthless.

In the moment of death, which we all must confront after seventy/ eighty/ninety years or so, wealth is worthless. It does you absolutely no good. We all know we must die, but according to Elisabeth Kübler-Ross's studies, when we are dying we all deny it. We refuse to acknowledge that we are dying. The Bible comes home to us with a very dark and yet very truthful and honest picture. You hear the same message in Thomas Gray's *Elegy Written in a Country Churchyard:*

> The boast of heraldry, the pomp of power,
> And all that beauty, all that wealth e'er gave
> Awaits alike th' inevitable hour:
> The paths of glory lead but to the grave.

None of it saves us. Were the sun a coin of gold in one pocket, were the moon a coin of silver in another, were the planets rubies on our fingers, were the milky-way cultured pearls around our neck, were the bright stars diamonds in our crowns or tiaras, at the day of death it is worthless; it cannot save you. We look for a different savior.

Verse 10 says that not only is death inevitable, it is universal: *For all can see that wise men die; the foolish and the senseless alike perish and leave their wealth to others. Their tombs will remain their houses forever, their dwellings for endless generations, though they had named lands after themselves.* The

435

kings of Egypt would bury themselves in their pyramids and the great kings of the ancient East would have lavish tombs. In the United States some of the rich bury themselves in coffins that I've heard cemeteries advertise as well drained — small comfort that is!

All of this is folly, and to try to find your immortality in something in this world, putting your name on a street or a city or some foolish thing like that, you might as well write your name on water. There is no security in this world. Only God and his church in Christ are immortal and eternal.

But man, despite his riches, does not endure; he is like the beasts that perish (v. 12). In other words, he is a consumer. He's like one big digestive tract — eating, eating, consuming, consuming. What the sage is saying is that to build your life around being a consumer is sheer folly. It is to be like a bull in the field titillating every appetite, gratifying every desire, and getting fatter and fatter — for what? For the butcher shop! That's a hard line. If it were not in the Scriptures I would hesitate to use that kind of language.

We now come to the second half of the psalm's body, verses 13-20. If the first stanza pertains to all humankind, the second distinguishes between the foolish and the wise. If the glory of all humankind is temporary, the doom of the foolish in contrast to the wise is eternal. The topic of the second stanza is defined in verse 13: *This is the fate of those who trust in themselves, and of their followers, who approve their sayings.* Great is the multitude that follow this kind of thinking and who live their lives independently of Christ. In spite of its absurdity and folly this is where the masses of humanity are. But the truth is, it is eternal doom. *Like sheep they are destined for the grave, and death will feed on them* (v. 14a). It is a macabre figure. As they have spent their lives consuming, now they are consumed and death grossly feeds on them.

The upright will rule over them in the morning; their forms will decay in the grave, far from their princely mansions (v. 14b). If all I had was this Psalm I might derive from it the doctrine of annihilation. I might say that's it — at death they are consumed, annihilated, they are no more; but I would do an injustice to Holy Scriptures. Jesus is even more severe. Jesus said there is eternal punishment for people who live their lives independently of him. It is the way to hell, an eternal condemnation.

Let us consider Matthew 25:31-46. When Jesus pictures the day of judgment he speaks of himself as the *Son of Man,* for only the Son of Man comes on the clouds of the air and only God comes on the clouds of the air. In this way Jesus alludes to his deity, for what man rides the clouds as described in Daniel 7?

When the Son of Man comes in his glory and all the angels with him, he will sit on his throne in heavenly glory. All the nations will be gathered before him, and he will separate the people one from another as a shepherd separates the sheep from the goats. He will put the sheep on his right and the goats on his left.

Then the King will say to those on his right, "Come you who are blessed by my Father; take your inheritance, the kingdom prepared for you since the creation of the world. For I was hungry and you gave me something to eat, I was thirsty and you gave me something to drink, I was a stranger and you invited me in, I needed clothes and you clothed me, I was sick and you looked after me, I was in prison and you came to visit me."

Then the righteous will answer him, "Lord, when did we see you hungry and feed you, or thirsty and give you something to drink? When did we see you a stranger and invite you in, or needing clothes and clothe you? When did we see you sick or in prison and go to visit you?"

The King will reply, "I tell you the truth, whatever you did for one of the least of these brothers of mine, you did for me."

Then he will say to those on his left, "Depart from me, you who are cursed, into the eternal fire prepared for the devil and his angels. For I was hungry and you gave me nothing to eat, I was thirsty and you gave me nothing to drink, I was a stranger and you did not invite me in, I needed clothes and you did not clothe me, I was sick and in prison and you did not look after me."

They also will answer, "Lord, when did we see you hungry or thirsty or a stranger or needing clothes or sick or in prison, and did not help you?"

He will reply, "I tell you the truth, whatever you did not do for one of the least of these, you did not do for me."

Then they will go away to eternal punishment, but the righteous to eternal life.

There are some today, even in evangelical circles, who are saying there is only annihilation. But Christ says, *they will go away to eternal punishment* (Matt. 25:46a). If that's not true then I have no guarantee the righteous go to eternal life (25:46b). One goes to eternal life and the other goes to eternal punishment, says Jesus. The issues are high; this is not just a minor proverb, it's profound. How do we respond in an unethical society? Are we simply competing, taking, and consuming, or do we use the opportunity to help others with what we have because of our faithfulness to Jesus, which is the proof of our regeneration? These are issues of life and death.

Turning back to Psalm 49:14: *Like sheep they are destined for the grave, and death will feed on them. The upright will rule over them in the morning; their forms will decay in the grave, far from their princely mansions.* The rich person, who finds his or her security and significance in money, needs to realize that not only is the glory temporary but it leads to an eternal damnation. We need now to distinguish between the outcomes for the righteous and the wicked because it said back in verse 10 *all can see that wise men die; the foolish and the senseless alike perish.* Where is the distinction then between the wise and the foolish, between the righteous and the wicked? It's after death — that's when separation is made; that's when the sheep are separated from the goats.

That's what he says in verse 15. *But God will redeem my life from the grave; he will surely take me to himself.* There are many who believe there is no doctrine of resurrection in the Old Testament. I cannot square such a view with a verse like this. What else could this mean, than that God will take us from the grave in resurrection? This is the Christian faith.

I said we have two stanzas for this proverb — verses 5-12 and verses 13-20 — and it is significant that in the third verse of the first stanza we are told that no man can redeem us. *No man can redeem the life of another or give to God a ransom for him* (v. 7). No matter how much money he or she may have, no person can save you from death. But what humans cannot do God can do. As I read in verse 15: *God will redeem.* No human could pay the price that would save us from death, but God paid the price.

The great masses of unbelievers believe that the end of life is death — there is no more. For the unbeliever, therefore, death is God. The one who has the last word in your life. The one who has the final verdict, the final control over your life, is God. For the unbeliever, the end of it all is that we go into the grave and the last word is that dirt is shoveled into our faces — that's the end of it. They worship death; they will spend their fortunes to live one more week or one more month because that's all they have: anything to ward off death. But death is not God; Christ is God. He swallowed up death itself. He conquered death and spoiled it by his resurrection from the dead, and we as Christians worship the Living Christ who conquered death.

In Israel's rituals they were constantly reminded that they belonged to life and not to death. Remember the strange ritual that if you came across a carcass you would have to go to the priest, take a hairy plant that contained lots of liquid and the ashes of the red heifer which included blood and water, and the priest would sprinkle you. If that were still a law today, with our road kill, we'd be going to the priest all the time to get sprinkled. Why was that ritual performed? Israel was being reminded that they did not belong to death but to life. They belonged in the temple of the Living God. That which transferred them from death to life was the precious blood, which was a type of the blood of Jesus, who sprinkles us and takes us out of the realm of the death that we deserve. The wages of our sin cause our death, but the gift of God is eternal life through Jesus Christ our Lord. It's his blood that pays the price that puts us into the realm of life.

Israel had the same ritual, you may recall, of sprinkling with hyssop the blood and water when they had been cleansed from leprosy, which was the picture of a living death. They were in the process of dying, and that's how you may feel about your life — mucked up in sin and in the process of dying. But the good news of the gospel is that the blood of Jesus can cleanse us; can wash our sins away and transfer us into the realm of life — eternal life — where Christ has conquered death itself. God will do what humans cannot do. God can save us from eternal death. Death is not God — it is not the last word in your life — Christ will have the last word and deliver you from death.

But God will redeem my life from the grave (v. 15a). What is not clarified here is the purchasing price. On what basis did he redeem us? How did he save us from the grave? The New Testament makes clear that it is with the precious blood of Jesus. Silver and gold could not redeem us. It was with the value that God put upon the blood of Christ that made that payment for our sins. Peter says in 1 Peter 1:18-19, "For you know that it was not with perishable things such as silver or gold that you were redeemed from the empty way of life handed down to you from your forefathers, but with the precious blood of Christ, a lamb without blemish or defect." The blood of Jesus made the purchase price — he paid for our sins so that God can and will redeem us.

He will surely take me to himself. The word translated "take" here is the same word used of Enoch in Genesis 5:24: *He walked with God and he was not, for God took him.* It was the word used for Elijah in 2 Kings 2:1 when God appeared in the chariots of fire to take him up to heaven. Jesus promises on all of his authority, I will "take" you from the grave; I will give you eternal life.

The Psalm says in conclusion: *Do not be overawed when a man grows rich, when the splendor of his house increases; for he will take nothing with him when he dies, his splendor will not descend with him* (vv. 16-17). It has been said with wry humor, "I've never seen an armored truck at a funeral."

Though while he lived he counted himself blessed — [this is true, foolish humans do this] *and men praise you when you prosper* — *he will join the generation of his fathers, who will never see the light of life. A man who has riches without understanding is like the beasts that perish* (vv. 18-20).

There is a tale of a man who was rich in the sense we have defined from the Bible. He was visited by an angel who said, "I'll give you anything you want." He thought about it and said, "Yes, I know what I want. I want the newspaper one year from today," and his wish was granted. He turned immediately to the stock market page and saw what the stocks would do one year from then and realized what a killing he could make in that market and the investments he was going to make. But as he was calculating the fortune he was about to amass he happened to glance across the page and saw his picture in the obituary column. Suddenly he lost all interest in the stock market page. What our psalmist is saying is, your picture is in tomorrow's obituary column. That's not too far off as the Word of God puts it, but there is more than that — our names can be written in the Lamb's Book of Life. Our pictures can be in heaven with the resurrected Jesus. Where is your picture — is it in tomorrow's obituary column, or is your picture in heaven with Jesus?

I like the way it's put there in verse 14, and with this I conclude: *The upright will rule over them in the morning.* Have you ever noticed how different God's calendar is from our calendar? God's calendar is day; it begins at night and it ends in the morning. Our day begins in the morning and ends at night; we think of morning and night and then we think of darkness and death, but God doesn't think that way. First comes the night and then comes the morning. It's the way Israel thought about a day. It was evening and it was morning — day one. First comes the cross and then comes Easter Sunday; first comes the deprivation and then comes the glory.

May God give us the grace to hear what the Psalmist had to say and what none of us can give to one another, but God's good gift to us enables us to see this, to hear it, and to understand. If you can see it, if you can hear it, if you can embrace it, then you are a child of God. May God give you the grace to embrace it, trust it, and believe in our precious Savior, Jesus Christ.

Righteousness in Proverbs

Thank you, Dr. Lillback, Dr. Edgar, and members of the Gospel and Culture Project, for inviting me to deliver the inaugural "endowed lecture on Biblical and Systematic Theology and their impact on culture in the global context of Christianity." This opportunity is a special privilege because the lectureship honors Professor Richard Gaffin. It is proper and good that we honor those whom God has honored.

Since I have written recently a commentary on the book of Proverbs, perhaps I can be most helpful by restricting my topic to the potential impact of Proverbs on culture. The key word in this connection is the book's term "righteousness." The title of this lecture is "Righteousness in Proverbs."

T. S. Eliot asked: "Where is the wisdom we have lost in knowledge? Where is the knowledge we have lost in information?"[1] In Eliot's worldview, wisdom implies an endeavor to interrelate differing levels of reality. His worldview is counter-cultural, for Western culture is technological — that is to say, it endeavors by the process of analysis to obtain knowledge and information about the constituent parts of different levels of reality. This process of analyzing, Eliot implies, is destructive to wisdom. In contrast to the process of analysis, he suggests that synthesis works in the opposite direction. In contrast to our technological society's aim to analyze the different levels of reality, wisdom seeks to interrelate them. Our technological culture hopes by

---

1. T. S. Eliot, "Choruses from 'The Rock'" (London: Faber & Faber, 1934).

Previously published in *Westminster Theological Journal* 70 (2008). This is a revised version of the first annual Richard B. Gaffin Lecture Series on Theology, Culture, and Missions, delivered at Westminster Seminary, March 5, 2008.

scientific knowledge to control the different levels of reality and so achieve salvation. By contrast, says Eliot, wisdom by the process of synthesis builds up a bigger picture to be admired. The consequences of seeking to control by analysis instead of integrating the levels of reality have been catastrophic, as our environmental crisis demonstrates. Wisdom can be described by the color "green," as environmentalists use this metaphorical color.

Wisdom in Proverbs and its correlative term "righteousness" are all about being rightly related to God, to other human beings, to all creatures, and to the environment. The wisdom and knowledge that our technological culture has lost and that T. S. Eliot was looking for is found in the book of Proverbs. In this lecture I hope to contribute to coloring our culture green.

The principal text in Proverbs that informs my lecture is the preamble to the book.

> [1]The proverbs of Solomon, son of David, king of Israel:
> [2]To know [literally, to know in experience] wisdom and instruction,
>   to understand words of insight;
> [3]to receive instruction in prudence,
>   in righteousness, justice, and equity [literally, uprightness];
> [4]to give prudence to the noncommitted [traditionally, simple],
>   knowledge and discretion to the youth —
> [5]let the wise listen and add to their learning,
>   and let the discerning get guidance —
> [6]to understand proverbs and parables,
>   the sayings of the wise and their riddles.
> [7]The fear of the LORD is the beginning of knowledge;
>   wisdom and instruction fools despise.

The preamble asserts that King Solomon aims through this book to instruct the covenant youth, both the wise and the as-yet uncommitted, "to know wisdom" (v. 2) and to give them the prerequisite knowledge to make them wise (v. 4). More specifically, I argue in this lecture that the book's wisdom and knowledge pertain to pursuing right relatedness. Before proceeding with the argument, however, by way of introduction, let me summarize some of the spiritual values of pursuing righteousness according to the book of Proverbs:

1. To profit self: "Whoever pursues righteousness and love finds life, prosperity, and honor" (21:21).

2. To promote a relationship with God: "*I AM* detests the way of the wicked but he loves those who pursue righteousness" (15:9).
3. To exalt the community: "Righteousness exalts a nation, but sin condemns any person" (14:34).

In this lecture I specifically aim to define the concept and the term "righteousness" in the book of Proverbs. The inspired sages' conception of righteousness is socially transformative; it transforms the City of Man into the City of God, from a culture that is metaphorically red, dripping with blood, to a culture that is green with life. Toward the conclusion of the lecture, after arguing the case, I venture to coin a proverb that encapsulates the sages' conception of righteousness. The proverb aims to make the concept of righteousness in Proverbs memorable, one that can be carried into every social situation. To justify the conceptualization and the proverb I will develop the argument as follows:

I. The Concept of Wisdom in Proverbs: What is the source of wisdom? And what does wisdom mean? How does the creation reveal God's wisdom?

II. Wisdom of Solomon and Law of Moses: How does the wisdom of Solomon compare or contrast with the law of Moses? Do the proverbs of Solomon teach the same thing as the Mosaic law or do their teachings differ?

III. Wisdom and Righteousness: Are wisdom and righteousness related? Is a person who is wise necessarily righteous? Can a person be wise and wicked, or be a fool and righteous?

IV. The Concept of Righteousness in Proverbs: What exactly does "righteousness" mean in Proverbs? Does King Solomon use righteousness in the same way as the Apostle Paul?

I will develop the lecture as an artist might paint Edward MacDowell's famous musical composition "To a Wild Rose." First, I will paint the background of the sky to give the wild rose its proper interpretative context, and then the landscape of a mountain to give it further context. Third, I'll paint the woodland that is more immediately in the foreground of our subject, and finally, having contextualized the wild rose, I'll paint our subject and highlight it. In this analogue, the sky represents the conception of "wisdom" in Proverbs with regard to its source and its meaning. This conception is necessary, for the literary context of righteousness in Proverbs is "to know wisdom." That context provides a necessary background for interpreting righteousness in this book. The mountain landscape represents the second point: the contrast between the wisdom of Solomon and the Mosaic law given on Mount Sinai. This contrast, hopefully, will further clarify the meaning of righteousness in Proverbs. The foreground woodland represents the third point: a demonstration that wisdom and righteousness are correlative terms. This reflection is necessary to show that wisdom and righteousness are inseparable notions. Finally, the rose refers to the culturally transformative concept of righteousness in Proverbs, and my proverb highlights that notion.

Wisdom: The Literary Context of Righteousness

Let us begin, then, by painting the sky: the conception of wisdom (*ḥokmâ*). The preamble asserts that the book aims to give Israel's youth wisdom: "The proverbs of Solomon, son of David, king of Israel, to know [literally, to know in experience] wisdom." To be sure, the preamble identifies Solomon as the human author, but other texts show that Israel's God, Yahweh in the Hebrew language (in God's own mouth his sentence name in English means, *I AM WHO I AM*), revealed this wisdom to Solomon and inspired his proverbs that convey this wisdom. If you will, let three texts suffice to validate the claim that God revealed to Solomon this wisdom and inspired him to set it forth in proverbs.

> "God gave Solomon wisdom and very great insight . . . [and so] Solomon spoke three thousand proverbs" (1 Kings 4:29-32). "For *I AM* gives wisdom; from his mouth come knowledge and understanding" (Prov. 2:6). Solomon's wisdom, personified as a heavenly mediatrix,[2] says of herself: "*I AM* brought me forth as the first of his works before his deeds of old" (Prov. 8:22).

Wisdom must begin with the ultimate reality, *I AM*, to assure the comprehensive embrace of wisdom and the right relationship of all levels of reality. Without *I AM*'s comprehensive knowledge, the finite mortal cannot attain to certain knowledge about what is good and bad by rightly relating all aspects

---

2. Bruce K. Waltke, *The Book of Proverbs: Chapters 1–15*, NICOT (Grand Rapids: Eerdmans, 2004), pp. 83-87.

of reality. Without revelation and inspiration, the finite mortal has only evaluations, not certain values. That is why Solomon personifies his wisdom as being with God before and when he created anything: "Then I [Woman Wisdom/Solomon's wisdom] was constantly at *I AM*'s side. I was filled with delight day after day, rejoicing always in his presence, rejoicing in his whole world and delighting in humankind" (Prov. 8:30-31). In sum and in short, without revelation from the Eternal, the finite mind cannot attain to infinite knowledge, the prerequisite of certain knowledge and wisdom.

Having identified the ultimate and immediate sources of wisdom, let us continue to paint the sky by asking, What does "wisdom" mean? In brief, "wisdom" *(ḥokmâ)* means "masterful understanding," "expertise," "skill." The NIV helpfully renders on occasion *ḥokmâ* by "skill."[3] The term is used in the Bible for all sorts of skills. Outside of Proverbs *ḥokmâ* is used, for example, of technical and artistic skill (Exod. 28:3; 31:6), of the arts of magic (Exod. 7:11; Isa. 3:3), of government (Eccles. 4:13; Jer. 50:35), and of diplomacy (1 Kings 5:7 [HB 5:21]). Let me illustrate only artistic and technical skill from Exodus 28:3.

In this text God directs Moses: "Tell all the skilled workers [*ḥakmê lēb*, woodenly, 'wise of heart') to whom I have given wisdom [*Ruaḥ ḥokmâ*, woodenly, 'spirit of wisdom'] in such matters that they are to make garments for Aaron, for his consecration, so he may serve me as priest." These skilled workers cut down the flax in the field, boiled the fibers of the stalks to soften them, spread them out on their flat roofs to dry in the hot sun, heckled the fibers to separate them, spun them together to make thread, wove the threads on a loom into broadcloth, and cut and sewed the broadcloth to fit Aaron's body. Moreover, they dipped some fabric into dyes of blue and purple and scarlet to adorn the garment. Perhaps a metallurgist had the skill to make Aaron's headpiece, the gold miter that read "Holy to *I AM*." By clothing Aaron in these rich garments, these skilled artists and technicians set him apart as a sacred person of *I AM*.

In Proverbs, *ḥokmâ* is used once of the survival skills of wee-creatures (30:24-28), but otherwise it refers to social skill: how to build a healthy society under God's rule and not a lethal one. In other words, "wisdom" in Proverbs refers to shaping a God-honoring culture under God's blessing, not one that stands under his curse. For example, many of the proverbs pertain to communication skills upon which all social relationships depend. The other dominant theme of Proverbs is on how to be money-wise, namely, to use money to create a community of friends and not to alienate people from one

---

3. Waltke, *The Book of Proverbs: Chapters 1-15*, p. 76.

another. As we shall see, righteousness in Proverbs is closely related to wisdom — that is to say, social skill.

Permit me for a moment to reflect as a systematic theologian. Orthodox theologians agree that God alone is eternal and has no associates. Now, since wisdom is a social concept pertaining to right relationships, for *I AM* to be eternally wise, he must be a unity of distinct personalities. Wisdom, which means social skill, must be exercised toward another person. Logic demands that for God eternally to exercise wisdom, God must be a unified plurality of persons in order to exercise and experience social skill.

Let me now reflect as an exegetical theologian upon *I AM*'s wisdom as displayed in the creation. "By *I AM*'s knowledge the clouds let drop the dew" (Prov. 3:22b). So consider raindrops. If raindrops were circular and not spheroids, falling from the height of the clouds, gravity would bring them down with such force that the rain would strip the foliage off all plants and trees in the same forceful way as water under pressure from a hose strips it. As spheroids, however, without an even distribution of weight, the drops of rain spin and keep splitting apart as they pick up speed in their descent to the earth and so become ever lighter and finally fall gently upon the fragile foliage. Such is the social skill of *I AM*.

Or consider apple trees. They reproduce enough food to feed many creatures and enough seed to feed an expanding population. For example, in summer a bear can eat about eighty pounds of apples per day. The fruit trees and seed-bearing plants do not simply reproduce themselves; they bear enough seed and vegetation to feed everybody when wisely managed. This too is exemplary of the wisdom, the social skill, of *I AM*.

Wisdom of Solomon and the Law of Moses

Let us now continue to prepare our canvas by painting the mountain landscape, namely, by contrasting Solomon's wisdom with the law given on Mount Sinai. Solomon, who authored the bulk of the book of Proverbs, found his knowledge of the law insufficient for his responsibility as the supreme and final judge of God's people. His role as king was similar to that of the chief justice of the Supreme Court of the United States. But unlike the American chief justice, who is *primus inter pares* (first among equals), Solomon was the supreme judge over all other judges. To fulfill his role as sole chief justice of the kingdom of God, which was founded to establish righteousness and justice on earth, he indirectly confesses that the Mosaic law was insufficient.

Upon ascension to the throne, Israel's kings had to copy by hand the book of the law mediated by Moses. (The book of the law comprises approximately all but fifty-six verses of the book of Deuteronomy.)[4] Moreover, the king was to read the book of the law daily. Moses ordained:

> When he [the king] takes the throne of his kingdom, he is to write for himself on a scroll a copy of this law, taken from that of the priests, who are Levites. It is to be with him, and he is to read it all the days of his life so that he may learn to revere *I AM* his God and follow carefully all the words of this law and these decrees and not consider himself better than his brothers and turn from the law to the right or to the left. Then he and his descendants will reign a long time over his kingdom in Israel. (Deut. 17:18-20)

Moreover, King David on his deathbed charged his son Solomon to keep the law of Moses:

> When the time drew near for David to die, he gave a charge to Solomon his son. "I am about to go the way of all the earth," he said. "So be strong, show yourself a man, and observe what *I AM* your God requires: Walk in his ways, and keep his decrees and commands, his laws and requirements, as written in the law of Moses, so that you may prosper in all you do and wherever you go, and that *I AM* may keep his promise to me: 'If your descendants watch how they live, and if they walk faithfully before me with all their heart and soul, you will never fail to have a man on the throne of Israel.'" (1 Kings 2:1-4)

Tragically, however, Solomon failed to read the law daily, and for this reason the once wisest of men died a fool. He hangs himself on his own gibbet: "Stop listening to instruction, my son, and you will stray from words of knowledge" (Prov. 19:27).

Nevertheless, Moses' instruction that the king copy the book of the law and David's deathbed charge to Solomon to keep it imply that Solomon knew the book of the law. This inference finds support in the theological unity between the book of the law and Solomon's proverbs.

As we shall see, Solomon's proverbs refine the law of Moses. The book

4. Bruce K. Waltke, *An Old Testament Theology: An Exegetical, Canonical, and Thematic Approach* (Grand Rapids: Zondervan, 2007), p. 57.

of the law, even without Solomon's refinement, on its own has had a profound influence for good to benefit cultures that have lived by faith according to its teachings. Indeed, that book has had greater consequences for human history than any other single book. Its continuing influence is one of the major forces shaping cultures. Its regulations are the first to establish universal education and healthcare for all members of a nation and to fix the only welfare system that was in existence in ancient times. It first formulates the greatest command of all Scripture: to love God (cf. Matt. 22:34-40). It also establishes a constitutional monarchy, a king subject to God's law.[5]

In spite of the great importance and profound influence of the book of the law, Solomon found that, in his role as supreme judge of the elect nation, he needed more discretion and wisdom than the book of the law provided. Shortly after his coronation he went to the high place at Gibeon, where after offering thousands of sacrifices to atone for his sin and to seek God's favor, he asked for a greater wisdom than he found in the Mosaic law:

> The king went to Gibeon to offer sacrifices, for that was the most important high place, and Solomon offered a thousand burnt offerings on that altar. At Gibeon *I AM* appeared to Solomon during the night in a dream, and God said, "Ask for whatever you want me to give you." Solomon answered, "You have shown great kindness to your servant, my father David, because he was faithful to you and righteous and upright in heart. You have continued this great kindness to him and have given him a son to sit on his throne this very day. Now, *I AM* my God, you have made your servant king in place of my father David. But I am inexperienced [*na'ar*] and do not know how to carry out my duties. Your servant is here among the people you have chosen, a great people, too numerous to count or number. So give your servant a discerning heart to govern your people and to distinguish between right and wrong. For who is able to govern this great people of yours?" The Lord was pleased that Solomon had asked for this. So God said to him, "Since you have asked for this and not for long life or wealth for yourself, nor have you asked for the death of your enemies but for discernment in administering justice, I will do what you have asked. I will give you a wise and discerning heart, so that there will never have been anyone like you, nor will there ever be. Moreover, I will give you what you have not asked for — both riches and honor — so that in your lifetime you will have no equal among kings.

5. Waltke, *An Old Testament Theology,* p. 479.

And if you walk in my ways and obey my statutes and commands as David your father did, I will give you a long life." (1 Kings 3:4-14)

With that gift of a wise and discerning heart Solomon coined his proverbs:

God gave Solomon wisdom and very great insight, and a breadth of understanding as measureless as the sand on the seashore. Solomon's wisdom was greater than the wisdom of all the men of the East, and greater than all the wisdom of Egypt. . . . And his fame spread to all the surrounding nations. He spoke three thousand proverbs and his songs numbered a thousand and five. (1 Kings 4:29-32)

Solomon's proverbs take up those social and cultural issues that are too fine to be caught in the mesh of the law, too small to be hit by the broadsides of the prophets. The refinement of the law of Moses by Solomon's proverbs may be compared to learning to drive a car. A driver first learns the comprehensive rule: "Drive carefully." But that abstract rule needs definition such as those provided by the road signs, such as "Stop," "Yield," "Speed limit 35 mph," and the signals of traffic lights. Before being granted a driver's license the applicant must demonstrate ability to follow these signs. But even knowing and following these more specific posted regulations do not qualify a driver to be granted a driver's license. Many states require the applicant for a driver's license to pass a written test before granting the license. To pass this test the applicant must know, for example, to park at least fifteen feet from a fire hydrant, to park at least fifteen feet from the corner of an intersection, to turn into the inside lane of a four-lane highway and to ease one's way over into the outside lane through the use of mirrors, and so forth.

In this illustration the general rule to drive carefully is like the comprehensive commandments "to love God with all your heart, soul, mind, and strength," and "to love your neighbor as yourself." But those abstract commands need further definition. What road signs are to the driver, the Ten Commandments are to the covenant people. To love your neighbor means more specifically, "not to murder," "not to commit adultery," "not to steal," and "not to bear false witness." But as essential as these commandments are, Solomon found them insufficient for taking to the road of life; they needed further refinement. The comprehensive rule, love your neighbor as yourself, more specifically defined as "do not murder," and so forth, is refined in the sages' hands by their proverbs.

The command "not to murder" in the Proverbs becomes to feed your enemy: "If your enemy is hungry, give him food to eat; if he is thirsty, give him water to drink" (25:21). The command "not to commit adultery" is refined to the husband's gesture to stand up in his noble wife's presence to give her honor and to praise her with public verbal praise: "Her husband [arises] and he praises her: 'Many women do noble things, but you surpass them all.' ... Give her the reward she has earned, and let her works bring her praise at the city gate" (31:28-31). "You shall not steal" becomes in Proverbs to be generous: "A generous man will himself be blessed, for he shares his food with the poor" (22:9). And the command "not to bear false witness" is sharpened by Proverbs, specified by "hatred stirs up dissension, but love covers over all wrongs" (10:12). The original translators of Proverbs for the NIV rendered the second half of that proverb by, "love draws a veil over all transgressions." In other words, the command not to bear false witness, in the hands of the sage becomes: "Protect your neighbor's reputation by drawing a veil over his or her wrongs; do not put them on the stage and then draw the curtain apart for all to see their faults."

If the book of the law in the past has had a greater impact for good on Western culture than any other book, how much more would be the impact of its refinement in the book of Proverbs? Furthermore, when these small details are learned and practiced, the Ten Commandments will be actualized.

The logic here is similar to that of "the broken window theory." That theory is based on an article titled "Broken Windows" by James Q. Wilson and George L. Kelling, which appeared in the March 1982 edition of *The Atlantic Monthly*. The article's title comes from the following example:

> Consider a building with a few broken windows. If the windows are not repaired, the tendency is for vandals to break a few more windows. Eventually, they may even break into the building, and if it's unoccupied, perhaps become squatters or light fires inside.
>
> Or consider a sidewalk. Some litter accumulates. Soon, more litter accumulates. Eventually, people even start leaving bags of trash from take-out restaurants there or breaking into cars.

A successful strategy for preventing vandalism, say the theory's authors, is to fix the problems when they are small. Repair the broken windows within a short time, say, a day or a week, and the tendency is that vandals are much less likely to break more windows or do further damage. Clean up the sidewalk every day, and the tendency is for litter not to accumulate (or for the rate of littering to be much less). Problems do not escalate, and thus respectable residents do not flee a neighborhood.

When Mayor Rudolph Giuliani applied the broken window theory to New York City, he significantly reduced crime in that great metropolis. So likewise when youth learn to feed their enemies, to honor those to whom honor is due, to be generous to the poor, and to protect another's reputation, the larger matters, such as those of the Ten Commandments, not to murder, not to commit adultery, not to steal, and not to bear false witness, will become a reality and society will become a place where people love one another as themselves. That sort of culture establishes the City of God and *I* AM's blessings crown it.

Wisdom and Righteousness as Correlative Terms

Having painted the sky (the literary context of knowing social skills) and the mountain landscape (the proverbs of Solomon intensify the commands in Moses' book of the law), let us now paint the immediate woodland foreground to give our wild rose more context. Here we reflect on the notion that wisdom and righteousness are correlative terms.

Correlative terms are like synonyms in that they refer to the same person, object, or situation. Unlike synonyms, however, correlative terms belong to different worlds of thought, different fields of meaning — what linguists call "semantic domains." As an example of synonyms, consider "wisdom" and "prudence." They are synonyms because both terms pertain to the same person and/or situation and both belong to the semantic domain of intelligence. But "wisdom" and "righteousness," though they pertain to the same person and/or situation, belong to different fields of meaning. Whereas wisdom pertains to the semantic domain of intelligence, righteousness pertains to the semantic domain of ethics. In Proverbs the same person and/or situation belongs inescapably to both fields of thought: of spiritual intelligence and of right behavior.

We can illustrate a correlative term by considering Dick Cheney. Dick Cheney is vice-president of the United States and president of the United States Senate. These are distinct roles, but they pertain to the same person and are inseparable. In relation to the president of the United States, Dick Cheney is his vice-president and in an emergency stands in his stead. In relation to the Senate, however, he governs that body. Nevertheless, these offices, though distinct, are inseparable. If he is vice-president of the United

States, he is president of the Senate, and vice-versa. Similarly, wisdom and righteousness denote different notions, but they are inseparable. If a person is wise, he or she is righteous; if righteous, they are wise.

"Wisdom" in Proverbs needs the correlative term "righteousness" because "wisdom" without qualification is a morally neutral term. The serpent was wise but a devil (Gen. 3:1). The Bible uses the term wisdom *(ḥokmâ)* of sorcery and of black magic. Consider, for example, its use in Exodus 7:11-12: "Pharaoh then summoned wise men and sorcerers, and the Egyptian magicians also did the same things by their secret arts: Each one threw down his staff and it became a snake. But Aaron's staff swallowed up their staffs." Outside Proverbs it is possible to be wise and wicked, but not in the book of Proverbs.

The preamble of the book of Proverbs carefully protects the morally vulnerable term "wisdom" and its synonyms by employing a chiastic structure that features the correlative term "righteousness." A chiastic structure (also called a chiastic pattern or ring structure) is a literary structure in which concepts or ideas are placed in a reversing symmetric order or pattern. For example, suppose that the first topic in a text is labeled A, the second topic is labeled B, and the third topic is labeled C. If the topics in the text appear in the order ABC X CBA so that the first concept that comes up is also the last, the second topic is the second to last, and so on, the text is said to have a chiastic structure. In this pattern, X, the pivot, has a special emphasis. A chiastic structure may be likened to throwing a rock into a pond. Where the rock strikes is X, and from that center the topics ripple outward in opposite directions. This structure can be discerned in the preamble.

¹The proverbs of Solomon, son of David, king of Israel:
²To know wisdom and instruction, to understand words of insight;
³to receive instruction in prudence: righteousness, justice, equity;
⁴to give prudence to the simple, knowledge and discretion to youth;
. . . .
⁶to understand proverbs and parables, the sayings of the wise and
    their riddles.
⁷The fear of *I* AM is the beginning of knowledge; wisdom and
    instruction fools despise.

Note how verse 2a: "to know [*da'at*] wisdom and instruction" matches verses 7: "The fear of *I* AM is the beginning of knowledge; wisdom and instruction fools despise." Though the syntax of the preamble's framing verses (2a, 7) differs, they repeat the same words in the same sequence, namely, know/knowledge [*da'at*], wisdom, and instruction. In the B pairing verses, verse 2b matches verse 6: "to understand the words of the wise" and "to understand a proverb and parable; the sayings of the wise and their riddles." In the C pairing, "prudent behavior" in verse 3a matches its synonym "prudence" in verse 4a. This concentric pattern highlights the pivot: "doing what is right, and just and fair." In other words, within this A B C C B A structure, X, righteousness, is where the rock hits, and from it ripple out the other notions pertaining to the semantic domain of wisdom.

Here is a schematic sketch of the preamble's chiastic structure:

A. Comprehensive, intellectual values: 2a
    To know [*da'at*] wisdom and instruction
  B. Literary Expression of Wisdom   2b
      to understand words of insight,
    C. Instrumental virtue: **prudent behavior**   3a
      X. Moral, communal virtues:
        righteousness, justice, equity   3b
    C'. Instrumental virtue: **prudence**, discretion, guidance   4-5
  B'. Literary expressions of wisdom   6
    to understand proverbs and parables
A'. Comprehensive, intellectual virtues: 7
  knowledge [*da'at*], wisdom and instruction

In addition to this revealing pattern that unites inseparably wisdom and righteousness, elsewhere in the book of Proverbs and other wisdom literature, wise/wisdom and righteous/righteousness constantly interplay with one another, and so do their antonyms, "fool/folly" and "wicked/wickedness." For example, consider the first unit of proverbs in the first collection of proverbs, titled "The proverbs of Solomon" (10:1a):

A **wise son** brings joy to his father, but a **foolish son** grief to his
    mother.
Treasures of wickedness are of no value, but righteousness delivers
    from death.
I AM does not let the *righteous* go hungry, but he thwarts the craving
    of the *wicked*.

. . . .

A **wise son** gathers crops in summer, but a disgraceful son sleeps
    during harvest. (10:1b-5)

In sum, if a person is wise he or she is righteous; if wicked, they are fools. Skillful living is invariably doing what is right.

Righteousness

Having given our wild rose (i.e., righteousness) its interpretative contexts of the sky (a definition of wisdom as social skill), and of its mountain landscape (the refinement of the Mosaic law by Solomon's proverbs), and of the woodland foreground (wisdom and righteousness are inseparable terms), we now paint the wild rose (the concept of righteousness in the book of Proverbs).

The Hebrew lexeme (that is to say, its lexical form) *ṣādaq* is universally glossed as "to be righteous." Some scholars, such as E. Kutzsch (1881),[6] define righteousness as subjection or obedience to a norm, to a standard.[7] If *ṣādaq* means conformity to a norm, in the Bible that norm is God's holiness. His holiness finds expression in part in the Bible's teachings, such as the law of Moses, the proverbs of Solomon, and the teachings of the Lord Jesus Christ in his Sermon on the Mount. Other lexicographers, however, such as H. Cremer (1899)[8] and E. Achtemeier,[9] define "righteousness" as socially acceptable behavior. According to the former notion — that is to say, that righteousness means to submit oneself to the norm of the Bible's teachings — the term righteousness belongs in the semantic domain of jurisprudence, of law. According to the latter conceptualization of right social behavior, it pertains to the semantic domain of sociology, of human relationships.

After studying in the book of Proverbs every use of the terms involving the lexeme *ṣādaq*, I drew the conclusion that the conceptualization of righteousness should be subsumed under the umbrella concept of doing what is right in a social relationship as defined by God's standard of what is right behavior. J. W. Olley similarly defined righteousness: "to bring about right and harmony for all, for individuals, related in the community and to the physical and spiritual realms. It finds its basis in God's rule of the world."[10]

---

6. E. Kautzsch, *Abhandlung über die Derivate des Stammes* ṣdq *im alttestamentlichen Sprachgebrauch* (Tübingen: L. F. Fues, 1881), p. 53.

7. H. H. Schmid, *Gerechtigkeit als Weltordnung* (Tübingen: Mohr, 1969).

8. H. Cremer, *Die paulinische Rechtfertigungslehre im Zusammenhang ihrer geschichtlichen Voraussetzungen* (Gütersloh: Bertelsmann, 1900).

9. E. Achtemeier, "Righteousness in the Old Testament," *IDB* 4:81.

10. J. W. Olley, "'Righteous' and Wealthy? The Description of *Ṣaddîq* in Wisdom Literature," *Colloquium* 22 (1990): 38-45.

I also drew the conclusion that according to Proverbs this socially acceptable behavior of doing what is right in social relationships as defined in the Bible's teachings entails depriving self to benefit others. As Solomon expressed it: "The righteous give without sparing [literally, 'without holding back']" (21:26b). This qualification of the book's aim to know wisdom entails feeding the enemy and the poor, protecting another's reputation, and so forth. Righteousness in the book of Proverbs is equivalent to the Mosaic teaching to love your neighbor as yourself (Lev. 19:18), for the one who loves self looks to be fed by capable and willing people when hungry and to be protected when slandered.

Having defined the concept of righteousness in Proverbs as expending oneself to serve one's neighbor, let me highlight the definition by coining a proverb:

The wicked advantage themselves by disadvantaging others,
but the righteous disadvantage themselves to advantage others.

Most English speakers, I suspect, when they think of wickedness, think in terms of the Ten Commandments. For most, wickedness refers to murder, adultery, stealing, and lying. But in Proverbs wickedness pertains to the finer points: of not feeding the poor when you have the power to do so, of not honoring the honorable, of not stopping gossip in its track, and so forth.

This proverb to disadvantage self to advantage others puts wisdom in shoe-leather. As is the case with proverbial sayings, it can be carried into many social situations. In the classroom, it means that when a professor assigns a book that is no longer in print, the student does not rush to the library to take the book out to earn an A and so deprive the rest of the class of that advantage. To selfishly possess the book is wickedness. Rather, the wise and righteous student makes sure that classmates have access to the book, even as he or she would desire in their same situation. This wisdom-in-shoe-leather can be applied to the highway. One does not cut into a line of cars to save one's own time at the expense of the time of the cut-off drivers. The proverb can be carried into a public rest room. The wise and righteous person leaves the facility clean for the next person.

This definition of proverbs also resolves troublesome sayings such as: "Do not be overrighteous, neither be overwise — why destroy yourself? Do not be overwicked, and do not be a fool — why die before your time?" (Eccles. 7:16-17). Let me explain this troublesome saying by a personal anecdote. When I lived in the snowy winters of Philadelphia, my proverb of disadvantaging myself to advantage others prompted me, after I had shoveled my own sidewalk, to shovel the sidewalk of my neighbors: a widow next door in her nineties and a couple across the street also over ninety years of age. But after shoveling their sidewalks, as well as mine, I also had to consider the neighboring widower, also in his nineties. I had already spent four hours shoveling sidewalks, when it occurred to me, "Do not be over-righteous, neither be overwise — why destroy yourself?" There is a limit to which one can disadvantage oneself to advantage others.

Conclusion

The church will put the proverb, "The wicked advantage themselves by disadvantaging others, but the righteous disadvantage themselves to advantage others," within her commitment to the Lord Jesus Christ. He is the supreme example of righteousness as conceptualized in Proverbs. He became poor that we might become rich; he gave up his life that we might have eternal life. Moreover, the church's catechism teaches that our Lord gave his church his Spirit to empower her to live his sort of life. Her best resolutions to live righteously will fail. Apart from God's grace, her best social efforts are splendid vices, for they are all tarnished by self-interests. Let the church look to the triune God from whom every good and perfect gift comes, including the gift to give one's life to serve others.

The Role of Women in the Bible

Introduction

In this essay I aim to offer as an exegetical theologian a broad survey of the role of women in "worship," with particular emphasis on the Old Testament, my area of expertise. I prefer to define the role of women in the Bible in terms of their "worship" because, from the biblical perspective, believers offer their entire lives as an act of worship to God, even as Adam and Eve offered theirs in the Garden before the Fall.

Since the church is not united in its understanding of the role of women in the church, in the home, and in society, let me say at the outset that I regard these matters as nonessentials for the unity of the church; our differences regarding the role of the sexes should not divide the church either spiritually or politically. Nevertheless, the topic is important. Godly men and women, as citizens of heaven, earnestly desire to play out their lives in a way that is worthy of the gospel (Phil. 1:27). Furthermore, the church must face the practical issue of whether to ordain gifted women to various ministries and/or to the office of ruler. I offer this essay to further our mutual endeavors to live godly lives, to handle rightly the Scriptures, and to attain to the unity of the faith regarding the role of women, though we all still see through a glass darkly.

Before looking at specific texts, however, the hermeneutical question of how texts conditioned by historical particularity can be normative for the contemporary church must be addressed.

Previously published in *Crux* 31, no. 3 (September 1995).

Hermeneutical Issues and the Method of Criticism

The order of creation is normative. To transcend the historically particular and culturally conditioned situation in which Scripture is given and to find what is normative for the practice of the covenant people I first examine the role of women in worship before the Fall. The two creation accounts, Genesis 1:1–2:3 and 2:4-25, represent God's design for men and women, husbands and wives. The rest of Scripture recounts a sacred story that to a large extent is moving toward the restoration of this ideal.[1] It treats this charter for humanity as normative for the covenant community, though sometimes concessions are made because of the hardness of the human heart (Matt. 19:8). Foundational to my view is my understanding that the situation represented in these first two chapters of Genesis is regarded as normative for humanity in the rest of Scripture. This ideal is not imposed upon men and women but presented to help them understand their natures and the roles for which they were created. Their sexuality lies deeper than their physical characteristics to reproduce, but in their very embodiment as human beings, in the way they view the world, and in the way they are perceived.[2] Men and women have distinctive "glories." In the light of this ideal for men and women I will examine the rest of the Old Testament and note, as necessary, its continuities and discontinuities with the New Testament.

The order of creation, which is set forth in these two accounts, stands behind the order of redemption, which is represented in the rest of Scripture. For example, the Fourth Commandment (Exod. 20:8-11) to refrain from work on the sabbath is based on the first creation account that God ceased his own work on that day (2:2-3). The Seventh Commandment (Exod. 20:14) to not commit adultery is founded on the institution of marriage in the Garden of Eden according to the second account (Gen. 2:18-25). The Sixth Commandment (Exod. 20:13) protects innocent life because every life is created in God's image (Gen. 1:26-28; cf. 5:1-3; 9:6).

Moreover, our Lord aimed to recapture for his church the Creator's original intention for marriage (Matt. 19:3-9), and the Apostle Paul based on these accounts his arguments concerning the roles of women in the home and in the church (1 Cor. 11:3-12; 1 Tim. 2:12-15).

In sum, the Bible is a story of Paradise lost in the first Adam and being

---

1. Revelation 21 and 22 present the end of that history in images representing the Garden of Eden as regained.

2. Stanley Grenz, *Sexual Ethics* (Dallas: Word, 1990), pp. 10-17.

regained in the Second. The Garden of Eden symbolically represents the ideal culture that was lost and that Moses restores in the Law and that Christ restores more perfectly in his church through the Spirit. These accounts present what is normative for the role of women in "worship."

Furthermore, the historically conditioned texts in the rest of the Old Testament cannot be ruled out of hand as not normative practices of the church in its worship before God, for at least three reasons:

God ordained Israel's culture. First, God sovereignly ordained the culture in which he became incarnate. The roles played by godly women in ancient Israel are due to his design, not chance. The Sovereign God, not Lady Luck, is Israel's Lord. Since his sovereignty extends even to assigning the pagans their gods and their cultures (Deut. 4:19), we may rightly suppose that the Sovereign did not hand over to chance either his representation of himself as Father, Son, and Spirit or the role of women in the nation that he chose to bless the world by embodying and disseminating his teaching (cf. Gen. 18:18-19).

Orthodox theology cannot consent to Krister Stendahl's comment, made while he was still dean of Harvard Divinity School, that God's numerous and strong masculine metaphors for himself are largely an accident.[3] According to Stendahl, "The masculinity of God, and of God-language, is a cultural and linguistic accident, and I think one should also argue that the masculinity of the Christ is of the same order. To be sure, Jesus Christ was a male, but that may be no more significant to his being than the fact that presumably his eyes were brown."[4] In truth, however, the biographies of Jesus in the New Testament curiously do not mention anything about our Lord's physical appearance apart from his masculinity, suggesting it has theological relevance. His incarnation occurred at the right time and in the right way according to God's own sovereign purposes (Gal. 4:2-4).

Prophets critique Israel's culture but not patriarchy. Second, Israel's prophets, God's mouth, were iconoclasts, not traditionalists, who called Israel into the dock for numerous injustices. Abraham Heschel in his justly praised work *The Prophets* makes the point:

---

3. God uses six feminine similes for himself (e.g., Isa. 42:14).

4. Krister Stendahl, "Enrichment or Threat? When the Eves Come Marching In," in *Sexist Religion and Women in the Church: No More Silence!* ed. Alice L. Hageman in collaboration with the Women's Caucus of Harvard Divinity School (New York: Association Press, 1974), p. 120, as quoted in *Words and Women,* ed. Casey Miller and Kate Swift (New York: Anchor Books, 1977), p. 67.

They challenged the injustices of their culture. The prophet is an icono-clast, challenging the apparently holy, revered and awesome beliefs cher-ished as certainties, institutions endowed with supreme sanctity. They exposed the scandalous pretensions, they challenged kings, priests, in-stitutions and even the temple.[5]

However, not one of these cultural revolutionaries regarded patriarchy as an unjust or oppressive form of government. Quite the contrary. They in-terpreted the rule by women as God's judgment against the sinful nation. Isaiah, for example, ridicules it: "Children are their oppressors, and women rule over them" (Isa. 3:12). They inveighed, however, against abuse of power that oppressed women: "The women of my people you cast out from their pleasant homes" (Mic. 2:9). They gave a voice for those too weak to have a voice, especially the fatherless and widows. Against unjust magistrates Isaiah complained: "They do not defend the fatherless, nor does the widow's cause come before them" (Isa. 1:23; cf. v. 7).

Practice of Christ Jesus confirms male rulership. Third, our Lord was a revolutionary in his own age with regard to the role of women in worship. He amazed his disciples by conversing with a woman because he violated the prejudice of both the Jews and the Romans against women (John 4:27). The Son of God bestowed dignity upon the Samaritan adulteress, "unclean" by Jewish standards, by revealing to her for the first time that worship would now be directed toward the Father in heaven, not toward "Mecca-like" Jeru-salem on earth (John 4:21-25). Moreover, our Lord entrusted women to be the original witnesses to his resurrection, the cornerstone of the Christian faith, though their testimony would have been discounted in a Roman court (Luke 24:1-4). He rewarded the devotion of Mary of Magdala, out of whom he had cast seven demons, by allowing her to be the first person to meet him after his resurrection (Mark 16:9-10; John 20:14-18). His disciples refused to believe Mary's report of the risen Lord. In fact, they dismissed it as an "idle tale" (Mark 16:11; Luke 24:11). Later Jesus rebuked them for their unwilling-ness to believe her (Mark 16:14). Yet he implicitly confirmed the role of men as rulers by not appointing a woman as an apostle, though women followed him, ministered to him, and were his close friends.

Does it make sense to argue that Jesus, who in these matters pertaining to theology was so counter-cultural with respect to women, only appointed male apostles, upon whom he founded his church, because he was culturally

5. Abraham J. Heschel, *The Prophets* (New York: Harper & Row, 1962), p. 10.

conditioned? Is it not more plausible to think that had he intended to empower women to have equality with men in government, he would have called a woman to be an apostle, either before or after his resurrection? The appointment of men or women to this important office is not a matter of theological indifference.

Forbidden Fruit

There are those today who would argue for a perspective about women, the world, and God that is based on human autonomy, the attempt to know truth apart from divine revelation.[6] Elsewhere in this journal I have argued that an adequate epistemology must be based on revelation, not on human reason, experience (e.g., so-called "callings"), and/or tradition (cf. Deut. 8:3; Ezek. 28:6, 15-17).[7]

This truth is symbolically represented in the second account by God's prohibition not to eat of the "tree of knowledge and good and evil." "The tree of knowledge of good and evil" represents knowledge that is God's prerogative. As Christians we know that the only accurate description of reality is that which is known to God. He is the maker of reality and our only clear interpreter of it. Therefore only the good Creator and moral Sovereign of the universe can legislate inerrantly what promotes life and social well-being and what harms them. Our first parents, by seizing this prerogative for themselves in order to become equal with God, died spiritually and lost Paradise. To be sure, eating the forbidden fruit (i.e., living independently from God's revelation) appeared good for food (i.e., of practical value), pleasant to the eye (i.e., having aesthetic appeal), and desirable to make one wise (i.e., provided intellectual gratification). The price, however, was too high. They lost a relationship with both God, symbolized by hiding among the trees, and with one another, symbolized by putting a barrier of clothing between them.

Some Christian feminists acknowledge the authority of the Bible, but they tend, I suggest, to interpret Scripture in a way that favors their social

6. It is not my purpose to critique specific advocates of the many and varied feminist positions. But I must take exception to those like Mary Daly who begin their analysis with human autonomy rather than biblical revelation. Cf. Mary Daly, *The Church and the Second Sex* (Boston: Beacon Press, 1968).

7. Bruce K. Waltke, "Exegesis and the Spiritual Life: Theology as Spiritual Formation," *Crux* 30, no. 3 (September 1994): 28-35.

agenda, *viz.:* the equality of women in authority and leadership. Regarding their zeal to ordain women rulers, we need to ask, are they projecting their system upon the Bible, as a better system, and thereby imposing their own will for power against God's design? Until the twentieth century the church universally understood Scriptures to teach male rulership in the church,[8] but I observe that many evangelical churches, certainly not all, have overthrown that heritage on the superficial basis that scholars are divided on the issue. The truth is that scholars are divided on most theological issues, including the Bible's trustworthiness. On that basis no doctrine is safe, and the more liberal perspective and practice must prevail. Anthony Thiselton, citing Robert Morgan, rightly advised pastors to be on guard that "some disagreements about what the Bible means stem not from obscurities in the texts, but from conflicting aims of the interpreters."[9]

Furthermore, we must guard ourselves against political correctness, conformity to a consensus, and demagoguery. To be sure, all of us interpret texts out of a tradition, a consensus, and/or under the influence of some authority. This is inevitable and rational, for, as Gadamer[10] explains, we are aware of our own limitations and accept that others have better understanding. As followers of Christ, however, we must always submit our heritage, consensus, and/or authority to Scripture lest we make Scripture void. Like the Bereans, we need to examine "every day" the Scriptures for ourselves to see what is the truth.

Marriage and Motherhood

Those who would urge married women to give priority to fulfillment in careers outside of the home over against fulfillment in childbearing within the marriage structure — in my understanding of the biblical text — are not offering sound advice.

According to the first creation account God created humanity as male and female (Gen. 1:26-28; cf. Matt. 19:4), whereupon he blessed them (i.e., filled them with potency to reproduce life and to triumph over enemies [cf.

---

8. See Bruce K. Waltke, "1 Timothy 2:8-15: Unique or Normative?" *Crux* 28, no. 1 (March 1992): 22-27.

9. Anthony C. Thiselton, *New Horizons in Hermeneutics* (Grand Rapids: Zondervan, 1992), p. 49.

10. H. G. Gadamer, *Truth and Method* (New York: Continuum, 1975), p. 248.

Gen. 22:17]) and commanded them to be fruitful and multiply. He intended that they procreate his image and similitude (cf. 5:1-3), thereby affording the opportunity to as many people as possible to sit at his banquet table of life. Humanity is grounded in being male and female, an immutably fixed, natural reality. It is my view that any form of feminism which, in a desire for freedom and power, depreciates this fundamental design is inconsistent with the biblical revelation. "Grace," as Pope John Paul II noted in his remarks to Roman Catholic bishops, "never casts nature aside or cancels it out, but rather perfects it and ennobles it."[11]

In the second creation account God gives Adam his bride and thereby institutes marriage, defining them now as husband and wife. By instituting marriage in the Garden of Eden, God represents marriage as an ideal and holy state, an act of worship (Heb. 13:4). We recall that the church restores the Garden. Therefore, believers commit themselves in marriage to one another in the presence of God. Marriage is the only social institution that precedes the Fall, and the homes established through marriage provide the foundation stones for society. After the Fall, God instituted the state to protect society from criminals and the church to promote a new community of love in a world of hating and being hated (Titus 3:3).

The Gift of the Bride story emphasizes the goodness of marriage. The Lord's statement that Adam's singleness "is not good" (Gen. 2:18) is highly emphatic. Instead of saying "it is lacking in goodness," a normal Hebrew way of saying that a situation is less than ideal, he emphatically calls it in effect "bad." God completes the man by the gift of a bride, not by placing him in a community, which is no surrogate for a wife. This account ends, with no trace of male chauvinism, with the coda that *the man* leaves his parents to cling to his wife (2:24). However, as we shall again note, the New Testament presents a singleness devoted to Christ as even better than marriage.

The rest of the Old Testament also defines marriage as a holy and an ideal state. Though certainly marriage was not required for holiness, it is instructive to observe that the holiest people in the Old Testament were married. The high priest, who alone could enter once a year with awe and trembling into God's presence in the Most Holy Place, was married.[12] Nazirites,

11. Richard John Neuhaus, "True Christian Feminism," *National Review,* November 25, 1988, p. 24.

12. The High Priest had to marry a virgin, not a widow or divorcee, to guarantee that the successor to his high and holy office was Aaron's offspring (Lev. 21:13-15), not because a formerly married woman was discarded as used property. In fact, the Old Testament looks with compassion on both widows and divorcees (Mal. 2:13-16; 3:5).

the holiest people in the Old Testament by their own choice, not by birth as in the case of the high priest, likewise were married (see Num. 6:1-21). By definition he or she (see v. 2) was "separated" to God, but Nazirites never fasted sexually. They showed their separation to the Creator by not cutting their hair, just as an orchard was set apart to God by not pruning it and an altar dedicated to God was not made of cut stones. They symbolized their separation from earthly pleasures by not eating the fruit of the vine that cheers both gods and people (Judg. 9:13), and they showed they belonged to the God of life by a total separation from death. However, they did not show their separation to God by celibacy. Marriage was part of their consecration, worship, and holiness.

Paul, as noted, elevates singleness for "gifted" individuals to an even higher state (1 Cor. 7). In regard to women who are called to singleness, however, his design is not to favor women's careers outside the home over motherhood within it, but, in addition to minimizing the dangers of an "impending crisis" (v. 26), to enable them to be fully devoted to Christ without distraction (vv. 32-35). Apart from this "giftedness," the apostle teaches as normative behavior that older women teach younger women "to love their husbands and be busy at home, to be kind, and to be subject to their husbands, so that no one will malign the word of God" (Titus 2:4-5).

God elevates godly mothers to a high status after the Fall. In sovereign grace he changed the fallen woman's affection to enmity against Satan: "I will put enmity between you [the Serpent] and the woman [who had earlier denied faith in the goodness of God and in the trustworthiness of his word]" (Gen. 3:15). By his promise to give this new woman a triumphant, though suffering, offspring, he implicitly assigned her the role of bearing the seed that would destroy the Serpent, the Adversary of God and humanity. The quintessential expression of that seed is Christ, who defeated Satan on the cross, but the mandate finds its fulfillment in every covenant child: "The God of peace," says the Apostle to the church at Rome, "will soon crush Satan under your feet" (Rom. 16:20). In response to the promise to give the woman seed to defeat Satan, believing Adam named his wife Eve, "because she would become the mother of all the living" (Gen. 3:20). Every Christian mother by being in Christ bears his holy children (1 Cor. 7:14; cf. Isa. 53:10). If a woman has suffered any loss of leadership through her creation (1 Tim. 2:12-13; cf. Gen. 2:18-25) and (Greek *kai*)[13] through her historical guilt by Satan's deception, in contrast to Adam, in connection with the Fall (1 Tim. 2:14;

---

13. *Pace* Grenz, *Sexual Ethics*, p. 29.

cf. Gen. 3:1-14), says the Apostle — if I understand him correctly — she will be saved from that loss through bearing children in Christ, if the children continue in the faith, love, and holiness with propriety (3:15; 1 Tim. 2:15). In short, the Apostle is saying, "The hand that rocks the cradle rules the world." Pastors need to hold before the women of their churches Mary's response to the angel's announcement that she would be with child: "I am the Lord's servant. May it be to me as you have said." Mary models for Christian women a most important aspect of woman in worship and ministry. Jonathan Mills[14] helpfully pointed out that Mary's submission is not a passive, unthoughtful, abject resignation, but an obedience she offered out of her freedom, her independence, her thoughtful commitment, so that her submission is meaningful and glorious.

The Equality of Men and Women

Most debated issues have the heuristic value of enabling one to see truth in a new way. The various contemporary versions of "feminism" have had the heuristic value of reasserting the equality of women with men. Unfortunately, as has been documented many times, both the synagogue and the church have not only failed to proclaim this glad truth but have shouted it down. It is a black mark in sacred history.

The error, however, lies in the interpreters of Scripture, not in the Holy Bible itself. In the first creation account both men and women are created in God's image (Gen. 1:26-28). An image of the deity in the Ancient Near East, as D. J. A. Clines has shown, entailed dominion.[15] He cites a cuneiform text dated about 675 BC: "It was said to Esarhaddon [the Assyrian king], 'A free man is as the shadow of god, the slave is as the shadow of a free man, but the king, he is like unto the very image of god.'"[16] God crowned men and women as kings and queens to rule over his entire creation, including the mysterious serpent who "was more crafty than any of the wild animals the LORD God had made" (Gen. 3:1). Together, as his image, they share this derivative authority to be culture makers.

The second account reinforces this equality and clarifies it. When the Lord says "I will make for Adam a helper suitable to him," he means that he

---

14. Jonathan Mills, "Notes on a Faithful Rebel Woman," *Et cetera*, November 8, 1994.

15. D. J. A. Clines, "The Image of God in Man," *TynBul* 19 (1968): 53-103.

16. Clines, "The Image of God in Man," p. 84.

will form a woman who is equal to and adequate for the man. She stands opposite him in her sexual differentiation but equal with him in her personhood and dignity. Adam's response to her formation from his own body is the only human speech preserved from before the Fall. Untouched by envy and/or a desire to dominate and control her, he celebrates with admiration her equality with him in elevated poetry, "This is now bone of my bones and flesh of my flesh." At the same time he recognized her sexual differentiation from him: "She shall be called 'woman' for she was taken out of man" (Gen. 2:23).

The rest of the Old Testament reinforces women's equality in being and in dignity with men. Let me cite a few of many illustrations to make the point. After Sarah overreacted to the arrogance of her maidservant, Hagar, and had driven her out of the house, the angel of the LORD found the runaway at a well. He said, "Hagar, servant of Sarai . . ." (Gen. 16:8). The modern reader misses the significance of that address. This is the only instance in all of the many thousands of Ancient Near Eastern texts where a deity, or his messenger, calls a woman by name and thereby invests her with exalted dignity. Hagar is the Old Testament counterpart to the Samaritan woman (see John 4). Both were women, both were not of Abraham's family, and both were sinners, yet God treated both with compassion, gave them special revelations, and bestowed on them unconventional dignity.

In the Old Testament women were called to be "prophetesses," God's mouth in the world, on an equal footing with prophets. Miriam (c. 1400 BC) (Exod. 15:20f.) was the first of several who are named, including Deborah (Judg. 4:4-7), Isaiah's wife (725 BC) (Isa. 8:3), Huldah (640 BC) (2 Kings 22:13-20), and the false prophetess Noadiah (c. 450 BC) (Neh. 6:14). Joel 2:28 predicts that in the last days the LORD will fulfill Moses' prayer that all the Lord's people, men and women alike, shall become prophets (Num. 11:29). At Pentecost the Holy Spirit was given to both men and women, young and old alike, to enable them to proclaim boldly the triumphant news that Jesus is Lord of all, and to build his church (Acts 1:8, 14; 2:1-4, 17-18).

Huldah is a most remarkable prophetess with regard to the question of women's roles in worship and ministry. During the reformation of Josiah, his workmen, who were repairing the temple, found the Book of the Law, which King Manasseh had neglected during the previous generation. Josiah directed five leaders to inquire of the LORD about the book. Instead of going to the now-famous prophets, Jeremiah and Zephaniah, they went to their contemporary, Huldah, to verify the book (2 Kings 22:3-20). Clarence Vos in his superb doctoral dissertation on our topic says:

That officials from the royal court went to a prophetess relatively unknown with so important a matter is strong indication that in this period of Israel's history there is little if any prejudice against a woman's offering of prophecy. If she had received the gift of prophecy, her words were to be given the same authority as those of men.[17]

Women and men were also equal in prayer. Covenant women prayed directly to God without the priestly mediation of their husbands. For example, when carnal Jacob defaulted in his responsibility to pray for his barren wife (Gen. 30:1-2), in contrast to his godly forefathers who prayed for their children and wives (cf. 24:7, 12-15; 25:21), Rachel petitioned God directly, and he listened to her and opened her womb (30:22-24). Barren Hannah also sought dignity and worth through childbearing. She too went directly to God in prayer, independently from her husband Elkanah and the high priest Eli, both of whom were insensitive to her need. In fact, when challenged by Eli, she spoke up and defended her right (1 Sam. 1:15-16). She named her boy, "Asked of God," and dedicated him to the LORD with the prayer that he would introduce kingship into Israel (2:10b). Hannah's prayer turned Israel around from the nadir of its spiritual history and political misfortune and started it on its upward ascent to its glory under David. A mother's prayer saved Israel and ruled it.

In addition to these prophetesses other women also received direct revelations from God. When Rebekah felt the twins struggling in her womb, she asked the LORD, "Why is this happening to me?" (Gen. 25:22), a question written large across the page of history. The LORD revealed to her Jacob's triumph over Esau.

Women sang and danced in worship, expressions of the acme of life. Miriam and Deborah composed the two oldest pieces of literature preserved in the Bible, which are regarded by scholars as literary masterpieces (Exod. 15 and Judg. 5). Women celebrated before the LORD with singing, dancing, and tambourines (e.g., 1 Sam. 18:6; Ps. 68:25), although they were not a part of the temple choir.

Mothers stood on equal footing with fathers in teaching children: "She speaks with wisdom, and faithful instruction is on her tongue" (Prov. 31:26). Israel's sages were also cultural revolutionaries with regard to the role of women teaching in the home. The father's command to the son, "do not for-

---

17. Clarence J. Vos, *Woman in Old Testament Worship* (Delft: N.V. Verenigde Drukkerijen Judels & Brinkman, 1968), p. 168.

sake your mother's teaching" (Prov. 1:8), seems unexceptional to the average reader. However, nowhere else in the wisdom literature of the Ancient Near East, from the Euphrates to the Nile, is the mother mentioned as a teacher. In order for the mother to teach Israel's inherited wisdom, she herself had first to be taught, suggesting that "son" in the Book of Proverbs is inclusivistic, not gender specific.

Women in the Old Testament offered sacrifices and gifts along with men (cf. Lev. 12:6). The laws for ceremonial cleansing in connection with bodily emissions were essentially the same for both sexes (chap. 15). Women as well as men consecrated themselves to God as Nazirites (Num. 6:2). Sarah, when wronged by her female servant and by the apathy of her husband to the injustice inflicted upon her, appealed to God for justice, but did not issue an ultimatum that either Hagar goes or she goes (Gen. 16:5).

The role of woman in ministry in the New Testament is better known. Luke takes pains to stress the important role that women played on Paul's second missionary journey when he established the church in Macedonia and Achaia (cf. Acts 16:13; 17:4, 12, 34; 18:2). The apostle had a vision of a man of Macedonia begging him to come and help him (16:9), and when he arrived he found women in prayer who became his first converts (vv. 11-15). Phoebe, Priscilla, Junia, Euodia, and Syntyche are celebrated as "minister" *(diakonos),* "co-worker" *(synergos),* and "missionary" *(apostolos).*[18] However, a woman was to keep silent in the church if she had a question about her husband's prophecy; she should ask him about it at home (1 Cor. 14:34-35).[19]

The mutual submission of men and women to one another is unique to the New Testament. However, their equality before God, in their nature, spiritual gifts, and prayer is found in both testaments. It is a dramatic irony that it has been some of the more radical feminists, who malign the Old Testament for its patriarchy, who have opened my eyes to this truth. Their perspective has had the heuristic benefit of bringing to the forefront these

18. Mardi Keyes, *Feminism and the Bible* (Downers Grove, IL: InterVarsity, 1995), p. 12, claims that Phoebe is also called "leader": "described in the Greek as a *gospel minister* [Greek *diakonos* (Rom. 16:1)] *and leader* [Greek *prostatis* (16:2)]. Using the same Greek root, Paul told *leaders* to *govern* [Greek *ho proistamenos*] diligently (Rom. 12:8)." Her argument, however, is flawed philologically. To be sure, *prostatis* derives from *proistēmi,* but in usage it never means "leader" but "protectress, patroness, helper" (BAGD, p. 718) (cf. "succourer" (KJV), "a great help" (NIV), "benefactor" (NRSV). Moreover, *ho proistamenos* in 12:8 may also mean "those who give aid" (BAGD, p. 707, entry 2); cf. "he who gives aid, with zeal" (RSV).

19. Wayne A. Grudem, *The Gift of Prophecy* (Westchester, IL: Crossway, 1988).

equalities. Thanks to this perspective, women are being liberated to use their gifts to enrich the church. This is a real gain.

In sum, we are now in a position to draw the conclusion from Scripture that the church should ordain women to various ministries according to the Spirit's gifts and callings.

We now turn again to the question whether the church should ordain women to the office of ruler (e.g., of priest, elder, and pastor of the Anglican, Presbyterian, and Baptist traditions respectively). Here we need to distinguish clearly between call to ministry and appointment of an office. They are not the same.

Male Priority in Government

There is a growing consensus within the church that rejects male government. Nevertheless, as best I can tell, male authority in the home and in the church is founded on the order of creation and reinforced in the order of redemption as presented in both the Old and New Testaments.

God established this pattern by creating Adam first and the woman to help the man (Gen. 2:18). As Paul noted in a passage dealing with the role of men and women, one that demands its own study: "For man did not come from woman, but woman from man, neither was man created for woman, but woman for man" (1 Cor. 11:8-9). If I understand Paul rightly, he gives priority to the man by the sequence of the creation of man and woman and by the purpose for which the woman was created. For these two reasons the man has a priority in government. Is it not plausible to assume, if this interpretation is valid, that had he intended equality in government he would have formed Eve and Adam at the same time and have said, "It is not good for the man or woman to be alone, I will make them to be helpers suitable to each other"? If he had wanted a matriarchy, would he not have formed Eve first and created the husband to be a suitable helper to his wife? However, he created a government in which the husband has authority.

As stated earlier, the "Gift of the Bride" story does not aim to impose an ideal upon us but to give us an insight into our natures. It is a truism of anthropology, I am told, that male leadership is normative in every culture and that there is no evidence of matriarchy. George Gilder says:

> Steven Goldberg's rigorously argued book *The Inevitability of Patriarchy*, described by Margaret Mead as "flawless in its presentation of data," re-

futes every anthropological claim that there has ever existed in human affairs either a society where women rule or a society where final authority resides with them in male-female relations.[20]

Hierarchy in government is not the result of the Fall. It existed eternally in the Godhead itself, wherein the Son was always voluntarily subservient to the Father's will and the Spirit to both. However, Christian hierarchy, it must be insisted, is unlike those of the world. It is a government of mutual, active, voluntary submission. Leaders, on the one hand, love and serve others, become their servants; they do not lord it over the governed. They abhor the worldly concepts of "having the last word" and of defining hierarchy as "a pecking order" (Matt. 20:25-28). Those who are led, on the other hand, actively, independently, and freely submit to this leadership. The mutual submission and ownership of each other's body in marriage (1 Cor. 7:4-5) probably offended the pride of the Greco-Roman male. "Patriarchy," "obedience," "submission," are red-flag words because we invest them with worldly meanings, not with biblical ones. We need to sanctify them or invent new vocabulary. A power struggle between the sexes, as we note again below, resulted from the Fall. Christ saves his people from seeking to lord it over one another into submitting themselves to one another in a way appropriate to their sexual differences.

God prepares the husband for leadership before giving him his bride by having Adam name the living creatures (Gen. 2:19-20). In the Ancient Near East, as today, naming is a form of leadership. For example, when the Israelites conquered Transjordan, they asserted their authority by renaming the rebuilt cities (Num. 32:38), and Pharaoh Neco asserted his rule over Eliakim by renaming Jehoiakim (2 Kings 23:34). After the Lord gives Adam his bride, Adam tactfully uses the passive form of construction, presumably not to dominate, for her generic name: "she shall be called woman . . ." (Gen. 2:23b). After the Fall, he calls out her personal name, "Eve" (3:20).[21]

Paul, as noted above in connection with 1 Timothy 2:14, forbids women to have authority over men in the church (1 Tim. 2:12) also because the woman, not the man, was deceived and became a sinner. We need not detain ourselves here, however, in an exegesis regarding Paul's reason for his ruling. What is important for our purposes is his ruling. Elsewhere I argued for the

20. George Gilder, *Wealth and Poverty* (New York: Basic Books, 1981), p. 136.
21. In the rest of the Old Testament both parents name the children: naming of children is ascribed to women twenty-six times, to men fourteen times, and to God five times.

traditional understanding that this text is normative for the church.[22] It will not do to obscure the New Testament teaching about husband-headship by appealing to Galatians 3:28: "there is neither male nor female." While in the eschaton, of which we are already members, that is true, until the redemption of our bodies we still participate in the first creation with its distinction between the sexes. The biblical instructions regarding the distinctive roles of men and women, of husbands and wives, address that obvious reality and serve the best interests of both sexes.

As a result of the Fall and God's judgment upon them, the woman desires to rule her husband and he seeks to dominate her (3:16b).[23] The solution to this tragic power struggle that divides the home is the new creation in Christ, in which the husband humbles himself and in love serves his wife, and the wife voluntarily submits herself to him in faithful obedience (Eph. 5:22). The rest of Scripture sustains hierarchy, not democracy or matriarchy.

God, who is over all, represents himself by masculine names and titles, not feminine. He identifies himself as Father, Son, and Spirit, not Parent, Child, and Spirit, nor Mother, Daughter, and Spirit. Jesus taught his church to address God as "Father" (Luke 11:2) and to baptize nations "in the name of the Father, and of the Son, and of the Holy Spirit" (Matt. 28:19). God's titles are King, not Queen; Lord, not Mistress.[24] God, not mortals, has the right to name himself. It is inexcusable hubris on the part of mortals to change the images by which the eternal God chooses to represent himself. We cannot change God's name or titles without committing idolatry, for we will have reimaged him in a way other than the metaphors and the incarnation by which he revealed himself. His representations and incarnation are inseparable from his being. Moreover, in contrast to male imagery, one cannot introduce feminine imagery without introducing sexual connotations. For example, in Hebrew grammar the masculine form is inclusivistic (i.e., with reference to animate beings it can be used of male and female), but the feminine form is marked (i.e., with reference to animate beings only the female is in view).[25]

In the mystery of Godhead, in which the three persons are both one

---

22. Waltke, "1 Timothy 2:8-15: Unique or Normative?"

23. I arrived at this interpretation, based on the same Hebrew expression in Genesis 4:7, independently from Susan T. Foh, *Woman and the Word of God: A Response to Biblical Feminism* (Phillipsburg, NJ: Presbyterian and Reformed Publishing Co., 1979), pp. 68f.

24. In Psalm 123:2 David uses the simile of a maid to a mistress, but he never uses "mistress" as a title for God.

25. Bruce K. Waltke and M. O'Connor, *An Introduction to Biblical Hebrew Syntax* (Winona Lake, IN: Eisenbrauns, 1990), p. 108.

and equal, the Son obeys the Father, and the Spirit obeys both. Paradoxically Jesus says both that "I and the Father are one" (John 10:30) and "the Father is greater than I" (John 14:28). Jesus veiled his own glory to follow the path of humble obedience (Phil. 2:6-11). The idea that hierarchy is an evil that can be transcended is a failed Marxist notion, not biblical teaching.

Although God gave Israel prophetesses, he did not give them priestesses in contrast to other religions in the ancient Near East. Recall it was the priests' duty to teach the Law of the Lord to the people (Deut. 17:11; 33:10) and the parents' duty to teach it in the home (6:7-8).

A woman had the right to make vows to the LORD independently from her husband, as in the case of Hannah, but the husband, in the case of a married woman, and the father, in the case of a young daughter living in her father's house (Num. 30:16), had the right to overrule it: "But if her husband overrules her on the day that he hears it, he shall make void her vow which she took . . . , and the LORD will release her" (30:8). A wife or daughter could not overrule the husband's or father's authority in the home by claiming she made a vow to the Lord, a higher authority than her male attachment, which she was obliged to fulfill. A direct vow to the Lord could not overrule their earthly authority. The Lord stands behind the authority of a husband or father. This is not because women are inferior, but to protect the male leadership of the home. That the ruling is based on male leadership, not on male superiority, can be seen in the provision that the vow of a woman who was without male attachment was as binding upon her as that upon a man (30:9).

It is on the spiritual foundation that husbands and wives submit to one another out of reverence for Christ that Paul specifies the relationship between a husband and his wife. They express their submission in ways appropriate to their sexuality. He expresses his submission to her by loving her as Christ loves the church, and she to him by obeying him in everything: "Wives, submit to your husbands as to the Lord. For the husband is the head of the wife as Christ is the head of the church, so also wives should submit to their husbands in everything" (Eph. 5:22-24). If, however, the husband denies God's authority over him, he undermines his own authority. His own authority is derivative and bestowed upon him to effect God's will on earth as it is in heaven. Should he seek to govern his home selfishly, not sacredly in accordance with God's revealed will, then the wife must obey God, the ultimate authority, not her husband (cf. Acts 5:29).

Peter holds up Sarah as an example of a godly wife. In her self-talk, not in polite address, she referred to Abraham as her lord (Gen. 18:12): "For this is the way the holy women of the past who put their hope in God used to make themselves beautiful. They were submissive to their own husbands, like Sarah, who obeyed Abraham and called him her master" (1 Pet. 3:1-6). These texts today in many circles are not politically correct, but they should not be neglected or explained away.

There are other texts in both testaments that teach that husbands have authority over their wives. For example, "the elder must be the husband of one wife" (1 Tim. 3:2), never ". . . the wife of one husband." One cannot appoint a wife as a leader of the church without upsetting this government, for if a wife were an elder her husband would be subject to her authority: "Obey your leaders and submit to their authority" (Heb. 13:17). Deborah, however, who was married, is one clear exception to "patriarchy" (Judg. 4:4-9). Probably, however, it is the exception that proves the rule. In addition to being a prophetess, Deborah was "judging" (i.e., "ruling") Israel. The narrator, however, makes his intention clear by carefully shaming the Israelite men at that time for their fear of assuming leadership. Note, for example, how Deborah shames Barak, the military commander of Israel's army, for his failure to assume leadership. After she mediated God's command to him to join battle with Sisera, commander of the Canaanite army, Barak replies: "If you go with me, I will go; but if you don't go with me, I won't go." To which Deborah responds, "Very well . . . I will go with you. But because of the way you are going about this [i.e., full of fear] the honor will not be yours; the LORD will hand Sisera over to a woman [i.e., to shame him]" (cf. Judg. 9:54). She did not seek to overthrow patriarchy through her gifts but to support it. Apparently, the LORD raised up this exceptional woman, who was full of faith, to shame the men of Israel for their lack of faith, as such faith is essential to leadership in the holy nation. If so, the story aims to reprove unfaithful men for not taking leadership, not to present an alternative norm to male authority. The story also shows, however, that the Spirit of the Lord is above culture and not restricted by normative patriarchy.

We are now in a position to draw the conclusion that the church ought not to appoint women to the office of ruler. The distinction between ordaining them to ministry, but not to office, is important, but too often neglected in the discussion about the role of women in the church.

Conclusion

According to my interpretation of Scripture the Bible commends the equality of women with men as equals in being, dignity, gifts, and ministry. The Spirit validates it by calling and gifting women to the same ministries as men.

However, Scripture condemns the arrogance of anyone, male or female, who autonomously names God, the world, and self. It also contends against those who see marriage as a galling bondage or who look down upon motherhood within the structure of marriage as a lesser ministry than ministries outside the home. Finally, we find the insistence on the equality of wives with husbands in authority and leadership as unbiblical. In my understanding of Scripture it is essential to the message of the gospel that husbands love their wives and that wives submit to the authority of their husbands. If husbands and wives are equal in leadership, how does the husband exemplify a new model of leadership wherein the ruler becomes a servant (Matt. 20:25-28)? And if a woman seeks to become empowered as an equal to her husband in authority, how does she show the submission of the church to its Lord (Eph. 5:24)? Tragically, the elders in the church and husbands in the home, often out of a distorted emphasis on their headship and their depreciation of the Spirit's gifts that empower women to minister, have both consciously and unconsciously suppressed women and quenched the Spirit. Feminist perspectives have rightly exposed this abuse. Again, however, the problem is our failure to interpret the Bible accurately. The model of leadership is that of a servant. Jesus models the servant King who so loved his queen that he died for her. The willingness to do the grand gesture of dying for a loved one becomes practical to the extent that one practices self-surrendering service as a way of life. C. S. Lewis wryly observes: "The real danger [in the Christian doctrine of man's *imitatio Christi* in marriage] is not that husbands will grasp [the crown of thorns] too eagerly, but that they will allow or compel their wives to usurp it."[26] The "servant" empowers his wife to use her spiritual gifts to their fullest potential. On the other hand, the Bible instructs the wife to respect her husband as her lord, which entails obeying him in everything as we have qualified it above. It is important to note the Bible neither instructs the woman to manipulate the man to serve her, to be the proverbial "neck that turns the head," nor the husband to have his wife in subjection, to be the head that lords itself over the body. Serving and obeying in mutual subjection are inward beauties worked in our hearts, consciences, behaviors, and customs by the Holy Spirit. These are ideals for which we strive, though recognizing they will never be fully attained any more than any of the other perfections of holiness. Our failure to attain them should be accompanied with repentance and renewed faith, not by cynicism, despair, or seeking new social structures.

26. C. S. Lewis, *The Four Loves* (London: Geoffrey Bles), p. 98, cited by Jonathan Mills in personal correspondence.

I am a member of a church where I submit to women leaders, whom I trust and respect, because, even though I disagree with the practice, I am called upon to endeavor to keep the unity of the Spirit until we come to the full knowledge of Christ (Eph. 4:1-13). It is wrong to divide the body of Christ, which confesses Jesus as Lord and believes in its heart that God raised him from the dead, on such nonmoral and nonessential issues for the unity of the church as modes of baptism, eschatology, forms of government, and belief in the continuation or cessation of gifts. However, I ask my church, as individual members and not as a political body, and others like it, because we "want to find out what is acceptable to the Lord" (5:10), to reassess for themselves whether our practice of ordaining women to rule us is biblically justified.

Birds

Origin

It is agreed that birds appeared on this planet before man and in connection with the fish, whether one argues the case for the theory of evolution, which places the origin of birds at roughly 125,000,000 years ago, or for the doctrine of a creation in seven literal days. Just as the Bible associates the fashioning of the luminaries on the fourth day with the making of light on the first day, and the creation of land creatures, beasts, and man on the sixth day with the making of land and vegetation on the third day, so also it parallels the bringing forth of the fish and fowl on the fifth day with the separation of the water from the atmosphere on the second day. The fossils *Archeopteryx* and *Archaeornis* are often regarded as connecting links in the evolution of the reptile to the bird. However, they must be classified as birds because they had feathers, wings for flying, feet for perching, and were warm-blooded. Their lizard-like tails, teeth, and claws on wings may be features only of extinct species of birds.

Because birds were created by God (Gen. 1:20f.) and continue to owe their fecundity to his blessings (v. 22), they are both owned and known by him (Ps. 50:10f.; Matt. 10:29), and they are called upon to praise him along with all his creation (Ps. 148:1-14).

Because God's spokesman in Genesis refused to reduce Yahweh to a nature deity, but rather insisted that he was the Creator of the cosmos, the Is-

Previously published in *The International Standard Bible Encyclopedia*, ed. G. W. Bromiley, vol. 1 (Grand Rapids: Eerdmans, 1979), pp. 511-13.

raelites avoided the folly of the priests of the surrounding nature religions, who reduced man to the point of worshiping birds (Exod. 20:3f.; Rom. 1:23). Moreover, by separating the Creator from his creation, the Hebrews described birds not as gods empowered to act in unpredictable, magical ways, but as creatures of an orderly, predictable universe. The modern ornithologists R. C. Murphy and D. Amadon have said: "To judge from the Old Testament, the inheritors of the Land of Canaan were extraordinarily good naturalists."[1] Concerning the description of the behavior of an ostrich in Job 39:13-18 they note: "Few readers of the Bible realize how exact is this passage" (Parmelee, p. 204).

Identification

Created in the image of the eternal Ruler, man is given the mandate by him to "have dominion" over the creation, including the birds (Gen. 1:26-28). To achieve this aim, God brought the creatures to man, and by naming them, presumably according to their unique qualities, man began the process of reducing the world to a conceptual order.[2] Unfortunately this catalog by the first naturalist, whose powers of observation were not jaded by the Fall, could not be recorded. But modern ornithologists of Palestinian birds resumed the task, beginning with Frederick Hasselquist in 1750. His list of fifteen birds was considerably expanded by Henry B. Tristram in his classic work, *Flora and Fauna of Palestine* (1884), to include 348 species. F. S. Bodenheimer (1953) listed 413 species and subspecies (cf. Ps. 104:24).

But the exegete's task of relating the birds mentioned in the Bible to these known species is complicated by two facts. First, the biblical writers speak of only some fifty birds, and therefore must have classified more than one species in some instances under one label. Second, the names mentioned once or twice with little clue as to their identity will always remain a difficulty.[3]

---

1. Cited by A. Parmelee, *All the Birds of the Bible* (New York: Harper, 1969), p. 20. Hereafter page references to this book are given parenthetically in the text.

2. G. von Rad, *Old Testament Theology*, trans. D. M. G. Stalker, vol. 1 (New York: Harper, 1962), p. 158.

3. For G. R. Driver's identification of the birds listed in Leviticus 11:13-19, see my article "Abomination, Birds of," in *ISBE*, 1:14.

In Legal Literature

The divine law specified that those too poor to offer animals from the herd or flock be allowed instead to offer turtledoves (Heb. *tôr*) or young pigeons (Heb. *yōnā*, covering all species of the large family designated *Columbidae*) as a burnt offering (Lev. 1:14; 14:22) — either as a sin offering or in connection with the reparation offering (Lev. 5:7), in the ritual cleansing of the leper (Lev. 14:22, 30), and for other purifications (Lev. 12:6, 8; 15:14, 29; Num. 6:10). The turtledove and young pigeons are cousins, but their habits are different. The turtledove is a wild bird, never domesticated like the pigeon, for it has strong migratory habits (cf. Song of Sol. 2:12). Only from April to October can turtledoves be obtained, for they spend the winter in Africa. Therefore the pigeon had to be authorized for winter sacrifices. The adjective "young" has significance. The common rock doves are extremely wary, fly fast, and cannot easily be trapped. But at any time of the year a search among the rocks discovers nests of these abundant birds with helpless young. In the rituals for cleansing a leper or a house, two birds (*ṣippōr*, meaning any little bird) were used (Lev. 14:4-7, 49-53). In each case one was killed and the other let go. Perhaps this is a picture of the one "who was put to death for our trespasses and raised for our justification" (Rom. 4:25).

The law also distinguished the cultically acceptable birds from those cultically unacceptable (Lev. 11:13-19, 46; 20:25; Deut. 14:11-18). Israel was enjoined to eat clean birds (Deut. 14:11), i.e., those that fed on grain; but they were forbidden to eat birds of prey that fed on carrion or blood, because both were cultically unclean (Lev. 17:10-14).[4]

Finally, the law forbade robbing a nest and taking the mother bird as well (Deut. 22:6-7). This commandment, like the fifth of the Decalogue (Exod. 20:12), also has the promise "that it may go well with you, and that you may live long." This law was not only humane but also prudent, for it helped to conserve the land's natural heritage.

In Narrative Literature

The accuracy with which birds are described in the historical literature is striking. The book of Genesis says that Noah used first the raven and then the dove to determine whether the water had subsided (Gen. 8:6-13).

4. See "Abomination, Birds of," in *ISBE*, 1:14-15.

Whereas the raven continued flying to and fro from the ark until the water subsided, the dove returned quickly to the ark the first time she was let go, returned with a newly plucked olive leaf in her beak the second time, and did not return the third time. A. Heidel noted the superiority of the biblical account to the parallel account in the Babylonian Gilgamesh Epic where Utnapishtim, called "the exceedingly wise," first sent a dove, then a swallow, and finally a raven.[5] Noah, whose wisdom is nowhere mentioned, showed much more knowledge about birds. Parmelee wrote: "In selecting the raven as his first scout Noah made an excellent choice, for [the raven] is a powerful and unusually astute bird. . . . With a wing spread of four feet and great strength and endurance, ravens survive where smaller, weaker birds perish . . . they can fly without rest for long periods of time, covering immense distances. . . . Because they have heavy beaks and can eat almost anything including carrion, Noah's raven would have found enough to eat in the floating wreckage of a flooded world" (Parmelee, pp. 54f.). The dove, believed to be the ancestor of the message-carrying homing pigeon, was an excellent second selection. "When it flies it attains remarkable speed in its first moments and can cover long distances very rapidly. It nests in cliffs and on ledges, preferring pleasant valleys to barren wastes or wind-swept mountains" (Parmelee, p. 55).

In the episode where Yahweh confirmed his promise to give Abram the land of Canaan, the relatively defenseless turtledove and fledgling lay exposed under the birds of prey that characteristically swooped down upon them (Gen. 15:9-12). The attack probably continued until nightfall, for the sudden dive of one is a signal to the others who in turn transmit the signal until hungry birds from miles around gather at the feast. Their arrival, however, would have ceased at sunset, for recent experiments have shown that carrion-feeding birds locate their food by sight rather than smell (Parmelee, p. 63). Throughout the attack Abram "blew" them away. Perhaps this incident is a cameo of Israel's future history in which foreign powers attempt to frustrate God's promise to give Israel the land, but by his vigilant care Israel possesses it.

The description of the very edible quail (undoubtedly the common quail, *Coturnix communis* or *Coturnix dactylisonans*) that provided meat for the Israelites in the wilderness also corresponds accurately to modern observation in its details — the great multitude of the birds, their use of wind in

---

5. A. Heidel, *The Gilgamesh Epic and Old Testament Parallels* (Chicago: University of Chicago Press, 1963), pp. 252f.

their migration (during March and April, and August and September), the lowness of their flight, the ease with which they are netted when weary. "Pliny told the story of a boat crossing the Mediterranean on which so many quails alighted that it sank" (Parmelee, p. 76).

Both references to birds in the description of Solomon's glory are of uncertain derivation and meaning. The "fatted fowl" (Heb. *barburîm* '*ăbûsîm*, 1 Kings 4:23 [MT 5:3]) may be derived from a root meaning "be white." L. Kohler proposed that it is cognate with Arabic *abu burbur* ("the cuckoo"), presumably referring to a tidbit like the Roman dish of larks' tongues. J. Gray suggested "geese." G. R. Driver offered the best suggestion in deriving it from Arabic *birbir*, "chicken." This prolific bird, valuable for its eggs, originated as a wild red jungle fowl in India, Burma, and Malaya and is believed to have become domesticated before 2700 BC. It was carried from its original home to all parts of the world and has become the world's most valuable bird (Parmelee, p. 122). The peacocks (Heb. *tukkiyîm*) mentioned in 1 Kings 10:22 may be baboons, according to W. F. Albright.[6]

Rizpah had to protect the carcasses of her sons from the birds of prey only by day, for, as stated, birds of prey depend on sight. At night she had to protect them from the beasts of the field (2 Sam. 21:10).

The ravens in the Elijah pericope (1 Kings 17:3-6) are also depicted according to the facts of their natural history. "It has been noted that ravens and other members of the crow family often store surplus food in rocky crevices or beneath a covering of leaves," and this habit may explain their action when commanded by Yahweh to feed Elijah (Parmelee, p. 149).

In accordance with the law (Lev. 12:6, 8; 15:14), Mary and Joseph, after the birth of Jesus, offered for Mary's purification two turtledoves or two young pigeons (Luke 2:24). This information indicates that Mary and Joseph had to avail themselves of the provision for those too poor to offer a lamb to substitute a bird.

It is also noteworthy that when Jesus cleansed the temple, the unscrupulous dealers and moneychangers — who were issued licenses by the Sadducees — were involved in the sale of pigeons, the sacrifice of the poor (Matt. 21:12; Mark 11:15; cf. Luke 19:45f. and John 2:14-16).

The Holy Spirit descended on Jesus at his baptism "in bodily form like a dove" (Luke 3:22) to symbolize his character. The dove, as indicated above, is wise and strong (cf. Isa. 11:2) but at the same time guileless (Gk. *akéraios*, lit. "unmixed," Matt. 10:16).

---

6. J. B. Gray, *1 and 2 Kings*, OTL (Philadelphia: Westminster, 1970), pp. 142f., 262-68.

The cock, which since the days of Solomon had become common in Palestine, appears in the account of Peter's denial of Christ (Mark 14:30, 66-72). True to its character, this bird welcomed the light of day on the morning mankind revealed the depth of its own darkness.

In Prophetic and Poetic Literature

The preachers and poets in the Bible made frequent use of the habits and habitat of birds to illustrate their message.

One of the most frequently mentioned birds is the griffon-vulture or golden eagle (Heb. *nešer*). The superb protection and care of Yahweh for his people is likened to that of a *nešer* (Exod. 19:4; Deut. 32:11-13). The nests of these birds are built in inaccessible places with great skill. The parent bird guards the nest with great ferocity, incubates the eggs by shielding them from too much sun and from cold winds, and feeds the nestlings until they are large enough to fly. Then the parent stirs up the nest and lures the fledglings out of it for their first flight. Sometimes the adult birds hover over them and flutter encouragingly around them. Although there is no reliable report of any bird actually flying with a smaller bird on its back, the fledglings sometimes appear to be carried, so that the poet speaks of the *nešer* bearing the young on its wings. The Hebrew poets also saw in the wings of these majestic birds a symbol of God's redeeming activity and of his care and protection of his people (Parmelee, pp. 99f.; cf. Ps. 17:8; 91:4; cf. Isa. 31:5). (The wings of God probably refer to the protective wings of the cherubim [Ps. 36:7; 57:1; 61:4; 63:7; Ruth 2:12].)

In likening the speed of Saul and Jonathan to the *nešer* David may have had in mind the golden eagle, which, pressing its wings against its sides, dives from great heights upon its victim, "usually taking it by surprise and striking it dead in an instant with its powerful, sharp talons" (Parmelee, p. 118; cf. 2 Sam. 1:23). "Jeremiah warned of a foe that would approach with an eagle's speed" (Parmelee, p. 157; cf. Jer. 4:13; cf. Hab. 1:8), and Job lamented that his days go by like an eagle swooping on its prey (Job 9:25f.).

The flight of other birds is also used in comparisons (cf., e.g., Jer. 48:9; Ezek. 13:20; Hos. 9:11). Birds' nests are used to illustrate security (Ps. 104:16f.; Prov. 27:8; Isa. 16:2; Jer. 49:16). "Birds were quick to notice that nests built within the sacred area of the Temple . . . were inviolate. Here both man and bird found peace and security in God's house" (Parmelee, p. 161; cf. Ps. 84:3f.). The proverb that compares the one who "gets riches but not by right" to "the partridge that gathers a brood which she did not hatch" (Jer. 17:11) refers to an erroneous popular belief widespread among the Israelites, without saying anything about its accuracy. The migratory habit of birds illustrates the return of Israel from the Diaspora (Hos. 11:11) and contrasts sharply with the ignorance of Israel (Jer. 8:7). Birds of prey feeding on carrion illustrate the fate of Israel (Deut. 28:26), of the northern kings (1 Kings 14:7-11; 16:4; 21:22-24), of the house of the Lord (Hos. 8:1), of Egypt (Ezek. 29:5; 32:4), of Babylon at the hands of Cyrus (Isa. 46:11), of Gog (Ezek. 39:4), and of God's enemies at the end of time (Ezek. 39:17-20).

Birds, as part of the ecology, also illustrate the physical conditions of Israel. Songbirds suggest a well-cared-for land (mentioned only in Ps. 104:1-12; Song of Sol. 2:11f.), but the absence of such birds indicates desolation (Jer. 4:25; 9:10; 12:4; Zeph. 1:3) and birds of prey indicate a state of chaos (Isa. 34:11, 13-15; Ps. 102:6f.). Likewise, the sounds of a dove or a raven suggest a melancholy or ominous situation (Isa. 59:11; Ezek. 7:16; Zeph. 2:14). Conditions during the times of the writing prophets can be inferred by their failure to refer to songbirds.

Job, an astute naturalist, saw the wisdom of the Creator in the ways of birds (12:7; 39:26-30). Job's poor opinion of the ostrich and the raven as parents was based on appearance rather than reality (39:14f.; 38:41).

The use of about a dozen different words for "net," "snares," "gins," and "traps" shows the popularity of this figure for destruction (cf. Hos. 9:8; Jer. 5:26-28). "Egyptian wall paintings illustrate the method of suddenly lowering a net over ducks resting on the water. Flocks of quails were often captured in nets thrown over the bushes in which they had taken refuge. When the birds flew up they became entangled in the meshes of the net" (Parmelee, p. 193). Birds were also hunted with bows and arrows (Ps. 11:1f.). When out in the wilderness David likened Saul's pursuit of him to the hunt for a partridge (1 Sam. 26:20), he probably had in mind Hey's sand partridge, whose range is almost confined to this area. Deliverance is portrayed as an escape from the fowler either by flight (Ps. 55:6), breaking his snare (Ps. 124:7; cf. Ps. 91:4), or being let loose (Prov. 6:5).

In Apocalyptic Literature and Visions

Birds appear in visions as symbols. The majestic, high-flying eagle symbolizes heavenly beings (Ezek. 1:5-11; 10:14; Rev. 4:7). The wings of the eagle and stork symbolize great speed and/or strength (Dan. 7:4; Zech. 5:9; Rev.

12:13f.). "Actually, even larger birds are able to lift only a little weight in addition to their own. It is believed that if the strongest eagles can lift as much as ten pounds, they cannot carry it far" (Parmelee, p. 156).

Birds in a tree symbolize the subject people in the kingdom and empire (Ezek. 31:6; Dan. 4:1-12). God's command to Peter to eat unclean birds in the vision in the house of the tanner (an unclean trade) at Joppa, the Jewish port, teaches him that he should no longer consider unclean the Gentiles he is about to meet at Caesarea, the Roman port (Acts 10).

In the Teaching of Jesus

Like the prophets and poets of the OT, Jesus used the birds to illustrate his teachings. He described the care he desired to provide by comparing it to the protection given by the wings of a hen over her brood (Matt. 23:37). He illustrated a disciple's life without earthly comfort by contrasting it with that of the bird that has a nest (Matt. 8:20). W. M. Thomson noted that the bushes in the area around Capernaum where he taught this lesson "are stuffed full of bird's nests."[7] Jesus also likened the destruction of the last day to the gathering of vultures (Matt. 24:28), and illustrated the day of judgment by a fowler's net (Luke 21:35).

He deduced God's care for man and the value he placed upon him from his care for the birds (Matt. 6:25f.) and from the value he placed on the common sparrow (Luke 12:6f.). His teaching contrasts markedly with Cicero's statement: "the gods care for the great, but they neglect the lowly" (cited by Parmelee, p. 245).

Bibliography

Candale, G. S. *NBD*, s.v.

Driver, G. R. "Birds in the OT," *PEQ* 87 (1955): 5-20.

————. "Once Again: Birds in the Bible," *Palestine Exploration Quarterly* 90 (1958): 56-58.

Gray, J. B. *1 and 2 Kings*, OTL (Philadelphia: Westminster, 1970).

Heidel, A. *The Gilgamesh Epic and Old Testament Parallels* (Chicago: University of Chicago Press, 1963).

7. W. M. Thomson, *The Land and the Book*, vol. 2 (New York: Harper and Brothers, 1882), p. 410.

Parmelee, A. *All the Birds of the Bible* (New York: Harper, 1969).

Thomson, W. M. *The Land and the Book,* vol. 2 (New York: Harper and Brothers, 1882).

von Rad, G. *Old Testament Theology,* trans. D. M. G. Stalker, vol. 1 (New York: Harper, 1962).

Theonomy in Relation to Dispensational and Covenant Theologies

In 1749 Jonathan Edwards said, "There is perhaps no part of divinity attended with so much intricacy, and wherein orthodox divines do so much differ as stating the precise agreement and differences between the two dispensations of Moses and Christ."[1] About a century later dispensationalism resolved the tension between them by divorcing them, and more than two centuries later theonomy remarried them. Meredith Kline observed:

> This theory of theonomic politics stands at the opposite end of the spectrum of error from dispensationalism. The latter represents an extreme failure to do justice to the continuity between the old and new covenants. Chalcedon's error, no less extreme or serious, is a failure to do justice to the discontinuity between the old and new covenants.[2]

In this chapter I aim to appraise critically the views of dispensationalism, Reformed theology, and theonomy with regard to the role of the law in social ethics, including its role to define the duty of government officials and to inform civil legislation. One cannot appraise these views without also taking into consideration their views of the church-state relationship and of es-

---

1. Jonathan Edwards, "Inquiry Concerning Qualifications for Communion," in *The Works of President Edwards*, 4 vols., 8th ed. (New York: Leavitt & Allen, 1858), 1:160. Cited by Daniel P. Fuller, *Gospel and Law: Contrast or Continuum?* (Grand Rapids: Eerdmans, 1980), pp. 5-6.

2. Meredith C. Kline, "Comments on an Old-New Error," *WTJ* 41 (1978): 172-73.

Previously published in *Theology: A Reformed Critique,* ed. William S. Barker and W. Robert Godfrey (Grand Rapids: Zondervan, 1990), pp. 59-86. Reprinted by permission.

chatology. I will present the views of each theology, a brief presentation of some arguments supporting it, and finally an evaluation of some of its strengths and weaknesses.

Dispensationalism

Views

Dispensationalists believe that God is pursuing three distinct programs: one for the Jews, one for the church, and one for the nations. Paul, they argue, by distinguishing these three groups in 1 Corinthians 10:32, implies these separate economies: "Do not cause anyone to stumble, whether Jews, Greeks, or the church of God." The touchstone of dispensationalism is its conviction that God's dealings with Israel are totally separate from his dealings with the church. According to dispensationalists, God administered Israel by the law, and the church by grace. C. I. Scofield wrote:

> The most obvious and striking division of the word of truth is that between Law and Grace. Indeed, these contrasting principles *characterize* the two most important dispensations — Jewish and Christian. . . . Scripture never, in *any* dispensation, mingles these two principles (emphasis his).[3]

According to dispensationalists, the law of Moses is a unity and was meant for *the distinct people,* Israel, for *a distinct* time, from Sinai (Exod. 19:1) until it was nailed to the cross and was canceled by the death of Christ (Col. 2:14), and for *a distinct place,* "in the sworn-land" (Deut. 6:1).

The grace-administered church, according to dispensationalists, began at Pentecost and will cease at its rapture prior to the millennial reign of Christ.

Opponents of dispensationalists often accuse them of being antinomian. The charge is largely both uncharitable and untrue.[4] Dispensationalists include the "higher teachings" of the New Testament for the church as

3. C. I. Scofield, *Rightly Dividing the Word of Truth* (Findlay, OH: Fundamental Truth Publishers, 1940), p. 5.

4. R. J. Rushdoony uses even more inflammatory, divisive, and un-Christian rhetoric when he falsely asserts: "dispensationalism is . . . either evolutionary or polytheistic or both," in *The Institutes of Biblical Law* (Nutley, NJ: Craig, 1973), p. 18.

part of the grace principle. R. Laird Harris rightly censures theonomist Greg Bahnsen on this point:

> It is hardly fair to charge dispensationalists with being antinomian. . . , for they speak of being "inlawed to Christ." Dispensationalists do emphasize the ethical teachings of the New Testament and the example as well as the commands of Christ. It is obvious also that dispensationalists, like other true Christians, lead lives of admirable probity and high moral standards. They are not against God's law in this age, but rather believe that God's law in Moses' age was a unified code which is transcended today.[5]

Dispensationalists normally do not discuss either the relationship of the church and the state or God's mode of administering the nations, a principal concern of theonomists and the focus of this chapter. Surprisingly, even in his essay "A Dispensational Response to Theonomy," Robert Lightner does not clearly set forth his own views on these matters.[6] It can be inferred, however, from their system of theology and from observation that dispensationalists separate church and state after the radical model of Roger Williams and regard states as being governed by the eternal moral law, which, in contrast to Reformed theologians, they do not equate with the Ten Commandments. In their view, though the nations are a part of God's universal kingdom, they belong to the "world," which stands in black-and-white opposition to the church and is under the rule of Satan (Luke 4:5-6). Using H. Richard Niebuhr's models of analyzing Christ and culture, many dispensationalists follow the model in 1 John and Tertullian, that of "Christ Against Culture."[7] Nevertheless, in this view, though the church and culture, including the state, stand in opposition to one another, the state is part of God's universal kingdom, administering justice according to natural law (Romans 13). In summary, dispensationalists are concerned with saving the church out of the world before the Rapture rather than with transforming culture. When a ship is sinking, they popularly argue, one does not shine the brass but puts out the lifeboats.

5. R. Laird Harris, "Theonomy in Christian Ethics: A Review of Greg L. Bahnsen's Book," *Presbyterion* 5 (1979): 4-5.

6. Robert P. Lightner, "A Dispensational Response to Theonomy," *BSac* 143 (1986): 228-45.

7. H. Richard Niebuhr, *Christ and Culture* (New York: Harper & Brothers, 1951), pp. 45-82.

Finally, with regard to eschatology, dispensationalists believe that after the church is raptured, God will once again restore Israel in the "sworn-land" for a thousand years. At this time the church will reign with Christ over the Jews, the subjects of the kingdom. This kingdom of God will be administered according to the provisions of the new covenant, which contains the substance of the unified Mosaic law, including its ceremonies, but differs from it in containing better promises and better provisions. In this millennial kingdom the nations will subject themselves to the rule of perfected Israel.

Argumentation

The dispensational system of theology is founded on the "plain, normal" sense of Scripture. Even the hermeneutical principle, the analogy of faith, cannot supplant this foundation. Charles Ryrie explains their rule: "This means interpretation which gives to every word the same meaning it would have in normal usage. . . ."[8] In Micah 4:1, for example, "the mountain of the LORD's temple" must refer to the mount dominated today by the Dome of the Rock and cannot refer to the heavenly Jerusalem. Likewise, "Israel" means Abraham's physical seed and not the church. With this hermeneutical tool dispensationalists discern God's distinct programs for Israel and the church. Ryrie says, "Normal interpretation leads to clear distinction between words, concepts, peoples, and economies."[9]

The distinction between Israel and the church now turns around to become itself the hermeneutical principle in rightly dividing the Word of truth. J. N. Darby wrote that the distinction between Israel and the church is the "hinge upon which the subject and the understanding of Scripture turns."[10] The whole is greater than the sum of its parts, and so specific Scriptures are "pigeonholed" as belonging to either Israel or the church. The law, it is concluded, belongs to the Jew and not to the church. Lewis Sperry Chafer taught:

> The Bible student must recognize the difference between a primary and a secondary application of the Word of God. Only those portions of Scripture which are directly addressed to the child of God under grace are to

8. Charles Caldwell Ryrie, *Dispensationalism Today* (Chicago: Moody, 1965), p. 86.

9. Ryrie, *Dispensationalism Today*, p. 98.

10. J. N. Darby, "Reflections Upon the Prophetic Inquiry," in *The Collected Writings of J. N. Darby, Prophetic*, no. 1, ed. William Kelly (London: CAPS, reprint 1962), p. 18.

be given a personal or primary application. . . . It does not follow that the Christian is appointed by God to conform to those governing principles which were the will of God for people of other dispensations.[11]

Strengths

One may commend dispensationalists for recognizing that laws are mutable according to the end for which they were designed. If the objectives and situations for which a law was originally designed cease or are changed, then the law either ceases or may be changed. The New Testament clearly teaches that Christ inaugurated a new age, an age in which God no longer deals primarily with the Jews in the sworn-land but with Gentiles in the world and that he no longer administers his elect by the law of Moses to the extent that it was written for Israel's existence in the land. The Apostle Paul clearly teaches in a number of passages that God is not administering the church by the law and that the law has been done away with (Rom. 6:14; 7:4-7; 2 Cor. 3:6-13; Gal. 3:17-25; 5:18). Moreover, our Lord implied the coming of the new situation when he set aside both divorce, which had been allowed by Moses (Matt. 5:31-32; 19:1-12), and Israel's dietary laws (Mark 7:18-19). The Jerusalem council set aside circumcision and "the law of Moses" (Acts 15:5 — probably a reference to Israel's judicial and ceremonial laws) except that the people were enjoined "to abstain from food polluted by idols, from sexual immorality [probably a reference to Israel's laws of consanguinity], from the meat of strangled animals and from blood" (15:20). Correlatively, dispensationalists are to be commended for carefully distinguishing the specific situations for which specific texts were written and for distinguishing carefully between their primary interpretation and their secondary application to other situations.

They are also to be applauded for not depreciating the role of natural law and conscience. Before the Law was given at Sinai, the *Torah* implies the operation of conscience. Cain was found guilty of murder and sentenced (Genesis 4), while Enoch and Noah were found righteous and rewarded (5:24; 6:8-9). Centuries before the Law was given at Sinai, Abraham asked in connection with the righteous people living in Sodom and Gomorrah: "Will not the Judge of all the earth do right?" (Gen. 18:25), and later in connection with the moral atmosphere of Abimelech's court, which he judged as subnor-

---

11. Lewis Sperry Chafer, *Major Bible Themes* (Philadelphia: Sunday School Times, 1926), pp. 97-98.

mal, he said, "There is surely no fear of God in this place, and they will kill me because of my wife" (20:11). In the New Testament Paul explicates the implication of these texts:

> Indeed, when the Gentiles, who do not have the law, do by nature things required by the law, they are a law for themselves, even though they do not have the law, since they show that the requirements of the law are written on their hearts, their consciences also bearing witness, and their thoughts now accusing, now even defending them. (Rom. 2:14-15)

Weaknesses

On the other hand, dispensationalists commit a fundamental hermeneutical blunder when they simplistically base their views on an ill-defined notion of "the normal, plain" meaning of Scripture and, even worse, against its own fundamental principle, disallow the analogy-of-faith principle that could correct their errors. Vern Poythress brilliantly perceives that they read the text not "plainly" but "flatly," failing to see adequately the symbolic import.[12] For example, the temple on Mount Zion always participated in the heavenly reality and cannot be distinguished from it (cf. Heb. 12:22). Moreover, dispensationalists fail to appreciate fully the significance that the church has become fellow heirs of Israel's covenants through its union with Abraham's Seed, Jesus Christ (cf. Rom. 4:16-17; 11:11-24; Gal. 3:26-29; Eph. 2:19). Paul's illustration of the one olive tree in Romans 11 suggests that the elect comprise one covenant community rooted in the Patriarchs, and not two, and that the covenant community is essentially not a national group, because the Gentiles, who are not treated as political states, are grafted into it.

With regard to their handling of the law, dispensationalists, while tacitly acknowledging such verses as Romans 3:21 and 7:12, in practice give inadequate attention to the truth that the law is "holy, righteous, and good." Furthermore, they tend to obscure the truth that today Christ is the mediator of the new covenant (Heb. 8:6), a covenant that assumes the provisions of the law (cf. Jer. 31:33-34) but is superior to it because, unlike the old covenant, which Moses wrote on stone depending on Israel's faithfulness, Christ with the Spirit of the living God writes on the fleshly tablets of the heart

12. Vern Poythress, *Understanding Dispensationalists* (Grand Rapids: Zondervan, 1987).

(2 Cor. 3:3). The new covenant is also superior because it depends on God's faithfulness to fulfill the law for his elect saints (Heb. 8:6). In this connection we should note that dispensationalists also slight the truth that the church, composed of both Jews and Gentiles, is baptized into our Lord Jesus Christ, who is Abraham's physical seed, and so, in a very real sense, both Jews and Gentiles are Abraham's seed (Gal. 3:26-29). The Lord Jesus Christ is the true "Israel" and "Judah" (cf. John 15:1), and so his body, the church, is the "Israel" and "Judah" with whom the new covenant is made (Jer. 31:31). Then, too, dispensationalists fail to note that "the law" itself distinguishes between the moral law, the judicial law, and the ceremonial law, as we shall see, and that only the last two types are conditioned in time and space. Finally, the New Testament strongly implies that the church is bound, albeit through the power of the Spirit, to fulfill the moral law (cf. Rom. 13:8-10; Eph. 6:2) and the general equity of its other laws (cf. 1 Cor. 9:8-10). The moral law condemns sinners — note Paul's application of the Ten Commandments to his sinful generation in 1 Timothy 1:8-10 — and so drives them to Christ for his justification that saves them from its condemnation and for his sanctification that fulfills its righteousness.

Dispensationalism is also to be censured for its lack of concern about the lordship of Christ over all society. This indifference can be seen in its failure to address the questions of church-state relationships and of the ethical principles that ought to guide the state. Following the model of Roger Williams, they relegate religion to the chapel and neglect the transforming power of Scripture to guide society in education, music, art, science, and politics. They restrict Christ's lordship because they fail to grasp the changing circumstances of the church from an oppressed minority in New Testament times to a reigning majority in later church history.

With regard to eschatology, dispensationalists commit the fundamental error of leaving the Reformed principle that unclear texts must be interpreted in the light of clear ones, and, instead, they interpret the clear texts of the New Testament epistles in the light of the unclear symbols of apocalyptic works such as Daniel and Revelation. Not one clear text in the New Testament teaches either that Israel will be restored to the land, or that Israel will be restored as a nation, or that there will be a millennial reign of Christ after this age, which is called by the apostles "the last days" (i.e., the last stretch of historical time) (Acts 2:16-17; Heb. 1:2). No word in Scripture depicts the consummate glory of Christ as an earthly King ruling over the restored nation of Israel. This silence, after the Lord had promised that the Spirit would guide the apostles into all truth and bring glory to Christ (John 14:26; 16:12-

15), is deafening! The New Testament teaches that the new covenant is in effect now (Hebrews 8) and that the shadows of the Old Testament law have been done away with forever (Hebrews 9–10). The attempt to link the Golden Age anticipated by the prophets with the millennium envisioned in Revelation 20 is a desperate one. None of the characteristics of the apocalyptic millennium — resurrected martyrs judging, living, and reigning with Christ in heaven — link it with the Old Testament kingdom promises, a remarkable absence in the New Testament book that shows more links with the Old Testament than any other book.

Reformed Theology

Views

Reformed theologians confess that the elect participate in a covenant of grace that transcends dispensations. In this covenant, according to the Westminster Confession of Faith, "God freely offered unto sinners life and salvation by Jesus Christ, requiring of them faith in him that they may be saved."[13]

Reformed theologians regard the nonelect as standing under condemnation for having failed to keep the covenant of works made with Adam, humankind's federal head. According to the Westminster Confession of Faith, "the first covenant made with man was a covenant of works, wherein life was promised to Adam, and in him to his posterity, upon the condition of perfect and personal obedience."[14] Humankind, however, fell in Adam and can find salvation only through the gift of faith whereby it accepts the covenant of grace.

In this system the law has a twofold purpose. On the one hand, for the nonelect, much like the covenant of works, it reiterates God's demands. The law says: "Keep my decrees and laws, for the man who obeys them will live by them" (Lev. 18:5). The Westminster Confession says,

> God gave Adam a law, as a covenant of works, by which he bound him and all his posterity to personal, entire, exact, and perpetual obedience; promised life upon the fulfilling, and threatened death upon the breach

---

13. "The Westminster Confession of Faith, AD 1647," in *The Creeds of Christendom*, ed. Philip Schaff, 4th ed. (New York: Harper & Brothers, 1877), 3:617; 7:3. Hereafter WCF.
14. WCF, 2:2.

of it. . . . This law, after his fall, continued to be a perfect rule of righteousness; and as such was delivered by God upon Mount Sinai in ten commandments. . . . The moral law doth forever bind all . . . to the obedience thereof.[15]

On the other hand, for the elect, whom the Spirit of Christ subdues and who are enabled "to do that freely and cheerfully which the will of God, revealed in the law, requireth to be done,"[16] the law functions as an aspect of the covenant of grace. The Confession puts it this way:

Although true believers be not under the law as a covenant of works, to be thereby justified or condemned; yet is it of great use to them, as well as to others; in that, as a rule of life, informing them of the will of God and their duty, it directs and binds them to walk accordingly; discovering also the sinful pollutions of their nature, hearts, and lives; so as, examining themselves thereby, they may come to further conviction of, humiliation for, and hatred against sin; together with a clearer sight of the need they have of Christ, and the perfection of his obedience.[17]

In summary, according to covenant theology, the law, on the one hand, cannot justify the ungodly on account of their sinful nature, but instead, condemning them, drives them to the covenant of grace; on the other hand, the law is useful in the sanctification of the elect in whom God works both to will and to do his good pleasure.

Moreover, Reformed theologians traditionally analyze the law as consisting of three parts: moral, ceremonial, and judicial. The moral law, summarized in the Ten Commandments, is eternal, but the ceremonial and judicial laws, though of eternal value for their typology and of eternal force to the extent that they express the moral law in relative situations, are abrogated. The Westminster Confession says,

Besides this law, commonly called moral, God was pleased to give to the people of Israel, as a church under age, ceremonial laws, containing several typical ordinances, partly of worship, prefiguring Christ, his graces, actions, sufferings, and benefits; and partly holding forth divers instruc-

15. WCF, 19:1, 2, 5.
16. WCF, 19:7.
17. WCF, 19:6.

tions of moral duties. All which ceremonial laws are now abrogated under the New Testament. To them also, as a body politick, he gave sundry judicial laws, which expired together with the state of that people, not obliging any other now, further than the general equity thereof may require.[18]

Since the ceremonial and judicial laws comprise most of the law, and Reformed theologians regard them as canceled, and since dispensationalists note that the Ten Commandments, with the exception of keeping the sabbath, are repeated in the New Testament, it may seem as though the difference between Reformed theologians and dispensationalists comes down to the fine point of whether or not to keep the sabbath. In fact, however, this is not so; the two theologies fundamentally differ in their attitudes toward the law. Dispensationalists, concentrating on its spiritually debilitating effects through man's sinfulness, negate it; Reformed theologians, moving beyond its weakness to its spiritual value in conjunction with the Spirit, validate it. Dispensationalists pit law against Spirit; Reformed theologians combine them.

With regard to the relationship of the church and the state, Reformed theologians are not agreed. Keith Pavlischek traces Reformed theology's development of thought regarding the relationship of church and state and the toleration of confessional pluralism into a "conquest-compromise-withdrawal" paradigm. The radical Presbyterians, who prevailed in the early seventeenth century, without reservation advocated a purely Calvinistic established church. The Independents and moderate Presbyterians, who had to contend with civil war and growing sectarianism in the middle of that century, compromised on the issue, making the issue of "toleration" dependent on their historical situation. The Baptists, represented by Roger Williams as the foremost Baptist theorist, rejected the notion of a National Establishment and advocated instead a withdrawal from the pollutions and corruptions of the political world.[19] Pavlischek himself advocates toleration along the lines laid out by the Reformed theologians Abraham Kuyper and Herman Dooyeweerd in their theory of sphere sovereignty. Nevertheless, although not agreed about church-state relationships, Calvinists are agreed that Christ is not to be pitted against culture but in Niebuhr's terms is "Christ the transformer of culture."[20]

18. WCF, 19:3-4.

19. Keith Pavlischek, "In Critique of Theonomy: A Reformational Case for Pluralism" (Th.M. thesis, Westminster Theological Seminary, Philadelphia, 1986), p. 97.

20. Niebuhr, *Christ and Culture*, pp. 190-229.

Reformed theologians are also not agreed with regard to eschatology. Amillennialists identify the church as the fulfillment of the Old Testament promises after Christ's advent into the world, first in the flesh at Bethlehem and then in the Spirit at Pentecost. Historic premillennialists see the kingdom promises of the Old Testament as being fulfilled in the church after the first advent of Christ and consummated in restored national Israel after the second advent of Christ. Postmillennialists believe the second coming of Christ will be after the millennium, which is to come as the result of the Christianization of the world without miraculous intervention. Nevertheless, all Reformed theologians agree that the law is binding today in the sense that it is a means used by the Spirit to sanctify the elect.

Argumentation and Strengths

Scripture consistently asserts that the moral law of God, which is embodied in the Ten Commandments, is eternal. "Long ago," says the psalmist, "I learned from your statutes that you established them to last forever" (Ps. 119:152). The positive Reformed attitude conforms to that of both Testaments. Psalm 119, the "golden ABC" (Luther), speaks of the law as righteous (v. 7, passim) and true (v. 142) along with many other spiritual virtues. The law from God's mouth is more precious to him than thousands of pieces of silver and gold (v. 72) and sweeter than honey to his mouth (v. 103). Paul also refers to the law as holy, just, good, and spiritual (Rom. 7:12ff.). Although it is a deadly sword for sinners (Rom. 7:9-11; 1 Cor. 15:56), the law transforms saints into living trees (Ps. 1:1-3).

Moreover, the law itself suggests the appropriateness of the Westminster Confession's tripartite analysis of it. In the Book of Exodus, the Ten Commandments (Exod. 20:1-17) are plainly distinguished from the judicial commands designed for the land and collected in the Book of the Covenant (20:18–23:19). Moses, reflecting on the two distinct revelations of the law on Mount Sinai, one to all Israel and the other to him (cf. Exod. 19:24–20:17 with 20:18–23:33), said of the former, "Then the LORD spoke to you out of the fire. You heard the sound of words but saw no form; there was only a voice. He declared to you his covenant, the Ten Commandments, which he commanded you to follow and then wrote them on the two stone tablets" (Deut. 4:12-13). Concerning the later judicial and ceremonial laws mediated to Israel through him he adds, "And the LORD directed me at that time to teach you the decrees and laws you are to follow in the land that you are crossing the Jordan to possess" (4:14). In Deuteronomy 5 Moses reinforces the distinction between the primary Ten Commandments, which are not restricted to time and place, and the secondary ordinances mediated through him and related to the land. After recounting the Ten Commandments, which are called the "covenant made at Horeb" (5:2), Moses says about them:

> These are the commandments the LORD proclaimed in a loud voice to your whole assembly there on the mountain from out of the fire, the cloud and the deep darkness; and he added nothing more. Then he wrote them on two stone tablets and gave them to me. (Deut. 5:22)

He thereupon supplements this covenant and relates it to the land in the rest of Deuteronomy. After rehearsing the people's request that God no longer speak directly to them but through a mediator (5:23-29), the lawgiver reminds them of God's instructions: "Go, tell them to return to their tents. But you stay here with me so that I may give you all the commands, decrees and laws you are to teach them to follow *in the land* I am giving them to possess" (vv. 30-31). Moses then warns the people to obey carefully "so that you may live and prosper and prolong your days *in the land* that you will possess" (vv. 32-33). He commences giving the commands for the land in Deuteronomy 6:1:

> These are the commands, decrees and laws the Lord your God directed me to teach you to observe *in the land* that you are crossing the Jordan to possess, so that . . . you may enjoy long life . . . so that it may go well with you and that you may increase greatly *in a land* flowing with milk and honey. . . . (Deut. 6:1-3; emphases mine)

To be sure, these commands are informed by the Ten Commandments and are consistent with them so that they have binding force to the extent that they represent "the general equity," but they are specifically for the time Israel was in the land. The Torah plainly distinguishes the Ten Commandments from the rest of the law in at least the following ways: They have priority through the chronology of revelation, through the manner of revelation, and through their unrestricted extension. The Ten Commandments are uniquely uttered by the voice of God himself out of smoke and fire on a mountain in the hearing of all, and are uniquely written with the finger of God (Exod. 31:18). They are uniquely housed in the Holy of Holies (Deut. 10:1-6), the copy of heaven itself (Exod. 25:9). Finally, they are uniquely to be kept without restriction to time or place.

The law also plainly distinguishes cultic legislation from the Ten Commandments and the judicial ordinances in three ways. First the cultic legislation is given in Exodus 25–40 and Leviticus, "The Handbook of the Priests," and not in Deuteronomy, addressed to the people as a whole, except to the extent that people are involved in the practice of this legislation, such as going up to Jerusalem three times a year. Second, the cultic legislation is given only after the Book of the Covenant had been ratified in a separate ceremony recorded in Exodus 24. Finally, throughout Scripture priority is always given to the religious and ethical laws over the cultic. In a chronology reflecting their relative importance, the covenant is first given, then the mostly judicial instructions in Exodus 21–23, and finally the cultic legislation in Exodus 25:1–40:38. When the people sin in connection with the Golden Calf (Exod. 32:1-6), God, interrupting his giving of instructions regarding the tabernacle, instructs Moses to get down off the mountain (v. 7). Samuel, the first prophet, expresses the prophetic ideal: "Does the LORD delight in burnt offerings and sacrifices as much as in obeying the voice of the LORD?" (1 Sam. 15:22).

In conclusion, laws are mutable or immutable relative to the abiding nature of the situation for which they were intended. Richard Hooker said:

> In a word, we plainly perceive by the difference of those three laws which the Jews received at the hands of God, the moral, ceremonial, and judicial, that if the end for which and the matter according whereunto God maketh his laws continue always one and the same, his laws also do the like; for which cause the moral law cannot be altered: secondly, that whether the matter whereon laws are made continue or continue not, if their end have once ceased, they cease also to be of force: as in the law ceremonial it fareth: finally, that albeit the end continue, as in that law of theft specified and in a great part of those ancient judicials it cloth; yet forasmuch as there is not in all respects the same subject or matter remaining for which they were first instituted, even this is sufficient cause of change: and therefore laws, though both ordained of God himself, and the end for which they were ordained continuing, may notwithstanding cease, if by alteration of persons or times they be found unsufficient to attain unto that end. In which respect why may we not presume that God doth even call for such change or alteration as the very condition of things themselves doth make necessary?[21]

21. *The Works of That Learned and Judicious Divine, Mr. Richard Hooker,* revised by R. W. Church and F. Paget (Oxford: Clarendon, 1888), 1:387; 3:x, 4.

Weaknesses

The fourth commandment calls into question the equation of the Ten Commandments with the eternal moral law. That command is mutable, for if the
Reformers are right, it has been changed from the seventh day to the first.
Nevertheless, the principle behind it is immutable. Also, Reformed theology should recognize the unity of the law, which, as a way of administration, has been changed. The New Testament, reflecting this change of administration, contains no collection of commandments such as are found in
the Torah. Finally, Reformed theologians need to stress the role of the Spirit
in keeping the new covenant, which has replaced the older, lest the un-
taught fall into legalism.

Reformed theology is also obviously weak in its failure to define convincingly church-state relationships and in deciding decisively the millennial question.

Theonomy

Views

"The theonomy movement," writes David Watson, "is composed of several
groups of people whose ultimate goal is to reconstruct 'Christian' nations according to the model of Old Testament Israel."[22] Watson tersely summarizes
the history of the movement:

> The first person to promote successfully this goal in the twentieth cen-
> tury was Rousas J. Rushdoony. . . . Rushdoony combined: 1) the philo-
> sophical presuppositionalism of Cornelius Van Til . . . ; 2) a "positive,"
> postmillennial eschatology; 3) and a belief that the civil laws of the Mo-
> saic covenant were still binding on the modern magistrate into his own
> unique blend of "Christian conservativism."

"In the early 1960's," Watson continues, "Rushdoony gained two brilliant young disciples, Gary North and Greg Bahnsen, and through the next
decade, these three prolific theonomic authors built up the movement's the-

22. David K. Watson, "Theonomy: A History of the Movement and an Evaluation of
Its Primary Text" (M.A. thesis: Calvin College, Grand Rapids, 1985), p. vi.

oretical foundations."[23] Although theonomists are not agreed in the details of their views and arguments, it is generally conceded that Bahnsen's book *Theonomy in Christian Ethics* lays the theory's cornerstone, and so I will interact primarily with this book.

Bahnsen states his view thus:

> Central to the theory and practice of Christian ethics, whether personal or social, is every jot and tittle of God's law as laid down *in* the revelation of the Older and New Testaments. The Christian is obligated to keep the whole law of God as a pattern of sanctification, and in the realm of human society the civil magistrate is responsible to enforce God's law against public crime.[24]

Like dispensationalists, theonomists insist on the integrity of the law, resisting any *relevant* distinction between the Ten Commandments and specific judicial ordinances. Against dispensationalists, however, Bahnsen writes, "The Older Testament commands are not mere artifacts in a religious museum, nor are they ideals suspended over an age of parenthesis. . . ."[25] Against the Westminster Confession's article that the judicial laws are binding only to the extent that they express "general equity," though Bahnsen in contrast to Rushdoony denies he is in conflict with the Confession, Bahnsen reasons that because God loves us in a very extensive and specific fashion, "He did not deliver to us merely some broad and general moral principles."[26] Rather, "*every* single stroke of the law must be seen by the Christian as applicable to this very age between the advents of Christ."[27] "Does Scripture . . . limit the law which is binding upon Christians to the ten commandments?" he asks. To which he replies: "Our Lord definitely did not; according to His word, *every jot* and *every tittle* has abiding validity (Matt. 5:17)."[28]

Bahnsen's specific agenda is to bring back the penal sanctions of the Older Testament. The civil magistrate, he argues, is responsible to discharge

---

23. Watson, "Theonomy: A History of the Movement," p. vi.

24. Greg Bahnsen, *Theonomy in Christian Ethics* (Nutley, NJ: Craig, 1979), p. xiii. His book *The Authority of God's Law Today* (Tyler, TX: Geneva, 1983) popularly explains theonomic ethics.

25. Bahnsen, *Theonomy*, p. 34.

26. Bahnsen, *Theonomy*, p. 35.

27. Cited by Rodney Clapp, "Democracy as Heresy," *Christianity Today*, February 20, 1987, p. 18.

28. Bahnsen, *Theonomy*, p. 314.

fully the specific details of the law, both the positive demands of the law and its penal sanctions. The law of God commands not only "the full discharge of its precepts but also the infliction of the appropriate penalty for all infractions." Unless both of these elements are heeded "the law of God is *not* being met," Bahnsen says.[29] This means the death penalty is to be applied by the civil magistrate to violations both against the purity of the God-man relationship (e.g., idolatry, witchcraft, sabbath breaking, apostasy, sorcery, blasphemy, and false pretension to prophecy), against the purity of the home (e.g., adultery and unchastity, homosexuality, rape, incest, and proven incorrigibility of children), and against the purity of person-to-person relationships (e.g., murder and kidnapping).[30]

Theonomists, however, do not think this theonomic ethic should be applied to politics immediately. "Most theonomists," explains Pavlischek, "maintain that these laws should only be enacted when there is some sort of Christian consensus."[31] Bahnsen, with Rushdoony, believing that "God's law should not be imposed with force on a recalcitrant people or society," holds that "only when those Christians work out their adherence to God's Son in their various life involvements — including political and social ethics — will the statutes of God's law become the law of the land."[32] Theonomists are not revolutionaries willing to overthrow legitimate governmental authorities in order to usher in their own view of government. For this reason theonomists are also postmillennialists, with the new twist that the future millennial kingdom will be administered according to the theonomic ethic. In theory postmillennialism is not essential to the system; in practice, however, it is, for otherwise the goal of theonomists appears hopeless. Like dispensationalists they see the Mosaic law once again in force in a millennium, not in a Jewish millennium, but in a Christian one.

Argumentation

What are some theses on which theonomy rests?[33] First, theonomists argue that the law in its entirety reflects the unchangeable, righteous character and

29. Bahnsen, *Theonomy*, p. 435.
30. Bahnsen, *Theonomy*, p. 445.
31. Pavlischek, "Critique of Theonomy," p. 3.
32. Bahnsen, "God's Law and Biblical Prosperity: A Reply to the Editor of the *Presbyterian Journal*" (privately distributed), 30, cited by Pavlischek, "Critique of Theonomy," p. 3.
33. Cf. Bahnsen, *Theonomy in Christian Ethics*, 2nd ed. (Phillipsburg, NJ: Presbyte-

standards of God for the actions and attitudes of all people in all areas of life, including politics. Bahnsen reasons:

> Since God is the living Lord over all creation and immutable in His character, and since all men are His creatures and morally accountable to Him, we are led to believe that God's law (as reflecting the righteousness of God) applies to every man irrespective of his position in life, situation in the world, nationality, or place in history.[34]

Elsewhere he says the law's "standards of justice have remained immutable."[35] When D. James Kennedy, who denies he is "a theonomist as such," was asked by *Christianity Today* whether it would be desirable for every nation to be theonomic, he replied, "Well, I think it would be presumptuous for me or anyone else to disagree with God, don't you?"[36]

Second, theonomists argue on the basis of Matthew 5:17, their Golden Text, that the Mosaic laws continue to be morally binding in the New Testament, unless they are rescinded or modified by further revelation. The new covenant, it is argued, does not abrogate the content of the older but reinforces it through its surpassing glory, power, and finality.

Third, Bahnsen recognizes a distinction between "positive" law, which is restricted to a specific situation such as God's command to Adam in the Garden not to eat the forbidden fruit, and "standing" law, which is unrestricted: he contends that the integrated Mosaic law is standing law. He discusses this important point, however, almost as an aside.

Fourth, theonomists are convinced that natural law is an unacceptable standard in guiding nations because it is "simply a projection of autonomy."[37] To be sure, Bahnsen tips his hat to the statements in Scripture about natural law,[38] but that concession is irrelevant to his thesis.

Fifth, theonomists agree with Reformed theologians that the law serves many functions, including, for example, declaring God's character and demands, defining sin, exposing infractions, inciting sin, and guiding sanctification. They uniquely argue, however, that it also functions as a per-

---

rian and Reformed, 1984), pp. xvi-xvii; *By This Standard: The Authority of God's Law Today* (Tyler, TX: Institute for Christian Economics, 1985), pp. 345-47.

34. Bahnsen, *Theonomy,* p. 339.
35. Bahnsen, *Theonomy,* p. 398.
36. Clapp, "Democracy as Heresy," p. 21.
37. Bahnsen, *Theonomy,* p. 399.
38. Bahnsen, *Theonomy,* pp. 279-306, 345-55.

fect model of social justice for all cultures, even in the punishment of criminals. Bahnsen finds support for this thesis in Moses' encouragement: "Observe the decrees and laws carefully, for this will show your wisdom and understanding to the nations, who will hear about all these decrees and say, 'Surely this great nation is a wise and understanding people' (Deut. 4:6)." Bahnsen also appeals to Isaiah's and Micah's vision in precisely the same words: "Many nations will come and say, 'Come, let us go up to the mountain of the LORD, to the house of the God of Jacob. He will teach us his ways, so that we may walk in his paths' (Mic 4:2; Isa 2:3)."[39]

Sixth, Bahnsen sees no difference between church-state relationships in the Older Testament and in the New. With regard to the Old Testament he radically divorces the priestly-cultic sphere (i.e., the Israelite "church") from that of the kingly-civil sphere (i.e., the Israelite "state"). With regard to the New Testament he just as radically unites the ecclesiastical sphere (i.e., "the church") and the civil sphere (i.e., "the state"). As a result there is no difference between Israel's kings and other nations' civil magistrates, and the Old Testament theocracy and the New Testament Christocracy both combine state and church in expressing God's kingdom. He recognizes that Israel is a theocracy, but that admission he notes is irrelevant to theonomic ethics. Among other arguments for equating Israel's king with the civil magistrates in the surrounding nations he notes seven characteristics identifying pagan kings as occupying the same position in God's theocracy/Christocracy as Israel's kings: God sovereignly appoints and removes both; neither in nor outside Israel are rulers to be resisted; both bear religious titles — for example, David's sons are called "priests" and the uncircumcised Cyrus is called "Messiah" and "Shepherd," while Paul refers to the civil magistrates of Rome as "ministers." Both vicegerents are avengers of his wrath, must deter evil but honor the good, and must rule according to God's law.

Finally, Bahnsen argues that the death penalties of the Older Testament are part of God's immutable, eternal law:

> Knowing that God's standard of righteousness (which includes temporal, social relations) is as immutable as the character of God Himself, we should conclude that crimes which warrant capital punishment in the Older Testament continue to deserve the death penalty today.[40]

39. Bahnsen, *Theonomy*, p. 362.
40. Bahnsen, *Theonomy*, p. 442.

Strengths

We commend theonomists for their conviction, with Reformed theologians, that the law is a compatible servant of the gospel, to be delighted in, and is a useful tool in the Spirit's hands for sanctification. We also celebrate the theonomists' efforts to give concrete expressions to the confession that Christ is Lord of all and their high regard for the written Word. Westminster folk applaud them for basing themselves squarely on Cornelius Van Til's apologetics. Moreover, we applaud their fresh insights into many texts of Scripture and for alerting us to the hubris of the state in deifying itself rather than recognizing its derivative authority from God. Finally, we commend theonomists for putting theologians in the heuristic position to think through both the entailments of "general equity," on the one hand, and their eschatology and their understanding of the church-state relationship, on the other.

Weaknesses

The theonomists' particular way of cutting through this briar patch of problems, however, is neither theoretically sound nor practically workable. First, they cannot carry through the theonomic ethic consistently. Bahnsen must agree in the light of the clear teachings of the New Testament (e.g., Acts 15 and Hebrews 7–10) that the ceremonial laws cannot be continued. He attempts to salvage his thesis by noting that "the meaning and intention of these laws is equally valid under the Older and New Covenants, even though the former manner of observation is now 'out of gear.'"[41] But this way of putting the matter does not do justice to the New Testament. Bahnsen disallows the full force of the apostle's words: "'How can you desire to be enslaved again to the weak and worthless rudiments of the [ceremonial] law?' (cf. Gal 4:9f.)."[42] The writer of Hebrews links the law with the Levitical priesthood and asserts in no uncertain terms that it has been replaced by the Melchizedekian priesthood of Christ. Moreover, although Bahnsen attempts to define ceremonial law and what is situationally conditioned, he fails to do so, as shown by the many differences among theonomists. Bahnsen damagingly admits, "Theonomists will not necessarily agree with each other's ev-

41. Bahnsen, *Theonomy*, p. 212.
42. Bahnsen, *Theonomy*, p. 211.

ery interpretation and ethical conclusion. For instance, like me, many do not affirm R. J. Rushdoony's view of the dietary laws, Gary North's view of home mortgages, . . . or David Chilton's attitudes toward bribery and 'ripping off' the unbeliever."[43] These differences, in fact, are only the tip of the iceberg once the various theonomists attempt to apply the law to hundreds of details. Rodney Clapp rightly noted:

> Reconstruction does not actually provide the clear, simple, uncontest-
> ably "biblical" solutions to ethical questions that it pretends to. . . . Re-
> constructed society would appear to require a second encyclopedic Tal-
> mud, and to foster hordes of "scribes" with competing judgments, in a
> society of people who are locked on the law's fine points rather than liv-
> ing by its spirit.[44]

Second, although Bahnsen acknowledges some difference between the Ten Commandments and other laws, that admission is irrelevant to his ethic. Also, although he makes a distinction between temporary positive law and enduring standing law, he fails to appreciate Hooker's point that the ju-dicial and ceremonial laws, in contrast to the Ten Commandments, are meant for a specific situation and therefore are mutable, relative to changing purposes and situations. As noted, these laws were meant for Israel as long as they were in the Promised Land.

Third, the Golden Text of theonomy, Matthew 5:17, cannot aim to es-tablish a theonomic ethic. Paul Fowler, Watson, Poythress, and others have pointed out Bahnsen's faulty exegesis of this verse.[45] Here I want to under-score that Bahnsen contradicts himself with regard to this text, for he must admit that in some cases Christ actually does abrogate the law. Although our Lord reinforces Moses when he says that the law is a matter of the heart, he replaces the older teaching of "eye for eye, and tooth for tooth" with his own authoritative teaching, "Do not resist an evil person. If someone strikes you on the right cheek, turn to him the other also" (Matt. 5:38-42). He also negates dietary laws (Mark 7:19; cf. Acts 15:19-20) and certain provi-sions for divorce (Matt. 19:3-9). Bahnsen will not concede the obvious point that in Matthew 5:38-42 Christ abrogates the principle of immediate justice;

43. Bahnsen, *Theonomy,* 2nd ed. (1984), p. xix.
44. Clapp, "Democracy as Heresy," p. 23.
45. Paul B. Fowler, "God's Law Free from Legalism: Critique of Theonomy in Chris-tian Ethics." Unpublished paper, n.d.

Christ will bring justice in the *parousia*. Bahnsen dodges the issue in Matthew 19:3-9. But our theonomist friend cannot shout down the obvious abrogation of the dietary laws in the New Testament. Here he appeals to the principle of the Reformers that distinguishes moral law from ceremonial law. With regard to Mark 7:19 he reluctantly concedes: "It is noted that the parenthetical inference of Mark 7:19 deals with the ritualistic law; hence this thesis suffers nothing in admitting that the ceremonies are no longer useful after Christ. The abiding validity of the *moral* law is our concern here."[46] Regarding Acts 15:19-20 he similarly concedes: "It does not imply that believers are obligated to keep the ceremonial provisions of the Mosaic law as such."[47] Bahnsen complains that his critics fail to note that he allows that "God has the authority and prerogative to discontinue the binding force of anything He has revealed,"[48] but what he fails to realize is that his concessions undermine his thesis. Jesus cannot be establishing every jot and tittle of the law, as Bahnsen's thesis declares, and at the same time abrogate some of the laws. The many specific changes of the law in the New Testament seriously undermine the thesis that the burden of proof rests on the interpreter to show that the law is not in force.

Fourth, Bahnsen distorts the purpose of the law when he alleges that one of its primary functions is to serve as a model of legislation for the nations. The law was written above all for the redeemed community to make them a treasured possession, a priestly kingdom, a holy nation (Exod. 19:5-6). The Sermon on the Mount was delivered not to the unbelieving world but to the disciples; in fact only Jesus' disciples can keep it. Christ summarizes his teaching in the abstract principle of the Golden Rule: "Therefore in everything, do to others what you would have them do to you, for this sums up the Law and the Prophets" (Matt. 7:12). As is well known, similar sayings, though in the negative, are found in the rabbis (Tobit 4:15 and Hillel) and in the philosophers (Isocrates, Philo, and the Stoics). What distinguishes it from these other precepts is the preceding *logion* to which the inferential particle *oun* introducing the Golden Rule partially points: "Ask and it will be given to you; seek and you will find; knock and the door will be opened to you. . . . If you . . . know how to give good gifts to your children, how much more will your Father in heaven give good gifts to those who ask him!" (Matt. 7:7-11). The morally good gift in view, as the parallel in Luke 11:13

46. Bahnsen, *Theonomy*, p. 228.
47. Bahnsen, *Theonomy*, p. 131.
48. Bahnsen, *Theonomy*, 2nd ed., p. xiv.

shows, is the Holy Spirit, who enables believers to keep his commandments. Our Lord intends nations to come under his sway, not apart from the gospel but through it (cf. Matt. 28:18-20). Isaiah and Micah present the nations as converts to the true religion by representing themselves as overhearing the strong nations exhorting one another to go up to the temple so that they may learn to walk in his paths. Moses' statement in Deuteronomy 4:6 entails little more than the fact that "righteousness exalts a nation, but sin is a disgrace to any people" (Prov. 14:34).

Fifth, as Meredith Kline brilliantly noted,[49] Bahnsen distorts Scripture by likening the separation of the ecclesiastical and civil roles with the separation of church and state in the New. In order to support his thesis, Bahnsen alleges, for example, that "the only time the *priests* were involved in *political* matters were *exceptional* cases" (emphasis his).[50] He goes on to argue that their involvement at Jericho is "exceptional." Elsewhere he argues that the succession of Israel's kings was based on popular choice: "The will of the people or human arrangements were foundational to the selection or election of a king."[51] In fact, however, the involvement of priests in battle was normative. The law instructed, for example, that the priest should encourage the army before battle, promising them the Lord's presence; and one of the ways God initiated battle was through the Urim manipulated by the priests (1 Sam. 28:6). To be sure, sometimes the *vox populi* put the king on the throne, but Yahweh complains, "They set up kings without my consent; they choose princes without my approval" (Hos. 8:4). God indicated his approval through prophetic oracles. Bahnsen also does violence to Scripture when he suggests that Cyrus's role as Messiah is representative of the surrounding nations. In fact, however, Cyrus was uniquely given his titles because, functioning in the place of Israel's exiled Shepherd-king, he miraculously led Israel in a second exodus back to the sworn-land and rebuilt its temple. Bahnsen throws together so many unexegeted texts in the chapter titled "Separation of Church and State" that the reader pushes away the indigestible potpourri.

His argument regarding church and state is not only exegetically flawed, it is also logically defective. Similarities between Israel's anointed kings and uncircumcised pagan kings do not establish their equivalence. One must also note the many dissimilarities between these kings. For exam-

49. Kline, "Comments on an Old-New Error," pp. 176-78.
50. Bahnsen, *Theonomy*, p. 405.
51. Bahnsen, *Theonomy*, p. 409.

ple, Israel's magistrates, participating in the holy redemptive nation in contrast to the civil magistrates of the merely preservative states, had to follow rules of holy war that radically distinguished them from pagan rulers. According to the rules of holy war, for example, Yahweh's warriors had to hamstring their military might to the extent that they could not win apart from Yahweh's help. The LORD, for example, reduced Gideon's army from 32,000 men to 300. By contrast, Jesus assumes that pagan kings must match troop for troop (Luke 14:31-33). A spiritual chasm, not a mere crack, separates Israel's kings from pagan rulers, disallowing Bahnsen's equation. His seven similarities between the rulers of Israel and the rulers of the surrounding nations do not support Bahnsen's thesis but illustrate that God is the ruler of the universe as well as Israel's ruler. Ockham's razor, the maxim that assumptions introduced to explain a thing must not be multiplied, validates my contention that no other explanation is necessary.

His thesis is also theologically marred. Kline cogently notes that the Chalcedon theory desacralizes Israel and sacralizes the nations.[52] In a brilliant essay on the politics of the kingdom — must reading for everyone in this debate — Edmund Clowney rightly notes:

> To suppose that the body of Christ finds institutional expression in both the church and state as religious and political spheres is to substitute a sociological conception of the church for the teaching of the New Testament. Christ does not give the keys of the kingdom to Caesar, nor the sword to Peter before the *parousia*. The church is the new nation (1 Pe 2:9).[53]

Sixth, Bahnsen underestimates the role of natural law, which is sufficient to either commend a person toward God or condemn him before God (Rom. 2:15). Harris has Scriptural warrant for his contention that common grace and general revelation are "not so fragile as Bahnsen supposes."[54] Harris also has historical warrant. In fact, the Book of the Covenant probably draws heavily from the Code of Hammurabi, and without controversy the Book of Proverbs finds inspiration in Egyptian sapiential literature. The Ten Commandments give cause for obeying the first four commandments — note "for" (= "because") in Exodus 20:5, 7, 11 — but none for the last five,

---

52. Kline, "Comments on an Old-New Error," p. 178.
53. Edmund P. Clowney, "The Politics of the Kingdom," *WTJ* 41 (1978-79): 306.
54. Harris, "Theonomy," p. 10.

probably because the former are unique in Ancient Near Eastern literature and the latter are found commonly. No society that does not protect the life, home, property, and reputation of its citizens can endure. I suggest, however, that Luther went too far in 1525 in his treatise *Against the Heavenly Prophets,* in which he maintained that whatever in the law of Moses exceeded natural law was binding only on the Jews and not on Christians.[55]

Seventh, the law explicitly states that capital punishment for various offenses is not part of an eternal law. Cain's blood was not shed in *lex talionis* for Abel's blood, which cried out for justice, but in fact was protected (Gen. 4:15). Capital punishment for religious offenses is specifically denied an unrestricted status with respect to the time and place of the offense and the people involved in it. When the son of Shelomith blasphemed, the people were confused as to what to do, showing that capital punishment for that crime did not exist before Israel became a nation. Only after they had put him in custody did the Lord make his will known to the people (Lev. 24:10-16). Similarly, the law did not stipulate what should be done in connection with breaking the sabbath. Once again, lacking prior precedent, the people put the unfortunate man who had gathered wood on the sabbath day into custody until the Lord gave direction that he must die (Num. 15:32-36). These religious laws were appropriate for Israel's unique situation; they are not appropriate in a pluralistic society.

Moreover, postmillennialists mistakenly hope for a kingdom of perfect justice apart from the *parousia.* Most Christians, however, do not expect to establish a perfectly just kingdom apart from the Lord's coming in power. May the church boast in its weakness, not in its might! "We boast," says Paul of the Thessalonians, "about your perseverance and faith in all the persecutions and trials you are enduring. . . . As a result you will be counted worthy of the kingdom of God, for which you are suffering. God is just: He will pay back trouble to those who trouble you. . . . This will happen when the Lord Jesus is revealed from heaven in blazing fire with his powerful angels. He will punish those who do not know God and do not obey the gospel of our Lord Jesus" (2 Thess. 1:4-8). May the church not hope for a kingdom apart from its sufferings with its Lord on the cross, lest it no longer have in mind the things of God but the things of men (Matt. 16:21-23).

Finally, and above all, theonomists err by putting saints back under ad-

---

55. Cited by Peter Alan Lillback, "The Binding of God: Calvin's Role in the Development of Covenant Theology" (Ph.D. dissertation, Westminster Theological Seminary, Philadelphia, 1985), 1:122.

ministration by the Mosaic law rather than leaving them under administration by the Spirit of Christ.

Conclusion

Dispensationalism, by its overzealous negation of the law and by its radical separation of church and state, has left the state without the light of the law. On the other hand, theonomy, by its overkill application of the law to the state and by its unholy alliance of church and state, would ultimately take the light of the church out of the world and would leave the world in its great darkness just as surely as Judaism did. The debate, however, has the heuristic effect of making the lamp of Reformed theology shine more brightly. Dispensationalism by its emphasis on the Spirit fills that lamp with oil, and theonomy by its attention to the specifics of the law trims its wick.

The New Testament Doctrine of "Land"

Thank you, President White, for honoring me with the invitation to deliver this year's lecture in honor of Johannes Geerhardus Vos, who for thirty years was Professor of Biblical Studies at Geneva. You noted perceptively in the preface to the Festschrift in honor of J. G. Vos, "Humanly speaking, the revival of interest in 'Vosian Biblical Theology' would not have occurred without J. G. Vos."

Old Testament theologians like the Vosians aim, among other distinctive goals, to identify the teachings of Old Testament books on themes associated with motifs such as "seed," "temple," "sabbath," "kingship," "land," etc. Having identified the motifs and themes, they chronologically trace the trajectory of those themes through the Old Testament corpus. The Vosians, however, are among the few *biblical* theologians who trace the trajectory of themes from the Old Testament into and through the New Testament.

In this lecture I trace the trajectory of the Old Testament theme "Promised Land" [hereafter Land] in the New Testament. In addition to honoring J. G. Vos, I hope my reflections will profit my audience with regard to hermeneutics, pedagogy and homiletics, theology, spiritual life, and politics. As for hermeneutics, the Hebrew word *'āreṣ,* "land"/"earth" is the fourth most-frequent word in the Old Testament. The Old Testament refers "Land" to Canaan, but the New Testament, I will argue, refers it to the whole earth and/or to spiritual, eternal realities. If one interprets the Old Testament in light of its canonical context, this redefinition of land affects most of the books of the Old Testament. As for pedagogy and homiletics, one cannot

---

Previously published in *Gift of the Land Part III: New Testament,* chap. 20.

teach or preach the whole counsel of God without taking into account this redefinition of Land in the New Testament. As for theology, the theologian's definition of "Land" validates or falsifies a premillennial system of theology. As for spiritual life, Christians will be nourished by understanding what the New Testament reveals about the Land, which the Old Testament conceals. As for politics, the validity of the Jewish state's claim to the Land of Palestine depends on the meaning of "Land" in the canon.

The trajectory of the Land motif is the most difficult biblical motif to track. This is so because the New Testament rarely uses the term "land" for salvation history after the death of Jesus Christ. In fact, the Lord Jesus intentionally changes the one Old Testament reference to the Land in the New Testament found in Matthew 5:5. Paul infers the term in Romans 4:13, but he too refers it to the whole earth.

Since the New Testament does not use the term Land, I have to work with equivalent terms that imply Land, such as "Jerusalem," "throne of David," "temple," "Zion," etc. Prophets use Jerusalem and Land in close connection with one another. The superscript to Micah says his words are addressed to Jerusalem and Samaria, but he opens his first sermon with: "Listen, Land, all who are in it" (Mic. 1:1-2). In the same sermon he asks and answers: "What is Judah's high place? Is it not Jerusalem?" (v. 5). In the postexilic period Jerusalem came to be used as a synecdoche for Judea. Within the Persian Empire Judea was a tiny province, only twenty-five miles east to west and thirty-five miles north to south, and Jerusalem was the center of the province's political, economic, and social life. The rabbis regarded the temple in Jerusalem as the center of the world. Israel's hope to rule the world at the End centered in Jerusalem. It comes as no surprise that in the second temple period Jerusalem and its equivalents are a synecdoche for the Land. As a convenient catchall for these coreferential terms I will use hereafter either "Land" or "Jerusalem."

In this lecture I argue that the New Testament redefines Land in three ways: first, spiritually, as a reference to Christ's person; second, transcendentally, as a reference to heavenly Jerusalem; and third, eschatologically, as a reference to the regenerated earth in the End. In short, "Land" in the Old Testament refers to Israel's life in Canaan, and in the New Testament "Land" is transmuted to refer to life in Christ. Christian theologians since Augustine have contended that the New is in the Old concealed, and the Old is in the New revealed. As for Land, I am arguing that the Old conceals and the New reveals that Land refers to these three truths. By applying this New Testament redefinition of Land to the Old Testament, I am not allegorizing Land in the Old Testament. Rather, I am arguing that the Author of the Old Testament intended from the first these concealed, spiritual truths regarding Land. These three realities referred to by "Land" usually overlap with one another, but by distinguishing them I hope to clarify our reflection upon the motif.

The New Testament redefines most Old Testament motifs, such as "people of God," sabbath, and purity. In the new dispensation the covenant people of God are not marked by circumcision but by their doing God's will and by baptism (Matt. 8:21-22 [Luke 9:59-60]; Matt. 12:46-50 [Mark 3:21, 31-35; Luke 8:19-21]; Luke 11:27). Jesus does away with sabbath-keeping as religious obligation and "redefines" it according to its true intent: as a time to heal, to do good, and to enjoy the spiritual rest he gives (Matt. 12 [Mark 2]; passim). As for the purity of food, Jesus taught in contrast to the rabbis that real purity pertains to the state of the heart, not to what goes into one's mouth (Matt. 15 [Mark 7]). As the Author of Torah, Jesus has the right to redefine Old Testament concepts according to the divine Author's intention.

Before analyzing the New Testament's three positive "useful" teachings regarding Land, we first consider its references to the Land as geopolitical territory.

"Land" as Geopolitical Territory

Salvation history in the New Testament opens with Jerusalem still being ruled by foreign powers. The seven times seventy years of God's judgment upon Israel, which Daniel prophesied and to which Jesus probably referred to as "the times of the Gentiles" (Luke 21:24), terminates in Messiah's death and resurrection. His death and resurrection fulfilled and inaugurated the six things God promised Daniel would happen at the end of the 490 years (Dan. 9:24): "to put an end to sin, to atone for wickedness, to bring in everlasting righteousness, to seal up vision and prophecy and to anoint the most holy."

The Jews, however, rejected Jesus as Messiah and with that rejection forfeited the six promises. Forced from the Land in AD 70, they have wandered the face of the earth and have traditionally hoped for the day that they will return to the Land, and that God's ancient promises to Abraham and to David for the Land will be realized at the end of history. Three times a day Jews remember Zion in prayer: "Merciful Father, Deal kindly with Zion, Rebuild the walls of Jerusalem." Rabbi Heschel affirms: "To abandon the land would make a mockery of all our longings, prayer, and commitments. To abandon the land would be to repudiate the Bible."[1]

The writers of the synoptic gospels, however, each in his own way discredits this Jewish hope for the Land.

In Matthew and Mark

Before looking at the discrediting of Jewry's expectations for the Land in Matthew and Mark, let us first consider Land prophecies literally fulfilled in Messiah's passion.

"Land" Prophecies Literally Fulfilled in Messiah's Passion

Matthew interprets Old Testament prophecies that locate Messiah's earthly career in the holy land as having a literal, geopolitical fulfillment. For example, Christ's birth in Bethlehem (2:1-12) fulfills Micah's prophecy that Israel's future ruler would come from Bethlehem (Mic. 5:2 [1]), and the escape of the holy family to Egypt (2:13-15) is represented as the fulfillment of Hosea 11:1, "Out of Egypt I called my son." After these and other fulfillments of the birth narrative, Matthew identifies John the Baptist as the one in Isaiah's vision who in the wilderness prepares the way of *I AM*" (Matt. 3:1-2; Isa. 40:3). Jesus begins his own preaching in Galilee in fulfillment of Isaiah's prophecy that the first territory of Israel to suffer the darkness of deportation and exile will be the first on which the light of the Messiah's salvation will shine (Isa. 9:1-3 [8:23–9:2]; Matt. 4:12-16).

These and other prophecies, such as the triumphal entry of the Lord Jesus into Jerusalem riding upon a donkey and her foal in fulfillment of Zechariah's prophecy (21:1-5; Zech. 9:9), find a literal fulfillment because they pertain to Christ's earthly ministry. It does not follow, however, that because Land prophecies that pertain to Christ's earthly passions find a literal fulfillment, prophecies that pertain to his glory also have a literal fulfillment. Rather, the apostles who wrote of Christ's present glory represent that glory as being fulfilled from Christ's throne in heavenly Jerusalem through his administration of the Holy Spirit. In other words, Old Testament prophecies that pertain to Messiah's glory, though couched in the language of the old

---

1. Abraham Heschel, *Israel: An Echo of Eternity* (New York: Farrar, Straus & Giroux, 1969), p. 44.

dispensation when Israel existed as a geopolitical kingdom, are redefined according to the spiritual realities of the kingdom where Messiah reigns from heaven by the Holy Spirit.

"Land" Prophecies Fulfilled Spiritually in Messiah's Glory

Although Matthew's and Mark's writings trace the life of Messiah Jesus only to his resurrection, they prepare the way for the apostolic teaching that the Land promises are fulfilled in the church spiritually. They anticipate this redefinition by predicting the annihilation of Jerusalem, and they discredit Jewish expectations for the holy city by exalting Galilee over Judea in the new age.

GALILEE: LOCUS OF BEGINNING THE NEW AGE

Matthew and Mark artificially divide the ministry of Jesus into three successive acts, each of which they carefully stage in different locations within the Land. I restrict my reflection here to Mark. Act 1 takes place in Galilee (1:14–8:21). Galilee is a place of "open proclamation and acceptance, with committed disciples and the enthusiastic crowds."[2] Act 2 takes place on the way from Galilee to Jerusalem (8:22–10:52). In this transitional act, Jesus for the first time tells his disciples that he must be rejected and crucified by the Jewish authorities in Jerusalem. Act 3 is staged in Jerusalem (11:1–16:8). This Act is "a dismal story of conflict, rejection, and death."[3]

After his crucifixion and resurrection in Jerusalem, both Gospels feature Galilee. In Mark, the angelic messenger at the tomb directs the disciples to return to Galilee, where they will meet and see the resurrected Christ (Mark 16:7). In Matthew, Christ and his disciples return to Galilee where on a mountain he authorizes them to proclaim the good news worldwide (Matt. 28:16-20).[4] In sum, Galilee is the place where the good news of Jesus was first preached and widely embraced, and the place from which the worldwide preaching of the good news will be launched.

2. Heschel, *Israel: An Echo of Eternity*, p. 34.

3. R. T. France, *The Gospel of Mark: A Commentary on the Greek Text*, NIGTC (Grand Rapids: Eerdmans, 2002), p. 34.

4. Of course, there are exceptions in this broad characterization of the gospel — the distinction is not absolute. W. D. Davies, *The Gospel and the Land: Early Christianity and Jewish Territorial Doctrine* (Berkeley: University of California Press, 1974), pp. 221-43, rejects this linking of doctrine with Land because he emphasizes the specks of exceptions and not the overall unique thrust of Mark's presentation.

JERUSALEM: THE LOCUS OF THE END OF THE OLD AGE

In striking contrast to this unexpected rhetorical exaltation of Galilee as playing the honored role of launching the new age, Jesus predicts Jerusalem will be annihilated during the generation that killed Jesus. His prediction was fulfilled in AD 70.

Let us reflect briefly upon Jesus' prediction in the so-called Olivet discourse as recounted in Matthew 24 (see also Mark 13).[5] Jesus symbolically leaves the temple for the Mount of Olives. His movement from Jerusalem to the Mount of Olives reprises Ezekiel's vision of the glory of the Lord leaving Solomon's Temple and stopping on the same mountain just prior to the destruction of Jerusalem in 586 BC. In this private teaching he tells them that Jerusalem will be destroyed in their generation. And no New Testament passage predicts or cites an Old Testament prophecy that it will be rebuilt. Pascal makes the point: "When Nebuchadnezzar carried away the people captive, in case they thought the scepter had been forever removed from Judah, God told [Israel] beforehand their captivity would not last long, and that they would be restored (Jer. 29:10). They were comforted throughout by the prophets, and their royal house continued. But the second destruction came [in AD 70] without any promise of restoration — without having prophets, without kings, without consolation and hope, because the scepter has forever been removed [from national Israel]" (Pascal, *Pensées*, 278).[6]

This characterization of Galilee as the place of proclaiming the new age and of Jerusalem as the place of annihilation marks a decisive change from the old age to the new. Matthew and Mark negate Jewry's expectation that Jerusalem will continue to play a role in salvation history after its de-

---

5. After Jesus' triumphal entry into Jerusalem (Matt. 21:1-11) and his clearing of the temple (21:12-17), Matthew anticipates the destruction of Jerusalem and the end of the old age by mixing the accounts of the rejection of Jesus by the Jewish authority (Matt. 21:23-27, 28-32; 22:15-22, 23-33, 34-46) with Jesus' symbolic cursing of the fig tree (21:18-22), his parables of the tenants (21:33-46), of the wedding banquet (22:1-14), and his seven woes upon the Jewish authorities in Jerusalem (23:1-36). The barren fig tree symbolizes the temple with its barren ritual, ripe for destruction. Similarly, the three polemical parables in 21:28–22:14 are all directed against the Jewish authorities in Jerusalem and aim to identify the true people of God as those who win his favor in contrast to the Jerusalem authorities, who gain his wrath. The passage in 23:37-39 forms a bridge between the denunciation of the Jerusalem leadership and the explicit prediction of the destruction of the temple in Matthew 24. In this bridging passage we have Jesus' last words to the people: "Your house is left to you desolate . . . and you will not see me again until you say, 'Blessed is he who comes in the name of the Lord.'"

6. Cited by James M. Houston, *The Mind on Fire* (Vancouver: Regent College Publishing, 1989), p. 200.

struction in AD 70. Implicitly, then, Old Testament prophecies about Jerusalem's future glory must find their fulfillment in ways that conform to the transmutation of the kingdom of God from an earthly kingdom into a spiritual kingdom.

In Luke-Acts

Turning to Luke's narrative in his gospel and its sequel, the Acts of the Apostles, we can trace Luke's redefinition of the kingdom of God from the birth of Messiah to a generation beyond Messiah's resurrection. Given that temporal extension, we can trace within Luke's narratives the definition of the Land by the primitive church according to their Jewish understanding to the Spirit-enlightened church's redefinition of the Land to refer to spiritual realities.

Jewish Misunderstandings of the Primitive Church

The opening scenes of Luke take place in Jerusalem (Luke 1:5-79). Here the pious characters of Luke's infancy narratives — Zechariah and Elizabeth, Joseph and Mary and Simeon — praise God for sending Israel's long-hoped-for Messiah. Not yet having heard the teachings of Jesus and not yet having experienced the gift of the Holy Spirit, they expressed their praise in terms they inherited from their Jewish context. For example, Mary probably understood Gabriel's announcement that Jesus would reign over the House of Jacob from David's throne in an everlasting kingdom as referring to David's throne in Jerusalem (Luke 1:32-33).

Jerusalem: The Locus of the End of the Old Dispensation

But as Luke continues his narrative the primitive church's Jewish expectations for the kingdom are reshaped. Jerusalem remains the center of God's kingdom during Messiah's earthly career but not after his resurrection. Upon his march to Jerusalem in order to fulfill his destiny, Jesus says sardonically: "I must keep going . . . for surely no prophet can die outside of Jerusalem" (Luke 13:33; cf. 18:31).

Jesus now subverts any future in salvation history for the "unholy" city through his parables, actions, and prophecies. Luke records that "when Jesus was near Jerusalem and the people thought that the kingdom of God was going to appear at once" (Luke 19:11), he told them the parable of the mina. In this parable the mina is taken away from the unfaithful servant and given to another. He concludes the parable with the ominous command: "But those enemies of mine who did not want me to be king over them — bring them here and kill them in front of me" (19:27). Following the telling of this parable, Luke records Jesus' triumphal entrance into Jerusalem, but instead of fulfilling Jewish hopes for the exaltation of Jerusalem, Jesus weeps for Jerusalem because the city is about to be annihilated for rejecting him. "The time is near," he says, when armies will lay it waste. Luke neither alludes to Old Testament prophecies that Jerusalem will be rebuilt nor does he cite any new prophecies to that effect.

Turning to Luke's sequel, in its first scene we find Jesus instructing his disciples to stay in Jerusalem until God empowers them from on high. Only after they have been clothed with the Holy Spirit are they to begin their worldwide witness to the gospel. In the second scene, which is set on the Mount of Olives, the disciples still think like the primitive church: "Are you at this time going restore the kingdom to Israel?" they ask (Acts 1:6; cf. Luke 24:22). Instead of promising to fulfill their Jewish expectations, Jesus again instructs them to stay in Jerusalem until Spirit-empowered to bear witness to the gospel from Jerusalem to the ends of the earth. With that, Luke shifts the scene to Christ ascending into the clouds and to an angel announcing that he will return in the same manner (Acts 1:1-11).

Jerusalem: Locus of the Beginning of the New Age

After Christ's ascension the disciples return to Jerusalem, where on Pentecost they are filled with the Holy Spirit and begin their preaching mission to the world (Luke 24:50–Acts 2:4). Luke reduces Jerusalem to become the starting point of the new age and divests it of ever again becoming the center of the world. The earthly city is no longer the center of the world in the everlasting End as the Jews had expected.

With Christ's ascension and the outpouring of the Holy Spirit, Luke explicitly redefines crucial terms regarding the kingdom of God. Peter locates David's throne in heaven. He explains the gift of the Spirit enabling Christ's disciples to bear witness to the gospel in many languages as evidence that he now sits on David's heavenly throne: "Exalted to the right hand of God, he has received from the Father the promised Holy Spirit and has poured out what you now see and hear." For David did not ascend to heaven, yet he said: "The LORD said to my lord: 'Sit at my right hand'" (Acts 2:33-35).

517

After witnessing to the ascended Christ, the apostle with the keys to the kingdom opens its gate to the Samaritans and then to the Roman centurion.

Luke now shifts his focus from Peter, the apostle to the Jews, to Paul, the apostle to the nations. Paul's conversion occurs on the Damascus road, not in Jerusalem. Shortly thereafter we learn that Antioch, not Jerusalem, becomes the center for gospel proclamation throughout the Roman Empire (Acts 13:1-3). Luke draws his narrative to conclusion with Paul in Rome. Here, at the political and religious center of his world, the great apostle "preaches the kingdom of God and teaches about the Lord Jesus Christ" (Acts 28:31).

This narrative background tracing the redefinition of Land from a reference to a Jewish kingdom ruled from Jerusalem to a universal kingdom ruled from heaven has prepared us to reflect upon the teachings of the apostles about the continuing role of the Land in salvation history.

In the Teaching of the Apostles

Land Jerusalem disappears entirely from the radar screen of salvation history in the New Testament teachings. The contrast between the Old Testament prophecies regarding the Land and the teachings of the apostles regarding the Land is so striking that it becomes such a *tour de force* that the New Testament redefines the concept. Land no longer refers to territorial space but to spiritual space that encompasses both universal space — on both the vertical and horizontal axes — and universal time (i.e., "forever more").

Jerusalem Intentionally Omitted from Salvation History

It is surely unsettling, if there is a continuing role for Jerusalem in salvation history, that the most formally educated apostle in Jewish literature never mentions it. At an unknown age Paul came to Jerusalem to study under Gamaliel. As a devout Pharisee who outstripped his classmates for zeal (Gal. 1:14; Phil. 3:4-5), Paul shared in and cherished the Diaspora Jews' apocalyptic hopes that the Messiah would rule the world from his glorious throne in Jerusalem. His failure to mention that role must be chalked up as a meaningful gap, not an insignificant blank. To be sure, in speaking of ethnic Israel's privileges, in contrast to the Gentiles, he says that theirs are the "promises" (Rom. 9:4), but he never singles out the Land for special mention (Galatians 3; 4:2; Romans 4; 9:7; 11:28). Davies says: "[Paul's] silence points not merely to the absence of a conscious concern with [the Land promises], but to his deliberate rejection of it. His interpretation of the promise is a-territorial."[7]

This is not an argument from silence. Jesus promised the apostles that the Spirit would guide them into *all* truth, presumably with reference to his kingdom (John 16:13). The logic is inescapable. If the Spirit will guide the apostles into all truth regarding his kingdom, and if the inspired apostles do not teach a future Jewish kingdom centered in Jerusalem, then the popular, evangelical eschatology that the Land will play a role in an intermediate Jewish kingdom between two comings of Christ is not true.

The writer of Hebrews confirms this logical inference. He explicitly teaches that the earthly sanctuary with its liturgy has been done away forever, and he forbids the church from going back to that shadow.

Two ambiguous passages, however, *may imply* a continuing role for Jerusalem in salvation history: 2 Thessalonians 2:4 and Romans 11:26.

2 Thessalonians 2:4

Commentators have proposed three identifications of the temple of God in Paul's prediction: "he [the Man of Lawlessness] takes his seat in the temple [*naos*, 'inmost shrine'] of God, proclaiming himself to be God": first, a future earthly temple; second, the church either corporately or individually; or third, the heavenly temple of God.[8] Time permits me only to defend the latter interpretation. Old Testament references to God's heavenly temple are also found in Psalms 11:4; 18:6 [7]; 103:19; Habakkuk 2:20. If the reference is to God's heavenly abode, "to sit" is a metaphorical way of saying that the

---

7. Davies, *The Gospel and the Land*, p. 179.

8. Two objections eliminate a reference to a third temple as the temple of God. First, the conjectured third temple entails the restoration of the Old Testament liturgy, but the writer of Hebrew says that its liturgy in God's economy has been *forever* done away with (Hebrews 8–10; see above). Second, and correlatively, the Lord Jesus replaced the Old Testament temple with his body (John 2:19-22), and Paul consistently uses the term *naos theou* for the church, collectively or individually, that is in Christ, never for a temple of this world.

Paul's consistent use of the term "the temple of God" for the church (1 Cor. 3:16f.; 1 Cor. 6:19; Eph. 2:21-22; cf. 1 Pet. 2:4-10) has led many commentators, both ancient and modern, to identify "the temple of God" with the church. In that case, "he takes his seat" would mean to snatch the primacy.

However, in all other cases where Paul refers to "the temple of God," Paul makes it perfectly clear that the term "temple of God" is being used figuratively for a spiritual reality. The physical activity of "he takes his seat" does not readily suggest a spiritual sense of "temple of God."

lawless man exalts himself to the place of god. Just as the king of Babylon aspired to set his throne in heaven (Isa. 14:13-14), and the king of Tyre proclaimed, "I am God, I sit in the seat of the gods" (Ezek. 28:2; cf. Acts 12:21-23), so this lawless ruler will boast that he has dispossessed God and taken his place. F. F. Bruce comments: "Had they (Paul, Timothy and Silas, 2 Thess. 1:1) said, 'so that he takes his seat on the throne of God,' few would have thought it necessary to think of a literal throne; it would have been regarded as a graphic way of saying that he plans to usurp the authority of God."[9] Jesus uses "sit/seat" in a similar figure with reference to the Pharisees: "they sit in Moses' seat" (i.e., they have taken Moses' authoritative place, Matt. 23:2).

Romans 11:26-27

In Romans 11:26-27 Paul points to Zion's role in ethnic Israel's future salvation from sin, citing Isaiah 59:20f. and 27:9: "The deliverer will come from Zion;[10] he will turn godlessness away from Jacob. And this is my covenant with them when I take away their sins." In saying "from [Greek *ek*] Zion," Paul intentionally changes the Hebrew text and its Greek paraphrase. The Hebrew text reads that "the deliverer will come to [Hebrew *lamed*] Zion," and its Greek paraphrase reads "the deliverer will come for the sake of [Greek *heneken*] Zion." If the deliver is still to come "to" or "for the sake of" Zion, Paul could be implying that Jerusalem will play a future role in God's salvation history. But by changing the text to "the deliverer will come from Zion," he diminishes that implication.

But in what sense does Israel's spiritual salvation come from Zion? Douglas Moo thinks it refers to salvation coming from heavenly Jerusalem,[11] but David Holwerda contends that "Zion" refers "to earthly Jerusa-

---

9. F. F. Bruce, *1 and 2 Thessalonians* (WBC 45; Waco, TX: Word), p. 169.

10. A poetic name for *I am*'s dwelling on the temple mount. See Peter J. Leithart, "Where Was Ancient Zion?" *TynBul* 53, no. 2 (2002): 161-76.

11. The former interpretation is unlikely for several reasons: (1) In that case Jesus would have to return to Zion before bringing salvation from Zion. Paul avoids this misunderstanding by changing the prepositions of the Hebrew text of Isaiah 59:20, which reads "to Zion," and the Greek translation of that text, which reads "for the sake of Zion," to "*from* Zion" (cf. Pss. 14:7; 53:6 [7]; 110:2). (2) The interpretation that connects Jesus' return to Zion with his bringing salvation to the Jews is without an eschatological horizon in the Pauline corpus. (3) Nowhere in Romans 9–11 does Paul make any reference to Israel's future salvation as having any connection with the Land or with a future Jewish kingdom. His point in the entire section and in this unit particularly is Israel's spiritual salvation — that is to say,

lem, from which the gospel has gone out to the entire world."[12] We need not decide here which interpretation is right. The important point for our purposes is that neither of these careful exegetes interprets Zion as referring to a continuing role for Jewish Jerusalem.

Land as Spiritual Territory

The Gospel writers remove the Old Testament literal husk of Land so that the church may feed on its hidden, spiritual manna. They reinterpret Land in ways appropriate to the new age of the Spirit: first, as a reference to the person of Jesus Christ; second, as a reference to his reign from heaven; and third, as a reference to his future reign in the regeneration of all things.

Land as "Christified"

In both the Gospel of John and in the apostolic teaching Land is "Christified." The New Testament replaces Israel's hope for life in the Promised Land (cf. Exod. 40:35; 1 Kings 8:11; Pss. 9:11; 76:2; 87:3; 132:13) with eternal life by baptism into Jesus Christ.

In the Gospel of John

John opens his Gospel with the glory of God appearing in Jesus Christ, perhaps an intertextual allusion to Ezekiel's vision of the glory of God departing

---

that God "will turn godlessness away from Jacob" and "when I take away their sins." Their salvation in Rom. 11:15 is equated with "life from the dead."

The following considerations favor this interpretation. (1) Paul uses the term "Jerusalem/Zion" of heavenly Zion/Jerusalem in Galatians 4:26. (2) Other apostles also transcendentalize Old Testament references to earthly Zion to refer to heavenly Zion (Heb. 12:22; Rev. 14:1-2). Peter and the writer of Hebrews do so explicitly with reference to the throne from which the Lord Jesus establishes his present and future rule on earth (cf. Ps. 110:1-2 with Acts 2:34f.; Heb. 8:1; 12:2). (3) Christ and his apostles clearly taught that the ascended Lord rules on earth from heaven (Matt. 28:18; 1 Cor. 15:27; Eph. 1:20-22; 1 Pet. 3:22); that upon his ascension he and the Father poured out the Holy Spirit on his church (John 16:7-14; Acts 2:33); and that believers are joined with him in his heavenly reign (Eph. 1:20; 2:6; 3:10; 6:12; Rev. 3:21-22).

12. David E. Holwerda, *Jesus and Israel: One Covenant or Two?* (Grand Rapids: Eerdmans, 1995), pp. 172-75.

from the temple before its destruction in 586 BC. Moreover, in John's Gospel the person of Jesus Christ replaces Jerusalem's earthly temple. Jesus said to those who challenged his authority: "Destroy this temple, and I will raise it again in three days." The Jews thought he meant the literal temple, but John says, "But the temple he had spoken of was his body," and that the disciples did not understand what he meant until after his resurrection (John 2:13-22). In other words, to anticipate W. D. Davies's coinage, John "Christifies" the Land.

In the Apostolic Teaching

By way of introduction to Paul's "Christification" of the Land, recall that Paul proclaims his gospel throughout the Roman Empire. Moreover, according to his gospel, Jews and Gentiles are equally coheirs of God's covenant promises to Abraham and David (Gal. 3:26; Eph. 2:11-22; 3:6). This worldwide equality of all believers, however, is not possible in the old age. In that dispensation each family of Israel inherited *in perpetuity* a piece of the turf in the Land, and none of the Land was left undistributed. In other words, that economy gave only the Jews an opportunity to own space in the Land. Gentiles, disenfranchised as they were, had no hope of possessing holy space. Davies draws the logical conclusion: "The logic of Paul's Christology and missionary practice, then, seems to demand that the people living in the land had been replaced as the people of God by a universal community which had no special territorial attachment."[13]

Moreover, Paul explicitly spiritualizes the Land promises. He replaces Abraham's physical seed attachment to the Land with Abraham's spiritual seed attachment to a life in Christ. This replacement of an attachment to the Land by an attachment to Christ has two aspects: first, the Land of Canaan is "Christified," and second, the stones of the Jerusalem temple are redefined as living, spiritual stones of the church.

LAND AS "CHRISTIFIED"

First, we reflect upon the redefinition of the Land of Canaan. Whereas old Israel found God's unique presence and her inheritance in the Land of Canaan, scores of New Testament texts assert that the New Israel finds God's unique presence and her eternal inheritance in Christ. Suffice it to cite one: "For you died, and your life is now hidden with Christ in God. When Christ, who is your life appears, then you all will appear with him in glory" (Col. 3:3-4). W. D.

---

13. Davies, *The Gospel and the Land,* p. 182.

Davies coins the term "Christified" for this new attachment: "The land has been for him [Paul] 'Christified.' It is not the land promised . . . that became his [Paul's] 'inheritance,' but the Living Lord, in whom was a new creation."[14]

TEMPLE AS LIVING STONES

We now reflect upon the temple. Whereas old Israel located the most holy space in the Jerusalem temple, in the new age sacred space is located in all believers by their baptism into Christ, the true temple of God. The holy space of the Jerusalem temple is redefined as a community of holy persons in the New Testament. In the teachings of Paul and Peter, the church, both corporately and individually, is the temple of God (1 Cor. 3:16-17; 6:14-20; 1 Pet. 2:4-10). The Spirit of God indwells directly every individual within the totality, so that the Spirit corporately indwells the whole. All believers are "fellow citizens with God's people and members of God's household, built on the foundation of the apostles and prophets, with Christ Jesus himself as the chief cornerstone. In him the whole building is joined together and rises to become a holy temple in the Lord. And in him you too are being built together to become a dwelling in which God lives by his Spirit" (Eph. 2:19-22).

LAND AS REST

The writer of Hebrews contrasts the temporary, physical rest that Joshua gave Israel with God's lasting and satisfying sabbath-rest that the elect enjoy by believing in the gospel of the Lord Jesus Christ (Heb. 4:1). "God swore on oath in his anger against Israel's unbelief, 'They shall never enter my rest'" (Heb. 4:3). God's rest refers to the rest he enjoyed upon his cessation from work on the sabbath day. However, "today" God offers his people that rest. "If Joshua had given them [God's sabbath] rest, God would not have spoken about another day." Today those who accept the gospel of the Lord Jesus Christ enter that rest (4:3).[15]

Land as "Transcendentalized"

The New Testament also "transcendentalizes" the Land. By "transcendentalize" I mean Jerusalem is redefined as heavenly Jerusalem.

14. Davies, *The Gospel and the Land*, p. 213.

15. Simon J. Kistemaker, *New Testament Commentary: Exposition of the Epistle to the Hebrews* (Grand Rapids: Baker, 1984), pp. 102-15.

In the Teaching of Jesus

Amazingly, Jesus revealed the transmutation of earthly Jerusalem to heavenly Jerusalem to a woman, a mixed-breed Samaritan, an adulteress. The unexpected recipient of this revelation points to the new administration of grace, where all people are allowed access to God in a heavenly Jerusalem that transcends land boundaries and cultural restrictions. In response to her contention, "Our fathers worshiped on this mountain [i.e., Gerizim], but you Jews claim that the place where we must worship is in Jerusalem," Jesus declared that the Jews until Messiah's appearing had it right, but now that he is here: "You will worship God neither on this mountain nor in Jerusalem. . . . Yet a time is coming and has now come when the true worshipers will worship the Father in Spirit and truth" (John 4:19-24). Because God is spirit, not flesh and blood, Jesus argues that his worshipers encounter him in the "Holy Spirit" who comes from God, not in an earthly locale (cf. Joel 2:28-29; 1 Cor. 2:10-16). By "truth" *(alēthē)* he refers to "reality" — that is to say, the earthly Zion is only a type or symbol of the heavenly reality (cf. Heb. 8:2; 9:24).

In the Apostolic Teachings

As we noted above, Peter relocates David's temporary throne in Jerusalem with his son's true throne in heaven. Seated now at God's right hand, Christ rules from heaven (Matt. 28:18; Acts 2:29-36; 1 Cor. 15:27; Eph. 1:20-22; 1 Pet. 3:22) and believers participate with him in his heavenly reign (Eph. 1:20; 2:6; 3:10; 6:12; Col. 3:1; Rev. 3:21-22).

According to the apostles, we are "blessed in the heavenly realms with every spiritual blessing in Christ" (Eph. 1:3). Paul contrasts the freedom offered in this heavenly Jerusalem with the bondage of earthly Jerusalem (Gal. 4:26-27). He also reckons that the church's citizenship is in heaven (Phil. 3:20). The writer of Hebrews also transfers the Christian hope from Jewish Jerusalem to the heavenly Jerusalem: Jesus entered "once and for all" into the heavenly sanctuary, not into a manmade one that was only a copy of the true (Hebrews 7–10; esp. 9:11-12, 24). Presently, he argues, the society of the New Covenant now convenes in Mount Zion with thousands upon thousands of angels in joyful assembly (Heb. 12:22). They come to this throne of grace to receive mercy and obtain hope in their time of need from their "great high priest who has gone through the heavens" (Heb. 4:14-16).

Land as Eschatologized

The New Testament also "eschatologizes" the Land. By "eschatological" I mean the everlasting End beyond Christ's Second Coming. The writer of Hebrews sees behind Abraham's quest for God's promised land a quest for a city with foundations, whose architect and builder is God (Heb. 11:10). Abraham's quest segues us into the New Testament's eschatologizing the Old Testament Land promises.

In the Teaching of the Apostles

The apostles refer to the Land in connection with the eschaton by the terms "to inherit," "heavenly country," and "times of refreshing" or "restoration of all things."

Let us look first at the term "to inherit." The apostles frequently encourage the suffering church with the promise of their imperishable inheritance (Rom. 8:16-17; 1 Cor. 4:8; 6:2; Eph. 2:6; Heb. 9:15). For example, Peter assures the elect saints that their new birth has brought them into "an inheritance that can never perish, spoil or fade — kept in heaven" (1 Pet. 1:3-4) and that this inheritance is their coming salvation to be revealed in the last time (1 Pet. 1:3-5). The imagery of "to inherit" derives from the Old Testament terminology associated with Israel's inheritance of the Land (Exod. 32:13; Lev. 20:24; Num. 26:3-56; Deut. 3:28). In other words, Israel's inheritance of the land of Canaan is a foretaste of the Christian's inheritance in the regeneration of all things.

The writer of Hebrews redefines Land in the eschaton as "a heavenly country." For him the Old Testament pilgrims were from the first "longing for a better country — a heavenly one. Therefore God is not ashamed to be called their God, for he has prepared for them a city" (Heb. 11:13-16). None of these pilgrims, he says, "received what had been promised. God had planned something better for us so that only together with us would they be made perfect" (Heb. 11:39-40). This perfection will appear at the *parousia* (12:26; 13:14; Rom. 8:18; Eph. 1:9-10). In other words, the spiritual meaning of Land was already present in the Old Testament.

Peter speaks of "times of refreshing" and "restoration of all things." He exhorts the Jews in Jerusalem: "Repent, then, and turn to God, so that your sins may be wiped out." And he motivates them with the promise "that times of refreshing [*anapsyxis*, 'relaxation, relief'] may come from the Lord, and that he may send the Christ. . . . He must remain in heaven until the time comes for God to restore everything [*apokatastaseōs pantōn,* 'restoring everything to perfection'[16]] as he promised long ago through the prophets" (Acts 3:19-21). The references to "times of refreshing," and "restoration of all things" to their perfection, presumably refer to the perfections of the eschaton. That "he must remain in heaven" until that time entails that the eschaton will come in conjunction with the Second Coming. As in Romans 11, the final end occurs in connection with Israel as a nation repenting, turning to God, and having their sins wiped away.

In Matthew

Two passages in Matthew about the Land *may imply* its role in an intermediate kingdom between Christ's *parousia* and his Second Coming: Matthew 5:5 and 19:27-28. More probably, however, the intended Land in these passages should be located in the eschaton.

MATTHEW 5:5

Christ's third beatitude in Matthew, "blessed are the meek, for they shall inherit the earth [*tēn gēn*]" is a direct quote of Psalm 37:11 (cf. LXX Ps. 36:11). Though *'āreṣ* in the Hebrew text of Psalm 37:11 probably refers to the Land, in Christ's citation of that text from the LXX, *gē* means either "land" or the "whole earth." Some commentators interpret "land" in this beatitude as a symbol for inheriting conditions under the Rule of God in the Kingdom of Heaven (cf. Matt. 5:3, 10, 20; 6:10, 33; 23:13). Two factors, however, should be borne in mind when interpreting this beatitude: *tēn gēn* has an obstinately territorial connotation and the beatitudes have an unmistakable eschatological dimension. More probably, then, Jesus means that the meek will inherit the earth when God will vindicate them by giving them the inheritance in the renewed earth (Matt. 12:27-28).

MATTHEW 19:27-28

The interpretation of Matthew 19:27-28 is the most difficult from the perspective of this lecturer. In response to Peter's question regarding a reward for the Twelve, Jesus replied: "At the renewal of all things [*palingenesia*], when the Son of Man sits on his glorious throne, you who have followed me will also sit on twelve thrones, judging the twelve tribes of Israel" (Matt. 19:27-28; cf. 20:20-28). *Palingenesia* is derived from *palin genesis* and etymo-

16. *BAGD,* p. 112, s.v. *apokatastasis.*

logically means "new genesis."[17] In the eschaton Jesus will be enthroned as king over all things (cf. Matt. 25:31-34). The highly symbolic Apocalypse also represents nations as having distinct roles when God lowers the heavenly Jerusalem to the new earth: "The nations will walk by the light of the glory of the Lord, and the kings of the earth will bring their splendor into it" (Rev. 21:24), and "the leaves of the tree of life are for the healing of the nations" (Rev. 22:2).

The language and thought of the twelve disciples sitting on thrones in the regeneration of all things are derived from Daniel 7. In Daniel's vision Israel rules the nations, but in Christ's teaching the Twelve, who represent the true people of God in contrast to unbelieving Israel, judge (i.e., rule) the twelve tribes of Israel.[18] France comments: "This remarkable transfer of imagery graphically illustrates the theme of a 'true Israel' of the followers of Jesus who take the place of the unbelieving nation, a theme which runs through much of the teaching of Jesus in this Gospel (cf. Matt. 8:11-12; 21:43)."

Conclusion

In conclusion let us apply these reflections upon the Land to see how the New Testament reveals what the Old Testament concealed. The promise to Abraham that his descendants will inherit a land flowing with milk and honey becomes a metaphor for the milk and honey of life in Christ, for participation in heaven itself, and for a world that is beyond what saints could

---

17. *Palingenesis* first acquired significance in Stoicism before passing into Judaism. Philo uses the word of the restoration to life of an individual (e.g., Abel in Seth) and also of the reconstitution of the world after the Flood. Büchsel comments: "When *palingenesia* passes from Stoicism into Judaism its meaning changes. The new existence to which the world and man come in the new aeon is not just a repetition of the form, as in Stoicism. It is an existence in which righteousness dwells (2 Pet. 3:13). In Judaism the cosmic catastrophe is the Last Judgment, and in contrast to that expected in Stoicism this is definitive (see Büchsel, *TDNT*, 1.688 s.v. *palingenesia*). Büchsel also says, "In Matthew 19:28 . . . the Jewish faith in the resurrection of the dead and the renewal of the world is clothed in this term." In other words, the word entails the final judgment and the renewal of individuals and of the earth in a definitive final end. R. T. France says, "The word effectively conveys the Jewish eschatological hope of 'new heavens and a new earth' in the Messianic age (Isa. 56:17 [actually, 65:17; 66:22]; etc.)." See R. T. France, *The Gospel of Matthew* (Grand Rapids: Eerdmans, 2007), p. 287.

18. For the identification of "Son of Man" see also Frank Thielman, *Theology of the New Testament* (Grand Rapids: Zondervan, 2005), pp. 68-71.

imagine or think. Isaiah and Micah predict that Mount Zion will be exalted above all mountains and all the nations will flow to it. This prophecy in its canonical context refers to the heavenly Jerusalem and/or to its being lowered to the new earth in the eschaton. Let the church rejoice that myriads of Christians from all over the world make their pilgrimage to heavenly Mount Zion to feed upon the hidden manna of Jesus Christ.